Fodor's Vietnam

First New Edition

The complete guide, thoroughly up-to-date

Packed with details that will make your trip

The must-see sights, off and on the beaten path

What to see, what to skip

Mix-and-match vacation itineraries

City strolls, countryside adventures

Smart lodging and dining options

Essential local do's and taboos

Transportation tips, distances and directions

Key contacts, savvy travel tips

When to go, what to pack

Clear, accurate, easy-to-use maps

Books to read, videos to watch, background essays

Fodor's Travel Publications, Inc.
New York • Toronto • London • Sydney • Auckland
www.fodors.com/

Fodor's Vietnam

EDITOR: Natasha Lesser

Editorial Contributors: Robert Andrews, David Brown, Andrew Chilvers, Pilar Guzman, Mai Hoang, Michael Mathes, Chelsea Mauldin, Peter Saidel, Heidi Sarna, Helayne Schiff, M.T. Schwartzman (Gold Guide editor), Jim Spencer, Dinah A. Spritzer, Russell Stockman, Nancy van Itallie, Susan Winsten, Felicity Wood
Editorial Production: Tracy Patruno
Maps: David Lindroth, *cartographer*; Bob Blake, *map editor*
Design: Fabrizio La Rocca, *creative director*; Guido Caroti, *associate art director*; Jolie Novak, *photo editor*
Production/Manufacturing: Mike Costa
Cover Photograph: Owen Franken

Copyright

ISBN 0-679-03543-5

First Edition

Special Sales

Fodor's Travel Publications are available at special discounts for bulk purchases for sales promotions or premiums. Special editions, including personalized covers, excerpts of existing guides, and corporate imprints, can be created in large quantities for special needs. For more information, contact your local bookseller or write to Special Markets, Fodor's Travel Publications, 201 East 50th Street, New York, NY 10022. Inquiries from Canada should be directed to your local Canadian bookseller or sent to Random House of Canada, Ltd., Marketing Department, 2775 Matheson Boulevard E., Mississauga, Ontario L4W 4P7. Inquiries from the United Kingdom should be sent to: Fodor's Travel Publications, 20 Vauxhall Bridge Road, London, England SW1V 2SA.

PRINTED IN THE UNITED STATES OF AMERICA

10 9 8 7 6 5 4 3 2 1

CONTENTS

	On the Road with Fodor's	*v*
	About Our Writers *v* New This Year *v* How to Use This Book *vi* Don't Forget to Write *vii*	
	The Gold Guide	*xiii*
	Smart Travel Tips A to Z	
1	**Destination: Vietnam**	*1*
	Vietnam Today: Motorbikes and Water Buffalos *2* New and Noteworthy *3* What's Where *4* Pleasures and Pastimes *5* Great Itineraries *9* Fodor's Choice *10* Festivals and Seasonal Events *12*	
2	**Hanoi**	*14*
3	**The North**	*81*
	Halong Bay, Sapa, Dien Bien Phu	
4	**The Central Coast**	*120*
	Hue, Hoi An, Danang	
5	**The South-Central Coast and Highlands**	*151*
	Nha Trang and Dalat	
6	**Ho Chi Minh City**	*169*
7	**The Mekong Delta**	*221*
8	**Portraits of Vietnam**	*238*
	Vietnam at a Glance: A Chronology *239* "Riding the Dream," by Jim Spencer *247* "Getting Down to Business," by Andrew Chilvers *253* Books and Videos *257*	
	Vietnamese Vocabulary	*259*
	Menu Guide	*264*
	Index	*267*

Maps

World Time Zones *viii–ix*
Southeast Asia *x–xi*
Vietnam *xii*
Hanoi *20–21*
The Old Quarter *23*
The French Quarter *27*
Around the Ho Chi Minh Mausoleum and West Lake *33*
Hanoi Dining *44–45*
Hanoi Lodging *52–53*
The North *88–89*
The Central Coast *124*
Hue *126*
Danang *138*
Hoi An *145*
The South-Central Coast and Highlands *154*
Nha Trang *156*
Dalat *162*
Ho Chi Minh City *176–177*
Cholon *185*
Ho Chi Minh City Dining *188–189*
Ho Chi Minh City Lodging *194–195*
Ho Chi Minh City Environs *207*
The Mekong Delta *226*

ON THE ROAD WITH FODOR'S

WE'RE ALWAYS THRILLED to get letters from readers, especially one like this:

It took us an hour to decide what book to buy and we now know we picked the best one. Your book was wonderful, easy to follow, very accurate, and good on pointing out eating places, informal as well as formal. When we saw other people using your book, we would look at each other and smile.

Our editors and writers are deeply committed to making every Fodor's guide "the best one"—not only accurate but always charming, brimming with sound recommendations and solid ideas, right on the mark in describing restaurants and hotels, and full of fascinating facts that make you view what you've traveled to see in a rich new light.

About Our Writers

Our success in achieving our goals—and in helping to make your trip the best of all possible vacations—is a credit to the hard work of our extraordinary writers.

Andrew Chilvers, who spent most of his life in London and Hong Kong, is a freelance journalist based in Ho Chi Minh City. He has written for newspapers and magazines in England, New Zealand, Vietnam, Thailand, and Japan, and hopes to extend his global reach. He reports to us on what's going on in Ho Chi Minh City and the Mekong Delta.

Pilar Guzman, a freelance writer and illustrator, did much of the original research for *Fodor's Vietnam*. After visiting the country, she is now devoting all of her spare time to accurately recreating the dishes she ate there.

Michael Mathes, our expert on exploring Hanoi and the northernmost reaches of Vietnam, is a freelance writer based in Hanoi. Vietnam has been his home since 1994, minus a brief hiatus in San Francisco. He is brave (or crazy) enough to travel around Hanoi by motorbike—wearing a helmet, of course—especially in search of the city's best *pho*, Vietnam's delicious noodle soup.

Sherrie Nachman, who covered the chapters on central Vietnam, is a freelance writer living in New York. Her articles have appeared in numerous publications including the *Wall Street Journal*, the *New York Times Magazine*, and *Travel Holiday*.

Felicity Taybalo Wood, a Kiwi-American who is fluent in Vietnamese, is the tenth member of her family to live in Vietnam. She first moved to Vietnam in 1989 and has been living there almost ever since. Before writing about Hanoi for Fodor's, she traveled hundreds of miles through the country by bicycle and worked to strengthen relations between the United States and Vietnam as executive director of the American Chamber of Commerce in Ho Chi Minh City.

We'd also like to thank Bill Hastings of the Pacific Asia Travel Association for helping us gather information.

New This Year

We're extremely proud of our 1st edition of *Vietnam*. Our writers and editors have worked very hard to put this guide together so your trip to Vietnam can be an adventurous, exciting, and enjoyable one.

We're also proud to announce that the American Society of Travel Agents has endorsed Fodor's as its guidebook of choice. ASTA is the world's largest and most influential travel trade association, operating in more than 170 countries, with 27,000 members pledged to adhere to a strict code of ethics reflecting the Society's motto, "Integrity in Travel." ASTA shares Fodor's devotion to providing smart, honest travel information and advice to travelers, and we've long recommended that our readers consult ASTA member agents for the experience and professionalism they bring to the table.

On the Web, check out Fodor's site (www.fodors.com/) for information on major destinations around the world and travel-savvy interactive features. The Web site also lists the 85-plus radio stations nationwide that carry the *Fodor's Travel Show*, a live call-in program that airs every weekend. Tune in to hear guests discuss their wonderful adventures, or call in to get answers for your most pressing travel questions.

How to Use This Book

Organization

Up front is the **Gold Guide,** an easy-to-use section divided alphabetically by topic. Under each listing you'll find tips and information that will help you accomplish what you need to in Vietnam. You'll also find addresses and telephone numbers of organizations and companies that offer destination-related services and detailed information and publications.

The first chapter in the guide, **Destination: Vietnam,** helps get you in the mood for your trip. New and Noteworthy cues you in on trends and happenings, What's Where gets you oriented, Pleasures and Pastimes describes the activities and sights that really make Vietnam unique, Great Itineraries helps you plan your trip, Fodor's Choice showcases our top picks, and Festivals and Seasonal Events alerts you to special events you'll want to seek out.

Chapters in *Fodor's Vietnam* are arranged geographically from north to south. Each city chapter begins with an Exploring section subdivided by neighborhood; each subsection recommends a walking or driving tour and lists sights in alphabetical order. Each regional chapter is divided by geographical area; within each area, towns are covered in logical geographical order, and attractive stretches of road and minor points of interest between them are indicated by the designation *En Route*. Throughout, OFF THE BEATEN PATH sights appear after the places from which they are most easily accessible. And within town sections, all restaurants and lodgings are grouped together.

To help you decide what to visit in the time you have, all chapters begin with **recommended itineraries**; you can mix and match those from several chapters to create a complete vacation. The A-to-Z section that ends all chapters, and some town and region sections, covers getting there and getting around. It also provides helpful contacts and resources.

At the end of the book you'll find **Portraits,** essays about Vietnam, followed by suggestions for any pretrip research you may want to do—from recommended reading to movies on tape with Vietnam as a backdrop.

Addresses and Telephone Numbers

We have used the English word *street* (abbreviated St.) throughout the book rather than the Vietnamese words: *pho* or *duong*. This was done to make sure street names are clear; in Vietnamese, the words pho and duong come before the name streets, which can prove very confusing when trying to find your way around. In addition, many Vietnamese refer to streets only by name (without adding pho or duong), so you may only see these words on street signs and maps.

You may notice, too, that listings in this guide do not always include a street address. In Vietnam's smaller and less developed cities and towns, systems of street naming and numbering are not always as rationalized as those in North America or Europe. Often an attraction—such as a temple or market—or a hotel is a large enough local landmark that a street number is superfluous, or the town is sufficiently small that the establishment is readily findable. When in doubt, ask a local or take a taxi.

As for telephone numbers, in Vietnam they have 6 or 7 digits; also, many places don't have phones. Numbers in this guide are listed with their city or regional code (04 for Hanoi, for example). For more information, *see* Telephones *in* the Gold Guide.

Icons and Symbols

★ Our special recommendations
✕ Restaurant
🏨 Lodging establishment
✕🏨 Lodging establishment whose restaurant warrants a special trip
🦆 Good for kids (rubber duckie)
☞ Sends you to another section of the guide for more information
✉ Address
☎ Telephone number
⏲ Opening and closing times
🎟 Admission prices (those we give apply to adults; substantially reduced fees for senior citizens, children, and students do not exist in Vietnam)

Numbers in white and black circles that appear on the maps, in the margins, and within our tours correspond to one another.

Dining and Lodging

The restaurants and lodgings we list are the cream of the crop in each price range. Price categories are as follows:

For restaurants:

CATEGORY	COST*
$$$$	over $25
$$$	$15–$25
$$	$7–$15
$	$2–$7
¢	under $2

**per person for a three-course dinner, including 10% tax and 5% service but not drinks*

For hotels:

The rates quoted below are for accommodations in summer. Reservations are recommended during July and August and during Tet, the lunar new year (January or February); prices sometimes fluctuate at that time. At more upscale accommodations, rates sometimes include breakfast.

CATEGORY	COST*
$$$$	over $200
$$$	$100–$200
$$	$50–$100
$	$25–$50
¢	under $25

**All prices are for a standard double room, including 10% tax and 5% service.*

Hotel Facilities

We always list the facilities available, but we don't specify whether they cost extra: When pricing accommodations, always ask what's included. In addition, assume that all rooms have private bathrooms unless otherwise noted; the majority of hotels in Vietnam, big and small, do. The main exception is guest houses in very rural areas.

Prices

Prices are listed in dong (abbreviated "d") when an item costs 120,000d or less; prices are listed in U.S. dollars when the cost is $10 or more. At press time (winter 1997) about 12,200d equaled $1. You can usually pay for most items in either dong or dollars, but it's always a good idea to carry both at all times. For a more detailed description *see* Money *in* the Gold Guide.

Restaurant Reservations and Dress Codes

Reservations are always a good idea; we note only when they're essential or when they are not accepted. Book as far ahead as you can, and reconfirm when you get to town. Unless otherwise noted, most upscale restaurants listed are open daily for lunch and dinner; less expensive restaurants often serve breakfast as well. We mention dress only when men are required to wear a jacket or a jacket and tie. For an overview of other local habits, *see* Dining *in* the Gold Guide.

Credit Cards

The following abbreviations are used: **AE,** American Express; **DC,** Diners Club; **MC,** MasterCard; and **V,** Visa.

Don't Forget to Write

You can use this book in confidence that all prices and opening times are based on information supplied to us at press time; Fodor's cannot accept responsibility for any errors. Time inevitably brings changes, so always confirm information when it matters—especially if you're making a detour to visit a specific place. In addition, when making reservations be sure to mention if you have a disability or are traveling with children, if you prefer a private bath or a certain type of bed, or if you have specific dietary needs or other concerns.

Were the restaurants we recommended as described? Did our hotel picks exceed your expectations? Did you find a museum we recommended to be a waste of time? If you have complaints, we'll look into them and revise our entries when the facts warrant it. If you've discovered a special place that we haven't included, we'll pass along the information to our correspondents and have them check it out. So send us your feedback, positive *and* negative: E-mail us at editors@fodors.com (specifying the name of the book on the subject line) or write the Vietnam editor at Fodor's, 201 East 50th Street, New York, New York 10022. Have a wonderful trip!

Karen Cure

Editorial Director

World Time Zones

+11 +12 - -11 -10 -9 -8 -7 -6 -5 -4 -3 -2

Numbers below vertical bands relate each zone to Greenwich Mean Time (0 hrs.). Local times frequently differ from these general indications, as indicated by light-face numbers on map.

Algiers, **29**
Anchorage, **3**
Athens, **41**
Auckland, **1**
Baghdad, **46**
Bangkok, **50**
Beijing, **54**
Berlin, **34**
Bogotá, **19**
Budapest, **37**
Buenos Aires, **24**
Caracas, **22**
Chicago, **9**
Copenhagen, **33**
Dallas, **10**
Delhi, **48**
Denver, **8**
Djakarta, **53**
Dublin, **26**
Edmonton, **7**
Hong Kong, **56**
Honolulu, **2**
Istanbul, **40**
Jerusalem, **42**
Johannesburg, **44**
Lima, **20**
Lisbon, **28**
London (Greenwich), **27**
Los Angeles, **6**
Madrid, **38**
Manila, **57**

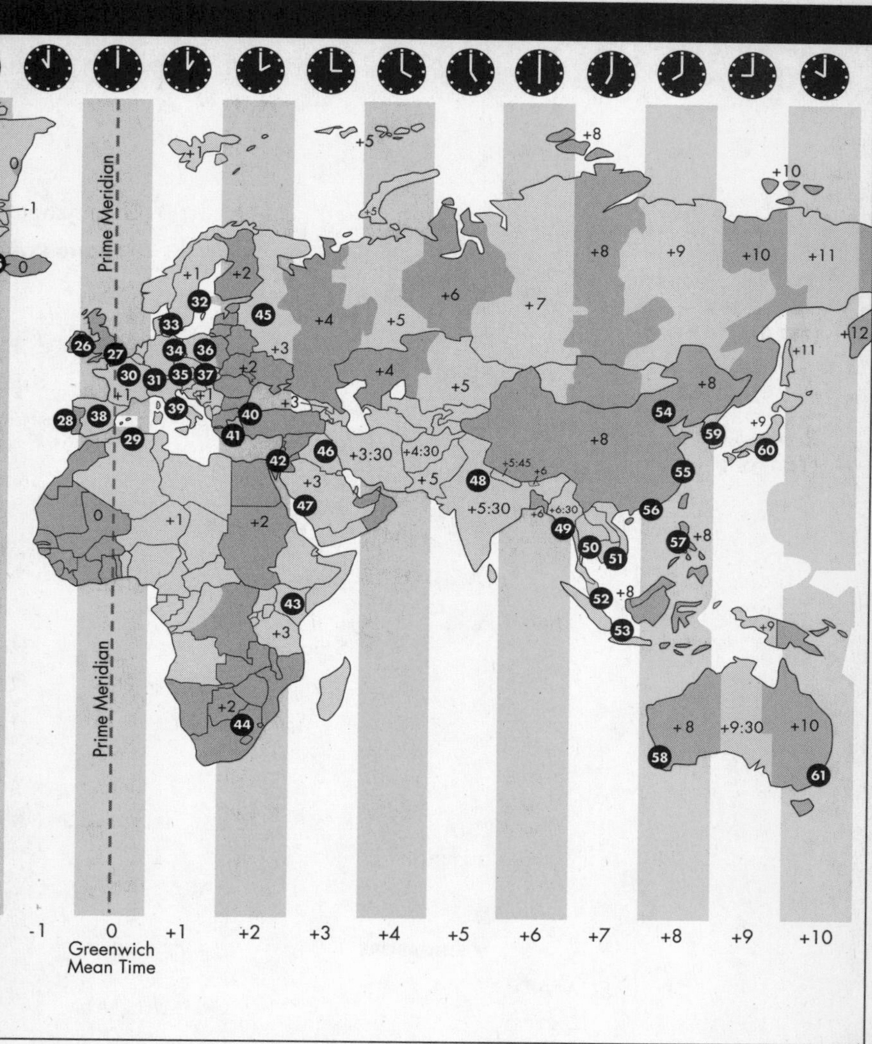

Mecca, **47**
Mexico City, **12**
Miami, **18**
Montréal, **15**
Moscow, **45**
Nairobi, **43**
New Orleans, **11**
New York City, **16**

Ottawa, **14**
Paris, **30**
Perth, **58**
Reykjavík, **25**
Rio de Janeiro, **23**
Rome, **39**
Saigon (Ho Chi Minh City), **51**

San Francisco, **5**
Santiago, **21**
Seoul, **59**
Shanghai, **55**
Singapore, **52**
Stockholm, **32**
Sydney, **61**
Tokyo, **60**

Toronto, **13**
Vancouver, **4**
Vienna, **35**
Warsaw, **36**
Washington, D.C., **17**
Yangon, **49**
Zürich, **31**

Southeast Asia

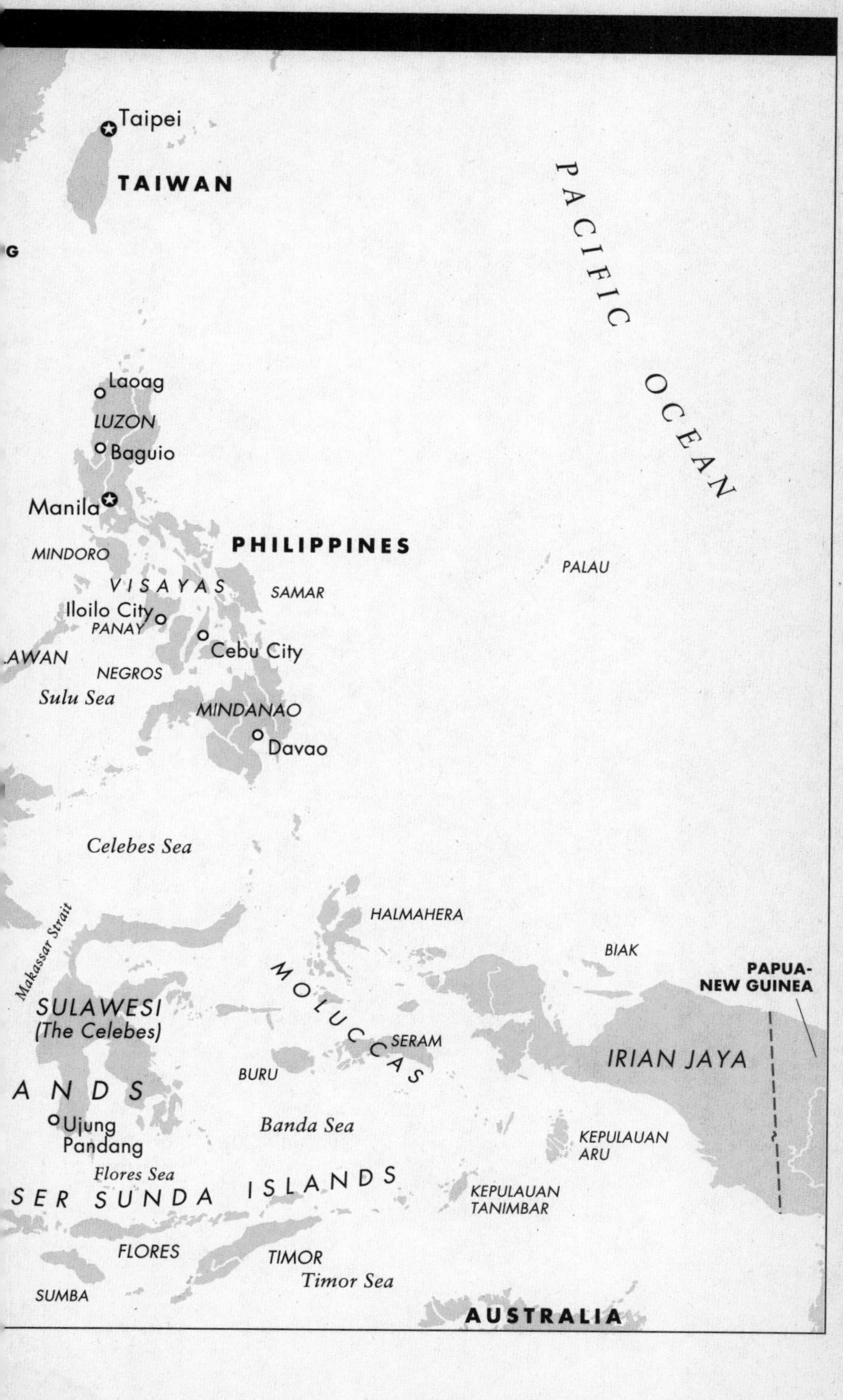

Taipei
TAIWAN
G
PACIFIC OCEAN
Laoag
LUZON
Baguio
Manila
PHILIPPINES
MINDORO
PALAU
VISAYAS
SAMAR
Iloilo City
PANAY
Cebu City
AWAN
NEGROS
Sulu Sea
MINDANAO
Davao
Celebes Sea
HALMAHERA
Makassar Strait
BIAK
PAPUA-
NEW GUINEA
MOLUCCAS
SULAWESI
(The Celebes)
SERAM
IRIAN JAYA
BURU
ANDS
Ujung
Pandang
Banda Sea
KEPULAUAN
ARU
Flores Sea
SER SUNDA ISLANDS
KEPULAUAN
TANIMBAR
FLORES
TIMOR
Timor Sea
SUMBA
AUSTRALIA

Vietnam

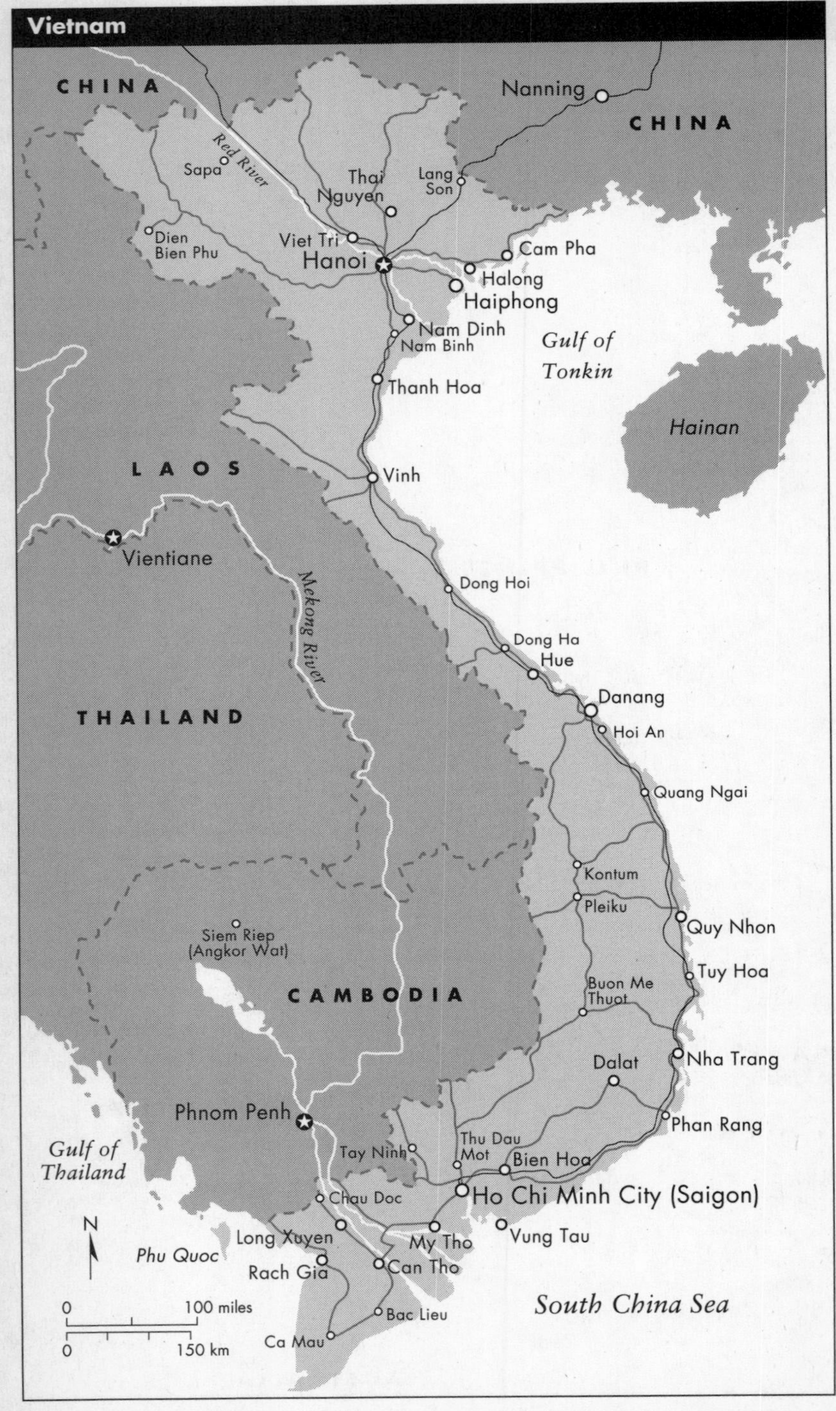
CHINA
Nanning
CHINA
Red River
Sapa
Thai Nguyen
Lang Son
Dien Bien Phu
Viet Tri
Hanoi
Cam Pha
Halong
Haiphong
Nam Dinh
Nam Binh
Gulf of Tonkin
Thanh Hoa
Hainan
LAOS
Vinh
Vientiane
Mekong River
Dong Hoi
Dong Ha
Hue
Danang
THAILAND
Hoi An
Quang Ngai
Kontum
Pleiku
Quy Nhon
Siem Riep (Angkor Wat)
Tuy Hoa
Buon Me Thuot
CAMBODIA
Nha Trang
Dalat
Phnom Penh
Phan Rang
Gulf of Thailand
Tay Ninh
Thu Dau Mot
Bien Hoa
Chau Doc
Ho Chi Minh City (Saigon)
N
Long Xuyen
My Tho
Vung Tau
Phu Quoc
Rach Gia
Can Tho
South China Sea
0
100 miles
Bac Lieu
0
150 km
Ca Mau

SMART TRAVEL TIPS A TO Z

Basic Information on Traveling in Vietnam, Savvy Tips to Make Your Trip a Breeze, and Companies and Organizations to Contact

A

AIR TRAVEL

International flights into Vietnam typically connect through hubs like Bangkok, Singapore, Manila, Hong Kong, Kuala Lumpur, and Taipei and fly into Ho Chi Minh City and Hanoi. Danang, in central Vietnam, has been under consideration as an international gateway for the past few years, but more than one timetable to open the huge American-built runways to foreign air traffic has come and gone. At present there are no direct flights to Vietnam from North America, but ongoing negotiations to offer direct U.S.–Vietnam service may bear fruit by the end of the millennium.

Note that two airlines may jointly operate a connecting flight from an Asian hub, so **ask if your airline operates every segment of your flight**—you may find that your preferred carrier flies only part of the way. For instance, if you purchased a ticket through an international carrier such as Air France, Cathay Pacific, or Thai International Airways, but are not flying direct into Hanoi or Ho Chi Minh City, it is possible that your connecting flight into Vietnam will be on Vietnam Airlines. Vietnam Airlines itself has direct routes from cities such as Paris (via Dubai) as well as Moscow and Sydney into Vietnam.

Some airlines' layovers are short; others, particularly those offering discounted fares, require an overnight stay in a connecting city. Before buying your ticket, **check to see who covers the cost of the hotel—you or the airline—if you have to stay overnight.** Flying time from Los Angeles to the Southeast Asian hub of Bangkok is approximately 18 hours, Chicago to Bangkok is 20 hours, and New York to Bangkok is 22 hours. Bangkok to Ho Chi Minh City takes 1 hour.

For domestic air travel major transportation hubs are Ho Chi Minh City, Hanoi, and Danang, but there is also service to Ban Me Thuot, Dalat, Dien Bien Phu, Haiphong, Hue, Nha Trang, Phu Quoc Island, Pleiku, Quy Nhon, and Vinh.

It is a good idea to **confirm both domestic flights and flights out of Vietnam a day or two in advance.** Flights are occasionally delayed or cancelled altogether. Also, **be sure to arrive at the airport early**: 45 minutes to 1 hour before domestic flights or 2 hours before international flights. Ticket agents have been known to give away seats if passengers are not present within 30 minutes of departure.

MAJOR AIRLINE OR LOW-COST CARRIER?

Most people choose a flight based on price. Yet there are other issues to consider. Major airlines offer the greatest number of departures; smaller airlines—including regional, low-cost, and no-frills airlines—usually have a more limited number of flights daily. Major airlines have frequent-flyer partners, which allow you to credit mileage earned on one airline to your account with another. Low-cost airlines offer a definite price advantage and fewer restrictions, such as advance-purchase requirements. Safety-wise, low-cost carriers as a group have a good history, but **check the safety record before booking** any low-cost carrier; call the Federal Aviation Administration's Consumer Hotline (☞ Airline Complaints, *below*).

Domestic routes in Vietnam are flown by Vietnam Airlines and its smaller semiprivate competitor, Pacific Airlines. Despite the appearance of competition, however, ticket prices for both airlines are set by the government. At press time (winter 1997) both Vietnam Airlines and Pacific Airlines were charging about $160 for a one-way ticket to Hanoi from Ho Chi Minh City. Combined, these airlines will get you to all major destinations and many smaller airports in the country. Breaking up a Ho Chi Minh City–Hanoi flight by stopping in, say, Hue or Danang for a few days will cost you only $10 extra.

A rule of thumb when traveling: **during rainy season avoid flying in late afternoon and early evening**, when storms generally occur. Note that since the fatal air crash in Phnom Penh, Cambodia, in September 1997, Vietnam Airlines has grounded all remaining Russian-made aircraft in its fleet. Planes now include 10 Airbus A320s, 3 Boeing 767s, and a few German Fokker 70s and French ATR 72s.

➤ MAJOR AIRLINES: **Asiana** (☎ 800/227–4262). **Cathay Pacific Airways** (☎ 800/233–2742 in the U.S., 800/268–6868 in Canada). **China Airlines** (☎ 800/227–5118). **Korean Air** (☎ 800/438–5000). **Singapore Airlines** (☎ 800/742–3333). **Continental** (☎ 800/231–0856), **Northwest** (☎ 800/225–2525), and **United Airlines** (☎ 800/241–6522) have flights into Tokyo, Singapore, and Bangkok, which then connect with regional carriers.

➤ FROM THE U.K.: There are no direct flights to Vietnam from the United Kingdom. Bangkok and Hong Kong are the easiest connection points, from which there are two daily flights to Ho Chi Minh City, and one daily to Hanoi. Contact **British Airways** (☎ 0345/222–111), **Cathay Pacific** (☎ 0345/581–581), or **Thai Airways** (☎ 0171/491–7953).

➤ DOMESTIC AIRLINES: **Pacific Airlines** (✉ 100 Le Duan St., Hanoi, ☎ 04/851–5356; ✉ 177 Vo Thi Sau St., District 1, Ho Chi Minh City, ☎ 08/820–0978). **Vietnam Airlines** (✉ 1 Quang Trung St., Hanoi, ☎ 04/825–0888; ✉ 116 Nguyen Hue St., District 1, Ho Chi Minh City, ☎ 08/829–2118).

GET THE LOWEST FARE

The least expensive airfares to Vietnam are priced for round-trip travel. Major airlines usually require you to **book far in advance and stay at least seven days** and no more than 30 to get the lowest fares. Ask about "ultrasaver" fares, which are the cheapest; they must be booked 90 days in advance and are nonrefundable. A little more expensive are "supersaver" fares, which require only a 30-day advance purchase. Remember that penalties for refunds—if you can get them—or scheduling changes are stiffer for international tickets, usually about $150. International flights are also sensitive to the season: **plan to fly in the off-season** for the cheapest fares. If your destination or home city has more than one gateway, **compare prices to and from different airports.** Also price flights scheduled for off-peak hours, which may be significantly less expensive.

To save money on flights from the United Kingdom and back, **look into an APEX or Super-PEX ticket.** APEX tickets must be booked in advance and have certain restrictions. Super-PEX tickets can be purchased at the airport on the day of departure—subject to availability.

USE AN AGENT

Travel agents, especially those who specialize in finding the lowest fares (☞ Discounts & Deals, *below*), can be especially helpful when booking a plane ticket. When you're quoted a price, **ask your agent if the price is likely to get any lower.** Good agents know the seasonal fluctuations of airfares and can usually anticipate a sale or fare war. However, waiting can be risky: The fare could go *up* as seats become scarce, and you may wait so long that your preferred flight sells out. A wait-and-see strategy works best if your plans are flexible, but if you must arrive and depart on certain dates, don't delay.

CHECK WITH CONSOLIDATORS

Consolidators buy tickets for scheduled flights at reduced rates from the airlines and then sell them at prices below the best fare available directly from the airlines, usually without advance restrictions. Sometimes you can even get your money back if you need to return the ticket. Carefully read the fine print detailing penalties for changes and cancellations and **confirm your consolidator reservation with the airline.**

➤ CONSOLIDATORS: **United States Air Consolidators Association** (✉ 925 L St., Suite 220, Sacramento, CA 95814, ☎ 916/441–4166, FAX 916/441–3520).

AVOID GETTING BUMPED

Airlines routinely overbook planes, knowing that not everyone with a ticket will show up, but sometimes everyone does. When that happens, airlines ask for volunteers to give up their seats. In return these volunteers usually get a certificate for a free flight and are rebooked on the next flight out. If there are not enough volunteers, the airline must choose who will be denied boarding. The first to get bumped are passengers who checked in late and those flying on discounted tickets, so be sure to **confirm your flight the day before, and get to the gate and check in as early as possible,** especially during peak periods. This is especially important if you're flying Vietnam Airlines.

ENJOY THE FLIGHT

Don't forget to **bring your passport with you to the airport,** even when flying domestic routes in Vietnam. You will be asked to show it before you are allowed to check in.

For more legroom, **request an emergency-aisle seat**; don't, however, sit in the row in front of the emergency aisle or in front of a bulkhead, where seats may not recline. If you don't like airline food, **ask for special meals when booking.** These can be vegetarian, low-cholesterol, or kosher, for example. To avoid jet lag, try to maintain a normal routine while traveling. At night **get some sleep.** By day **eat light meals, drink water (not alcohol, which dehydrates), and move about the cabin** to stretch your legs. Many carriers have prohibited smoking throughout their systems; others allow smoking only on certain routes or even certain departures from that route, so **contact your carrier regarding its smoking policy.**

COMPLAIN IF NECESSARY

If your baggage goes astray or your flight goes awry, complain right away. Most carriers require that you file a claim immediately.

➤ AIRLINE COMPLAINTS: U.S. Department of Transportation **Aviation Consumer Protection Division** (✉ C-75, Room 4107, Washington, DC 20590, ☎ 202/366–2220). **Federal Aviation Administration (FAA) Consumer Hotline** (☎ 800/322–7873).

AIRPORTS

The major gateways to Vietnam are Ho Chi Minh City's Tan Son Nhat Airport and Hanoi's Noi Bai Airport. Tan Son Nhat Airport was the U.S. military airport in Saigon and was once the busiest landing strip in the world. As the main gateway for thousands of *Viet Kieu,* returning overseas Vietnamese who still raise suspicion among the country's government workers, Ho Chi Minh City's airport has procedures that can involve more in-depth immigration checks and baggage searches—if customs (☞ Customs & Duties, *below*) has any reason to be suspicious.

Hanoi's Noi Bai Airport, despite the aging Soviet MiGs resting on the runway, feels less like an airport serving the capital of a nation of 80 million people and more like a regional landing strip. The crumbling terminal brings to mind 1970s utilitarian Soviet chic, but at least the arrival procedures are relatively painless.

In general, at both airports you are more than likely to get through immigration, pick up your waiting bags, and breeze in and out of customs before you break a sweat.

➤ AIRPORT INFORMATION: **Noi Bai Airport** (✉ 35 km/22 mi north of Hanoi, ☎ 04/821–6660). **Tan Son Nhat Airport** (✉ Hoang Van Thu Blvd., Tan Binh District, 7 km/4 mi from central Ho Chi Minh City, ☎ 08/844–3179).

AIRPORT TAXES

Every time you fly into or out of an airport in Vietnam, whether on a domestic or international flight, you must pay an airport tax. The airport tax for domestic flights is either 15,000d or $2. For international flights you must pay either 70,000d or $7 if you depart from Hanoi and either 80,000d or $10 if you depart from Ho Chi Minh City. You must get your boarding pass and airport tax receipt before going through the security check.

AIRPORT TRANSFERS

Figuring out how to get into Hanoi or Ho Chi Minh City from the airport can be a little overwhelming when you first arrive. There are a few options: Either **have your hotel or tour company arrange to pick you up, or take a taxi or shuttle bus** into the city center. Outside both the Hanoi and Ho Chi Minh City airports, a crush of taxi drivers waits, all jockeying for your business. Don't be put off: Just choose an official-looking one and be on your way. *See* Chapters 2 and 6 for more information about traveling between the airport and the city center.

B

BICYCLING

In scenic cities like Hanoi and Hue, biking can be an ideal way to get around town, see the sights, and in the case of Hoi An and Nha Trang, head to the beach. However, **bicycling is generally not recommended in Ho Chi Minh City** because of the smog and heavy traffic; the city is also much more spread out than others in Vietnam. You can rent Vietnamese-made bicycles or the sturdier Phoenix bicycles from China for 25,000d–35,000d per day from most tourist cafés and some hotels and tourist agencies. Make sure the bike has an attached wheel lock or borrow a lock from the owner.

Hardy travelers have been known to bring their own mountain bikes and cycle the length of the country. Bikes can be placed on ferries, buses, and trains at an added cost, which varies by destination. A few tour operators organize bike trips across the country (☞ Tour Operators, *below*).

BOAT TRAVEL

For many riverside or seaside towns in Vietnam, boat rides are a natural attraction, sometimes the only way to get around, and a great way to get a view of life on, in, or near the water. Areas like the Mekong Delta are only worthwhile if you travel by boat. Even if you do not go through a travel agency or tourist office, cheap boats for hire will certainly find you—probably before you even get to the water's edge. With a bit of bargaining you can negotiate yourself a deal, and apart from paying more than the locals for the same trip, you can count on being delivered safely back to your starting point. Just **make absolutely sure you agree on a price before you set off.** In northern Vietnam and in the Mekong Delta ferries are often the only way to get to destinations where bridges have not yet been built or have been destroyed, or to get to islands such as Cat Ba. Bicycles, cars, and motorbikes can usually be brought on board for a fee.

BORDER CROSSINGS

Air travel is the recommended way to go between Vietnam and other points in Asia. You must **get a visa to visit most countries near Vietnam**—Laos, Cambodia, and China—which can be difficult; you're best off trying to make visa arrangements before you go to Vietnam. The exception is Thailand, which generally automatically grants short-term-stay visas to most Western visitors.

Going overland from Vietnam to other points is not recommended because it is arduous and risky, though border crossings with China have been simplified in the past few years. To go to China you need to get a standard tourist visa for entry into the country from Vietnam, as well as the appropriate exit permit attached to your visa to Vietnam; inquire about this procedure when applying for your visa to Vietnam and at the Chinese embassy. Vietnam–China border crossings include Mong Cai, Dong Dang (north of Lang Son), and Lao Cai (near Sapa). Two trains per week run from Hanoi to Beijing, crossing at Dong Dang. The trip takes 55 hours.

➤ VISA OFFICES: **Chinese Embassy Visa Section** (✉ 520 12th Ave., New York, NY, 10036, ☎ 212/330–7409; ✉ 40 Tran Phu St., Hanoi, ☎ 04/845–3736, FAX 04/823–2826). **Cambodia** (✉ 4500 16th St. NW, Washington, DC 20011, ☎ 202/726–7742); ✉ 71 Tran Hung Dao St., Hanoi, ☎ 04/825–3788, FAX 04/826–5225).

BUS TRAVEL

Though an extensive and dirt-cheap public bus system services every nook and cranny of the country, these buses are the most uncomfortable way to travel in Vietnam. Buses are often overcrowded, cramped, unbearably hot, and notoriously loud, and roads can be rough. They also break down like clockwork and operate under arbitrary schedules. Departure times depend on when they fill up, and arrival times depend on how many times they stop to pick up passengers—who are sometimes carrying pigs, chickens, snakes, goats, or fish—by the roadside.

Air-conditioned minibuses are a better alternative and are only slightly more expensive; these are often available at or near most bus stations. An even better option is to **take the more convenient, reliable, and infinitely more comfortable privately-run tour buses** organized by travel agencies, tourist offices, and travel cafés to most destinations. Even the most budget-conscious backpackers opt for the minivans or the reasonable tourist buses.

Sinh Café Travel, based in Ho Chi Minh City (☞ Chapter 6), has created a niche market with its privately run, open tour bus schedules. For $35 you **get an open-ended ticket on the Sinh Café bus** that enables you to break your journey at several points—Ho Chi Minh City, Nha Trang, Dalat, Hoi An, Hue, and Ninh Binh—en route to Hanoi. You can stop for as much time as you can spare at each stop on this tour itinerary; the Sinh Cafe's 45-seat air-conditioned bus leaves daily from these stops. Service is run in partnership with several smaller agencies that have their own buses. Since the service is not a tour but a private means of transportation, you have the flexibility to stay (or not) in any of the stops for any number of days before hooking up with the next available seat arranged by the Sinh Café office at each of these points. The buses also stop at various sights along the way.

➤ PRIVATE BUSES: **Sinh Café Travel** (✉ 179 Pham Ngu Lao St., District 1, Ho Chi Minh City, ☎ 08/835–5601). *See* individual chapters for information on travel agencies and other tourist cafés that organize bus trips around the country.

➤ STATE-RUN BUS COMPANIES: *See* individual chapters for information on services.

BUSINESS GROUPS & COMMERCE OFFICES

Many international business groups and chambers of commerce have opened offices in Hanoi and Ho Chi Minh City to serve the growing community of foreigners living in Vietnam and doing business there. You are usually welcome at monthly meetings, forums, and business lunches put on by these organizations. There may be a fee for certain functions, especially if a meal is involved.

➤ LOCAL GROUPS: **American Chamber of Commerce** (✉ 17 Ngo Quyen St., 1st floor, Hanoi, ☎ 04/934–0325, FAX 04/934–0323; ✉ New World Hotel, 76 Le Lai St., Room 357, District 1, Ho Chi Minh City, ☎ 08/824–3562, FAX 08/824–35720. **British Business Group** (✉ British Embassy, 31 Hai Ba Trung St., Hanoi, ☎ 04/825–2510, FAX 04/826–5762; ✉ 25 Le Duan St., ground floor, District 1, Ho Chi Minh City, ☎ FAX 08/822–5172). **Canadian Vietnam Business Association** (✉ IMAC,103 Pasteur St., District 1, Ho Chi Minh City, ☎ 08/822–9632, FAX 08/822–9633). **United States Foreign Commercial Office** (✉ 31 Hai Ba Trung St., 4th floor, Hanoi, ☎ 04/824–2422, FAX 04/824–2421).

BUSINESS HOURS

Small family-run shops seem to stay open indefinitely, primarily because living and working quarters are often one and the same. Many offices, museums, and government-run agencies are open weekdays and Saturday in the morning from 7:30 or 8 until 11:30 and from 1 or 1:30 to 4 or 5 in the afternoon but are generally closed on Sunday.

Banks are open on weekdays and on Saturday morning until 11. Post offices are open seven days a week. Cafés and restaurants are open all day, almost every day. Most sidewalk stalls serving breakfast and lunch finish by 2 and don't reopen for dinner until 4. By 10 PM in Hanoi and 11 PM in Ho Chi Minh City activity starts slowing down; smaller cities die down even earlier. In bigger cities more popular venues stay open much later. You can always find late-night noodle stands. Bars and nightclubs usually close at about 1 AM or whenever the last customer leaves.

Vietnam has a tradition of afternoon siestas (especially in the countryside), which means that all activities except eating tend to stop during lunch, between 11:30 and 2. Urban life is changing rapidly in Vietnam, however, and as free-market economics affect Ho Chi Minh City and Hanoi, more and more businesses are staying open during lunchtime to accommodate the increasing number of tourists and office-bound Vietnamese who use their midday break as a time to catch up on shopping or chores.

C

CAMERAS, CAMCORDERS, & COMPUTERS

Always keep your film, tape, and computer disks out of the sun. Carry an extra supply of batteries, and **be prepared to turn on your camera, camcorder, or laptop** to prove to security personnel that the device is real. Always **ask for hand inspection of film,** which becomes clouded after successive exposure to airport X-ray machines, and **keep videotapes and computer disks away from metal detectors.**

If you're bringing a laptop, check to see whether your computer's adapter can take 220 volts, the electrical voltage used in Vietnam. It is also advisable to **use an electrical surge protector** because power surges can cause permanent damage to your computer. Internal modems are particularly susceptible to power surges, especially when electricity returns after a power cut. Also, be sure to unplug your equipment after use. For longer stays, consider investing in a voltage stabilizer.

➤ PHOTO HELP: Kodak Information Center (☎ 800/242–2424). *Kodak Guide to Shooting Great Travel Pictures,* available in bookstores or from Fodor's Travel Publications (☎ 800/533–6478; $16.50 plus $4 shipping).

CUSTOMS

Before departing, consider registering your camera, camcorder, or laptop computer with U.S. Customs (☞ Customs & Duties, *below*). Upon arrival in Vietnam it is a good idea to **declare your camera, camcorder, laptop computer, and any other expensive electronics** that you want to take into and then out of the country.

CAR RENTAL

At present, **you (as a tourist) are not permitted to drive a car yourself.** The only foreigners allowed to drive are those with business or diplomatic visas who have registered with the Ministry of Transportation and obtained a Vietnamese driver's license (exceptions are made for Laotian and Chinese nationals). These cumbersome procedures—and the hectic state of the country's traffic—assure that very few foreigners find themselves behind the wheel. A few American car-rental companies, such as Hertz, Thrifty, and Avis have been negotiating with authorities to set up car-rental agencies in Hanoi and Ho Chi Minh City, but as yet no licenses have been signed. Even if a deal is inked, the first step is likely to be chauffeur-driven rental cars, not self-driven ones.

A rented car automatically comes with a driver who will, hopefully, speak some English. Cars and minivans with drivers are readily available from private and state-run travel agencies, tourist offices, and through most hotels in bigger cities like Ho Chi Minh City, Hanoi, Hue, Danang, Nha Trang, and Vung Tau. You are charged either by the kilometer or by the day, or both. A daily rate runs anywhere from $30 to $60 per day, depending on the city in which you rent the vehicle, whether the vehicle has air-conditioning, the make of the car, and your bargaining skills. The agreed-on price should include gas and tolls (but clarify all this before you set off). Travel agencies can also arrange for English-speaking guides to accompany you and the driver.

The most common type of vehicles for rent are Japanese-made sedans and minivans, though some older Russian Volgas and small, new Korean Kias (some made through a Vietnamese joint venture) are available from smaller agencies. Four-wheel-drive vehicles such as Toyota Landcruisers and Mitsubishi Pajeros are ideal for major forays into river deltas, highlands, or mountains, but there aren't many of these available for rent, and they are often twice the price of a sedan. Remember that you must **negotiate a price in advance and check out the vehicle before you rent**

it. Note that the name *Landcruiser* is overused in Vietnam, especially in Hanoi. Too many people consider a Landcruiser—made only by Toyota—to be any four-wheel-drive vehicle that's not a Russian Jeep. For more information on getting around by car in Vietnam, *see* Driving, *below.*

CHILDREN & TRAVEL

Traveling with very young children to Vietnam is not recommended, especially because of health considerations—young children's immune systems are not as developed as those of adults, and Vietnam doesn't have emergency children's medical care up to international standards. One hospital that does treat children, however, is the Olaf Palme Swedish Hospital (Vien Nhi Thuy Dien Olaf Palme), in Hanoi (☞ Emergencies *in* Chapter 2).

Few restaurants have high chairs, although diapers, baby bottles, and canned milk are available at minimarkets. Hotels, particularly those of international standard, are usually happy to add a cot or small bed to your room to accommodate children. Some hotels offer this service free for children under 12 and at only 10%–20% of the room rate for those over 12 years old. Separate rooms for children are likely to be cheaper; when making reservations, **ask if you can get a discount for your children and what the cutoff age is for these.**

If you do travel to Vietnam with young ones, brace yourself—and your child—for an interesting trip. Foreign youngsters, particularly Caucasians and especially blondes, are the center of attention almost everywhere they go in Vietnam—even in the major cities. People may want to hold your baby and may even take him or her across the street to show a friend—often without asking. Toddlers get pinched, poked, hugged, squeezed, and even grabbed between the legs or, worse, have their pants pulled down to see if they're "cut from the same cloth" as Vietnamese children. Of particular annoyance is the regularity with which fawning bystanders or complete strangers touch Western babies, especially on the face and mouth. Intestinal parasites can be transmitted by hands, so be sure people's fingers are clean before they start poking and prodding. No malice is intended by any of this, but it can be stressful.

Overall, be sure to plan ahead and **involve your youngsters** as you outline your trip. When packing, include things to keep them busy en route. On sightseeing days try to schedule activities of special interest to your children.

FLYING

As a general rule infants under 2 not occupying a seat fly at greatly reduced fares and occasionally for free. If your children are 2 or older, **ask about children's airfares.** Vietnam Airlines issues half-price tickets for children 12 or under; infants up to 2 years old are charged only the airport tax.

In general the adult baggage allowance applies to children paying half or more of the adult fare. When booking, **ask about carry-on allowances** for those traveling with infants. In general, for babies charged 10% of the adult fare you are allowed one carry-on bag and a collapsible stroller, which may have to be checked; you may be limited to less if the flight is full.

According to the FAA it's a good idea to use safety seats aloft for children weighing less than 40 pounds. Airlines, however, can set their own policies: U.S. carriers allow FAA-approved models but usually require that you buy a ticket, even if your child would otherwise ride free, since the seats must be strapped into regular seats. Airline rules vary regarding their use, so it's important to **check your airline's policy about using safety seats during takeoff and landing.** Safety seats cannot obstruct any of the other passengers in the row, so get an appropriate seat assignment as early as possible.

When making your reservation, **request children's meals or a free-standing bassinet** if you need them; the latter are available only to those seated at the bulkhead, where there's enough legroom. Remember, however, that bulkhead seats may not have their own overhead bins, and there's no storage space in front of you—a major inconvenience.

CONSUMER PROTECTION

Whenever possible, **pay with a major credit card** so you can cancel payment if there's a problem and you can provide documentation. This is a good practice whether you're buying travel arrangements before your trip or shopping at your destination.

If you're doing business with a particular company for the first time, **contact your local Better Business Bureau and the attorney general's offices** in your state and the company's home state, as well. Have any complaints been filed?

Finally, if you're buying a package or tour, always **consider travel insurance** that includes default coverage (☞ Insurance, *below*).

➤ LOCAL BBBS: **Council of Better Business Bureaus** (✉ 4200 Wilson Blvd., Suite 800, Arlington, VA 22203, ☎ 703/276–0100, FAX 703/525–8277).

CUSTOMS & DUTIES

When shopping, **keep receipts** for all your purchases. Upon leaving Vietnam and reentering your country, **be ready to show customs officials what you've bought.** Keep in mind that **it is illegal to export antiques and wooden furniture** unless you get special permission to do so (☞ Shopping, *below*). If you purchase an item that looks like an antique, be sure to get a note from the store owner stating that it is not.

If you feel a duty is incorrect, appeal the assessment. If you object to the way your clearance was handled, get the inspector's badge number. In either case, first ask to see a supervisor, then write to the port director at the address listed on your receipt. Send a copy of the receipt and other appropriate documentation. If you still don't get satisfaction, you can take your case to customs headquarters.

ENTERING VIETNAM

When you enter Vietnam, you will be given a yellow customs declaration slip and a green departure slip. You need these to get out of the country, so **do not lose your customs forms** (if you do, a customs search, a fine, and a long delay are likely when you try to leave the country). Do not attempt to bring any weapons, pornographic materials, or anything that could be considered subversive into Vietnam, as you may receive a hefty fine, be detained, or in extreme cases, jailed. It is a good idea to **declare cameras, camcorders, laptop computers, and any other expensive electronics** that you want to take out of the country again, though it's not required.

ENTERING THE U.S.

You may bring home $400 worth of foreign goods duty free if you've been out of the country for at least 48 hours and haven't already used the $400 allowance or any part of it in the past 30 days.

Travelers 21 and older may bring back 1 liter of alcohol duty free. In addition, regardless of your age, you are allowed 200 cigarettes and 100 non-Cuban cigars. (At press time a federal rule restricting tobacco access to persons 18 years and older did not apply to importation.) Antiques, which the U.S. Customs Service defines as objects more than 100 years old, enter duty free, as do original works of art done entirely by hand, including paintings, drawings, and sculptures.

You may also send packages home duty free: up to $200 worth of goods for personal use, with a limit of one parcel per addressee per day (and no alcohol or tobacco products or perfume worth more than $5); label the package PERSONAL USE and attach a list of its contents and their retail value. Do not label the package UNSOLICITED GIFT, or your duty-free exemption will drop to $100. Mailed items do not affect your duty-free allowance on your return.

➤ INFORMATION: **U.S. Customs Service** (Inquiries: ✉ Box 7407, Washington, DC 20044, ☎ 202/927–6724; complaints: ✉ Office of Regulations and Rulings, 1301 Constitution Ave. NW, Washington, DC 20229; registration of equipment: ✉ Resource Management, 1301 Constitution Ave. NW, Washington, DC 20229, ☎ 202/927–0540).

ENTERING CANADA

If you've been out of Canada for at least seven days, you may bring in C$500 worth of goods duty-free. If you've been away for fewer than seven days but more than 48 hours, the duty-free allowance drops to C$200; if your trip lasts 24–48 hours, the allowance is C$50. You may not pool allowances with family members. Goods claimed under the C$500 exemption may follow you by mail; those claimed under the lesser exemptions must accompany you.

Alcohol and tobacco products may be included in the seven-day and 48-hour exemptions but not in the 24-hour exemption. If you meet the age requirements of the province or territory through which you reenter Canada, you may bring in, duty-free, 1.14 liters (40 imperial ounces) of wine or liquor *or* 24 12-ounce cans or bottles of beer or ale. If you are 16 or older you may bring in, duty-free, 200 cigarettes and 50 cigars; these items must accompany you.

You may send duty-free to Canada an unlimited number of gifts worth up to C$60 each. Label the package UNSOLICITED GIFT—VALUE UNDER $60. Alcohol and tobacco are excluded.

➤ INFORMATION: **Revenue Canada** (✉ 2265 St. Laurent Blvd. S, Ottawa, Ontario K1G 4K3, ☎ 613/993–0534, 800/461–9999 in Canada).

ENTERING THE U.K.

From countries outside the EU, including Vietnam, you may import, duty-free, 200 cigarettes or 50 cigars; 1 liter of spirits or 2 liters of fortified or sparkling wine or liqueurs; 2 liters of still table wine; 60 milliliters of perfume; 250 milliliters of toilet water; plus £136 worth of other goods, including gifts and souvenirs.

➤ INFORMATION: **HM Customs and Excise** (✉ Dorset House, Stamford St., London SE1 9NG, ☎ 0171/202–4227).

CYCLOS

Cyclos (pedicabs), the bicycle-drawn buggies that are unfortunately on the verge of becoming outlawed, provide the most entertaining and cheapest means of transportation in Vietnam. In Ho Chi Minh City the cyclos are too narrow to seat two healthy Westerners; in Hanoi the cyclos are wider and may be able to accommodate more than one person. Although cyclo drivers are supposed to charge 2,000d per kilometer, they definitely deserve more since many double as informed English-speaking tour guides. Plan to pay 10,000d–25,000d per hour. Bargaining is advised, but it's worth giving the guys a break (and a tip).

D

DINING

A variety of eateries exists in Vietnam: small, basic Western-style restaurants serving Vietnamese food; upscale Western-style restaurants (including hotel restaurants), which can be surprisingly elegant and hip, serving Vietnamese, Chinese, Japanese, French, American, Italian, or other international cuisines; tourist cafés, which cater primarily to budget travelers, serving mediocre Western and Vietnamese dishes; stalls or stands on the street, surrounded by small plastic stools, serving very cheap and often quite good rice and noodle dishes; and peddlers selling food or coconut milk from their hand-carts or shoulder poles. As a rule the only restaurants that accept credit cards and perhaps traveler's checks are the more upscale places. However, if you do pay with plastic, these places may add a 4%–5% service charge to your bill.

For information on the types of cuisine available in Vietnam, *see* Pleasures and Pastimes *in* Chapter 1.

MEALTIMES

Breakfast is served beginning at 6 at most sidewalk stalls and 7 at most restaurants, lunch is served anywhere between 11:30 and 2, and dinner is available any time after 5 and usually before 8. Restaurants are generally open daily (except major holidays), and although Vietnamese eat dinner fairly early, most restaurants remain open well into the night, even after they are supposed to close.

PRECAUTIONS

It's important to **be careful of what you eat and drink** in Vietnam. Fresh, leafy vegetables are known to carry parasites, so avoid those of dubious origin or those likely to have been washed in tap water. Also, try to only eat fruit that has a peel. If you don't want some ingredient to be included, just ask (or gesture) for it not be added.

That said, dining at street-side food stands can be as safe or safer than eating in restaurants, especially in cities. The stands often serve fresher food than many restaurants because they have a faster turnover; they also prepare the food in front of you. Be more careful of food stalls once you are out of urban areas. Most of all, use common sense when choosing where to eat: pick a food stand, restaurant, or café that looks clean, is crowded, and has fresh food.

It is imperative that you **avoid drinking tap water as well as beverages with ice,** which is often made from local water. Most decent restaurants either make their own ice using boiled water or buy ice in bulk from huge freezer warehouses. You're best bet is to **drink bottled water,** particularly the La Vie and Evian brands.

Keep in mind that monosodium glutamate (MSG) is used in many dishes in Vietnam, particularly in the ubiquitous *pho* (noodle soup). If you don't want MSG in your food, ask—the cooks may not have already added it to the dish.

DISABILITIES & ACCESSIBILITY

Very few places in Vietnam, including hotels, restaurants, sites, and offices buildings, are fully wheelchair accessible. In many hotels makeshift ramps provide sufficient access into the building, but service areas such as restaurants, business centers, and rest rooms are up or down flights of stairs not serviced by elevators. Most elevators in larger hotels can accommodate wheelchairs, but very few guest rooms are equipped with large enough bathrooms or sufficient grab bars. Vietnam's newer hotels are the ones most likely to conform somewhat to international standards regarding wheelchair access and services for guests with disabilities.

City planning has largely ignored the requirements of the wheelchair-bound: There are virtually no curb cuts or permanent ramps, public transportation is inaccessible, and most office buildings have no elevators or escalators (some new office buildings, where many expatriates conduct business, have large elevators and temporary ramps). Taxi drivers often help passengers get from chair to backseat and back again. Cyclo drivers can also be helpful.

Vietnam Airlines claims it has the facilities and equipment to handle passengers using wheelchairs. The reality proves otherwise, however. When flying Vietnam Airlines, call ahead to be sure the appropriate equipment will be available at your departure and arrival points.

Health-care issues for travelers with disabilities should be well thought out before coming to Vietnam. Equipment of international-standard quality is for the most part unavailable, and hygiene is a concern.

➤ LOCAL RESOURCES: **Bright Futures for People with Disabilities** (✉ 190 Lo Duc St., Hanoi, ☎ 04/971–2894). **Vietnam Blind Association** (✉ 139 Nguyen Thai Hoc St., Hanoi, ☎ 04/845–2060, FAX 04/845–2682). **Vietnam Sports Association for the Disabled** (✉ 1B Le Hong Phong St., Hanoi, ☎ 04/843–2287, FAX 04/825–3172).

TIPS & HINTS

When discussing accessibility with an operator or reservationist, **ask hard questions.** Are there any stairs, inside *or* out? Are there grab bars next to the toilet *and* in the shower/tub? How wide is the doorway to the room? To the bathroom? For the most extensive facilities meeting the latest legal specifications, **opt for newer accommodations,** which are more likely to have been designed with access in mind. Older buildings or ships may offer more limited facilities. Be sure to **discuss your needs before booking.**

➤ COMPLAINTS: **Disability Rights Section** (✉ U.S. Department of Justice, Box 66738, Washington, DC 20035-6738, ☎ 202/514–0301 or 800/514–0301, FAX 202/307–1198, TTY 202/514–0383 or 800/514–0383) for general complaints. **Aviation Consumer Protection Division** (☞ Air Travel, *above*) for airline-related problems. **Civil Rights Office** (✉ U.S. Department of Transportation, Departmental Office of Civil Rights, S-30, 400 7th St. SW, Room 10215, Washington, DC 20590, ☎ 202/366–4648) for problems with surface transportation.

TRAVEL AGENCIES & TOUR OPERATORS

The Americans with Disabilities Act requires that travel firms serve the needs of all travelers. That said, you should note that some agencies and operators specialize in making travel arrangements for individuals and groups with disabilities.

➤ TRAVELERS WITH MOBILITY PROBLEMS: **Access Adventures** (✉ 206 Chestnut Ridge Rd., Rochester, NY 14624, ☎ 716/889–9096), run by a former physical-rehabilitation counselor. **Accessible Journeys** (✉ 35 W. Sellers Ave., Ridley Park, PA 19078, ☎ 610/521–0339 or 800/846–4537, FAX 610/521–6959), for escorted tours exclusively for travelers with mobility impairments. **Hinsdale Travel Service** (✉ 201 E. Ogden Ave., Suite 100, Hinsdale, IL 60521, ☎ 630/325–1335), a travel agency that benefits from the advice of wheelchair traveler Janice Perkins. **Wheelchair Journeys** (✉ 16979 Redmond Way, Redmond, WA 98052, ☎ 425/885–2210 or 800/313–4751), for general travel arrangements.

DISCOUNTS & DEALS

Be a smart shopper and **compare all your options before making a choice.** A plane ticket bought with a promotional coupon may not be cheaper than the least expensive fare from a discount ticket agency. For high-price travel purchases, such as packages or tours, keep in mind that what you get is just as important as what you save. Just because something is cheap doesn't mean it's a bargain.

DIAL FOR DOLLARS

To save money, **look into 1-800 or 1-888 discount reservations services,** which use their buying power to get a better price on hotels and airline tickets. When booking a room, always **call the hotel's local toll-free number** (if one is available) rather than the central reservations number—you'll often get a better price. Always ask about special packages or corporate rates.

When shopping for the best deal on hotels, **look for guaranteed exchange rates,** which protect you against a falling dollar. With your rate locked in you won't pay more even if the price goes up in the local currency.

You may also be able to **make a deal on room rates;** many of the newer, large hotels are not fully booked and may be willing to negotiate about room prices. It's worth asking about when you call.

➤ AIRLINE TICKETS: ☎ 800/FLY–4–LESS.

➤ HOTEL ROOMS: **Steigenberger Reservation Service** (☎ 800/223–5652). **Travel Interlink** (☎ 800/888–5898).

JOIN A CLUB?

Many companies sell discounts in the form of travel clubs and coupon books, but these cost money. You must use participating advertisers to get a deal, and only after you recoup the initial membership cost or book price do you begin to save. If you plan to use the club or coupons frequently, you may save considerably. Before signing up, find out what discounts you get for free.

➤ DISCOUNT CLUBS: **Entertainment Travel Editions** (✉ 2125 Butterfield Rd., Troy, MI 48084, ☎ 800/445–4137); $23–$48, depending on destination. **Great American Traveler** (✉ Box 27965, Salt Lake City, UT 84127, ☎ 800/548–2812); $49.95 per year. **Moment's Notice Discount Travel Club** (✉ 7301 New Utrecht Ave., Brooklyn, NY 11204, ☎ 718/234–6295); $25 per year, single or family. **Privilege Card International** (✉ 237 E. Front St., Youngstown, OH 44503, ☎ 330/746–5211 or 800/236–9732); $74.95 per year. **Sears's Mature Outlook** (✉ Box 9390, Des Moines, IA 50306, ☎ 800/336–6330); $14.95 per year. **Travelers Advantage** (✉ CUC Travel Service, 3033 S. Parker Rd., Suite 1000, Aurora, CO 80014, ☎ 800/548–1116 or 800/648–4037); $49 per year, single or family. **Worldwide Discount Travel Club** (✉ 1674 Meridian Ave., Miami Beach, FL 33139, ☎ 305/534–2082); $50 per year family, $40 single.

LOOK IN YOUR WALLET

When you use your credit card to make travel purchases, you may get free travel-accident insurance, collision-damage insurance, and medical or legal assistance, depending on the card and the bank that issued it.

American Express, MasterCard, and Visa provide one or more of these services, so **get a copy of your credit card's travel-benefits policy.**

SAVE ON COMBOS

Packages and guided tours can both save you money, but don't confuse the two. When you buy a package, your travel remains independent, just as though you had planned and booked the trip yourself. Fly/hotel packages, which combine airfare and accommodations, are often a good deal.

DRIVING

As a tourist you are currently not allowed to drive cars yourself, though you may drive motorbikes (☞ Motorbikes & Scooters, *below*). For more information on renting a car with a driver, *see* Car Rental, *above*.

BREAKDOWNS

If you have hired a car and driver for the day or longer and the car breaks down, you should not be held responsible for the cost of repairs. Make sure everyone is clear about this before you take off on a long journey. Your exemption from financial responsibility may be little consolation when your vehicle does break down, however. Mechanical and engine problems with Japanese-made sedans, Toyota Landcruisers, or Mitsubishi Pajeros, for instance, are rarer. But expect breakdowns in Russian-made Jeeps and cars. Most mechanical problems can be fixed, and there are mechanics on virtually every block in the cities.

As for motorbikes, the Japanese-made ones are quite dependable. If there's a problem in the cities, repair shops for these are also ubiquitous. In the countryside old East German Simsons and Soviet-era Minsk motorcycles are the standards. They break down regularly, but everyone claims to know how to fix them (though it's not always true), and parts—at least for the Minsks—are readily available.

GAS

Unleaded gasoline is sold by the liter in Vietnam. There are about 4 liters to the gallon. Gas stations sell at a government-regulated price of about 4,800d per liter. But **be careful: some gas station pumps issue a gas/oil mixture** (between 2% and 4% oil) for two-stroke motorcycles such as Minsks. Make sure you are getting the right gas for your vehicle. If communication proves impossible, find someone with a similar vehicle and watch what they pump into their vehicle. Gas is also sold by vendors on the street and at just about every corner in the cities—a fortunate option when stations are closed. Their price is slightly higher, however, and it's not unheard of for watered-down gas to be sold on the street.

MAPS

City maps and maps of Vietnam and Southeast Asia can be purchased from sidewalk vendors, hotel gift shops, bookstores, tourist cafés, and the ubiquitous postcard sellers who roam the city streets seeking out visitors. Detailed road atlases and topography maps of rural regions are, however, rare; they're also notoriously inaccurate.

PARKING

Any traveling by car you do will be with a hired driver, so he (drivers are rarely women) will be the one responsible for finding adequate parking. On many streets in Ho Chi Minh City and Hanoi it is now illegal to leave an unattended car; the streets are simply too narrow or crowded. Instead, cars—and motorbikes and bicycles—are often parked in guarded lots, driveways, even on roped off pieces of sidewalk. A few streets now have marked automobile parking, and some of the newer high-rises in Ho Chi Minh City and Hanoi have underground or elevated garages.

ROADS

The backbone of Vietnam's road system is Highway 1 or as its French builders called it, La Route des Mandarins. This narrow, crumbling road extends from near the Chinese border, north of Hanoi, through Ho Chi Minh City and to the heart of the Mekong Delta in the south. Other major roadways include: Highway 5 from Hanoi to Haiphong; Highway 6 out to Dien Bien Phu; Route 70, which bisects the northwest; Highway 7, the Nghe An Province route into Laos; Route 14 through the Central Highlands; Route 22, west out of Ho Chi Minh City toward Tay Ninh and the Cambodian capital of Phnom Penh; and Route 80, through the upper Mekong Delta.

Vietnam's major roads are for the most part paved. But all roads, except for a few spots such as the 16-km (10-mi) stretch on Highway 5, are slow going (96 km/60 mi takes about 90 minutes–2 hours, depending on the condition of the road). Thoroughfares labeled national roads cover only 12,000 km (7,500 mi) of Vietnam's transportation system; only 60% of these roads are paved. The lowest category of roads, called provincial or district roads, account for 40,000 km (25,000 mi) of the system. Only 8% of these are paved. Most dirt roads turn to mud during the rainy season and become impassable.

Highways are the main transport route for cars, public buses, transport trucks, tractors, motorbikes, bicycles, pedestrians, oxcarts, and a host of farm animals. Highway 1, for example, is the primary north–south commercial route.

Road conditions in the north are far worse than in the south, where the U.S. war effort built or paved many of the roads. But even these routes are suffering due to lack of maintenance or repair. Since the embargo was lifted on Vietnam, however, the World Bank and the Asian Development Bank have approved soft loans to upgrade much of Highway 1 and other roadways. So major progress has been made on certain stretches of Highway 1 and Highway 5.

When driving around the country, **try to travel during the day.** Driving at night can be hazardous since many vehicles don't have lights and it is difficult to see bad spots in the road.

RULES OF THE ROAD

Bicyclists, motorcyclists, and pedestrians take note: The romantic notion that Vietnamese city traffic is a crowded but mysterious ballet dance in which all parties approach each other in a calculated frenzy and then magically weave through to safety is, in a word, nonsense. Vietnam's traffic fatalities per capita per vehicle are among the highest in the world. Yes, there seems to be a vague understanding among riders, drivers, and pedestrians that they're all in it together. But this doesn't make the streets much safer.

When riding a motorbike or bicycle, **use your skills of prediction, timing, weaving, and of course honking.** And *always* give trucks, army jeeps, and buses the right-of-way. It's not that they won't necessarily *want* to stop for you—they just might not have any brakes. The best way to get through traffic on foot is to **walk at a steady pace across the street and, of course, watch out**; the oncoming vehicles will have a better chance of avoiding you if the drivers can get a sense of where you will be going next. If you stop suddenly, it is harder for drivers to judge where you are in relation to them.

In case of an accident, remember that the foreigner is always at fault. So, in minor accidents, even if you are not at fault it's a good idea to stay in the car and let your driver do the talking or to try to get out of the situation as quickly as possible without involving the police. Unless the case is crystal clear, you will probably be fighting a losing battle and will probably be asked to pay damages immediately even if you are not to blame.

E

ELECTRICITY

To use your U.S.-purchased electric-powered equipment, **bring a converter and adapter.** The electrical current in Vietnam is 220 volts, 50 cycles alternating current (AC); in the north and other parts of the country wall outlets take the continental European type, with two round plugs; they use the flat-pin type in much of the south. Many of the international hotels can provide you with converters and adapters. If your appliances are dual-voltage, you'll need only an adapter. Don't use 110-volt outlets, marked FOR SHAVERS ONLY, for high-wattage appliances such as blow-dryers. Most laptop computers operate equally well on 110 and 220 volts and so require only an adapter and a surge protector (☞ Cameras, Camcorders & Computers, *above*).

E-MAIL & THE INTERNET

Vietnam has had E-mail service since 1992, when the Institute of Information Technology, in Hanoi, linked up with a dial-back system at Coombs University in Australia. In Vietnam the main server is Netnam. For information on Netnam or VAREnet, another hopeful Internet service provider, contact the Institute of Information Technology. You can also **try the business centers in larger international hotels,** which often have E-mail you can use for a fee. You may also be able to hook up to your own server through the phone lines (though some hotels don't allow it), but this is very expensive—the cost of an overseas call.

There are dozens of Web sites dedicated to Vietnam and issues of interest to Vietnamese nationals, overseas Vietnamese, tourists to the country, and Vietnam War veterans. To find these, just run a search on your browser.

➤ LOCAL RESOURCES: **Institute of Information Technology** (✉ Hoang Quoc Viet St., Hanoi, ☎ 04/834–6907, FAX 04/834–5217, admin@netnam.org.vn).

EMBASSIES & CONSULATES

Embassies are in Hanoi and consulates in Ho Chi Minh City. If your passport is stolen or lost or you are in need of any other kind of emergency assistance, contact your country's embassy or consulate.

➤ CONSULATES: **Australia** (✉ 5B Ton Duc Thang St., District 1, ☎ 08/829–6035, FAX 08/829–6031). **Canada** (✉ 203 Dong Khoi St., District 1, Ho Chi Minh City, Room 102, ☎ 08/824–2000, ext. 1209; FAX 08/829–4528). **New Zealand** (✉ 41 Nguyen Thi Minh Khai St., District 1, 5th floor, ☎ 08/822–6907, FAX 08/822–6905). **U.K.** (✉ 25 Le Duan St., District 1, Ho Chi Minh City, ☎ 08/829–8433, FAX 08/822–1971). **U.S.** (✉ 51 Nguyen Dinh Chieu St., District 3, Ho Chi Minh City, ☎ 08/822–9433, FAX 08/822–9434).

➤ EMBASSIES: **Australia** (✉ Van Phuc Compound, Hanoi, ☎ 04/831–7755, FAX 04/831–7711). **Canada** (✉ 31 Hung Vuong St., Hanoi, ☎ 04/823–5500, FAX 04/823–5333). **New Zealand** (✉ 32 Hang Bai St., Hanoi, ☎ 04/824–2481, FAX 04/824–1480). **U.K.** (✉ 31 Hai Ba Trung St., Hanoi, ☎ 04/825–2510, FAX 04/826–5762). **U.S.** (✉ 7 Lang Ha St., Hanoi, ☎ 04/843–1500, FAX 04/843–1510).

EMERGENCIES

If something has been stolen from you, contact the police or your embassy (☞ Embassies & Consulates, *above*), especially regarding more costly items such as expensive jewelry or laptop computers. Also contact your embassy if your passport has been stolen or lost. For medical emergencies, seek assistance from local hospitals or clinics or from your hotel in more rural areas (☞ Health, *below, and* Emergencies *in* individual chapters).

➤ EMERGENCY NUMBERS: **Ambulance** (☎ 15). **Police** (☎ 17).

ETIQUETTE

Vietnamese people rarely say "no." Usually they answer in the positive—a way of avoiding confrontational situations. If a situation is unpleasant, most people simply stay quiet and ignore it until it passes. Anger is generally viewed as a sign of weakness and its display in public is considered ill-mannered. It is better to **remain calm and good-natured while trying to work out a disagreement with someone.**

Keep in mind that pointing at people and beckoning to them with your hand facing up is thought to be the height of rudeness. So remember to **call people with your hand facing down.** Patting children on the head is considered to be a bad omen and best avoided. In many pagodas you are required to remove your shoes before entering.

When hosting Vietnamese guests, be sure to offer drinks and food as soon as they arrive. It's considered impolite to simply ask if they would like anything. Also, Vietnamese women seldom drink beer or coffee, so have some green tea or soft drinks on hand. Don't be surprised if a social event ends quickly; they usually don't drag on too long in Vietnam unless you have gone out drinking or are doing business (☞ Getting Down to Business *in* Chapter 8, for more information about business practices).

Giving gifts to Vietnamese can be an unfulfilling affair for someone from the West. Often the recipient simply acknowledges the gift and carries on as before. But this is not a sign of disrespect; any gift is always highly appreciated.

H

HEALTH

As with any trip to a developing country, you should **check with the Centers for Disease Control and your physician** about current health risks in Vietnam and recommended vaccinations before you go.

Tetanus-diphtheria and polio vaccinations should be up to date—if you haven't been immunized since childhood, **consider bolstering your tetanus and polio vaccinations.** If you have never contracted measles, mumps, or rubella, you should also be immunized against them. Also note: **Immunizations for hepatitis A and typhoid fever are advised.** According to the Centers for Disease Control (CDC), there is a risk of contracting malaria only in rural areas of Vietnam, except in the Red River Delta and the coastal plain north of Nha Trang, which are safe. The CDC recommends taking mefloquine (brand name Larium) for malaria. Dengue fever occurs in Vietnam, though the risk for travelers is small except during periods of epidemic-size transmission; there is no vaccine to prevent it, therefore you should **take precautions against mosquito bites.** Malaria- and dengue-bearing mosquitoes bite at dusk and at night. No matter where you go, it's a good idea to protect yourself from mosquito-born illnesses with a good insect repellent containing Deet, and if you're in susceptible regions, use aerosol insecticides indoors, wear clothing that covers the body, and take mosquito nets. If you're staying for a month or more and are traveling to rural areas, you should be vaccinated against Japanese encephalitis; for six months or more, against hepatitis B as well. Some of these vaccinations require staggered treatments, so plan ahead.

A first-aid kit with antacids, antidiarrheal, cold medicine, Band-Aids, antiseptics, aspirin, and other items you may need is a good idea. Also, know your blood type and **bring enough medication to last the entire trip;** you may be able to get common prescription drugs in Vietnam, but don't count on their availability or their quality. Just in case, however, have your doctor write you a prescription using the drug's generic name because brand names vary from country to country. It also makes sense to **bring an extra pair of eyeglasses or contact lenses.**

Contamination of drinking water and fresh fruit and vegetables by fecal matter poses a major health risk in Vietnam; this contamination causes the common intestinal ailment known as traveler's diarrhea and sometimes is responsible for visitors contracting typhoid fever, hepatitis A, and parasites. Traveler's diarrhea can also be caused simply by a change of diet. It usually only lasts a few days; **if symptoms persist or worsen, seek medical assistance.** Two drugs recommended by the National Institutes of Health for mild cases of diarrhea can be purchased over the counter: Pepto-Bismol and loperamide (Imodium).

If you come down with the malady, rest as much as possible and **drink lots of fluids** (such as tea without milk, especially herbal tea). In severe cases rehydrate yourself with a salt-sugar mixture added to purified water (½ teaspoon of salt and 4 tablespoons of sugar per quart/liter of purified water). It's recommended you **avoid eating unpeeled fruit and uncooked vegetables or those you suspect have been washed in unboiled water** and drinking unbottled or unboiled water or ice made from unbottled or unboiled water. **Drink bottled water** such as Evian or La Vie; it's even a good idea to brush your teeth with it.

➤ HEALTH WARNINGS: **National Centers for Disease Control** (CDC; ✉ National Center for Infectious Diseases, Division of Quarantine, Traveler's Health Section, 1600 Clifton Rd., M/S E-03, Atlanta, GA 30333, ☎ 404/332–4559, FAX 404/332–4565, http://www.cdc.gov).

HOLIDAYS

The traditional lunar new year, known as Tet in Vietnam and celebrated throughout much of Southeast Asia, falls in January or February, depending on the lunar calendar. Other national holidays include: New Year's Day (January 1), the anniversary of the founding of the Vietnamese Communist Party (February 3); Liberation Day

(April 30), commemorating the day the North Vietnamese army took Saigon; International Workers Day, or May Day (May 1, the date following Liberation Day, which means a two-day holiday); Ho Chi Minh's birthday (May 19); National Day (September 2); and Christmas Day (December 25).

I

INSURANCE

Travel insurance is the best way to **protect yourself against financial loss.** The most useful policies are trip-cancellation-and-interruption, default, medical, and comprehensive insurance.

Without insurance you will lose all or most of your money if you cancel your trip, regardless of the reason. It's essential that you **buy trip-cancellation-and-interruption insurance,** particularly if your airline ticket, cruise, or package tour is nonrefundable and cannot be changed. When considering how much coverage you need, look for a policy that will cover the cost of your trip plus the nondiscounted price of a one-way airline ticket, should you need to return home early. Also **consider default or bankruptcy insurance,** which protects you against a supplier's failure to deliver.

Medicare generally does not cover health-care costs outside the United States, nor do many privately issued policies. If your own policy does not cover you outside the United States, **consider buying supplemental medical coverage.** Remember that travel health insurance is different from a medical-assistance plan (☞ Health, *above*).

Citizens of the United Kingdom can buy an annual travel-insurance policy valid for most vacations during the year in which it's purchased. If you are pregnant or have a preexisting medical condition, make sure you're covered.

If you have purchased an expensive vacation, particularly one that involves travel abroad, comprehensive insurance is a must. **Look for comprehensive policies that include trip-delay insurance,** which will protect you in the event that weather problems cause you to miss your flight, tour, or cruise. A few insurers sell waivers for preexisting medical conditions. Companies that offer both features include Access America, Carefree Travel, Travel Insured International, and Travel Guard (☞ *below*).

Always **buy travel insurance directly from the insurance company**; if you buy it from a travel agency or tour operator that goes out of business, you probably will not be covered for the agency or operator's default, a major risk. Before you make any purchase, **review your existing health and home-owner's policies** to find out whether they cover expenses incurred while traveling.

➤ TRAVEL INSURERS: In the U.S., **Access America** (✉ 6600 W. Broad St., Richmond, VA 23230, ☎ 804/285–3300 or 800/284–8300), **Carefree Travel Insurance** (✉ Box 9366, 100 Garden City Plaza, Garden City, NY 11530, ☎ 516/294–0220 or 800/323–3149), **Near Travel Services** (✉ Box 1339, Calumet City, IL 60409, ☎ 708/868–6700 or 800/654–6700), **Travel Guard International** (✉ 1145 Clark St., Stevens Point, WI 54481, ☎ 715/345–0505 or 800/826–1300), **Travel Insured International** (✉ Box 280568, East Hartford, CT 06128-0568, ☎ 860/528–7663 or 800/243–3174), **Travelex Insurance Services** (✉ 11717 Burt St., Suite 202, Omaha, NE 68154-1500, ☎ 402/445–8637 or 800/228–9792, FAX 800/867–9531), **Wallach & Company** (✉ 107 W. Federal St., Box 480, Middleburg, VA 20118, ☎ 540/687–3166 or 800/237–6615). In Canada, **Mutual of Omaha** (✉ Travel Division, 500 University Ave., Toronto, Ontario M5G 1V8, ☎ 416/598–4083, 800/268–8825 in Canada). In the U.K., **Association of British Insurers** (✉ 51 Gresham St., London EC2V 7HQ, ☎ 0171/600–3333).

L

LANGUAGE

Vietnamese, or *kinh,* is written in a Roman-based script, called *quoc ngu,* created by a French Jesuit scholar in the 17th century. Before that the Vietnamese created their own system, called *nom,* which drew on the Chinese system of characters. Although letters may look familiar, the language is tonally based and therefore quite foreign to Western ears. Barring a few exceptions in tones and words, written Vietnamese is homogenous throughout the country. However, accents differ dramatically, particularly between north and south. *See* the Vocabulary and Menu Guide at the end of this book for more information.

It's best to **use a phrase book as a point-and-show device,** though a little Vietnamese goes a long way. With a few Vietnamese words, you may find daily interchange—such as bargaining with cyclo drivers—much easier, so **attempt to learn at least numbers and some important pronouns and verbs.** (Some helpful phrases and words are listed in our Vocabulary and Menu Guide.) In large cities English is practically a second language; in the countryside, particularly outside tourist spots, communicating your desires or intentions can be difficult if you don't speak any Vietnamese. French is still spoken among an elite but shrinking crowd of older Vietnamese. A surprisingly large number of Hanoians can speak Russian, though there is hardly any opportunity for most of them to use it these days. English is by far the most widely used language in Vietnam's tourist trade.

LODGING

Graham Greene did much to romanticize hotel life in Vietnam in his book *The Quiet American.* But aside from the Continental Hotel in Ho Chi Minh City, immortalized in Greene's book, and a handful of other older institutions including the Sofitel Metropole in Hanoi, hotels in Vietnam have little old world mystery. The focus today is on newness; the vast majority of joint-venture, international-standard hotels in the nation are less than five years old. And unfortunately many of the older hotels that have survived the wrecking ball have fared poorly from years of neglect, bad management, and lack of funds.

The Vietnam National Administration of Tourism has instituted its own rating system, which vaguely conforms to international standards of quality. Yet hotels billed as five star in Vietnam are often more like three- or four-star hotels in the United States. Although hotel staffers are generally enthusiastic and some have received training in Korea or the West, really good service is still a rarity. A few hotels, however, are as luxurious and have as high standard of service as any international establishment in the world. Beach resorts are being developed along the coast, and two particular standouts are in Nha Trang and China Beach near Danang; another resort option is the majestically restored Sofitel Palace in the mountain town of Dalat.

In Hanoi, Ho Chi Minh City, and other major tourist destinations the hotel industry continues to grow, and more and more international and smaller-size hotels are opening up. Many of the larger, international hotels often aren't fully booked and may be ready to give you a better room rate than listed; when calling to make reservations, **ask if you can get a deal on the price of a room.**

Besides the surprisingly pricey international properties, Vietnam has a selection of other accommodations. Mid-size, mid-level hotels and guest houses are generally state run and are usually perfectly acceptable for a night's sleep, especially in cities and popular tourist areas. Yet another good option is minihotels. Unique to Vietnam, these privately-owned, often family-run operations range from the utilitarian to the plush; they usually provide friendly service, spotless if basic rooms, and a homey environment. Although such facilities as discos, swimming pools, and exercise facilities are rare at these hotels and their restaurants are often bland and lifeless, guest rooms generally have air-conditioning and sometimes include satellite TV, IDD telephones, refrigerators, and bathtubs. Unfortunately, sometimes they also include lots of street noise.

In smaller towns or rural areas expect much more basic accommodations. Phones, televisions, and fax machines are the norm at most hotels outside the major cities, even the smaller ones, but don't expect luxury in anything but the country's most popular destinations. If you are going to very off-the-beaten-path places you may not have much choice in the kind of place in which you stay—the one or two guest houses in town, which may not be up to your usual standard, may be your only lodging option.

M

MAIL

When mailing packages into and out of Vietnam, be aware that your parcels will probably be scrutinized at the post office. **Note that videotapes, books, and compact discs are especially sensitive items to ship or mail** to and from Vietnam. Delivery times for mail going into and out of the country have been shortened substantially over the last few years. Expect about two weeks, sometimes longer, for mail to arrive in the West from Vietnam.

EXPRESS MAIL SERVICES

The U.S. Postal Service, DHL, FedEx, and UPS all have express mail services to Vietnam. Unfortunately the service isn't always that fast: It can take from four to seven days, depending on how long the package sits in customs.

➤ LOCAL ADDRESSES: **DHL** (✉ 150 Lang Rd. or 1 Le Thach St., Hanoi; 2 Cong Xa Paris St., District 1, Ho Chi Minh City). **FedEx** (✉ 6 Dinh Le St., Hanoi, ☎ 04/824–9054; ✉ 1 Nguyen Hau St., District 1, Ho Chi Minh City, ☎ 08/829–0747). **UPS** (✉ 4C Dinh Le St., Hanoi, ☎ 04/824–6483; 80F Nguyen Du St., District 1, Ho Chi Minh City, ☎ 08/824–3597).

POSTAL RATES

Postage is based on weight. On average, a postcard or letter to the United States costs about 13,000d; one to Europe costs about 11,000d. Stamps are sold at post office (*buu dien*) branches, which are generally open daily 6 AM–8 PM, and at many hotels and shops. Usually the postal clerk will cancel the stamps on your letter and give it back to you to put into the mail slot. This policy exists in part to eliminate any possibility of stamps being peeled off your letter for resale and your letter thrown away.

RECEIVING MAIL

Don't be surprised if you receive an already-opened parcel—just be grateful it arrived at all. Most parcels are opened as a matter of course, and sometimes the recipient in Vietnam is charged for the "service" of checking the parcel. In lieu of the parcel, you may receive a note providing information on where to collect a particular piece of mail. Items such as videos, books, compact discs, and cassettes should not be sent through the mail, as they rarely arrive at their destination. Because such packages make many stops along the way, they become too tempting to resist, and opportunities abound for theft or loss. And even if they do arrive, they're sometimes confiscated or checked for subversive material. Such "quarantines" for videos sometimes provides opportunity for replication by unscrupulous postal clerks or customs officials before they're handed over to you. Most letters and postcards will arrive within about two weeks of being mailed from abroad.

The main post offices in Hanoi and Ho Chi Minh City (☞ individual chapters for addresses) have Poste Restante, where you can have mail sent to you from abroad.

MEDICAL ASSISTANCE

MEDICAL CARE

Vietnam's medical infrastructure is not up to international standards. Hospitals and pharmacies are often undersupplied and out of date. Only a handful of Vietnamese doctors have top-quality Western training. Foreign insurance is very rarely accepted, so you should **expect to pay immediately in cash on completion of treatment.** The larger hospitals in Hanoi and Ho Chi Minh City have experience treating foreigners (mainly due to motorcycle accidents, the biggest cause of injury or death of Westerners in Vietnam), but there are few, if any, Western physicians based at these institutions. Blood supply is a serious problem in Vietnam: The nation's blood banks are small and, say Western doctors, insufficiently screened.

Foreign-run medical clinics offering basic treatment and 24-hour on-call services can guide you to local hospitals for more serious operations and can arrange for emergency medical evacuation to better hospitals in other countries in the region—Medevac planes dedicated to Vietnam are on standby in Singapore. Embassies have duty officers on call who can assist with logistics. If you get sick outside Hanoi or Ho Chi Minh City, get yourself to those cities as soon as possible. For more information on medical care, *see* individual chapters.

MEDICAL PLANS

No one plans to get sick while traveling, but it happens, so **consider signing up with a medical-assistance company.** Members get doctor referrals, emergency evacuation or repatriation, 24-hour telephone hot lines for medical consultation, cash for emergencies, and other personal and legal assistance. Coverage varies by plan, so **review the benefits carefully.**

➤ MEDICAL-ASSISTANCE COMPANIES: **International SOS Assistance** (✉ Box 11568, Philadelphia, PA 19116, ☎ 215/244–1500 or 800/523–8930; ✉ 1255 University St., Suite 420, Montréal, Québec H3B 3B6, ☎ 514/874–7674 or 800/363–0263; ✉ 7 Old Lodge Pl., St. Margaret's, Twickenham TW1 1RQ, England, ☎ 0181/744–0033). **MEDEX Assistance Corporation** (✉ Box 5375, Timonium, MD 21094-5375, ☎ 410/453–6300 or 800/537–2029). **Traveler's Emergency Network** (✉ 3100 Tower Blvd., Suite 1000B, Durham, NC 27707, ☎ 919/490–6055 or 800/275–4836, FAX 919/493–8262). **Worldwide Assistance Services** (✉ 1133 15th St. NW, Suite 400, Washington, DC 20005, ☎ 202/331–1609 or 800/821–2828, FAX 202/828–5896).

MONEY

CURRENCY

The Vietnamese unit of currency is the dong (abbreviated as *d* throughout this guide), which comes in 100d, 200d, 500d, 1,000d, 2,000d, 5,000d, 10,000d, 20,000d and 50,000d notes. Since a 50,000d note is worth less than $5, you have to lug around quite a few notes. It's a good idea to **keep plenty of 5,000d, 10,000d, and 20,000d notes handy for cyclos, cabs, and snacks.** Pulling out 50,000d for a bowl of noodles that costs 5,000d is viewed by many Vietnamese like paying with gold bullion. Familiarize yourself with the 5,000d and 20,000d notes, as they are the same color. The many zeros on bills sometimes makes it difficult to see the difference between 5,000d and 50,000d notes, as does the appearance of Ho Chi Minh's countenance on every banknote.

EXCHANGING MONEY

The official exchange rate at press time was about 12,300d to the U.S. dollar, 8,600d to the Canadian dollar, and 19,700d to the British pound. The Vietnamese dong has been impressively stable over the last few years, though perhaps artificially stable. Between 1994 and mid-1997 the value of the dong changed less than 5% against the U.S. dollar. But in late 1997 the dong dropped 5% in *four weeks,* forcing investors to speculate about a further deflation. It is advisable to **keep tabs on the exchange rate.**

Although traveler's checks are accepted for exchange at many places, cash—in the form of U.S. dollars or dong—is much more widely accepted (☞ Forms of Payment, *below*). It's best to **bring at least a few hundred dollars in cash** or as much as you feel comfortable carrying. A money belt is good idea.

The Bank for Foreign Trade of Vietnam, or Vietcom Bank, has numerous branches all over the country and gives the official government rate. International banks have a presence in Vietnam and offer extensive banking services, including currency exchange, cash transfers, and cash advances on credit cards. Although they don't often have the best exchange rates, hotels are convenient places to change money. You can usually get the highest exchange rates in gold or jewelry shops, which are eager to convert their business profits into dollars. Although there was no visible police crackdown on black marketers in Hanoi or Ho Chi Minh City at press time, using the services of black-market money changers is a high-risk option. Plus they don't always really give you the best rate, and they have been known to cheat customers. Note that at many places you may **get a better exchange rate using higher-denomination bills** (i.e., a $50 instead of a $10).

➤ EXCHANGE SERVICES: **International Currency Express** (☎ 888/842–0880 on the East Coast or 888/278–6628 on the West Coast for telephone orders). **Thomas Cook Currency Services** (☎ 800/287–7362 for telephone orders and retail locations).

FORMS OF PAYMENT

Credit cards have yet to catch on as a form of payment by Vietnamese, but they are accepted at most large international hotels, upscale restaurants, better shops, large tour operators such as Saigon Tourist, and airline agencies. Hotels and shops sometimes insist on a service charge of up to 4% if you pay by credit card, however. MasterCard and Visa are the most widely accepted cards. Some locations also accept American Express and Diners Club.

Traveler's checks are also accepted in Vietnam but not by every place and especially not in rural areas and small towns. You should **ascertain from an individual establishment whether it accepts traveler's checks,** particularly the type you are carrying, before assuming you can use them. (Banks that issue traveler's checks will tell you every place should take them, which may be correct but isn't always true.) Banks in Vietnam charge a fee, usually 1%–2%, for cashing traveler's checks into dollars. The fee is lower if you cash the checks for dong. If your checks are lost or stolen, they can usually be replaced within 24 hours. To ensure a speedy refund, buy your checks yourself (don't ask someone else to make the purchase). When making a claim for stolen or lost checks, the person who bought the checks should make the call.

Technically it is illegal for many smaller establishments to receive payments in anything but Vietnamese dong, but such rules are widely ignored. U.S. dollars are accepted at almost every private business, but many state enterprises—including trains—only accept dong. It's recommended that you **carry both dong and dollars** with you at all times, especially in smaller denominations. Consider bringing $50–$100 in $1 and $5 denominations with you to Vietnam. Twenty- and fifty-dollar bills are good for exchanging money and for paying hotel bills. You should **take cash if your trip includes rural areas** and small towns.

Although rare, you can find a few ATMs in Hanoi and Ho Chi Minh City. For information about specific bank and ATM locations, *see* individual chapters.

WHAT IT WILL COST

Although Vietnam is not as much of a bargain as other Southeast Asian countries, it is still a relatively inexpensive destination. However, some upscale international hotels in Ho Chi Minh City and Hanoi command prices exceeding $200 per night. But this is far from average. Reasonably priced minihotels and guest houses (☞ Lodging, *above*) are abundant and can run under $35 per night in Hanoi or Ho Chi Minh City. Elsewhere they're even cheaper.

Food can be a steal. If you eat at small local restaurants, street-side cafés, food stalls, or markets, you'll pay between $1 and $5 and save hundreds over your counterparts. A meal at an upscale restaurant, including wine, costs an average of $15–$20.

Be aware that Vietnam has an official dual-pricing system, so **foreigners often are expected to pay more than double what locals do** for trains, buses, flights, and other goods and services. Admission to temples or tourist sites can be ten times more expensive for foreigners than for Vietnamese.

Sample Costs: Unless you are at a five-star hotel, a cup of coffee in a street café will cost you 2,500d (20¢); a cyclo ride will generally cost from 5,000d to 10,000d (from 45¢ to 75¢) per kilometer; a liter of *bia hoi* (fresh draft beer) is 2,500d (20¢); bottled beer goes for between 12,000d and 25,000d (about $1–$2); and a bowl of noodles from a food stall is 5,000d (45¢).

MOTORBIKES & SCOOTERS

One of the quickest ways to get around Vietnam's major cities is to ride on the back of a motorbike taxi, known as an *Honda om* or a *xe om.* This service usually costs about 20,000d. Motorbike drivers are often ex-cyclo drivers who have saved up enough money for a bike. They'll drive up alongside you and ask where you're going and whether you're interested in a ride. It's relatively safe to travel on motorbikes; unfortunately, the same can't be said for the roads, especially at rush hour.

You can also rent motorbikes and scooters in major cities at most tourist cafés and some hotels and guest houses for about 45,000d to 80,000d a day. A deposit is usually required along with a passport or a photocopy of one. Although automobile driving is off-limits for tourists, motorbike riding by tourists is generally accepted by the police; it is technically illegal, but few Vietnamese police seem to enforce this rule. Temporary insurance for tourists is basically nonexistent, and your own auto insurance generally does not apply. It's a good idea, however, to **make sure your medical insurance covers you in case of a motorbike accident,** even if you are only a passenger.

Driving a motorbike in Hanoi is easier than doing so in hectic Ho Chi Minh City, but traffic skills remain poor throughout the country. Traffic lights are often ignored, traffic police are treated with contempt, pedestrians seem oblivious to the flow—and danger—of vehicles, late-night construction workers play cards in the intersections, and children have been known to dart into streets without warning. It is imperative that you **use the horn** since most drivers rarely glance around before changing lanes. Unfortunately, since everyone uses the horn at every opportunity, it has become less of a warning and more of an announcement of one's status as a motorcycle rider. You should **wear a helmet.**

O

OUTDOOR ACTIVITIES & SPORTS

Sports such as badminton, martial arts, and Ping-Pong remain popular pastimes in Vietnam. In line with the old Soviet imperative of athletic prowess, Vietnamese schools stress gymnastics. The uneven parallel bars doesn't pack in the crowds, however, like Vietnam's new sport to watch: soccer. A national semiprofessional league fills stadiums during its autumn-to-spring season. There is a local team in almost every city and town in the nation. Vietnam considers the Southeast Asian Games, held every two years, to be a gauge of their success and competitiveness in the international sports arena.

Hanoi and Ho Chi Minh City have plenty of tennis courts, though rarely are they free. Golf courses are more popular in the south, although there is a course outside Hanoi and a driving range in the suburbs. Swimming pools can be found at many luxury hotels—inquire about one-day memberships. Some sports clubs in the cities also have pools, but they are not always clean or adequately treated—or even full of water.

Tourist cafés in Hanoi and Ho Chi Minh City have begun organizing trekking tours. Mountain biking has a bright future as an adventure activity, but in-country orchestration has proven difficult so far. Contact tour organizations for more information (☞ Tour Operators, *below*).

The coast has good spots for surfing, particularly Danang (the site of an international surfing competition in 1994). But for now, with the exception of hotel-affiliated diving clubs in China Beach near Danang and in Nha Trang, you need to bring your own surfboarding, snorkeling, and scuba-diving gear. Jet-skiing and paragliding clubs have opened in the resort towns of Vung Tau and Nha Trang, which also have a few scuba-diving schools.

For information on outdoor activities and sports in particular cities and regions, *see* individual chapters.

P

PACKING FOR VIETNAM

Since you never know where you will have to lug your bags, it is always a good idea to **pack light.** Bring luggage that is easy to carry and makes the most sense for your travel plans, whether that means a backpack (especially one that doubles as a bag), rolling suitcase, or duffle bag. Be sure to leave room in your suitcase or bring expandable totes for all your bargain purchases. A lock for your suitcase can come in handy, as can a cable lock if you are planning to travel by train (to secure your bag).

For warm weather, bring cotton, linen, and any other natural-fiber clothing that allows your skin to breathe and is easy to wash. (You can get your laundry done very inexpensively at most hotels, though you may not want to give them your delicate items—they've been known to get ruined.) Avoid manmade or other hard to clean fabrics, as you may have difficulty getting them laundered. Pack a light raincoat or umbrella during rainy season and warmer clothing in winter and early spring. Dress in Vietnam is generally informal, except during meetings. Shorts are acceptable for both men and women, though women may feel more comfortable in longer shorts or skirts.

Sandals, nylon or canvas sneakers, and walking shoes are fine for the cities and more developed parts of the country. Hiking boots are recommended if you're going to head into the hills or onto trails or if you are traveling during rainy season. Keep in mind that you must remove your shoes when entering most temples, so you may want to bring ones that are hassle free. A hat and some suntan lotion are always good ideas.

Bring an extra pair of eyeglasses or contact lenses in your carry-on luggage, and if you have a health problem, **pack enough medication** to last the entire trip. But just in case, have your doctor write you a prescription using the drug's generic name, because brand names vary from country to country (☞ Health, *above*). It's important that you **don't put prescription drugs or valuables in luggage to be checked** since it might go astray. To avoid problems with customs officials, carry medications in the original packaging.

And **don't forget mosquito repellent and a first-aid kit** (with, perhaps, antacids, antidiarrheal, cold medicine, Band-Aids, antiseptics, etc.). Other items to consider are a Swiss-army knife, feminine hygiene items, packs of tissues (toilet paper is not always supplied in public places), moist towelettes, and your favorite toilet articles (in plastic containers, to avoid breakage and reduce the weight of luggage). Finally, be sure to bring the addresses of offices that handle refunds of lost traveler's checks.

LUGGAGE

In general, you are entitled to check two bags on flights within the United States and on international flights leaving the United States. A third piece may be brought on board, but it must fit easily under the seat in front of you or in the overhead compartment.

If you are flying between two foreign destinations, note that baggage allowances may be determined not by piece but by weight—generally 88 pounds (40 kilograms) in first class, 66 pounds (30 kilograms) in business class, and 44 pounds (20 kilograms) in economy. If your flight between two cities abroad *connects* with your transatlantic or transpacific flight, the piece method still applies.

Airline liability for baggage is limited to $1,250 per person on flights within the United States. On international flights the limits are $9.07 per pound or $20 per kilogram for checked baggage (roughly $640 per 70-pound bag) and $400 per passenger for unchecked baggage. You can purchase insurance for losses exceeding these amounts from the airline at check-in for about $10 per $1,000 of coverage; note that this coverage excludes a rather extensive list of items, which is shown on your airline ticket.

Before departure **itemize your bags' contents** and their worth, and label the bags with your name, address, and phone number (if you use your home address, cover the information so potential thieves can't see it readily). Inside each bag, put an address label and **pack a copy of your itinerary.** At check-in, **make sure each bag is correctly tagged** with the destination airport's three-letter code. If your bags arrive damaged or fail to arrive at all, file a written report with the airline before leaving the airport.

PASSPORTS & VISAS

To get into Vietnam, **a passport is required and a visa is generally necessary,** though it depends on your country of origin; check with the Vietnam Embassy. Once your travel plans are confirmed, **check the expiration date of your passport.** It's also a good idea to make photocopies of the data page; leave one copy with someone at home and keep another with you, separated from your passport. Travel restrictions on foreigners were lifted in 1993, so you are not required to carry your passport with you at all times. Most hotels will ask you for your passport when you check in, however; so if you are going on overnight trips, bring it with you. It makes sense to **carry a photocopy of your passport** with you, if you leave the real thing at your hotel. If you lose your passport, promptly call the nearest embassy or consulate and the local police; having a copy of the data page can speed replacement.

U.S. CITIZENS

American citizens are required to have a passport and a visa to enter Vietnam. You can obtain a visa from the Vietnamese embassy. The standard processing fee is $65 for a two-week turnaround and $80 for a four- or five-day rush turnaround. Although officially the embassy is only supposed to grant 30-day visas (that you may be able to extend once you're in Vietnam), persistent callers have been known to receive two-month visas.

➤ INFORMATION: **Office of Passport Services** (☎ 202/647–0518). **Vietnam Embassy** (✉ 1233 20th St. NW, Suite 400, Washington, DC 20036, ☎ 202/861–0694, FAX 202/861–1297, www.vietnamembassy-usa.org/).

CANADIANS

Citizens of Canada need a valid passport and a visa to enter Vietnam.

➤ INFORMATION: **Passport Office** (☎ 819/994–3500 or 800/567–6868). **Vietnam Embassy** (✉ 226 Maclaren St., Ottawa, Ontario, Canada, K2POL9, ☎ 613/236–0772, FAX 613/236–2704).

U.K. CITIZENS

Citizens of the United Kingdom need a valid passport and a visa to enter Vietnam.

➤ INFORMATION: **London Passport Office** (☎ 0990/21010) for fees and documentation requirements and to request an emergency passport. **Vietnam Embassy** (✉ 12–14 Victoria Rd., London W8-5RD, U.K., ☎ 0171/937–1912, FAX 0171/937–6108).

PRECAUTIONS

CRIME

Although it is widely accepted that Vietnam is safe for tourists, pickpocketing and bag snatching are becoming serious problems in Ho Chi Minh City, and even Hanoi is beginning to see more petty crime. You may want to **remove any jewelry that stands out.** The rest of Vietnam's cities are safer, except from intense curiosity and a temptation to double prices for you. You should take standard precautions, however.

In the big cities **do not walk with your bag or purse on your street-side shoulder or leave it at your feet in a cyclo,** as the snatch-and-ride (on a motorbike or bicycle) is a common stealing method. Put your wallet in your front pocket or in a zipped-up bag or purse, and be extra alert when you enter busy markets or crowds. Also, watch out for children or elderly people who may be acting as decoys or pickpocketing you themselves. When sitting in a street café or in a cyclo, make sure you **either hold your bag in your lap with your hands through the straps or put the straps around your neck**; if you do put it at your feet, wrap its handles around your ankles so no one can grab it. If someone does steal your bag, don't pursue the thief; assailants often carry knives. As for cyclos, be sure to negotiate a price before you get in, don't go with a driver you don't feel comfortable with, and don't travel by cyclo after dark, especially in cities.

You want to **avoid leaving passports, cameras, laptop computers, and other valuables in your hotel room,** except if the room has a safe. If it doesn't, consider leaving your valuables in the hotel's safe or with the front desk. It is advised that you leave your passport in your hotel and only carry a photocopy with you while out exploring. A lock for your luggage can come in handy—even one for other purposes such as for added protection on doors and windows.

Minihotels in popular tourist areas such as Halong Bay seem to be thief magnets, so **always be sure your doors *and windows* are locked.** If you've hired a boat for a tour of the bay, have someone trustworthy watch your things if you take a dip in the water. And be extra cautious if you decide to spend the night on the boat.

HEALTH

☞ Health *and* Dining, *above*.

SAFETY

Dozens of Vietnamese are killed every year by unexploded war ordnances. However, it is very unlikely you will visit any area where there are still unexploded ordnances. If you are going someplace where you believe you may be in danger, be sure to travel with a very experienced guide.

PUBLIC TRANSPORTATION

There are no subways in Vietnam, nor is there much of a mass transit system to speak of. Public bus service is spotty and unreliable, and the buses are generally unsafe and overcrowded. They do go almost everywhere, however. Nonetheless, you are better off taking one of the private tour buses run by travel agencies and tourist cafés (☞ Bus Travel, *above*). The train is a better option as a mode of public transportation for getting across the country, or at least from north to south (☞ Train Travel, *below*). But the easiest way to get around the country is on tourist buses, minivans, or in a car with a driver (☞ Car Rental, *above*).

S

SENIOR-CITIZEN TRAVEL

To find out about age-related discounts, **mention your senior-citizen status up front** when booking a room at international hotels (not when checking out); Vietnamese-owned hotels don't usually offer age-related discounts, nor do museums. Note that discounts may be limited to certain days or months.

➤ ADVENTURE TRAVEL: **Overseas Adventure Travel** (✉ Grand Circle Corporation, 625 Mount Auburn St., Cambridge, MA 02138, ☎ 617/876–0533 or 800/221–0814, FAX 617/876–0455).

➤ EDUCATIONAL TRAVEL PROGRAMS: **Elderhostel** (✉ 75 Federal St., 3rd floor, Boston, MA 02110, ☎ 617/426–8056). **Folkways Institute** (✉ 14600 Southeast Aldridge Rd., Portland, OR 97236-6518, ☎ 503/658–6600, FAX 503/658–8672).

SHOPPING

Bone up on your bargaining skills. The fixed-price standard of America and Western Europe is out the window in Vietnam, where paying the asking price on the street is just not done. Major exceptions include state department stores, restaurants, post offices, and transportation tickets—basically, the government-run businesses. Also, plenty of Western-style shops have opened, such as minimarts and even small supermarkets, and prices in these are usually marked and non-negotiable. However, in other shops and markets and in minihotels, motorbike rental agencies, and some art galleries, **bargaining is almost always expected**; when dealing with anybody selling goods on the street (postcard and coconut sellers, boys who want to shine your shoes, cyclo drivers, etc.), it's positively de rigueur.

It's important to **keep the bargaining process good natured**; shopkeepers generally don't respond kindly to aggressive haggling. If you have time, comparison-shop for similar items in several stores to get a feel for prices. The final price will depend on your bargaining skill and the shopkeeper's mood but generally will range from 10% to 40% off the original price. If you don't have much time or really like an item, don't hesitate to buy it—you may not see it again (or you may see it for half the price, though you probably won't have paid that much for it to begin with). Also, **don't assume that all tourist-oriented shops are a rip-off**—some actually sell very nice items, but you need to use your judgment about whether a shop seems good.

Knowing numbers in the Vietnamese language puts you in a better position than if you go in armed with nothing but English and cash; they'll respect your attempt at learning the language, and/or they'll think you've been in Vietnam more than 20 minutes. One expression that's good to know if you're going on a buying spree is *dat qua!* It means "too expensive," and it's a good opening to negotiations if someone's quoted you a steep price. Step 2: Shake your head and feign disinterest. Step 3: Express interest in *another* shop or person selling the same item. If that doesn't get the price down, start walking away. If they've gone as low as they can you won't hear from them; if they haven't, they'll call you back. One trick the Vietnamese are not fond of is "testing" the price: seeing how low the merchant will lower his or her price but then not buying. If you name a price, be prepared to honor it if or when they agree to sell.

It's very important to **make sure an item can be legally taken out of the country before you buy it.** If you are interested in buying antiques, be aware that many items of historic or cultural value to Vietnam may not be exported. Wooden furniture also may not be exported. If you do buy antiques or wooden furniture, you will need approval from the Ministry of Culture to take any pieces out of the country; often this can be arranged by the merchant. Also check on customs and shipping fees to make sure your bargain doesn't turn costly.

With any purchase **make sure to get a receipt** for the amount paid, both for potential returns and for customs. If you are purchasing an item that looks like it could be an antique, be especially sure to get a receipt stating when it was made. Many lacquer and stone statues are designed to resemble antiques but are relatively new. The best of these replicas should have a Ministry of Culture label affixed to them that states they are not antiques; or get a note and bill from the shop stating the same thing. Note that some of the Vietnam War memorabilia for sale in Ho Chi Minh City is real, but much of it is mass produced in Vietnam or China. There are very few antiques in Vietnam's tourist shops.

STREET ADDRESSES

To find addresses in Vietnam, it helps to know a few local practices. You may see addresses with numbers separated by a slash, such as "361/8 Nguyen Dinh Chieu St." This means you should head for No. 361 on Nguyen Dinh Chieu Street, and then look for an alley next to the building; you want No. 8 in this alley. When you see addresses with a number followed by a letter, such as "97A," this means there is more than one No. 97 on the street and you need to find the one numbered specifically with an "A." If you see "54 bis," this is a leftover from the French that means 54½, so look for a building adjacent to No. 54.

STUDENTS

To save money, **look into deals available through student-oriented travel agencies.** To qualify you'll need a bona fide student ID card. Members of international student groups are also eligible. For now, Vietnam has no international youth hostels.

Keep in mind that Vietnam's small population of university students is not as well organized as in America or Europe. But the average student group is very interested in learning English or studying abroad. The result is a community of intelligent young locals who for the most part are thrilled to practice their English with you.

➤ STUDENT IDs AND SERVICES: **Council on International Educational Exchange** (CIEE; ✉ 205 E. 42nd St., 14th floor, New York, NY 10017, ☎ 212/822–2600 or 888/268–6245, FAX 212/822–2699), for mail orders only, in the United States. **Travel Cuts** (✉ 187 College St., Toronto, Ontario M5T 1P7, ☎ 416/979–2406 or 800/667–2887) in Canada.

T

TAXES

AIRPORT

See Air Travel, *above,* for information about airport taxes on international and domestic departures.

DINING & LODGING

State-run and joint-venture restaurants and major hotels often charge a 10% government tax and a 5% service charge; smaller, family-owned places may not charge for tax or service. Many hotels charge tax and service on top of the room rate; others include such charges in the price of the room. When you make your reservation, be sure to **ask about the tax and service charges.**

TAXIS

Metered taxis are common in Hanoi and Ho Chi Minh City and are becoming more common in Vietnam's smaller cities. In Hanoi, the moment you step into a cab the meter reads 14,000d—the rate for the first 2 kilometers or any part thereof; after that the rate runs about 6,000d per kilometer. Taxis in Ho Chi Minh City are less expensive: the meter starts at 5,000d–6,000d for the first 2 kilometers, and then costs 2,000d per kilometer. Fares are always quoted in dong, though you can always pay in U.S. dollars. Although tipping is not required, some cabbies have developed a habit of "not having change" in the hope you'll tell them to keep it.

Though many cabbies act like reckless kings of the road, **taxis are the safest way to get around Vietnam's cities.** For information about specific cab companies, *see* individual chapters. A faster but less safe option is motorbike taxis (☞ Motorbikes & Scooters, *above*).

TELEPHONES

The country code for Vietnam is 84. Some city codes follow:

Dalat, 063; Danang, 0511; Hoi An, 0510; Haiphong, 031; Halong Bay, 033; Hanoi, 04; Ho Chi Minh City, 08; Hue, 054; Nha Trang, 058; Phan Thiet, 062; Vung Tau, 064.

CALLING HOME

To call overseas from Vietnam, dial 00 + the country code (1 for the United States) + the area code + the number. Remember that the time difference between Eastern Standard Time (i.e., in New York) and Vietnam is 12 hours ahead, and the time difference between Pacific Standard Time and Vietnam is 16 hours ahead.

International phone calls from Vietnam cost a small fortune. Many hotels have international direct-dial (IDD), which they advertise as a selling point and which you need in order to call overseas. The connection can be surprisingly clear. The hotel will charge you for your call when you check out.

Another option is to buy phone cards at the telephone companies that are usually in or near post offices. These phone cards can be used on special phones inside the phone company offices or in hotel lobbies. Cards are available in the following denominations: 30,000d, 60,000d, 150,000d and 300,000d. Card calls to the United States, Europe, and Canada cost about $4 for the first minute and about $3 for each additional minute.

As of press time, **access numbers for reaching U.S. long-distance operators do not work in Vietnam,** though the phone companies claim otherwise. It's worth a try, but don't count on being successful. The hope is that this situation will change in the near future.

➤ TO OBTAIN ACCESS CODES: **AT&T USADirect** (☎ 800/874–4000). **MCI Call USA** (☎ 800/444–4444). **Sprint Express** (☎ 800/793–1153).

CALLING VIETNAM

To call Vietnam from overseas, dial the international access code (011 in the United States) + the country code 84 + the area code without the first 0 + the number.

MAKING CALLS IN VIETNAM

To make an intercity or interregional telephone call, dial the city's area code + the number. For instance, to call Danang from Hanoi, dial 0511 + the number. When making a local call, omit the area code.

You can make local calls for free from most hotels. Even if your hotel room doesn't have a phone, you can usually make calls from the reception desk. Once in a while you will be charged around 1,000d–2,000d to make a call.

TIPPING

Tipping at restaurants is not common in Vietnam, although many upscale places are starting to add a service charge and/or 10% gratuity to bills. If this hasn't been done and the service is good, you might **consider leaving 5%–10%.** You might also consider tipping other people in the service industry including bellboys and cyclo drivers. As you go farther north, however, you may find that some hotel employees will refuse tips, waving them off with a perplexed grin. Others, especially those working for the private sector, are learning to appreciate gratuities. Although it is not necessarily expected, tour guides are more than happy to receive a tip if you enjoyed their services.

You may feel almost embarrassed *not* tipping in some situations, such as for the women who row you to and from Perfume Pagoda or around the bay in Hoi An. But be aware that if 10 tourists each tip a rower 5,000d, that amount will match her daily wage. Taxi drivers can be aggressive in their demand for tips. A common ploy among drivers is to claim he doesn't have the 2,000d or 5,000d note you're expecting as change. Whether you challenge him on this scheme is up to you. Many cyclo drivers will request in English a "souvenir" after you've paid the agreed amount, to which you might feel compelled to answer, "But *I'm* the tourist." Of course, he's really requesting a tip.

TOUR OPERATORS

Buying a prepackaged tour or independent vacation can make your trip to Vietnam less expensive and more hassle free. Because everything is prearranged (including visas, domestic air and ground transportation, meals, hotels, English-speaking guides, and sometimes airfare), you spend less time planning and less time organizing transportation and lodging once you have arrived.

Operators that handle several hundred thousand travelers per year can use their purchasing power to give you a good price. Their high volume may also indicate financial stability. On the other hand, small companies provide more personalized service; because they tend to specialize, they may also be more knowledgeable about a given area.

A number of small, international companies have offices in Vietnam or are based there. Others have offices elsewhere in Southeast Asia or work with Vietnamese partner agencies. These companies can also arrange nationwide tours or one-day excursions for you from overseas, or they can make arrangements for you once you arrive (☞ Travel Agencies, *below*). The trips vary from upscale to rugged, backpacker-oriented travel.

Another option is to have one of the state-run tourist agencies, which are in every city and almost every province of Vietnam, organize a tour or even just a few day trips for you from abroad or in Vietnam. Unfortunately, these state-run agencies are often overpriced and not that helpful (☞ Travel Agencies, *below*).

Note that most tour operators can arrange all kinds of customized tours for groups of four or more.

A GOOD DEAL?

The more your package or tour includes, the better you can predict the ultimate cost of your vacation. Make sure you know exactly what is covered, and **beware of hidden costs.** Are taxes, tips, and service charges included? Transfers and baggage handling? Airfare? Entertainment and excursions? These can add up.

If the package or tour you are considering is priced lower than in your wildest dreams, **be skeptical.** Also, **make sure your travel agent knows the accommodations** and other services. Ask about the hotel's location, room size, beds, and whether it has a pool, room service, or programs for children, if you care about these. Has your agent been there in person or sent others you can contact?

BUYER BEWARE

Each year consumers are stranded or lose their money when tour operators—even very large ones with excellent reputations—go out of business. So **check out the operator.** Find out how long the company has been in business, and ask several agents about its reputation. **Don't book unless the firm has a consumer-protection program.**

Members of the National Tour Association and United States Tour Operators Association are required to set aside funds to cover your payments and travel arrangements in case the company defaults. Nonmembers may carry insurance instead. Look for the details, and for the name of an underwriter with a solid reputation, in the operator's brochure. Note: When it comes to tour operators, **don't trust escrow accounts.** Although the Department of Transportation watches over charter-flight operators, no regulatory body prevents tour operators from raiding the till. You may want to protect yourself by buying travel insurance that includes a tour-operator default provision. For more information *see* Consumer Protection, *above.*

It's also a good idea to choose a company that participates in the American Society of Travel Agents' Tour Operator Program (TOP). This gives you a forum if there are any disputes between you and your tour operator; ASTA will act as mediator.

➤ TOUR-OPERATOR RECOMMENDATIONS: **American Society of Travel Agents** (☞ Travel Agencies, *below*).

National Tour Association (NTA; ✉ 546 E. Main St., Lexington, KY 40508, ☎ 606/226–4444 or 800/755–8687). **United States Tour Operators Association** (USTOA; ✉ 342 Madison Ave., Suite 1522, New York, NY 10173, ☎ 212/599–6599, FAX 212/599–6744).

SINGLE TRAVELERS

Prices for packages and tours are usually quoted per person, based on two sharing a room. If traveling solo, you may be required to pay the full double-occupancy rate. Some operators eliminate this surcharge if you agree to be matched with a roommate of the same sex, even if one is not found by departure time.

USING AN AGENT

Travel agents are excellent resources. In fact, large operators accept bookings made only through travel agents. But it's a good idea to **collect brochures from several agencies** because some agents' suggestions may be influenced by relationships with tour and package firms that reward them for volume sales. If you have a special interest, **find an agent with expertise in that area**; ASTA (☞ Travel Agencies, *below*) has a database of specialists worldwide. Do some homework on your own, too: Local tourism boards can provide information about lesser-known and small-niche operators, some of which may sell only direct.

GROUP TOURS

Among companies that sell tours to Vietnam, the following are nationally known, have a proven reputation, and offer plenty of options. The classifications that follow represent different price categories, and you'll probably encounter these terms when talking to a travel agent or tour operator. The key difference is usually in accommodations, which run from budget to better, and better-yet to best.

➤ SUPER-DELUXE: **Abercrombie & Kent** (✉ 1520 Kensington Rd., Oak Brook, IL 60521-2141, ☎ 630/954–2944 or 800/323–7308, FAX 630/954–3324). **Travcoa** (✉ Box 2630, 2350 S.E. Bristol St., Newport Beach, CA 92660, ☎ 714/476–2800 or 800/992–2003, FAX 714/476–2538).

➤ FIRST CLASS: **Global Spectrum** (✉ 1901 Pennsylvania Ave. NW, Suite 204, Washington, DC 20006, ☎ 800/419–4446 or 202/293–2065, FAX 202/296–0815). **Mountain Travel-Sobek** (✉ 6420 Fairmount Ave., El Cerrito, CA 94530, ☎ 510/527–8100 or 800/227–2384, FAX 510/525–7710). **Orient Flexi-Pax Tours** (✉ 630 3rd Ave., New York, NY 10017, ☎ 212/692–9550 or 800/545–5540, FAX 212/661–1618). **Pacific Bestour** (✉ 228 Rivervale Rd., River Vale, NJ 07675, ☎ 201/664–8778 or 800/688–3288, FAX 201/722–0829). **Pacific Delight Tours** (✉ 132 Madison Ave., New York, NY 10016, ☎ 212/684–7707 or 800/221–7179, FAX 212/532–3406).

PACKAGES

Like group tours, independent vacation packages are available from major tour operators and airlines. The companies listed below offer vacation packages in a broad price range.

➤ AIR/HOTEL/SIGHTSEEING: **Orient Flexi-Pax Tours** (☞ Group Tours, *above*). **Pacific Bestour** (☞ Group Tours, *above*). **Pacific Delight Tours** (☞ Group Tours, *above*). **United Vacations** (☎ 800/328–6877).

➤ FROM THE U.K.: **Abercrombie & Kent** (✉ Sloane Square House, Holbein Pl., London SW1W 8NS, ☎ 0171/730 9600). **Kuoni Travel** (✉ Kuoni House, Dorking, Surrey RH5 4AZ, ☎ 01306/740–500). **Imaginative Traveller** (✉ 14 Barley Mow Passage, London W4 4PH, ☎ 0181/742–8612).

THEME TRIPS

➤ ADVENTURE: **Asian Pacific Adventures** (✉ 826 S. Sierra Bonita Ave., Los Angeles, CA 90036, ☎ 213/935–3156 or 800/825–1680, FAX 213/935–2691). **Himalayan Travel** (✉ 110 Prospect St., Stamford, CT 06901, ☎ 203/359–3711 or 800/225–2380, FAX 203/359–3669).

➤ BICYCLING: **Butterfield & Robinson** (✉ 70 Bond St., Toronto, Ontario, Canada, M5B IX3, ☎ 416/864–1354 or 800/678–1147, FAX 416/864–0541).

➤ CUSTOMIZED PACKAGES: **Absolute Asia** (✉ 180 Varick St., New York, NY, ☎ 212/627–1950 or 800/736–8187, FAX 212/627–4090). **Pacific Experience** (✉ 185 Spring St., Newport, RI 02840, ☎ 800/279–3639, FAX 203/618–0121).

➤ LEARNING VACATIONS: **Smithsonian Study Tours and Seminars** (✉ 1100 Jefferson Dr. SW, Room 3045, MRC 702, Washington, DC 20560, ☎ 202/357–4700, FAX 202/633–9250).

➤ VIETNAM VETERANS: **Global Spectrum** (☞ Group Tours, *above*). **Vietnam Veterans of America Foundation** (✉ 1224 M St. NW, Washington, DC 20005, ☎ 202/628–2700, FAX 202/628–5880) organizes tours to Vietnam at least once a year.

LOCAL OPERATORS

Most state- and privately-run travel agencies in Vietnam organize tours of the whole country. Privately-run companies are more likely to be able to customize trips, have better English-speaking guides, and offer you a wider range of restaurant and hotel choices. The state-run operators are generally much less flexible and provide many fewer options. The main drawback to organizing your trip through tour operators in Vietnam is that you generally don't have the same recourse to consumer protection as you do with many larger, American-based companies.

➤ LOCAL AGENCIES: *See* Travel Agencies, *below,* and individual chapters for more information on local tour operators and travel agencies.

TRAIN TRAVEL

The 2,600-km (1,612-mi) rail system, built by the French, goes north–south, servicing coastal towns between Hanoi and Ho Chi Minh City. The trains' main drawback is that they're slow. The quickest train from Ho Chi Minh City to Hanoi, the Reunification Express, takes about 36–44 hours, depending on how many stops it makes.

Train travel is better for the 12–14 hour hops between Hanoi and Hue (daily, $57 for a soft berth); Hanoi and Lao Cai, which gets you to Sapa (daily, with the soft sleeper leaving on Friday night, 11 hours, $10–$20); or Ho Chi Minh City and Nha Trang (15–22 hours, $25–$35). It is also possible to take a train from Hanoi to Beijing (twice weekly, 55 hours, $58–$88). The northeastern border crossing is at Dong Dang, just north of Lang Son.

Fares vary based on the length of trip and the class of travel, and you'll need separate tickets for each destination. You can purchase tickets at train stations; travel agencies can also help you book tickets. It's a good idea to **book ahead,** especially for overnight travel, although for some trips you can only reserve a few days in advance.

Train travel through Vietnam can be an enjoyable experience, not to mention a time-saver if you take overnight trips, provided you can get a soft sleeper or at least a soft chair. There are a number of seating and sleeping options on the train: the best are soft-berth sleepers, which generally have comfortable, 4-inch-thick mattresses and contain only four bunks; next are the mid-range soft sleepers, which also have only four bunks but with 2-inch-thick mattresses (Vietnamese nationals are allowed in these cabins but not in the soft-berth sleepers); then come hard-berth sleepers, which have reed mats instead of mattresses and six bunks (the top ones are cheapest); after that are soft seats, which are wooden seats with a soft cushion but no space to lie down; and finally, hard seats, which are just what they sound like. Don't skimp: **when traveling long distances by train, always reserve the soft-berth sleeper.**

You probably want to **bring food and water with you,** although you can sometimes get some on the trains or from vendors in stations.

➤ TRAIN STATIONS: **Hanoi Railway Station** (Ga Hanoi; ✉ Le Duan St. at Tran Hung Dao St., ☎ 04/825–3697 or 04/825–3949). **Ho Chi Minh City Railway Station** (Ga Saigon; 1 Nguyen Thong St., District 3, ☎ 08/823–0105).

TRAVEL AGENCIES

A good travel agent puts your needs first. Look for an agency that has been in business at least five years, emphasizes customer service, and has someone on staff who specializes in your destination. In addition, **make sure the agency belongs to the American Society of Travel Agents** (ASTA). If your travel agency is also acting as your tour operator, *see* Buyer Beware *in* Tour Operators, *above.*

➤ TRAVEL AGENT REFERRALS: **American Society of Travel Agents** (ASTA; ☎ 800/965–2782 for 24-hr hot line, FAX 703/684–8319). **Alliance of Canadian Travel Associations** (✉ 1729 Bank St., Suite 201, Ottawa, Ontario K1V 7Z5, ☎ 613/521–0474, FAX 613/521–0805). **Association of British Travel Agents** (✉ 55–57 Newman St., London W1P 4AH, ☎ 0171/637–2444, FAX 0171/637–0713).

TRAVEL AGENCIES IN VIETNAM

Almost every city and province has a state-run tourist agency that does everything from book trains, planes, and automobiles to arrange guided tours and extend visas. These state-run agencies are often pricey, slow, and not that helpful, but in some smaller provinces they're the only game in town. Hotels, big and small, are frequently affiliated with a state-run or private agency, or they have their own travel services that can organize excursions for you.

The larger firms (Vietnam Tourism, Saigon Tourist, Hanoi Tourism) are huge state-owned agencies with fingers in many pies. If you book a tour outright through, for example, Saigon Tourist, expect to be shuttled every step of the way from the Saigon Tourist hotel to the Saigon Tourist bus to the Saigon Tourist restaurant to the Saigon Tourist reed boat that floats down the river at Perfume Pagoda. And you'll pay for the privilege: As an example, Hanoi Tourism's superior-class 15-day/14-night nationwide bonanza costs $3,150 per person. These companies are not known for their flexibility; they *are* known as cash cows for the Vietnamese government, and many people find that their services and accommodations don't match their prices. On the other hand, they've got connections absolutely everywhere.

In organizing travel around the country, don't write off "Backpackerville" completely. In Ho Chi Minh City, you'll find numerous, well-informed, privately-owned travel agencies that cater to budget travelers around Pham Ngu Lao Street in District 1, including those run out of tourist-oriented restaurants such as Sinh Café or Kim Café (☞ Chapter 6). There is no specific congregation of such agencies in Hanoi, but some are in the Old Quarter, around Hang Be Street and Hang Bac Street (☞ Chapter 2).

These tourist cafés, as they're called, have many of the services large travel agencies do and generally some of the best information, the widest selection of adventure tours and day trips, and the lowest prices. Some extend visas; a number double as hotels and restaurants. (Tourist cafés are referred to throughout this guide in this context—primarily as good travel agencies but also as good spots to meet other travelers over a cup of coffee.) Most are not equipped to handle tour bookings from overseas; they're mainly walk-in businesses.

Tourist cafés have their travel itineraries posted on the walls, with photographs of the destinations, prices of each tour, and departure days clearly visible. Accommodations are usually in average minihotels. Occasionally you may want to question their policies: Queen Café's six-day, five-night Jeep adventure through the northwest is $65 per person with a "good driver" but $75 per person with an "experienced driver"—makes you wonder what the terms mean.

In Hanoi and Ho Chi Minh City travel agencies can provide English-speaking guides for about $15 a day. You may also be approached on the street by former interpreters or by cyclo drivers who want to make 50,000d for a full day's work guiding you around the city. Although this is just as viable an option as any, make sure you understand their English by conducting an informal interview before you agree on an amount. Tourist agencies in cities like Hue, Danang, Halong Bay, and Haiphong all claim they can provide English-speaking guides. But outside the main cities, it's definitely hit or miss.

➤ LOCAL AGENCIES: *See* individual chapters for specific information on local travel agencies and tourist cafés.

TRAVEL GEAR

Travel catalogs specialize in useful items, such as compact alarm clocks and travel irons, that can **save space when packing.** They also offer dual-voltage appliances, currency converters, and foreign-language phrase books.

➤ MAIL-ORDER CATALOGS: **Magellan's** (☎ 800/962–4943, FAX 805/568–5406). **Orvis Travel** (☎ 800/541–3541, FAX 540/343–7053). **Travel-Smith** (☎ 800/950–1600, FAX 800/950–1656).

U

U.S. GOVERNMENT

The U.S. government can be an excellent source of inexpensive travel information. When planning your trip, **find out what government materials are available.**

➤ ADVISORIES: **U.S. Department of State** (✉ Overseas Citizens Services Office, Room 4811, N.W., Washington, DC 20520); enclose a self-addressed, stamped envelope. **Interactive hot line** (☎ 202/647–5225, FAX 202/647–3000). **Website** (www.state.gov/).

➤ PAMPHLETS: **Consumer Information Center** (✉ Consumer Information Catalogue, Pueblo, CO 81009, ☎ 719/948–3334) for a free catalog that includes travel titles.

V

VIETNAM VETERANS

The office of the Vietnam Veterans of America Foundation (VVAF) in Vietnam is involved in building long-lasting ties and increasing understanding between Vietnamese and Americans. VVAF organizes cultural exchange programs and a much-needed prosthetics clinic. Veterans returning to Vietnam are encouraged to contact VVAF, either in Hanoi or at its Washington, D.C., office. At least once a year VVAF organizes tours to Vietnam; contact the Washington office for information.

➤ VETERANS' RESOURCE: **Vietnam Veterans of America Foundation** (✉ 1224 M St. NW, Washington, DC 20005, ☎ 202/628–2700, FAX 202/628–5880; ✉ 51 Ly Thai To St., Hanoi, ☎ 04/934–1607, FAX 04/934–1606).

VISITOR INFORMATION

As of yet, there is no official source of tourist information abroad, but you might try calling the Vietnam embassy or consulate (☞ Passports & Visas, *above*). There are a couple of business magazines available internationally, such as the *Vietnam Business Journal* or *Vietnam Economic Times,* which provide some business information of interest to tourists. The local Vietnamese papers provide slanted news coverage with little emphasis on the arts or leisure. In Vietnam, privately and state-run travel agencies, tourist cafés, and hotels are your best sources of information (☞ Travel Agencies *and* Tour Operators, *above and in* individual chapters).

W

WHEN TO GO

Vietnam has a number of annual festivals and holidays (☞ Holidays, *above, and* Festivals and Seasonal Events *in* Chapter 1). The biggest, Tet, the lunar new year, falls in January or February, depending on the lunar calendar. Although it is a very picturesque and lively time of year in Vietnam, accommodations are scarce; museums, offices, and shops tend to close for days at a time; and the weather in the north can be cold and drizzly.

CLIMATE

Vietnam's climate varies widely from region to region during different times of the year. The best time of year in northern Vietnam is from October to December, when the weather is cool and the least rainy. Chilly, wet weather starts in December and continues through March, when a clammy mist descends on the region; the northern mountains get even colder. Sweltering heat is common from May to early October. Flooding can be expected during the rainy summer months.

The Central Highlands are cool year-round and dry from December to March. Along the central coast, the rainy season brings wet weather from December to February; dry heat is the norm from June to October.

In the south the best weather is from December to April when it is dry. May to November generally brings the wet season and sporadic showers, usually during lunchtime. The rain shouldn't discourage you from visiting the south during this time (especially in late fall), though flooding in the Mekong Delta can make traveling there difficult.

Overall, the best time of year to visit all of Vietnam is from late September to December and from March to April.

The following are average daily maximum and minimum temperatures for Hanoi and Ho Chi Minh City.

Climate in Vietnam

HANOI

Jan.	66F	19C	May	84F	29C	Sept.	82F	28C
	54	12		72	22		68	20
Feb.	66F	19C	June	88F	31C	Oct.	81F	27C
	55	13		73	23		68	20
Mar.	70F	21C	July	86F	30C	Nov.	75F	24C
	59	15		73	23		63	17
Apr.	77F	25C	Aug.	84F	29C	Dec.	70F	21C
	66	19		73	23		59	15

HO CHI MINH CITY

Jan.	84F	29C	May	88F	31C	Sept.	88F	31C
	74	23		74	23		74	23
Feb.	84F	29C	June	88F	31C	Oct.	88F	31C
	74	23		74	23		74	23
Mar.	85F	30C	July	88F	31C	Nov.	85F	30C
	74	23		74	23		74	23
Apr.	86F	30C	Aug.	88F	31C	Dec.	85F	30C
	74	23		74	23		74	23

1 Destination: Vietnam

VIETNAM TODAY: MOTORBIKES AND WATER BUFFALOS

VIETNAM is a country on the move. The introduction of economic reforms—known as *doi moi*—more than 10 years ago acted as a catalyst, releasing the energies of the nation left behind after decades of war and isolation. Now wherever you travel in Vietnam—in the towns, the cities, and the countryside—you will see people on the go.

From the rows of *pho* (noodle soup) stalls lining the sidewalks to the numerous vendors selling postcards to the huge neon signs advertising Western chic, it is apparent that this drive to make it in this new era cuts across social boundaries. Billboards hawk everything from Lifebuoy soap to Heineken beer to the newest luxury apartments, and tower above streets jammed with motorbikes, bicycles, and more and more cars.

It seems as if, once day breaks, the entire population is up within an hour rushing headlong into another day. The roads are often gridlocked with motorbikes by 6:30 AM, making you wonder just where so many people are going so early in the morning. The answer is in frantic pursuit of advancement, which ends each day only when everyone is too exhausted to continue. Most Vietnamese are in bed by 10 PM. All this goes on despite the continued presence of the old Communist Party cadres, who have by no means completely embraced the gung-ho, American-style capitalism that they themselves initiated.

It is especially in the main cities—Hanoi, Haiphong, Danang, and most of all Ho Chi Minh City (Saigon)—that you see this rush to make money. But travel just 30 mi from the heart of downtown Ho Chi Minh City or Hanoi and you still see farmers sowing rice seeds with water buffalos, and duck herders wooing their flocks across roads where the only hazards are passing bicycles. These scenes are no less exhilarating than those in the booming cities.

For Vietnam is a country of stunning beauty, its pristine coastline of golden beaches stretching 2,000 mi from tip to tail along the South China Sea. To the north Vietnam borders China along the rugged Hoang Lien mountain chain, a breathtaking landscape of deep valleys and tall, mysterious peaks shrouded in mist. Down the country's enormous arched spine are forest-covered highlands, which can be as deliciously cool as a European spring. These mountains, as well as those in the north, are home to Vietnam's ethnic minority groups—the Black Tai, Flower H'mong, Ede, and Muong—whose traditional way of life has been basically preserved despite the passing centuries and the ravages of war. The majority of Vietnamese, however, live along the coast, and in the country's two major deltas—the Red River Delta in the north and the Mekong Delta in the south. Here the land fans out into patchworks of vivid-green, wet rice paddies, fruit orchards, and fishing hamlets—inhabited by a thousand generations of farmers and fishermen.

In the midst of this beautiful country, stark reminders of the high price paid by the Vietnamese people for their independence is never far away. Although few visible signs of the damage sustained by Vietnam remain, every town has its monument to war, be it a captured American jet fighter or a victorious North Vietnamese tank. And dotting the cities and countryside are huge Soviet-style memorials recording the millions that died in the country's most recent struggle against outside forces.

For 2,000 years the country has been fending off foreign invaders, most notably the Chinese, Japanese, French, and Americans (☞ Vietnam at a Glance: A Chronology *in* Chapter 8 for more information on Vietnam's history). The Chinese were the first to invade, and by the time they were finally driven out by Ngo Quyen in 938 AD they had ruled the country for 1,000 years. During the following centuries the Vietnamese migrated south in ever increasing numbers, battling with the kingdoms of Champa and Angkor as they went. These expansionist ambitions lead to conflicts between competing Vietnamese lords—the Nguyen and the Trinh—vying for control of the country.

The French inititially entered the scene at the beginning of the 19th century by invitation from the Nguyen lords who sought assistance in crushing a rebellion against them. But by the mid-19th century, the French had taken over by force, annexing large parts of Vietnam to create the colony of Cochin China. The Japanese occupation during World War II interrupted the French monopoly, briefly. With Japan's surrender, the French returned to rule Vietnam, but not without conflict: By 1946 anti-French sentiments developed into the French-Indochina War.

The French were defeated at Dien Bien Phu in 1954, and the country was split into two under the Geneva Accords that same year. Cold-War concerns drew the American military into Vietnam, which lead to full-scale U.S. involvement in the Vietnam War. But American firepower only reinforced the conviction among many Vietnamese that they would not be defeated. And the 1968 Tet Offensive was the turning point. By 1973 most U.S. troops had left the country, and the Saigon regime soon fell.

But strife did not end there for the Vietnamese. Following Khmer Rouge border incursions in 1978, Vietnam became involved in armed conflict with Cambodia until 1989, effectively ending the "killing fields" of Pol Pot. In response to Vietnam's involvement in Cambodia, the Chinese invaded northern Vietnam in 1979, devastating much of the countryside and many towns and villages. But the Vietnamese army repulsed the Chinese and for the first time in decades lived in relative peace. They were not, however, without a new set of visitors: the Soviets.

Now that the Soviets have departed, what becomes evident is the Vietnamese's amazing resilience after so many thousands of years of conflict. From each of their foreign rulers they have taken what appealed to them and melded the most dissonant elements of foreign cultures into a way of life uniquely their own. When you visit Vietnam, you can't help but marvel at the Vietnamese people's endurance. Waifish, silk-clad women bear yokes hung with baskets of rice weighing 10 times their own weight. Or build roads, protected only by a conical hat and a perfectly white handkerchief tied over nose and mouth. You also can't help but admire their panache: Do not be surprised to encounter a pair of bareheaded men careening on a motorbike through city traffic at the height of a midday downpour, the driver tooting his horn with a soggy cigarette in his mouth, his companion, arms outstretched, balancing a large pane of glass on his knees. That mixture of practicality and bravado is in some ways the essence of Vietnam, and it is what's taking the country into the future.

NEW AND NOTEWORTHY

From the days of the colonizing French to those of the occupying American troops, Saigon's hotels and restaurants have a history of catering to foreigners, and today Vietnam is surprisingly travel-friendly. Even the government in Hanoi, zealous guardian of all things Vietnamese, has reversed its famed xenophobia and virtually eliminated domestic travel restrictions at the same time it has beefed up travel facilities and agreed to a number of joint-venture hotels with foreign companies and investors. The result is the current boom in **new high-rise luxury hotels** and the development of more beach resorts along the coast, though the frenetic results can be unsightly. The international chains going up overnight seem to homogenize the cityscapes—but they also lower the average hotel rates, as does any fluctuation in currency. Some luxury properties have officially dropped their rates by 30% or more. If you have not yet booked your trip, consider calling the hotels directly to see if they'll make you a deal. All but the busiest hotels will probably be willing to listen to an offer.

The **currency crisis** that beset Southeast Asia in 1997 seriously affected all economies in the region. Although Vietnam has no convertible currency, it's economy will inevitably suffer as a result of the region's downturn. However, what this means for you, the traveler, is that you may be able to negotiate with hotels for significant discounts on the price of rooms.

Most hotels—from mom-and-pop mini-hotels to five-star palaces—have a wide range of **travel services.** Tours in particular are widely available, as everyone from the central government bureaucrat to the corner café owner runs or organizes excursions. The result? Nearly every attraction in every corner of the country is accessible—provided, of course, you have a wide-open schedule and heaps of patience.

Though the country is undergoing a **major road-improvement program,** precarious road conditions and suicidal driving habits persist, making car travel nerve-racking. A road in the Central Highlands may wash out, stranding villagers (or you) for a week. A typhoon, or even the threat of one, could shut down Halong Bay or Mekong Delta tourism for days. Nature is hardly the only impetus for a change in travel plans in Vietnam. **Unrest** rocked Thai Binh, a coastal province southeast of Hanoi, in mid-1997. The disturbances, generally considered the worst since national reunification in 1975, prompted the government to bar all foreign journalists and tourists from travel to the region.

The government's various **campaigns against corrupting foreign influences,** known by the appellation "social evils," seem to take hold of the nation and then gradually release. Foreign advertisements in vogue one month are deemed offensive or inappropriate the next and are removed. A month later they're back. Nightclubs steer clear of trouble for 18 months, then a dozen are raided. This cycle isn't fixed, but it isn't random either: Crackdowns often coincide with official gatherings, such as a Communist Party congresses and international conferences. These conferences also bring good results: Before a 1997 meeting in Hanoi of representatives of French-speaking countries, the Vietnamese government beautifully renovated the glorious opera house, built in 1911.

The government has put a lot of money into **reliable air service,** and state-run Vietnam Airlines has seen considerable improvements. Planes seem to run efficiently and frequently to destinations throughout Vietnam and to certain international cities. The fatal September 1997 crash of a Vietnam Airlines plane in Phnom Penh, Cambodia, caused the Civil Aviation Administration of Vietnam to ground all remaining Russian aircraft in its fleet and only use its new Boeing, Air Bus, and Fokker planes.

WHAT'S WHERE

Central Coast

Two of Vietnam's finest cities, Hue and Hoi An, are in the central coast region. Both places provide a fascinating look into Vietnam's past. Hoi An is an ancient trading and fishing town with a heavy Chinese influence. Ancient homes, temples, and meeting houses remain as they were 200 years ago. Hue, the former capital of Vietnam, was once the home of the country's emperors. Though much of Hue was destroyed during the Vietnam War, its Imperial City and palatial royal tombs are still impressive reminders of Vietnam's regal past. In between Hue and Hoi An is Danang, the region's major transportation hub and home to the splendid Cham Museum.

Hanoi

Quieter and more reserved than brash, bustling Ho Chi Minh City, Hanoi is the self-appointed capital of Vietnamese culture. This city of majestic lakes, wide tree-lined boulevards, and hauntingly familiar colonial French architecture is one of the most charming cities in Southeast Asia. Hanoi oozes history and legend: Ho Chi Minh declared Vietnamese independence here in 1945 in Ba Dinh Square; the Old Quarter, a dense 15th-century collection of the original 36 Streets, beckons you into its maze; the Lake of the Restored Sword, the physical, emotional, and legendary heart of the capital, enthralls; and the many makeshift sidewalk cafés invite you to sip green tea and share your tales of the city. Hanoi is the home base for touring parts of the north; use it as a jumping off point to other sites in the area, such as the Perfume Pagoda or Halong Bay, and destinations farther afield, such as Sapa or Dien Bien Phu.

Ho Chi Minh City (Saigon)

Ho Chi Minh City, still called Saigon by most (and both names used interchangeably throughout this book), is a lively—some might say hectic—city with French colonial architecture, broad boulevards, and a busy waterfront on the Saigon River where barges and sampans load up with freight. It is also a city that is changing overnight: A plethora of new high-rise buildings are rapidly transforming the skyline, and an ever-increasing number of motorbikes compete for space on the streets with a sea of bicycles. The city is filled with history—from the French-built Notre Dame Cathedral and the former U.S. embassy to the War Remnants Museum and the Reunification Palace. And its streets are alive with activity. For a good view of it all, head up to the rooftop bar at the Hotel Rex or Hotel Majestic. The city also offers a wide-range of cuisines—not only Vietnamese but also French, American, Russian, and Thai. It makes a good base for daylong excursions to the northernmost part of the Mekong Delta and the infamous Cu Chi Tunnels.

Mekong Delta

The Mekong Delta is a patchwork of waterways, tropical fruit orchards, mangrove swamps, and brilliant green rice paddies that run their way into the emerald-color South China Sea. It's a land touched by ancient and modern cultures, from the Funanese to the Khmer, Cham, and Vietnamese, all living side by side today after centuries of strife. Running through the upper delta is the Mekong River, dotted with small, fertile islands where fruit grows in abundance. In the lower delta are crocodile-infested swamps and cajeput forests teeming with monkeys and wild pigs. The farther south you go, the more untamed the delta becomes. If you're looking for wild frontiers, take time to explore the farthest reaches of the Mekong Delta—it doesn't get much more isolated than this.

The North

A world away from Hanoi, the rest of northern Vietnam is home to more than 50 ethnic minorities, most of whom live in the fiercely beautiful highlands of the Tonkinese Alps. Take the overnight train to the enchanting trading outpost of Sapa and spend a long weekend in Montagnard country, trekking to the remote villages of the Dao, the H'mong, and the Thai. Jump into a Jeep for a bumpy weeklong circuit through the idyllic valley village of Mai Chau and out to Dien Bien Phu, site of the doomed French garrison that surrendered to the Vietminh in 1954. To the east lies the grandeur of Halong Bay, a dramatic region of limestone islets and secluded coves that has earned official World Heritage status. Northeast of Hanoi up Highway 1 is Lang Son, a frontier town where Vietnamese and Chinese residents have put aside the animosity generated by a brief but fierce border war in 1979 in order to proceed with the business of doing business. Here is where people gather to buy and sell everything from monkeys to Mercedes Benzes.

South-Central Coast and Highlands

If you want to take time out to relax, make sure to visit the south-central coast and highlands. Here you will find Vietnam's two main resort towns—Nha Trang, by the ocean, and Dalat, in the mountains. On the South China Sea, Nha Trang has a glorious palm-lined boulevard running the length of its beach, flanked by hotels and ocean-side restaurants. Though not as developed as other beach resorts in Southeast Asia, it is a nice place to spend a couple of days. If it's mountains and lakes you're after, head to temperate Dalat, the country's number one destination for Vietnamese newlyweds. In Dalat the pace is slow, and activities include strolling along the lake, visiting waterfalls, paddleboating on the lake, playing a round of golf on Southeast Asia's oldest course, touring Emperor Bao Dai's summer palace, and sipping the local specialty—artichoke tea.

PLEASURES AND PASTIMES

Architecture

Vietnamese architecture is as eclectic as its culture. A host of invading and vanquished civilizations—the Cham, the Chinese, the French, the Americans, and the Russians—have left their marks on the nation in a hodgepodge of contrasting styles.

Historically, the Vietnamese themselves were not big builders. The oldest existing buildings in the country are temples built by the Cham, the Indianized Hindu culture occupying south-central Vietnam around the area of present-day Nha Trang from the 4th to the 15th centuries (many Vietnamese from this region are descendants of the Cham people). Temple sites such as the Po Ro Me Tower and the Ra Thap Towers outside Phan Rang on the central coast are still centers of annual Cham pilgrimages. Khmer influence (descendants of the Kingdom of Angkor, now Cambodia) can be seen in the Po Klong Garai Towers built in the 12th century at Thap Cham.

Most temples and pagodas around the country reflect the Chinese influence on Vietnamese culture. But because the Vietnamese mainly built using wood, many ancient pagodas and temples "still standing" have actually been rebuilt, often many times. The layout and foundations of the Temple of Literature in Hanoi, for example, may be 900 years old, but many of the wooden structures of the pagoda and entrance gate are renovations. In Hue, the impressive Imperial City, though modeled on its Chinese counterpart, the Forbidden City in Beijing, is actually relatively modern—it was constructed in the early 19th century by French architect Olivier de Puymanel. Sadly much of this exquisite palace was destroyed during the 1968 Tet Offensive. Hue also has an incredible collection of tombs—vast and beautiful temples to emperors, constructed in an array of architectural styles reflecting the wealth of Vietnam's royal families. Some structures have been around for centuries, for example, the ancient, 10th-century capital of Hoa Lu, southeast of Hanoi.

French architecture has probably had the most pervasive foreign influence on Vietnamese building. In Hanoi you still find such classic French colonial architectural treasures as the Governor-General's Palace, the National Assembly, and the exquisite Opera House, modeled on its counterpart in Paris. The city also possesses treasure troves of various styles that would excite any student of architecture—for instance, beautiful Art Deco blocks that seem to step straight out of 1920s Le Corbusier–influenced designs.

In the south much of the French architecture was bulldozed to make way for American-style urban planning, though plenty of it still exists. Many colonial villas were demolished in the 1960s for what has been irreverently described as "bunker architecture"—buildings reflecting a city under siege. The best example of this in Ho Chi Minh City is the former U.S. embassy. The former Presidential (now Reunification) Palace is also a model of '60s-style building design. However, classic colonial buildings like the ornate and rather flamboyant Hôtel de Ville (now the People's Committee Building) and the Central Post Office are vivid reminders of the romance of what the French once called the "Paris of the East."

One of the last architectural influences to take hold in Vietnam was, unfortunately, Russian. Apart from an imposing monolith, the Ho Chi Minh Mausoleum, there is very little to commend about most Soviet-era structures, which generally dominate the suburbs of most towns and cities. They usually are residential tower blocks that would not be out of place in a Moscow suburb.

Both Hanoi and Ho Chi Minh City have an amalgam of this overwrought Communist Bloc nostalgia, early 20th-century Art Deco, French colonialist chic, mandarin Chinese elegance, and a fast-growing array of high-rises, all sprinkled with a healthy dose of kitsch. In Hanoi's Old Quarter and Ho Chi Minh City's Cholon district, a certain rhythm and style are at least maintained. But as residents turn to remodeling or rebuilding their homes, chaos has come to rule in the once-uniform 36 Streets that make up the Old Quarter and the old, Chinese-style houses of Cholon. Tacky plastic and aluminum-framed house exteriors now abut 100-year-old wooden homes or pagodas. Others who don't have the cash to renovate add to their century-old storefronts a hideous blinking neon sign advertising *pho* (noodle soup), or iron smelting, or gas cookers.

The race for space and the astronomical rise in real estate values are forcing new builders to head skyward with the funkiest and foulest of plans. This is also true in the areas outside the old quarters of both cities, where newfound wealth (or more accurately, newfound nonpoverty) is precipitating a residential construction boom that has even the most avid reformers worried about the new Hanoi and the new Ho Chi Minh City. The soothing ochre-color walls of the French villas are being replaced with cheap concrete, aluminum, and plate glass. The result is houses that look centuries old about three months after they're built. You will also see these old-looking new houses along the highways throughout the country—just look for the date of construction on top of the house. Only time will tell what a new Vietnam will look like—but no one can deny that the architectural face of the country is rapidly changing.

Art

Whether you're a seasoned collector or just like pretty pictures, you can appreciate the explosion of Vietnamese art splashed onto canvases throughout the country. Much of the work is derivative (copies of French Masters, for instance) or clichéd, but some is truly impressive and unique. A handful of painters, including members of the loosely knit but hiply and cleverly named "Gang of Five," are treated as conquering heroes by expatriates, collectors, and international artists. The undisputed art capital is Hanoi, where dozens of galleries line their walls with the latest by Vietnam's rising stars. An afternoon meandering through the galleries is a must. Lacquerware (a Chinese creation, which the Vietnamese have embraced as their own) and stone and wood sculptures are for sale everywhere. Many pieces are painstaking replicas of ancient figures or statues, while others are chintzy knockoffs. A trained eye will easily distinguish the trash from the treasure. And if you're in the country to make major art purchases, it is crucial you work with a respected dealer; fakes of the more famous artists are sprouting like weeds.

Beaches

Unlike Thailand and other Southeast Asian countries, Vietnam's beach culture is still very underdeveloped. The country's endless stretch of pristine coast is still a working shoreline, home to thousands of fishing families who row daily into the surf in tiny, oval-shaped boats woven from reed and rattan. Some towns along the coast, however, are beginning to be developed with the influx of tourists. Nha Trang is home to the Thai-style Ana Mandara resort, and China Beach, near Danang, has the Furama Resort, an international hotel opened in 1997. Other new resorts are opening in Phan Thiet and Vung Tau.

These resorts are so new they still retain an air of glorious isolation, and it will be a few years yet before they attract the international tourist set. For now, for the most part, there are few restaurants or bars along the waterfront, no boutiques selling designer surf wear, and no lifeguards. And though the coral reefs and sea life are incredible and the surf is excellent, particularly in Danang (the site of an international surfing competition in 1994), very few places, if any, rent gear or give lessons. Check with your hotel or bring your own snorkeling, scuba diving, boating, or surfing equipment. Jet skiing and paragliding clubs have opened in Vung Tau and Nha Trang, which also has a scuba diving club, as does China Beach. For some of the most beautiful, untouched beaches in Vietnam, you'll need to head north to Halong Bay or south to Phu Quoc Island.

Dining

Though it may not look it at first glance, Vietnam is a nation obsessed with its culinary traditions. Rule 1: Vietnamese food is not "Chinese food without the spices." Sophisticated cuisine, distinct from what is north of its border, has evolved in Vietnam over the last few thousand years. Soy sauce is not as common in Vietnam as in China, for instance; instead, the nearly universal seasoning of choice in the country is *nuoc mam*—inadequately translated as fish sauce—a clear amber liquid pressed out of large barrels of anchovies and salt. This exquisitely complex condiment submerges itself in the flavors of other ingredients—it's truly a remarkable concoction. Don't be put off by the smell of this potent liquid; skeptical foreigners have been known to become converts after a couple of experiences. But do take care not to overdo, as a little bit goes a long way.

The cuisines in the south and the north differ subtly. Southern Vietnamese cooking uses a great variety of greens, fruits, meats, and seafood. The French, ever the gourmands, left their mark on the region in the form of elaborate vegetable dishes (French transplants such as asparagus are still grown in the southern highlands). The Indian influence is also apparent in the south, judging by the number of curries.

Central Vietnam is known almost as much for its culinary presentation—exquisitely displayed dishes are small but varied and numerous—as for its use of spices. Here the seafood and fresh fish are adorned with plenty of chili. Shrimp sauce is also a favorite, as are different forms of *banh,* rice pancakes with all kinds of fillings.

In the more temperate latitudes of the north, dishes are traditionally lighter and consist of fewer ingredients. Stir-fry is more popular in the north than elsewhere—understandable given China's proximity. But the dish that reigns supreme in Hanoi and the north (though also commonly found in the south) is *pho,* the ubiquitous noodle soup that can safely be called Vietnam's national dish. Served at all hours but especially at breakfast, this chicken (or beef or pork or shrimp) soup for the soul is a work of art that is a perfect balance of texture and taste.

To taste pho and other favorites, you only need to step out of your hotel and into the streets. Vietnam's best eating isn't found in elegant restaurants or hotel dining rooms but at stalls on every street corner and in every marketplace. These soup, rice, noodle, and seafood kitchens are usually run by several generations of a single family, and sitting down on the low plastic chairs at one of these self-contained sidewalk operations for a bowl of *bun cha* (chopped grilled meat and pork over vermicelli-style rice noodles) feels like joining in a family gathering.

In addition to pho, noodles, and spring rolls (called *nem* in the north, and *cha goi* in the south), rice is another staple, served with anything and everything. In Vietnam rice is food, food is rice. There is one word for both: *com.* Seafood is also delicious, abundant, and cheap all over Vietnam, but particularly in coastal towns such as Nha Trang, Danang, and Halong Bay, where large crabs and prawns are grilled to perfection. Beef and pork are also generally of high quality, but chicken tends to be somewhat tough in Vietnam. Dog meat isn't as inexpensive or plentiful as you might think, and the chance of encountering it shouldn't deter you from exploring Vietnam's back-alley food scene; just watch out for dishes that contain *thit cho.* Be sure to wander the markets in search of the dozens of incredible indigenous fruits, including rambutans, litchis, kumquats, papayas, pineapples, star fruit, and the spiky olfactory overload known as durian.

As for international cuisine, Vietnam's major cities have reentered the modern age. Upscale restaurants to suit nearly all palates have opened in Ho Chi Minh City and Hanoi. The nation's top hotels are winning over expatriate clientele with their superb cuisine. French, Italian, Indian, Chinese, Korean, Mexican, Middle Eastern, Thai, and, yes, certain configurations of fast food are all represented in the northern and southern hubs. And if *onigiri* are your favorite, you're in luck; Ho Chi Minh City alone has more than 20 Japanese restaurants. As soon as you venture outside Hanoi and Saigon, finding top-notch Western food is difficult. However, family-run restaurants and cafés with fresh seafood offerings, delicious meats, and tasty *an chay* (vegetarian dishes) are nearly everywhere.

Drinks include local beers—Ba Ba Ba (333), Halida, and Tiger—and rice wine (similar to sake), though you may want to skip the snake rice wine (with a cobra in the bottle) made "especially for men." You can also get French, Australian, and Californian wines at the better international restaurants, as well as beers such as Heineken (made in Vietnam) and Foster's. Tap water—and ice—are not potable for foreigners, so be sure to ask for bottled water like La Vie or Evian, which are widely available. Another option is a Coca-Cola or 7-Up (both also now made in Vietnam). Good, strong coffee and Vietnamese tea are served with breakfast, after dinner, and any time of day at local cafés.

Golf

With the influx of international businesspeople and tourists, golf courses have been opening—or reopening, as the case may be—after a long period of "anti-bourgeois" dormancy. These days most fairways are in the south. There are two 18-hole golf courses outside Saigon: the Vietnam Golf and Country Club, in the outlying district of Thu Duc, 10 km (6 mi) north of Saigon, and the Song Be Golf Resort, 20 km (12 mi) outside the city. Another delightful course is in Phan Thiet, 200 km (125 mi) east of Saigon. In the north, there is one golf course 40 km (25 mi) from Hanoi. One of the nicest, and oldest, courses in the country (dating from the 1920s) is in Dalat, in central Vietnam. Two others major courses are on the way, but with a government imperative to keep as many rice paddies as possible from succumbing to new development projects, it is unlikely you'll see a million Vietnamese kids wanting to be Tiger Woods anytime in the next decade.

Shopping

There is plenty to buy in Vietnam, though perhaps not of as high quality as elsewhere in Asia. Custom-made clothing in silks and linens, and unique handicrafts such as delicate blue-and-white ceramics, elegant black-and-red lacquerware, colorful textiles made by ethnic minority groups, and intricate woodcarvings of Buddhas and animals, can be found at rock-bottom prices. You can also find all kinds of items at the local markets, from aluminum kitchenware, straw baskets and bags, and lacquer chopsticks to plastic barrettes, velvet slip-on shoes, conical hats, and baseball caps. In addition, Vietnam—particularly Hanoi—has a booming contemporary arts scene, though paintings can get pricey. The asking price might be as little as $30, but don't be surprised if it's $1,000.

Hanoi is less expensive than Ho Chi Minh City and is a better place to find silks and have clothes tailor made. Ho Chi Minh City, however, has better markets and chicer shops filled with more contemporary-looking goods appealing to expatriates and Vietnam's growing moneyed class. In the rest of the country shopping is more tourist oriented and is centered around the major sights in the towns. One exception is the colorful outdoor weekend market in Sapa, in northern Vietnam. Here hill tribes from around the area convene to sell and exchange their beautifully embroidered, indigo-dyed clothing, as well as other handicrafts and food staples.

GREAT ITINERARIES

The itineraries that follow suggest ways in which destinations can be combined and give an idea of reasonable (minimum) amounts of time needed in various destinations. Other suggested itineraries are in every chapter.

Hanoi to Ho Chi Minh City

Length of Stay: 1–2 Weeks

If you have one to two weeks in Vietnam, you can divide your time between the country's two major urban centers, Hanoi and Ho Chi Minh City, and take short trips to the surrounding areas. For instance, from Ho Chi Minh City you could make a daylong foray into the Mekong Delta or to the Cu Chi Tunnels and the Caodai Holy See in Tay Ninh. From Hanoi you could take a day trip to the Perfume Pagoda or make an overnight excursion to beautiful Halong Bay.

With two weeks, you can probably also fit in a visit to one or maybe two destinations in the middle of the country—Hue, Danang, Dalat, or Nha Trang, for instance. You might begin in Ho Chi Minh City, fly to Danang, take a train, bus, or car to Hue, and from there fly to Hanoi. Or fly directly to Hue for a night and then fly on to Hanoi. Another option is to stop briefly in Danang, then drive to China Beach and on to beautifully-preserved Hoi An for a day. This itinerary doesn't give you much time to explore each region, but it does give you a chance to see more of the country.

TRANSPORTATION➤ Air travel to Ho Chi Minh City, Danang or Hue, and Hanoi is the best way to make use of limited time. Note that not all routes are flown every day and that Vietnam Airlines does not have service between every city (for instance, there is no service between Dalat and Nha Trang, between Danang and Hue, or between Hanoi and Haiphong). Check with your travel agent and confirm the availability of flights with Vietnam Airlines as soon as you are in the country. Once at your destination, rent a car and driver to get to places that are close enough to be easily reached by road.

Length of Stay: 3 Weeks or More

If you have three weeks or longer, you can travel the length of the country; plan on spending even more time in Vietnam if you want to get to more off-the-beaten spots. Seeing the whole country will give you a sense of its diversity—from the Mekong Delta's floating markets to the beaches of central Vietnam, from the former imperial capital of Hue to northern Vietnam's rugged highlands. Start either in Hanoi or in Ho Chi Minh City—and spend a couple of days exploring. Then use the city as a base for making one- to three-day excursions to points nearby (to the Mekong Delta in the south, for instance, or to Halong Bay in the north). After seeing the region, head north or south, depending on the city you began in; along the way, stop in such places as Phan Rang, Dalat, Nha

Trang, Danang, and Hue. Two or three days in each destination should be sufficient to see the sights, but who knows: You may find a delightful hotel on a secluded beach and decide to stay much longer.

TRANSPORTATION➢ If you're set on seeing as much as possible in the shortest amount of time, it makes the most sense to fly between major cities and towns—just be prepared to either backtrack a bit or skip a city or two since Vietnam Airlines doesn't fly between every destination in the country (☞ Transportation *in* Length of Stay: 1–2 Weeks, *above*). A series of flights from town to town up the coast from Ho Chi Minh City to Hanoi doesn't take much longer than the direct flight between the two. Only one destination in the highland north—Dien Bien Phu—is serviced by Vietnam Airlines. The rest you'll have to cover by land unless you'd like to charter a helicopter (☞ Chapter 2 for more information). To get to more inaccessible areas like the central highlands and the DMZ (Demilitarized Zone), be ready to brave the roads with a Jeep and driver or minibus tour (☞ Chapter 5 for more information).

A slower and less comfortable but perhaps more romantic way to get across the country is by train. The Reunification Express (☞ Train Travel *in* the Gold Guide) travels the length of the country from Ho Chi Minh City to Hanoi (and vice versa), stopping at most major towns along the coast. The scenery is often spectacular, sometimes drab, but the experience itself is never boring. (Depending on how long you wish to stay in each place, this trip could even be managed in two weeks or less.) You can also quite easily combine air travel with your train journey. For example, from Ho Chi Minh City you could fly to Nha Trang, then to Danang, and from there take a train or bus or hired car to Hue. From Hue fly to Hanoi, and from there explore northern Vietnam.

A third option is to hire a car or minibus with a driver to drive you the length of the country from Ho Chi Minh City to Hanoi, or vice versa (☞ Car Rental *in* the Gold Guide). Keep in mind that when driving around Vietnam you should set aside more time than you think to get from place to place. A distance of 100 km (62 mi) can take from 90 minutes to 2 hours, depending on road conditions.

FODOR'S CHOICE

No two people agree on what makes a perfect vacation, but it's fun and helpful to know what others think. We hope you'll have a chance to experience some of Fodor's Choices yourself in Vietnam. For detailed information about each entry, refer to the appropriate chapter.

Cultural Landmarks

★ **Central Post Office, Ho Chi Minh City.** Completed in 1891, this classic colonial building, with a huge map of old Indochina inside, is one of the best examples of the French architectural presence in Vietnam.

★ **Cham Museum, Danang.** Savor the glories of the ancient kingdom of Champa at the impressive Cham Museum.

★ **Hotel Continental, Ho Chi Minh City.** The setting for Graham Greene's *The Quiet American* and the meeting place for journalists and diplomats during the Vietnam War, the Continental is one of most historic hotels in town.

★ **Emperor's Tombs, Hue.** Vietnam's emperors were laid to rest in these elaborately constructed, extraordinarily beautiful, and peaceful tombs.

★ **Temple of Literature, Hanoi.** An oasis in the middle of Hanoi, the country's first university is an example of 11th-century Vietnamese architecture.

Dining

★ **Café des Amis, Hoi An.** Five heavenly courses of seafood or vegetarian ambrosia are served nightly; come again the next night, as the unwritten menu changes daily. *$*

★ **Hoa Sua, Hanoi.** The food is good, but what makes this place really special is the terra-cotta patio surrounded by palms—a great place for a calm lunch or brunch. *$$*

★ **Hue Restaurant, Hanoi.** Wonderful pork-wrapped sugarcane and other delicious Vietnamese standards are served at this casual sidewalk café. *$*

★ **Khazana, Hanoi.** Surprisingly delicious Indian cuisine made in a real Tandoor oven is served in an opulent setting. *$$*.

★ **Le Camargue, Ho Chi Minh City.** Unique Eurasian cuisine is accented by an elegant open-air villa setting. *$$$$*

★ **Lemongrass, Ho Chi Minh City.** Masterful Vietnamese standards and tasteful Franco-Viet decor make this an expat standard. *$$$*

★ **Ngoc Suong, Ho Chi Minh City.** Seafood perfection is served in a tree-house setting. *$*

★ **Ngoc Suong, Nha Trang.** Try some of the world's freshest and finest seafood while dining in a delightful garden. *$$*

Lodging

★ **Auberge, Sapa.** Until recently the only game in town, this expanded yet delightful hotel has hardwood floors, grand views, and great prices. *$$*

★ **Dalat Sofitel Palace, Dalat.** On the cool slopes of rolling green hills, this perfectly restored old-world resort is an ideal retreat, especially for golfers. *$$$–$$$$*

★ **Hotel Majestic, Ho Chi Minh City.** New restorations have uncovered a slice of colonial Saigon in its heyday. *$$$*

★ **New World Hotel Saigon, Ho Chi Minh City.** Presently the best international hotel in the city, it may soon be supplanted by one of the new luxury accommodations opening at a rapid rate. *$$$$*

★ **Sofitel Metropole, Hanoi.** Its beautifully renovated French colonial architecture and central location make this one of the most popular hotels in Hanoi. *$$$$*

★ **Stilt house, ethnic minority village.** A night in a traditional stilt house (such as those in Mai Chau or outside Sapa), a world away from fax machines and honking Honda Dreams, may be your most relaxing downtime in Vietnam. *¢*

The Natural World

★ **Hai Van Pass, north of Danang.** This stretch of Highway 1, perched on top of the Truong Son mountain range, has an unforgettable panorama of the startlingly limpid South China Sea.

★ **Halong Bay, northern Vietnam.** Jutting dramatically out of the South China Sea, Halong Bay's limestone archipelago is a water-bound sculpture garden.

★ **Mekong Delta, southern Vietnam.** Traveling along Mekong River tributaries on a boat to a tropical fruit orchard may be one of your most memorable excursions in Vietnam.

★ **Nha Trang, south-central coast.** Catch this beautiful resort beach on the South China Sea before it becomes overdeveloped.

★ **Sapa, northern Vietnam.** Hill-tribe cultures thrive in the magnificent verdant highlands shadowed by Vietnam's tallest mountain, Fansipan.

Shrines and Places of Worship

★ **Caodai Holy See, Tay Ninh.** South of Ho Chi Minh City, this colorfully decorated temple is devoted to Caodaism, a religion based on an amalgamation of Eastern and Western thought.

★ **Jade Emperor's Pagoda, Ho Chi Minh City.** A Vietnamese "It's a Small World," this pagoda is lined with carnival-like sculptures and reliefs of gods and mythical figures.

★ **Marble Mountains, south of Danang.** Remarkable cave temples house dozens of statues of the Buddha, some said to have magical powers.

★ **Perfume Pagoda, near Hanoi.** After a bus ride, a boat ride, and a two-hour hike to get here, this holy temple complex and mountaintop cavern inspire all who enter.

Shopping

★ **Heritage, Ho Chi Minh City.** The beautiful contemporary-looking lacquerware and outstanding replicas of antique Buddhas and statuary will leave you wishing you had bought more.

★ **Hoi An.** The whole town, a perfectly preserved ancient port, is almost entirely dedicated to seamstress boutiques and to souvenir shops that sell pottery and paintings by local artists.

★ **Tax Department Store, Ho Chi Minh City.** Some of the city's best bargains—from designer clothes to handmade bags to custom-made clothes—can be found at this huge store.

★ **Tien Dat, Hanoi.** The best tailor in town for casual custom clothing makes items to order using the finest silks and cottons.

★ **Weekend Market, Sapa.** Hill tribes from around Sapa convene at this colorful outdoor market to sell and exchange their beautiful handicrafts and food staples.

FESTIVALS AND SEASONAL EVENTS

There are nearly 400 major festivals throughout the country and countless smaller celebrations. Every festival is dedicated to something: a legendary event, a supernatural being, or quite often a famous ancestor. Most of Vietnam's festivals originated in the north or central regions and migrated southward; many events are celebrated differently in each locale. The dates of most festivals are based on the lunar calendar, as are weddings, funerals, and other important occasions. For exact festival dates, check with your tour operator or travel agency.

WINTER

EARLY–MID-JAN.➢ **Ong Tao,** the Festival of the Kitchen God, falls on the 23rd day of the 12th and last month of the lunar year, right before Tet. During this festival, every family buys a carp for the kitchen god, who watches over the house throughout the year, so he can ride to heaven on it. For a bon voyage, houses are cleaned and gifts offered. When the kitchen god returns home, new year celebrations begin.

MID-JAN.–MID-FEB.➢ By far Vietnam's largest and most important festival, **Tet,** the celebration of the lunar new year, takes place for a week usually between mid-January and mid-February. Many travelers to Vietnam plan their trips around Tet—either they come for the holiday or try to avoid it. Tet is a complex weeklong holiday whose themes are renewal, spiritual growth, ancestral reverence, and family ties. It's like Christmas, New Year's, Thanksgiving, Easter, Rosh Hashanah, and Yom Kippur all rolled into one. In many cases, entire communities shut down and take a few days off from their busy lives. Many museums, markets, restaurants, shops, and offices are closed for a four- or five-day weekend. Major hotels stay open, although some fine dining establishments may be closed for the first day of Tet but will open on Day 2 or 3.

Traditional Tet food, particularly *banh chung* (gelatinous sticky rice cakes with fatty pork), is consumed by the pound. Peach blossom branches ornament newly cleaned homes, and *mung tuoi* (small red envelopes of money) are presented to youngsters for good luck. Vietnamese love asking, "Where will you *an Tet?*"—literally, "Where will you eat Tet?" If you say you've got no plans, don't be surprised if you receive half a dozen invitations to celebrate at someone's house.

But passing Tet with some new friends is more than throwing on a pair of slacks and rapping on the door. Timing is crucial. Unless you are Bill Gates, it is not advisable for you to be the first person to cross the threshold of a Vietnamese house as the clock strikes midnight and ushers in the new year. This role of honor is reserved, usually well in advance, for a distinguished guest such as a party official, a university professor—or these days a successful businessperson. If the wrong person stumbles through the door first, it could mean disaster for the household.

House calls are positively required during Tet. Day 1 is reserved for close family relatives. Day 2 is for distant relatives, intimate relations, and important colleagues or bosses. Days 3 and 4 are for friends and newer acquaintances. If you are invited to *an Tet,* it is generally understood that you will show up on one of these days. A gift such as fruit or flowers and mung tuoi for the children will be greatly appreciated. But if you are going to sit down for a meal, you'll score major points with a bottle of cognac.

SPRING

MAR.–APR.➢ Early spring, in the middle of the second lunar month, is the time of the Buddhist **pilgrimage to the Perfume Pagoda** near Hanoi. The crowds at this time can clog the winding river with rowboats and make ascending the slippery stairs to the mountaintop a bit of a traffic nightmare, but you'll be welcomed with open arms by the thousands of pilgrims. There are plenty of peaceful spots to break up your boat ride and walk.

APR.➢ **Thanh Minh** is celebrated on the fifth day of the third month and is a day of ancestor worship; ceremonies usually involve burning incense over the graves of diseased loved ones. The **H'mong Spring Festival** is celebrated in the northwest mountain town of Sapa.

SUMMER

LATE MAY–EARLY JUNE➢ A three-day celebration in the fourth lunar month brings some colorful and oversize mythology to the village of **Phu Dong,** just across the Red River from Hanoi. The event commemorates the legendary exploits of the genie Thanh Giong, an ancient warrior born in Phu Dong who helped ward off Chinese invaders. Two hundred men hoist a massive centuries-old likeness of the local hero—he was said to be gargantuan—in a spectacular procession on the final day, when a Giong-led victory over the Chinese is reenacted.

Tet Doan Ngu, the celebration of the summer solstice, falls on the fifth day of the fifth month. Historically the festival takes place during the hottest time of year when fevers and malaria are most common. Fruit, rice, cakes, and liquor are served to ward off these diseases, and effigies are burned to satisfy the god of death.

AUG.–SEPT.➢ **Tet Trung Nguyen or Vu Lan,** the second most important festival after Tet, takes place on the 14th or 15th day of the seventh lunar month. It is a time to give thanks and praise to parents and ancestors. But its most important function is to help lost souls by pardoning and looking after them. These homeless spirits, Buddhists believe, include those who died unnatural deaths: soldiers killed in war, murder and accident victims, and ancestors whose graves are not properly tended by the living.

On **Ram Thang Bay,** the 15th day of the seventh lunar month, the portals of hell are allegedly thrown open, and its souls ascend to the material world for a day, where offerings of fruit, sticky-rice cakes, flowers, and sweetened rice cookies are intended to ease their transition to heaven. Captured animals, in particular birds and fish, are released to signify the liberation of lost souls, and it is not uncommon to see a Vietnamese throw a cupped bird skyward or let a carp slither out of his or her hands and into a lake or stream. Burning paper models of material objects, called *hang ma,* is also common, and though this tradition has ancient origins, modern times are providing a curious twist—paper models of motorcycles, mobile phones, luxury cars, and even new homes are set ablaze in the hope of providing comfort for the damned. This festival is a favorite for parents, who bring children to the pagodas to teach them about gratefulness, piety, and respect. On the night before Vu Lan, big pagodas in Hanoi and Saigon are jammed with people.

AUTUMN

A 4,000-year dependence on the rice harvest has generated an abundance of harvest festivals. Each locale or region celebrates differently, so you may want to ask your tour guide or tour operator about specific harvest festivals throughout Vietnam.

SEPT.➢ Ten thousand screaming, chanting, gambling Vietnamese gather in the muddy northern beach town of Do Son in the 8th lunar month for what is the most spectacular animal battle in the country: the **Do Son Bullfighting Festival.** This intensely popular clash of the titans has lost much of its original legendary mystery, but that's not why people flock here. It's the crashing of buffalo horn on skull, the deep reverberating thud of 2,000-pound beasts racing toward each other from a distance of 250 yards, and perhaps more than anything, the glory that comes with a victory. The hometown of the winning bull and its trainers earns bragging rights for an entire year. A buffalo meat feast follows the competition.

SEPT.–OCT.➢ **Trung Thu, or the Mid-Autumn Festival** (also known as the Moon-Watching Festival), on the 14th or 15th day of the eighth lunar month, is especially for children. Families throw parties for their children and friends. Parading around with gongs and drums and doing dragon dances is the order of the day, as is eating fruits and cakes.

NOV.–DEC.➢ **Trung Thap,** which falls on the 10th day of the tenth lunar month, is a festival surrounding the traditional harvesting of herbal plants.

2 Hanoi

Ancient lore and postmodern kitsch collide in Vietnam's capital. Experience both in the sensory feast of Hanoi's Old Quarter, where traditional guilds are juxtaposed with modern glitter. Wander around the city's lakes and along its wide, tree-lined boulevards where French colonial architecture and age-old temples meet. Explore its lively art and café scenes, and breeze through its quirky museums. Then head out of town on excursions to some of northern Vietnam's highlights.

By Michael Mathes and Felicity Wood

HANOI, THE SELF-APPOINTED STRONGHOLD of "true" Vietnamese, anti-imperialist culture, has learned to covet satellite TV and blue jeans. The country's leaders let in a flood of overseas investment from China, Malaysia, Singapore, Taiwan, and even the United States and Australia, and now the capital of the Socialist Republic of Vietnam relishes its newfound economic liberalization despite itself. Although Western fashions, music, and food have managed to elbow their way into the once-impenetrable north, Hanoi is appealing because it retains its ancient culture, French colonial architecture, broad tree-lined boulevards, and beautiful lakes.

The city dates to the 7th century, when Chinese Sui dynasty settlers occupied the area and set up a capital called Tong Binh. In 1010 King Ly Thai To is said to have seen a golden dragon ascending from Hoan Kiem Lake. The dragon is a traditional Chinese symbol of royal power, and the king took the omen literally: He relocated his capital to the shores of the lake, the site of present-day Hanoi, and named his new city Thang Long, or "City of the Ascending Dragon." During the 11th century the old citadel was built, and 36 villages, each with its own specialized vocation, sprang up to service the royal court. This is the origin of the 36 streets that define the city's Old Quarter.

In 1428 King Le Loi is said to have driven Vietnam's Chinese overlords from the country with the help of a magic sword. Celebrating his success after the war with a boating excursion on Hoan Kiem Lake, Le Loi was confronted by a gigantic golden tortoise that retrieved the sword for its heavenly owner. Thus the lake became known as the Lake of the Restored Sword, or Ho Hoan Kiem. In 1789 the Chinese reconquered Hanoi but not for long. Nguyen Hue, leader of a rebellion in Tay Son (in the south), drove the Manchu invaders out of the country and crowned himself King Quang Trung. Officially, however, by then the country was led by the Nguyen dynasty, which moved the capital to Hue under the rule of Gia Long in 1802. This chapter in northern Vietnam's history was in part orchestrated by the French, who began to play a stronger role in the political and commercial fabric of the country.

The French usurped more and more control, setting up the protectorate of Annam in 1883–84, which meant the Hue royalty held the reins but only under the auspices of French rule. In the following years the French set up its administration and used Hanoi as the Eastern Capital, or Dong Kinh (the origin of *Tonkin*), of French Indochina. The Chinese character of the city was basically eliminated as the French filled in canals between Hanoi's many lakes and created a plain on which to remake the capital in its own mold. They constructed the large villas and administrative buildings that cluster in the streets around the present-day Presidential Palace and the Ho Chi Minh Mausoleum and that continue to give the city a somewhat dilapidated but still striking colonial-era feel.

Once the French were defeated by the Vietminh at Dien Bien Phu, in 1954, the city was again declared the capital of Vietnam. From 1954 until 1975 it was the seat of the Democratic Republic of Vietnam, or North Vietnam, from which Ho Chi Minh initiated his struggle to reunify the country, which had been split by the 1954 Geneva Accords. Despite American attempts to smash the Communist administration by bombing it from the air, the city survived the war with most of its grandeur remarkably intact. Given the country's experience with foreign rulers, it is not surprising that the post-1975 socialist order sought to seal off the city and, after the war with China in 1979, expel ethnic Chinese from Vietnam, although many of these predominantly mercantile families had lived in Vietnam for generations.

In the decades after 1975 relations with the Soviet Union were strengthened. Tens of thousands of Russian advisers came to live in Hanoi and other parts of the country, leaving their mark in such buildings as the Viet Xo Cultural Palace. But the '80s were a tough time for Hanoians and everyone else. Natural disasters and international isolation lead to near mass starvation. Then in 1986 the government proclaimed *doi moi,* the move to a market economy. Foreign investors started preliminary explorations, and the Soviet Union dissolved, taking with it foreign assistance to Vietnam. But more and more foreign investment started coming, especially after the American embargo was lifted in 1993.

More than a decade of economic reforms has changed the attitudes of the ruling party members considerably, and reformist city leaders are learning the ways of capitalism quickly—perhaps too quickly, according to some of the aging Communist Party cadres and conservative critics who pride themselves on their city's being the seat of Vietnam's socialist revolution. Although they are loathe to admit it, their once-firm hold on the past and its ideals of solidarity are loosening quickly. The sanctimonious concept known as market socialism is intended to strike a delicate balance between socialist ideals and economic prosperity, but while most young Hanoians are familiar with the former, it is the latter they crave.

But few can argue that the last decade of change in Hanoi has been anything short of a godsend. Hanoi is now cordially welcoming both billions of dollars of foreign investment and the many foreign visitors eager to see this city—this nation—in the midst of renewal. In the past three years, as the economy has continued to open and the people have increasing amounts of disposable income, the city has modernized rapidly. Less than a decade ago the predominant sound at an intersection was the delicate ring of bicycle bells. Today motorcycles and cars are taxing the city's antiquated road system. Life for a pedestrian is, in short, dangerous. But the chaos has its own attraction. Dust hangs heavy in the air as a side effect of the construction boom, and you can see changes that took years to happen in the West occurring literally before your eyes. Where the prison commonly referred to by U.S. soldiers as the Hanoi Hilton once stood is now a 20-story office building. Where once a small lake sat is now a gas station.

Nonetheless, Hanoi remains a city of academics, artists, diplomats—and contradictions. Although you will see people carrying their new TVs on the back of their Honda Dream motorbikes, you will also see people carrying hundreds of pounds of rice on bicycles. People may zoom around all day doing business, but they also take time out for discussions over a cup of coffee in a café. Pete Peterson, once a prisoner in the Hanoi Hilton, is now the U.S. ambassador to Vietnam. On a Sunday you may see him cruising to a noodle shop on his motorbike. Eighty-year-old General Giap, the commander of the Vietminh forces at Dien Bien Phu, is involved in Vietnam's developing telecommunications industry. Like everyone else in Hanoi and all over Vietnam, General Giap is aware of his history but is moving on with the times.

Pleasures and Pastimes

Art Galleries

Hanoi is Vietnam's undisputed fine arts capital, with dozens of art galleries happily partaking in an artistic renaissance. At least half a dozen are serious venues and not just wall space for souvenir art. A tour of the finer galleries—showing the works of young painters like Dinh Y Nhi, Truong Tan, and Le Thiet Cuong—offers a glimpse into the modern Vietnamese psyche. Exhibits at government-sponsored galleries show Vietnam's awkward transformation from communism to "free-market socialism." Here, idyllic portraits of village life hang next to political propaganda posters. The burnished inlay of lacquer, a Chinese creation embraced by Vietnam as its own; extraordinary watercolors on rice paper; the multifarious weavings of the ethnic minority groups—all have emerged from hibernation to create a national oeuvre surprisingly palatable to Western sensibilities. With the burgeoning reputation of Vietnamese art in both domestic and international circles, however, prices have risen remarkably in the past five years.

Cafés

More than any other city in Vietnam, Hanoi has a flourishing café society, a legacy of French colonial days. Now historic haunts compete with trendy cafés serving imported coffee to the sounds of jazz and MTV. At the humbler end of the spectrum, myriad sidewalk spots—often consisting of just a few tiny stools and tables—play host to students, artists, Communist Party cadres, and philosophical types who sip *ca fe den,* or black coffee, sometimes with a whipped egg on top. Park yourself at one of these places, and—who knows—you could find yourself sitting beside the next Vietnamese Hemingway or Einstein, or the chairman of the Hanoi People's Committee.

Dining

Hanoi's cuisine offers plenty of excitement if you're an adventurous diner. What it doesn't have in color or spice, it makes up for in outlandish offerings—from eight-course meals of dog meat (*thit cho*) to barbecued songbirds and snake-penis wine. (In the outlying snake village of Le Mat, your dinner is skinned alive and its blood mixed with rice wine for a 100-proof shot of virility!)

If you're looking for a dinner a bit less provocative, you should know that Hanoi is also home to Vietnam's most famous dish—*pho* (rice noodles in chicken or beef broth). This and other northern specialties are best enjoyed at the bustling sidewalk food stalls lining many streets. Hanoi also has a wide array of good international restaurants, and new ones are opening all the time. (They also close frequently, so some listings may be gone by the time you get to Hanoi; check in advance before setting out.)

Cuisine options range from Vietnamese to Japanese, French, and Italian. Prices range from the incredibly cheap to the just plain inexpensive—even in more upscale restaurants you'll pay less than in other big cities around the world (except perhaps at the big international hotels). In Hanoi restaurants usually close by 10 PM. Sidewalk eateries stop serving breakfast and lunch by 2 and don't reopen for dinner until about 4. You can always find a late-night noodle stand.

The capital is also a city for beer drinkers. Pints of *bia hoi* (fresh but weak draft beer tapped from kegs) are enjoyed with snack foods like boiled peanuts, dried squid, and pork rolls beginning in the late morning. It's a wonder how Hanoians get any work done, judging from the number of hours they spend at the hundreds of bia hoi sites around the city. This quintessential Hanoi pastime should not be missed.

Lakes

Hanoi's network of lakes is perhaps its most romantic asset. A byproduct of the Red River floodplain, Hanoi's biggest lake, West Lake (Ho Tay), resembles Lake Geneva from its southern edge (except for the absence of mountains). In the evenings groups of Vietnamese of all ages line the shores of West Lake and central Hoan Kiem Lake to soak up the calming breeze off the water. With such an abundance of water, it is surprising that boating is not really part of Hanoi life. Apart from the canoes used by fisherman and a few low-budget paddleboats popular with courting couples, the lakes are free of nautical traffic. You can, however, hire cruise boats on West Lake for large parties. And with the recent opening of the upscale Hanoi Club on the lake's southeast fringe, speed boats, jet skis, and catamarans are appearing for the first time.

Lodging

Over the last five years, many quite luxurious (and surprisingly expensive) joint-venture international hotels have opened in Hanoi—and they are continuing to open every year. These hotels are in the early years of their existence, which is reflected in the sometimes haphazard service. Patience may be required. Minihotels are another good option; they are reasonably priced and generally have such amenities as cable TV, IDD telephones, and air-conditioning. These smaller properties are often a better option than the huge state-run hotels, many of which were built in the '60s and haven't been properly maintained or renovated since.

Most hotels are in the historic, crowded, and central Hoan Kiem District, which includes the bustling Old Quarter, or in the Ba Dinh District, around Ho Chi Minh's Mausoleum and on West Lake. Though hotels in the Ba Dinh District may seem a little far away (you may need to take a taxi to get into the center of town), they are out of the hustle and bustle of downtown and closer to most of the embassies and corporate offices.

Shopping

It is often said the average working Hanoi woman spends more than 50% of her salary on clothing. And judging by the activity around the vendors selling both bolts of cloth and ready-to-wear fashions, it's more than just an urban myth. The Vietnamese—both men and women—are generally sharp dressers (if they can afford to be), mixing classic European style and retro '70s items. You can easily get clothing—in silk, linen, or any other fabric—tailor made in a day. Hanoi offers some of Vietnam's best selections of silver jewelry, pottery, hand-woven textiles, embroidery, and art, as well as traditional prints, bright wooden water puppets, pottery, and baskets from nearby villages. Finding quality gifts may take some hunting, however, as standards of work vary greatly. Markets are generally better for sightseeing than for finding a treasure trove of souvenirs.

EXPLORING HANOI

Hanoi is divided into four main districts, or *quan*. The **Hoan Kiem District,** named after the lake at its center, stretches from the railway tracks to the river, north of Nguyen Du Street, and is the hub of all local and tourist activity. Just north of the lake is the Old Quarter, a charming cluster of ancient streets. South of the lake you'll find the modern city center, once the French Quarter, which houses grand colonial-style villas that have been turned into hotels and offices; the best examples of French-era architecture are around Dien Bien Phu Street and Le Hong Phong Street, where embassies line the road.

The **Ba Dinh District** includes the zoo, Ho Chi Minh's Mausoleum, and areas around West Lake. Big buildings, fine hotels, and open spaces define the area. North of both Ba Dinh and Hoan Kiem is picturesque West Lake. The **Hai Ba Trung District,** which covers the southeast part of Hanoi, is a calm, elegant residential area; the primary attraction here is Lenin Park, in the northwest corner of the district. The **Dong Da District,** to the southwest, is where the Temple of Literature can be found (along its northern edge).

Unlike Ho Chi Minh City, Hanoi does offer a few places where you can have a very pleasant stroll, particularly around the edges of its many lakes. The escalating traffic congestion along its narrow streets, where the footpaths are already crowded with sidewalk vendors, often forces you back out into the melee, however. Anyone thinking to take a wistful walk along the banks of the Red River should take a taxi toward the Thang Long Bridge (the road to the airport) and get off just south of the imposing concrete span, where there is a small green fringe bordering the waterway.

Getting around Hanoi on foot can be tiring, so if you're intending to stick within the Old Quarter or elsewhere in Hoan Kiem District, break up your walks with a cyclo ride or two. Otherwise consider taking taxis, or if the weather is good and you're feeling a little more gung ho, hop on the back of a *xe om* (motorcycle taxi). Although the traffic may look a little daunting, once you learn to trust your driver, you will (perhaps) realize there actually is a knack for navigating what seems like streams of vehicular anarchy. If you're feeling really brave, consider renting a Chinese bicycle for a day and pedaling yourself around.

Once you have seen the sights in Hanoi, it's time to jump off into the "real" Vietnam: the countryside. Not one hour out of Hanoi in any direction brings you to stretches of rice paddies interrupted only by villages and jagged rocky outcrops, which makes taking day trips, with the capital as a base, a very viable option.

Great Itineraries

IF YOU HAVE 2 DAYS

If you'll just be passing through, your time would be best spent exploring the Old Quarter and visiting Ho Chi Minh's Mausoleum and the adjacent museum. On your second day take in a show at the water-puppet theater and browse the city's many art galleries.

IF YOU HAVE 5 DAYS

Spend two days wandering the Old Quarter and exploring the Ba Dinh District, where you'll find such interesting sights as the Ho Chi Minh Mausoleum, One Pillar Pagoda, and the Temple of Literature. Then devote your remaining time to side trips from the city: to Halong Bay (☞ Chapter 3), where you can easily spend two days exploring the limestone grottoes by boat; or a one-day trip to the Perfume Pagoda (☞ Side Trips from Hanoi, *below*); or an overnight stay in a Thai minority family's stilt house in Mai Chau Valley (☞ Chapter 3).

IF YOU HAVE 10 DAYS

Spend a few days seeing the major sights described above while making arrangements to travel to Sapa (☞ Chapter 3) by car or train (allow a day or an overnight for traveling either way). Sapa's mountain trails and ethnic-minority villages will occupy you for at least two full days. Upon your return to Hanoi, take in the sights you may have missed, such as Lenin Park or the recently refurbished Opera House and the nearby History and Revolutionary museums. Your next excursion could be to the mist-covered islets of Halong Bay or a shorter trip to the Perfume Pagoda or the ancient Vietnamese capital of Hoa Lu. If you have time, make your way to the nearby professional craft villages such as Bat Trang, just 12 km (7 mi) on the east side of the Red River, the source of most ceramics sold in Hanoi.

Hanoi

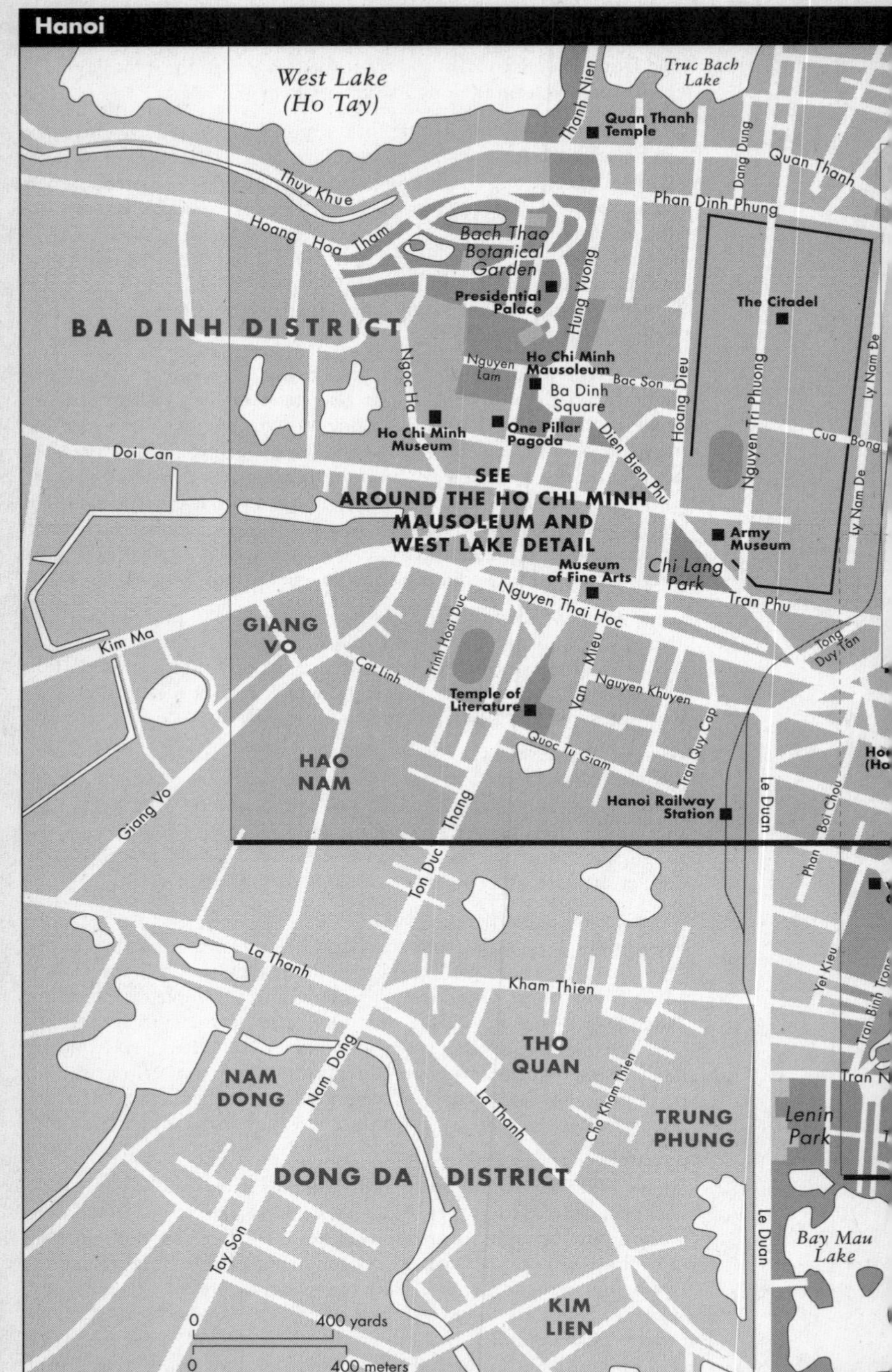
West Lake
(Ho Tay)
Truc Bach
Lake
Thanh Nien
Quan Thanh
Temple
Dang Dung
Quan Thanh
Thuy Khue
Phan Dinh Phung
Hoang Hoa Tham
Bach Thao
Botanical
Garden
Presidential
Palace
Hung Vuong
The Citadel
BA DINH DISTRICT
Ngoc Ha
Nguyen
Lam
Ho Chi Minh
Mausoleum
Bac Son
Ba Dinh
Square
Hoang Dieu
Nguyen Tri Phuong
Ly Nam De
Ho Chi Minh
Museum
One Pillar
Pagoda
Dien Bien Phu
Cua Bong
Doi Can
SEE
AROUND THE HO CHI MINH
MAUSOLEUM AND
WEST LAKE DETAIL
Army
Museum
Museum
of Fine Arts
Chi Lang
Park
Tran Phu
Nguyen Thai Hoc
GIANG
VO
Kim Ma
Trinh Hoai Duc
Van Mieu
Tong
Duy Tan
Cat Linh
Nguyen Khuyen
Temple of
Literature
Quoc Tu Giam
Tran Quy Cap
HAO
NAM
Giang Vo
Hanoi Railway
Station
Le Duan
Ton Duc Thang
Phan Boi Chau
La Thanh
Kham Thien
Yet Kieu
Tran Binh Trong
THO
QUAN
NAM
DONG
Nam Dong
La Thanh
Cho Kham Thien
TRUNG
PHUNG
Lenin
Park
DONG DA DISTRICT
Le Duan
Bay Mau
Lake
Tay Son
KIM
LIEN
0
400 yards
0
400 meters

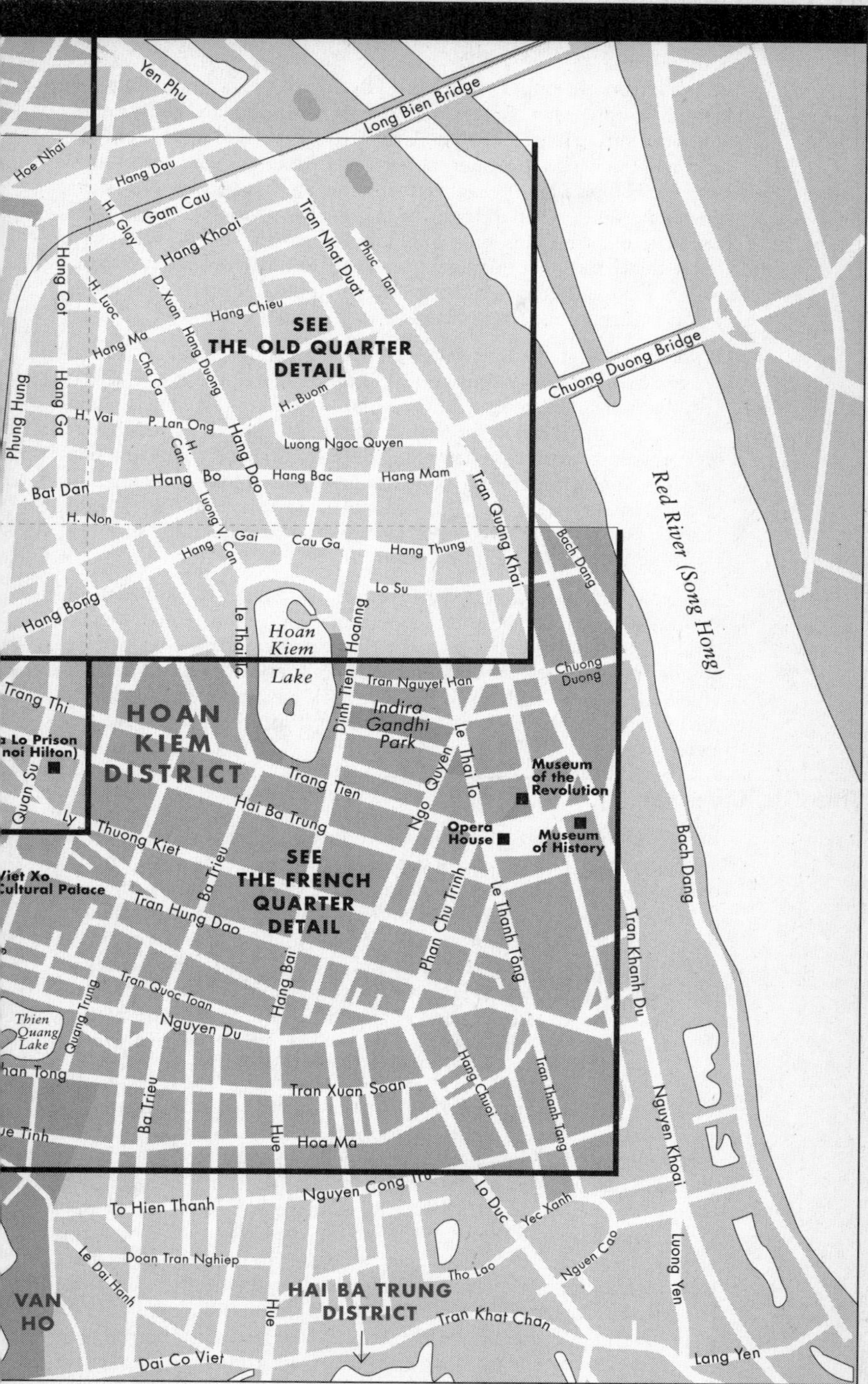
Yen Phu
Long Bien Bridge
Hoe Nhai
Hang Dau
Gam Cau
H. Giay
Hang Khoai
Tran Nhat Duat
Phuc Tan
Hang Cot
H. Luoc
D. Xuan
Hang Chieu
SEE
THE OLD QUARTER
DETAIL
Hang Ma
Cha Ca
Hang Duong
Chuong Duong Bridge
Phung Hung
Hang Ga
H. Vai
P. Lan Ong
H. Buom
Luong Ngoc Quyen
H. Can.
Hang Dao
Bat Dan
Hang Bo
Hang Bac
Hang Mam
Tran Quang Khai
Red River (Song Hong)
H. Non
Luong V. Can
Hang Gai
Cau Go
Hang Thung
Bach Dang
Lo Su
Hang Bong
Le Thai To
Hoan Kiem Lake
Dinh Tien Hoanng
Tran Nguyet Han
Chuong Duong
Trang Thi
HOAN KIEM DISTRICT
Indira Gandhi Park
Le Thai To
Museum of the Revolution
Trang Tien
Ngo Quyen
Quan Su
Ly
Hai Ba Trung
Opera House
Museum of History
Thuong Kiet
Bach Dang
Viet Xo Cultural Palace
Ba Trieu
SEE
THE FRENCH
QUARTER
DETAIL
Phan Chu Trinh
Le Thanh Tong
Tran Hung Dao
Tran Khanh Du
Tran Quoc Toan
Hang Bai
Thien Quang Lake
Quang Trung
Nguyen Du
Tran Xuan Soan
Hang Chuoi
Tran Thanh Tang
Nguyen Khoai
Ba Trieu
Hue
Hoa Ma
Nguyen Cong Tru
Lo Duc
Yec Xanh
To Hien Thanh
Le Dai Hanh
Doan Tran Nghiep
Tho Lao
Nguen Cao
Luong Yen
VAN HO
HAI BA TRUNG DISTRICT
Hue
Tran Khat Chan
Dai Co Viet
Lang Yen

When to Tour Hanoi

The ideal time to visit Hanoi weatherwise is between October (with temperatures averaging 80°F) and mid-December (with temperatures ranging from the upper 60s to mid-70s), when the heat and humidity are not so oppressive. But be prepared for cold snaps and chilly nights. The brief spring from March to April is also a pleasant time. From January to March a layer of clammy mist—the infamous *mua phun*—hovers over Hanoi. The city begins its summer swelter in May and sweats through August, when the monsoons bring heavy downpours and sudden flooding. This continues until late September, so if you choose to brave the elements at this time, bring rubber footwear and rain pants or buy them in Hanoi—because you could be in it up to your knees. Temperatures range from the mid-70s to the high 90s.

With an eye on the festival calendar, from late January to early February is a good time to visit if you want to breathe in the excitement of Tet, the lunar new year, a movable date based on the Chinese lunar calendar. In preparation for Vietnam's largest festival, the Old Quarter comes alive with floor-to-ceiling displays of moon cakes, red banners, joss sticks, and red envelopes for giving lucky money (*mung tuoi*) to children. Beware: When Tet does arrive, most shops and restaurants close for up to a week. If you are planning to conduct any business, this is definitely not the time to do it.

February is also the time to join the mass Buddhist pilgrimage to the Perfume Pagoda, but be prepared to deal with serious crowds—many thousands each day—if you make the trip during this peak season. Smaller religious festivals take place at Hanoi's temples and outlying villages in March and April. Because all Vietnamese festivals follow the lunar calendar, check with your tour operator or travel agency for exact dates.

The Old Quarter

Between Hoan Kiem Lake, Long Bien Bridge, a former city rampart, and a citadel wall lies the oldest part of the city. The area was unified under Chinese rule, when ramparts were built to encircle the city. When Vietnam gained its independence from China in the 11th century, King Ly Thai To built his palace here, and the area developed as a crafts center. Artisans were attracted from all over the northern part of the country and formed cooperative living and working situations based on specialized trades and village affiliation. In the 13th century the various crafts—silversmiths, metal workers, potters, carpenters—organized themselves into official guilds.

This area is referred to as the 36 Streets—actually there are nearly 70. To this day the streets are still named after the crafts practiced by the original guilds, and they maintain their individual character despite the encroachment of more modern lifestyles. Note the slim buildings called tunnel or tube houses—with narrow frontage but deceiving depth—which combine workshops and living quarters. They were built this way because each business was taxed according to the width of its storefront. In addition to the specialty shops you'll still find here, each street has religious structures reflecting the beliefs of the village from which its original guilds came. Some are temples dedicated to the patron saint of a particular craft. Hang Bong and Hang Dao, as examples, each have five of these pagodas and small temples. Many are open to the public and offer welcome relief from the intensity of the streets.

Numbers in the text correspond to numbers in the margin and on the Old Quarter map.

Dong Xuan Market, **1**
Hang Bac Street, **3**
Hang Dao Street, **2**
Hang Gai Street, **6**
Hang Ma Street, **8**
Hang Quat Street, **7**
Hoan Kiem Lake, **4**
Ngoc Son Temple, **5**

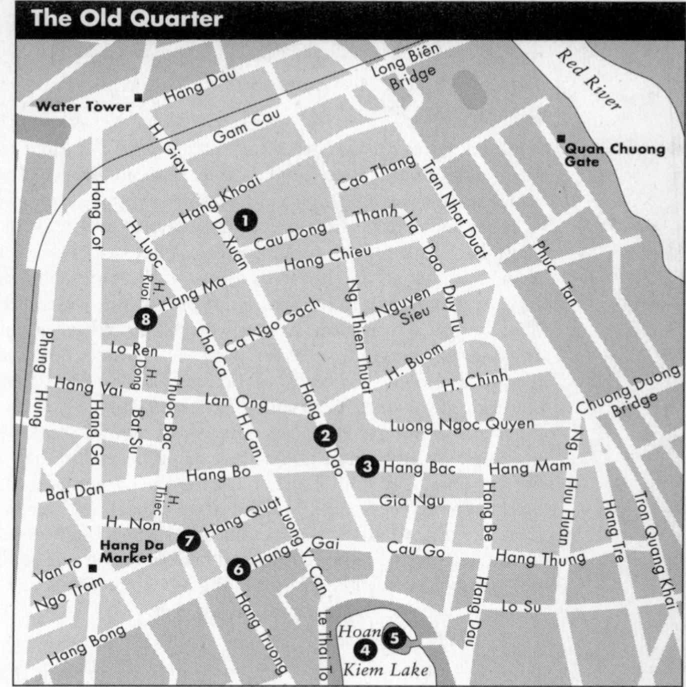

A Good Walk

Begin your walking tour of the Old Quarter in the northern section of the Hoan Kiem District, at the **Dong Xuan Market** ① on Hang Chieu Street. From here you can dive right into the bustle of the ancient streets—but be careful in the traffic! These streets are narrow, and the main roadways are clogged with motorbikes, fruit sellers, street sweepers, endless mercantile activity, even funeral processions. Also be aware that many streets in Hanoi—and throughout Vietnam—bear different names in different sections. The main artery north through the Old Quarter, for example, is 1½-km (1-mi) long and changes name six times. This is the street on which you'll start.

From the intersection of Hang Chieu and Dong Xuan streets, head south on Dong Xuan, which immediately turns into Hang Duong (Sugar) Street and then into Hang Ngang Street. Spare a moment for 48 Hang Ngang Street, where President Ho Chi Minh wrote his country's Declaration of Independence. He then read the document (which borrows liberally from Thomas Jefferson's American declaration) to a massive crowd gathered at Ba Dinh Square on September 2, 1945, when he declared Vietnam's independence from France. Continue south, to **Hang Dao Street** ②. Hang Dao Street divides the Old Quarter and serves as a convenient corridor from which to venture down any of the appealing side streets. Once you come to busy **Hang Bac Street** ③, turn left.

Turning right down Hang Be Street brings you to the historic boat-building district. The bamboo rafts, called *cai mang,* that you see here were designed especially for the shallow rivers, lakes, and swamps of Hanoi. From Hang Be Street take a right on Cau Go Street, the southeast border of the Old Quarter. This neighborhood was known for its flower market in colonial times, a vestige of which can be found at the intersection with Hang Dao Street. Just beyond this flower mart and to the left is the northern tip of **Hoan Kiem Lake** ④. On the left, or east, side is the distinctive red footbridge that leads to **Ngoc Son Temple** ⑤, the focal point for legends surrounding King Le Loi's encounter with the Ho Guom turtle. This is a good place to have a rest and enjoy the lake.

Walk back to Cau Go Street and through the chaotic intersection here. Beyond this roundabout, Cau Go Street becomes **Hang Gai Street** ⑥, where you'll want to spend some time if you're shopping for embroidery, silk, or other souvenirs or if you want to wander through some art galleries. From here turn north on Hang Hom Street, which leads to **Hang Quat Street** ⑦. This area is home to a few of the oldest musical instrument shops still standing in the Old Quarter. A quick jog to the left on Hang Non Street will bring you to Hang Thiec Street, where utilitarian tin chests and utensils dangle from every doorway. Notice the crumbling, plank-fronted house at 65 Hang Thiec Street; this kind of structure was a more common site around the ancient city streets 10–15 years ago and is a reminder that not everyone has the cash to rebuild yet. Given the pace of development in Hanoi, however, it could be a glittering new minihotel by the time you visit. Farther north, this street becomes Thuoc Bac Street. The street has maintained quite a bit of its French-era Art Deco frontage. Eventually this street becomes **Hang Ma Street** ⑧, which gets its name from the paper goods and fake money made for burning to appease ancestral spirits. East on Hang Ma Street leads you back to Hang Chieu Street and the Dong Xuan Market.

TIMING

One walk will not be enough to acquaint you with the various specialties of the maze-like Old Quarter. Be prepared to get distracted by the activity, honked at by motorbikers, approached by beggars, hounded by cyclo drivers, repulsed by the food stalls vending all kinds of dishes, and accept that you will lose your way at least twice—no matter what time of day. Since the Old Quarter is filled with shops, this is the kind of walk that could take two hours or ten, depending on how much of a browser you are. If you use a landmark such as Dong Xuan or Hang Da market, or the northern edge of Hoan Kiem Lake, you could complete a circuit in two to three hours.

Sights to See

❶ **Dong Xuan Market.** Once conveniently accessible by riverboat, this market, the oldest and largest in the city, has seen trading with the whole of Southeast Asia. The huge structure, to which the French added a number of features including a new facade, was destroyed by a massive fire in 1994—ironically enough on July 14, Bastille Day. The fire displaced 3,000 workers, caused millions of dollars in damage and losses, and took five human lives, not to mention the lives of thousands of exotic and endangered animals. The market reopened in December 1996 with a bit of a stir: Hundreds of women, livid over unfair stall allocations, took to the streets in anger, inducing the prime minister's office to intercede. Today the market looks more like a concrete shopping mall but continues to offer all manner of local and Western goods. ✉ *Dong Xuan and Hang Chieu Sts.* ⏲ *Daily 7–7.*

❸ **Hang Bac Street.** This street was originally dominated by silversmiths and money changers and still has a wide variety of jewelry shops. The Dong Cac jewelers' guild was established here in 1428, and it later erected a temple (now gone) in tribute to three 6th-century brothers whose jewelry skills, learned from the Chinese, made them the patron saints of Vietnamese jewelry.

❷ **Hang Dao Street.** Since the 15th century, when it was one of the original silk-trading centers, Hang Dao Street has been known for its textiles. It first specialized in lovely pink silk, always in particular demand because the color symbolizes the Vietnamese lunar new year. By the 18th century the street had branched out into a whole spectrum of colors. When the French colonized Vietnam, Hang Dao Street became the center for all traffic in silk, with massive biweekly trade fairs. Indians who settled here at the turn of the century introduced textiles from the West, and today the street features ready-made clothing in addition to bolts of silk.

★ ❻ **Hang Gai Street.** The Street of Hemp now offers a variety of goods, including ready-made silk, lovely embroidery, and silver products. Those who don't have qualms about buying bootleg recordings smuggled from China can also acquire a wide range of compact discs for about 25,000d each.

❽ **Hang Ma Street.** Here you can find delicate *ma,* paper replicas of material possessions made to be burned in tribute to one's ancestors. These faux luxury villas and Honda motorbikes can be found alongside more practical merchandise such as imported party decorations.

★ ❼ **Hang Quat Street.** The Street of Fans now features a stunning array of religious paraphernalia, including beautiful funeral and festival flags. It is one of the most atmospheric streets in Hanoi.

★ ❹ **Hoan Kiem Lake** (Ho Hoan Kiem or Ho Guom). The spiritual, legendary, and social heart of Hanoi, Hoan Kiem Lake, the Lake of the Restored Sword, is one of the most enchanting spots in the city. In the early morning mist locals come to the lakeshore to swing their arms and legs in exercise, play a little badminton, and practice tai chi. The lake serves as a gathering point during major festivals such as Tet and for holidays like Vietnam National Day, but it's also a relaxing lunchtime escape or evening rendezvous point for friends and lovers. Vietnamese of all ages delight in recounting the legend of how the Lake of the Restored Sword got its name: 15th-century war hero Le Loi used a magic golden sword from heaven to vanquish Chinese invaders. While Le Loi was boating on the lake in celebration of his successful martial exploits, a gigantic tortoise rose from the depths and retrieved the blade for its heavenly owner. The legend may owe some of its universal popularity to the real turtles still living in the lake. The apparently unique species, known as *rafetus swimhoei,* are a city favorite—some estimate they're the largest freshwater turtles on earth, but no one knows for sure. Huge crowds gather at the water's edge whenever one of these near-mythical creatures comes up for air, which herpetologists (yes, they're the reptile experts) say is happening with increasing frequency as the lake becomes more polluted.

❺ **Ngoc Son Temple** (Den Ngoc Son). Quiet and well-manicured, this 18th-century shrine, whose name means "jade mountain," sits on an island in Hoan Kiem Lake and is one of Hanoi's most picturesque temples. This shrine is dedicated to 13th-century military hero Tran Hung Dao, scholar Van Xuong, and to Nguyen Van Sieu, a Confucian master who assumed responsibility for repairs made to the temple and the surrounding areas in 1865. He helped build both Pen Tower (Thap But), a 30-ft stone structure whose tip resembles a brush, and the nearby rock hollowed in the shape of a peach, known as the Writing Pad (Dai Nghien). To get to the temple, walk through Three-Passage Gate (Tam Quan) and across the Flood of Morning Sunlight Bridge (The Huc). The island temple opens onto a small courtyard where old men, oblivious to visitors, are engrossed in spirited games of *danh co tuong,* or

Chinese chess. In the pagoda's anteroom is a 6-ft-long stuffed tortoise that locals pulled from Hoan Kiem Lake in 1968. ✉ *Dinh Tien Hoang St., Hoan Kiem District.* 🎫 *12,000d.* ⏲ *Daily 8–5, later for festivals and 1st and 5th days of every lunar month.*

The French Quarter

Regardless of your opinion of their colonial policies, the French certainly can be applauded for thoroughly transforming this once-swampy southern suburb of Hanoi. In order to reflect the grandeur and aesthetic befitting the capital of their protectorate (the French called it Tonkin, from the Vietnamese *Dong Kinh,* or Eastern Capital), French developers rebuilt much of southern Hanoi from the ground up. The wide tree-lined boulevards combine with the majesty of Parisian-style villas and the shuttered elegance of government buildings to form an unusually handsome seat of colonial power. The French have long gone, of course, and for decades Hanoians lacked the affluence to renovate or further build on the architectural contributions of their colonial masters. Villas fell into disrepair, and only those buildings appropriated for state offices were even moderately maintained. This part of the city was caught in a 1920s- and '30s-style time warp.

Although much of the French Quarter's appeal lies in its grand but aging architecture, the area is fast becoming a leading diplomatic and commercial section of the city. As you walk through this airy, surprisingly green district, note the considerable international presence here: More than a dozen embassies occupy renovated villas or compounds in the grid of avenues south of Hoan Kiem Lake, and 20-story office buildings have begun to shadow the streets of this lovely part of town.

Numbers in the text correspond to numbers in the margin and on the French Quarter map.

A Good Walk

This 3- to 4-km (2- to 2½-mi) walk, beginning southeast of Hoan Kiem Lake, ends not where it begins but on the west side of the lake, still in the heart of the city. If you've arranged for a driver to pick you up afterward, tell him to meet you in front of the Nha Tho Lon, the Grand Cathedral, also known as St. Joseph's.

Start on the steps of the downtown area's grandest building, the newly restored **Opera House** ⑨. In front of you is Tran Tien Street, which leads straight out to the southern edge of Hoan Kiem Lake. The area behind and to the south of the Opera House is Nhuong Dia, site of the original Thang Long naval base, which protected the city from enemies attacking via the Red River. By 1875 the French had filled this area with their own military barracks and hospitals. The sprawling villa of the French commander of the armed forces in Indochina was here, on Pham Ngu Lao Street; it's now the Ministry of Defense Guest House. From the Opera House steps turn sharply to the right and follow Trang Tien Street east to its end. Here, at No. 1, is the **Museum of History** ⑩, which houses some of Vietnam's dearest artifacts. This often empty landmark is in a tranquil garden whose only fault is its proximity to the honking, smoke-belching trucks on Tran Quang Khai Boulevard. Just up Trang Tien Street, at 25 Tong Dan Street, is the **Museum of the Revolution** ⑪.

Return to the huge intersection in front of the Opera House. From here head south on Phan Chu Trinh Street—that's the second road on the left if you're looking west from the Opera House steps. As you walk down this street, you'll pass buildings housing the Algerian embassy (✉ 12 Phan Chu Trinh St.) and its stately ambassador's residence, the Union of Vietnamese Youth, and the Vietnam Students Association.

Ambassador's Pagoda, **14**
Hoa Lo Prison (Hanoi Hilton), **15**
Museum of History, **10**
Museum of the Revolution, **11**
Opera House, **9**
St. Joseph's Cathedral, **16**
Tran Hung Dao Street, **12**
Viet Xo Cultural Palace, **13**

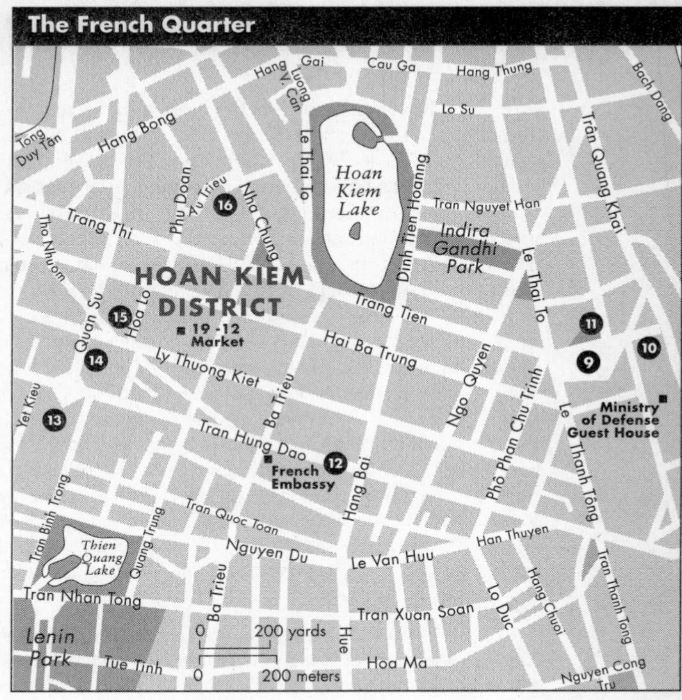

Turn right onto **Tran Hung Dao Street** ⑫. If you're pressed for time or want to rest your legs, hop into a cyclo here for a 1-km (½-mi) ride down Tran Hung Dao Street to Quan Su Street (it should cost a maximum of 10,000d, but you could try to bargain it down to 5,000d). If you choose to walk, you'll discover that this stretch of Tran Hung Dao Street is an embassy row of sorts: You'll pass by the well-positioned Indonesian embassy at the corner of Ngo Quyen Street (taking a right here brings you up to the Hotel Sofitel Metropole and the Government Guest House, the former Palace of the Governor of Tonkin), as well as the Finnish and German ambassadors' residences. Also here are the embassies of Cambodia, at 71A Tran Hung Dao Street; India, at Nos. 58–60; Iraq, at No. 66; and the massive French embassy, at No. 57.

At the intersection of Tran Hung Dao and Quan Su streets, on your right-hand side very close to the police headquarters, is a large shuttered building that houses the Ministry of Transportation and Communication. To the left is the **Viet Xo Cultural Palace** ⑬, the Soviet Union's most striking architectural contribution to this district of the city. At the end of Tran Hung Dao Street is the dreary Ga Hanoi, the main railway station. Opposite the west side of the Viet Xo Cultural Palace, at 17 Yet Kieu Street, is the Fine Arts College. Founded by the French as an Indochina-wide arts academy in 1924, the college has regained its fine reputation and today trains many of Vietnam's best young artists. Next door to the college is the Alliance Française, a popular center for learning French and a vibrant western cultural hub.

Now travel north on Quan Su Street to the nearby **Ambassador's Pagoda** ⑭. At Ly Thuong Kiet Street, turn right, then left about 300 ft later at Hoa Lo Street. This is the site of the infamous **Hoa Lo Prison** ⑮, the turn-of-the-century "fiery furnace" that the French euphemistically called La Maison Centrale and that American prisoners of war sardonically nicknamed the Hanoi Hilton. Only about a third of the prison is intact, as a 22-story office tower and 14-story hotel complex was built in its place.

From Hoa Lo continue east on Ly Thuong Kiet Street for another block and a half. On the left is the entrance to a bustling market with CHO 19–12 (19-12 Market or December 19th Market) on rusting iron gates. Some of Hanoi's most intense street commerce goes on in here, especially in the early morning. (If you want to skip the market, continue down Ly Thuong Kiet Street and take a left on Quang Trung Street.) The market spills out onto Hai Ba Trung Street, named after the rebellious and heroic Trung sisters, who led a short-lived revolt against the Chinese in AD 40. Turn right on this street and then left on Quang Trung Street; at No. 1 is the main Vietnam Airlines ticketing office. Beyond Trang Thi Street, the road merges with Nha Chung Street. Just above this small triangular park is the Green Bamboo Café, one of Hanoi's best tourist cafés (☞ Travel Agencies *in* Hanoi A to Z, *below*). Continuing north on Nha Chung Street brings you to the Hoan Kiem District Culture Center (Nha Van Quan Hoan Kiem), a Soviet-style dance hall. Another 650 ft or so and you've reached **St. Joseph's Cathedral** ⑯, a proud but tired-looking stone-and-cement edifice that fronts a small square. From here it's just a two-block walk east to Hoan Kiem Lake or two blocks north to busy Hang Gai Street in the Old Quarter.

TIMING

This is a full-morning walk that could extend into the afternoon if you're keen on Vietnamese history or would like to comb through the many photographs, captions, and other exhibits outlining Vietnam's modern-day revolutions. The museums, including the one at Hoa Lo Prison, are closed on Monday and at lunchtime. If you *must* see all three museums on this walk and you have other afternoon plans, then start early: Go to the Revolutionary Museum first, as it opens at 8. The History Museum opens its doors at 8:45, and the Hoa Lo Museum closes for lunch at a frustratingly early 11. You can also save time by hopping in a cyclo or taxi on Phan Chu Trinh Street, at the Opera House, and going straight to the Viet Xo Cultural Palace. The December 19th Market slows down in midafternoon, but by 5-ish it's lively again with an after-work crowd. Rush hour is not the loveliest of times to roam the city, however, as the mass of motorbikes in narrow arteries like Nha Chung Street turns pedestrians into second-class citizens.

If you're in Hanoi on a Sunday night, you may want to wind up at the cathedral by 7 or 7:30, when Mass lets out and throngs of churchgoers, particularly elderly Vietnamese women in traditional outfits, throng the streets and the square in front.

Sights to See

⑭ **Ambassador's Pagoda** (Chua Quan Su). This stately prayer house once served the many ambassadors who called on the Le kings. A hall named Quan Su was built in the 15th century to receive these guests, mostly Buddhists, and a pagoda was built for them in which they could comfortably worship. The hall burned to the ground, but the pagoda was saved. The Ambassador's Pagoda escaped destruction a second time, as it was the only pagoda not burned or ransacked in the final chaotic days of the Le dynasty. This pagoda sees more action than most in town: As the pagoda is in part dedicated to a monk who is said to have saved King Ly Than Tong from his deathbed, many older women come here to pray for good health. Dozens of young monks come here for daily study in the classrooms directly behind the pagoda. ✉ *73 Quan Su St., Hoan Kiem District,* ☎ *04/825–2427.* 🎫 *Free.* ⏲ *Daily 7:30–11:30 and 1:30–5:30.*

15 **Hoa Lo Prison (Hanoi Hilton).** There's not much left of the infamous "Hanoi Hilton," the prison that once housed captured American servicemen during the Vietnam War, including U.S. Air Force pilot Douglas "Pete" Peterson, now the first American ambassador to Hanoi. These days it's the focal point of what the government plans as the central business district of the emerging metropolis of Hanoi—much to the chagrin of local residents: The Hanoi Towers, a twin-tower structure that now occupies the site, is not one of the world's more aesthetically pleasing buildings. What does remain, however, is a small section of the old prison, which is now a museum, and the tree under which Do Muoi, the aging former General Secretary of the Communist Party, used to sit while writing epithets on the backs of leaves during his imprisonment by the French during the years of Vietminh resistance.

Opened in late 1997, the **Hoa Lo Prison Museum** is a blunt reminder of the horrors of colonialism and wartime imprisonment. Here, through the front gates of the old French Maison Centrale (Central House, or Prison), built in 1896, you can get a handle on what life was like for Vietnamese prisoners held during France's occupation of Vietnam. (The number of prisoners under the French grew from 615 in 1913 to 2,000 in 1953.) A number of small cells still exist, though many—particularly on the north side of the museum, where political prisoners were held—are repainted in a dull, inauthentic black-and-grey. The real thing can be found in the southern hall, beyond the grisly guillotine and body basket, where death row prisoners, including Hoang Van Thu, Tran Dan Ninh, and Nguyen Van Cu (who escaped and became a powerful early leader of modern Vietnam), were held. These cells are dank, dark, and anything but welcoming.

On exhibit upstairs are Vietnamese propaganda photos of American POWs, including U.S. Senator John McCain and Ambassador Peterson, cheerily shooting pool, cooking, and writing letters. You won't be able to see the building where the American pilots were kept since it has been torn down, as has the cell from which General Secretary Do Muoi escaped in 1945 with 100 prisoners. This was accomplished through the maze of sewers that ran under the prison, parts of which are on display in the courtyard. Also on display are present-day photos of some of the last prisoners held by the French before their defeat in 1954, when the government of the newly formed Democratic Republic of Vietnam took over the prison.

If you're looking for historical detail about the prison, bring your own well-informed guide; those available at the museum are far more inclined to talk about the size of the cells than reveal any nuggets about what once took place behind the musty yellow walls. Note, too, that at press time there was no information in English at the museum. ✉ *1 Hoa Lo St.* 🎫 *Free.* ⏲ *Tues.–Sun. 8:30–11 and 1:30–4.*

10 **Museum of History** (Bao Tang Lich Su). Opened in 1932 as the museum of the École Française d'Extrême Orient, this building has served in its present capacity since 1958, when the French finally handed it back to Hanoi authorities. It houses treasures from early history, particularly Vietnam's Bronze Age. Of special interest are the Ngoc Lu bronze drums, vestiges of this period some 3,000 years ago that have become enduring national Vietnamese symbols. Tools from the Paleolithic Age are on display, as are ceramics from the Ly and Tran dynasties. Painstakingly elaborate but somewhat cheesy dioramas depict various Vietnamese victories over hostile invaders. Note the depiction of the victory of Ngo Quyen over Nam Han troops in 938 and the 1861 attack on the French ship *L'Espérance* (*The Hope*). Upstairs are a few sparse exhibits focusing on more modern Vietnamese culture:

Standouts include a beautiful 18th-century sedan chair made of lacquered wood and inlaid with gold and a model of a Tay Nguyen stilt house.

Visiting the Museum of History can be a frustrating experience. You get the impression that preserving Vietnam's distinct identity is the focus here—like in so many institutions in this country—despite the looming and often invasive presence of foreign cultures, particularly China. There is far too little explanatory text, even in Vietnamese, and English-language translation is pitifully lacking. You would be best served accompanied by a translator and, if possible, a historian. The English-language brochure is often out of print, and English-speaking guides are only occasionally available. ✉ *1 Trang Tien St., Hoan Kiem District,* ☎ *04/825–3518.* 🎟 *10,000d.* ⏲ *Tues.–Sun. 8:45–11:45 and 1:15–4:30.*

11 **Museum of the Revolution** (Bao Tang Cach Mang). History buffs will do better here, at the Museum of the Revolution, than at the Museum of History, just across the street. Built in 1926 to house the French tax office, this cavernous museum opened its doors in 1959 and now has 29 halls, individual rooms that focus on specific events or periods in Vietnam's arduous road to independence. The focus naturally lands on the country's efforts against French colonialism, Japanese fascism, and American imperialism. The photographs from the August 1945 Revolution are particularly interesting. Fortunately, just about all the exhibits have English and French commentary, so a few hours in here can actually be a learning experience. On the other hand it may be difficult to swallow some of the museum section titles, such as "The Peaceful Struggle for National Reunification, 1954–1957." English-language guided tours must be arranged in advance. ✉ *25 Tong Dan St., Hoan Kiem District,* ☎ *04/825–4151.* 🎟 *10,000d.* ⏲ *Sat. 8–11:30, Tues.–Fri. and Sun. 8–11:30 and 1–4.*

9 **Opera House** (Nha Hat Lon). The centerpiece of French architecture in Hanoi and one of the grandest buildings in the city, the Hanoi Opera House is a small-scale version of the Paris Opéra designed by Charles Garnier and completed in 1875. The Hanoi structure, finished in 1911, incorporates the same grand elements of Napoleonic architectural style. Despite (or because of) the theater's French history, its steps were the site of frequent denunciations against colonial rule. Immediately following World War II, in August 1945, Vietminh troops commandeered the Opera House and announced from its balcony the triumph of the August Revolution.

Today the Opera House is positively glowing after a three-year, $17 million restoration. Complete with enhanced orchestra pit for 60 musicians and a movable stage, the 400-seat, three-tiered theater is once again set to host national celebrations, ballet, symphonies, pop and rock concerts, and, hopefully, opera. The renovation included extensive redesign of the surrounding gardens. Seeing a show may be the only way to get into the Opera House, however, as its doors are usually closed; unfortunately, there aren't many performances yet. ✉ *Trang Thien St.,* ☎ *04/824–8029.*

16 **St. Joseph's Cathedral** (Nha Tho Lon). The imposing square towers of this century-old cathedral rise up from a small square near Hoan Kiem Lake on the edge of the Old Quarter. French missionaries built the cathedral in the late 19th century and celebrated the first mass here on Christmas Day 1886, and it feels like absolutely nothing's changed since then—the liturgy has not been modernized since the cathedral was built. The small but beautiful panes of stained glass were created in Paris in 1906. Also of note is the ornate altar, with its high gilded side walls.

Seventy-something Father Do Tong presides here; he conducts Mass mostly in Vietnamese but will attempt to intersperse English or French when he sees foreigners in attendance. Sunday Mass is a popular event here, and the pews—men and women are separated—are often full. On major holidays like Christmas and Easter it can be positively chaotic, with 5,000 people either trying to cram their way in or trying to follow along with the service from the front steps. The creaky wooden front doors open for Mass, but if you're visiting at midday, you'll have to walk through the iron gates to the left of the main entrance and enter through the side door, which is up the steps near the back of the structure. ✉ *Nha Tho St., Hoan Kiem District,* ☎ *04/828–5967.* ⏲ *Mass Sun. at 4:30 AM, 6:30 AM, 10 AM, and 6 PM; Mon.–Tues., Thurs., and Sun. at 5:30 AM; Wed. and Fri.–Sat. at 5:30 AM and 6 PM.*

NEED A BREAK? **Café Moca** (✉ 14–16 Nha Tho St., ☎ 04/825–6334) opposite the Cathedral, offers excellent international coffees at a reasonable price. The striking two-story brick interior—those wrought-iron chandeliers were custom made—could belong to a student coffeehouse in Cambridge or Berkeley.

12 **Tran Hung Dao Street.** Once called Rue Gambetta, Tran Hung Dao Street is now named after the revered 13th-century Vietnamese warrior who repulsed Kublai Khan's Mongol hordes at a legendary battle on the Bach Dang River, near present-day Haiphong. This long tree-lined boulevard is the southern border of the French Quarter and a marked example of the stateliness with which the French imbued these east–west streets. Today the boulevard is lined with a number of diplomatic missions; among them, fittingly, is the **French embassy,** which takes up an entire city block. Because an imposing wall has been erected around the compound, little can be seen of the glorious embassy garden with centuries-old banyan trees.

13 **Viet Xo Cultural Palace** (Cung Van Hoa Viet-Xo). Never one to downplay its influence, the Soviet Union assisted with the design and construction of this "workers' cultural palace." Inaugurated September 1, 1985, the rigid 120-room white colossus stretches from Yet Kieu Street to Tran Binh Trong Road. The palace actually is three structures: The performance building houses a 1,200-seat concert hall, while the study and technology buildings contain a library, a conference hall, and an observatory. The palace is noted for hosting a variety of clubs where Hanoians gather to share ideas on everything from biochemistry and chess to billboard usage in the Old Quarter. Most documents in the library are in either Vietnamese or Russian and have particular relevance to labor and trade issues, as it was specifically the Soviet Trade Union that contributed aid in honor of its Vietnam counterpart. The Vietnam Trade Union headquarters is just across the street, next to the Ministry of Transportation and Communication. The broad open space here known as May 1 Square is conducive to commemorating the past and present glories of the Communist Party, and you'll invariably see propaganda posters and waves of dangling street lights consisting of blinking yellow stars and red hammers and sickles. ✉ *91 Tran Hung Dao St.,* ☎ *04/825–3787.* 🎫 *Free.* ⏲ *Daily 8–noon, 1–4:30.*

Around Ho Chi Minh's Mausoleum

Ask a cyclo or taxi driver to take you from Hoan Kiem Lake to the Ho Chi Minh Mausoleum, in the Ba Dinh District. This once-forested area west of the citadel—which is still a military base and essentially off-limits to foreign tourists—is an expansive and refreshingly tranquil district whose stalwart buildings and monuments seem to revel in the glories of Ho Chi Minh and the Communist cause. As you travel northwest on Dien Bien Phu Street, you'll leave the tightly woven fabric of the Old Quarter behind and find yourself surrounding by sweeping French-era villas and massive ochre-color government buildings, most newly painted and all well protected from the sun by a phalanx of tall tamarind trees. Many of these villas house the embassies of socialist (or once-socialist) nations that have stood fast by Vietnam over the last few decades. Scattered among these gems are occasional anomalies of Soviet-era architecture.

At the end of Dien Bien Phu Street is the minimally landscaped Ba Dinh Square, in the center of which flutters Hanoi's largest Vietnam flag. One can almost hear the echoes of Ho Chi Minh's voice ringing out over loudspeakers to the half million northern Vietnamese who gathered to hear Uncle Ho's Declaration of Independence on September 2, 1945. A quarter century later, six days after Ho's death on September 3, 1969, another 100,000 Hanoians gathered here to pay homage to their late president. On the west side of the square is the mausoleum itself, a cold and squat cubicle that's nonetheless arresting in its simplicity and grandeur. In the days leading up to Vietnam National Day (September 2) and Ho Chi Minh's birthday (May 19), thousands of curious citizens—many of them students from nearby districts and provinces—and loyal party members line up to pay their respects to the patriarch, preserved for eternity behind bullet-proof glass.

Across the square from the mausoleum and slightly to the left is Ba Dinh Meeting Hall, the four-story headquarters of the Communist Party and where the National Assembly convenes. Across the square and to the right, where Dien Bien Phu Street meets the square, stands the huge and graceful Ministry of Foreign Affairs. Directly opposite the mausoleum and at the end of short Bac Son Road is the monument to Vietnam's revolutionary martyrs. The palm- and willow-shaded mansion to the right of the monument is the home of former minister of defense and national treasure General Vo Nguyen Giap, who orchestrated the brilliant siege at Dien Bien Phu in 1954. Behind the mausoleum are the Ho Chi Minh Museum and One-Pillar Pagoda; directly to the north is Ho's house on stilts, and beyond that the Presidential Palace and then West Lake (Ho Tay). The underrated Fine Arts Museum as well as the Army Museum and the famed Temple of Literature are also within easy walking distance.

Numbers in the text correspond to numbers in the margin and on the Around the Ho Chi Minh Mausoleum and West Lake map.

A Good Walk

Start at the **Ho Chi Minh Mausoleum** ⑰, in the heart of the Ba Dinh District. Once you have passed by the unflinching guards and through the mausoleum itself, you'll be directed through large iron gates and toward **Ho Chi Minh's Residence** ⑱, which is in the tranquil wooded compound of the **Presidential Palace** ⑲. Although visitors are welcome to Uncle Ho's house, the palace itself is off-limits, as is much of the surrounding parkland. Behind the Presidential Palace, however, is the large **Botanical Garden** ⑳, which *is* open to the public, although the entrance is a bit far away, on Hoang Hoa Tham Street. A short pathway leads from Ho Chi Minh's house to **One-Pillar Pagoda** ㉑, the reconstructed Buddhist tower in the center of a small square lake. To the left is Dien Huu Pagoda; this charming but seldom-visited temple sits in the shadow of the architecturally disorienting **Ho Chi Minh Museum** ㉒.

From the museum walk out the front doors and down the steps toward Ba Dinh Square. Turn right on Huong Vuong Road, the street in front

Around the Ho Chi Minh Mausoleum and West Lake

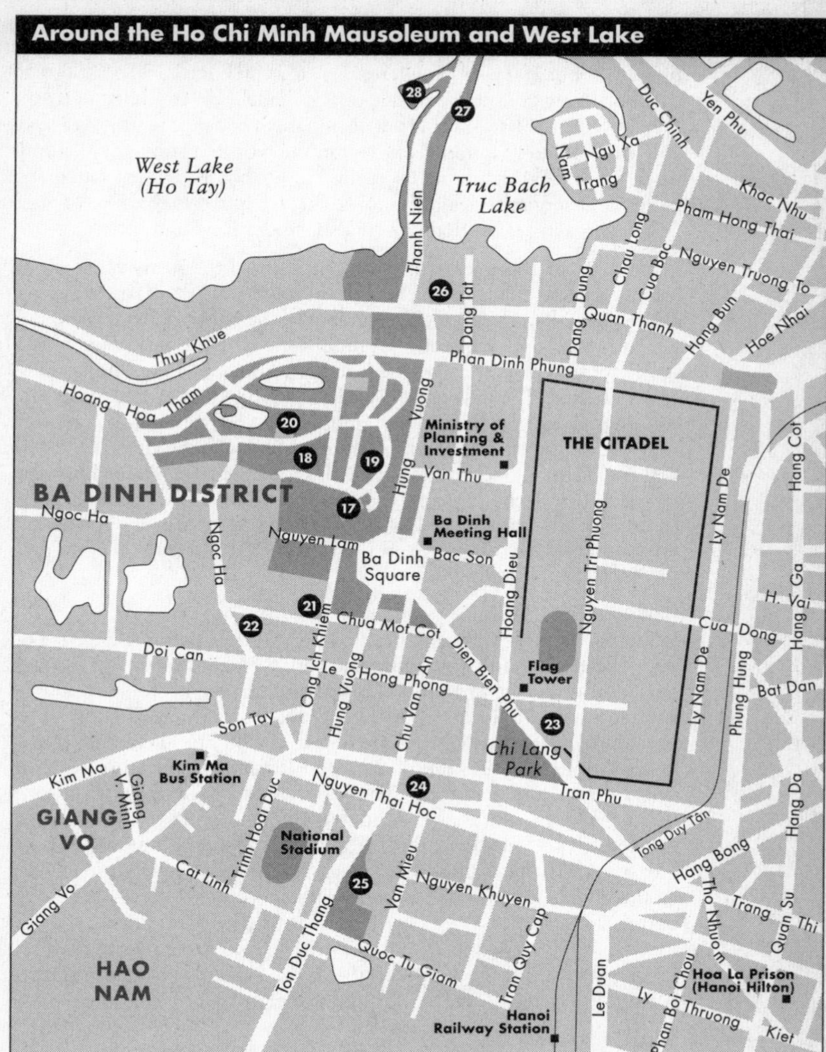

Army Museum, **23**
Botanical Garden, **20**
Fine Arts Museum, **24**
Ho Chi Minh Mausoleum, **17**
Ho Chi Minh Museum, **22**
Ho Chi Minh's Residence, **18**
One-Pillar Pagoda, **21**
Presidential Palace, **19**
Quan Thanh Temple, **26**
Temple of Literature, **25**
Tran Quoc Pagoda, **28**
War Memorial, **27**

of the mausoleum, then left on Le Hong Phong Street. This wide, shaded boulevard leads back to Dien Bien Phu Street, where you should bear right. In about 200 yards you'll reach shady Chi Lang Park, once a small lake bordering the southern edge of the citadel but later filled in by the French. Here, set back behind a wide square of polished marble, is a sight you are not likely to find elsewhere in the world: a statue of Vladimir Ilyich Lenin. Though long discredited in his home country, Lenin still looms large in Vietnam, and Hanoi's aging party cadres continue to place flowers here in celebration of Lenin's October Revolution.

Lenin appears to be leaning resolutely toward the **Army Museum** ㉓, just across Dien Bien Phu Street. To the left is the 100-ft tower known as the Flag Pillar, the surviving remnant of the Nguyen dynasty citadel, which has become a historic symbol of the city. From the Army Museum, retrace your steps to the intersection of Le Hong Phong, Dien Bien Phu, and Hoang Dieu streets. Turn left on Hoang Dieu Street and continue, going past the Chinese embassy on your right, until you reach very busy Nguyen Thai Hoc Street. One block to the right is the **Fine Arts Museum** ㉔, back in a courtyard. From here the **Temple of Literature** ㉕ is just across the street, secluded behind a low stone wall. To get to the entrance, proceed south down Van Mieu Street, opposite the art museum, and turn right on Quoc Tu Giam Street. You can't miss the entrance, on the right.

TIMING

Taking in all these sights within a comfortable time frame depends on your preferences and how long you want to spend traversing through museums or gazing at architectural anomalies. Three hours should be enough to get from Ho Chi Minh's Mausoleum to the Fine Arts Museum, provided you don't venture over to the Botanical Gardens. Leave at least another 30–40 minutes for the Temple of Literature. Or conversely, you could start at the Temple of Literature—it opens in the summer at 7:30, in winter at 8—and make your way up to the Botanical Gardens or to West Lake, taking in the sights along the way. Generally speaking, this walk is more pleasant during the week, but so long as there's no special holiday, weekends are quite fine, too. The only real delay is lining up to view Uncle Ho (keep in mind, too, that his mausoleum is closed in the afternoons). If you are an early riser, the dawn patrol of people doing calisthenics and tai chi in front of the mausoleum in Ba Dinh Square is a sight to behold.

Sights to See

㉓ **Army Museum** (Bao Tang Quan Doi). Although not as provocative as its Ho Chi Minh City counterpart, the Army Museum is nonetheless an intriguing example of Vietnam's continuing obsession with publicizing its past military exploits. At the southern edge of what was once the Thang Long citadel, which housed the imperial city, the museum buildings were once used as French military barracks. In the courtyard of the museum, Chinese- and Soviet-made weaponry—including MiG fighters, antiaircraft guns, and the tank that smashed through the gates of the Presidential Palace in Saigon on April 30, 1975—surround the wreckage of an American B-52 shot down over Hanoi. (Regardless of how you feel about the bombastic zeal behind such a display, standing next to this mountain of twisted metal is a humbling experience.) Other, far-less-arresting displays include depictions of the Trung sisters' revolt against Chinese overlords in 40 AD, sound-and-light shows highlighting battles and troop movements during the wars against the French and Americans, bicycles known as steel horses that were used on the Ho Chi Minh Trail, captured French and American firearms and uniforms, field maps and tables of major attacks, and the dreaded *pungee* sticks.

Adjacent to the museum is the **Hanoi Flag Pillar,** a 100-ft tapered hexagonal guard tower atop a three-tier square base. Built in 1812, the pillar escaped destruction by the French when they leveled much of the citadel; instead they used the tower as an observation and communication station—much like the Vietnamese military before them. The intricate fan- and flower-shape holes allow light into the tower, which has a crisp red-and-yellow Vietnamese flag fluttering from its flagpole. ⊠ *Dien Bien Phu St., Ba Dinh District,* ☎ *04/823–4264.* 🎫 *10,000d.* ⏲ *Tues.–Sun. 8–11:30 and 1:30–4:30.*

20 **Botanical Garden** (Vuon Bach Thao). This 50-acre park behind the Presidential Palace was designed by French landscape engineers in 1890. After defeating the French in Hanoi in late 1954, the state rebuilt the gardens and opened the grounds and its extensive network of cement trails to the public. Athletes in search of exercise congregate here for pickup soccer games, badminton, tai chi, and jogging. Lovers looking for seclusion cross the bridge to an island in the middle of the lake. Between dusk and closing time—10 PM—this island retreat is definitely rated R. ⊠ *Entrance on Hoang Hoa Tham Rd.* 🎫 *1,000d.* ⏲ *Daily 7 AM–10 PM.*

★ 24 **Fine Arts Museum** (Bao Tang My Thuat). The evolution of Vietnamese art is sparingly, if not lovingly, chronicled in this musty three-story museum, which opened in 1966 after serving as a boarding house for French girls living in Indochina. The architecture, sculpture, drawing, and fine arts of Vietnam are displayed in a series of exhibits, mainly organized chronologically, starting with Stone Age and Bronze Age artifacts on the third floor. Also on the top level are examples of lacquer and wood sculpture, including a fantastical bodhisattva with 1,000 eyes and arms, a 16th-century statue from the Hoi Ha Pagoda.

Several yard-high stone statues and wooden sculptures lining the open-air hallways reflect the wide range of artistic styles incorporated into Vietnamese art. Note the intrusion of the Soviet aesthetic on mid-20th-century sculpture: the martial, even superhuman forms are a far cry from the elegance and lightheartedness of Dong Ho folk art or the centuries-old evocative lacquered-wood depictions of *arhats,* or enlightened monks, from the Tay Phuong Pagoda. On the lower floors are oil and watercolor paintings by such Vietnamese masters as Nguyen Tu Nghiem, Bui Xuan Phai and To Ngoc Van. The central exhibition rooms on the first floor contain some of Vietnam's most stunning lacquer painting, much of it excellent examples of socialist realism and so-called combat art—these should not be missed.

Conspicuously absent are the most recent works of art from Vietnam's bold young painters. The unfortunate reality is these artists are busy showing their works in stylish Hanoi and Saigon galleries and selling to eager collectors, while the Ministry of Culture, which is ultimately responsible for the art museum, doesn't have the financial resources to buy their works. ⊠ *66 Nguyen Thai Hoc St.,* ☎ *04/823–3084.* 🎫 *10,000d.* ⏲ *Tues.–Sun. 8–noon and 1–4.*

★ 17 **Ho Chi Minh Mausoleum** (Lang Chu Tich Ho Chi Minh). It is hard to overstate Ho Chi Minh's heroic stature among the Vietnamese and how significant his mausoleum and the surrounding area are in Vietnam's ideological consciousness. Respected as a determined revolutionary patriot and loved as a public figure who empathized with the people, particularly of the North, Ho Chi Minh has reached icon status in the minds of most Vietnamese. Perhaps it's because schools throughout the country focus almost exclusively on the man's positive exploits, deferring any responsibility for failed economic policies or mismanagement onto

Ho's successors, that the youth of Vietnam, though often frustrated by the limitations of the rigid communist system, continue to admire and venerate the man. Many of the faithful who visit the tomb are, in fact, school children on field trips; some of them walk past Ho's reclining body with tears in their eyes, others suppress giggles, but mostly they appear mystified at the pinkish-yellow glow that seems to emanate from the frail, wispy-bearded corpse. Although the number of citizens queuing up to see their late president has dropped significantly in the last few years, thousands of Vietnamese still visit the revered site—and Ba Dinh Square, where independence was declared in 1945—each year to pay homage to "Uncle Ho." During the country's major national holidays, Vietnam's power troika—the general secretary of the Communist Party, the prime minister, and the president—line up in front of the mausoleum with other national leaders to review columns of parading ethnic minorities, rolling tanks, and goose-stepping soldiers.

Had officials followed the president's wishes, this structure may never have been built, as Ho Chi Minh had expressed in his will his desire to be cremated. But the preservation of the Vietnamese leader and his memory has gone the way of such other communist figureheads as Lenin, Stalin, and Mao. Ho's embalmed body, touched up now and again in Russia, is virtually the only thing inside the mausoleum. Just inside the entrance is Ho's famous quotation, "Nothing is more precious than independence and freedom," etched in bright red lettering, followed by his signature. The structure itself is a squat, cold, gray cubicle ringed by columns and topped by a flat square frieze adorned with the words "Chu Tich (President) Ho Chi Minh" in red plum marble. Built using materials native to Vietnam, such as marble from Marble Mountain outside Danang, the mausoleum stands out as an exception to the graceful architectural environment that is Hanoi.

When you enter the mausoleum, be aware of the strict propriety expected of visitors. Although you will see Vietnamese pilgrims moving in a solemn single-file procession, foreigners must sign in at an office on Chua Mot Cot Street, south of the mausoleum, then leave their possessions at another checkpoint closer to the actual tomb, where uninformative brochures are for sale. Your purchase of them amounts to your entrance donation. No cameras, hats, or bags of any kind may be brought in the building, and you are expected to behave respectfully. This means not wearing shorts or tanktops or putting your hands in your pockets while inside. Talking is also forbidden, and once inside the chilly room containing Ho's corpse you are discouraged from lingering for more than a few moments in front of the glass. ✉ *Enter at corner of Hung Vuong and Le Hong Phong Sts.* 🎫 *Donation expected.* 🕐 *Sat.–Mon. and Wed.–Thurs. 8 AM–11 AM; usually closed Oct. and/or Nov., when Ho's body is in Russia for maintenance.*

22 **Ho Chi Minh Museum** (Bao Tang Ho Chi Minh). Opened on May 19, 1990, on what would have been Ho's 100th birthday, this complex was established, in the language of the brochure that you can take on entering, "to satisfy the Vietnamese people's desire to express their deep gratitude to the President." In 1997 officials finally scraped together funding to add English commentary to the bizarre exhibits, making this museum a must-stop—if only for 15 minutes—on the Uncle Ho circuit. A collection of manifestos, military orders, correspondence, and photographs from the Communist Party's early days to the present are mixed with historical exhibits covering the October and August revolutions, the fight against fascism, Ho's revolutionary world movement, and Vietnam's struggle against imperialism.

Close-Up

MEET UNCLE HO

ORIGINALLY NAMED Nguyen Sinh Cung, Ho Chi Minh (literally "bringer of light") is the final and most memorable pseudonym in a series of more than 50 that Vietnam's intrepid leader acquired during the course of his remarkable life. Born in 1890 in the central Vietnamese province of Nghe An, Ho received traditional French schooling and became a teacher. However, he inherited from his father (who abandoned the family early on) a wanderlust that became fueled by a lifelong obsession with Vietnamese independence.

In 1911 Ho signed on to the crew of a French freighter; two years later a stint aboard another French ship took him to the United States, where he settled for a year in Brooklyn, New York, and found work as a laborer. Ho then left for London, where he became an assistant pastry chef. He mastered several languages—among them English, French, German, Russian, Cantonese, and Japanese. He moved to Paris for six years and became increasingly active in socialist, communist, and nationalist movements. After helping to found the French Communist Party, Ho left for Moscow in 1924. It soon became clear that to successfully foment a workers' revolution in Vietnam, he would have to dedicate himself to organizing his countrymen.

By the end of the 1920s, a number of poorly organized revolts had incited aggressive French retaliation, which was only compounded by economic depression. In 1930, while based in Hong Kong, Ho consolidated a number of rebellious factions under the umbrella of the Indochinese Communist Party. However, it was not until 1941—after escaping arrest in Hong Kong, forging documentation "proving" his death, shuttling between China and the Soviet Union, and disguising himself as a Chinese journalist—that he was able to sneak back into Vietnam.

Shortly thereafter Ho founded the Vietminh Independence League. In July 1945, U.S. OSS officers met with Ho; impressed with Ho's operation, they agreed to supply him with arms. In August, Ho called for a general uprising, known as the August Revolution. Ho proclaimed himself president of the Democratic Republic of Vietnam in the north. The following year, Ho, in order to rid northern Vietnam of Chinese troops, agreed to an accord with the French: Vietnam would be a "free state" within the French Union and 25,000 French troops would be stationed there. Tensions between the Vietminh and the French escalated, however, and soon led to the French-Indochina War.

By 1950 the United States was supplying military aid to the French and Ho's government was recognized by the Soviet Union and China. The French-Indochina War ended in 1954 with the Vietminh's defeat of the French at Dien Bien Phu. American involvement in Vietnam escalated rapidly.

Ho died of natural causes in September 1969 at the age of 79. After his death the fighting continued, though in 1970 Henry Kissinger began secret talks with the North Vietnamese. By 1975 the Vietnam War had ended and the country was reunited.

Ho never married—he asserted that the Vietnamese people were his family—thus he preferred the familiar "Uncle Ho." Though he died over 30 years ago, Uncle Ho is still present, from his embalmed body in the Ho Chi Minh Mausoleum to his portrait on Vietnamese currency.

Like many museums in Hanoi, you're encouraged to start at the top and wind your way down. The centerpiece on the top floor is a gargantuan gold lotus flower that itself contains smaller exhibits about Ho's revolutionary activities. Labyrinthine murals and installations lead from the section called "Past" into the "Future," where you'll find everything from space-age conceptual representations of peace to models of automobiles symbolizing America's military failure. A red "volcano" surrounded by national totems symbolizes the various national liberation movements. Under the banner "Ho Chi Minh and Young People," huge plastic fruit sits atop a slanting table framed by a backdrop black-and-white photo of nuclear reactors, a display that would look more at home on the set of *Dr. Strangelove*. At one point you stumble into a small but disorienting house of mirrors. Dark TV screens hang from the corners. The few Vietnamese who wander the floors seem less interested in the exhibits and more curious about the specifics of the overwrought Soviet architecture. It is indeed eerie.

You must leave your cameras and bags at the reception area. There is an interesting gift shop. ✉ *3 Ngoc Ha St. (also accessible from Chua Mot Cot St.), Ba Dinh District,* ☎ *04/846–3752.* 🎫 *5,000d.* ⏲ *Tues.–Sun. 8–11:30 and 1:30–4.*

18 **Ho Chi Minh's Residence** (Nha Bac Ho). After 1954 Ho Chi Minh had the run of the Presidential Palace, but the ostentation was too much for the austere president, who openly shunned luxury and preferred the humble former home of the palace's electrician, where he lived for four years. Then, the story goes, in 1958 Ho Chi Minh moved to this simple but tastefully designed wooden house on stilts, which served as his living quarters and work space until his death in 1969. An elegant but spare study—some books, his small typewriter, a few newspapers, and an electric fan presented to him by a group of Japanese communists are visible—adjoins his equally spare bedroom. Downstairs he received his guests: foreign dignitaries, Politburo members, army cadres, and schoolchildren. The well-manicured gardens surrounding the house are home to flame trees, willows, mango trees and the aromatic milkweed. Cyprus trees thrive on the edge of the pond, which Ho had stocked with carp. A crisp clap of the hands apparently still brings the fish to the surface.

Regardless of Ho Chi Minh's faith in the accuracy of the city's antiaircraft gunners, some doubt must be thrown on the claim that Ho Chi Minh spent so much time in this open-air sanctum, with only the various trees, his wooden house, and a trusty old war helmet as protection. American bombers targeted Hanoi during the war, and they surely would have emptied their loads on Ba Dinh District had they known their archnemesis was feeding fish and conferring with his generals in the unprotected confines of his stilt house. Indeed, Ho's Politburo ordered the construction of a nearby bomb shelter, later dubbed House No. 67. Legend holds that Uncle Ho refused to use the shelter as a home, preferring to confer with the Politburo in this fortified bunker but to sleep in his stilt house.

A tip: Before visiting Ho's residence, wait for the rest of the group that accompanied you through the mausoleum to go on ahead; it's much more enjoyable to walk through the jasmine-scented compound unhurried and without the inevitable chatter of other tourists. You may want to purchase a 20,000d booklet entitled *The Living Quarter and Working Place of President Ho Chi Minh,* available at the entrance gate to the house. Though overwrought, it's actually quite informative.

The area around Ho's house is quite serene; linger by the carp-filled pond lined with blossoming flame and cypress trees and take in the strains of traditional music often played here during the day. You'll exit this area via a pebbled pathway to the south of the mausoleum. As if they were themselves sites on the tour, older Vietnamese intellectuals wearing bifocals and striped cotton pajamas sit on park benches and read the Communist Party mouthpiece, *Nhan Dan* (*The People*), or sip green tea and smoke cigarettes. ✉ *Huong Vuong Rd., Ba Dinh District.* 🎫 *3,000d.* ⏲ *Daily 7:30–11 and 1:30–4.*

21 **One-Pillar Pagoda** (Chua Mot Cot). The French destroyed this temple, once known as Lien Hoa Tower but now exclusively referred to as One-Pillar Pagoda, on their way out in 1954. It was reconstructed by the new government and still commemorates the legend of Emperor Ly Thai Tong. It is said that the childless emperor dreamed that Quan Am, the Buddhist goddess of mercy and compassion, seated on a lotus flower, handed him a baby boy. Sure enough, he soon met and married a peasant woman who bore him a male heir, and in 1049 he constructed this monument in appreciation. The distinctive single pillar is meant to represent the stalk of the lotus flower, a sacred Vietnamese symbol of purity. The pillar was originally a single large tree trunk; today it's made of more durable cement. The tiny 10-ft-square pagoda is covered by an ornate curved roof and rises out of a square pond. Steps leading to the pagoda from the south side of the pond are usually blocked off, but if there aren't too many people around, a monk may invite you into this miniature prayer room.

Just a few yards from the One-Pillar Pagoda is **Dien Huu Pagoda,** a delightful but often-overlooked temple enclosing a bonsai-filled courtyard. A tall and colorful gate opens out onto the path leading to the Ho Chi Minh Museum, but the entrance is opposite the steps to the One-Pillar Pagoda. ✉ *Ong Ich Kiem St., Ba Dinh District, no phone.* 🎫 *Free.* ⏲ *Daily 7–5:30.*

19 **Presidential Palace** (Cung Chu Tich). This imposing three-story palace just north of the mausoleum is testament to France's dedication to architectural elegance in Indochina. Constructed from 1900 to 1906, the bright, mustard-yellow building served as the living and working quarters of Indochina's general governors. When Ho Chi Minh returned to Hanoi after the defeat of the French in 1954, he refused to live in the palace itself but chose the more modest quarters of the palace electrician. He did, however, offer use of the palace to distinguished guests during their visits to the capital. Today the building is used for formal international receptions and other important government meetings. Surrounding the building are extensive gardens and orchards, as well as the famed Mango Alley, the 300-ft pathway from the palace to Ho Chi Minh's stilt house (☞ *above*). ✉ *Huong Vuong Rd. and Hoang Van Thu St., Ba Dinh District.* ⏲ *Not open to public.*

★ 25 **Temple of Literature** (Van Mieu). An unusually well-preserved example of Vietnamese architecture, this monument to Confucius was built in 1070 by Emperor Ly Thanh Tong and is widely considered the most important historic site in the Dong Da sector of Hanoi. Soon after its construction, it became the site of Vietnam's first university, Quoc Tu Giam, which specialized in training students—many of them sons and daughters of emperors and other high-ranking dignitaries—to pass the rigorous examinations for government and civil-service posts. The achievements of several centuries of the university's doctoral recipients are recorded on 82 stelae (stone slabs), which rest on stone tortoises. The oldest of these, the Dai Bao Stele, dates to 1442. It wasn't until 1802 that Emperor Gia Long moved his capital and the national university to Hue. The French later used the building as, appropriately, their school of civil administration, dubbing it the Temple of the Crows because of the birds that tended to gather here.

Van Mieu is divided into five courtyards. The first two, now bare of buildings, used to house the wooden hostels and dormitories for students. A central walkway once reserved for the king runs down the center of these open sections between two square lotus-flower ponds. Separating these courtyards from the middle section of the compound is an elaborate two-story gate, the second floor of which is called the Poet's Balcony. University examinations eventually came to include poetry competitions, introduced by Emperor Le Loi, and poetry readings still take place from this balcony on special occasions—as do concerts of traditional and classical music. The gate opens onto a large square fish pond, which is bracketed on either side with the stone stelae. Through an ancient wooden doorway is the fourth area, containing the temple dedicated to Confucius and his disciples. On the far side of this temple is the site of what was the Van Mieu Library, destroyed by bombing raids in 1954. If you come before 3:20, there is a water-puppet show that's worth seeing. Traditional music plays throughout the day. A number of stalls sell books, temple trinkets, and ethnic-minority handicrafts. ✉ *Quoc Tu Giam St., Dong Da District,* ☎ *04/845–2917 or 04/823–5601.* 🎫 *12,000d; 20,000d for an English-speaking guide.* ⏲ *Summer, daily 7:30–6; winter, daily 8–5.*

West Lake

About 3 km (2 mi)—10 minutes by taxi or motorbike—northwest of Hoan Kiem Lake is West Lake (Ho Tay), another body of water that's steeped in legend. It is said a giant golden calf from China followed the peals of a monk's bronze bell to this spot. When the ringing stopped, the calf lost its direction and kept walking in circles, creating the basin of West Lake. Like Hoan Kiem's turtle, the calf is said to still dwell in the lake. If so, it likely feeds on the snails that are considered a local delicacy.

West Lake's wealth of history takes more tangible form in the temples and war memorials that line its shores. Development is changing the face of the shore, however, as luxury hotels and high-rent villas eat away at the land of traditional flower villages like Nghi Tam, where wealthy expatriates seclude themselves behind walls of bougainvillea.

The lake itself is a weekend boating spot for Vietnamese families, which paddle around the murky waters in boats shaped like ducks and dragons. Afterward they stop in one of the floating restaurants for snails boiled in lemon leaves or *banh tom* (deep-fried toast with a shrimp on each side). You can also rent boat houses made of bamboo for an afternoon of fishing (although eating what you catch is not recommended).

Numbers in the text correspond to numbers in the margin and on the Around Ho Chi Minh's Mausoleum and West Lake map.

A Good Walk

Start your walk at the beginning of the wide causeway of Thanh Nien Street that divides West Lake from the smaller Truc Bach Lake, created when fishermen closed off the southeast section of West Lake. Thanh Nien means "youth"; the causeway was so named in honor of the young "volunteers" who helped build this roadway between the two lakes. Along the way note the floating seafood restaurants and the neon signs of the times—billboards for Carlsberg and Compaq. At the very beginning of Thanh Nien duck into ornate **Quan Thanh Temple** ㉖. Sidewalk vendors in front will offer you incense and flowers. This is a marvelous spot to take a rest and soak up the atmosphere, though try to ignore the street noise beyond the walls.

Staying on the same side of the street, walk for about five minutes to reach an unnamed **War Memorial** ㉗ to antiaircraft gunners stationed on the roof of a nearby factory who shot down 10 American planes in 1967. Walk about 650 ft, then cross the street to Hanoi's oldest pagoda, the delightful **Tran Quoc Pagoda** ㉘, on an islet jutting into West Lake. The West Lake side of the causeway is often crowded with picnicking students, many of whom may make attempts at communicating in English with you. From there it's a 10- to 15-minute walk back to the beginning of Thanh Nien Street, where you will find a small flower garden (*vuon hoa*) bearing the name of Ly Tu Trong, a revolutionary martyr whose white-plaster statue faces the Presidential Palace to the south. Older women gather here to exercise and perform tai chi, while the busy park across the street plays host to badminton games.

If you're up for walking back into the center of town from here, or at least want to walk part of the way before getting a cyclo or taxi, then go along Phan Dinh Phung Street. This beautiful shaded avenue leads past sprawling French villas and Chinese mandarin mansions (many occupied by long-serving party members) as well as the gracious but seldom-used Gothic North Door Cathedral (Cua Bac). The large wheel of stained glass is reminiscent of Renaissance-era artwork in Europe and enchanting from the inside; try the large front doors or ask around for a caretaker to let you in. On the right side of the street are the tall ramparts of the citadel, the military compound that once protected the Imperial Palace of Thang Long. Phan Dinh Phung Street ends about 1 km (½ mi) from the edge of West Lake, near a rectangular park and Hanoi's own version of the Leaning Tower of Pisa: the old water tower and critical military fortification built by the French. This is the northern edge of the Old Quarter, and cyclos are everywhere. Some taxis should be waiting near the Galaxy Hotel, to the right of the park.

TIMING

The causeway can be traversed in about 20 minutes, but allow for an hour if you want to peek around the temples. Allow 90 minutes if you want to rent a paddleboat from the quay on the Truc Bach side. The walk from the southeast corner of West Lake to the water tower is another 15–25 minutes.

Sights to See

26 **Quan Thanh Temple** (Chua Quan Thanh or Chan Vu Quan). It's worth seeing the four-ton, 13-ft-tall black bronze statue of the Taoist god Tran Vu housed in the shrine here. Built by King Ly Thai To in the 11th century, this much-made-over temple was once known as the Temple of the Grand Buddha. An important collection of 17th-century poems can be seen in the shrine room. Above the ornamented main gate is a 1677 replica of the bronze bell that supposedly lured the West Lake's legendary golden calf from China. Huge trees drape over the courtyard, keeping the temple and its environs cool and somewhat dark, even in midday. On your way out note that the rock formation in the goldfish pond hosts a number of very loud cicadas. A pair of brightly painted plaster tigers protect the entrance. ✉ *Quan Thanh and Thanh Nien Sts.,* ☎ *04/823–4378.* *5,000d donation.* ⏲ *Daily 8–4:30.*

28 **Tran Quoc Pagoda** (Chua Tran Quoc). Hanoi's oldest temple dates from the 6th century, when King Ly Nam De had a pagoda, named Khai Quoc, built on the bank of the Red River. More than a thousand years later excessive erosion of the river bank caused King Le Kinh Tong to move the pagoda to Goldfish Islet (Ca Vang) on West Lake, and a subsequent Le king renamed it Tran Quoc. This modest temple is noted for its stele dating from 1639, which recounts the history of the pagoda and its move from the Red River, and the lovely brick stupa adjacent

to the main temple. Tran Quoc is an active monastery where resident monks in brown robes hold daily services. Architecturally distinct from other Hanoi pagodas, Tran Quoc maintains a visitors hall in front and various statues including a gilded wooden depiction of Shakyamuni Buddha. In the main courtyard is a giant pink-and-green planter holding a bodhi tree, purportedly a cutting from the original bodhi tree beneath which the Buddha reached his enlightenment. The bodhi was a gift from the president of India, who visited the pagoda in 1959. The Vietnamese government recognized the site as a national historic relic in 1989. It is a popular spot for Vietnamese tourists and Hanoi couples, and street vendors and photographers gather here to cash in on the business. ✉ *Thanh Nien St.* *5,000d donation.* *Daily 8–4:30.*

27 **War Memorial.** If you're interested in Vietnam War history, head for this small memorial between West Lake and Truc Bach Lake; it marks the capture of one of the war's most famous prisoners of war. On October 26, 1967, Navy lieutenant commander John McCain's plane was shot down, sending him into Truc Bach Lake. Suffering from badly broken bones and severe beatings, he was imprisoned in Hoa Lo, the infamous "Hanoi Hilton," for over four years. He went on to become an Arizona senator and a vocal advocate of reconciliation between the United States and his former captors. In 1997 he traveled to Hanoi to meet the old man who allegedly plucked him from the lake and near-certain death. The red-sandstone memorial features a bound and suspended prisoner and the letters U.S.A.F. ✉ *Thanh Nien St.*

DINING

Most of Hanoi's international restaurants are found in the Hoan Kiem District, as are many places serving Vietnamese cuisine. Local specialties, such as *banh cuon* (a rice pancake with savory stuffing) and *mi xao* (Chinese egg noodles), can be found on Ngo Cam Chi Street (off Hang Bong Street) in the Old Quarter. Goat meat is the specialty of Lang Ha Street, south of the U.S. embassy, and dog meat (if you're really an adventurous eater) is served in restaurants on Nghi Tam Road between West Lake and the Red River.

Tong Duy Tan Street, where the king's food was cooked in ancient times, and the junction of Dien Bien Phu and Hang Bong streets is busy with noodle shops serving seafood dishes and *ga tan,* a chicken soup cooked with eight Chinese herbs, including lotus seed; it is considered especially good for women's health. Men may want to try *pin tan,* the same soup made with bull parts, instead. Toasted bread soaked in honey is served with the soup—you are charged by the slice. Make sure to avoid dishes with "scallops"; they are actually tough, bitter periwinkles. Eat upstairs at the restaurants in this area for a better view of the street—and the inside of someone's house.

Another excellent food street, known as "Xoi Alley," tees off Tong Duy Tan Street towards Trang Thi Street. *Xoi,* or sticky rice, is a glutinous grain served with sausage, boiled egg, dried shredded pork, or cucumbers and fish sauce. Here you can find sticky rice, fried noodles, or pho any time of day and late into the night. The "fast food" advertised in café windows actually means cheap rice, omelettes, and noodle dishes.

Keep in mind that Hanoi's dining scene is in constant flux. Though the establishments listed below have staying power, it is recommended you call before heading out to a particular restaurant, as places may close as suddenly as they open. In addition, it's not uncommon for owners and managers to change, transforming the whole restaurant for better or worse.

Hoan Kiem District

Cafés

$ ✕ **Au Lac Café.** It's the perfect spot for breakfast, an afternoon break, or after dinner coffee—at a table on the outdoor terrace of this café across from the Hotel Metropole. Cappuccinos, biscotti, and even bagels are served. Don't confuse it with the copy next door, the Mai La Café. ✉ *57 Ly Thai To St.,* ☎ *04/825–7807. No credit cards.*

¢ ✕ **Café 252.** This is the famous breakfast spot where Catherine Deneuve hung out while filming *Indochine*. It's no frills but serves good pastries and the best yogurt in town. ✉ *252 Hang Bong St.,* ☎ *04/825–0216. No credit cards.*

French

$$$ ★ ✕ **Le Splendide.** This French restaurant is, as the name claims, truly splendid. Mussels in white wine sauce are sublime, as is the crème brûlée. The Gallic cuisine and ambience are authentic enough that it can come as a shock to step outside and find cyclos and Honda motorbikes, not the Eiffel Tower. ✉ *Hoa Binh Hotel, 27 Ly Thuong Kiet St., Hoan Kiem District,* ☎ *04/826–6087. Jacket and tie. AE, MC, V. No lunch.*

$$ ★ ✕ **Hoa Sua.** Walk through a front courtyard off the street to find this restaurant, a favorite of Francophiles and French expatriates. More than a restaurant, it's a humanitarian project: young people in need of assistance are trained as waiters and cooks. The latter project seems to have turned out better than the former, as service can be slow. But the food—both French and Vietnamese—is good and the atmosphere very pleasant. Try the goat cheese on toast, the avocado salad, or the vegetable terrine (skip the chicken). The fruit tarts make a good end to the meal. Outdoor seating is available on a terra-cotta patio surrounded by palms; indoors is equally charming, with wrought-iron furniture. Reservations are recommended for Sunday brunch; if you can't get in, try the adjoining pastry shop, which serves a reasonable selection of breads, cakes, and pastries. ✉ *81 Tho Nhuom St., Hoan Kiem District,* ☎ *04/824–0448. No credit cards.*

Indian

$ ✕ **Tandoor.** This small Indian restaurant in the Thuy Loi minihotel makes up for its lack of ambience with a wonderful yet inexpensive menu. Food is prepared fresh, with Tandoor's cooks going so far as to hand-grind their own spices. You honestly cannot go wrong with any choice, but do try the fluffy garlic nan bread, the tender chicken *masala*, and eggplant curry. The fish *tikka* in red sauce and the chicken kebab marinated in yogurt are also sensational. Service is very friendly, though it can become chaotic at dinnertime. ✉ *24 Hang Be St., Hoan Kiem District,* ☎ *04/824–5359. No credit cards. No lunch Sun.*

International

$$$ ✕ **Club Opera.** One of Hanoi's top all-around restaurants, Club Opera serves both Western (downstairs) and Vietnamese food (upstairs). The imported Australian beef tenderloin or T-bone steak, grilled salmon, and New Zealand lamb chops are excellent, as are such Vietnamese dishes as the "steamboat," a boiling pot of meat-and-vegetable soup, and the shrimp compote served on a stalk of sugarcane. Mr. Son, the manager, is proud of his collection of jazz, and the atmospheric bar is one of the best places in town to hear recordings from the '40s through '60s. ✉ *59 Ly Thai To St., Hoan Kiem District,* ☎ *04/826–8802 (downstairs), 04/824–6950 (upstairs). AE, MC, V.*

$$$ ✕ **Miró.** The American-run Miró (named after the painter—prints of his work covers the walls) is Hanoi's most fashionable and stylish restaurant. Bryce Lamb, the American chef, cooks up impressive contemporary

Al Fresco, **29**
Au Lac Café, **22**
Café Moca, **13**
Café 252, **35**
Cha Ca La Vong, **7**
Club Opera, **18**
Da Tano, **9**
Dac Kim Bun Cha, **12**
Edo, **2**
Five Royal Fish, **16**
Galleon Steak House, **28**
Ha Thanh Restaurant, **8**
Hoa Sua, **33**
Hue Restaurant, **24**
Il Grillo, **30**
Il Padrino Wine Bar and Delicatessen, **15**
Indochine, **36**
Khazana, **3**
Madison's, **31**
Mediterraneo, **14**
Miró, **19**
Nam Phuong, **20**
La Paix, **1**
Piano Restaurant and Bar, **6**
Press Club, **17**
La Primavera, **26**
Quan Gio Moi, **4**
Saigon Sakura, **34**
Sampan, **25**
Seasons of Hanoi, **5**
Smiling Café, **10**
Soho Café and Deli, **27**
Le Splendide, **23**
Tandoor, **11**
Vegetarian Restaurant Com Chay Nang Tam, **32**
The Verandah, **21**

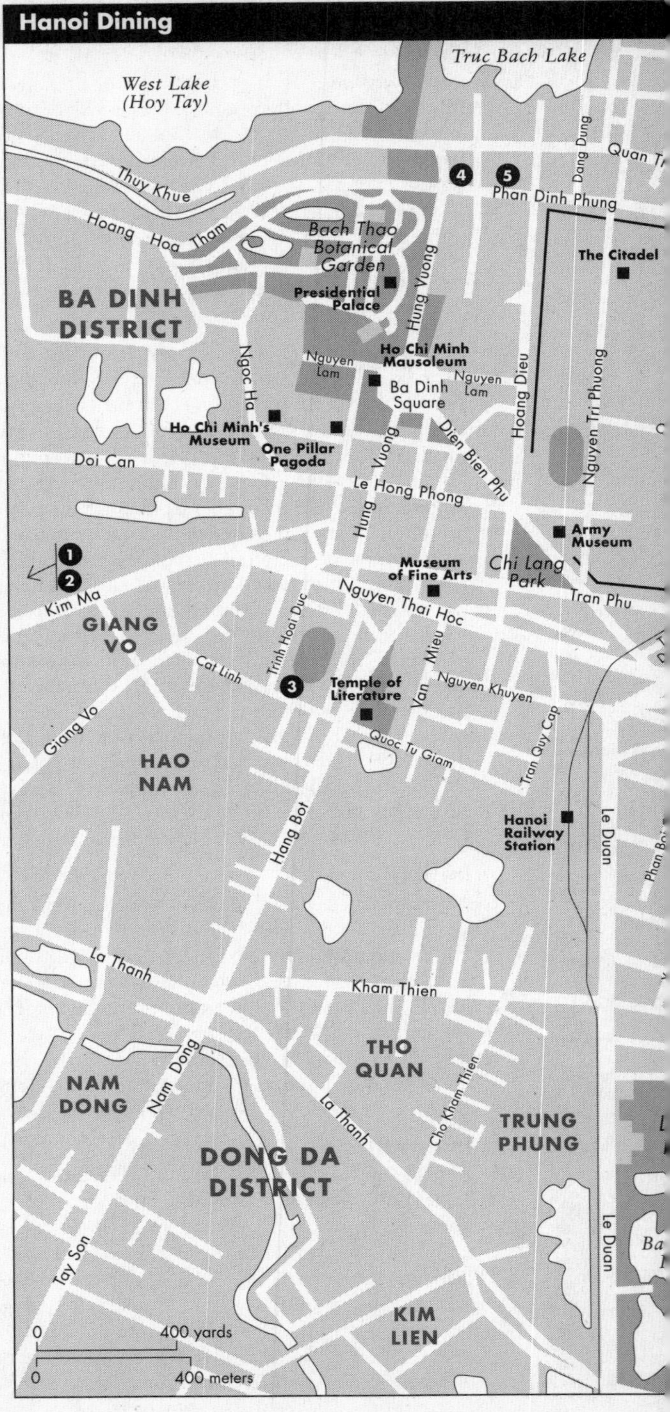

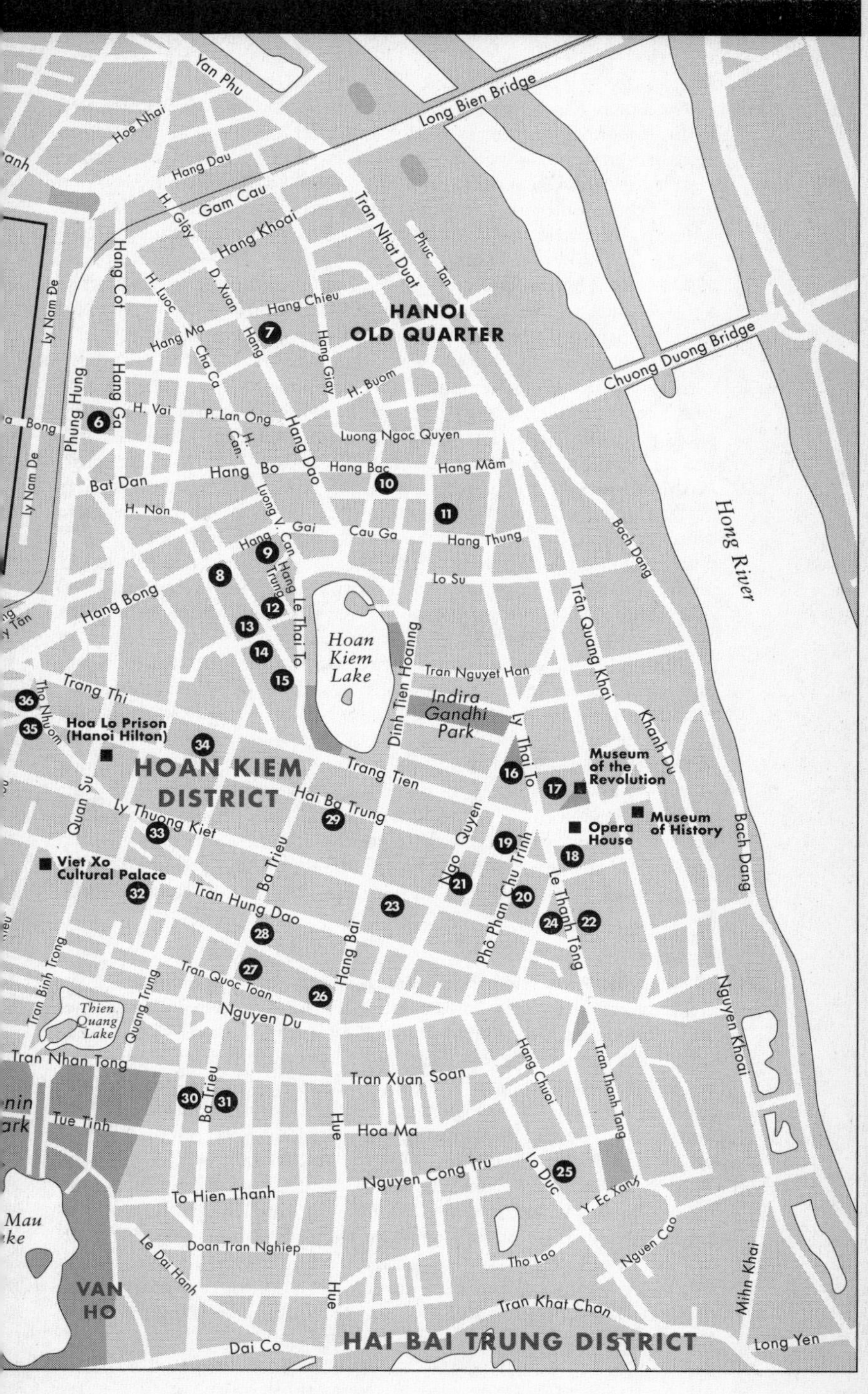

Long Bien Bridge
Chuong Duong Bridge
HANOI
OLD QUARTER
Hong River
Hoan Kiem Lake
Indira Gandhi Park
HOAN KIEM
DISTRICT
Hoa Lo Prison (Hanoi Hilton)
Museum of the Revolution
Museum of History
Opera House
Viet Xo Cultural Palace
Thien Quang Lake
HAI BAI TRUNG DISTRICT
VAN HO
Yan Phu
Hoe Nhai
Hang Dau
Gam Cau
Hang Khoai
Tran Nhat Duat
Phuc Tan
Hang Chieu
Hang Ma
Hang Cot
Ly Nam De
Phung Hung
Hang Ga
H. Vai
P. Lan Ong
H. Buom
Hang Giay
Luong Ngoc Quyen
Hang Bo
Hang Bac
Hang Mâm
Bat Dan
H. Non
Cau Ga
Hang Thung
Bach Dang
Lo Su
Hang Bong
Le Thai To
Trang Thi
Tran Nguyet Han
Dinh Tien Hoanng
Trân Quang Khai
Khanh Du
Ly Thai To
Trang Tien
Hai Ba Trung
Ly Thuong Kiet
Quan Su
Ngo Quyen
Phô Phan Chu Trinh
Le Thanh Tông
Ba Trieu
Tran Hung Dao
Hang Bai
Tran Quoc Toan
Tran Binh Trong
Quang Trung
Nguyen Du
Nguyen Khoai
Tran Nhan Tong
Tran Xuan Soan
Hang Chuoi
Tran Thanh Tang
Tue Tinh
Hoa Ma
Hue
Nguyen Cong Tru
Lo Duc
Y. Ec Xanh
To Hien Thanh
Doan Tran Nghiep
Le Dai Hanh
Tho Lao
Nguen Cao
Mihn Khai
Tran Khat Chan
Dai Co
Long Yen

cuisine, including ginger chicken with sesame seeds, and a fruit-filled filo-dough pastry for dessert. The staff, however, can be overattentive, and drinks are too expensive. ✉ *3 Nguyen Khac Can St., Hoam Kiem District,* ☎ *04/826–9080. MC, V.*

$$$ ✕ **Press Club.** Modern Mediterranean cuisine and fine wines are served at this elegant restaurant evoking the 1930s. Eat inside in the tasteful dining room or outside on the terrace surrounded by palms. Be sure to sample the calamari appetizer and the moussaka, if available. Don't be upset if they don't have the wine you wanted; every bottle needs to be inspected by customs officials; if they don't do it, the wine can't be sold. ✉ *59A Ly Thai To St., Hoan Kiem District,* ☎ *04/934–0888. MC, V.*

$$ ✕ **Al Fresço.** This colorful south-of-the-border-cum-pizza restaurant/bar a block south of Hoan Kiem Lake gets high marks from expats and travelers. Run by a friendly Aussie, the eclectic East-meets-West dining is coupled with a casual open-air ambience. The Mexican rolls, filled with avocado and chicken, are highly recommended. Al Fresco's may be the most popular foreign restaurant in Hanoi because of its jumbo portions of ribs, pasta, T-bone steak, Mexican salad, and pizza. ✉ *23L Hai Ba Trung St., Hoan Kiem District,* ☎ *04/826–7782. No credit cards.*

$$ ✕ **The Verandah.** This English-run restaurant and pub offers tasty meals and a chance to wind down in style. Housed in a villa near the center of town, the Verandah has an attentive staff, high ceilings, and minimal but elegant decor. The chicken in green curry is deliciously tender, and the green-pepper quiche with the accompanying salad and zingy dressing makes a good meal. The best reasons to dine here, however, are the rich potato-and-leek soup and the fried Camembert with walnuts. The namesake verandah provides for pleasant al fresco dining, and at night the cozy bar area is crowded with expatriates sipping gin and tonics. ✉ *Nguyen Khac Can St., Hoan Kiem District,* ☎ *04/825–7220. AE, V.*

$ ✕ **Five Royal Fish.** The shaded, second-floor outdoor terrace overlooking Hoan Kiem Lake, and the food and people-watching make up for the unremarkable decor. Homesick Westerners enjoy pizzas, sandwiches, and hamburgers, but there's also a good Vietnamese menu. Barbecued pork, beef, chicken, and seafood are served, though you should skip the curry. ✉ *16 Le Thai To St., Hoan Kiem District,* ☎ *04/824–4368. No credit cards.*

Italian

$$$ ✕ **Il Padrino Wine Bar and Delicatessen.** This peppy, Italian-run eatery is a pleasant spot to cool down and fuel up. Floor-to-ceiling windows face Hoan Kiem Lake and at night allow you to look inside to see the socializing foreigners eating here. After having an espresso brewed on the Rizenerazione machine, you may feel up to seeing all of Hanoi's sights in a day. The iced coffee, yogurt, good-sized sandwiches, tasty pasta carbonara, and the midnight closing time may keep you coming back. 🏨 *42 Le Thai To St., Hoan Kiem District,* ☎ *04/828–8449. AE, V.*

$$$ ✕ **La Primavera.** The American chef here creates very good contemporary Italian-American dishes. Sample the excellent grilled sirloin of tuna with mushrooms and pesto or the shrimp and lobster fra diavolo. For dessert try the fruit with ice cream combo or a crepe with vanilla ice cream and chocolate sauce. Finish off your meal with a cup of good, strong coffee. ✉ *12 Pho Hue St., Hoan Kiem District,* ☎ *04/826–3202. MC, V.*

$$ ✕ **Da Tano.** Let the friendly patron, Paulo, welcome you to this charming, no-frills trattoria where the checkered tablecloths carry you to the Mediterranean. The attentive staff serves up a good lasagna and noteworthy ravioli. Other pan-regional pasta dishes are cooked to al dente perfection, and the Italian chef also rolls out a delicious thin-crust pizza.

✉ *10 Hang Hanh St., Hoan Kiem District,* ☏ *04/828–7936. No credit cards.*

$$ ✕ **Mediterraneo.** Really delicious, reasonably-priced Italian food is served in a California-like atmosphere at Mediterraneo. The spinach pie is surprisingly good, as are an interesting array of home-made grappas—try licorice or peach. ✉ *23 Nha Tho St., Hoan Kiem District,* ☏ *04/826–6288. MC, V.*

Japanese

$$ ✕ **Saigon Sakura.** Frequented by expats, this take-off-your-shoes Japanese restaurant has clean zen decor and a good-value fixed-price lunch. Try the excellent calamari with vinegar marinade or what appears on the menu as risotto with shrimp, actually a very tasty cream rice that comes sizzling in a clay pot. Service is enthusiastic—staff yell a traditional Japanese greeting to approaching customers—if not altogether professional. ✉ *17 Trang Thi St., Hoan Kiem District,* ☏ *04/825–7565. MC, V.*

Steak

$$$ ✕ **Galleon Steak House.** With beef imported from Australia and the U.S., the meat here can satisfy most any carnivorous hankerings. Sizzling-hot steaks and ice-cold draft beer bring customers back again and again. The Galleon was cited for the "Best Steaks in Hanoi" by the Vietnam Investment Review two years running. The restaurant is housed in an uninspirational narrow building; inside you'll find a nautical theme, chevron-pattern wood floors, and a lugubrious wooden bar in back. ✉ *50 Tran Quoc Toan St., Hoan Kiem District,* ☏ *04/822–8611. AE, DC, MC, V.*

Vegetarian

$$ ✕ **Vegetarian Restaurant Com Chay Nang Tam.** An unusual array of vegetarian dishes, many prepared to resemble meat, are served in a dimly lit villa. The warm corn squares are a pleasing starter, and the "ginger fish," made of tofu, is a good main course. The restaurant fills up, so reservations are recommended, especially for larger parties. ✉ *79A Tran Hung Dao St., Hoan Kiem District,* ☏ *04/826–6140. No credit cards.*

Vietnamese

$$$ ✕ **Indochine.** One of the better upscale Vietnamese dining establishments in town, Indochine is set back from a small street in a worn but elegant house. Antiques from the region set the mood, though interior lighting is somewhat dim. Live traditional music plays some nights, and staff members wear colorful traditional costumes. Choose from seating inside upstairs or downstairs, or outside in the small but pleasant courtyard. Favorite dishes include banana-flower salad, prawns in coconut milk, crab spring rolls, and beef in bamboo with lemongrass. ✉ *16 Nam Ngu St., Hoan Kiem District,* ☏ *04/824–6097. Jacket and tie. Reservations essential. AE, MC, V.*

$$ ✕ **Cha Ca La Vong.** Right in the thick of the Old Quarter is Hanoi's most famous purveyor of *cha ca* (grilled boneless fish cubes marinated in dill and served with rice noodles and peanuts). Watch out! Cha ca is cooked at your table on a brazier that can send hot grease flying. (On a warm evening, you may feel like you're being grilled along with the fish.) Portions are small, but that doesn't seem to dissuade the tourists who pack the upstairs restaurant. Fewer people sit downstairs. The grease-covered walls add to the authentic, pungent experience. ✉ *14 Cha Ca St., Hoan Kiem District, no phone. No credit cards.*

$$ ✕ **Nam Phuong.** Upscale Vietnamese cuisine is served in a stylish-but-elegant French villa setting. Portions of the tasty and beautifully presented dishes (like the beef in coconut milk served in a coconut) are disappointingly scanty, however. The owl-like manager, an older Hanoian gentleman, keeps a watchful eye over customers and the staff, who wear tasteful traditional costumes. Traditional instruments are played, though the tunes can be modern and even experimental. ✉ *19 Phan Chu Trinh St., Hoan Kiem District,* ☎ *04/824–0926. AE, MC, V.*

$$ ✕ **Piano Restaurant & Bar.** A piano-and-violin duo creates a pleasant mood, while the high-ceilinged French-colonial architecture, soft lighting, and antique yellow walls recreate turn-of-the-century charm. The food is less exceptional, though you can expect a good, traditional Vietnamese meal. Stick to the very fresh boiled crab. Don't expect the best English skills, especially on the telephone. ✉ *50 Hang Vai St., Hoan Kiem District,* ☎ *04/828–4423. No credit cards.*

$ ★ ✕ **Dac Kim Bun Cha.** After souvenir shopping on Hang Bac, consider having lunch at this four-story Old Quarter institution. The first floor is tiny and used for food preparation, but staff will eagerly lead you up. . . and up. . . and up the winding tiled stairs until enough empty plastic stools can be found for your party. You may be planted cozily among other customers. Ordering shouldn't be hard: The restaurant offers only two dishes, and locals say both are tops: *Bun cha* (grilled pork patties with rice noodles) are served with heaping plates of herbs and lettuce; as a side, try the huge pork- and crab-filled spring rolls. Wash both down with *bia lanh* (cold beer) or *che da* (iced Vietnamese tea). ✉ *1 Hang Hanh St., Hoan Kiem District, no phone. No credit cards. No dinner.*

$ ★ ✕ **Hue Restaurant.** If you want the best food in Hanoi, come here for imperial Hue cuisine and other traditional Vietnamese fare in a rustic outdoor/indoor setting. Pork Pie is a poor translation for culinary nirvana—a some-assembly-required platter of sugarcane-wrapped ground pork that you roll with greens and vegetables in rice paper and dip into a delicious peanut sauce. For those who wince at this carnivorous frenzy, vegetarian delights are plentiful. A warning: It's advised not to drink too much since the rest room here is essentially a sloping floor. ✉ *6 Ly Thuong Kiet St., Hoan Kiem District,* ☎ *04/826–4062. No credit cards.*

¢ ✕ **Ha Thanh Restaurant.** Packed with locals at lunchtime, this Vietnamese equivalent of a greasy-spoon diner serves tasty heaping portions of Vietnamese and Chinese dishes. ✉ *15A Hang Hanh St., Hoan Kiem District,* ☎ *04/828–5829. No credit cards.*

¢ ✕ **Smiling Café.** Brimming with young travelers, the Smiling Café not only serves some of Hanoi's cheapest Vietnamese fast food but also doubles as a tourist agency that books boat and bus day trips out of the city. As a hub of tourist activity, the Smiling is a great place to meet other travelers and exchange information over a refreshing fruit shake. ✉ *10 Dinh Liet St., Hoan Kiem District,* ☎ *04/828–2109. No credit cards.*

Around Lenin Park

Chinese

$$ ✕ **Quan Gio Moi.** The best part about this plain-looking restaurant is its perfect location overlooking a lake in Lenin Park. The food is good, though not superb. Try the hot-and-sour soup, the chili prawns, or the sweet-and-sour chicken. Eat here if you're in the area, but it's not worth a special trip. ✉ *63 Le Duan St., Lenin Park, Hai Ba Trung District,* ☎ *04/822–9839. No credit cards.*

International

$$$ ✕ **Madison's.** Under the discerning eye of Australian manager Joshua Quinn, Madison's has established itself in Hanoi's nascent fine-dining scene. In Madison's Hotel, this understated restaurant manages an elegant blend of Continental cuisine and Asian flavors. The decor is upscale and refined, like a British gentlemen's club. The menu, which changes periodically, includes the highly recommended chicken schnitzel,

crab soufflé, and pork medallions with mango chutney. Every dish is special, but Director's Crab is a hit. The wait staff is attentive but not overbearing. Sample the fine selection of Australian wines. ✉ *16 Bui Thi Xuan St., Hai Ba Trung District,* ☎ *04/822–8164. AE, DC.*

$$ ✕ **Sampan.** Go upstairs for delicious pan-Asian food served in a green and sunny setting. The restaurant has windows on all sides, making the elegant interior seem light and bright; traditional Vietnamese cultural items, including a whole boat, decorate the space. A lovely courtyard is shaded by bushy trees and bamboo. Try the Thai barbecued chicken, a sizzling dish with Asian-Cajun sauce, or the succulent curry coconut scallops and chili garlic prawns. ✉ *125 Lo Duc St., Hai Ba Trung District,* ☎ *04/821–4138. Reservations essential. No credit cards.*

$$ ✕ **Soho Cafe and Deli.** Black and white tiles, salmon-color walls, a high ceiling, and large windows make this a very pleasant lunch spot. So do the light, tasty food, and the stock of international newspapers and magazines. Grilled red snapper with coriander and lime butter is a good warm-up for the real taste sensation: the lemon cheesecake. Also recommended are such Mediterranean dishes as hummus or beef, bacon, and red-wine filo pie. The terrace balcony overlooks Ba Trieu Street's classic French architecture, in turn overlooked by new office towers in the distance. ✉ *57 Ba Trieu St., Hoan Kiem District,* ☎ *04/826–6555. AE, MC, V.*

Italian

$$ ✕ **Il Grillo.** This very popular Italian-run eatery serves authentic prosciutto and grappas. The rib-eye steak is highly recommended, as are the homemade pasta dishes. Ask Luca, the proprietor, for the day's specials. The restaurant has cheerful, cozy decor—like a cabin in the Dolomites. It's the perfect place for a hearty meal and a well-earned beer after a day of sightseeing. Reservations are recommended, especially for Sunday night. ✉ *116 Ba Trieu St., Hai Ba Trung District,* ☎ *04/822–7720. No credit cards.*

Around the Ho Chi Minh Mausoleum/Ba Dinh District

Indian

$$ ★ ✕ **Khazana.** Manager Shankar Dutta runs this opulent tribute to North Indian cuisine near the Temple of Literature. Its classy decor and succulent meat dishes from a real Tandoor oven make it popular. Paintings from Rajasthan decorate the walls, and miniature musical instruments hang from the three central pillars. Intricately carved doors and windows grace the main hall and three private rooms. Curries, soups, and chutney, all served with aplomb by the wait staff, are worthy of the higher-than average prices. Portions are good-sized, however, and the prix-fixe lunch is a good value. For a mild, sweetish vegetarian dish, try *malai kofta,* balls of cottage cheese filled with nuts, deep-fried, then cooked with saffron gravy. At press time the restaurant was set to move to an as yet unspecified address; check in the Vietnam Economic Times for information. ✉ *27 Quoc Tu Giam St., Dong Da District,* ☎ *04/843–3477. MC, V.*

Italian

$$$–$$$$ ✕ **Edo.** People go out of their way to this place in the Hanoi Daewoo Hotel, the most expensive restaurant in Hanoi and also the best. Have the $12 lunchbox, try the especially good grilled salmon, or go all out with the extravagant $110 "Swellfish Course." ✉ *Hanoi Daewoo Hotel, 360 Kim Ma St., Ba Dinh District,* ☎ *04/831–5000. AE, MC, V.*

$$$ ✕ **La Paix.** The ceiling here is painted sky-blue to complement the broad windows looking out to the real sky. Southern Italian and Mediterranean dishes are artfully prepared by chef Avelino Aniello. Try the veal cut-

let sautéed with wild mushrooms in an herb sauce laced with grappas, or the green salad and smoked chicken with mayonnaise dressing. The fish fillet pan-fried with prawns tarragon and American sauce is especially fresh. Finish off with a double-strength espresso. ✉ *Hanoi Daewoo Hotel, 360 Kim Ma Street, Ba Dinh District,* ☎ *04/831–5000, ext. 3245. AE, MC, V.*

Around West Lake

Vietnamese

$$ ✕ **Seasons of Hanoi.** In a beautifully restored villa dating from 1902, Seasons is filled with antiques from Indochina. Young British expatriate Justin Wheatcroft has given his restaurant a classic feel, with French elegance meeting Vietnamese charm. The coconut and lemongrass chicken curry is a rich choice, and the fish baked in a clay pot is tasty but salty. Highly recommended is the soft-shell crab tempura. Sunday brunch is popular. ✉ *95B Quan Thanh St., Ba Dinh District,* ☎ *04/835–5444. AE, MC, V.*

LODGING

Hanoi's hotels range from charming and idiosyncratic to some of the most luxurious in the region (although even the swankiest properties tend to have spotty service; managers are working hard to develop more professional staffs, but for the time being, it's a good idea to cultivate patience). The general character of hotels varies somewhat by district: Hoan Kiem offers the greatest proportion of minihotels and state-run places, where you'll find the most Vietnamese flavor. Ba Dinh District and the shores of West Lake are home to larger and more upscale facilities.

Hoan Kiem District

$$$$ ★ **Metropole Hotel Sofitel.** The exquisitely renovated Metropole, built by the French at the turn of the century, combines old-world European grandeur with modern convenience. And you can't beat the central location in the heart of Hanoi. The bar-side pool is a nice option on a sunny day or warm evening, and the lobby bar is a good bet any day of the week. You're better off going out for meals, however. The impeccably decorated rooms with French-style shuttered windows are luxurious if not incredibly spacious. Just keep in mind that though this is an internationally-managed hotel, service is not always consistently up to par. ✉ *15 Pho Ngo Quyen St., Hoan Kiem District,* ☎ *04/826–6919,* FAX *04/826–6920. 244 rooms. Restaurant, 2 bars, air-conditioning, in-room safes, minibars, refrigerators, room service, pool, laundry service and dry cleaning, concierge, business services, meeting rooms, travel services, airport shuttle, car rental. AE, DC, MC, V.*

$$$ **Hanoi Opera Hilton.** At press time (winter 1997), this Hilton was set to open at the end of 1998 next to the Opera House. The building was designed to complement the original French colonial architecture. It will have all the amenities that you would expect from this international hotel chain. ✉ *Just off Trang Tien St.,* ☎ *800/445–8667 in the U.S., no local phone at press time. 300 rooms. 2 bars, 3 restaurants, pool, health club, business services, meeting rooms. AE, MC, V.*

$$$ ★ **Saigon Hotel.** A joint venture between Saigon Tourist (which manages the Rex Hotel in Ho Chi Minh City) and the Hanoi Railway Service, this property offers superior-quality service and, despite the concrete '60s architecture, a pleasant ambience. Rooms are standard hotel-style. The rooftop garden is a terrific place for an evening drink; from here you can see the Hanoi Towers office complex, on the site of

the former "Hanoi Hilton" prison. The hotel is not far from the train station, opposite the United Nations Vietnam headquarters, and near the Fansland Cinema, the only theater in Hanoi with movies in English. The professionally-run restaurant serves Vietnamese, French, and American food. ✉ *80 Ly Thuong Kiet St., Hoan Kiem District,* ☎ *04/826–8499,* FAX *04/826–6631. 44 rooms. Restaurant, 2 bars, air-conditioning, in-room safes, minibars, refrigerators, room service, TVs, massage, sauna, laundry service and dry cleaning, business services, meeting rooms, travel services, car rental. AE, DC, MC, V.*

$$–$$$ **Chains First Eden Hotel.** Completed in 1996, this establishment has all the makings of a first-class luxury hotel, except decent management. Ideally located in the Old Quarter, the Chains First Eden is an excellent point of departure for walking tours through Hanoi. Rooms have all the amenities, but unfortunately they also have bright orange curtains. Deluxe rooms with fax machines are available. ✉ *2 Phung Hung St., Hoan Kiem District,* ☎ *04/828–3897,* FAX *04/828–4066. 42 rooms. Restaurant, bar, air-conditioning, in-room safes, minibars, refrigerators, room service, TVs, health club, laundry service and dry cleaning, business services, travel services, car rental. AE, DC, MC, V.*

$$–$$$ **Dan Chu Hotel.** The partial renovations here have not quite done justice to the lovely French architecture, which dates from the early part of the 20th century. Rooms are spacious, with high ceilings, although their charms are compromised by ersatz Louis XV decor and synthetic bed covers sporting roses. The staff tries but isn't always up to par. Still, the location is great, and an open, airy, verdant back area commands a certain grand elegance. ✉ *29 Trang Tien St., Hoan Kiem District,* ☎ *04/825–4937,* FAX *04/826–6786. 56 rooms. Restaurant, bar, air-conditioning, minibars, refrigerators, room service, TVs, laundry service and dry cleaning, concierge, business services, travel services, car rental. AE, DC, MC, V.*

$$–$$$ **Hoa Binh Hotel.** In a grand old building, the three-star Hoa Binh is poised to accommodate an upscale crowd but seems to be lacking an experienced staff. The spacious rooms are clean and have high ceilings, but they betray sloppy renovations. However, the hotel is efficient and well maintained, and it houses one of the best French restaurants in town, Le Splendide (☞ Dining, *above*). Clocks in the lobby tell you what time it is in Moscow and Beijing, not just London, New York, and Hanoi. ✉ *27 Ly Thuong Kiet, Hoan Kiem District,* ☎ *04/825–3315,* FAX *04/826–9818. 102 rooms. Restaurant, bar, air-conditioning, minibars, refrigerators, TVs, barbershop, laundry service and dry cleaning, business services, car rental. AE, DC, MC, V.*

$$–$$$ **Prince Hotel** (Hoang Tu). This posh minihotel offers comfortable and elegant rooms, very nice bathrooms, and a very enthusiastic English-speaking staff. The balconies block the noise from the street. Views range from a peek at the beautiful Hai Ba Trung Pagoda, the havoc of apartments, and the Hanoi Towers. Conveniently near the train station, the Prince is also not too far from the city center. The restaurant, which has formal straight-back chairs, serves all meals. ✉ *96A Hai Ba Trung St., Hoan Kiem District,* ☎ *04/824–8314,* FAX *04/824–8323. 25 rooms. Restaurant, bar, air-conditioning, minibars, refrigerators, TVs, laundry and dry cleaning, business services, car rental. AE, DC, MC, V.*

$$–$$$ **Thang Long Hotel.** The freshly-painted rooms have high ceilings and new bathroom facilities; many have balconies overlooking a lovely courtyard. Unfortunately, the otherwise elegant 1920s French structure suffers from puckering industrial red carpeting. ✉ *5 Nguyen Bieu St., Hoan Kiem District,* ☎ *04/823–1437,* FAX *04/823–1436. 18 rooms. Restaurant, bar, air-conditioning, minibars, refrigerators, laundry service, travel services, airport shuttle, car rental. AE, DC, MC, V.*

Chains First Eden Hotel, **23**
Dan Chu Hotel, **17**
Eden Hotel, **21**
Galaxy Hotel, **9**
Hanoi Daewoo Hotel, **1**
Hanoi Horison Hotel, **3**
Hanoi Hotel, **2**
Hanoi Opera Hilton, **18**
Hanoi Sheraton Hotel, **5**
Hawaii Hotel, **20**
Ho Tay Villas, **4**
Hoa Binh Hotel, **19**
Lien Westlake Resort, **6**
Metropole Hotel Sofitel, **16**
Nam Phuong Hotel, **13**
Phan Thai Hotel, **11**
Planet Hotel, **8**
Prince Hotel, **15**
Saigon Hotel, **22**
Thang Loi Hotel, **7**
Thang Long Hotel, **14**
Vinh Quang Hotel, **10**
Win Hotel, **12**

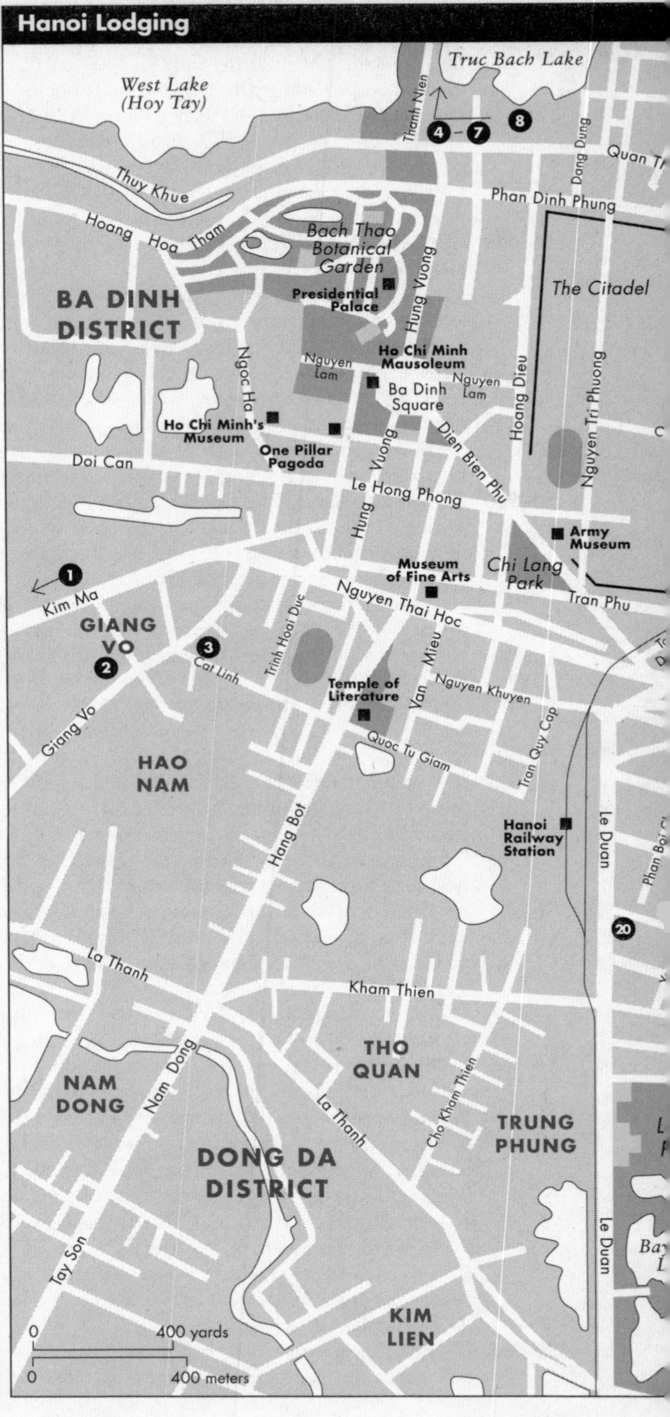

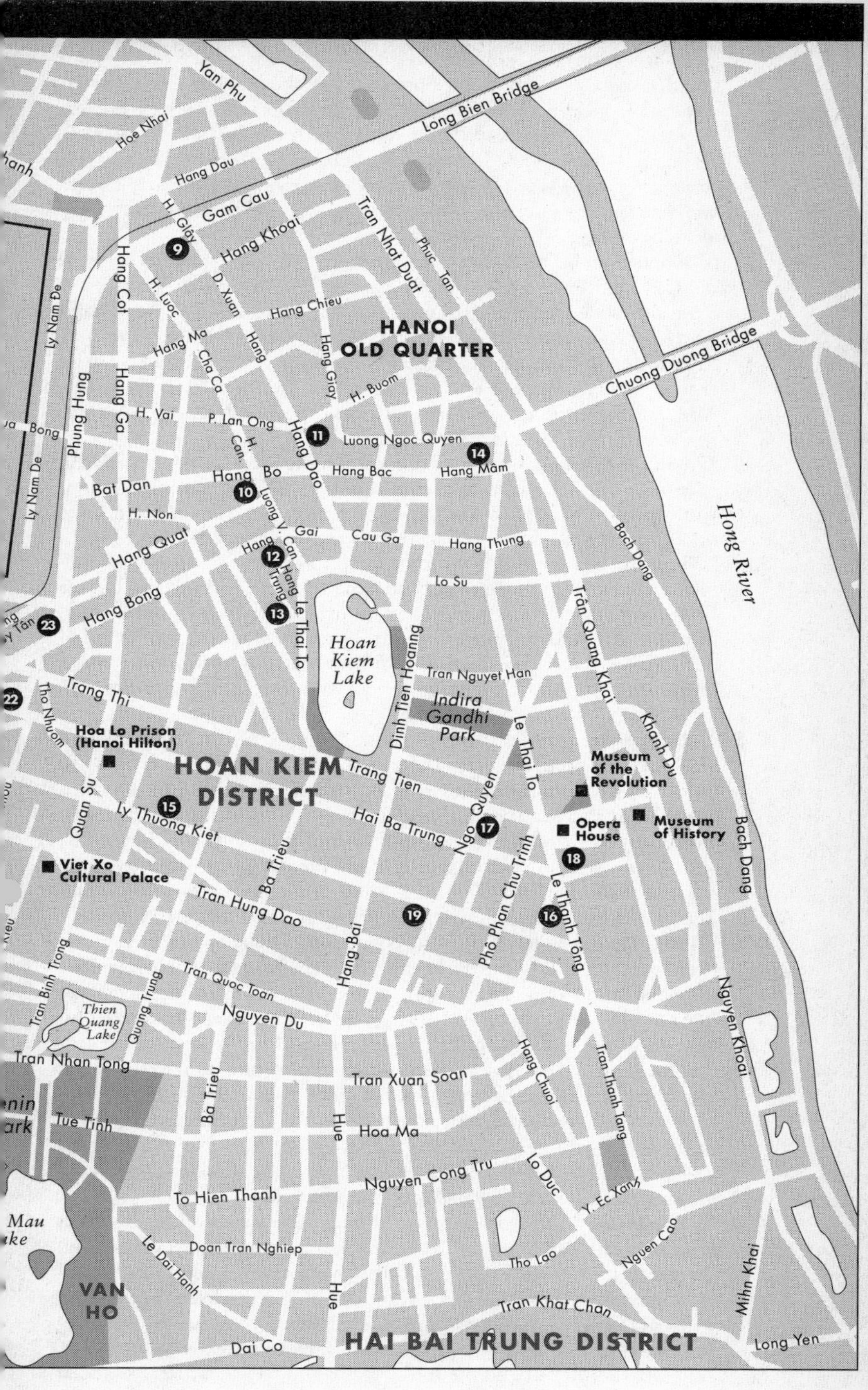

HANOI
OLD QUARTER
HOAN KIEM
DISTRICT
HAI BAI TRUNG DISTRICT
Hong River
Hoan Kiem Lake
Indira Gandhi Park
Thien Quang Lake
VAN HO
Hoa Lo Prison (Hanoi Hilton)
Museum of the Revolution
Opera House
Museum of History
Viet Xo Cultural Palace
Long Bien Bridge
Chuong Duong Bridge
Yan Phu
Hoe Nhai
Hang Dau
Gam Cau
Hang Khoai
Tran Nhat Duat
Phuc Tan
Hang Cot
Hang Chieu
Hang Ma
Ly Nam De
Phung Hung
Hang Ga
H. Vai
P. Lan Ong
Hang Giay
H. Buom
Luong Ngoc Quyen
Hang Bo
Hang Bac
Hang Mâm
Bat Dan
H. Non
Hang Quat
Cau Go
Hang Thung
Lo Su
Hang Bong
Le Thai To
Dinh Tien Hoanng
Tran Nguyet Han
Tran Quang Khai
Bach Dang
Khanh Du
Trang Thi
Tho Nhuom
Trang Tien
Quan Su
Ly Thuong Kiet
Hai Ba Trung
Ngo Quyen
Le Thai To
Phô Phan Chu Trinh
Le Thanh Tông
Ba Trieu
Tran Hung Dao
Hang Bai
Tran Binh Trong
Quang Trung
Tran Quoc Toan
Nguyen Du
Tran Nhan Tong
Tran Xuan Soan
Hang Chuoi
Tran Thanh Tang
Nguyen Khoai
Tue Tinh
Hoa Ma
Hue
Nguyen Cong Tru
Lo Duc
Y. Ec Xang
To Hien Thanh
Doan Tran Nghiep
Le Dai Hanh
Tho Lao
Nguen Cao
Tran Khat Chan
Mihn Khai
Dai Co
Long Yen

$$ ★ **Galaxy Hotel.** Although built in 1918, this granite-faced hotel has been fully renovated to accommodate business travelers and seems wholly modern. The comfortable rooms have typical hotel decor and are quieter than you'd suspect given the hotel's proximity to the bustling Old Quarter; some have garden views. The attentive staff members speak English very well. ✉ *1 Phan Dinh Phung St., Hoan Kiem District,* ☎ *04/828–2888,* FAX *04/828–2466. 48 rooms. Restaurant, bar, air-conditioning, in-room safes, minibars, refrigerators, room service, TVs, laundry service and dry cleaning, concierge, business services, meeting rooms, travel services, car rental. AE, DC, MC, V.*

$$ **Planet Hotel.** The Planet offers plush rooms and a great location in the Old Quarter overlooking West Lake. Wooden touches offset the ultraslick modern edge and the profusion of granite. ✉ *120 Quan Thanh St., Hoan Kiem District,* ☎ *04/843–5888,* FAX *04/843–5088. 53 rooms. Restaurant, 2 bars, air-conditioning, in-room safes, minibars, refrigerators, room service, TVs, hot tub, sauna, health club, laundry service and dry cleaning, concierge, business services, travel services, car rental. AE, DC, MC, V.*

$ **Phan Thai Hotel.** Modern minihotel conveniences, inoffensive decor, balconies, and a friendly staff make this a very decent accommodation. Conveniently located in the Old Quarter, it's near Hoan Kiem Lake on a biscuit- and candy-selling street, a stumble from the Roxy Disco. Follow the bellman's gold-trimmed cap to the top floors for a fabulous view of Old Quarter roofs and the Long Binh train and bicycle bridge. Also upstairs is a family altar, featuring tiled dragons and a many-armed goddess. ✉ *44 Hang Giay St., Hoan Kiem District,* ☎ *04/824–3667,* FAX *04/826–6677. 16 rooms. Restaurant, air-conditioning, minibars, refrigerators, TVs, laundry service, travel services, car rental. AE, DC, MC, V.*

¢–$ **Nam Phuong Hotel.** Just off Hang Trong Street on the northwest side of Hoan Kiem Lake, this hotel has old but charming rooms with balconies overlooking a state newspaper agency. The lobby is musty, but there is a sweet, if petite, central atrium. Rooms feature the traditional carved-wood furniture usually found in established homes. The staff is very accommodating. ✉ *16 Bao Khanh St., Hoan Kiem District,* ☎ *04/825–8030,* FAX *04/825–8964. Air-conditioning, fans, minibars, refrigerators, laundry service, travel services. No credit cards.*

¢–$ **Vinh Quang Hotel.** This hotel is on Hang Quat, or Fan Street, one of the most charming and lively streets in the Old Quarter. Now instead of selling fans, stores here specialize in red-velvet banners with messages like GOOD LUCK IN YOUR NEXT LIFE. Aside from the cheap East-West fusion decor, the Vinh Quang offers neat, efficient rooms and a great central location. Front rooms overlook the color and activity of Hang Quat Street, while back rooms have a more placid view of terra-cotta-tile roofs and green-and-white-tile courtyards. Tremendous carp swim in the lobby pool. ✉ *24 Hang Quat St., Hoan Kiem District,* ☎ *04/824–3423,* FAX *04/825–1519. Restaurant, bar, air-conditioning, fans, minibars, refrigerators, laundry service, travel services. AE, MC, V.*

¢–$ ★ **Win Hotel.** At the top end of the budget accommodations, the Win is immaculate and homey all at once. On a quiet street just off Le Thai To Street, it's also just a stone's throw from Hoan Kiem Lake. Floor-to-ceiling one-way windows let Hanoi in, or you can keep the light out with lace and red-velvet curtains. Carved hardwood furniture, tastefully arranged fake flowers, high ceilings, clean baths, satellite television, and a fluffy dog in the lobby make you feel at home. An added bonus is its location next to Café Nhan, which is the size of a mansion and is famous for its avocado shakes. ✉ *34 Hang Hanh St., Hoan Kiem District,* ☎ *04/828–7371 or 04/828–7150,* FAX *04/824–7448. 8* *rooms. Air-conditioning, fans, minibars, refrigerators, laundry service, travel services, car rental. No credit cards.*

Around Lenin Park

$$$ **Hawaii Hotel.** Ignore the name: This comfortable minihotel has spacious and tasteful rooms as well as a helpful, sweet staff that takes good care of guests from all over the globe. It's not too far from Thien Quang Lake and Lenin Park, and the huge rooms overlook the National Press Security and Ministry of Foreign Affairs buildings. (The roof has 360-degree views but, unfortunately, no chairs.) ✉ *77 Nguyen Du St., Hoan Kiem District,* ☎ *04/822–7517,* FAX *04/822–8698. 25 rooms. Restaurant, bar, air-conditioning, minibars, refrigerators, TVs, laundry service, business services, travel services, car rental. AE, DC, MC, V.*

$$–$$$ **Eden Hotel.** The Eden—not to be confused with the Chains First Eden Hotel on Tho Nhuom Street—offers minihotel luxury and service at its finest in a decent location near Thuyen Quang Lake. Bright rooms with carved-wood furniture have all of the conveniences—carpeted floors, big baths, and 10 television channels. Happily absent are neon and nylon, especially in the low-lighted, wood-paneled dining area. In the lobby, birds sing over a tremendous fishtank, and an altar stacked with fake gold, oranges, beer, and Cokes for the ancestors. ✉ *94 Yet Kieu St., Hoan Kiem District,* ☎ *04/822–7465,* FAX *04/822–8235. 22 rooms. Restaurant, air-conditioning, minibars, refrigerators, TVs, laundry service and dry cleaning, concierge, travel services, car rental. AE, DC, MC, V.*

Around the Ho Chi Minh Mausoleum/Ba Dinh District

$$$$ ★ **Hanoi Daewoo Hotel.** The pool here—the longest in Southeast Asia—is just one example of how sumptuous (almost over the top) the Daewoo is. Even its impressive collection of more than 1,000 paintings by contemporary Vietnamese artists, hanging in public spaces and guest rooms, is worthy of a book. Space is abundant—from the open marble lobby that spills into a large two-story lounge overlooking the pool to the four restaurants serving Chinese, Japanese, Vietnamese, and Western cuisine. Rooms are big and tastefully decorated in better-than-average hotel-style furnishings; some overlook the zoo, West Lake, or downtown Hanoi. The main drawback is needing to take a taxi to get downtown; although there is a shuttle service, it doesn't run very frequently. ✉ *360 Kim Ma St., Ba Dinh District,* ☎ *04/831–5000,* FAX *04/831–5010. 411 rooms. 4 restaurants, 2 bars, air-conditioning, in-room safes, minibars, refrigerators, room service, TVs, pool, hot tub, sauna, aerobics, exercise room, dance club, laundry service and dry cleaning, concierge, business services, meeting rooms, travel services, car rental. AE, DC, MC, V.*

$$$$ **Hanoi Hotel.** This charmless Western-style hotel seems to cater to businesspeople who have no interest in knowing they are in Vietnam. It's quite a distance from the city center but close to Ho Chi Minh's Mausoleum. Some rooms overlook Giang Vo Lake. ✉ *D8 Giang Vo St., Ba Dinh District,* ☎ *04/825–4603,* FAX *04/825–9209. 224 rooms. 2 restaurants, 2 bars, air-conditioning, in-room safes, minibars, room service, massage, dance club, laundry service and dry cleaning, concierge, business services, meeting rooms, travel services, car rental. AE, DC, MC, V.*

$$ **Hanoi Horison Hotel.** Known as the "Emerald City" because of its impressive green glass-fronted facade, the Horison is a joint Vietnamese-Indonesian project. The spacious lobby has a marble floor and Indonesian artwork. Rooms are luxurious if not overly large and are done in soothing pastels. Chinese and international fare is served in the restaurants; occasional live music is featured at the Chimney Pub and Bistro. ✉ *40 Cat Linh St., Ba Dinh District,* ☎ *04/733–0808,* FAX *04/733–0688. 350 rooms. Bar, 3 restaurants, lobby lounge, air-conditioning, in-room safes, minibars, room service, pool, tennis court, exercise room, laundry service, business services, meeting rooms, travel services. AE, DC, MC, V.*

Around West Lake

$$$$ **Hanoi Sheraton Hotel.** The Sheraton has one of the most striking entrances in Hanoi—a Chinese-style pagoda at the top of a curving driveway. The hotel sits right on West Lake—it's not the closest accommodation to the center of town, but it is undoubtedly one of the finest. Restaurants include Asian and Western options, and the gym's energetic manager is sure to help you work off your dessert. ✉ *K5 Nghi Tam, Tay Ho, Ba Dinh District,* ☎ *04/829–1923,* FAX *04/829–1815. 299 rooms. Restaurant, bar, air-conditioning, pool, tennis court, health club, laundry services, business services, meeting rooms. AE, MC, V.*

$$$ **Lien Westlake Resort.** Manager Achim Ihlenfeld is seeing to it that guests are well taken care of at this property set to open in mid-1998. Built on a fan of pontoons over West Lake, this hotel/resort offers luxury rooms and dining, as well as lakeside facilities. Visitors from all over the world, but especially the Southeast Asian region, will get to take advantage of one of the best uses of West Lake in Hanoi. ✉ *Nghi Tam, Quang An, Tay Ho District,* ☎ *04/826–4847,* FAX *04/826–4846. 375 rooms. AE, MC, V.*

$$$ **Thang Loi Hotel.** Built during the '60s with help from the Cuban government, the "Victory Hotel" was the first Western-style hotel in Hanoi. The Thang Loi has charm and appeal if you're a connoisseur of the Eastern bloc style: it literally floats on pontoons in West Lake. Tranquil views of all the construction activity around the lake comes with the room. ✉ *Yen Phu St., West Lake District,* ☎ *04/826–8211,* FAX *04/825–2800. 178 rooms. 2 restaurants, 2 bars, air-conditioning, fans, minibars, refrigerators, room service, TVs, pool, barbershop, beauty salon, massage, sauna, tennis court, shop, laundry service and dry cleaning, business services, meeting rooms, travel services, airport shuttle, car rental. AE, DC, MC, V.*

$$ **Ho Tay Villas.** If you are interested in complete silence, these villas, 5 km (3 mi) outside Hanoi on West Lake, offer peaceful accommodations that feel like a cross between an elegant estate and a socialist summer camp. Rooms are clean with all the amenities but perhaps a little musty from age and proximity to the lake. ✉ *Dang Thai Mai St., Quan Tay Ho,* ☎ *04/845–2393,* FAX *04/823–2126. 10 villas. Restaurant, bar, air-conditioning, fans, minibars, refrigerators, TVs, laundry service, meeting rooms, travel services. No credit cards.*

NIGHTLIFE AND THE ARTS

Nightlife

Hanoi has enough bars and clubs to keep you busy, and more are opening all the time. They range from the low-key Met Pub to the eclectic R&R Pub to the popular Apocalypse Now dance club.

Bars and Pubs

Bat Dan Café (✉ 10 Bat Dan St., Hoan Kiem District, ☎ 04/828–6411) is a bright, cozy wood-paneled bar run by a Frenchman and an Italian photographer. Expatriates gather here for the cheap alcoholic and coffee drinks and to play chess, checkers, or Trivial Pursuit. Photo exhibits are held here periodically.

Le Club (✉ 15 Ngo Quyen St., Hoan Kiem District, ☎ 04/826–6919), in the Hotel Sofitel, has a very pleasant ambience and good finger food. Clusters of couches fill up the expanded lounge, where patrons sip strong but expensive cocktails.

Met Pub (✉ 15 Ngo Quyen St., Hoan Kiem District, ☎ 04/826–6919), on the Ly Thai To Street side of the Hotel Sofitel, is where high-rolling businesspeople hang out at the wood-paneled bar watching satellite TV and middle-aged expats drink martinis and listen to live jazz. An after-work crowd comes for the lively happy hour, despite the rather pricey snack foods and drinks.

Pear Tree (✉ 78 Tho Nhuom St., Hoan Kiem District, ☎ 04/825–7812), a pub in the Eden Hotel dominated by wrought iron. Satellite TV, a free pool table, and good bar food draw a loyal clientele of French and Americans. Drinks are moderately priced.

Polite Pub (✉ 5 Ngo Bao Khanh St., Hoan Kiem District, ☎ 04/825–0959) is one of the nicer, quieter bars in town. A piano in the corner and movie-star posters on the walls add a nostalgic touch to the home of Hanoi's tastiest frozen margaritas. Upstairs is a large snooker table. Next door is its sister establishment, the Gold Cock.

Stone Elephant (✉ 2 Cua Dong St., Hoan Kiem District, ☎ 04/828–4545) is a trendy expat hangout with loud, live jazz on Fridays. Proprietor Mr. Manh will pour you a draft beer himself at this friendly pub, where stucco walls, arches, and pink neon strike a different note than most Vietnamese-run establishments.

Sunset Pub (✉ 31 Cao Ba Quat St., Ba Dinh District, ☎ 04/823–0173), a Finnish-run establishment near the Temple of Literature, serves a cheap and filling lunch buffet. Live jazz is performed most Thursday nights in the pub upstairs, where you can also admire—and buy—local art.

Tin Tin Pub (✉ 14 Hang Non St., Hoan Kiem District, ☎ 04/826–0326) is a backpackers' hangout with good food, ice-cold beer, and a casual ambience.

Dance Clubs

Apocalypse Now (✉ 338 Ba Trieu St., Hai Ba Trung District, ☎ 04/821–6416) trades on the mystique of the Francis Ford Coppola movie with Vietnam War and Hollywood props—movie posters, sandbags, and helicopter propeller ceiling fans. Black walls and no windows adds to the bomb-shelter atmosphere, where expatriates hunker down for drinking and dancing to rock oldies until almost dawn. The place has a sweaty, meat-market feel. It's very popular on weekends after 11 PM, but it can get rowdy, so watch your wallets. On weeknights, play a game on the free pool tables.

Club Q (✉ Daewoo Hotel, 360 Kim Ma St., Ba Dinh District, ☎ 04/831–5000) has unrivaled sound and lighting, plus live music nightly. Sing in English in the five, elegant, private karaoke rooms—a truly Vietnamese (and Asian) experience. The club could do with some more clientele to fill up the dance floor, however.

Dong Da Magic (✉ 3 Thai Thinh St., Dong Da District, ☎ 04/563–0257) is not just a disco: it also features a 100-seat cinema, a video arcade, a high-tech disco, a party room, cheap beer and drinks, and a wild atmosphere. Multiple levels of glitzy dance rooms will keep your adrenaline pumping until the bread vendors start shouting, "*Banh me nao!*"

Mai La Club (✉ 23 Quang Trung St., Hoan Kiem District, ☎ 04/825–7799) is packed most nights with mobile-phone-wielding, Calvin Klein–

clad hipsters and their fashion-model girlfriends. A sprinkling of expatriates and businessmen round off the clientele, who dance to everything from the cha-cha to the Macarena. There's a cover charge.

Metal (✉ 57 Cua Nam St., Dong Da District, ☎ 04/824–1975) has the stainless-steel panels and rivets to back up its name. The music, however, is not metal but Asian techno. Local young people pack the place on Fridays, when there's no cover charge.

Queen Bee (✉ 42 Lang Ha St., Ba Dinh District, ☎ 04/835–0938), one of Hanoi's most established discos, is popular with the embassy crowd and Korean businessmen. A choice music selection nearly guarantees a good time.

Sparks (✉ 88 Lo Duc St., Hai Ba Trung District, ☎ 04/825–7207) is Hanoi's attempt at mass-scale hipness. Singaporean investors reportedly spent more than $1 million turning this old theater into a dance palace. It has a cavernous entrance and Hanoi's most sophisticated sound system. A cover is charged.

Vortex (✉ 336 Ba Trieu St., Hai Ba Trung District, ☎ 04/978–0121), is a vibrant, American-run club. The bright tomato red and eggplant purple walls provide a fun background for dancing to good music or just hanging out for a drink.

The Arts

The arrival of television has dealt a serious blow to Hanoi's once-vibrant performing-arts scene, and it is unclear whether or not it will ever recover. Throughout the city, once-thriving movie houses have gone dark as Hanoians tune in to Vietnam Television and satellite TV, and for the past few years, VCRs have been flying out of the stores, further jeopardizing the fate of film and performing arts in Vietnam.

Nonetheless, some Hanoians remain firm in their belief that nothing beats a live performance. With the multi-million dollar restoration of the Opera House (☞ Exploring Hanoi, *above*) finally finished, Hanoi's performing arts scene may reemerge. The imposing French-built arts palace is going to feature Vietnam's top traditional musicians and pop stars—and the occasional Western performer. Elsewhere in the city, you can catch a performance of Vietnamese folk opera, traditional music, or enchanting water puppetry. If you want a peek at the results of years of Eastern European physical training, go to the circus at the northern edge of Lenin Park.

Circus

Vietnam Circus (Rap Xiec; ✉ Tran Nhan Tong and Tran Binh Tong Sts., at north end of Lenin Park, Hoan Kiem District, ☎ 04/822–0268) was founded 45 years ago in the mountains, along with the Communist Party. The troupe's jovial director, Nguyen Quang Vinh, has spend time in Las Vegas with Ringling Brothers, Barnum & Bailey Circus, with which the circus has an exchange program. Besides an evening of guaranteed entertainment—the elephants, horses, monkeys, and bears are accompanied by the antics of 160 human performers—the Vietnam Circus is also a significant bit of architecture: the distinctive 1,500-seat, round-topped building was constructed in 1985. In winter, bring a jacket. Shows are two hours and held Tuesday–Sunday at 8 PM; ticket prices range from 15,000d to 30,000d.

Film

Alliance Française (✉ 42 Yet Kieu St., Hoan Kiem District, ☎ 04/826–6970) sponsors weekly viewings of French films, as well as art exhibits.

Fansland Cinema (✉ 84 Ly Thuong Kiet St., Hoan Kiem District, ☎ 04/825–7484) occasionally shows non-Vietnamese films; check the listing outside the theater to see if an English-language movie is playing. Screenings are usually at 8 PM.

Theater and Opera

Hanoi's performing-arts legacy is impressive. As in Europe, the emperors often kept acting guilds and musicians in or around the Imperial Palace. Roving drama and musical troupes entertained citizens in the countryside. The arrival of the French and the 20th century saw an explosion of theater culture in the capital, the lingering remnants of which can be experienced at a handful of small drama houses that host troupes performing traditional folk arts.

Tuong is a classical art form developed in central Vietnam. It uses very few stage props, and the actors must conform to age-old rules of behavior concerning their specific characters. Content usually focuses on Vietnamese legends, and music is minimal. The northern folk art known as *cheo* is more of a "people's opera," incorporating both comic and tragic elements. Music and singing are prominent, as it developed into a loud and lively art form in order to outdo the noise and distractions of the marketplace, where it was originally performed. *Cai luong,* the "renovated opera" that emerged in the early 20th century, is more similar to Western dramas and operas than the other styles. Music and singing are an important feature of these performances. Although cai luong is a southern creation, the form has endeared itself to Hanoians. The following Hanoi theaters stage productions (none prints schedules in English, so call or drop by the theater to see if there's something on for an evening when you're in town).

Central Cheo Theater of Hanoi (✉ 199 Son Tay St., at Kim Ma, ☎ 04/845–7403), once the quintessential cheo stage in the north, rarely has performances these days. The theater needs major renovation, which may begin as early as 1998. Tickets go up to 55,000d, depending on the show.

Cheo Theater (✉ 15 Nguyen Dinh Chieu St., Ba Dinh District, ☎ 04/826–7361), a tiny, simple drama house, seats 50 guests. Shows are usually on Monday, Wednesday, and Friday, but call or stop by to confirm. Ticket prices go up to 45,000d.

Cheo Traditional Opera (✉ Hong Ha Theater, Le Thai To St., Hoan Kiem District, no phone) features the typical screaming performers in neon-bright costumes and make-up who perform true village drama. One can follow the story line as the actors' faces are contorted into the most amazing expressions, giving you a sense of exactly what they are singing about.

Chuong Vang Theater of Hanoi (✉ 72 Hang Bac St., Hoan Kiem District, ☎ 04/825–7823) has performances of cai luong- and tuong-style shows. Tickets are usually 20,000d for foreigners, and the curtain generally goes up at 8. Check for dates.

Municipal Theater (✉ Intersection of Le Thanh Tong, Phan Chu Trinh, and Trang Tien Sts., no phone) offers mediocre government-sponsored shows in the evening rather than the opera for which this 1911 structure was built.

Youth Theater (Nha Hat Tuoi Tre; ✉ 11 Ngo Thi Nham St., Hoan Kiem District, ☎ 04/825–4673), a 650-seat facility, is one of the larger theaters in the city and focuses mainly on contemporary drama, although music and dance are sometimes performed. Many of the 300 shows per year are for children. About a dozen foreign theater groups perform here annually. Tickets are 20,000d–50,000d for foreigners.

Traditional Music

As much of Vietnam's dramatic performances are closely linked with the strains of Vietnamese music, there are very few concerts of exclusively traditional music in the city. Your best bet is to see a water-puppet performance or go to the theater to watch cheo, tuong, or cai luong (☞ Theater and Opera, *above*).

If you happen across an old man or woman on the street who's playing a one-stringed instrument in an impromptu fashion, consider yourself extremely lucky. *Xam,* a type of melancholy folk music, is a dying art in Vietnam—and not because it's the music played at funerals, although xam artists are often invited to perform at such functions. Xam artists are simply dying off, and no one's replacing them. Four professional xam musicians were on hand throughout the day and evening at Hoan Kiem Lake in Hanoi—one at each corner—in the xam heyday of the early 1940s. A half century later there's not a single true xam master plying his or her trade on the streets of the capital. One aging xam professional, the unflagging Hoang Thi Cau of Ninh Binh Province, has done much to save her art from extinction by teaching xam to some cheo performing groups in and around Hanoi and by recording her performances for future generations. But the prospects for this ancient art are bleak; cheo artists are understandably concerned with preserving their own beloved art, and experts say that true xam music cannot be performed by anyone but a bona fide xam master.

Water Puppetry

The thousand-year-old art of *roi nuoc,* or water puppetry, is unique to northern Vietnam and easily ranks as one of Southeast Asia's most beautiful and complex art forms. Long considered an art of the common people, water puppetry gained acceptance at royal celebrations and was often performed for reigning emperors and kings. Water puppetry is performed on—and under, in particular—a small pond whose surface conceals the flurry of action beneath it. Through the near-magical use of bamboo rods and a system of pulleys and levers, master puppeteers stand waist deep at the back of the pond (usually behind a curtain) and make their lacquered marionettes literally walk on water. Shows usually depict scenes from rural life and Vietnamese legend, and the experience is positively delightful.

Municipal Water Puppet Theater (✉ 57 Dinh Tien Hoang St., on northeast shore of Hoan Kiem Lake, Hoan Kiem District, ☎ 04/825–5450) is the best place to see water puppetry performed in Hanoi. From seven to eight puppeteers pull the strings from behind elaborate stage sets while half a dozen musicians play soothing traditional folk music. The resident Thang Long Water Puppet Troupe has been performing in this 300-seat building since 1990; it is also the only troupe that has toured Europe and North and South America in the past. If you're in Hanoi on a package tour, it's highly likely you're already scheduled for a show here. If not, get your tickets early, as they do sell out. Tickets are 40,000d, including a cassette of the music, or 20,000d without. The curtain goes up at 8 every night but Monday, and there's a 9:45 AM matinee on Sunday. Occasionally there are 6 PM shows as well. There's a 10,000d fee to use your camera; videotaping costs 50,000d. Souvenir puppets are available to buy.

You can also catch an afternoon performance at the **Temple of Literature** (☞ Around Ho Chi Minh's Mausoleum *in* Exploring, *above*).

OUTDOOR ACTIVITIES AND SPORTS

Participant Sports

Basketball

U.S. citizens in Hanoi hoop it up on the half-court of the **American Club** (✉ 19–21 Hai Ba Trung St., Hoan Kiem District, ☎ 04/824–1850) on Monday and Wednesday evenings at 7:30. There's an outdoor barbecue on Friday nights as well, and live music every other Friday night. The club has a membership policy, but Americans passing through town are more than welcome.

Somewhat serious full-court action can be found at the **Hanoi Sports Center** (Trung Tam The Duc The Thao Hanoi; ✉ 115 Quang Thanh St., at the southeast corner of West Lake, Ba Dinh District, ☎ 04/845–5193) most days, particularly weekends, from 2 to 4. You might end up being paired with someone from the Vietnam women's team, which practices here regularly. As referees are used, small monetary contributions are expected.

Biking

Memory Cafe (✉ 33 Tran Hung Dao St., Hoan Kiem District) rents bicycles. Ms. CoCo will show you on a map where to go. One of the best trips is simply to head south along the river. Another more ambitious trip is to head over the Long Bien bridge into the countryside. Go south from the bridge, under the car bridge, and continue south along the river. After two hours you may reach Bat Trang, a village where pottery is sold.

Boating

In Hanoi, sailing—and water- and jet-skiing—are, for the most part, reserved for members of the elite **Hanoi Club** (✉ 76 Yen Phu St., Tay Ho District, ☎ 04/823–8115), a once-troubled international project that has finally opened its doors and docks. If you're not a member or the guest of a member, the only way you'll be able to use the club's catamarans and other goodies (including tennis, racquetball, squash, and exercise facilities, and a swimming pool) is if you stay at the hotel or apartment facilities managed by the club.

Paddleboating and sculling are the en vogue forms of boating in Hanoi. You can rent dragon-shape paddleboats on **Truch Bach Lake** at a few spots, one on the southwest corner of the lake and another on the causeway. Thien Quang Lake, just north of Lenin Park, also has paddleboats for rent. Go to the **Student Culture Center** (Nha Van Hoa Hoc Sinh Sinh Vien) on the small island that is connected by bridge to Tran Nhan Tong Street. Boats are from 6,000d to 10,000d per half hour. The newer plastic boats are more expensive than the rusting metal hulks.

A **boat house** on the southern edge of Bay Mau Lake, in the middle of Lenin Park, rents old racing sculls for 12,000d per hour. If you're looking for a thrill, they also rent Yamaha Waverunners—similar to jet skis—for an eye-popping $30 per hour. Access is via Dai Co Viet Road.

Golf

King's Valley Golf Resort & Country Club (✉ Dong Mo, Son Tay town, Ha Tay province, about 45 km/28 mi west of Hanoi, ☎ 034/846–373, Hanoi office ☎ 04/826–0342) has an 18-hole course designed by Robert McFarland, as well as a new upscale hotel and villa complex; greens fees are $50 for guests. Clubs are extra. Other recreational possibilities here include tennis, horseback riding, boating on the reservoir, and trekking excursions in nearby Ba Vi National Park and up Tan Vien

Mountain. For information, ask at the Metropole/Hotel Sofitel in Hanoi (☞ Lodging, *above*), which runs a weekly shuttle to the course.

Lang Ha Golf Driving Range (✉ 16A Lang Ha St., Ba Dinh District, ☎ 04/835–0908) offers diehards a chance to practice their shots.

Health Clubs

A few major hotels in Hanoi allow you to purchase one-day memberships to their exercise facilities, even if you aren't staying at the hotel.

Clark Hatch Fitness Center (✉ Metropole/Hotel Sofitel, 15 Ngo Quyen St., Hoan Kiem District, ☎ 04/826–6919, ext. 8881) has all your basic workout equipment—weights, a few machines, treadmills, and stationary bicycles—which you can use while watching the activity on the street below. They also have the best trainers in town as well as whirlpools and saunas. A one-day membership costs $17.

Daewoo Hotel Fitness Center (✉ Hanoi Daewoo Hotel, 360 Kim Ma St., Ba Dinh District, ☎ 04/831–5000, ext. 3309) has treadmills, stationary bikes, machines, and now yoga classes. You can also use the 50-meter pool and the saunas, all for $20 a day. Guests go free (except for an additional charge to use the saunas).

Hanoi Private Club (✉ ASEAN Hotel, 41 Chua Boc St., Dong Da District, ☎ 04/852–9108) has a variety of exercise machines, as well as a sauna and massages; the daily fee is $10.

Planet Hotel (✉ 120 Quan Thanh St., Hoan Kiem District, ☎ 04/843–5888) charges 55,000d for use of its gym.

Jogging

The best place to run in the city is around spacious **Lenin Park,** a favorite sports and exercise locale for Vietnamese and foreigners tired of the exhibitionist nature of a Hoan Kiem Lake workout (although that's not a bad place for a run, too). The **Botanic Gardens** is another place to run. Or, if you're an early riser, join the throngs of runners that pack the city streets at 5 AM. It is understood by everyone that runners are off the roads by 6:30 AM, however. Jogging is definitely not recommended in the streets of Hanoi during the day or evening, even though you may see some expatriates huffing and puffing through the center of town.

The **Hash House Harriers** (ask at the Sunset Pub, the Hanoi Daewoo Hotel, or the Metropole/Hotel Sofitel for locations and times) run every Saturday afternoon at 3 or 4 PM depending on the season. The throngs of expatriates running through the capital's suburbs always garner lots of attention.

Swimming Pools

Hanoi Daewoo Hotel pool (☞ Lodging, *above*) is an arched 80-meter affair that costs $20 for a day pass, including use of the gym, sauna, and whirlpool.

Metropole/Hotel Sofitel Pool (☞ Lodging, *above*) is small but lovely; it's available for non-guests with the purchase of drinks from the outdoor bamboo bar.

Tay Ho Hotel pool (✉ Ho Tay Villas, Quang An, Tu Liem, Ba Dinh District, ☎ 04/825–8241), on a spit of land jutting into West Lake, offers unparalleled views and prime sunbathing opportunities. The pool is empty, however, of people *and* water from late November to early April. The cost for nonguests is about 35,000d per person per day.

Thang Loi Hotel pool (✉ Yen Phu St., Ba Dinh District, ☎ 04/826–8211), out on West Lake, is an inviting place to swim; Fidel Castro stays at the hotel when he visits. A day pass runs 50,000d.

Tennis

The **Thang Loi Hotel** (✉ Yen Phu St., Ba Dinh District, ☎ 04/829–8211, ext. 391 for tennis courts) out on West Lake, has two courts that you can rent for 40,000d to 66,000d per hour, depending on the time of day (evening is most costly due to the lights). Hours of operation are 6 AM to 10 PM. Sporting goods shops carry racquets and balls in case you left yours at home.

Spectator Sports

Sports have been an integral and institutionalized part of the Hanoi educational system for years. Competition on an international level, however, has only recently taken off, though financial strains severely limit the number of meets or tournaments in which Vietnam can participate. Many resources are still committed to the study and improvement of martial arts such as tae kwon do and *wushu,* two disciplines in which Vietnam is world renowned. Ping-Pong and badminton are also determinedly pursued.

The **General Department of Physical Culture and Sports of Vietnam** (✉ 36 Tran Phu St., Ba Dinh District, ☎ 04/825–3158) and the **Hanoi Sports Department** (✉ 10 Trinh Hoai Duc St., Ba Dinh District, ☎ 04/826–4639) can provide information on sporting events in the city, including dates of the annual Hanoi Marathon, charity races, major tournaments, and so on.

Soccer

No sport captures the attention and hearts of the Vietnamese quite like soccer. The game's biggest crowds are down in Saigon, but the religiously followed semi-professional national league packs them in at the new 20,000-capacity **National Stadium** (✉ corner of Nguyen Thai Hoc and Trinh Hoai Duc Sts., Ba Dinh District). The season runs roughly from October to May, and when the Hanoi Police face off against the Ho Chi Minh City Police in the capital, you can bet the stadium is rocking. Smaller matches are held at the Army Stadium, in the southern portion of the citadel, with access from Hoang Dieu Street. Nearly every Vietnamese bar in town has a soccer schedule, and with a bit of gesturing and pointing you'll be able to figure out whether or not a huge match is going to be played while you're in town.

SHOPPING

Hanoi offers plenty of shopping options: The area north of Hoan Kiem Lake is bustling with tiny shops carrying everything from shoes to clothes to antique timepieces. Hanoi is Vietnam's fine arts capital, and running along the southern part of Hoan Kiem Lake, where Hang Khai Street turns into Trang Tien Street, are a number of arts-and-crafts galleries and antiques shops (note, however, that it is illegal to take antiques out of the country without permission from the government; ☞ Shopping *in* the Gold Guide for more information). You can find paintings and watercolors, as well as crafts such as lacquerware and puppets, on Trang Tien and Hang Khai streets. Any number of shops along Hang Gai and Duc Loi streets, not far from Hoan Kiem Lake, can inexpensively produce custom-made clothes. Hang Gai is also good for souvenirs and antiques. If you fancy beautiful hand-embroidered linens check out Hang Gai Street, which turns into Hang Bong Street. Most souvenir and silk shops in the tourist area of the Old Quarter are open to about 10 PM on weekends. Note: A 1997 law designed to protect Vietnam's forests made it illegal to export wooden furniture.

Markets

19–12 Market (Cho 19–12; ✉ Ly Thuong Kiet St. between Hoa Lo and Quang Trung Sts., Hoan Kiem District), the December 19th Market, has items for everyday use: vegetables, meat (even dog meat), poultry, clothes, pots and pans, toilet paper, etc.

Hom Market (Cho Hom; ✉ Pho Hue St. and Tran Xuan Soan Sts., Hai Ba Trung District) is the biggest and most crowded market in town. Upstairs is a Western-style market with air-conditioning, and downstairs is a Vietnamese-style open market. If you need plastic tubs, candles, or padded bras, this is the place to go.

Specialty Shops

Art

When buying art in Vietnam, be careful of fakes. Paintings by Vietnam's most famous painters—Bui Xuan Phai, Nguyen Tu Nghiem and Le Thiet Cuong—are the most widely copied. Serious art collectors should consult the well-respected high-end galleries. If you're serious about seeing Hanoi's art scene, consider contacting fine arts consultant **Suzanne Lecht** (☎ 04/862–3184, FAX 04/862–3185), who can lead you on studio tours, advise you on major purchases, and so on.

ATC Art Gallery (✉ 48 Lang Ha St., Dong Da District, ☎ 04/835–3179; ✉ 22 Le Van Huu St., Hoan Kiem District, ☎ 04/825–0821) has paintings, lacquerware, and sculpture by contemporary Hanoi artists on display and for sale; the gallery is also represented in Ho Chi Minh City, Vung Tau, and Danang.

Co Xanh (Green Palm Gallery; ✉ 51 Hang Gai St., Hoan Kiem District, ☎ 04/826–7116) is the top end of souvenir art galleries, with a good selection of paintings by graduates of the Hanoi Fine Arts College. Prices are determined by the stature of the painter and size of the piece, but can exceed $200. Mr. Ha, the owner, is very reputable and easygoing and speaks excellent English.

Hanart (✉ 43 Trang Tien St., Hoan Kiem District, ☎ 04/825–3045) is an excellent arts and crafts gallery.

Mai Gallery (✉ 3B Phan Huy Chu St., Hoan Kiem District, ☎ 04/825–1225) is run by the daughter of Vietnam's leading art critic, Duong Tuong. Down an alley, it is largely a showcase for Hanoi painters and is very popular with more serious collectors. The father is a charming old man who speaks French.

Red River Gallery (✉ 71A Nguyen Du St., Hai Ba Trung District, ☎ 04/822–9064) is the gallery that put the Gang of Five painters—Ha Tri Hieu, Hong Viet Dung, Dang Xuan Hoa, Pham Quang Vinh, and Tran Luong—on the map. Red River exhibits the most established Vietnamese artists and is a must-see for serious art collectors willing to shell out thousands of dollars.

Salon Natasha (✉ 30 Hang Bong St., Hoan Kiem District, ☎ 04/826–1387), the avant-garde hub of Hanoi's art scene, is run by a Russian expatriate and her husband, artist Vu Dan Tan. It exhibits and sells some of the most provocative art in Vietnam today. Natasha, a respected and trusted art dealer, sells painted vases and unframed oil paintings by well-known artists at reasonable prices.

Son Ha Art Gallery (✉ 35 Hang Than St., Hoan Kiem District, ☎ 04/826–9198) has a nice selection of works by Vietnamese artists.

Trang An Gallery (✉ 15 Hang Buom St., Hoan Kiem District, ☎ 04/826–9480) is an impressive, well-designed gallery with three rooms and a courtyard. Proprietor Trang An is the new kid on the gallery scene but offers the most comprehensive representation of Vietnam's contemporary art, with internationally recognized young painters and their avant-garde installations. If you can make it to only one gallery, make it this one.

Clothing and Accessories

It's possible to have clothes made to order with enough time (1 day to 3 weeks, depending on what you want made and how busy the tailor is). You may also need to return a couple of times to have the clothes fitted.

Cao Minh (✉ 47 Tran Hung Dao St., Hoan Kiem District, ☎ 04/825–1287) is a good but expensive tailor from Saigon, where tailors are generally considered to be more talented.

Huong Giang (✉ 58 Tue Tinh St., Hai Ba Trung District, ☎ 04/826–9372) speaks almost no English but is famous for her quality work. Her popularity means it may take a while to get things done, as seemingly every woman in Hanoi is having her next ao dai made here.

Ipa-Nima (✉ 30B Nguyen Huu Huan St., Hoan Kiem District, ☎ 04/934–0876) is the place to get beautifully designed, funky, and fashionable handbags made of rattan, brocade, crochet, beads, and all kinds of other materials. It also sells accessories like cufflinks.

Kenly Silk (✉ 102 Hang Gai St., Hoan Kiem District, ☎ 04/826–7236) has even better and less expensive silk and linen clothes than Khai Silk.

Khai Silk (✉ 121 Nguyen Thai Hoc St., Ba Dinh District, Hoan Kiem District; 96 Hang Gai St., Hoan Kiem District, ☎ 04/823–3508) is where the Princess of Thailand shops for fine silk blouses, sweaters, scarves, lingerie, sheets, and more. Linen is also available as are men's clothes.

Phuong Anh (✉ 56 Hang Hom, Hoan Kiem District, ☎ 04/826–1556) is a small, crowded shop where you can get a dress and other clothes made for you in three days (even faster if you are really pressed for time).

Tan My (✉ 66 Hang Gai St., Hoan Kiem District, no phone) features the skills of Ms. Hoang, who creates dresses from material made by the shop. She speaks very little English, however, so be ready to illustrate or gesture what you want made.

Tien Dat (✉ 75 Hang Gai St., Hoan Kiem District, ☎ 04/824–6244) is where the speedy, English-speaking Mr. Dat and his team custom-make clothes and hats for men, women, and children. The shop is not air-conditioned like some of the more expensive silk and clothing shops, but the work is of equal quality. A made-to-order woman's silk dress runs around $15–$20.

Tien Thanh (✉ 48 Le Thai To St., Hoan Kiem District, ☎ 04/825–6257) has nice dressing rooms and friendly tailors and seamstresses; note that they speak little English.

Thanh Ha (✉ 114 Hang Gai St., Hoan Kiem District) does a nice job on women's suits, which cost about $26.

Embroidery

Tan My (✉ 109 Hang Gai St., Hoan Kiem District, no phone) is the most famous embroidery shop in Hanoi. Employees from Thuong Tin province, which is known for its rich embroidery tradition, adorn table cloths, silk clothing, and wall hangings with intricate designs. Ready-made work depicts everything from traditional Vietnamese floral patterns and dragon designs to scenes from Western fairy tales, or you can custom-order. Ms. Huong, the manager, is very comfortable dealing with foreigners and her English is excellent.

Tuyet Lan (✉ 65 Hang Gai St., Hoan Kiem District, ☎ 04/825–7967, FAX 04/826–5816) does beautiful embroidery, especially children's bed sheets, and accepts credit cards. They do not offer discounts. This place is good competition to Tan My, but there's no air-conditioning.

Handicrafts

Craft Link (✉ 43 Van Mieu St., Ba Dinh District, ☎ 04/843–7710) is a terrific place to buy local handicrafts. Proceeds go to the ethnic minority women who make these crafts.

Ngo Thu Huong's Souvenir Shop (✉ 62 Hang Ngang St., Hoan Kiem District, ☎ 04/828–1046) is a good place to find real and imitation antiques.

Pan Flute (✉ 42 Hang Bac St., Hoan Kiem District, ☎ 04/826–0493) is a small, cute shop selling ethnic clothing and crafts. Ms. Ngan Ha speaks some English and offers better prices than other shops selling items made by hill tribes.

Housewares and Silver Items

Co Xanh (Green Palm Gallery; ☞ Art, *above*) sells boxes and figurines made of silver. The owner, Tran Thanh Ha, speaks English and is very reputable.

DOME (✉ 10 Yen The St., Ba Dinh District, ☎ 04/843–6036) has well-designed, modern home furnishings—linens, furniture, lamps, candles, and more. Simple, curved designs in wrought iron are a signature style, one you'll see in restaurants and hotels throughout town.

Ngo Thu Huong (✉ 62 Hang Nhang St., Hoan Kiem District, ☎ 04/828–1046) is a reliable vendor of good-quality, 90%-silver and silver-plated items. She has antiques, lacquer boxes, and gifts upstairs.

Musical Instruments

Hanoi Music Center (✉ 42 Nha Chung St., Hoan Kiem District, ☎ 04/824–3058) sells guitars, metronomes, keyboards, and pianos.

Pham Bich Huong (✉ 11 Hang Non St., Hoan Kiem District, no phone) carries a great selection of traditional Vietnamese instruments, but she speaks almost no English.

SIDE TRIPS FROM HANOI

Although Hanoi is the cultural and historic centerpiece of northern Vietnam, much of the city's history and many of its legends and traditions are rooted in the region surrounding the capital. Citadels, temples, art guilds, and festival focal points ring the city, and a few hours' drive in any direction will bring you to points of interest ranging from pagodas to idyllic valleys and national parks. Hanoi serves as a base for day trips or short excursions to the Perfume Pagoda, the Thay (Master's) Pagoda, Tam Dao hill station, the ancient capital of Hoa Lu, Phat Diem Cathedral, and the primeval beauty of Cuc Phuong National Park.

Tours organized by Hanoi's tourist cafés and travel agencies (☞ Travel Agencies *in* Hanoi A to Z, *below*) cover all of the sights and are the most time-efficient way to see this region. Tourist café tours are less expensive than those run by travel agencies: a group trip to Perfume Pagoda or Hoa Lu through a tourist café costs about $20 per person, including entrance tickets and meals. If a daily group tour isn't available to the site you want, these companies can arrange a private car and driver for the day. A good example is the "Suburbs of Hanoi" tour: This full-day trip goes to the silk-making village of Ha Dong, the Bat Trang pottery village, a snake farm in Gia Lam across the Red River, and the village of Dong Ho, where the ancient folk art of wood-block printing is still practiced. The trip averages $35 for an air-conditioned car and driver for the whole day. An English-speaking guide costs from $10 to $20 per day.

For history, religion, and a bit of hiking, head west to the Thay and Tay Phuong Pagodas. Combine a trip here with Co Loa Citadel (these sites are described below), and you've got a full day of exploring. Go with a group tour or rent a private car with a driver for between $30 and $50 for the trip.

Co Loa Citadel

15 km (9½ mi) north of Hanoi.

Less than 20 minutes north of Hanoi is a series of large earthen ramparts that once protected one of the country's earliest capitals from Chinese invaders. Co Loa, or "snail," so named for the spiral-shape protective walls and moats that resembled the spiral design of a nautilus, was built by An Duong Vuong more than 2,000 years ago and remains one of northern Vietnam's important historical relics.

At the end of the Bronze Age, in the 3rd century BC, King Vuong decided to move the power seat of the Lac Viets—a sophisticated society of indigenous northern Vietnamese, considered by many Vietnamese to be their direct ancestors, who eventually were incorporated into the Chinese empire. They relocated north of the Red River Delta, where Chinese looking for fertile land had been increasingly settling. The fortress was designed to be the ultimate protection from the invading Chinese. Nine large earthen ramparts guarded the inner palace of Co Loa. Carefully designed gates were built at angles to each other, and defense mounds created further obstacles for attackers. A series of moats fed by tributaries of the Red River lent an air of medieval invincibility to the place.

According to one of Vietnam's oldest legends, certain forces conspired against King Vuong and his well-protected citadel. After decades of failed attempts to defeat King Vuong's armies, Chinese general Trieu Da ordered his own son to surrender to King Vuong and then propose marriage to King Vuong's daughter, My Chau. Against the advice of his ministers, the king accepted. The new son-in-law lived harmoniously in his new home for three years, eventually coercing his wife into revealing defense secrets and helping him steal a magic crossbow—a gift to King Vuong from the gods, which held all the military secrets to the citadel. With their newfound knowledge, Trieu Da and his troops immediately invaded Co Loa and conquered the Lac Viets. King Vuong had his daughter beheaded. The son-in-law, Trong Thuy, realized his betrayal and threw himself into Ngoc Pond.

Only three of the earthen ramparts are extant today. The rectangular inner wall has a perimeter of 1½ km (1 mi); a middle rampart is in the shape of a polygon with a perimeter of 6½ km (4 mi); the outer wall is 8 km (5 mi) long. The remains of the towers are 40 ft high and up to 120 ft wide. You are invited to walk through the village gate, which once served as the gate of the inner citadel, and explore the site of the ancient imperial palace. Nearby, under an old banyan tree, is Ba Chua, a temple dedicated to Princess My Chau. Inside, there is a headless stone statue of the princess. A temple to An Duong Vuong has also been built on the site of the inner palace. In front of this temple is Ngoc Pond, where the evil son-in-law, Trong Thuy, allegedly killed himself.

A large and colorful festival on the sixth day of Tet, the lunar new year, celebrates King An Vuong Duong, now considered the guardian spirit of Co Loa. To the beating of drums and gongs and the melody of flutes, old men elegantly robed in tunics of the mandarin era march toward Co Loa bearing a tablet with the story of Co Loa, as well as gifts of incense, flowers, fruit, and rice cakes. An elaborate ceremony follows, held by the eight surrounding villages, in which the story of Co Loa is read to the public. The ceremonial palanquins of each village are aligned in the courtyard outside An Duong Vuong temple, cult objects and traditional weapons are displayed before a large incense table, and flags and banners head the procession as it winds its way around the site of the imperial palace. Communists banned this and other festivals after taking power in 1954, proclaiming that such superstitious rituals had no place in the new socialist order. But by the late 1980s Hanoi was no longer so eager to squelch such celebrations, and the Co Loa Festival and others like it have enjoyed a revival of sorts in the past decade.

Arriving and Departing

You should be able to hire a car with driver for about $50 to go from Hanoi to Co Loa Citadel as well as the Thay Pagoda and Tay Phuong Pagoda (☞ *below*). A round trip and a visit to Co Loa alone takes about two hours. Tourist cafés and travel agencies can arrange minivan tours to the three sites if there is enough interest. This trip takes about two-thirds of a day, depending on how long you linger at the sites.

Thay Pagoda and Tay Phuong Pagoda

40 km (25 mi) southwest of Hanoi in Hay Tay province.

Two lovely pagodas can be combined with the Co Loa Citadel to make an enjoyable day trip from Hanoi. (Admission to the pagodas is 10,000d each.)

The **Thay Pagoda,** or Master's Pagoda, is named in honor of Tu Dao Hanh, a 12th-century monk. A statue of Master Hanh is to the left of a large central altar that supports the statues of 18 *arhats,* monks who have reached enlightenment. To the right is Ly Nhan Tong, a king who was the supposed reincarnation of Tu Dao Hanh. The Thay Pagoda is the site of one of two ancient water-puppetry stages remaining in Vietnam. Constructed during the 15th century, this small stage is built on stilts in the middle of a pond and was used during elaborate pagoda ceremonies and royal visits. Water-puppetry shows still take place here, particularly on the annual festival of the pagoda, which is from the fifth through the seventh days of the third lunar month.

Numerous caves provide opportunities for exploring around the hillsides near Thay Pagoda. A few hiking trails also crisscross the landscape. Twenty kilometers (12 mi) to the northwest is **Ba Vi Mountain.** This 4,250-ft peak affords a spectacular view of the Red River Valley and the mountains to the west.

The **Tay Phuong Pagoda,** or Western Pagoda, is comprised of three sanctuaries built into a hillside and surrounded by a square enclosure. Each ancient wooden structure is separated by a small pool of water that reflects an eerie soothing light into the temples. Begun in the 3rd century, the pagoda was rebuilt in the 9th century and eventually expanded to its present size. The centuries-old curved rooftops are particularly noteworthy, as are the masterpieces of wood sculpture. About six dozen figures carved from jackfruit wood are the pagoda's primary features. The originals of the most beautiful figures, most of them arhats, or enlightened monks, are on display on the upper floors of the Fine

Arts Museum in Hanoi. The pagoda's rafters are elaborately carved with bas-reliefs of dragons and lotuses, and ceramic animal statues grace the rooftops.

Arriving and Departing

Trips organized by tourist cafés and travel agencies usually cover the admission fees for these sites. It's easy to combine a trip to these two pagodas with a visit to Co Loa Citadel (☞ *above*), north of Hanoi.

Perfume Pagoda

60 km (37 mi) southwest of Hanoi.

Considered Vietnam's most important Buddhist site, the Perfume Pagoda (Chua Huong) is the largest of a cluster of shrines carved into the limestone of the Huong Tich Mountains. In the late spring the trails leading up to the shrines are clogged with thousands making their pilgrimage to pray to Quan Am, the goddess of mercy and compassion.

According to a Vietnamized version of the Chinese legend, Quan Am was a young wife falsely accused of trying to kill her newlywed husband. She had been trying to clip a hair growing out of a mole in his neck. Thrown out of her mother-in-law's house, she took refuge in a monastery posing as a monk. A reckless girl one day blamed her pregnancy on the monk, not knowing he was a she. Without a word in self-defense, the vilified monk took the child in and raised him. Only after Quan Am died did villagers discover her silent sacrifice. In the past, pilgrims came to the grottoes to pray for Quan Am's help in bearing sons and in fighting unjust accusations.

From the shores of the Yen River, you are ferried to the site, 4 km (2½ mi) away, on sampans that seem to be made of flimsy aluminum. It is a spectacular ride through the flooded valley, past boats laden with fruit and farmers at work in their fields. You are let off at Chua Tien Chu. From there, follow a stone path uphill to the various pagodas and shrines. Three kilometers (2 mi) later you reach the Perfume Pagoda. A steep set of stairs takes you inside the impressive cavern, where gilded Buddhas and bodhisattvas sit nestled in rocky recesses. The air is misty from incense and the cooking fires of Buddhist monks who tend the shrines.

In early spring, from just after Tet to the middle of the second lunar month, thousands of Buddhists make their pilgrimage to the Perfume Pagoda. This is an intense—and sometimes stressful—time to visit, as the crowds of Vietnamese faithful clog the Yen River with extra boats and make navigating the slippery stairs more of an exercise in caution than a journey of discovery. The atmosphere at this time of year is positively electric with thousands of Buddhists crowding into the cavern to leave offerings, catch a droplet of water from a holy stalactite, or buy Buddhist trinkets and mementos from the dozens of stall owners.

Arriving and Departing

Day trips from Hanoi to the Perfume Pagoda, leaving at about 6:30 AM, are available from any number of travel agencies such as Vietnam Tourism, Vinatour, and O.S.C. Travel, as well as from tourist cafés such as the Green Bamboo Café (☞ Visitor Information *in* Hanoi A to Z, *below*). These tours run $20 or more per person, including all transport and entrance fees, which is a good deal considering that the officials at Perfume Pagoda now charge an exorbitant $10 per person for the boat ride and full access to the pagodas. You can also rent a car for about $30, and a guide for $10 to $20, but then you'll still have to pay the $10 per person to get to the pagoda itself. If you're feeling brave, go by motorbike.

Hoa Lu

113 km (70 mi) south of Hanoi.

Hoa Lu, the first capital of independent Vietnam, is known as "Halong Bay without the water." Both the stunning natural surroundings and Hoa Lu's status as a former seat of power make for an interesting excursion.

After three decades of internal strife following the expulsion of the Chinese by Ngo Quyen in the year 938, Dinh Tien Hoang unified the country (a colorful festival on the 12th day of the third lunar month commemorates this successful reunification). The new king moved the capital to Hoa Lu, in a valley whose maze of narrow streams and inhospitable limestone outcroppings served as natural protection for the fledgling nation; he had numerous fortifications built around his citadel in order to avert another Chinese invasion, and word quickly spread of his ruthless treatment of prisoners. (The king reportedly fed enemies to tigers and then boiled their bones in ceremonial urns.) Despite such tactics, the Dinh dynasty was short-lived; Dinh Tien Hoang was assassinated by bodyguards in 979. The killers were discovered and put to death, and General Le Dai Hanh ascended to the throne, establishing the Early Le dynasty. Upon Le Dai Hanh's death in 1009, Ly Thai To became first king of the Ly dynasty and moved the capital to Thang Long, the site of present-day Hanoi.

Much of the ancient capital of Hoa Lu has been destroyed or has succumbed to the forces of nature, but the two sanctuaries that do survive hint at the tastes of the emperor and his court. The first temple honors Dinh Tien Hoang and houses statues of the king and his three sons. Outside, all that remains of an elaborate throne is the stone base. The main hall has been heavily restored, and much of the wood construction you'll see here is from renovations done in the 17th century. The second temple is named after Le Dai Hanh, the general who became the first emperor of the Le dynasty in 980. A series of elaborate swords and spears are arranged in front of incense bowls and corner altars.

A short bus or car ride away—drivers and group tour operators know exactly where to go—from Hoa Lu is a **trio of caves** accessible by a traditional boat ride down the Hoang Long River, a peaceful stream that winds through rice paddies after cutting its path through the steep limestone cliffs around Hoa Lu. Lithe village women row you the 2 km (1 mi) through the three caves, one of which has a cement plaque on its far side commemorating Nguyen Cong Cay, a Vietnamese weapons maker who lived in Hoa Lu from 1947 to 1950 and plotted with other resisters against the French. At the far end of the boat ride, other women in similar boats are waiting to sell you soft drinks, bananas, even embroidery. It's a hard sell and somewhat ruins the idyllic moment.

Arriving and Departing

Tourist cafés and travel agencies have minibus tours to Hoa Lu for about $20 per person—entry tickets, boat ride, and lunch included. You can also rent a car. It makes sense to combine an excursion to Hoa Lu with a trip to nearby Phat Diem, an enclave of Catholic churches (☞ *below*). This trip takes the good part of a day.

Phat Diem

121 km (75 mi) southeast of Hanoi.

On your way back to Hanoi from Hoa Lu, make a stop at Phat Diem. You can tell you're headed in the right direction, as you pass one stone church after another. Though tensions between organized religions and the Vietnamese central government still exist, relations have improved considerably between officials and Vietnam's Catholic order. Many of these structures have been built in the last few years with financial assistance from American organizations.

All these churches pale in comparison to the massive complex known as **Phat Diem Cathedral**, built in 1891 in Kim Son village, one of the first landfalls of Portuguese missionaries in the 16th century. The cathedral itself is a hulking stone edifice with an enormous bell atop its tallest tower and is surrounded by a courtyard, which in turn is surrounded by a huge moat. The curved eaves are a nod to Sino-Vietnamese architecture, but the crosses and saints (all sitting in the lotus position) reflect the fervor of the 150,000-strong congregation. Many of Phat Diem's Catholics fled south in 1954, when Vietnam was divided into north and south.

Catholicism is definitely experiencing a comeback in these parts, and because a more liberal tone has been adopted by Hanoi, **Sunday Mass** is now extremely popular. It's also extremely early. Services are at 4:30 and 6:30; by 9 everyone's already out in the fields. On holidays like Christmas and Easter, expect crowds of 10,000 or more.

Arriving and Departing

Some tours that go to Hoa Lu do not stop at Phat Diem, so ask ahead. If you can't find one that stops on the day you wish to go, you can certainly find an organization that will rent you a car to go there—although finding one who'll get you there for 7 AM Mass might be tough. It shouldn't run more than $70 round-trip.

Cuc Phuong National Park

140 km (87 mi) southwest of Hanoi. The park entrance is in Ninh Binh, province, 40 km (25 mi) from Ninh Binh town.

Outside the general loop of tourist traffic in the north is secluded and prehistoric-looking Cuc Phuong, one of Vietnam's most important national parks. Established in 1962 as Vietnam's first national park, Cuc Phuong is 54,320 acres (about 85 square mi) of heavily forested subtropical lowlands that is home to 64 mammal species, including the red-bellied squirrel, the pig-tailed macaque, the three-striped palm civet, and a kind of barking deer called the muntjac. Leopards and tigers have also been spotted. More than 250 bird species and 33 types of reptiles live here as well, along with an array of nearly 2,000 species of flora.

Though this habitat would seem to be the perfect place to see Vietnam's wildlife in full splendor, mammal- and bird-watching are sadly not particularly successful pastimes in the park. Despite Cuc Phuong's status as a protected preserve, the primary forest habitat has been heavily denuded over the past few decades, and officials believe the park's wildlife numbers are dwindling. The low-key Endangered Primate Rescue Center is in the park and can be visited if the staff isn't too busy.

Despite the misfortunes of northern Vietnam's animals, Cuc Phuong is absolutely beautiful. April is especially lovely, and the swarms of butterflies that gather here would be enough to amaze Nabokov. Dozens of miles of trails lead to such highlights as cascading Giao Thuy waterfall, a 1,000-year-old tree, and Con Moong Cave, the "cave of early man," where evidence of prehistoric humans has been discovered. Longer hikes lead to some Muong villages. Many trails are well marked, but traveling this thick forest would be foolish without a guide.

Lodging

You'll probably end up in one of two areas: the **park headquarters** (☎ 030/866–085), just beyond the main gates, and **Bong,** a tiny village 20 km (12 mi) into the park. Overnighters can stay at either location, but tour operators usually guide guests to the facilities at park headquarters. Air-conditioned bungalows here are pricey at $40 per night, and double rooms in the nearby guest house run from $30 to $35, with air-conditioning and bathrooms inside. Call the park headquarters for information and reservations. The staff is quite helpful.

In Bong two stand-alone bungalows are available, also for $40, as well as nine simple rooms in a guest house. These run from $10 to $20. There are only four hours of electricity per night in Bong, and bathrooms are shared. Reservations are recommended for either location. You may wish to consider going on a weekday, as Cuc Phuong's proximity to Hanoi makes it a favorite weekend retreat among Vietnamese student groups. Bong, secluded as it is, occasionally fills with a boisterous crowd of between 100 and 200 students. Especially if you're staying the night, bring lots of mosquito repellent and cover-up.

Arriving and Departing

Cuc Phuong is an easy 2½-hour drive down Highway 1 from Hanoi and can be visited as a day trip if you leave early in the morning. If you've rented a car from Hanoi, it is possible to drive with a guide into the center of the park and hike out to the road to the west of the park, where your driver will meet you. You then drop your guide off at the headquarters on your way back to Hanoi. Tour operators in Hanoi are loathe to recommend this outright, claiming the road is too dangerous and difficulty in finding you should anything happen to you in the park, so you'll have to arrange it once at Cuc Phuong. Air-conditioned cars to Cuc Phuong can be arranged for $80 to $90. Hanoi Tourism charges $118 for transportation and driver's expenses, as well as an overnight stay in a double room at park headquarters.

Tam Dao Hill Station

85 km (53 mi) northwest of Hanoi in Vinh Phuc province.

High in the clouds, at an elevation of 3,050 ft, the damp hill station of Tam Dao feels like the mountain town that time forgot—almost. In 1907 French developers scaled the rugged 4,590-ft peaks (there are three of them) north of Hanoi and decided the cool weather of a nearby mountain retreat could serve the French well. The result was a graceful town of elegant villas surrounded by lush vegetation and sweeping views of the valley below. Since the French left in 1954, however, little grace has been bestowed on Tam Dao, whose chalet charm took a decided turn for the worse (perhaps it was the lack of oxygen up there) when Soviet-era architecture announced itself in the form of a monstrously square 40-room hotel. (You're welcome to stay here, but try one of the more intimate minihotels first.) Most villas—and the town church—have fallen into disrepair, though a few developers remain confident that Tam Dao could be resuscitated as a tourist resort; they've bought up some crumbling lodges and have begun to build.

Few people, even locals, realize that Tam Dao and the surrounding peaks are in a national park, which may be one reason why logging remains a problem for the area. But for the most part, a hike up to the radio transmitter above the town is a walk into dense jungle. Small Buddhist temples line the concrete steps up to the tower, and a spring bubbles up from beneath the underbrush and splays out into a small waterfall.

If you're spending the night up in these mountains, bring a sweater and some rain gear.

A guard station has been set up at the base of the mountain, and vehicles are charged a few dollars to get up to the hill station. The 15-km (9-mi) climb is a fascinating ride from subtropical vegetation up to more temperate flora such as pine trees. People have been known to ride mountain bikes up to Tam Dao and spend the night, but the climb is extreme. Less active riders put their bikes in minivans on the way up and then careen down the extremely winding and dangerous—but ultimately exhilarating—route to the guard station.

Arriving and Departing

There are no organized group tours to Tam Dao, but you can easily arrange a trip here on your own through a travel agency or tourist café.

HANOI A TO Z

Arriving and Departing

By Bus

Bus schedules are quite arbitrary. Few station attendants speak any English or French, and they aren't much help. Buses leave when full, and arrival times depend on how many times a bus stops along the road to cool off its overheated engine or pick up more passengers. Contact the **Hanoi Bus Company** (✉ 32 Nguyen Cong Tru St., ☎ 04/971–4590) for information.

Try to take minivans instead, as full-size buses are cramped, hot, and notoriously loud, uncomfortable, and unsafe. Pseudo-independent minibus service, particularly to Haiphong, is available from the alleyway called Hang Trung, adjacent to the Royal Hotel. These buses are more expensive than their hulking counterparts, yet they're usually just as crowded.

Three major bus stations—none of which is in the center of town—service the capital, in addition to a few express minibus services:

Gia Bat Bus Station (Ben Xe Gia Bat; ☎ 04/864–1462) is 7 km (4 mi) south of the Hanoi Railway Station, on Gia Phong Street, opposite the Giap Rat Railway Station; it serves most southern routes, including Vinh, Hue, and ultimately Ho Chi Minh City.

Gia Lam Bus Station (Ben Xe Gia Lam; ☎ 04/827–1529) is across the Red River and just beyond the tollbooth, 100 yards off Nguyen Van Cu Street on Ben Xe Street; it serves northern routes, such as Hanoi–Lang Son. A seat to Haiphong costs 18,000d. It's best to buy your ticket ahead of time.

Kim Ma Bus Station (Ben Xe Kim Ma; ☎ 04/845–2846), at the intersection of Nguyen Thai Hoc and Giang Vo streets, in the Ba Dinh District, is the closest of Hanoi's stations to downtown. It serves most routes to the northwest, including Dien Bien Phu.

By Car

As Hanoi is the largest city and tourist center in northern Vietnam and a major international gateway, few Western visitors actually arrive in Hanoi by car. Those who do are usually coming from Ho Chi Minh City via Highway 1 or from Danang or Hue after flying there from Ho Chi Minh City. A much more common method is to tour the south by land, say, by car or train from Ho Chi Minh City to Hue and then fly from there to Hanoi.

It's quite easy to arrange leaving Hanoi by car for side trips (☞ Getting Around by Car, *below*). Only a few road tolls are charged, and the cost is minimal—about 5,000d per car.

By Minibus

Make arrangements for travel by minibus—either independently or with group tours—through travel agencies, tourist cafés, and hotels.

By Plane

Many international airlines fly into Hanoi (☞ Air Travel *in* the Gold Guide).

Pacific Airlines (✉ 100 Le Duan St., Dong Da District, ☎ 04/851–5350) is Vietnam's smaller domestic carrier; ticket prices are comparable to those of Vietnam Airlines.

Vietnam Airlines (✉ 1 Quang Trung St., Hoan Kiem District, ☎ 04/826–9294) has nonstop international flights between Hanoi and Bangkok, Seoul, Hong Kong, Taipei, Guangzhou, Dubai, Paris, Vientiane, and Phnom Penh. Domestic destinations served from Hanoi include Danang, Dien Bien Phu, Ho Chi Minh City, Hue, Nha Trang, and Vinh. Flight schedules are often different each day of the week.

AIRPORT

Noi Bai International Airport (☎ 04/821–6660) is about 35 km (22 mi) north of the city. For international flights you must pay an airport tax of 70,000d or $7 (you can pay in either currency) and for domestic flights 15,000d or $2.

BETWEEN THE AIRPORT AND THE CITY CENTER

By Bus: Vietnam Airlines runs a bus service into Hanoi; tickets are 45,000d per person; it takes about 40 minutes. Buses leave when full, which can sometimes mean a wait. The bus usually drops people off at their hotel if it's not too far from the center of town. Buses to the airport depart from the Vietnam Airlines office (☞ *above*). Book a seat in advance for about 45,000d per person.

By Taxi: There are plenty of official taxis at the airport; the price into Hanoi should be $20 or less. Don't worry about finding a taxi stand—the drivers will find you inside the terminal, often before you've even gone through customs. Many unofficial taxi drivers hover at the terminal's exit, and they will tug at your sleeve or luggage cart in order to get your business. They'll get you into town for less than the official taxis if you bargain well, but they don't offer receipts and often drive clunking, steering-challenged Russian Volgas. They'll also try to get you to pay for the tolls into town. A bit of complaining usually gets you off the hook.

To get out to the airport, hire an official taxi with other travelers and split the fare, which should be between $15 and $20. Travelers looking to share taxis congregate in front of the Vietnam Airlines office, as do enterprising private drivers. Be prepared to bargain hard—some will make the trip for $10.

By Train

DOMESTIC TRAVEL

The ticket office at the main Hanoi train station, **Ga Hanoi** (✉ Opposite 115 Le Duan St., at west end of Tran Hung Dao St., ☎ 04/825–3549), is open 7:30–11:30 and 1:30–3:30. You'll find a special counter where foreigners buy tickets, and some of the schedules are even in English. Another, smaller train station, up the tracks from the main one, services northern routes; the foreign booking agents at the main station will direct you.

Trains leave four times daily for Ho Chi Minh City (soft berth $97–$125, 40 hours), but only one is an express. The express makes stops at most major cities, such as Vinh, Hue, Danang, and Nha Trang. Purchase a day in advance if you want to ensure a seat. Other destinations include Lang Son ($4, twice daily, 5 hours); Lao Cai (hard berth $17, soft sleeper $22; once daily; 11 hours); and Haiphong ($4, 4 times daily, 2 hours).

INTERNATIONAL TRAVEL

Trains connect Beijing with Hanoi twice weekly, and the trip takes 55 hours. The northeastern border crossing is at Dong Dang, just north of Lang Son in the northeast (☞ Chapter 3). The closest Chinese city to the Vietnamese border crossing is Nanning, the capital of Guangxi Province. A second international route leads from Hanoi through the border town of Lao Cai, to the northwest, and on to the Chinese provincial capital of Qunming. This train departs every Friday night—and is the same sleeper train many tourists take to go to Sapa. Standard tourist visas to China allow entry into the country from any port but Nepal. On the Vietnamese side, however, you'll have to have the appropriate overland exit permit stamped into your visa. This should be done before you arrive in Vietnam, although it is feasible to have your visa amended after you've arrived.

Getting Around

By Bicycle

Bikes can be rented at hotels and cafés in the center of town for around 10,000d per day. Make sure the bike you get has a lock. You can get the tires pumped up at just about any street corner for from 300d to 500d per tire.

By Car

These days in Hanoi it seems as if everybody with four wheels wants to rent you their car. This has caused rental rates to drop slightly, but you can still count on paying from $30 to $35 per day in the city for an air-conditioned sedan and a driver. Expect to pay $40 or more per day for a minivan.

To hire a car and driver, contact any hotel, a large operator such as Vietnam Tourism, one of the tourist cafés, or any other travel agency. If you play your cards right—i.e., don't rent from a large hotel—you can probably rent a coffin-black Russian Volga for $25 per day or less. These clunkers aren't so reliable, however, so you'd best not be heading off to sign a $20 million joint-venture agreement in one.

You can almost certainly arrange for a pickup at your hotel, although a deposit—usually 50% of the fare and some form of identification, like a photocopy of your passport—is often expected. There is no need for you to leave your passport with the agency renting you the car. The general time frame for day rentals is from 8 AM until dusk. If you keep the car beyond 5:30 or 6, the rates will rise. Make sure it is clear *exactly* how much the rate will rise if you keep the car longer.

See The Northwest A to Z *in* Chapter 3 for information on renting four-wheel-drive vehicles.

By Cyclo

Cyclo drivers in Hanoi are less likely to speak English than their Saigon counterparts, so definitely bring a map and be prepared to gesture. On the upside, cyclos here are wider than anywhere else in Vietnam, so two medium-size Westerners can squeeze into one; the fare is usually from 5,000d to 10,000d, depending on the distance. A cyclo driver will also be more than happy to take you around for the whole day for as little as 35,000d. Make sure you're both on the same wavelength when you're talking money: unsuspecting travelers have been known to agree to a fare of 10,000d, only to have the cyclo driver later claim the agreed-upon figure was $10. *See* Cyclos *in* the Gold Guide for more information.

By Motorbike

Motorbike taxis, known as *xe om* or *Honda om,* are one way to get around the city—if you're brave. Although the traffic may look a little daunting, drivers (hopefully) know how to navigate the traffic.

If you decide to rent a motorbike yourself and drive around the city, realize the traffic *is* busy, loud, and crazy. And though the streets may be less intimidating in Hanoi than Ho Chi Minh City, the consensus is that drivers are worse. And Westerners are paying the price: Vietnam's number one cause of injuries and death of foreigners is accidents involving a motorcycle. You can purchase helmets on Pho Hue and Lo Duc streets. Don't become a Vietnam traffic statistic—wear one. That said, many hotels and tourist cafés rent motorcycles. Prices start at about 60,000d per day. A deposit is usually required, as is a passport or a photocopy, and you sign a short-term contract (be sure you're aware of the stipulated value of the bike in the contract). And speaking of contracts, you would be wise to consult your insurance policy; many companies refuse to cover motorcycle drivers or riders.

Memory Café (✉ 33bis Tran Hung Dao St., ☎ 04/826–5854) has motorcycles available. **Tourist Service Office** (✉ 18C Ngo Quyen St., ☎ 04/824–7391) is a good place for rentals.

By Taxi

Though Hanoi's cabbies act like reckless kings of the road, taxis are still the safest way to get around town. The moment you step into a cab, the meter (all cabs in Hanoi should be metered) reads 14,000d; after that rates run about 5,600d per km. A trip across town will cost you about 25,000d.

Taxis tend to congregate at the northwest corner of Hoan Kiem Lake, on Trieu Viet Vuong Street, and outside most major hotels. You can also call for a cab, as all taxi dispatchers speak English. Competition is intense; a cab will be probably be at your doorstep in under three minutes if you're somewhere downtown. And don't be surprised if the cab that shows up is from a different company than the one you called; it means they've intercepted your request. Order a taxi by phone from the following: **Airport Taxi** (☎ 04/825–4250); **Hanoi Taxi** (☎ 04/853–5252); **Red Taxi** (☎ 04/856–8686); **Taxi CP** (☎ 04/824–1999); and **Taxi PT** (☎ 04/856–5656).

Contacts and Resources

Currency Exchange

The dollar has proven almighty, even in the capital of communist Vietnam, and exchanging greenbacks for Vietnamese dong is easy. Most major international banks in Hanoi have a currency exchange and other financial services such as money transfers, credit-card withdrawals, and cashing traveler's checks. Vietnamese banks, such as Vietcom Bank and VID Public Bank, also have such services. The rates of exchange at the international banks are controlled by the State Bank of Vietnam, so you'll likely find one is as good as the other. Hotels, too, can change money.

The dong has been stable for the past three years, though the currency crisis that beset the rest of Southeast Asia in 1997 has had some effect. This means that black market rates in Hanoi may now be high enough to justify the stress usually brought on by haggling over the money changers who gather around the General Post Office (GPO), at the corner of Dinh Tien Hoang and Dinh Le streets. (Beware, however: They always try to leave you shortchanged.) A better bet is generally the gold and jewelry shops around town. Jewelry shops have exchange bureau licenses; exchanging with the women at the GPO is illegal but rarely enforced.

Many of Hanoi's shops and upscale restaurants will accept both dollars and dong. Their exchange range for dollars is usually poor, however. Some shops, such as art galleries, already list all their prices in U.S. dollars.

Major banks in Hanoi include the following: **ANZ Bank** (Australia New Zealand Bank; ✉ 14 Le Thai To St., ☎ 04/825–8190, FAX 04/825–8189), **ABN-AMRO Bank** (✉ 360 Kim Ma St., Daeha Business Center, ☎ 04/831–5250, FAX 04/831–5275), **Bank of America** (✉ 27 Ly Thuong Kiet St., ☎ 04/824–9316, FAX 04/824–9322), **Citibank** (✉ 17 Ngo Quyen St., ☎ 04/825–1950, FAX 04/824–3960), **Standard Chartered Bank** (✉ 49 Hai Ba Trung St., 8th floor, ☎ 04/825–8970, FAX 04/825–8880), **VID Public Bank** (✉ 2 Ngo Quyen St., ☎ 04/826–6953, FAX 04/826–8228), and **Vietcom Bank** (Bank for Foreign Trade of Vietnam; ✉ 78 Nguyen Du St., ☎ 04/826–8035, FAX 04/822–8039).

Doctors and Hospitals

Medical facilities in Hanoi are not up to international standards. A few foreign-run medical clinics offer basic treatment—at Western prices—and can arrange for emergency medical evacuation in the region.

AEA International (✉ 31 Hai Ba Trung St., Hoan Kiem District, ☎ 04/934–0555) arranges emergency medical assistance, with referrals or evacuations. Routine health care is also available from a staff comprised of Vietnamese and international personnel.

Emergency Viet Duc Hospital (Benh Vien Viet Duc; ✉ 48 Tranh Thai St., Hoan Kiem District, ☎ 04/825–3531) is open 24 hours for emergency surgery; the staff speaks English, French, and German.

Hanoi Family Medical Practice (✉ A-1 Bldg., Van Phuc Diplomatic Compound, Suite 109–112, Kim Ma Rd., ☎ 04/843–0748 or 09/040–1919 for emergency mobile phone) is the creation of quirky Israeli Dr. Rafi Kot, who has one of the best and busiest practices in Hanoi. An expert staff of foreign doctors offers X rays, ultrasound, blood screening, inoculations, and pediatric care.

Olaf Palme Swedish Hospital (Benh Vien Olop Panmo; ✉ Lang Trung St., Dong Da District, ☎ 04/835–7533) treats children and adults.

Vietnam International Hospital (Benh Vien Quoc Te Viet Nam; ✉ Phuong Mai Rd., next to Bach Mai Hospital, Hai Ba Trung District, ☎ 04/574–0740 or 04/574–1111 for emergencies) opened in 1997 with much fanfare and hope. Gynecology, dentistry, and accident and emergency treatment are among the services; English-speaking doctors are available.

Embassies

If you have passport problems while in Hanoi, have had something very expensive stolen, or are extremely ill, contact your embassy.

Australia (✉ Van Phuc Quarter, Ba Dinh District, ☎ 04/831–7755, FAX 04/831–7711). **Canada** (✉ 31 Hung Vuong St., Ba Dinh District, ☎ 04/823–5500, FAX 04/823–5333). **New Zealand** (✉ 32 Hang Bai St., Hoan Kiem District, ☎ 04/824–2481, FAX 04/826–5760). **United King-**

dom (✉ 31 Hai Ba Trung St., Hoan Kiem District, ☎ 04/825–2510, FAX 04/826–5762). **United States** (✉ 7 Lang Ha St., Ba Dinh District, ☎ 04/843–1500, FAX 04/843–1510).

Emergencies

Ambulance (☎ 15). **Fire** (☎ 14). **Police** (☎ 13).

English-Language Books

The selection of English-language reading material—or even Vietnamese-language books, for that matter—is notoriously bad in Hanoi. All bookstores are state-run, and censorship is heavy. But in some you will be able to find a selection of international newspapers and magazines, provided none has infuriated Xunhasaba, the state-owned book distributor that occasionally yanks an issue off the shelves if a story portrays Vietnam too harshly.

The **Gioi Publishers Bookshop** (✉ 46 Tran Hung Dao St., Hoan Kiem District, ☎ 04/825–4086) has a varied selection of books on Vietnamese history, language, culture, and military exploits.

Hien Sach Hanoi (✉ 34 Trang Tien St., near the Metropole/Hotel Sofitel, Hoan Kiem District, ☎ 04/824–1616) has a selection of books in English and is open daily 8–7.

The **National Library** (✉ 31 Trang Thi St., ☎ 04/825–2643) is in a lovely compound. There are books in English, but you're not allowed to comb through the stacks; locate the number of the book you want in the card catalog (there are no computers), and an assistant will bring it to you.

The **State Bookshop** (✉ 40 Trang Tien St., Hoan Kiem District, ☎ 04/825–4282) has a wide range of newspapers and magazines, as well as plenty of books about Vietnam.

Xunhasaba (✉ 32 Hai Ba Trung St., Hoan Kiem District, ☎ 04/825–4067), or the State Enterprise for the Import and Export of Books and Periodicals, if you're feeling formal, has a wide selection of mainly technical titles, like computer-instruction manuals. The staff is not helpful, and the store closes for lunch.

Film Developing and Camera and Watch Repair

For the best film developing, try the storefronts at 1 Trang Thi Street and 19 Ba Trieu Street. Cameras can be fixed at any of the many camera repair shops on Trang Thi Street, on the south side of Hoan Kiem Lake, but for serious repairs, you're better off buying an Instamatic in Hanoi and fixing your trusty SLR when you get home.

For watch repair, try **Phuc Hung** (✉ 13 Hang Phen St., Hoan Kiem District, ☎ 04/828–1247). Expect minimal English but fast service. **Tuan Dung** (✉ 51 Hang Dao St., Hoan Kiem District, ☎ 04/826–4758) has a good selection of unusual batteries.

Guided Tours

☞ Travel Agencies and Visitor Information, *below*.

Late-Night Pharmacies

☞ Viet Duc Hospital *in* Doctors and Hospitals, *above*.

Post Office

The **General Post Office** (Buu Dien Trung Vong; ✉ *75 Dinh Tien Hoang St., Hoan Kiem District,* ☎ *04/825–7036*) occupies most of a city block across from Hoan Kiem Lake. Phone, fax, and telex services are available, as is express-mail service from companies such as Federal Express and UPS. It's open daily from 6:30 AM to 8 PM. Dozens of other small post-office branches dot the city.

Precautions

☞ Precautions *in* the Gold Guide.

Travel Agencies

The following travel agencies operate in Hanoi—some in many other parts of the country as well. They offer visitor information, transportation and hotel bookings, car and bus rentals, guided tours, private tour guides, and visa extensions. If you've signed on to a package tour from the United States, Europe, or Australia, it is highly likely you'll be cared for by one of these companies. *See* Tour Operators *and* Travel Agencies *in* the Gold Guide for a further discussion of your options.

Ann's Tourist (⊠ 26 Yet Kieu St., Hoan Kiem District, ☎ FAX 04/822–0018), headquartered in Saigon but with another office in Hanoi, is a private company that coordinates package and private tours and can assist with air or train reservations, car rentals, and so on.

Especen Travel Agency (⊠ 79E Hang Trong St., Hoan Kiem District, ☎ 04/826–6856, FAX 04/826–9612) was one of the first private tour operators in Hanoi.

Exotissimo Travel (⊠ 26 Tran Nhat Duat St., Hoan Kiem District, ☎ 04/828–2150, FAX 04/828–2146), an international wholesale inbound tour operator for more upscale travelers, now offers retail and walk-in services as well.

Hanoi Toserco (⊠ 8 To Hien Thanh St., Hai Ba Trung District, ☎ 04/825–2924, FAX 04/822–6055), a large state-run office, arranges travel services, books hotels, finds housing, and coordinates package tours.

Hanoi Tourism (⊠ 18 Ly Thuong Kiet St., Hoan Kiem District, ☎ 04/826–1627, FAX 04/824–1101; marketing office, ⊠ 1 Ba Trieu St., Hoan Kiem District, ☎ 04/824–2330 or 04/826–5244, FAX 04/825–6418) is one of the city's biggest state-run travel agencies.

Mansfield Toserco (⊠ 102 Hang Trong St., Hoan Kiem District, ☎ 04/826–9444, FAX 04/826–9485), a joint venture between Hanoi Toserco and Mansfield of Malaysia, can arrange package tours and standard travel services, as well as limousine service.

OSC First Holiday (⊠ 22 Phan Chu Trinh St., Hoan Kiem District, ☎ 04/824–0464, FAX 04/826–9219), a joint venture between OSC and a Malaysian tour agency, works mainly with international package tours.

OSC Vietnam Tours (⊠ 38 Yet Kieu St., Hoan Kiem District, ☎ 04/826–4500, FAX 04/825–9260) is the travel arm of the gargantuan Oil Services Company of Vietnam, headquartered in Vung Tau.

Saigon Tourist (⊠ 55 Phan Chu Trinh St., Hoan Kiem District, ☎ 04/825–0923, FAX 04/825–1174 for tours), the largest tour agency in Vietnam, is based in Saigon but has an office in the capital. Service is sometimes impersonal, but they can arrange everything.

Vidotour (⊠ 28 Hoa Ma St., Hoan Kiem District, ☎ 04/821–5682, FAX 04/972–1107), one of the largest private tour agencies in Vietnam, is stronger in the south.

Vietnam Tourism (⊠ 30A Ly Thuong Kiet St., Hoan Kiem District, ☎ 04/825–6916, FAX 04/825–7583) is another one of the country's large state-run travel agencies.

Vinatour (⊠ 54 Nguyen Du St., Hoan Kiem District, ☎ 04/825–5963, FAX 04/825–2707) is a mid-sized state-run agency.

TOURIST CAFÉS

These (mainly) private companies offer many of the services of large travel agencies but usually at lower prices. A number double as hotels and restaurants. Most are not equipped to handle tour bookings from overseas; it's mainly a walk-in business.

Price-wise, the tourist cafés' group tours can't be beat. For instance, a full-day guided tour to the Perfume Pagoda, including transportation, lunch, entrance fees, and boat rides, costs about $20 per person. To Halong Bay it's an even better deal (ranging from under $25 to $30 per person for a boat ride and an overnight stay, everything but drinks included), but the accommodations are usually in average minihotels. (*See* Travel Agencies *in* the Gold Guide for more discussion of tourist cafés.)

Green Bamboo Café (✉ 42 Nha Chung St., Hoan Kiem District, ☎ 04/826–8752, FAX 04/826–4949) is the best-organized tour café in town.

Lonely Planet Travel Café (✉ 33 Hang Be St., Hoan Kiem District, ☎ FAX 04/825–7002) has no affiliation with the guidebook company.

Meeting Cafe (✉ 59 Ba Trieu St., Hoan Kiem District, ☎ 04/825–8813) says it's "probably the best meeting place for you"—if it's not sure, we're not sure.

Memory Café (✉ 33bis Tran Hung Dao St., Hoan Kiem District, ☎ 04/826–5854) is a tiny café run by a friendly couple.

Old Darling Cafe (✉ 4 Hang Quat St., ☎ 04/824–3024) was the second café run by the original owner of the Darling; he's since left, but the café soldiers on.

Queen Cafe (✉ 65 Hang Bac St. Hoan Kiem District, ☎ 04/826–0860, FAX 04/825–0000) is one of the more serious rivals to the Green Bamboo's café crown.

Real Darling Cafe (✉ 33 Hang Quat St., ☎ 04/826–9386, FAX 04/825–6562) is the original Darling organization.

Sinh Café (✉ 56 Hang Be St., ☎ 04/934–0535, FAX 04/822–6055) is affiliated with the Saigon heavy hitters of the same name. It's hard to take a tour group seriously when they set up in the living room of somebody's house, but this is Vietnam.

Tin Tin Pub (✉ 14 Hang Non St., Hoan Kiem District, ☎ 04/826–0860, FAX 04/825–0000) was once one of the busiest tourist cafés in town, but business has slowed.

Tourist Smiling Café (✉ 22 Cau Go St., Hoan Kiem District, ☎ 04/824–4554) is yet another tourist café option.

3 The North

Halong Bay, Sapa, Dien Bien Phu

Northern Vietnam's stark beauty lies in its mist-shrouded islets and rice-terraced mountains. Fishing boats ply the magnificent waters of Halong Bay, while diligent farmers harvest crops on the steep slopes of the Tonkinese Alps, and fluttering rice stalks whisper the rhythm of Mai Chau Valley. In the shadow of Fansipan, the country's tallest peak, are the villages of northern Vietnam's ethnic minority groups. This region of imposing mountains bore witness to French ignominy at Dien Bien Phu—and at the same time nurtured Ho Chi Minh's revolution.

By Michael Mathes

THE SPECTACULAR TOPOGRAPHY OF THE NORTH includes the Hoang Lien Mountains—or Tonkinese Alps, as they are commonly called—the sprawling Red River Delta, and Halong Bay's limestone islets jutting out of the South China Sea. Even though the region has borne the brunt of centuries of war—first the Chinese invaders, then the French colonialists, the Americans, and once again the Chinese—and bomb craters still pockmark the Red River Delta, much of northern Vietnam has maintained its austere beauty.

The Red River Delta is the most densely populated area of Vietnam, with more than 1,000 people per square mile, compared with approximately 400 per square mile in the Mekong Delta. Many of these inhabitants of the Red River Delta, and those in the mountains to the north and west, are very poor. Extreme weather patterns—too much rain and too many damaging storms in the wet season, too little rain in the dry season—make living off the land more difficult than in the south. Years of postcolonial isolation, xenophobia, and ruinous collectivization programs also drove the north to the brink of disaster. Although forced collectivization and other such socialist land schemes have been confined to the dustbins of history, there are new threats and concerns for the indigenous people of northern Vietnam.

In the remote highlands and valleys north and west of Hanoi, ethnic minority populations continue to live as they have for centuries—despite the government's attempts at cultural integration. The history of these unique ethnic minorities is still the subject of some dispute, but many anthropologists now believe the largest of these ethnic groups, the Muong, as well as smaller groups like the Kho-mu, the Khang, the Mang, and the La Ha, have been living in the Hoang Lien Mountains and the northern foothills for thousands of years, preceding even the arrival of the Kinh—the ethnic Vietnamese who now make up 87% of the country's population.

Most other groups migrated from China or Laos—some as late as the 19th century—as a result of war or lack of land. (Communities of a number of these ethnic minorities can still be found in the countries from which they came, including China, Laos, Thailand, Cambodia, and Burma; migration across national borders is common.) Living in the highest elevations, near the climatic limits of hill rice cultivation, are the H'mong and Dao (pronounced "zao"). The clothing and jewelry of these two groups, particularly the women, are among the most colorful and elaborate in the north. The Muong and Thai (with distinct Black Thai and White Thai subgroups) are two of the larger minorities, each numbering about a million. They practice wetlands cultivation on the middle and lower slopes and generally live in airy, comfortable stilt houses in village clusters ranging from a handful of houses to several dozen.

Slash-and-burn agriculture, the traditional mainstay of ethnic minority economies, was for centuries an ideal form of natural resource management. Over the last decade or more, however, as the land available for such cultivation shrinks, this method has begun to generate heated controversy in Vietnam and has been blamed for just about every natural calamity that has befallen the north. Indeed, northern Vietnam is the most deforested region of Indochina, with as much as 90% of its primary forests lost to the encroachment of humans. Acres of trees are cut down every day for use as fuel or for wood for construction. A migration of Kinh Vietnamese from the Red River Delta farther inland

and into the distant valleys is also displacing many nomadic farmers as land privatization plans take hold.

Vietnam's growing energy needs are also wreaking havoc on minority life. The Hoa Binh Dam, Vietnam's first hydroelectric power project, 70 km (44 mi) southwest of Hanoi, displaced 60,000 people from the Da River valley. Most were ethnic minorities who were pushed into higher elevations, geography in which they had little farming experience or expertise. Another, larger hydro project, farther up the Da River in Son La Province, has already been approved. Feasibility studies estimate that 170 square mi of forest and farming area will be sacrificed, and anywhere from 110,000 to 143,000 people displaced.

From the mid-19th century until their departure in 1954, French colonialists had varied and extensive contact with these ethnic minority groups, all of whom they referred to as Montagnards ("mountain people"). Some of these groups sided with the French against the Kinh Vietnamese, while others helped foment rebellion against the French.

Only in the last few years have large numbers of tourists begun to seek out ethnic minority villages in northern Vietnam. For the villagers it has been a mixed blessing. A booming business of selling handicrafts, clothing, and textiles to tourists has sprung up in many communities, and around Sapa in particular. Increased contact between these ethnic minorities and tourists has created a flurry of interest in their cultures and lives but has also cost them some privacy. For instance, one unfortunate casualty has been the near disappearance of Saturday-night "love markets," where young Red Dao men and women in search of a spouse or lover would pair off for an evening of socializing and possible romance. In Sapa there is no sign of this market, which was once the highlight of the trip for visitors. Too many flashbulbs and curious foreign faces have driven the love market out of the spotlight and into more remote areas of the north.

Pleasures and Pastimes

Dining

Except for Hanoi and the coastal regions, dining in the north is more of a necessity than a delight. Seafood dishes in Haiphong, Cat Ba, Halong Bay, and farther up the coast are delicious. The mountains provide few opportunities for gourmands, however. Rice is a staple, of course, as well as corn, cassava, and green vegetables. Pond stocking ensures an ample fish supply. Although beef is now readily available in mountain towns, pork is the more common meat. Chicken, pork, and beef are usually tough, however, and little of the animals goes to waste. In the homes of poorer villagers especially, keep an eye out for meat dishes; they're usually accompanied by offal, and your hosts may not realize that most people from the West steer clear of such fare. By the same token, understand that meats are still a delicacy in many poor communities; as foreign visitors are still extremely rare in some areas, your hosts may splurge and butcher a pig or a few chickens in your honor. Deciding what to eat and what to pass up is an issue to treat with some sensitivity.

One "pleasure" that you most likely will be unable to avoid while traveling through the highlands is rice wine, or *ruou* (pronounced "zeeoo"). Distilled locally, ruou is everywhere, and is used as a welcoming drink. It is also drunk at lunch, before, during, and after dinner, while gathering with friends, when meeting with officials, at small and large celebrations, and as a good-luck send-off. Refusing it outright is difficult, stopping once you've started is nearly impossible, and getting sick from drinking too much is easy.

A communal twist on the ruou standard is *ruou can* (straw-rice wine), which is consumed by up to a dozen people at the same time through bamboo straws stuck into an earthenware jar. First half-filled with manioc and rice husks, the jar is sealed tight and left to ferment for 17 days. On the day of consumption, a water-sugar mixture is added. The sweet, slightly fetid alcohol is downed at weddings and other major celebrations—such as a couple of foreigners stepping into a remote village. It's beneficial that ruou can is more diluted than its bottled brother, which can be anywhere from 60- to 110-proof.

Hiking

One of the best ways to experience northern Vietnam is tackling the trails that lead out of the towns and into more remote areas of the highlands. Whether you're stepping into a national park (Cuc Phuong, Ba Be, and Cat Ba Island national parks all have spectacular hiking) or onto a Montagnard trail, these footpaths lead through more pristine terrain than you would be able to see from the back seat of a bouncing Jeep. Wildlife sightings are more likely (but still rare) the farther you are from busy roads and towns. Villages throughout the mountains are connected by trails, and it may not be long before someone produces a publication documenting and mapping a network of the best hiking trails in the north. Until then, however, your best bet is to pick up local maps when you arrive at a destination. Dozens of trails lead out of the hillside town of Sapa, for instance, and into H'-mong villages. Minority peoples have a vast knowledge of local routes, but communication may be a problem. You may want to have a guide along, especially if you intend on trekking to the foot—or if you've got three or four days, to the top—of Mt. Fansipan, Vietnam's highest peak.

The tourist cafés in Hanoi (☞ Hanoi A to Z *in* Chapter 2) have begun organizing tours that combine four-wheel transportation and serious hiking. It won't exactly be a one-on-one experience with nature, but the tour operators have researched the hikes with knowledgeable locals and are pretty familiar with the needs and desires of Western travelers.

If you're going hiking but are concerned about land mines and unexploded ordnance in the north, keep in mind that there is little to fear if you stay on marked trails or on clear footpaths. However, unless you're with an experienced guide, you should not hike along Vietnam's border region with China, specifically in the area around Lang Son and Mong Cai. Minelaying was common during the 1979 border war, and it's best to skip unmarked hillside exploring.

Jeep Trips

Adventure awaits on the roads of the north. Mud slides, breakdowns, and teeth-rattling stretches of "highway" compete for your attentions with spectacular scenery, revolutionary history, and ethnic minority culture. Only in a rented Russian Jeep—or in a far more civilized Toyota Landcruiser or Mitsubishi Pajero—are you in complete control of where and when you stop. The no-nonsense drivers speak little English, but they're also quite familiar with the terrain and can lead you to sights left alone by the big tour companies. By far the most popular multiple-day Jeep route is northwest from Hanoi, including overnight stops at Mai Chau, Dien Bien Phu, and Sapa. Some villages just a mile or two off the road haven't seen Westerners since the French left in 1954. Arrange a Jeep tour of any length from a Hanoi hotel, tour operator, or tourist café (they can also book your hotels). You'll pay by the kilometer and by the number of nights your driver is away from home.

Lodging

Except in the major cities such as Hanoi and Haiphong and established tourist destinations like Halong Bay and Sapa, accommodations in the north lack many basic amenities. If you're looking for comfort, stick close to Hanoi. In other small cities and towns such as Dien Bien Phu, Lang Son, or Lao Cai, expect hot running water in your hotel room, but don't count on having IDD phones, heaters, or bath tubs. In more remote areas, such as ethnic minority villages near Yen Phu or small coastal communities in the far northeast, expect to share a mat or roll-away mattress in the living room of a host family—with a bathroom that's a curtained shack next to a well where you draw your own water. Don't write such an experience off, however; many of the stilt houses in ethnic minority villages are exquisitely built, cool, and comfortable, and you may find the owners to be your most gracious hosts.

Shopping

If you've got an eye for indigenous style, northern Vietnam can be your mecca. The region's ethnic minority communities, particularly the women of these groups, have developed sophisticated trading networks, not just among themselves but for tourists as well. And what's trading hands is positively beautiful: richly dyed textiles; hand-loomed silk scarves, headdresses, and broadcloth; brocaded vests and dresses; woven bamboo baskets of all shapes and sizes; and traditional silver jewelry. The "industry" has even internationalized, and savvy distributors in Hanoi and Saigon are scrambling to send Vietnam's ethnic minority styles to overseas markets.

Exploring the North

A trip to the north is difficult to rush because traveling around often takes a long time, and changing weather can make some roads quite dangerous—even impassable. Roads for the most part are in bad shape. The major highways of the lowlands (Highway 5 to Haiphong, Highway 1 to Lang Son, Highway 6 to Hoa Binh) are being continuously upgraded, and the construction itself slows down traffic flow. In the mountains of the north and northwest, heavily traveled routes are paved but are still in lousy condition. Routes to distant villages like Muong Te or remote destinations like Ha Giang town are rutted dirt roads that wash out with the first heavy rain. Traveling them can be physically exhausting.

With this in mind, there are two ways to travel through the north. The most challenging is to cover the region by car, from Hanoi to Son La to Dien Bien Phu to Lai Chau to Sapa and back to Hanoi. This route is adventurous and allows for some great exploring, but it's a challenge: five or more days on rutted mountain roads is not for everyone. Make a run to the Chinese border near Lang Son, or stop at Ba Be Lake on the way back to Hanoi for a leisurely few days in this stunningly remote nature preserve. You'll have to have some idea of your itinerary before leaving Hanoi, however; your driver will want to know how long he'll be away from home.

The easiest way to see the north is to base yourself in Hanoi (☞ Chapter 2) or Haiphong, from which you can take two- or three-day trips. Using this method is highly recommended because it gives you a way to appreciate northern Vietnam without the discomforts of one endless, grueling road trip. You can either arrange these trips yourself or sign up with one of a variety of tour operators. Some destinations are too far for day trips, but you can easily hire a car or Jeep to head there and back, or to get to Sapa, you can hop on the relatively comfortable overnight train from Hanoi.

Around Haiphong, visit Cat Ba Island and northern Vietnam's most famous attraction, Halong Bay. Twenty-three kilometers (14 mi) south of Haiphong is the seaside village of Do Son, home to Vietnam's only official casino and the famous Do Son Buffalo Fighting Festival. Take a trip northeast of Hanoi to Lang Son. Farther east, beyond the boomtown of Mong Cai, lies Tra Co, the longest stretch of uninterrupted pristine beach in northern Vietnam. The far reaches of the north are home to dozens of ethnic minority groups, around Sapa and Bac Ha in the northwest, Dien Bien Phu in the westernmost province of Lai Chau, and Cao Bang in the central north.

Tours organized by Hanoi's tourist cafés (☞ Hanoi A to Z *in* Chapter 2) cover the more popular destinations and are the most inexpensive and time-efficient way to see this region. Large travel agencies in Hanoi such as Vietnam Tourism, Saigon Tourist, and Exotissimo Travel (☞ Hanoi A to Z *in* Chapter 2) arrange tours that are more expensive and, perhaps, more comfortable. Lodging, transportation, entrance fees to sites, and most meals are usually included. If you don't want to be stuck with a group of strangers (tourist cafés usually fill up a minivan or larger—from 6 to 20 people; international tour companies and the large tour operators inside the country try to fill up coach buses—from 15 to 40 people), you're better off renting a car with a driver from your hotel or a tour agency. If you'd like to be in control of every single aspect of the trip, including driving, your best bet is to rent a motorbike.

Numbers in the text correspond to numbers in the margin and on the North map.

Great Itineraries

Destinations in the north can be grouped into two geographic categories: the lowland areas in and around the Red River Delta; and the Hoang Liem Mountains, or Tonkinese Alps. Unless you're in the north for only four days or less, it's quite easy to venture into both the lowlands *and* the mountains. You can reach the delightful scenery on the coast, specifically Halong Bay and Cat Ba, from Hanoi in as little as four hours. Travel in the mountains is usually slower and requires more patience, but you'll soon discover that heading up into the northern highlands brings you into another world: a world of rugged and austere beauty, fascinating ethnography, and timeless traditions.

IF YOU HAVE 3 DAYS

If you don't have much time in the north, start with **Halong Bay** ③. From Hanoi you can easily get to this jewel in northern Vietnam's topographical crown. Hire a car from the capital or go with an organized trip and head east to Halong City, where you can hop on one of dozens of tour boats that can shuttle you around the thousands of limestone islands. Stay in one of the many hotels in town, or if adventure is your modus operandi, spend the night on the boat. From there catch a ferry to **Cat Ba Island** ④, the largest in the Halong Bay region and site of one of Vietnam's most beautiful national parks. Either return to your car in Halong City or take the high-speed ferry back to Haiphong, where you can catch the train or a minibus back to Hanoi.

IF YOU HAVE 6 DAYS

Travel from Hanoi to **Sapa** ⑫ and spend three days exploring the mountain trails that lead to ethnic minority villages. Head to the popular Saturday market, where members of ethnic groups such as the Red Dao and the H'mong gather to buy provisions and sell fabrics and clothing. You can see Sapa in a day's travel to and from Hanoi—or book a soft sleeper on the night train from the capital. If you've hired a four-wheel-drive vehicle to Sapa, consider an overnight side trip to the remote but incredibly beautiful **Ba Be Lakes** ⑦.

IF YOU HAVE 9 DAYS

If you have more than a week and can stand being in a car for many hours on rough roads, traveling through the farthest reaches of the north can be a real adventure. Rent a four-wheel vehicle (driver included), and do a circuit of this dramatic highland region. From Hanoi head for **Mai Chau** ⑨; you'll pass the impressive Hoa Binh Hydroelectric Power Dam on the way. Stay overnight in the lovely minority villages near Mai Chau or push on to **Son La** ⑩. From here head through spectacular valleys to infamous **Dien Bien Phu** ⑪, near the Laotian border, to explore the ruins of the French garrison. Wind your way over the bumpy roads past Lai Chau to **Sapa** ⑫ and **Bac Ha** ⑬, and then take a full day's drive back to Hanoi. Or break up the journey back by stopping at the **Ba Be Lakes** ⑦. An alternative itinerary is to take the return train from Hanoi to Sapa, take a two-day jaunt to Mai Chau from the capital, and fly from Hanoi to Dien Bien Phu. For the last few days head to the crystal-clear waters of **Halong Bay** ③.

When to Tour the North

The best time to tour the northern highlands is from late October to mid-December, after the August–October monsoons have abated and any mud slides are likely to have been cleared. As for Halong Bay, the season runs from early summer to mid-autumn. From July to September beware of tropical typhoons; flooding in Haiphong and Hanoi is common during these storms. The capital is hot and extremely humid in summer, which makes it a popular time for residents to head for the hills or the coast.

Beach season—which occurs mainly south of Haiphong at Do Son—is mid-summer, when hotels are filled with vacationing Hanoians who for some reason seem to love the extremely narrow and dirty beaches. The season culminates with the spectacular Do Son bullfights. By late October the place is virtually deserted. If you want the beach resort entirely to yourself, go to Do Son in November.

Northern Vietnam has a clearly defined winter, with a cold and clammy mist settling in for a few months starting in January. January and February are quite cold in the mountains, and Mt. Fansipan, Vietnam's highest peak, is occasionally dusted with snow. Peach and apricot trees blossom. If you're heading into the highlands in winter and intend to do some trekking, come prepared: a light sweater, a waterproof jacket, a wool hat, long johns, and some insulated hiking boots should keep you warm.

During Tet, the lunar new year, you'll find northern Vietnam cold and drizzly but extremely festive. If you're coming during this time, make plane and hotel reservations very early. Also understand that many tour operations, such as trips to Halong Bay, are severely limited or suspended during this period.

THE NORTHEAST

Natural beauty and nationalized industry share the spotlight in Vietnam's northeast. Take Quang Ninh Province as an example. Halong Bay and the rest of coastal Quang Ninh are battling with the province's expanding coal-mining industry over precious natural resources. Designated a World Heritage Site by UNESCO in 1995, Halong Bay is a breathtaking collection of limestone islands and secluded coves that

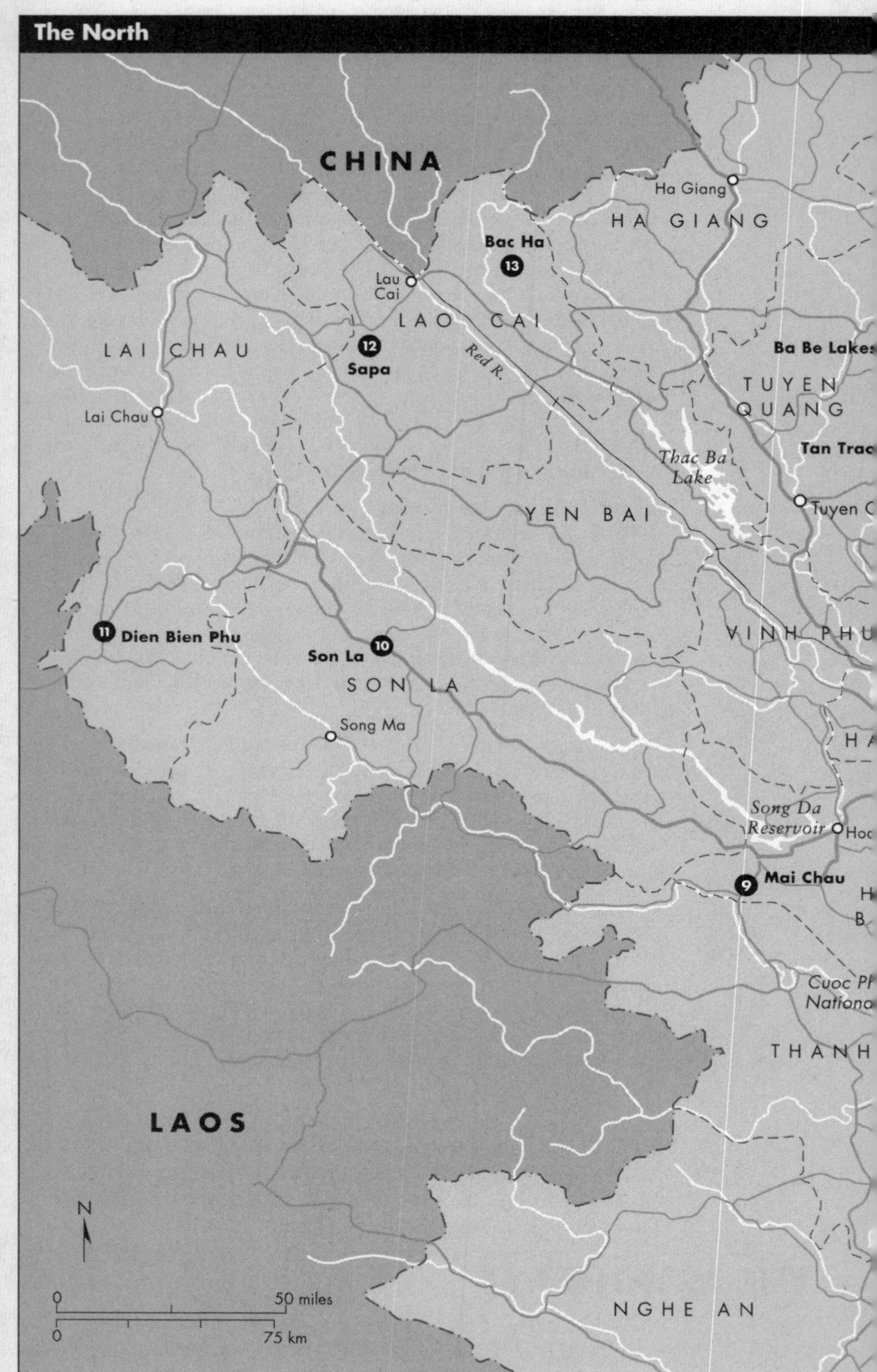
The North
CHINA
Ha Giang
HA GIANG
Bac Ha
13
Lau Cai
LAO CAI
Red R.
Ba Be Lakes
LAI CHAU
12
Sapa
TUYEN QUANG
Lai Chau
Tan Trao
Thac Ba Lake
Tuyen Q
YEN BAI
VINH PHU
11
Dien Bien Phu
10
Son La
SON LA
Song Ma
Song Da Reservoir
Hoa
9
Mai Chau
Cuoc Ph
Nationa
THANH
LAOS
N
0
50 miles
0
75 km
NGHE AN

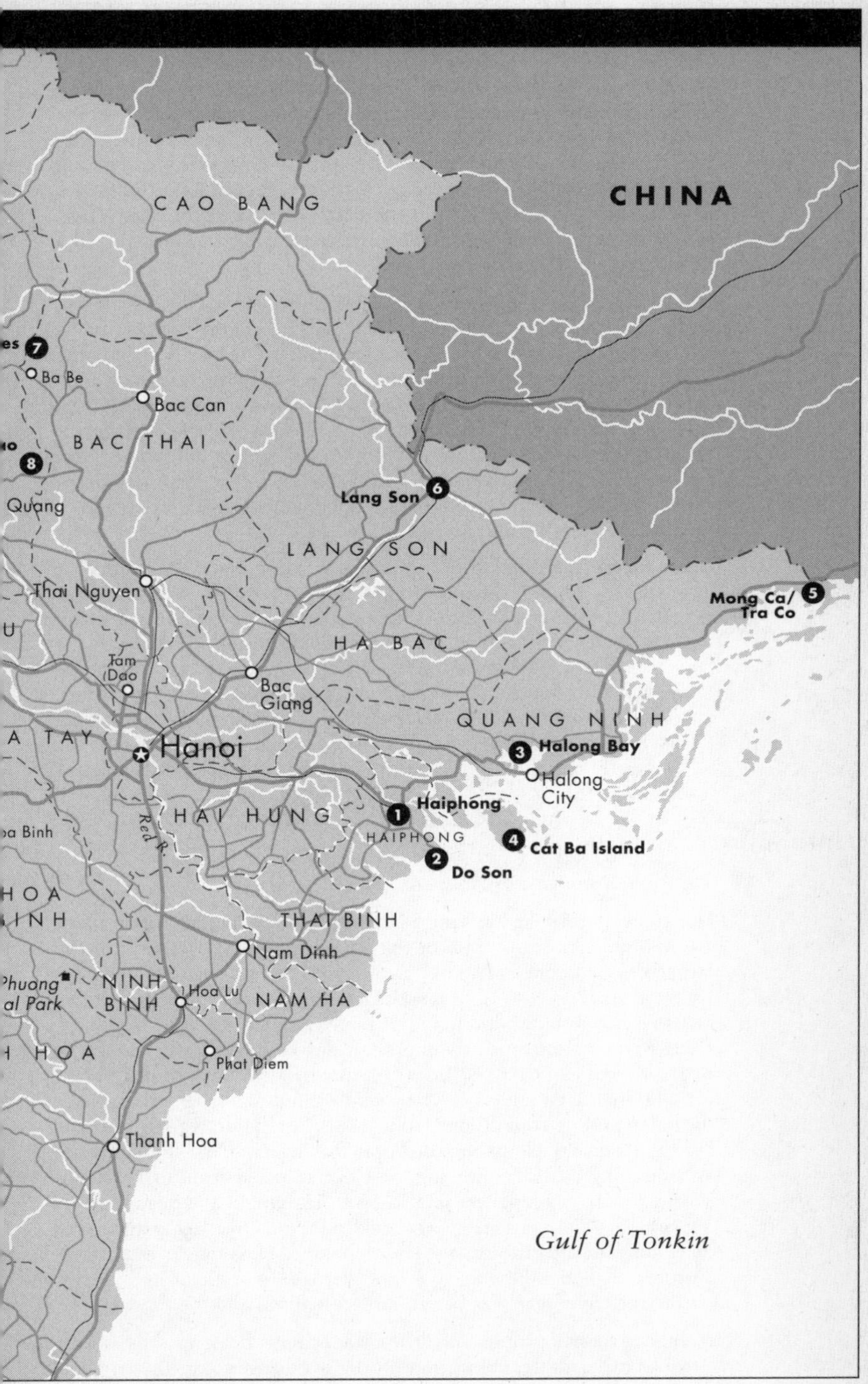
CHINA
CAO BANG
Ba Be
Bac Can
BAC THAI
Quang
Lang Son
LANG SON
Thai Nguyen
Tam Dao
HA BAC
Bac Giang
Mong Ca/ Tra Co
QUANG NINH
Hanoi
Halong Bay
Halong City
Haiphong
HAI HUNG
HAIPHONG
Red R.
Cat Ba Island
Do Son
THAI BINH
Nam Dinh
NINH BINH
Hoa Lu
NAM HA
Phat Diem
Thanh Hoa
Gulf of Tonkin

captured the imagination and the fancy of millions who saw the movie *Indochine,* starring Catherine Deneuve.

What was once a poor, struggling fishing village catering primarily to Communist Party officials has become the premier vacation spot in the north. Horsepower has long since replaced wind as the means of transport through the bay, and hotels have sprouted like weeds in Halong City, but the emerald waters and mysterious caves of this natural wonder continue to enchant. Just north of Halong Bay lies the gritty, soot-coated town of Cam Pha, the center of Vietnam's coal industry and a threat to the fragile ecosystem of the coast.

Similar destinies and dilemmas face Haiphong. Once the sleepy second cousin to the booming port of Saigon, Haiphong is emerging as more than just Vietnam's second-largest port. The city is awakening to the prospect of both tourism and the rapid development of import-export channels. Tree-lined boulevards, expansive green parks, and impressive if crumbling French colonial architecture fill the downtown. To the north of the city center, 10,000-ton freighters unload containers bound for Hanoi and load up with Vietnamese exports. A new deep-sea port, farther downstream from Haiphong, will be operational after the turn of the millennium.

International trade of a slightly different sort dominates the Wild West atmosphere of Lang Son and Mong Cai, two boomtowns on the Chinese border northeast of Hanoi. Nearly abandoned after retreating Chinese troops leveled them during a brief border war in 1979, the towns have risen again. Little animosity seems to remain between the two nations, which have normalized relations and opened border crossings, and cross-border trade—much of it illicit—is bustling. East of Mong Cai is Tra Co, northern Vietnam's most pristine stretch of beach. It's well off the beaten path, but the unruffled serenity of this coastline makes it worth the trip.

Haiphong

❶ *103 km (64 mi) east of Hanoi on Hwy. 5.*

Haiphong, today Vietnam's third-largest city, with a population of about 1.6 million, has been a hub of the north's industrial activity for the last century and one of its most significant seaports since the Tran dynasty ruled (1224–1400). Because of its strategic location, this port city has seen the comings and going of many foreign invaders. The Bach Dang River, on the outskirts of present-day Haiphong, was the site of one of Vietnam's greatest victories over forces from China: Kublai Khan's 300,000-man army and navy were soundly trumped by Vietnamese under the command of Tran Hung Dao in 1288. Six hundred years later the French settled into Haiphong and began turning it into a major industrial and shipping center. Following the German occupation of France in World War II, the Japanese muscled into Haiphong and began directing valuable Vietnamese exports back to Japan. Once again in control of the port city after the war, the French bombed Haiphong over a bizarre customs dispute, killing up to 1,000 Vietnamese civilians and precipitating the eight-year war between the Vietminh and the French.

Haiphong figured prominently in the war against the Americans as well. Because of its strategic location on the northeast coast, the city was often bombed during the Vietnam War and suffered particularly devastating attacks during the 1972 holiday season that became known as the Christmas bombings. President Richard Nixon ordered the mining of Haiphong Harbor in May 1972. The U.S. Navy was asked to help clear the mines as part of the agreement between the U.S. government and Vietnam in the Paris peace talks of 1973.

In 1979, following conflicts between Vietnam and China, as many as 100,000 ethnic Chinese who had lived for generations in the Haiphong area piled into barely seaworthy boats and fled from what they expected to be deadly reprisals by their Vietnamese neighbors. Few acts of retribution took hold, but the damage had been done. Haiphong has struggled to gain back much of its economic power lost because the large section of the merchant class that was Chinese left the city.

Now there is little visible evidence of Haiphong's troubled past, except perhaps the French architecture—much of it delightful—which can be spotted throughout the city center. The city's powerful People's Committee is too busy finding funding for a new deep-sea port and other massive projects to linger over past sentiments.

Today you are most likely to use Haiphong as a transfer point to destinations like Cat Ba, Do Son (both actually part of greater Haiphong), and Halong Bay. Here you can catch a cyclo to the port, and take the first boat out. If you have time, however, settle into an enjoyable two-day stay in Haiphong before moving farther afield. Some say it is what Hanoi was like four years ago: a sleepy northern city with less traffic and less nightlife, but bursting with potential. Even if you're in town for a half day, make the best of your time by picking up the excellent Haiphong Tourist Map at one of the major hotels and then walking around downtown. Or head to Vietnam Tourism (☞ The Northeast A to Z, *below*), a somewhat helpful operation that can find you a hotel, hire a car and driver, and answer questions about ferry and train schedules.

Haiphong's reputation as a dingy industrial port is not entirely justified. This is indeed the largest and busiest port in the north, and container trucks rumble through town on the way to Highway 5 and Hanoi. But the port itself is on the northern edge of the city and hugs the Cam River, away from the heart of the city. As you cross the Lac Long Bridge into the city center, you leave the dusty and bustling outskirts (where most of the industry with its factories is based) and slip into a quaint, clean downtown. Here huge banyan trees and blossoming magnolias line wide boulevards, and Vietnamese play badminton in the stately Central Square (Quang Truong). A walk through the city center feels like stepping into a time warp: Portraits of revolutionary heroes, especially Ho Chi Minh, hang elegantly from the eaves of buildings; socialist realist propaganda posters announce the latest health-awareness campaign; and swarms of bicycles fill the streets.

It's very easy to navigate central Haiphong. Purchase the well-designed Haiphong Tourist Map at one of the hotels in town. If you've come to Haiphong by car and plan to spend a leisurely day sightseeing, have the driver park at a hotel and then go for a long walk. Sidewalks on the main boulevards are wide, traffic is not as hectic as in Hanoi or Saigon, and the parks and gardens provide ample room to roam. Boat trips around the city are not available since the river is dominated by the city port, and the Tam Bac tributary to the southwest is not particularly scenic.

Shady, green **Children's Park** (Cong Vien Thieu Nhi), framed by Tran Phu and Tran Hung Dao streets, is the site of tai chi classes in the morning, children making the best of the playground during the day, and strolling couples and roller skaters in the evening. Many locals come down to the park after dinner to sit at sidewalk stalls and drink fruit shakes or eat sweets.

★ At the intersection of Hoang Van Thu and Tran Hung Dao streets stands one of the most beautiful buildings in Haiphong: the **City Theater** (Nha Hat Thanh Pho). Built by the French in 1907, this theater has all the exterior designs of a classic, except for its coat of splendidly pink paint. Once the site of lavish French and Vietnamese productions, the 400-seat theater was taken over by the Vietminh following World War II. President Ho Chi Minh addressed the world's youth in a June 1946 speech from the steps. A huge likeness of Uncle Ho now hangs above the wooden front doors—the painting is visible from hundred of yards away and feels eerily like the focal point of the city. In a way it is; the Haiphong People's Committee now holds its major meetings and assemblies here. Stage productions and concerts do take place, but they're rare. If you're not attending a show, you'll need written permission from the People's Committee to step inside. ✉ *Between Hoang Van Thu St. and Dinh Tien Hoang St.* ⏲ *Not open to public except for performances.*

A structure that rivals the City Theater in "pinkness" is the **Haiphong Museum** (Bao Tang Thanh Pho Hai Phong), an underrated gem of a building, which unfortunately is open only two and a half days per week. In the heart of the city, the museum is housed in a huge shuttered French villa with creaky wooden staircases, musty corners, and occasionally rotating ceiling fans. Though it attempts to cover all of the history, geography, archaeology, agriculture, and wildlife of the region (the stuffed owl with a rodent in its claws is rather macabre), the museum focuses on Vietnam's struggle for independence from various forces. Make sure you see the Bach Dang stakes, those sharp wooden poles driven into the riverbed that impaled Kublai Khan's boats in 1288, as well as the room dedicated to the Vietnam War. Here you can inspect a (presumably deactivated) MK-52 mine pulled from the waters of Haiphong Harbor in 1973, the lighthouse lantern that warned of impending bombing raids, and the antiaircraft gun that brought down a dozen U.S. planes. Nothing is in English, so bring a good guide or be prepared to do a lot of guesswork. ✉ *66 Dien Bien Phu St.* 🎫 *No official entrance fee; pay what you wish.* ⏲ *Thurs. 2–6, Sat. 5–9, Sun. 8–6.*

Haiphong's pagodas are tucked into the city's alleyways or off in the suburbs; no major religious structures except the **Large Cathedral** (Nha Tho Lon; ✉ 46 Hoang Van Thu St.) stand out in the middle of town.

★ Some beautiful pagodas are found in the southern and eastern districts of the city. The most impressive and moving of these is the **Du Hang Pagoda** (Chua Hang). Follow Cat Cut Street south until you hit Chua Hang Street. After a few alleyways you'll see the pagoda set back on the left. This 300-year-old temple is a good example of traditional Vietnamese architecture. A gate and three buildings surround a stone courtyard crowded with flowers, statues, and bonsai plants. In front and to the right of the compound is a round pond with lotus flowers encircled by white statues of the Buddha and scholars. One of the 10 monks who live here may be chanting his daily prayers and tapping on a round wooden drum in the richly gilded main sanctuary. Occasionally in the afternoons, the senior monk holds one-on-one healing sessions with the sick or mentally unbalanced. Hundreds of Buddhists fill the courtyard on the first and fifth of every lunar month. ✉ *Just off of Chua Hang St.* 🎫 *5,000d contribution.*

Closer to downtown is **Nghe Temple** (Den Nghe), a quiet place dedicated to Le Chan, a heroic peasant woman who helped organize the popular revolt against the Chinese that was led by the two Trung sisters in 40 AD. Later Le Chan helped lay the foundation for the city of Haiphong. Ceramic reliefs at the top of the front wall depict the Trung sisters in royal carriages. Two huge red-and-gold wooden carriages (built in 1916), similar to those used by the Trung Sisters and by royalty, are on display. Ancestral altars and chapels are to the right, through the courtyard. ✉ *Corner of Me Linh and Le Chan Sts.*

A few miles east on Danang Street is the Holiday Mansion Hotel, behind which you'll find the **Ve (Drawing) Pagoda** (Chua Ve). Emperor Ngo Quyen allegedly gathered his armies here before repulsing invaders in 938 AD. Similarly, General Tran Hung Dao spied on enemy Chinese troops from a perch on the pagoda grounds and then drew the battle maps that would help him orchestrate a commanding victory in 1288—hence the pagoda's name. ✉ *Behind Holiday Mansion Hotel on Danang St.*

Dining and Lodging

For a city of a million people, Haiphong doesn't have many upscale restaurants. Local seafood is excellent and cheap, however, and available at any number of nondescript, small family-run establishments. A few of the better-known ones are listed here, as are the handful of international restaurants on Dien Bien Phu Street. Restaurants specializing in fish are clustered around the north end of Rau Bridge (Cau Rau), a few miles from the city center on the road south to Do Son. Most restaurants close by 10 PM.

Haiphong has little of the style or variety of accommodations available in Hanoi and Saigon—yet. A couple of standard international hotels (the Royal Garden Hotel by Harborview is one; Accor Asia is assisting on another) are under construction, with an estimated opening date in late 1998 or early 1999. Until then, the lack of choice makes it easy to decide where to stay (on Dien Bien Phu Street, most likely). It also increases the likelihood that your first choice will be booked. Call ahead if you know your travel dates. If you're shopping around for hotels in person, *definitely* ask to see the room before you hand them your cash; a peculiarly arbitrary pricing system seems to have taken hold in Haiphong, and smaller $20 rooms are often much more pleasant than larger $35 rooms in the same hotel. And keep in mind that almost none of the rates are written in stone (meaning: you may be able to make a deal). Unless noted otherwise, every room comes with a private bath.

$$ ✕ **Chie Japanese Restaurant.** Chie Hara, owner and chef at Chie Restaurant in Hanoi, has opened a second restaurant in Haiphong. He trained the chef himself, and the result is the best Japanese food in the city. The 11-page menu makes ordering an ordeal, but the staff is patient and won't hesitate to suggest a favorite. Recessed tables and cushioned seating help make you feel a little closer to Tokyo than northern Vietnam. Take your shoes off and relax for a while. ✉ *97 Dien Bien Phu St.,* ☎ *031/823–327. MC, V.*

$$ ✕ **Han Kook Kwan.** Yong Ho Shin's authentic and down-to-business Korean restaurant captures the taste of Seoul with none of the bustle or passion. But Asian businessmen flocked here since it's the only Korean restaurant in town. Spicy barbecue dishes are cooked right at your table, but the sterility and fluorescent lights of the dining areas are suggestive of a charmless hotel lobby—perhaps because that is exactly where the restaurant is. ✉ *62 Dien Bien Phu St., 1st floor of Hotel du Commerce,* ☎ *031/822–092. MC, V.*

$$ ✕ **Quan Sake.** Owned and operated by the same people who run Quan Sake Hanoi, this Japanese restaurant cashes in on the growing market of Japanese expatriates living in Haiphong. Traditional fare—minus sushi—is served by a Vietnamese chef trained in Japan. Prix-fixe menus are available at lunch and dinner. As for ambience and decor, consider this: Quan Sake advertises take-out and delivery service. You may want to take them up on it. ✉ *55 Dien Bien Phu St.,* ☎ *031/823–659. No credit cards.*

$ ✕ **Saigon Thien Bao.** This lively restaurant north of the train station serves excellent seafood prepared by the Saigonese-born chef-proprietor. Salads are also a specialty. ✉ *6 Tran Binh Trong St., no phone. No credit cards.*

$ ✕ **Trung Hoa Restaurant.** Dine on Chinese at this hotel restaurant serving the best Peking duck in town. ✉ *In Hoa Binh Hotel, 104 Luong Khanh Thien St.,* ☎ *031/846–909. No credit cards.*

$$$ **Huu Nghi Hotel.** The decor in Haiphong's most sophisticated hotel of the moment ranges from dungeonlike to gaudy and is impersonal in character, yet the place is often full. Even during the day anywhere but the ground and top floors can be spooky, dark, and even depressing—if only they'd turn on the lights. At $300, the Superior Suite is the most overpriced room in town. ✉ *60 Dien Bien Phu St.,* ☎ *031/823–244 or 031/823–310,* FAX *031/823–245. 126 rooms. Restaurant, bar, air-conditioning, IDD telephones, minibars, satellite TVs, laundry service, business services, meeting rooms, travel services. AE, DC, MC, V.*

$$ **La Villa Blanche.** The three small buildings of this guest house are unexciting and overpriced but clean. There is little distinction between the $50 standard room and the $70 superior, so you may want to opt for the less expensive room. Breakfast is included in the price. ✉ *5 Tran Hung Dao St.,* ☎ *031/842–863,* FAX *031/841–113. 18 rooms. Air-conditioning, IDD telephones, refrigerators, satellite TVs. AE, MC, V.*

$$ **Navy Guest House.** Very popular with Asian businessmen, this small hotel is busy by 7:30 AM. The more expensive the room, the larger the "living area" and the more layers of lacquer on the furniture. ✉ *27C Dien Bien Phu St.,* ☎ *031/823–713 or 031/823–714,* FAX *031/842–278. 60 rooms. Restaurant, café, air-conditioning, IDD telephones, satellite TVs. DC, MC, V.*

$ **Dien Bien Hotel.** Despite the wedding banquets that are occasionally thrown in its cheesy restaurant, there's little excitement at this hotel. Rooms are small and clean, and the English-speaking staff is more than happy to help with anything you may need. ✉ *67 Dien Bien Phu St.,* ☎ *031/842–264,* FAX *031/841–743. 20 rooms. Restaurant, air-conditioning, minibars, refrigerators, satellite TVs. MC, V.*

$ **Hoa Binh Hotel.** Function rules over form in this Soviet-era hotel across from the railway station. The restaurant serves Chinese food (☞ *above*). ✉ *108 Luong Khanh Thien St.,* ☎ *031/859–029,* FAX *031/846–907. 45 rooms. Restaurant. Air-conditioning, satellite TVs. MC, V.*

$ **Hotel du Commerce (Thuong Mai).** This creaky, aging hotel is run by Vietnam Tourism—nothing except the quirky French colonial exterior suggests otherwise. Most rooms have satellite TV. Rooms in front have nice views and arched hallways but let in too much street noise. Korean food is served in the restaurant (☞ *above*). ✉ *62 Dien Bien Phu St.,* ☎ *031/842–706,* FAX *031/842–560. 35 rooms. Restaurant, air-conditioning. MC, V.*

$ **Thang Nam Hotel.** Two things stand out at the otherwise nondescript Thang Nam: The staff is quiet, thoughtful, and know what you need before you do; and one of the only tennis courts in town is right out back. It's not free, but hotel guests get a discount. The hotel doesn't have IDD phones. ✉ *55 Dien Bien Phu St.,* ☎ *031/823–460,* FAX *031/841–019. 20 rooms. Air-conditioning, satellite TVs. No credit cards.*

Nightlife

If you've got a good set of lungs, you'll be the hit of Haiphong. Every block has its requisite half-dozen **karaoke clubs,** and many hotels are blessed with them as well.

Cola Disco (✉ 53 Lach Tray St., ☎ 031/844–910) is the biggest and silliest disco going in Haiphong; there is a 40,000d cover for men, less for women. **Do Son Casino** (✉ Zone 3, Do Son, ☎ 031/861–189) is close enough that you may want to make the trip (☞ Do Son, *below*). The **Saigon Café** (✉ 107 Dien Bien Phu St., ☎ 031/822–195) is Haiphong's version of the corner pub and is popular with locals, expatriates, and travelers.

Getting Around

BY BICYCLE

Seeing downtown Haiphong by bike is almost idyllic. Unfortunately there are few places to rent them. Try Dien Bien Phu Street or cross streets like Dinh Tien Hoang Street and Minh Khai Street. You could probably get a sturdy Chinese bicycle for the day for about a dollar. Ask at your hotel as a last resort.

BY CYCLO

Haiphong cyclos are often large enough for two Westerners. They're great during the calm of midday or later in the evening when the streets are empty; riding one in the hectic and slow evening rush hour is not advised. Cyclo riders will be happy to cart you around this flat city for an entire day for about 30,000d.

BY MOTORBIKE TAXI (XE OM)

If you're here without wheels and want to see some pagodas outside the city center, a lift on the back of a motorbike may be your best option—especially if you're pressed for time. Prices are comparable with cyclos. You'll arrive quicker than in a three-wheeler but probably more frazzled.

BY TAXI

You probably won't need to take a taxi except to get from the train station to your hotel or to the ferry landing. Taxi companies have figured this out, and plenty wait outside the Haiphong Railway Station and at the ferry landing. Try **Taxi 84 Company** (☎ 031/848–484) to arrange a ride by phone.

Do Son

❷ *21 km (13 mi) southeast of Haiphong, 124 km (77 mi) southeast of Hanoi.*

This rapidly overbuilt seaside resort was but a quaint fishing village just five years ago. Today the oceanfront is packed with dozens of hotels or what are soon to be hotels. Vietnamese, particularly Hanoians, flock to this resort in midsummer to escape the sweltering heat. Many come to soak up some sun, meander on the promenade, and feast on fresh seafood. Others come for what is euphemistically called "Thai massage," a growing industry in Do Son that has yet to be clamped down. And still others come to swim in the murky waters. The ocean here isn't so much polluted as it is discolored by river silt wash making its way down the coast from Haiphong. But it doesn't make for great beach bathing. Nevertheless, in June, July, and August rooms can be hard to come by. Nearly the entire town is booked up for one week in September during the buffalo fights (☞ *below*). By late autumn beachgoers have completely vacated the place.

The promontory that rises above the finger of land on which Do Son sits provides wonderful views of the fishing harbor on the inland side and of the village itself to the north. But the major presence atop the hillside is the **Do Son Casino** (✉ Zone 3, Do Son Town, ☎ 031/861–189), the only casino in a country where gambling is technically illegal. The way around this rule is to limit entry to only those with a foreign passport. Slot machines fill the first of two rooms. In the back hall, roulette, blackjack, baccarat, and *tai siiu* (big and small) are offered. There are few people playing; the staff usually outnumbers the guests. Apparently the developers had—and perhaps still have—high hopes for the place. At the edge of the lot a billboard advertises a future project: The Garden Resort & Hotel, planned for just below the casino on the water's edge, will have 350 rooms when completed.

The Vietnamese of Do Son are hardly left out of the gambling loop, however. Each year the village gears up for its famous **Do Son Buffalo Fighting Festival,** a semireligious festival honoring local patron saint Diem Tuoc Dai Vuong, also known as the Great Footprint King. The event takes place on the ninth day of the lunar month, usually in about mid-September. Legend has it that on that date in the 1400s, two old men sat playing chess on nearby Nghe Mountain while two buffalos fought below. One of the men turned out to be a saint who left his bird-like footprint on an altar tray, thus identifying himself as the Great Footprint King. This tale may not have much to do with buffalos, but it was enough to start a tradition that draws thousands of visitors to Hai Phong and Do Son to gamble on the fights.

Villagers spend months priming up the best buffalos, which in part means depriving them of sexual activity in order to increase their aggressiveness. On the day of the fight, the buffalos are led into the stadium in a procession with gongs and drums. After opening ceremonies the clash of titans begins. Two buffalos face off against each other, their masters releasing them so they can thunder toward each other from a distance of 650 ft. The fights last anywhere from 10 seconds (sometimes the hit from a first charge is deadly) to 15 minutes. This continues all day until only two bulls remain. The thousands of spectators place their own secret bets. Others are not so clandestine; entire villages, which come to see bulls groomed by their neighbors, may put communal bets of up to $10,000 on the line. After the final battle all the participating buffaloes are slaughtered for a victory feast, and the winner's head is paraded around the town.

Dining and Lodging

The fresh seafood in Do Son is superb. Most family restaurants lining the beach road in Zones 1 and 2 serve the day's fresh catch. The same cannot yet be said for the hotels, which for the most part serve mediocre food. Most of the hotels were built quickly in the mid-'90s to accommodate growing numbers of visitors.

$ ✕ **Tri Huong Restaurant.** Tri and his wife, Huong, run the best-placed restaurant in town, right at the northern edge of the promenade in Zone 1. A lively, almost crazed atmosphere exists in summer. Perversely, what would be the loveliest location for dining—a terrace that juts out into the sea—is actually the parking lot. The seafood is simple but tasty. ✉ *At the northern edge of the promenade in Zone 1,* ☎ *031/861–244. No credit cards.*

$$ 🏨 **Hai Au Hotel.** This uninspiring structure is where the Do Son Casino shuttles its patrons after an evening of vice (you can continue your evil ways at the hotel by taking advantage of free karaoke). Rooms are musty, and it's never a good sign when the porter looks down and scans the floor the moment he turns on the lights. One plus: It's only 150 yards from the beach. Breakfast is included in the room rate. ✉ *In Zone 2,* ☎ *031/861–272,* FAX *031/861–176. 54 rooms. Restaurant, air-conditioning, IDD phones, satellite TVs. AE, DC, MC, V.*

$ **Khu Biet Thu Garden Resort.** Across the street from the Hai Au is a five-villa complex that dates from the 1970s. The most recently remodeled building is nearest the ocean. Ask for one of the second-floor rooms facing the water. Huge trees, a volleyball court, and no in-room phones give it a pseudo-rustic feel. ✉ *In Zone 2,* ☎ *031/861–226,* FAX *031/861–186. 21 rooms. Air-conditioning. No credit cards.*

$ **Lam Nghiep (Forestry) Hotel.** Set back from the coast road, this large Vietnamese favorite will do in a pinch. Note the stuffed leopard (not indigenous, presumably) in the lobby. ✉ *In Zone 1,* ☎ *031/861–304,* FAX *031/861–105. 76 rooms. Air-conditioning. MC, V.*

Halong Bay

★ ❸ *160 km (99 mi) east of Hanoi, 55 km (34 mi) northeast of Haiphong.*

Halong Bay's 3,000 islands of dolomite and limestone cover a 1,500-square-km (579-square-mi) area extending across the Gulf of Tonkin nearly to the Chinese border. According to Chinese legend this breathtaking land- and seascape (similar to the Guilin area of China) was formed by a giant dragon that came barreling out of the mountains toward the ocean. Geologists are more likely to attribute the formations to sedimentary limestone that formed here between 300 and 500 million years ago, in the Paleozoic Era. Over millions of years water receded and exposed the limestone to winds, rain, and tidal erosion.

Today the limestone formations are exposed to hordes of tourists—but don't let that discourage you. Hundreds of fishing trawlers and tour boats share space on these crystal waters, yet there seems to be room for everyone. The eons of erosion have left countless nooks and crannies to explore: Secluded half-moon beaches at the base of steep untouched forest canopies and grottoes of all shapes and sizes—some well-trampled, others virtually unknown—are open jaws of stalactites and stalagmites. One of the largest and most visited is the **Grotto of the Wooden Stakes** (Hang Dau Go), claimed to be the 13th-century storage spot for the stakes that General Tran Hung Dao planted in the Bach Dang River in order to repel the invasion of Kublai Khan. This cavernous grotto has three distinct chambers and is reached by climbing 90 steps.

Most people use the main population center, **Halong City,** as a base from which to venture into the bay. Although it's now officially one municipality, Halong City was until 1996 two separate towns: Bai Chay is now Halong City West, where Halong Road winds its way around the coast and past the lifeless central beach; Hon Gai is the grimier Halong City East, where a coal transportation station dominates the center of town and covers nearby roads and buildings with a sooty film. Locals still refer to the towns by their old names. A five-minute ferry ride (500d per person, 7,000d per car) across the mouth of a large inlet links the two communities. Plans for a bridge have been tossed around, but construction has yet to begin.

If you think the mouth of this inlet is a busy place now, just wait a few years, when construction is likely to be going full speed ahead on massive Cai Lan, a deep-water port to be built inside Bai Chay Bay. Millions of tons of coal will be delivered on barges through the straits of Bai Chay to a nearby thermal-power plant. It all sounds like an environmental nightmare, and there has been discussion about UNESCO possibly revoking Halong Bay's status as a World Heritage Site.

Boat trips through Halong Bay are the main attraction. Little of the majesty of this region can be found in the city, so head out onto the water and start exploring. Ten- and 30-ft fishing boats have been converted by the dozen into Halong Bay's tourist-boat fleet. Hotels or travel agencies in Halong Bay or Hanoi (☞ The Northeast A to Z *below, and* Hanoi A to Z *in* Chapter 2) can arrange boat trips for you (often they are part of organized tours from Hanoi), or you can go down to the wharf and bargain yourself onto a boat for the day. Boats can be had for anywhere from $4 to $20 per hour; if you're going to be out on the bay all day, see if they'll knock 20% off the hourly rate. Unfortunately, if you are making arrangements yourself you may find it's not that simple. It seems an organized ring of boat masters does its best to guide you onto their boats of choice and charge you what they want—even if the creaky dinosaur looks like it's already seen its last three-hour tour. Self-sufficient travelers have fallen victim to the old bait-and-switch: They've arranged a next-day boat tour with local fishermen, only to be told in no uncertain terms the following morning that they could not board their chosen boat, but they could take a different one for quite a bit more money. You may have no choice in the end. Usually travel agencies, however, have their tried-and-true favorites.

Dining and Lodging

Few restaurants distinguish themselves in Halong. It seems that restaurateurs figure you're a captive audience, and they all basically serve up the same dishes: boiled or grilled shrimp, sweet-and-sour fish, and fried squid, washed down with beer. Crabs, sautéed beef with vegetables, and chicken dishes are also readily available. Halong Road and the center of town are crowded with these nondescript eateries.

Halong City West is where most visitors bed down for an evening or two. The city appears to have divided its buildings into two main camps: minihotels and karaoke bars. The larger hotels, some of which are listed below, are slightly less tacky than the average downtown minihotel, which can be had for $20 or less. Sleeping on a fishing boat in Halong Bay is au courant among today's adventure travelers. Tourist companies are hesitant to arrange such overnight accommodations, however, as past incidents with bandits and extortion-happy police have tainted the image of this destination. These days tour groups need permission from the local police; a "permit" runs anywhere from $50 to $100, more if you've got a large group.

$$$ ★ 🏨 **Halong I Hotel.** The grande dame of Halong properties, a French colonial-era restoration, is evocative of a more sublime era. Pull up on the circular gravel driveway and walk down arched open-air passageways toward the reception area. The front verandas are great for sipping tea and playing cards after dinner. Don't expect fawning service here, however; thankfully the whole place is quiet—except for the strains of karaoke wafting up from the roadside below. Book the Catherine Deneuve Room if you can. The quarters that the French über-star stayed in while filming *Indochine* is the priciest of them all, but it has an in-room fax and two toilets. ✉ *Halong Rd.,* ☎ *033/846–320,* FAX *033/846–318. 23 rooms. Restaurant, air-conditioning, IDD phones. AE, MC, V.*

$$$ 🏨 **Halong Bay Hotel.** Also known as Halong II, this modern hotel has more amenities than Halong I, but without all the charm and élan. An outdoor swimming pool and bar add a dash of comfort. ✉ *Halong Rd.,* ☎ *033/845–210,* FAX *033/846–856. 42 rooms. Bar, air-conditioning, IDD phones, satellite TVs, pool. MC, V.*

$$$ 🏨 **Halong Plaza Hotel.** Opened in 1997, this modern luxury hotel has a spacious front lobby with a glass-fronted entryway looking out onto the bay. Most of the rooms, too, have views of the bay, though some face the more industrial back side. They are fairly large and are decorated with standard but tasteful hotel furnishings. The staff aims to please, but they still don't always quite get it right. ✉ *8 Halong Rd.,* ☎ *033/845–810,* FAX *033/846–867. 200 rooms. 2 restaurants, bar, air-conditioning, IDD phones, in-room safes, minibars, satellite TVs, non-smoking rooms, pool, massage, exercise room, dance club, laundry service, business services, meeting rooms. AE, MC, V.*

$$$ **Heritage Halong.** This eight-floor glitzy international hotel soaks up much of the package-tour business in Halong Bay. Rooms are clean; those on the top floors in front have lovely views of the distant islands. ✉ *88 Halong Rd.,* ☎ *033/846–888,* FAX *033/846–999. 101 rooms. Café, restaurant, air-conditioning, IDD phones, satellite TVs, pool. AE, MC, V.*

$ **Vuon Dao Hotel.** Ask for one of the top-floor rooms with a view of the sea at this three-story hotel run by Halong Tourist Company, the state-run travel agency. Breakfast is included in the room rate. ✉ *Halong Rd.,* ☎ *033/846–427,* FAX *033/846–287. 77 rooms. Restaurant, air-conditioning, IDD phones, satellite TVs. MC, V.*

Cat Ba Island

❹ *At southern end of Halong Bay, 30 km (19 mi) east of Haiphong by boat.*

One of Halong Bay's most remarkable formations is Cat Ba Island, 354 square km (138 square mi) of wildly steep spines of mountains, narrow valleys and waterfalls, lush wetlands, golden beaches, and one of Vietnam's most beautiful national parks. The park was established in 1986 to protect about half of the island. The sea life in much of the surrounding inshore waters is also protected. Included in these ecosystems are tropical evergreen forests, 15 kinds of mammals (including wild boars and hedgehogs), 200 species of fish, 21 species of birds, and 640 species of plants.

In 1938 a French archaeologist found traces of an ancient fishing culture on the island dating from the end of the Neolithic Era. Human bones alleged to be 6,000 years old were also found. More recently, American bombers targeted the military and naval station here, causing numerous casualties and forcing hospitals to set up in nearby caves on the island to avoid the bombings. An ethnic Chinese community numbering about 10,000 settled on Cat Ba over the years, only to leave en masse in 1979 after Chinese troops invaded Vietnam in the brief but bloody border war of that year. The ethnic Chinese, or Hoa, sailed in dinghies to Hong Kong or other Asian ports, many dying along the way. Few ethnic Chinese have returned to Cat Ba.

Today the population of more than 12,000 continues to subsist on fishing and rice and fruit cultivation, but tourism is quickly becoming Cat Ba's new cash crop. The beaches, particularly the lovely curved stretch of sand just over the hillside from the southeast corner of the wharf, are infinitely nicer than Do Son's, and Vietnamese tourists have begun to take note of them. Walk off your seafood dinner by heading to the nearest beach, where you can sip iced coffee and watch the shooting stars. Splendid caves, just off the road to the national park, offer great opportunities for exploring.

Tour packages usually include minibus transportation to the national park, where a guide leads a hike through it, down to a nearby village in a lovely cove, and over to a bay where a boat is waiting to bring you back to town. This runs about $10 per person, with a seafood lunch included. Ask at your hotel; most can book this tour. Or you can head down to the wharf and arrange for a boat yourself—just make sure they know what you're asking, and you know what they're offering. Rates are not set in stone, so be sure to bargain.

Hiking through Cat Ba can be marvelous but strenuous: The mountain ridges are steep, trails are poorly marked, and roads are narrow, making blind crests somewhat dangerous. Talk to your hotel owner or one of the many local tour operators about the best hiking trails for your level. A hike through the park—through the tropical forest to a rocky peak overlooking much of the island—is best done with a guide.

A high-speed ferry has been added to the schedule of two slower ferries to and from Haiphong, cutting the travel time by two-thirds. In 1997 at least 10 minihotels sprouted in the town of Cat Ba, the island's main commercial center, in order to accommodate the growing numbers of tourists. They're all relatively clean and incredibly cheap. New bars blare Caribbean pop music and serve chilled margaritas. Just about any of the hotels can arrange for car or minibus tours of the island and rides to the national park. You can also get to the park on your own (rent a Soviet-era Minsk or take a motorbike taxi, if you're really adventurous) and hire a guide there. But it's much easier to go along on one of tours, where the park and guide fees are prepaid and a hike is mapped out. The park is a favorite spot for Vietnamese as well. Yet despite the park's protected status, many Vietnamese tourists—who seem to be able to scale the slippery rocks in stiletto heels—litter the trails with empty beer cans and junk-food wrappers.

Note that Cat Ba's crash course in tourism management is failing to address one major issue: the relentless pursuit of you, the tourist, by the local populace and its adverse effect on the sanity of visitors to the island. Being treated like a walking dollar sign is bad enough in Hanoi and Ho Chi Minh City; out here in paradise it's downright annoying. But until officials—or concerned hoteliers or restaurateurs—do something about it, motorbike taxi drivers, boat rowers, seafood sellers, second-rate tour guides, and minihotel hawkers will be in your face from the moment you step off the ferry.

Dining and Lodging

The sudden plethora of dining and lodging facilities in Cat Ba means one thing: cheap prices. The seafood here is simply prepared but incredibly fresh. Most restaurants and hotels are right in the middle of town and are easy to find. You may want to try one of the many new minihotels in town; they are all about the same. You'll be tempted to sleep with the room's big windows open to allow in the cool ocean breezes. Be careful, though—you could also allow in some uninvited guests.

¢ ✕ **Coca Cola Restaurant.** A huge soft-drink sign on the roof makes this tiki house on stilts hard to miss. Seafood is the specialty. ✉ *Le Thanh Tong St.,* ☎ *033/821–330. No credit cards.*

¢ ✕ **Restaurant Gaulois.** At this popular spot the proprietor will make special seafood dishes if the restaurant is not too busy and you ask nicely. ✉ *Le Thanh Tong St., no phone. No credit cards.*

¢ 🏨 **People's Committee Guest House.** On the southeastern tip of land at the end of the promenade (to the right as you face the town), this old French resort was converted into a state-run hotel long ago, and it feels like it. Avoid the rooms on the ground floor, as they don't have private bathrooms. ✉ *At the end of Le Thanh Tong St.,* ☎ *033/835–190. 47 rooms, most with private baths. No credit cards.*

Mong Cai and Tra Co

5 *193 mi (310 km) northeast of Hanoi, 128 km (80 mi) northeast of Halong City.*

The relatively subdued coastal province of Quang Ninh explodes in a flurry of trade and cross-border activity at Mong Cai (sometimes called Hai Ninh), a boomtown on the Chinese border that has literally risen from the ashes. There is little in this city that speaks of the Chinese invasion in 1979 that left Mong Cai a smoldering, mine-strewn wasteland. Today it's a dusty but bustling city of 50,000, whose population nearly doubles every day as Chinese cross the border to do business with their southern neighbors.

Much of the activity in town centers around the customs quay on the Ka Long River, where porters heave boxes and bulging sacks onto small wooden boats bound for China on the opposite bank. The boats return with goods destined for Hanoi and ports south. A footbridge linking Vietnam with the Chinese city of Dongxing opened in 1995. The Vietnamese border patrol has set up a checkpoint a few hundred yards south of the bridge. Chinese flash their identity cards and are waived into Vietnam, but the officials are reluctant to let Westerners past the guard station—even if it's just to look—without the appropriate exit permit or a valid visa into China. Vietnamese dong and Chinese renminbi are used interchangeably. Needless to say, Vietnam's antismuggling police units are very active here.

The main reason you would want to make the trip into these far reaches of Quang Ninh Province is to experience the loveliest beach in northern Vietnam. Nine kilometers (6 mi) east of Mong Cai, on an island separated from the mainland by a sea channel, is Tra Co, a tiny fishing village on a largely uninhabited 16-km (10-mi) stretch of golden sand. You could conceivably walk up the beach into China; a few military guardhouses face the South China Sea just north of the fishing village, but the military personnel are often snoozing in hammocks strung between the knobby evergreens that come down to the beach. During the day most of the village is deserted; the men are offshore fishing in their boats, and the women and children are hauling in the catch from lengthy nets strung up along the coastline.

If you spend the night in Tra Co, wake up before sunrise and walk down to the water's edge to watch the fishermen slip into their boats. On the main north–south road an older man with a regal bearing builds and repairs the wooden fishing boats used by the village. Farther up the road is a once-resplendent Catholic church. A tacky red-tin roof replaced the one bombed out by the Chinese in 1979. A few miles farther south is **Mui Ngoc,** an equally beautiful spit of a beach known locally as a smuggler's haven.

Dining and Lodging

Hotels are cheap and basic in Mong Cai; the ones listed below have rooms with private bathrooms. The seedy Tra Co Hotel is right on the sand, while a few other guest houses line the north–south road. Some family homes double as restaurants on this stretch of asphalt. Many restaurants serve authentic southern Chinese dishes as well as fresh seafood. In the breezy evenings young couples and friends gather by the roadside at the Mong Cai Bridge to have fruit shakes, sticky-rice ice cream, or coffee.

¢ 🏨 **Binh Minh Hotel.** Like most of the hotels in Mong Cai, this one is very basic. ✉ *Huu Nghi Rd.,* ☎ *033/881–185. 14 rooms. No credit cards.*

¢ **Dong A Hotel.** This no-frills place is one of the few hotels in town. ✉ *Hung Vuong Rd.,* ☎ *033/881–151. 18 rooms. No credit cards.*

Lang Son

❻ *150 km (93 mi) northeast of Hanoi.*

North of Hanoi and the Red River Delta, Highway 1 weaves and wends its way through narrow valleys and past jagged cliffs into the mountains of Lang Son Province. Vietnam's major north–south artery officially ends at the provincial capital of Lang Son, another booming trade outpost near the Chinese border. Like Mong Cai, Lang Son was nearly destroyed by retreating Chinese troops in 1979, but the town has quickly resurrected itself. Blinking neon lights advertise the central post office, new minihotels and trading companies abound, and Chinese can be heard in the markets.

Though there is little of beauty in Lang Son, the atmosphere is electric. Traders and smugglers convene in corner cafés and hammer out deals with everyone from local shop owners to border guards. Foot porters hustle down the dusty streets bound for rendezvous points farther south. Market stalls in the winding streets of central Lang Son are bursting with cheap Chinese goods, mostly plastic toys and appliances. Lang Son Province is home to many ethnic minorities, including the Nung and the Tay, who often come into town to load up on provisions.

Lang Son is the terminus for trains from Hanoi, except for two days per week, when the train continues into China and eventually on to Beijing. Nineteen kilometers (12 mi) north of Lang Son is the border village of Dong Dang, the site of the **Friendship Gate.** Despite the name, there were sporadic exchanges of gunfire here between Vietnam and China until 1992. Relations are far more friendly today, but smuggling is a major concern in this province (a vast network of foot trails makes monitoring border crossings extremely difficult), and the border guards here are serious and often surly. However, visiting the border at Friendship Gate is possible. You may have to leave your passport at the guardhouse on the Vietnamese side before you walk the few hundred yards to the border. Chinese and Vietnamese guards are separated by a 600-yard no-man's-land of sorts.

Numerous caves and grottoes a few miles from Lang Son are worth exploring. The most beautiful are in an area known as **Nhi Tam Thanh,** overlooking which is Waiting Woman Mountain. Legend says a woman waited here so long for her husband to return from battle that she turned to stone. A guard at the mouth of the caves can escort you through, or, if you want to go yourself, provide flashlights for a small fee.

About 30 km (19 mi) south of Lang Son on Highway 1, a spring—known locally as the **Pissing Cow Waterfall**—sputters out of the hillside. It is reached through a private garden and is a favorite spot for local children to play.

On the desolate plateau above Lang Son, southeast of the town on Route 4 heading toward Quang Ninh Province, is a **military cemetery.** The few hundred grave sites face ominously toward China and the ring of steep mountains to the north. The gates to the cemetery are usually locked, but the watchman will lead you up the 100 or so stairs to let you in.

The Northeast A to Z

Arriving and Departing

BY BUS

State-run public buses travel from Hanoi to Haiphong, Mong Cai, and other points in the area, but they are ancient, unsafe, and usually packed to the gills—basically, not worth your trouble. If you do choose to take the bus to Haiphong, it leaves Hanoi from Gia Lam Station when full, mostly in the early morning or late afternoon. Much more comfortable are private minibuses (though still not as comfortable as those run by travel agencies and tourist cafés in Hanoi), which leave from Bac Co Street in the old quarter, near the Royal Hotel. You can also hitch a ride on a minivan that shuttles tourists to and from Haiphong on their way to Cat Ba Island or Halong Bay. Reserve your seat at one of the many tourist cafés in Hanoi (☞ Hanoi A to Z *in* Chapter 2).

BY CAR

Hiring a car and driver from one of the many travel agencies and tourist cafés in Hanoi (☞ Hanoi A to Z *in* Chapter 2) or going with an organized tour on a minivan are the easiest ways to get around the northeast. This doesn't always mean that is the most pleasant, however, as many of the roads are in bad condition.

To get to Haiphong from Hanoi, for instance, you must take Highway 5, one of the most hectic stretches of road in the north. In addition to the traffic, the road is constantly under construction or expansion, and the divided highway often shrinks down to a single lane in each direction. A 16-km (10-mi) stretch just outside the Ford Motor Company manufacturing plant, which contributed to the road's upgrading, seems like the most comfortable road in Vietnam. But be prepared for a stressful ride during the other 86 km (54 mi). Riding to Haiphong by motorbike is not recommended. Renting an air-conditioned car for a day's drive to Haiphong and back to Hanoi will run from $50 to $70. Of note on your way are the half-dozen pagodas set back in the rice fields along Highway 5. Cars or minivans traveling on to Halong Bay from Haiphong must cross the Cam River by ferry at Binh Station (Ben Binh), at the north end of Cu Chinh Lan Street. Access is easiest from Ben Binh Street, one block east. Ferries leave every 10 or 15 minutes. Passenger tickets cost 5,000d, more for cars.

Halong Bay is a four-hour drive from Hanoi. There are two routes, but your driver will most likely head east on Highway 5. Halfway to Haiphong, just before the city of Hai Duong, he'll turn left onto Highway 18. Much of this road is new or repaved and feels like the Autobahn compared to the rest of the country's roads. Renting an air-conditioned car with driver from Hanoi costs between $112 and $150 for a two-day, one-night trip to Halong, including all car and driver expenses. A travel agency such as Vietnam Tourist may charge more. If it's not the weekend or if it's in the dead of winter, bargain hard—you can usually get a better deal.

Hiring a car is really the only way to get to Mong Cai. To get there from Halong Bay, take the highway east from Halong City. The road winds up the coast 40 km (25 mi) to Cam Pha, a dingy coal-mining town. Beyond Cam Pha the road traverses gorgeous valleys and provides some majestic ocean views. About 60 km (37 mi) beyond Cam Pha, the road to Mong Cai turns to the right in the quiet trading post of Tien Yen. It's another 97 km (60 mi) or so to Mong Cai.

Lang Son is a relatively painless four or so hours from Hanoi. Road improvements on Highway 1 allow for easy access by car, though a four-wheel-drive vehicle is necessary if you're going beyond Lang Son, such as on a longer loop into Cao Bang Province (☞ The Far North, *below*) or east to Quang Ninh Province.

BY FERRY

There is no boat service from Hanoi to Haiphong, but ferries from Haiphong to other destinations abound. Five boats leave the Haiphong port for Halong each day. Four of them (the 6 AM, 11 AM, 1:30 PM, and 4 PM) dock in Halong East, and only one (the 9 AM) goes to Halong West. If you land on the east side, you'll want to catch the ferry across the inlet. The companies serving Halong East and Halong West are different, but they both charge 45,000d, and both trips take four hours.

The only way in and out of Cat Ba Island is by boat, unless you're a guest of the Vietnamese military. There is ferry service from Halong City to Cat Ba, but the more common route is from Haiphong. Three ferries leave Haiphong's Binh Station (Ben Binh) for Cat Ba town every day. The standard ferries leave at 6:30 and 1:30 and arrive in Cat Ba three hours later, after a brief stopover in Cat Hai. The fare is 55,000d. Beware, however: Do not take the 11 AM ferry! It stops at Cat Hai and does not continue on to Cat Ba town; you'll be stuck at Cat Hai until the 1:30 ferry arrives a few hours later. There is now a high-speed jet boat, the **Limbang Express passenger ship** (✉ Binh Station Ferry Landing, Haiphong, ☏ 031/838–311 in Haiphong, or ☏ 04/851–2918 in Hanoi), which makes one trip per day from Haiphong to Cat Ba. It leaves at 9 AM, takes an hour, and costs 85,000d. The Cat Ba–Haiphong return trip is at 3 PM every day. If you're coming from Hanoi, you could take the 6 AM train to Haiphong, catch a cyclo or taxi from the train station to the ferry landing, and take the 9 AM express to Cat Ba. This has become a popular alternative to the slow boats, so you'll need a reservation. The Limbang Express is often overbooked, and some passengers holding tickets for the one air-conditioned cabin are shifted back to the engine room.

BY HELICOPTER

If you want to be the first on your block to say you've flown in a Russian helicopter and lived to tell the tale, see Halong Bay in style on the MI70, the 20-seat chopper owned by state-run Northern Service Flight Company. The Hanoi–Halong Bay trip takes 50 minutes, and you get 10 minutes of bliss circling the emerald waters before the pilot touches down and ushers you onto a boat that cruises the bay. Seats on the bird run $175 each—with $20 extra for the boat, food, and an English-speaking guide. Departure is 7:15 AM Saturday from Hanoi; you'll be back in Hanoi by tea time—or rent the helicopter outright for $3,500, boat trip included. Inquire at the Metropole/Hotel Sofitel in Hanoi (☞ Lodging *in* Chapter 2) about reservations.

BY ORGANIZED TOUR

A number of travel agencies and tourist cafés in Hanoi (☞ Hanoi A to Z *in* Chapter 2) organize trips to various points in the region. This is one of the best—and by far the easiest—ways to see the area.

BY PLANE

Vietnam Airlines (☞ Hanoi A to Z *in* Chapter 2) flies to Haiphong from Ho Chi Minh City at least once a day. On Monday, Wednesday, Friday, and Sunday, there are two flights a day. Danang–Haiphong flights are twice a day on Monday, Wednesday, and Friday and once a day on other days. Nha Trang–Haiphong flights are once a day on Monday, Wednesday, and Saturday. At press time, there was no air service to Haiphong from Hanoi.

BY TRAIN

Four trains per day (from 6 AM to early evening) leave Hanoi bound for Haiphong from one of two stations: Hanoi Railway Station and Long Bien Station. Tickets for all trains can be purchased at the Hanoi Railway Station, but you must ask at the ticket booth if your train leaves from there or from Long Bien Station. There is only one fare: 45,000d. The unspectacular trip takes just over two hours. There are two stations in Haiphong. The first, **Thuong Li Railway Station**, is west of the city. You want to detrain at the **Haiphong Railway Station** (☏ 031/846–433), which is the end of the line on the Hanoi route. In the Reception Room for Tourists, the attendant can book ferry tickets, explain the schedules to Cat Ba and Halong Bay and train times back to Hanoi, and even recommend a hotel or restaurant. There's also a left-luggage service.

One train per day departs from Hanoi for Lang Son. The picturesque ride takes six hours and costs 67,000d one-way. Two trains per week continue on to the Dong Dang border crossing and then into China. It's likely that you'll have to change trains in Pinxiang, 20 minutes north of the border, and then again in Nanning, the capital of China's Guangxi Province. To take advantage of this, you must have the appropriate exit permit, your Vietnam visa, and a visa to China.

Getting Around

Most likely you will be traveling around this area with an organized tour or with your own car and driver. Getting from place to place in this region by other means is not easy.

BY FERRY

☞ Arriving and Departing by Ferry, *above*.

BY MINIBUS

Air-conditioned minibuses travel from Haiphong to Halong Bay. These line up at the Binh Car and Bus Station (Ben O To Binh), which is just on the north side of the Cua Cam River in Haiphong. The ferry from the Haiphong port to the north bank is 5,000d and runs every 10 or 15 minutes. The minibuses cost about 55,000d per person and leave when full (and they can get very full). Ask the ticket seller about minibuses back to Hanoi from Halong Bay, if that's where you're headed.

Contacts and Resources

CURRENCY EXCHANGE

Money can be exchanged at most hotels in larger towns in the area. If you're going to smaller towns, however, it's a good idea to exchange money before you go.

In Haiphong, **Vietcom Bank** (✉ 11 Hoang Dieu St., ☏ 031/842–658) is a full-service branch of the state bank that can exchange your dollars into dong, cash traveler's checks, and allow cash withdrawals on credit cards. **Asia Commercial Bank** (✉ 69 Dien Bien Phu St., Haiphong, ☏ 031/823–389) has similar services to Vietcombank except it doesn't cash traveler's checks. **VID Public Bank** (✉ 56 Dien Bien Phu St., Haiphong, ☏ 031/823–999) is another option.

EMERGENCIES

There are no medical facilities of international standard in the region. In case of a major medical emergency, try to get to Hanoi or Saigon as quickly as possible. For immediate attention in Haiphong, try the **Vietnam-Czech Friendship Hospital** (Benh Vien Viet-Thiep), on Nha Thuong Street, or the **Traditional Medicine Hospital** (Benh Vien Dong Y), on Nguyen Duc Canh Street.

POST OFFICE

Stamps can be bought at most hotels. In Haiphong, the brightly-painted main **Post Office** (✉ at the corner of Nguyen Tri Phuong St. and Dinh Tien Hoang St.) has international-access phones, mail, and fax services.

GUIDED TOURS

The easiest way to see northeast Vietnam is to arrange trips at a travel agency or tourist café in Hanoi (☞ Hanoi A to Z *in* Chapter 2). The trips generally include transport in a tour bus or minivan, accommodation (double occupancy; standard depends on price of tour), and an English-speaking guide. Tours to Halong Bay usually include a five-hour (or longer) boat trip and lunch on the boat. Tour packages to Cat Ba Island often include minibus transportation to the national park, where a guide leads a hike through the park, down to a nearby village in a lovely cove, and over to a bay where a boat is waiting to bring you back to town.

TRAVEL AGENCIES

See Hanoi A to Z *in* Chapter 2 for information about travel agencies and tourist cafés in Hanoi.

In Haiphong, **Vietnam Tourism Haiphong** (✉ 57 Dien Bien Phu St., Haiphong, ☎ 031/829–052) can get you a local English-speaking guide, hire a car, find you a hotel room, and arrange trips to Halong Bay, Cat Ba Island, and other points. **Haiphong Toserco** (✉ 40 Tran Quang Khai St., ☎ 031/841–415) provides services similar to Vietnam Tourism.

In Halong Bay, there are two main agencies: **Halong Tourist Company** (✉ 1 Halong Rd., ☎ 033/846–272, FAX 033/845–176) and **Quang Ninh Tourism Company** (✉ 7 Halong Rd., ☎ 033/846–350 or ☎ 033/846–320). They're both government-owned, and though they have experience setting up boat trips in the bay, and guiding package tours to the hotels owned by their companies, they're not experts at dealing with actual people. Don't be surprised if you're bounced around from one person to another if you call them; the man who usually answers the phone can be gruff. They can also provide an English-speaking guide for $15 per hour; call ahead.

THE FAR NORTH

Ethnic minority villages and natural splendor abound in Vietnam's northernmost region. Cao Bang Province is home to the Dao and Tay groups; Ha Giang Province, the country's farthest north, is populated by the H'mong, the small but distinct group called the Bo Y, and the even smaller Pu Peo group. The terrain in this northernmost area is rugged, and it is one of Vietnam's poorest regions. In the remote districts near the Chinese border the illiteracy rate surpasses 90%. The rocky, inhospitable mountains leave little room for rice cultivation. Corn and fruit are more common crops here, and honey production is on the rise. Although Ha Giang Province is extremely beautiful, there are still hardly any facilities for tourists. But if you're an adventurous traveler who delights in finding your own way—even if it means hitching a ride on an oxcart for eight hours—then Vietnam's far north is for you.

The provincial capital of Cao Bang is linked to Lang Son, 120 km (75 mi) to the east, by windy and rutted Highway 4. The road, which essentially follows the Chinese border from the coast westward, was the site of numerous skirmishes in the late 1940s between French colonial troops and Vietminh guerrilla forces. The French tried to maintain garrisons at Lang Son and Cao Bang, but by 1950 the Vietnamese had ousted them from the area.

Ba Be Lakes

7 *240 km (150 mi) north of Hanoi.*

Idyllic Ba Be Lakes, in newly expanded Bac Can Province, is home to one of Vietnam's oldest national parks. The lake environs are beautiful and peaceful; monkeys can even occasionally be heard as you float down the lake in a wooden longboat. It's quite possible you'll find no other visitors here, which leaves you to explore the breathtaking mountains and caves, El Capitan–like limestone cliffs, gurgling streams, and rushing waterfalls all on your own.

The 9-km (6-mi) fjordlike lake is too big to explore in its entirety in one day, but you can see as much of it as possible if you start out early in the morning, before the mist has burned off, on a motorized wooden longboat (which you can rent). Foreign visitors are rare (for now), so the boatman may see dollar signs in his eyes. But you should be able to hire a boat for about 30,000d per hour. Pack a lunch and have the boatman head to the waterfall (*thac nuoc*), a lovely spot for a picnic. Toward the far end of the lake (a good three hours by boat) is the remarkable Hang Puong Cave, where the Nam Nang River has carved a 300-ft grotto out of the hillside. Bats and swallows swoop through the darkness. At the far end of the lake are villages of the Thai ethnic minority, which could conceivably host visitors, although accommodations would be *very* rustic. Otherwise try the state-owned guest house.

Lodging

¢ ✕ **Ba Be Guest House.** This state-owned guest house beneath forested hills near the water's edge used to be the only game in town. Now there is also a hotel. If you stay here, you can choose between accommodations in one of the eight brick houses or in one of the eight stilt houses with attached bathrooms. ✉ *Ask for directions in town,* ☎ *0281/876–127. No credit cards.*

¢ ✕ **Ba Be Hotel.** About 30 minutes away from Ba Be Lakes in Ba Be townlet is this hotel, where cheery manager Nguyen Quynh will set you up with a clean room with a private bathroom. ✉ *In Ba Be town,* ☎ *0281/876–115. No credit cards.*

Tan Trao

8 *130 km (81 mi) north of Hanoi.*

The region's isolated mountains and once-lush jungles provided Ho Chi Minh and his forces with sufficient cover from the French and Japanese. In early 1945 Ho Chi Minh set up headquarters for the Communist Party in the remote village of Tan Trao, high in the mountains west of Thai Nguyen town. Tan Trao was also the birthplace in 1945 of what became known as the August Revolution, when General Vo Nguyen Giap led Vietminh troops eastward to attack a garrison occupied by the Japanese at Thai Nguyen. General Giap's attack inspired similar uprisings throughout the country. Nine years later he would lead the Vietminh to glory at Dien Bien Phu (☞ The Northwest, *below*).

Currently no organized tours visit Tan Trao. But if you do make it here, there are a few sights to see: a museum dedicated to Ho Chi Minh, a giant banyan tree where General Giap rallied his troops, Ho Chi Minh's simple jungle hut (*nha lua*), and the Tay minority communal house (*dinh*) where the first National Congress met. If you have hired a Jeep or car to Ba Be Lakes (☞ *above*), have a day to spare, and don't mind bedding down in an amenityless guest house, consider an excursion to Tan Trao. But be sure to ask ahead about road conditions; the road west from Thai Nguyen can wash out during heavy rains.

The Far North A to Z

Arriving and Departing

BY CAR OR FOUR-WHEEL-DRIVE VEHICLE

The drive from Hanoi to Ba Be Lakes takes you past green-tea plantations, stunning mountain vistas, and ethnic minority stilt houses. The road was repaved in 1997, so a four-wheel-drive vehicle is no longer needed—unless you are planning to see more off-the-beaten-path areas such as Tan Trao. You should be able to hire a car and driver from travel agencies in Hanoi—including two nights' lodging for the driver—for about $180 (☞ Hanoi A to Z *in* Chapter 2).

BY TOURIST CAFÉ TOUR

A number of Hanoi tourist cafés have tours of north-central Vietnam, with Ba Be Lakes as the centerpiece. **Lonely Planet Café** (☞ Hanoi A to Z *in* Chapter 2) has a four-day, three-night tour for about $45 per person, with a four-person minimum. A Landcruiser costs about $60 a person, with a four-person minimum. The route is generally as follows: Day 1, Hanoi to Lang Son; Day 2, Lang Son to Cao Bang; Day 3, Cao Bang to Ba Be Lakes; Day 4, return to Hanoi. The driver knows to stop at a variety of sites, including waterfalls and caves, ethnic minority villages, and local markets. **Queen Café** (☞ Hanoi A to Z *in* Chapter 2) has a five-day, four-night tour following a route similar to the Lonely Planet Café tour, except it includes an extra day in Ba Be Lakes. The price of $60 includes a "normal" driver; it's $65 with an "experienced" one. The distinction doesn't exactly instill confidence, but the café has a good reputation.

THE NORTHWEST

Vietnam's staggering beauty and ethnic diversity are perhaps most evident in the northwest, where the imposing highlands are inhabited by dozens of ethnic minority groups as well as the Kinh, the ethnic nationality of the majority. Physically and culturally removed from Hanoi, many communities in the remote far west have lived as they have for generations, harvesting terraced rice fields or practicing slash-and-burn agriculture on the rocky hillsides. Babbling mountain streams wind their way through deep, extended valleys.

Many of these streams join up with the Song Da, the once-rushing Da River that has been tamed by Hoa Binh Dam, Vietnam's first hydroelectric power project, about 74 km (46 mi) southwest of Hanoi. Here in the shadow of this Soviet-built hydroelectric marvel, some farmers still live without electricity. The winding, hilly roads beyond Hoa Binh offer panoramic views. Dusty crossroads towns like Man Duc leave little to smile about, but there are exquisite nearby caves and brick homes built right into the limestone rock at the base of towering cliffs. Make sure your driver stops at the picturesque first view of Mai Chau. Here the valley spreads out before you in its remarkable greenness and the tap-tap-tapping of carpentry signals the building frenzy currently enveloping the district.

Rising majestically above the region is Mt. Fansipan, Vietnam's tallest peak. In its shadow lies the sleepy hill town of Sapa, the tourist mecca of the northwest, where Dao and H'mong women converge at the local market to buy, sell, and trade.

The northwest is very conducive to adventurous four-wheel-drive tours. The Hanoi–Mai Chau–Son La–Dien Bien Phu–Lai Chau–Sapa–Hanoi loop is the most interesting of all, and it's the one followed by most tour operators. It's equally popular with small groups that have rented Jeeps or Landcruisers on their own and want a multiple-day excursion. If you're comfortable with the thought of a four- to seven-day Jeep trek, you'll want to spent plenty of time here. If not, there are still some wonderful options for you to consider. Idyllic Mai Chau is only 4–5 hours by car from Hanoi; you could push off early one morning and be back the next evening. Sapa is accessible by a fairly comfortable overnight train ride from Hanoi; you may wish to head there for a weekend to see various ethnic minority groups. Or if you would prefer to fly, Vietnam Airlines has five flights per week to Dien Bien Phu, the only northwestern town reachable by air.

The towns and sites below are listed in the order you'd reach them if you took the above-mentioned Jeep trek clockwise through the northwest.

Mai Chau

❾ *170 km (106 mi) southwest of Hanoi, south of Hwy. 6., in Hoa Binh Province.*

The Brigadoon of Vietnam, Mai Chau is nestled in a serene valley that has been called one of the most beautiful spots in the country. Like the fictitious town that rises every 100 years, Mai Chau appears out of the mist as if in a dream. The town itself is inhabited mainly by the majority Kinh Vietnamese. White Thai villages dot the paddy-rich valley, however, and this is where you're likely to spend most of your time.

The White (and later the Black) Thai migrated to Vietnam from what is now Thailand about 2,000 years ago. Today they incorporate elements of both cultures. The Mai Chau valley is home to a number of Thai villages whose hospitality is genuine and memorable. If you are staying overnight in a stilt house, expect your host family to offer you a roll-up mattress and mosquito net, unlimited use of a tobacco bong (*thuoc lao*), and giant vats of rice wine.

On Sunday the Mai Chau market teems with villagers selling everything from hand-carved opium pipes to flayed pigs. Except for some women, most villagers have given up wearing traditional garb. Although many villagers still farm, tourism and panning for gold have become the most lucrative industries. A tourist alley of sorts has sprung up in the village, accessible from the dirt road just beyond the large guest house (☞ Lodging, *below*). The de facto mayor of the Thai villages lives on this road, and his house is frequented by visitors and villagers. Baskets, old crossbows, and lovely weavings are laid out on tables in front of the stilt houses. Many other silk scarves and textiles hang from the windows. And they're all for sale.

Buy some bottled water in town before heading out on a long hike through the green (or golden, depending on when you go) rice fields and into the nearby hills. Countless footpaths head off into the mountains from the main valley routes and are used by Montagnards (usually women) who gather wood for cooking fires or for construction. Their baskets are usually extremely heavy, and it takes more than brute strength and simple coordination to balance more than 200 pounds, using only shoulder straps or a head brace.

The mountainsides have been so largely denuded of their primary forest cover, forcing the villagers to hike more than a day to reach the larger trees needed for building stilt houses. The White Thai villagers here are very friendly and will often invite you into their homes to watch TV together or to share some homemade rice wine or even lunch.

Lodging

¢ **Mai Chau Guest House.** Just beyond the center of town is this large and unfortunate-looking guest house. Each of the nine rooms is as sterile as the next; ask for one with a private bathroom. Though the place tries to create some atmosphere by hanging fabrics made by ethnic minorities (for sale, of course) throughout the lobby, it feels forced. ✉ *Ask for directions in town,* ☎ *018/851–812. 9 rooms, some with bath. No credit cards.*

¢ ★ **White Thai Villages.** Many people prefer to stay in one of the White Thai villages behind the guest house, where any of 60 households will put you up. Immaculately clean and surprisingly airy and comfortable, the traditional Thai longhouse sits on stilts about 7 ft up—and not a single nail is used in the construction. The split-bamboo floor is soft, smooth, and springy under foot. The going rate is 50,000d per person per night. Your hosts would accept less, but a hefty portion of the money goes to district coffers. ✉ *Ask for directions in village. No phone. No credit cards.*

En Route Northwest of Mai Chau in southern Son La Province, the road rises to a sheltered plateau. As the road sweeps downward, you'll see one of the few remaining primary forests in northern Vietnam. The old trees are huge, a sign of how the entire northern highlands once looked when tigers, leopards, and elephants reigned. This forest stretches for only a few miles, but the drive through is spectacular. Farther up Highway 6 are the rolling tea plantations and steep escarpments of the Moc Chau district in Son La Province. This area is famed for its tea as well as for the productive dairy industry, supported in part by UN assistance. But locals, oddly, don't seem to ever enjoy the two together. Beyond Moc Chau the road sweeps down vast valleys and past Black Thai villages, through the town of Yen Chau and eventually to the town of Son La.

Son La

10 *320 km (199 mi) west of Hanoi on Hwy. 6, 160 km (100 mi) northwest of Mai Chau.*

Son La is a convenient overnight stop on the journey to Dien Bien Phu. Even if you're not bedding down in Son La, take some time to explore the immediate environs. Many hill tribes reside in the area, which until 1980 was considered part of the Tay Bac Autonomous Region. The Tay Bac's support of the French during the French Indochina War led to repressive government measures against them.

For a commanding view of the town and the surrounding area, climb the stone steps to the lookout tower known as **Cot V3.** Just outside the town you can visit a former **French penal colony,** destroyed by American bombers but partially rebuilt. Or if you're feeling like soaking your tired bones for a while, have your driver or a motorbike taxi take you to the **hot springs** a few miles south of the main road. West of town are the small but intriguing **Tam Ta Toong Caves.** And 6 km (4 mi) southeast of Son La is the **Forestry Research Center,** which runs an animal-breeding program and studies deforestation and habitat loss. Son La is an ideal place to conduct such research; the province is one of the most deforested regions of the country, with over 90% of its primary forests already destroyed.

Dining and Lodging

¢ ✕ **Thit De Restaurant.** Goat meat—*thit de*—is the local delicacy here, so why not try some goat kebabs or *tiet canh,* goat's-blood curd soup if you're a really an adventurous eater? One of the better spots to enjoy such a culinary experience is this restaurant. ✉ *Dien Bien Rd.,* ☎ *022/852–394. No credit cards.*

$ **Hoa Ban Hotel.** More than a dozen minihotels are found in Son La, but one of the nicest is the Hoa Ban Hotel. Unfortunately, the staff can be unhelpful at times. ✉ *Hoa Ban Rd.,* ☎ *022/852–395. 23 rooms. No credit cards.*

¢ **Phong Lan Hotel.** Although more basic than the Hoa Ban Hotel, the people working at this place are friendlier. ✉ *Chu Van Thinh Rd., Chuong Le District,* ☎ *022/853–516. No credit cards.*

Dien Bien Phu

⓫ *470 km (292 mi) west of Hanoi, 150 km (93 mi) west of Son La, 16 km (10 mi) from Laos.*

The dream of reestablishing colonial rule throughout Indochina turned into an all-too-vivid nightmare for the French at Dien Bien Phu. History has documented General Vo Nguyen Giap's stunning victory over Colonel Christian de Castries and his 13,000 French and Vietnamese troops (as well as Foreign Legion volunteers) as one of the greatest military achievements of the modern era: a surprise 57-day siege culminating in the surrender of the French garrison on May 7, 1954. The Vietminh army had been on the offensive for much of 1953, and General Henri Navarre, commander of French forces in Indochina, was intent on regaining the initiative throughout the region by building up a series of bases from which his troops could mount offensive action. One of these bases, in the far northwest of Vietnam near the Laotian border, had been overrun by the Vietminh in 1952, but Navarre had ordered its recapture (the French took it back in 1953). The ethnic Thai minority called this centuries-old trading post on the Burma–China–Vietnam road Muong Thanh; the Vietnamese named it Dien Bien Phu.

Such a remote garrison ringed by inhospitable mountains would make it unlikely, thought the French, that General Giap would infiltrate the valley with ground troops. The French clearly controlled the skies and used two landing strips in the valley to shuttle in supplies, reinforcements, and batteries of howitzers and other field guns. But by late 1953 Giap had encircled the French garrison with 50,000 men and had accomplished a feat of near-impossible logistics: dragging into offensive position dozens of 105-millimeter artillery cannon and antiaircraft guns up steep and densely forested slopes, all under the nose of French surveillance planes and scout missions.

The surprise assault began on March 13. Two weeks later the airstrips were within Vietminh artillery range, forcing the French to turn to parachute drops for resupplying the base and cutting off the base from vital troop reinforcements. While the French were waiting, the Vietminh were digging. An elaborate tunnel system crisscrossed the valley and gave Giap's soldiers the necessary element of surprise over the French. The French solicited assistance from their longtime allies the Americans and the British, but to no avail. The defenders were steadily dwindling, and the injured began piling up in the French underground hospital. Morale collapsed, and on May 7, after a series of attacks by the Vietminh, the white flag was raised over the command bunker.

Coincidentally, the next day an international conference (whose initial purpose one month earlier was the completion of a peace treaty for the Korean conflict) opened in Geneva. The result was a declaration temporarily partitioning Vietnam along the 17th parallel and calling for elections in 1956 (they were never held). Tellingly, the agreement was never signed, partly because of the refusal by the United States to actively participate because of the presence of the Communist Chinese at the convention.

Today's Dien Bien Phu (population 14,000), in the immense Muong Thanh Valley, serves as the remote capital of the Dien Bien district and since 1993, the capital of westernmost Lai Chau Province. The shift in provincial power anticipated the erection of a second massive hydro project on the Da River, which will leave the former provincial seat of Lai Chau, 110 km (68 mi) north of Dien Bien Phu, at the bottom of an 800-ft deep reservoir. But Lai Chau is no stranger to water woes. Deforestation in the surrounding ring of mountains has caused catastrophic flooding of the Da River. This means major new construction in Dien Bien, a district whose primary attraction for tourists is history. The gaudiest example of these new buildings is the ostentatiously ornate provincial party headquarters.

The informative **Dien Bien Phu Museum** has been built on the site of the battle with the French. There is a section dedicated to the region's ethnic minority communities, but French ignominy and Vietnamese glory are the main topics here. The main hall recounts the events of the siege and the battle itself, with blinking maps and legends synchronized with a recorded loop outlining the battle's chronology. Outside is a collection of weapons used in and around the garrison: the Vietnamese tanks and guns look as if they were polished yesterday afternoon; the rusting French Jeeps are riddled with bullet holes, and the remains of a French plane lie in a twisted heap. (English-language guides are available.)

The **command bunker** of Colonel de Castries has been recreated, in walking distance of the museum, this time with makeshift sandbags filled with concrete. Overhead is a far-too-shiny reproduction of the corrugated roof from which a lone Vietminh soldier waved a victory flag—the image became Vietnam's enduring symbol of victory over colonial oppression.

Across the street from the museum is a **memorial cemetery,** the final resting place for many unknown Vietminh soldiers (there were about 25,000 Vietminh casualties). Here in bas reliefs are scenes of the battle depicted in near life-size socialist realism.

Some of the battle's most intense combat took place at nearby Hill A1, a position labeled **Eliane** by the French. A monument to Vietminh troops now stands here.

Lodging

More minihotels are opening in Dien Bien Phu; ask at travel agencies in Hanoi for the most up-to-date information (☞ Hanoi A to Z *in* Chapter 2).

¢ **Hotel Phuong Huyen.** Rooms at this minihotel close to the airport are clean, and the service is friendly. There are no phones in the rooms, but there is IDD service from reception. ✉ *8 Cau Moi St.,* ☎ *023/824–460. 8 rooms. No credit cards.*

Sapa

12 *35 km (22 mi) south of Lao Cai, 170 km (105 mi) northeast of Dien Bien Phu, 350 km (217 mi) northwest of Hanoi.*

Ringed by Vietnam's tallest peaks, Sapa is an enchanting hill-tribe village that has become the de facto tourist capital of the far northwest. Sapa is part of the northwestern province of Lao Cai, which means "town of sand," and is a 90-minute drive from the provincial capital. A pilgrimage to Sapa offers a glimpse of some of the country's most breathtaking mountain scenery as well as its ethnic minority cultures. The hill tribes cultivate rice and ginger and hunt wild game by traditional methods; they continue as they always have to worship the soul of rice, their ancestors, and the spirits of earth, wind, fire, rivers, and mountains. To see them in their traditional style of dress—layers of indigo-dyed, brilliantly embroidered cotton, elaborate headdresses, and silver adornments—is to feel yourself caught in a time warp.

The French dubbed the area around Sapa the Tonkinese Alps. In 1922 colonial authorities displaced the minority residents and began building villas for themselves in the town, turning it into a kind of health resort and a retreat from the oppressive heat of Hanoi as well as having it serve a nearby ore mine. Between the end of French colonial rule in 1954 and national reunification 21 years later, the North Vietnamese government made weak attempts to grant the ethnic minorities political representation and the same constitutional rights as the majority Kinh population—provided they took up the struggle against the U.S.-backed Saigon regime. Since 1975 the government has pursued "integration" programs in which the state provides limited education and health care for free. At the core of these programs were and are settlement and resettlement strategies. Since the late 1980s Sapa has been one of the regions where the government is encouraging relocation.

The protection of Sapa's cultural diversity and the environment seems to have little place on the state agenda, however. It appears that tourism may corrupt the integrity of the local populace and upset the area's fragile ecology. Some of the minority groups practice slash-and-burn agriculture, and along with the depredations of two centuries of outside interests, this has already reduced the virgin forest to a mere 12-square-km (4½-square-mi) area. Further destruction would be tragic, considering the area's remarkable natural gifts.

The local population is made up of the H'mong, the Dao, the Tay, the Giay, the Muong, the Thai, the Hoa (ethnic Chinese), and the Xa Pho, and is divided into 18 local communes with populations of between 970 and 4,500 inhabitants. These hill tribes, known as Montagnards by the French, convene every Saturday in Sapa to exchange everything from staples and handicrafts to live snakes. Be sure to plan your trip to Sapa so that it coincides with this colorful weekend market.

The town of Sapa is charming, but economic development has already put a strain on the small but growing community. Before 1954 there were 248 luxury villas throughout town and in the surrounding hillsides. The vast majority of these buildings have disappeared—they were either destroyed by invading Chinese troops during the 1979 border war (fires spread to the surrounding mountains, wreaking environmental havoc) or by the wrecking balls that are making way for new minihotels, marketplaces, a roller rink, and an international-style hotel sprouting up or in the final stages of completion. The lovely stone church has been spared, however, and services are still held here on Sunday morning and on Christian holidays.

The center of town is a street below the muddy soccer field, but here ★ you'll find the pulse of the community. The **Sapa Market** convenes on Saturday on the slippery stone stairway that crosses this narrow, bitumen-flecked street. A drab but roomy new marketplace-on-stilts has recently been completed, and plans are afoot to move this congregation indoors—which will be a shame. H'mong and Red Dao women come into town with the rising sun. Most walk in from surrounding villages, while a few catch rides on the back of motorcycles. They are often dressed in their finest traditional garb: richly embroidered vests and dresses, aqua-and-black cotton shirts, finely detailed silver necklaces and bracelets, and elaborate headdresses that tinkle with every movement. These women are well aware of Westerners' fondness for ethnic minority wares and are eager to sell to you. Many have picked up a few French and English words or phrases. Part of the fun is bargaining with them, but don't express too much initial interest, or you may be labeled a sucker. Hold out for as long as you can, then ask to see the good stuff. Invariably an elderly Dao woman will understand what you're looking for, dig deep into her bamboo basket, and produce fabric of quality superior to what she'd been showing you only moments before.

Sapa is part of the **Nui Hoang Lien Nature Reserve,** a mountainous 7,400-acre landscape covered by temperate and subtemperate forests. The reserve provides a habitat for 56 species of mammals—including tigers, leopards, monkeys, and bears—17 of which (the Asiatic black bear, for example) are considered endangered. An impressive 150 species of birds, including the red-vented barbet and the collared finch bill, can be found only in these mountains. Among the area's geological resources are minerals from sediments deposited in the Mesozoic and Paleozoic periods. From the Muong Hoa River to the peak of Mt. Fansipan, the eastern boundary of the reserve is formed by a ridge of marble and calcium carbonate. Also found in this region is kaolinite, or China clay, used in the making of porcelain.

Guided walking tours of the nature reserve are recommended and are easily arranged through hotels and guest houses in town. Pick up a very helpful copy of *Sapa,* which has detailed but somewhat crude maps outlining treks to nearby minority villages. Minsk or Jeep drivers will be happy to take you down the rutted road from Sapa past the Auberge Hotel (☞ Dining and Lodging, *below*) for a full day of hiking, swimming in waterfall pools, and visiting H'mong and Thai villages. Hoteliers can also make arrangements for you.

A **30-minute hike** from the center of town to the radio tower above Sapa gives you a spectacular panoramic view. Climb the stone steps from the main road. Next to the Ham Rong Hotel is a guard house where you may or may not have to pay 5,000d to hike to the top; it depends on the watchman's mood. The steps lead up past well-manicured gardens and through rocky fields. A path breaks off to the right and winds around boulders to the tower. The town of Sapa is laid out below, and across the valley is Mt. Fansipan.

Hiking **Mt. Fansipan,** Southeast Asia's tallest peak at 10,372 ft, requires little technical expertise. What it does take is three or four days, as you must depart from Sapa and hike *down* into the valley, then back up the other side. Bring your own tent and sleeping bag; there currently is no place to rent camping or mountaineering equipment. You'll also want an experienced guide to help you navigate the wet, chilly mountainside and suggest the best route and places to camp. If you're serious about hiking Mt. Fansipan, ask for more details at the Auberge Hotel or the Green Bamboo Hotel. It can get very cold in Sapa and ever colder on the mountain, so you need to dress accordingly (☞ When to Tour the North, *above*).

Dining and Lodging

Although it may seem like two-thirds of Sapa's buildings are hotels, clearly compromising the town's rugged charm, the result is a wider range of options. You can find rooms here for as little as 45,000d per night, although you may want to opt for something a bit more upscale. Note, however, that even most of the dirt-cheap minihotels have private bathrooms with hot water.

$ ✕ **Fansipan Restaurant.** This large restaurant (for Sapa, that is), 100 yards up the main road from the Auberge Hotel (☞ *below*), is a favorite meeting place for travelers. Expect quite a bit of attention from ethnic minority vendors. Simple but filling food is served: stir-fried vegetables, noodle soups, and pork and fish dishes. All other restaurants lining the main road are equally mediocre—at least this one has some atmosphere. ✉ *On the main road, no phone. No credit cards.*

¢ ★ ✕ **Auberge Hotel.** A Hanoi transplant, owner Dang Trung has the best thing going in Sapa: a lovely, popular hotel with exquisite views of the mountains. Rooms, particularly on the third floor, are cozy and clean, and have functioning fireplaces. In the restaurant, feast on standard Vietnamese fare—and excellent spring rolls—while soaking up rays out on the terrace. There's plenty of indoor seating as well. Mr. Trung and his son can help with all sorts of travel information. Competition for these rooms is fierce, so reservations are a must. One major fault: Mr. Trung can't say "no," so overbooking is a serious problem. He rarely leaves anyone in the lurch, though you may find yourself with a room in an Auberge annex or in another minihotel altogether. ✉ *On main road,* ☎ *020/871–243,* FAX *020/871–282. 12 rooms. Restaurant, laundry service, travel services, car rental. No credit cards.*

$$ **Hotel Victoria Sapa.** This international hotel is scheduled to open in early 1998. A French-designed pleasure palace on a hilltop overlooking town, it will have all the amenities, including a pricey restaurant and bar, room service, and plush rooms with bathtubs. No contact details were available at press time (Winter 1997), but ask for information at one of Hanoi's many travel agencies. ✉ *Overlooking town, no phone at press time. 81 rooms. Bar, restaurant, air-conditioning, room service. AE, MC, V.*

¢ **Cau May Hotel.** Overpriced but quiet, this out-of-the-way sleeper is a good place to find some solitude. Nothing but fruit orchards and mountains appear out the front windows. Note that power cuts, like in most other hotels here, can be a problem. As you drive into town from Lao Cai, take a right as soon as you reach the end of the soccer field. Turn left after 100 yards, the hotel is on the right. ✉ *Ask for directions in town,* ☎ *020/871–293. 8 rooms. No credit cards.*

¢ **The Green Bamboo.** Run by the Green Bamboo Café in Hanoi, this mountainside accommodation sprung up almost overnight and already has taken much of the pressure off the Auberge. The small, rather sunny rooms are decked out with televisions, new but simple furniture, and private bathrooms. If you're looking for a quiet getaway, stay elsewhere on the weekends. The Green Bamboo sends its backpacker tour groups here, and the bar downstairs is popular. The hotel is 100 yards past the Auberge on the main road. Reservations, which are suggested, can be made at the Green Bamboo Café in Hanoi (✉ 42 Nha Chung St., ☎ 04/826–8752). ✉ *On the main road,* ☎ *020/871–214,* FAX *020/871–411. 13 rooms. Bar, café, satellite TVs, laundry services, travel services. No credit cards.*

¢ **Ham Rong Hotel.** This imposing, faux chateaux-style hotel is in a large compound 100 yards above the town church. There are two main buildings with clean double rooms that have televisions and decent bathrooms. Concrete is a recurring theme in the hotel's gardens. You'll need earplugs to block out the blare of the town's nearby loudspeaker, which doesn't get going until 7:30 AM or so. ✉ *100 yards above the church,* ☎ *020/871–251,* FAX *020/871–303. 31 rooms. Restaurant, air-conditioning, travel services. No credit cards.*

Bac Ha

13 *100 km (62 mi) northeast from Sapa, 350 km (217 mi) northwest of Hanoi.*

Northeast of Sapa is Bac Ha, a small town built on a desolate highland plain northeast of Lao Cai. The main reason for venturing here is the century-old Sunday-morning market, one of the largest in the northwest. Ethnic minority villagers such as the Dao and the Flower H'mong (related to the H'mong but wearing brighter and more elaborate clothing) come from miles around to buy, sell, and trade everything from horses and dogs to medicinal herbs and beautiful handmade tapestries. Tourists are definitely in the background at this market; you will be tolerated and respected, but rarely approached by sellers. One thankful deviation from this function-over-form mentality is the lovely, high-pitched songs performed by Flower H'mong singers. If the market manager hasn't been able to arrange singers for that day, he plays a cassette of their songs over the public address system. The market gets going at about 9 AM, but early birds can be seen setting up their stalls and sipping *pho* (noodle soup) for breakfast as the sun comes up. A 3- to 6-km (2- to 4-mi) walk up the road past the Sao Mai Hotel (turn left at the fork) brings you to some ethnic minority villages that will be more than happy to see you.

Many minihotels in Sapa (☞ *above*) arrange day trips to Bac Ha, which leave at about 6 AM. The going rate is $10 per person in a Russian Jeep. The road is bumpy, and the trip takes three hours each way. If you're heading back to Hanoi, you may want to travel to Bac Ha on a Sunday morning and then get dropped off at the Lao Cai train station in the afternoon so that you can take the train that evening (☞ The Northwest A to Z, *below*).

Dining and Lodging

¢ ✕ **Cong Fu Restaurant.** This hole-in-the-wall does a brisk business with lunching tourists. Very basic Vietnamese fare is served: pho, and noodle, meat, and chicken dishes. Service can be painfully slow—simple orders like a cold beer sometimes take more than five minutes to arrive. ✉ *Just off main road, about 200 yards from entrance to market, no phone. No credit cards.*

¢ **Sao Mai Hotel.** If you're staying the night in Bac Ha, the Sao Mai is the ritziest accommodation in town—compared to local homes, that is—which isn't saying much. ✉ *On same road as market but on other side of highway,* ☎ *020/880–288. No credit cards.*

The Northwest A to Z

Arriving and Departing

BY CAR OR FOUR-WHEEL-DRIVE VEHICLE

A sedan is a perfectly viable way to get around much of the northwest if you're traveling in the dry season. Cars, however, are not recommended for the remote and difficult stretches of road; you will need a Jeep or four-wheel-drive vehicle to get you through the trouble spots. You can rent cars in dozens of spots in Hanoi (☞ Hanoi A to Z *in* Chapter 2), and you'll be able to book a two-day, one-night car trip to Sapa for about $80, all driver's expenses included. A longer excursion in a four-wheel drive vehicle is more expensive: The going rate for the popular six-day, five-night excursion through the northwest (Hanoi to Mai Chau to Son La to Dien Bien Phu to Sapa to Hanoi) in a Russian Jeep is $300. A Toyota Landcruiser can be rented for between $590 from the Green Bamboo Café in Hanoi and $830 from Vidotour (☞ Hanoi A to Z *in* Chapter 2) in Hanoi for the same tour. The price is a bit steep, but the more modern four-wheel-drive vehicles are safer and nicer.

The trip to Mai Chau from Hanoi can be treacherous in the rain, especially beyond Hoa Binh city, where the road rises into the steep mountains and sharp curves give way to long cliff drop-offs. However, the condition of the road is decent enough to manage without a four-wheel-drive vehicle. If you're on a motorbike, pay extra attention on the mountain roads: The trucks that run this route are notoriously stingy when it comes to giving adequate room to two-wheelers.

Set aside at least five days to visit Dien Bien Phu from Hanoi: two days traveling each way and one full day to see what you came for—although the remarkable scenery makes the trip as interesting as the history of the place. If you're coming from Mai Chau and Son La, the natural next step is to continue clockwise: through Lai Chau, on to Sapa, and then back to Hanoi. The Dien Bien Phu–Sapa road is in worse condition than the Hanoi–Dien Bien Phu road, so a high-clearance four-wheel-drive vehicle is necessary. The journey from Dien Bien Phu to Sapa is a hard day's trip on narrow, rutted roads through beautiful scenery. This round-trip route adds a day or two to your journey but is much more interesting than following the same route back and forth. If saving time is your goal, take the plane instead.

The 35-km (22-mi) stretch of road from Sapa to the border town of Lao Cai, to the north, is in better condition than the Dien Bien Phu–Sapa route. You may prefer to go directly to Sapa, bypassing Dien Bien Phu, Son La, and Mai Chau, and heading up and down Highway 2 and Route 70.

BY MOTORBIKE

The Hanoi–Dien Bien Phu–Sapa route is only for adventurous motorcyclists. You'll need a 150-cc engine or larger, and you should have some knowledge of engine mechanics, though locals are adept at fixing ailing Russian Minsks. Also, be prepared to get wet in mud puddles. At some larger washout spots, however, enterprising locals set up ferry services on small boats for motorcycles. These roads are very remote, and adequate emergency care is virtually nonexistent. Wear a helmet, take a sheet of important words and phrases (such as the Vietnamese expressions for "My clutch is broken"), and go with someone else. You'll need high clearance and maneuverability, however, so doubling up on bikes is not recommended.

BY MOUNTAIN BIKE

If you've got the legs, lungs, and equipment, mountain biking is a formidable but fantastic way to experience the steep mountain ranges of Hoa Binh Province. Most people who do the Mai Chau route find alternate transportation to the provincial capital of Hoa Binh, such as an early morning public bus. From there it's about 100 km (62 mi) up and down two major sets of mountains. Hardy bikers reach Mai Chau by evening, exhausted. Slower riders spend the night in a home in one of many roadside villages.

BY PLANE

Dien Bien Phu is the only town in the northwest accessible by commercial jet. There is a 10:30 AM **Vietnam Airlines** (☞ Hanoi A to Z *in* Chapter 2) flight Monday–Tuesday and Thursday–Saturday from Hanoi. The one-way fare is $53. Note that at press time the airport at Dien Bien Phu had no X-ray machines, and all bags were being inspected by hand—and not necessarily in front of you. If you don't want someone rifling through your things without your being there, lock your bags so that the inspector will need you to open your bags and will then do an inspection in your presence.

Consider flying to Dien Bien Phu and returning to Hanoi via some form of ground transportation, either down Highway 6 or up to Sapa and down Route 70 and Highway 2. Talk with one of the travel agencies or tourist cafés in Hanoi to see if they have contacts in Dien Bien Phu who could book you a one-way trip back to the capital. They may insist, however, that you pay for the mileage for the driver's return to Dien Bien Phu.

BY TRAIN

If you don't want to lose a whole day driving to Sapa, take the overnight train from Hanoi to Lao Cai, a dreary border town of 30,000 people that was leveled when the Chinese stormed it in 1979. The most comfortable trip to Lao Cai is on Friday night, when you get a soft sleeper in a four-person compartment on the "luxury" train. The one-way ticket costs about $20. The train leaves the Hanoi railway station at 8:15 PM and takes 11 hours. Currently tickets *cannot* be purchased more than two days in advance (in order to prevent agents from selling them at inflated rates). So get to the Hanoi railway station by Thursday morning to be assured of getting on the Friday-night train.

Don't lose your ticket after boarding the train. You need to present it to the station guards in Lao Cai when arriving at the station and again when departing the station upon returning to Hanoi. You can purchase your return ticket in Sapa (and check train and bus schedules) at the small post office next to Phan Xi Pan Hotel. Unfortunately, the night train from Lao Cai back to Hanoi doesn't have soft sleepers, and the hard sleepers ($17) are basically straw mats on a slab of wood. There are six in one compartment, and the top bunks are cheapest.

Minibuses waiting at the Lao Cai train station can take you the 35 km (22 mi) to Sapa for 25,000d. The buses leave when full and usually drop you off in front of the Auberge Hotel. From Sapa buses return to the Lao Cai train station twice daily, at 6:30 AM and 2 PM, but you can join with other travelers and share a bus or Jeep that will leave at the time you want. If you'd like to combine a one-way train to Sapa with a return to Hanoi by Jeep or car, you can arrange that in Sapa at the Auberge Hotel.

BY TRAVEL AGENCY OR TOURIST CAFÉ TOUR

Most travel agencies and tourist cafés in Hanoi (☞ Hanoi A to Z *in* Chapter 2) organize two kinds of trips to the northwest: an overnight to Mai Chau, and a six-day, five-night excursion loop by Jeep (☞ By Car or Four-Wheel-Drive Vehicle, *above*). On the very popular Mai Chau tour, you travel either on a 12-seat minibus or in a 30-seat tour bus, and you generally stay at the White Thai village behind the guest house. This tour costs about $20 per person, lodging included. The six-day loop tour, which is also popular, costs about $80 per person, with a minimum of four people. That makes it pretty crowded in a Russian Jeep. Lodging is not included on this tour, but you don't have to find it yourself. The driver does that for you; you just need to pay for it.

Contacts and Resources

Car and Motorbike Rental

Cars with drivers can be hired from travel agencies and tourist cafés in Hanoi. For more information, *see* Hanoi A to Z *in* Chapter 2.

Currency Exchange

It's best to exchange money in Hanoi before your trip; however, if you need to, you can usually exchange money (generally cash, not traveler's checks) at your hotel.

Emergencies

In case of medical emergency, try to get to the larger towns in the region. If you are really ill, get to Hanoi as quickly as possible.

Guided Tours

Guided tours of the region can be arranged through travel agencies and tourist cafés in Hanoi. For more information *see* Hanoi A to Z *in* Chapter 2.

Precautions

Make sure you hire a good driver who you can trust, as roads can be bad. Don't drink tap water or eat raw vegetables, and make sure meat is well cooked. Bring the right clothing; it gets chilly in the mountains—even in spring and autumn—and downright cold in winter.

4 The Central Coast

Hue, Hoi An, Danang

In Hue, explore the endless, grandiose tombs of emperors and the partially destroyed Imperial Enclosure, and absorb the almost eerie quiet of the long-gone ruling families' weighty presence. In perfectly preserved Hoi An, see how ordinary Vietnamese traders and fishermen lived in centuries past. In Danang learn about the history and culture of the Cham people. Then take a trip to famous China Beach and to the temple-caves of the Marble Mountains.

By Sherrie Nachman

EXTENDING 108 KM (67 MI) along the emerald-colored South China Sea from the former Imperial City of Hue (pronounced "hway") south to the town of Hoi An is Vietnam's scenic central coast. Here you will find the sandy Lang Co and China beaches, the dramatic peaks of the Truoung Son Mountains, and the cave temples of the Marble Mountains. Along National Highway 1—which, like all roads in Vietnam, is in rough shape—are numerous unnamed small towns consisting of clusters of homes. Families dry their rice in their front yards only inches from the road. But the highlights of the region are Hue and Hoi An, two of Vietnam's most interesting cities. Although Hanoi and Ho Chi Minh City may give you a taste of contemporary Vietnam and its recent history, Hue and Hoi An put you in a seemingly mythical Vietnam of centuries past.

Once the capital of Vietnam and home to its emperors, Hue is now largely in ruins, the consequence of both French attacks in the late 19th century and American bombings during the Vietnam War. Nonetheless, the Imperial City, as Hue is known, continues to evoke the grandeur of its royal past. In contrast, the tiny city of Hoi An, originally a Chinese trading village on the sea, is incredibly well-preserved. Families live in 200-year-old homes—amazing landmarks incorporating architectural elements from traditional Chinese, Vietnamese, and Japanese styles, reflecting those who populated Hoi An over the centuries.

The third major city in this region is Danang, which may be familiar to you as an important U.S. Air Force base during the Vietnam War. Today, it is a port town that offers little in the way of sights except for the fabulous museum of Cham culture. The ancient Kingdom of Champa existed from the 2nd to the 18th centuries around present-day Danang, Nha Trang, and Phan Rang (☞ Chapter 5), though its power was significantly weakened by the Viet and the Khmer in the 15th century. The city's other attribute is that it has the region's largest airport, which makes it a convenient starting point for Hue (which itself has a small airport), Hoi An, and other points of interest in the region.

In between Danang and Hoi An are the Marble Mountains, where there are temples built in the caves, and China Beach, made famous by the television show of the same name. As you drive between Hue and Danang on National Highway 1, be sure to stop at Lang Co Beach and the dramatic Hai Van Pass, which runs across the Truong Son Mountain range and overlooks the South China Sea below. (Unfortunately, the mountains' natural beauty is slightly spoiled by the hordes of postcard vendors who try to sell you packets of coconut cookies and chewing gum.)

Pleasures and Pastimes

Art and Architecture

Because this area served as the seat of the Kingdom of Champa from the 2nd to the 18th centuries, it has the greatest concentration of Cham art and architecture in the country. Savor the glories of Champa at the excellent Cham Museum in Danang. Soak in the history of Vietnam's emperors while exploring the grand remnants of the Imperial City and the magnificent Imperial Tombs. Get a feel for 17th- and 18th-century Vietnamese life in Hoi An, where the well-preserved houses and pagodas have hardly changed in the last 200 years. Hoi An's streets are also lined with art galleries, small shops selling all kinds of artifacts, and small cafés.

Dining

Along the central coast you can find outstanding regional cuisine. Hoi An's specialties include White Roses, a delicious and beautiful shrimp dumpling that resembles a rose (if you squint a little). Imperial Hue's cuisine, distinguished by the elegant radial symmetry of its presentation, is said to be the most sophisticated in Vietnam. One specialty of Hue is *banh khoai,* a rice pancake filled with shrimp and pork and topped with sprouts, fresh mint, and spicy star fruit. Be sure to also try the peanut dipping sauce that accompanies this dish. Another popular regional dish, served in both Hue and Hoi An, is *bun bo Hue,* a dish of rice noodles and broth topped with pork, beef, and pork rinds. There aren't many formal restaurants in this area, but there are plenty of small, pleasant family-run places with truly outstanding food. Imagine the Vietnamese version of a really good diner—nothing fancy, but decent portions of good, cheap food.

Almost all hotels and "real" restaurants post costs in dollars and accept both dollars and dong. Roadside cafés and smaller restaurants post prices in dong, but they also accept dollars. Almost no establishment in this region accepts credit cards or traveler's checks.

Lodging

You won't find any place close to a five-star, luxury hotel in this region. But there are many clean, comfortable accommodations, including some with tennis courts or swimming pools. Most have private bathrooms, unless otherwise noted. Hotel choices, especially in Hue, are numerous, and new minihotels are popping up every year in Hue and Hoi An. Almost all hotels post costs in dollars and accept either dollars or dong. Very few hotels in this region accept credit cards or traveler's checks.

Outdoor Activities

The entire region is excellent for bicycling and motorcycling, because the traffic hysteria that reigns in Ho Chi Minh City does not exist here. There aren't many cars in Hoi An and there are very few in Hue, although Danang is much more of a city with the concomitant traffic. The beaches in Hoi An, like everything about the town, are exceedingly pleasant places to relax in or to use as departure points for boat trips to the surrounding islands. Close to Danang is the famous China Beach, which is pleasant but doesn't quite live up to its acclaimed glory from the eponymous television program.

Exploring the Central Coast

It's relatively easy to travel around the fascinating and culturally rich central coast region. Hue and Hoi An are only about three hours from each other by car; Hoi An is about one hour south of Danang, and Hue is about two hours north. The best plan is probably to fly into Danang, travel to Hoi An, and leave from Hue. Trips to the Marble Mountains and China Beach usually originate or end in Danang or Hoi An.

Numbers in the text correspond to numbers in the margin and on the Central Coast, Hue, Danang, and Hoi An maps.

Great Itineraries

IF YOU HAVE 3 DAYS

Fly from Hanoi, Ho Chi Minh City, or Nha Trang to Danang, but bypass the city itself. Instead head straight for **Hoi An** ⑱–㉜, and spend a day to a day and a half seeing the city. Have dinner overlooking the river at Café des Amis, and stay in the Hoi An Hotel, the city's largest and friendliest. From Hoi An it is a quick three-hour drive to **Hue** ①–⑭; spend your remaining time exploring the Imperial City and the tombs and pagodas that line the banks of the Perfume River.

IF YOU HAVE 5 DAYS

Spend one day in **Danang** ⑮ exploring the treasures of the Cham Museum. That same day head out to the **Marble Mountains** ⑯ and return to Danang to spend a night at the Marco Polo Hotel. Spend part of your second day at nearby **China Beach** ⑰. On the afternoon of your second day, go on to **Hoi An** ⑱–㉜ for a day and a half. See its treasures at a leisurely pace, but be sure to take an afternoon to visit the nearby Cham and Cam Kim islands. You'll probably have time to have a shirt, dress, pants, or just about anything else you desire made in the silk shops that line the market; any clothing item can be made in less than 24 hours. Spend your last two days in **Hue** ①–⑭.

When to Tour the Central Coast

Unfortunately, the central coast is plagued by Vietnam's worst and most unpredictable weather. Rain can strike at any moment, especially in Hue. The official rainy season begins in November and ends in March, so the best time to go is from April to October (though it still may be rainy or overcast). Like the rest of the country, the area comes alive during Tet, the celebration of the lunar new year, which takes place in January or February.

HUE

Bisected by the Perfume River and 13 km (8 mi) inland from the South China Sea in the foothills of the Annimite Mountains (Truong Son Mountains), Hue—pronounced "Hway"—stands as a reminder of Vietnam's imperial past. The seat of 13 Nguyen dynasty emperors between 1802 and 1945, Hue was once Vietnam's splendid Imperial City. Although it was devastated by the French in the 19th century and again by the Americans in the 20th, the monument-speckled former capital has a war-ravaged beauty. One can still imagine its former splendor, despite gaping holes in its silhouette.

As early as the 2nd century BC, Hue was home to rulers: it was the seat of command for the Chinese Han army and was called Tay Quyen. By the 2nd century AD, Hue was captured by local chieftains, who renamed it K'ui Sou. Between the 10th and 14th centuries, the Cham and the Vietnamese fought over control of the city. By the 15th century, the Vietnamese had successfully captured the city from the Cham and renamed it Phu Xuan. In 1558 the city became the capital of a region ruled by Lord Nguyen Hoang, which established control of South Vietnam by the Nguyen lords. (During this time, two warring factions—the Nguyen lords, who controlled South Vietnam, and the Trinh lords, who controlled North Vietnam—were fighting for control of the whole country.)

With the Tay Son rebellion in the 18th-century, the Nguyen lords were temporarily defeated. Led by the sons of a wealthy merchant, the Tay Son rebels were acting on a general sentiment of discontent with both Nguyen and Trinh rule. The Tay Son emperor, Quang Trung, was installed in Hue from 1786 to 1802, until the ousted Lord Nguyen Anh returned, with French backing. At the same time, Nguyen Anh captured Hanoi from the Tay Son rebels, who had defeated the Trinh and the Chinese-backed Ly Dynasty based in the northern capital. In 1802, Nguyen Anh anointed himself Emperor Gia Long and made Hue the capital of a newly united Vietnam. Twelve Nguyen dynasty emperors followed him to the throne until 1945, and their impressive tombs, Imperial City, and pagodas are reminders of the important role the city once played.

It was under Emperor Gia Long's rule that the city's architectural identity was established—and the prospect of French colonial rule in Vietnam initiated. With guidance, ironically, from the French architect

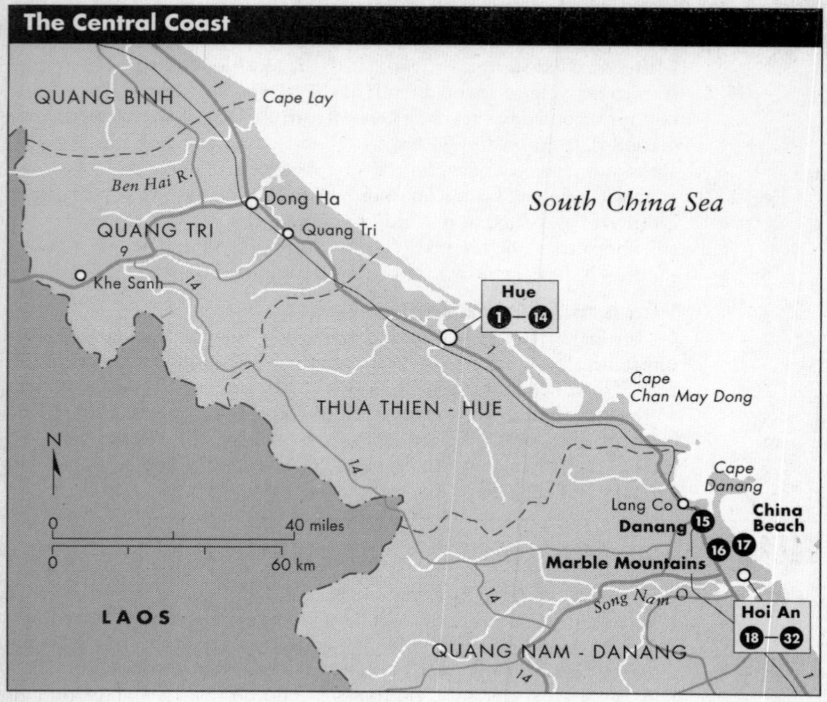

Olivier de Puymanel, Gia Long designed and built the city's surrounding fortress in the style of the Forbidden City in Beijing. The result is a fairly modern structure that looks centuries old. Enclosed within the thick walls of the Chinese-style citadel is the Imperial City (Hoang Thanh), where all matters of state took place and which was off limits to all but mandarins and royal family. Within the Imperial City was the Forbidden Purple City (Tu Cam Thanh), where the emperor and his family lived; very little of it remains today.

In the 1830s, voices of dissent arose against the French presence in Vietnam. The French responded by attacking Hue in 1833 (they had been looking for an excuse to assert their claims to the country in exchange for assisting Gia Long to the throne) and making the country—particularly, Tonkin and Annam—into a protectorate. During this time, a Western-style city was established across the river from the citadel to accommodate the French forces; some of these old French colonial buildings are still standing. In 1885, after repeated disagreements between the French and the emperors of Hue, the French pillaged the Royal Court, burned the Royal Library, and replaced Emperor Ham Nghi with the more docile Emperor Dong Khanh.

It was the Tet Offensive of 1968, however, that really destroyed large parts of the Imperial City. During one of the fiercest battles of the Vietnam War, the North Vietnamese army occupied the city for 25 days, flying its flag in defiance and massacring thousands of supposed South Vietnamese sympathizers. The South Vietnamese and the Americans moved in to recapture the city with a massive land and air attack and in doing so further destroyed many of Hue's architectural landmarks. Overall, more than 10,000 people died in the fighting, many of them civilians.

Though much of the Imperial City was reduced to rubble, many sections still exist and Hue's main draw continues to be the remnants of its glorious past. Today tourists keep the city thriving. There are many hotels and numerous cyclo drivers who can give you a tour of the Imperial City for only 50,000d. On top of it all, Hue is known for its outstanding cuisine.

Exploring Hue

Hue itself is quite small, and you can easily get around the Imperial City on foot. Within walking distance, too, are the local market and the Imperial Museum. To visit the sprawling tombs and pagodas on the outskirts of Hue, you will need to hire a car and driver—or a motorbike if you're more adventurous. Several of the tombs and pagodas, most notably Minh Mang Tomb and Thien Mu Pagoda, sit along the banks of the Perfume River and can be reached by boat. Don't feel obligated, however, to take one of those slow-moving boat trips up the Perfume River—you may find the scenery far from spectacular and the pace very slow.

The Citadel

A GOOD WALK

Most likely you will be staying on the east bank of the Perfume River, so it is best to begin your walk at the Phu Xuan Bridge and Le Loi Street. Over the bridge, a little to the right is the **Central Market** ①. Head west toward **The Citadel** ② and cross the bridge over the river. Once you have reached the west bank, turn left and make your first right. Continue west toward the citadel, circled by a moat and ramparts. Cross the moat and pass through the Ngan Gate (Cua Ngan). Along the entrance to the Imperial City, on your left, is the 122-ft **Flag Tower** ③. After entering through the Ngan Gate, you will see four of the Nine Holy Cannons on your right. These bronze cannons depict the four seasons; the other five depict the Chinese elements—water, soil, wood, metal, and fire. Make your way along 23 Thang 8 Street (it's not a specific address) and take a left, then an immediate right into the entrance of the **Imperial City** ④.

The Imperial City, once a large royal complex, is now mostly in ruins. Enter through the Noontime, or Royal, Gate (Cua Ngo Mon) and take an immediate left toward the **Nine Dynastic Urns** ⑤, which symbolize the formidable Nguyen dynasty. Head back toward the entrance to the Imperial City and turn left across the Golden Water Bridge (Trung Dao Bridge), once used only by the emperor. Straight ahead is one of the few still-intact structures in the Imperial City: the intricately decorated **Palace of Supreme Harmony** ⑥.

Exit the palace through the back of the gift shop. On either side of the path leading to the entrance of the **Forbidden Purple City** ⑦ are the Halls of the Mandarins, where mandarins (court officials) dressed in special attire before paying homage to the emperor. Through the courtyard in front of the halls, you can see the vast empty expanse on the threshold of the Forbidden Purple city—a result of the Tet offensive. To your right, the Royal Theater or Festival Hall is largely intact. Behind it is the intimate and partially restored **Royal Library** ⑧.

Heading east from the Royal Theater, exit the Imperial Enclosure through the beautiful and ornate Eastern Gate (Hung Khan Mon). Make a right on Doan Thi Diem Street and then take the first left on Le Truc Street to get to the **Imperial Museum** ⑨. In a beautifully preserved building that was formerly part of the palace, the museum houses a fine collection of imperial objects. Across the street are the unimpressive Military Museum

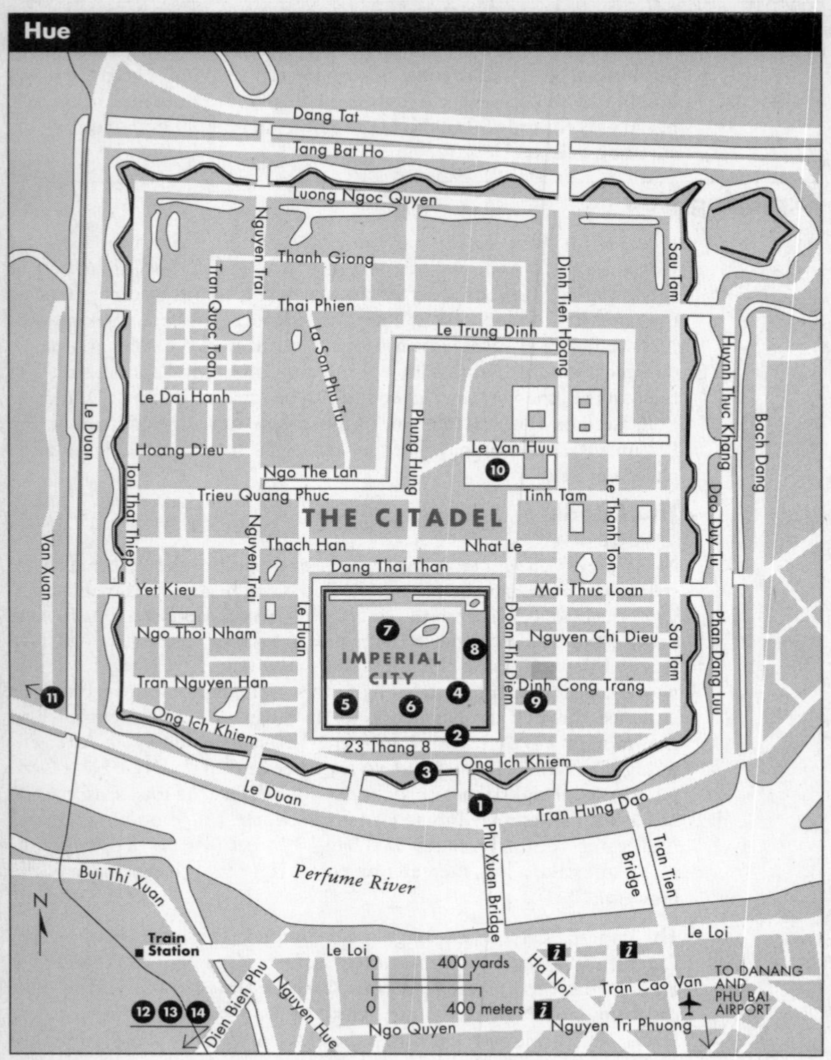

Central Market, **1**
The Citadel, **2**
Flag Tower, **3**
Forbidden Purple City, **7**
Imperial City, **4**
Imperial Museum, **9**
Nine Dynastic Urns, **5**
Palace of Supreme Harmony, **6**
Royal Library, **8**
Thien Mu Pagoda, **11**
Tinh Tam Lake, **10**
Tomb of Khai Dinh, **14**
Tomb of Minh Mang, **13**
Tomb of Tu Duc, **12**

and Hue's Archaeological Center, once a kind of prep school for male members of the royal court and now closed to the public.

Make a left out of the Imperial Museum and then another left onto Dinh Tien Hoang Street. Follow the street through what feels like a quiet suburban residential neighborhood for about 1 km (¾ mi). At the intersection with Tinh Tam Street is **Tinh Tam Lake** ⑩, overgrown with lotus flowers in spring and summer. Across Dinh Tien Hoang Street is another lake, Tang Tau, with a small island, once the location of the Royal Library and the current home of the small Ngoc Huong Pagoda. This is a very peaceful place to take a break.

TIMING

This walk should take you about four hours at a very leisurely pace. Early morning and late afternoon are the best times to explore Hue because it can get quite warm in the middle of the day, especially from April to October. Also many tour guides insist they need a two- to three-hour break in the middle of the day.

SIGHTS TO SEE

❶ **Central Market** (Cho). Hue's large Central Market has the usual collection of fresh fruits, dried fish, and motor parts. It's the best place to pick up two local specialties: conical hats, which can be decorated to order, and sesame-seed candy. It's also a good spot to see Hue daily life. ✉ *On citadel side of riverfront, across from Phu Xuan Bridge.* ⏲ *Daily 7:30–dusk.*

❷ **The Citadel** (Kinh Thanh). Seeking to secure his empire, Emperor Gia Long built this 1½-square-mi citadel with a 65-ft-wide moat in the heart of Hue in 1804. Gia Long was assisted in the design by the French architect Olivier de Puymanel, and the result is a combination of French military architect Vauban's work and classical Chinese-style architecture. The citadel was initially built of earth and later reinforced by 6 ft of bricks and fortified by 10 gates. Enclosed in the citadel is the **Imperial City or Imperial Enclosure** (Hoang Thanh; ☞ *below*), where official government activity took place. Within it is the **Forbidden Purple City** (Tu Cam Thanh; ☞ *below*), which was the private sanctuary of the emperors and their families. 🎫 *10,000d.* ⏲ *Daily 7–5.*

❸ **Flag Tower** (Cot Co). This 112-ft structure is one of the symbols of Hue and Vietnam's tallest flagpole. It was originally built in 1809 to serve as the Imperial Palace's central observation post. Like much of Hue, it has a history of being destroyed. The Flag Tower was toppled during a typhoon in 1904. It was rebuilt in 1915, destroyed again in 1947, and rebuilt anew in 1949. When the city was occupied by the North Vietnamese during the Tet offensive of 1968, the National Liberation Front flag flew from the Flag Tower. The interior is closed to the public. ✉ *In front of 23 Thang 8 St., facing Ngo Mon Gate.*

❼ **Forbidden Purple City** (Tu Cam Thanh). Built at the beginning of the 19th century, the Forbidden Purple City, which is inside the **Imperial City** (☞ *below*), was almost entirely destroyed during the Vietnam War; now it's largely a wide-open field. At its threshold is a vast expanse of spotty vegetation and rubble. In its glory days the Forbidden Purple City housed members of the imperial family and the concubines and eunuchs who served them. Anyone else who entered was executed. After the 1968 Tet offensive, only the **Royal Theater** (Duyet Thi Duong), on the right-hand side, and the intimate and partially restored **Royal Library** (Thai Binh Lau; ☞ *below*) behind it remained intact. These structures can be visited. ✉ *In Imperial City.* 🎫 *10,000d admission to citadel includes Forbidden Purple City.* ⏲ *Daily 8–5.*

4 **Imperial City** (Hoang Thanh). The Imperial City, also known as the Imperial Enclosure, was once a complex of palaces and pavilions where civil and religious ceremonies took place. Inside it was the Forbidden Purble City, where the royal family lived. Now the Imperial City betrays disappointingly few remnants of its past glory beneath the sporadic vegetation that has taken over the ruins. Nonetheless, it still conveys a sense of splendor. There are four gateways into the Enclosure: the **Gate of Peace** (Cua Hoa Binh), **the Gate of Humanity** (Cua Hien Nhian), the **Gate of Virtue** (Cua Chuong Due), and the **South Gate** (Ngo Mon). You can only get to the Imperial City after you have entered the citadel. ✉ *Inside citadel.* 🎫 *10,000d admission to citadel includes Imperial City.* ⏲ *Daily 8–5.*

9 **Imperial Museum.** This beautiful wooden structure was constructed in 1845 and houses miscellaneous royal knickknacks such as wooden incense boxes, many inlaid with mother-of-pearl. The museum's walls are inscribed with Vietnamese poetry. There is also a good collection of ceramics, traditional musical instruments, and old weapons. ✉ *On Dinh Cong Trang St., close to intersection of Doan Thi Diem St.* 🎫 *10,000d.* ⏲ *Daily 7–noon and 1:30–5.*

5 **Nine Dynastic Urns** (Cuu Dinh O The-Mieu). Cast in 1835 and weighing approximately 5,000 pounds each, every one of these urns is dedicated to a ruler of the Nguyen dynasty. Emperor Gia Long, the founder of this dynasty, is featured on the central urn, the most elaborately decorated of the nine. The urns are covered with nature motifs, including the sun and moon, rivers and mountains, and various landscapes. Many of the designs are Chinese in origin, dating back 4,000 years. ✉ *To left of entrance to Imperial City, when entering through Ngo Mon Gate.* 🎫 *10,000d admission to citadel includes Nine Urns.* ⏲ *Daily 8–5.*

6 **Palace of Supreme Harmony** (Thai Hoa Dien). This richly decorated wooden palace painted gold and red was constructed in 1803. In its imperial glory in the 19th century, it was where the emperor held special events, ceremonies, and festivals for the new moon. This is also where the emperor received dignitaries. Throngs of mandarins paid their respects to his highness while he sat on his elevated throne. Now the palace houses a gift shop where 10,000d will get you an imperial tune from the authentically outfitted minstrels. ✉ *In the citadel.* 🎫 *10,000d admission to citadel includes Palace of Supreme Harmony.* ⏲ *Daily 8–5.*

8 **Royal Library** (Thai Binh Lau). The Royal Library is one of the few largely intact buildings in the citadel. The wooden structure is on the right side of the Forbidden Purple City in a field of grass and rubble. The delicate carved architecture has survived, although there are no books or other librarylike objects left. 🎫 *10,000d admission to citadel includes Royal Library.* ⏲ *Daily 8–5.*

10 **Tinh Tam Lake** (Ho Tinh Tam). In spring and summer this little lake is covered with lotus flowers. Do as the emperors once did and walk across one of the bridges to the island for a little respite. ✉ *Intersection of Dinh Tien Hoang and Tinh Tam Sts.*

The Imperial Tombs and the Thien Mu Pagoda

A GOOD BOAT RIDE OR DRIVE

Many of the prearranged boat rides organized through hotels or tourist offices provide you with an all-day tour of the Imperial Tombs as well as of the Thien Mu Pagoda. These boat trips are worth taking if you have the time, although a faster way to visit the tombs is by car. The tombs and pagodas of Hue are extraordinarily beautiful and peaceful. At the tombs you won't just find a small tombstone: The emperors were laid to rest in elaborate pine forests and gardens with their own islands amid minilakes and pagodas. Boat tours generally stop at any combination of the following places: the Tomb of Tu Duc, the Tomb of Minh Mang, and the Thien Mu Pagoda. The Tomb of Khai Dinh is more easily accessible by car. You can also get to each of the other tombs by car—or by motorbike or bicycle, if you are more adventurous.

The price of admission for each tomb and pagoda is generally about 50,000d. Many boat trips, such as those arranged through Thua Thien–Hue Tourism, DMZ Tour Office, and other government agencies (☞ Travel Agencies *in* Hue A to Z, *below*), are advertised at a cost of $15 or so. But the agencies neglect to inform you of the additional 50,000d you must pay at each stop. One exception is the Thien Mu Pagoda, which is free. Other boats, holding up to 10 people, cost $10–$35, depending on whether you rent the boat yourself for only three or four people or if you join a preexisting group. You can arrange both options at the pier opposite the train station or through your hotel. The Huong Giang Company's tours give you the terrific option of going by boat and returning by car. Another option is to hire a car and driver to take you by land to the tombs.

Many boat tours follow this route down the Perfume River: Heading west along the river, you approach the **Thien Mu Pagoda** ⑪ on the right-hand side. After about 6 km (4 mi), you come to the **Tomb of Tu Duc** ⑫. You then must proceed on foot 1½ km (1 mi) inland to the **Tomb of Minh Mang** ⑬, on the west side of the river.

To get to the **The Tomb of Khai Dinh** ⑭, 1½ km (1 mi) inland on the other (east) side of the river, you're better off going by car on a separate trip, though some boat trips will take you here.

TIMING

It takes about a day to visit most of the tombs and pagodas by boat. Going by car to all of the pagodas will take you about half a day. You may, however, be happy to see just a couple of them; set aside about an hour for each (not including transportation time). Organized tours begin in the morning at about 8 and return at around 3 PM. These trips are available daily throughout the year.

SIGHTS TO SEE

⓫ **Thien Mu Pagoda.** At this Mahayana Buddhist temple is one of Hue's most famous monuments, the seven-story, octagonal Phuoc Nguyen Tower. It was built in 1844 by Emperor Thieu Tri and is a peaceful spot, overlooking the Perfume River. Each of the tower's tiers is dedicated to a different human incarnation of Buddha. Across the temple's main entrance is the famed Austin car that in 1963 delivered the Buddhist monk Thich Quang Duc to Saigon, where he set himself on fire in an act of pacifist protest against President Diem's regime. The main sanctuary, behind the tower, houses a splendid, large Laughing Buddha; it's open daily 7–11 and 2–5. The temple is still a training center for monks, so you may see the young novices with their mostly shaved heads going about their daily activities. Behind the temple compound is a large cemetery stretching over the hills. ✉ *About 2½ km (1½ mi) southwest of citadel on left bank of Perfume River.* ⏲ *Daily 7–5.*

⓮ **Tomb of Khai Dinh.** An unbelievable concoction of glitzy elements, the Tomb of Khai Dinh, completed in 1931, is well worth a visit. Khai Dinh became emperor in 1916 at the age of 31 and died in 1925. Climb the few flights of steps, flanked by dragons, to enter a surprisingly colorful tomb heavily decorated with tile mosaics. Scenes from the four seasons welcome you into the main building. It is best to visit this tomb by car, since it is not directly on the river. ✉ *About 16 km (10 mi) south* *of Hue and about 1½ km (1 mi) inland on right bank of Perfume River.* 🎫 *50,000d.* ⏲ *Daily 8–5.*

13 **Tomb of Minh Mang.** Another Hue classic, the Tomb of Minh Mang, emperor from 1791 to 1841, was completed in 1843 by his successor. His tomb is one of the most palatial, with numerous pavilions and courtyards in a beautiful pine forest. The burial site is modeled after the Ming tombs in Beijing. The route to the burial site is bordered with sculptures of mandarins, elephants, and lions. ✉ *About 11 km (7 mi) south of Hue and 1½ km (1 mi) inland on left bank of Perfume River.* 🎫 *50,000d.* ⏲ *Daily 8–5.*

★ 12 **Tomb of Tu Doc.** One of Hue's most visited tombs, the Tomb of Tu Doc, emperor from 1829 to 1883, has its own lake and pine forest. Built in 1867 by thousands of laborers, the tomb was once Tu Doc's second residence. He escaped here to relax and write poetry. One of his favorite spots was the Xung Khiem Pavilion on the pond filled with lotus blossoms. It's easy to see why he chose this place as a retreat—you may end up spending an hour just to wander around the grounds. ✉ *About 5 km (3 mi) south of Hue, on right bank of Perfume River.* 🎫 *50,000d.* ⏲ *Daily 8–5.*

OFF THE BEATEN PATH

TU HIEU PAGODA – You have to walk through a junglelike path from the road and pass a crescent-shape pool to get to one of Hue's most beautiful and peaceful pagodas. This temple, built in 1843, houses a large gold Buddha flanked by gladiolas. It is another good place for quiet meditation. The monks live in simple rooms off to the side. ✉ *About 3 km (2 mi) south of Hue.* ⏲ *Daily 8–5.*

DMZ – About 100 km (62 mi) north of Hue is the DMZ (Demilitarized Zone), site of some of the heaviest fighting of the Vietnam War. Some names that may be familiar from the war are Con Thien, Camp Carroll, the Rockpile, Hamburger Hill, Quang Tri, and Khe Sanh. The DMZ was established following the terms of the 1954 Geneva Accords, in which Vietnam was split in two along the 17th parallel at the Ben Hai River; it consisted of an area extending 5 km (3 mi) on either side of the line. The DMZ was supposed to have been a temporary measure, enforced only until the Democratic Republic of Vietnam in the north and the Republic of Vietnam in the south could be reunited following elections in 1956. The elections never took place, so the DMZ continued to exist until the country was reunified in 1975. Almost as soon as it was created, the DMZ was militarized, and by 1965 it had become a key battleground in the fight between north and south. One of the biggest battles of the war—and one of the most significant American losses—took place at Khe Sanh in 1968. The U.S. base became the target of intense North Vietnamese army attacks meant to divert American resources from Hue. There isn't much to see in Khe Sanh today, though the battleground itself remains a pockmarked terrain. About 20 km (12 mi) north of the DMZ are the 3-km-long (2-mi-long) Vinh Moc Tunnels, built by villagers in the area from 1966 to 1968 to escape American bombing and later used by the North Vietnamese army to transport goods to Con Co Island. The DMZ Tour Office (☞ Travel Agencies *in* Hue A to Z, *below*) organizes trips to the area.

Dining and Lodging

Most of Hue's hotels are on the east bank of the Perfume River. You have an excellent selection from which to choose in all price ranges. The larger hotels even have (small) swimming pools and tennis courts. Most have travel services and can arrange for a car and driver for a customized tour. Hotels of all sizes arrange boat tours to the tombs and pagodas as well as guided tours in and around Hue.

$$$ ★ ✕ **Century Riverside Hotel Restaurant.** Perhaps the most upscale dining establishment in Hue, the Century is decorated in traditional Vietnamese style with many Western touches, such as white-linen tablecloths. Diners are exclusively tourists from the Century Riverside or the adjacent Houng Giang Hotel. Two particularly tasty dishes are the grilled fish in banana leaves and the superb spring rolls. ✉ *49 Le Loi St.,* ☎ *054/823–390. AE, DC, MC, V.*

$$ ★ ✕ **Club Garden.** A dimly lighted street leads to you the entrance of this small restaurant, where a string of hanging lights welcomes you. One of Hue's most upscale spots, the Club Garden is primarily filled with tourists. Outside is a large garden, although the air-conditioned, fly-free interior is nicer. This is the place to get a fabulous fixed-price five-course dinner for under $10. A friendly family of waiters serves outstanding Vietnamese food. The seafood and fish dishes are particularly good, as are the pork buns. ✉ *12 Vo Thi Sau St.,* ☎ *054/826–327. No credit cards.*

$$ ✕ **Huong Giang Hotel Restaurant.** From the windows of this spacious third-floor restaurant you get great views of the Perfume River. Large portions of very solid Vietnamese food and Western dishes, such as chicken and french fries, are served. Make a reservation if you want a seat by the window. The service is excellent; the only down side is the occasional large tour group that takes over the place. ✉ *51 Le Loi St.,* ☎ *054/822–122. AE, DC, MC, V.*

$$ ✕ **Ngoc Anh.** This open-air restaurant, which is the Vietnamese version of a sidewalk café, serves high-quality Vietnamese and Chinese food in a relaxed atmosphere. The sizzling-hot clay-pot seafood special is exceptional. ✉ *29 Nguyen Thai Hoc St.,* ☎ *054/822–617. No credit cards.*

$$ ✕ **Ong Tao.** Ong Tao means "God of the Kitchen," and this restaurant exemplifies imperial cuisine. There are two locations. The citadel site serves lunch and dinner in an outdoor setting amid trees and ruins. Although swarming with tourists, it is still a pleasant place for lunch. The other location is less crowded. The garlic prawns are delicious here, as are the spring rolls. ✉ *Inside Hien Nhou Gate, opposite College of Fine Arts,* ☎ *054/823–031;* ✉ *134 Ngo Duc Ke,* ☎ *054/822–037. No credit cards.*

$ ✕ **Am Phu.** Excellent traditional Vietnamese cuisine is served at this restaurant. The nonglamorous atmosphere keeps this place relatively tourist free. Whether groups or individuals, everyone eats at large tables covered with red-plastic tablecloths. Although there are no prices listed on the menu, most dishes are about 30,000d. ✉ *35 Nguyen Thai Hoc St.,* ☎ *054/825–259. No credit cards.*

$ ✕ **Lac Thanh Restaurant.** Packed with tourists and teeming with postcard and cigarette vendors, this dive (and its next-door copycat) serves the tastiest and cheapest meals in Hue. Some notable dishes include Asian basics like shrimp and vegetables over crispy noodles and tofu or beef and vegetables wrapped in rice paper and dipped in peanut sauce. For dessert, try the delicious coconut ice cream topped with chocolate sauce and peanuts. ✉ *6A Dien Tien Hoang St., no phone. No credit cards.*

$ ✕ **Mai Huong.** Although it may not live up to your fantasy of a patisserie, this small "coffee shop" is still a good place for a slice of coconut cake and a cup of tea. Just keep in mind that the ice cream doesn't even vaguely resemble Carvel's. ✉ *6 Nguyen Tri Phuong St., no phone. No credit cards.*

$ ✕ **Tong Phuoc Nen.** Although soup is the specialty of the house, you can also order a variety of fish dishes. Different types of eel soup are some of the more popular dishes. Try *lau luon,* a tangy eel-and-vegetable concoction served over noodles, or *chao luon,* a more traditional soup prepared with mushrooms and lotus seed. Upstairs, the terrace seating has a kind of rustic charm with its whitewashed walls. Diners include more adventurous tourists and lots of Vietnamese teenagers. ✉ *20 Ba Trieu St.,* ☎ *054/825–264. No credit cards.*

¢ ✕ **Banh Khoai.** This two-table, family-run food stall serves some of the best banh khoai in town. The meat-filled rice pancake (three for 10,000d) topped with bean sprouts comes to the table piping hot. Break it up with chopsticks into your small rice bowl, add the greens and sauce, and eat. This place is a great dining experience if you don't mind eating in what is essentially this family's kitchen. You may have to share your table with the cook, who will need the space to peel shrimp. ✉ *2 Nguyen Tri Phuong St., off Hanoi St., no phone. No credit cards.*

¢ ✕ **Bun Bo Hue.** Close to the center of Hue, this very downscale sidewalk food stall serves some of the best bun bo Hue, the Hue noodle specialty made with beef and pork. This is the only dish served, and there is no menu. Order by pointing unless you can find a translator. ✉ *11b Ly Kiet St., no phone. No credit cards.*

$$$ **Century Riverside Inn.** This large Western-style hotel on the river is the most luxurious one in town. Still, the Century is not opulent by Western standards, but it is very clean and comfortable. The public rooms are tastefully decorated, and there is even a gift shop, albeit overpriced. About half the rooms, which are done in fairly standard hotel-style decor, have river views. After a long day of sightseeing, relax by the small riverfront swimming pool. Don't bother with the exercise room, however; none of the equipment works. ✉ *49 Le Loi St.,* ☎ *054/823–390,* FAX *054/823–399. 138 rooms. 2 restaurants, bar, air-conditioning, minibars, refrigerators, room service, TVs, pool, massage, tennis courts, exercise room, shop, laundry service and dry cleaning. AE, DC, MC, V.*

$$$ ★ **Huong Giang Hotel.** Large rooms with traditional Vietnamese-style decor and the most helpful staff in Hue make the Huong Giang, on the north end of the east bank, the most pleasant hotel in town. Bamboo furniture fills the rooms, and there is an almost palatial feel to the lobby. Ask for one of the renovated older rooms—they're better than the newer ones, which are around the pool. The hotel also has a very good restaurant and rooftop bar-garden with panoramic views of the river. The travel office in the hotel is exceptional. ✉ *51 Le Loi St.,* ☎ *054/822–122,* FAX *054/823–102. 102 rooms. 2 restaurants, 2 bars, outdoor café, air-conditioning, pool, tennis court, dry cleaning and laundry service, travel services. AE, DC, MC, V.*

$$ **Hoa Hong Hotel II.** Almost as comfortable as its more expensive neighbors, the Century Riverside and the Huong Giang, this new hotel has similarly styled semiluxurious rooms. It is one of the tallest buildings in town and has the reassuring air of a Western Holiday Inn. The decor is nondescript, but everything is new and tasteful. All rooms have TVs and minibars. Though the hotel is not on the water, it is tall enough so that many rooms have excellent views of the river. In the hotel's restaurant there are nightly shows of traditional music and dance. Credit cards are not accepted, but you can use traveler's checks. ✉ *1 Pham Ngu Lao St.,* ☎ *054/824–377,* FAX *054/826–949. 60 rooms. Restaurant, air-conditioning, dry cleaning and laundry service, travel services. No credit cards.*

$$ **Huong Giang Tourist Villa.** It's just as clean and pleasant as its hotel counterpart (☞ *above*), but the villa has larger rooms and a more intimate environment. The cozy and sunny rooms are arranged in a

horseshoe shape around a small garden; all are on the first or second floor. Staying here you sacrifice having access to a restaurant or recreational facilities, but you get the feel of a small inn and easy access to the center of town. ✉ *3 Hung Vuong St.,* ☎ *054/826–070,* FAX *054/826–074. 12 rooms. Restaurant, air-conditioning, fans, minibars, refrigerators, laundry service, travel services, car rental. AE, MC, V.*

$$ **Dong Da Hotel.** This spacious hotel on a quiet street corner falls somewhere between a minihotel—one of the new, privately-owned small places popping up all over Vietnam—and a Western-style accommodation. Rooms are clean and modern and have simple Japanese-style furnishings, including rice-paper room dividers. All have TVs. ✉ *15 Ly Thuong Kiet St.,* ☎ *054/823–071,* FAX *054/823–204. 37 rooms. Restaurant, bar, air-conditioning, TVs, dance club, laundry service, travel services, car rental. No credit cards.*

$$ **A Dong Hotel 1.** This pleasant, clean, and airy minihotel is a great budget alternative. There is nothing particularly charming about this place, but it does a great job of providing large, basic, immaculate rooms. It scores big, however, with fresh fruit and flowers delivered daily to your room. The staff speaks very little English but is very eager to please. ✉ *1 Chu Van An St.,* ☎ *054/824–148,* FAX *054/823–858. 10 rooms. Restaurant, bar, air-conditioning, minibars, refrigerators, TVs, laundry service, travel services, car rental. AE, MC, V.*

$$ **A Dong 2 Hotel.** The cheaper of the A Dong hotels, this one is a fine example of a small, clean, well-run minihotel. Rooms are plain, though all have TV and private bathroom. ✉ *7 Doi Cung St.,* ☎ *054/822–765,* FAX *054/828–074. 15 rooms. Restaurant, air-conditioning, TVs, laundry service, travel services, car rental. AE, MC, V.*

$$ **Binh Minh.** The small Binh Minh is another good choice if you're traveling on a budget. Rooms are sunny, and some have sliding doors that lead to balconies. The staff is very knowledgeable and speaks English. ✉ *12 Nguyen Tri Phuong St.,* ☎ *054/825–526,* FAX *054/828–362. 22 rooms, most with bath. Restaurant, air-conditioning, fans, minibars, refrigerators, laundry service, travel services. No credit cards.*

$$ **Dong Loi Hotel.** Though this hotel looks slightly worn, it is very reasonably priced and in the downtown area. Rooms are tidy, no-frills accommodations, with unmatched curtains, bedding, and towels. The staff will arrange city tours and excursions outside Hue for you. ✉ *11A Pham Ngu Lao St.,* ☎ *054/822–296,* FAX *054/826–234. 30 rooms. Restaurant, air-conditioning, minibars, refrigerators, TVs, laundry service, travel services. No credit cards.*

$$ **Duy Tan Hotel.** Despite its large and semigrand appearance, this hotel functions as a glorified minihotel. Rooms are bright and spacious, though the renovation job is pretty spotty. But the new bathrooms with tubs are a plus. ✉ *12 Hung Vuong,* ☎ *054/825–001,* FAX *054/826–477. 58 rooms. Restaurant, air-conditioning, minibars, refrigerators, laundry service, meeting rooms, travel services, car rental. No credit cards.*

$–$$ **Hue City Tourism Villas.** Just because they are called villas doesn't mean these state-run hotels resembles anything in the Italian countryside. But if you find something charming about decaying French colonial architecture, then these villas are for you. Though the buildings are slightly run-down, the rooms are quiet, peaceful, clean, and reasonably priced. Make arrangements through Hue City Tourism (☞ Travel Agencies *in* Hue A to Z, *below*) or just show up. The best one is at 13 Ly Thuong Kiet Street, which has five clean rooms for $15 each a night, as well as a small dining room and an eager-to-please staff. ✉ *13 Ly Thuong Kiet St.,* ☎ *054/823–064;* ✉ *11, 16, and 18 Ly Thuong Kiet St. and 5 Le Loi St.,* ☎ *054/823–753,* FAX *054/822–470. 8–10 rooms with bath in each villa. Air-conditioning, minibars, refrigerators, laundry service. No credit cards.*

$–$$ **Hue Hotel.** Run by and adjacent to Thua Thien–Hue Tourism, this refurbished property has two types of rooms. The more expensive rooms are clean but sparse and have superb air-conditioning. The cheaper rooms, which have fans only, are not as clean as the pricier ones, though they are still acceptable. Oddly, the cheaper rooms look out over the river, but the more expensive ones are set back closer to Le Loi Street. The staff speaks very little English and is not very helpful. ✉ *15 Le Loi St.,* ☎ *054/822–369,* FAX *054/824–806. 11 rooms. Air-conditioning, fans. No credit cards.*

$ **Hoa Hong I.** The smaller and less luxurious of the Hoa Hong family of hotels, this place has comfortable rooms and bathrooms with tubs. Just ignore the fake-flower finishing touches and the overly cutesy pastel decor. ✉ *46C Le Loi St.,* ☎ *054/824–377,* FAX *054/826–949. 56 rooms. Restaurant, air-conditioning, IDD phones, minibars, refrigerators, TVs, laundry service, travel services. No credit cards.*

$ **Huan Vu Hotel.** Slightly off the beaten path, this new and bright white minihotel has modest, clean rooms at decent though not exceptional prices. The staff does not speak a word of English, so you'll have to make do with a little sign language. ✉ *16 Dong Da St.,* ☎ *054/821–560,* FAX *054/821–561. 20 rooms. Restaurant, air-conditioning, fans, minibars, refrigerators, laundry service, travel services. No credit cards.*

$ **Le Loi Hue Hotel.** A little run-down but passable, this hotel has rooms with many amenities. It often has vacancies when other places fill up and is very close to the train station. *2 Le Loi St.,* ☎ *054/824–668,* FAX *054/824–527. 150 rooms, most with bath. Restaurant, air-conditioning, IDD phones, minibars, refrigerators, TVs, laundry service, travel service, car rental. No credit cards.*

$ **Saigon Hotel.** Don't be put off by the strangely decorated restaurant (for instance, the neon backlit cow's head) in this new minihotel. Rooms are sunny and squeaky clean, and the bathrooms are in excellent condition and have tubs. ✉ *32 Hung Vuong St.,* ☎ *054/821–007,* FAX *054/821–009. 20 rooms. Restaurant, air-conditioning, fans, laundry service, travel services, car rental. No credit cards.*

¢–$$ **Hung Vuong Hotel.** Both backpackers and nonbackpackers, especially those taking the Sinh Café Bus (☞ Arriving and Departing *in* Hue A to Z, *below*), which drops off and picks up passengers here, stay here because of the wide price range of rooms. All are clean, and the most expensive ones overlook the river and are a terrific bargain at $25. The hotel adjoins the Thua Thien–Hue Tourism office and is centrally located near downtown Hue. You can also get information from the Sinh Café representative here. ✉ *2 Hung Vuong St.,* ☎ *054/823–866,* FAX *054/825–910. 70 rooms, most with bath. Restaurant, air-conditioning, minibars, refrigerators, laundry service, travel services, car rental. No credit cards.*

Shopping

There aren't many places to shop in Hue, though you can pick up some nice souvenirs—including wood carvings and replicas of antique compasses and teapots—at the stands inside the Imperial City and along Le Loi Street. The central market isn't filled with spectacular finds, except for conical hats, decorated to order, and sesame-seed candy—two Hue specialties.

Hue A to Z

Arriving and Departing

Hue is 108 km (67 mi) north of Danang; 140 km (87 mi) north of Hoi An; 1,097 km (680 mi) north of Ho Chi Minh City; and 689 km (427 mi) south of Hanoi.

BY BUS

The **Sinh Café Bus** (✉ At Hung Vuong Hotel, 2 Hung Vuong St., Hue, ☎ 054/823–866) stops in Hue on both its northbound and southbound routes. The one-way fare from Hanoi to Hue is about $8 and takes about 12 hours; the one-way fare from Ho Chi Minh City is $14 and takes about 3 days (the trip is made in segments from Ho Chi Minh City to Dalat to Nha Trang to Hue). You can also purchase an open-ended ticket (☞ Bus Travel *in* the Gold Guide) that allows you to make as many stops as you want. The Sinh Café bus usually departs, both northbound and southbound, between 7 AM–8 AM. Call for details, as the schedule changes.

BY CAR OR MINIBUS

You can rent a minibus with a driver to take you to Hoi An, Danang, or other points near Hue; the cost is approximately $25–$50 for the trip, depending on the kind of vehicle, its age, and whether it has air-conditioning.

BY PLANE

Vietnam Airlines (✉ 12 Hanoi St., ☎ 054/823–249) flies to Hue's **Phu Bai Airport,** 15 km (9 mi) south of the city center, from Ho Chi Minh City (1 hr; $85 one way; 3 times a week); Hanoi (50 min; $80 one way; 3 times a week); and Dalat (1 hr 20 min; $105 one way; 2 times a week). The Vietnam Airlines office in Hue is open Monday–Saturday 7–11 and 1:30–4:40. The schedule changes frequently, so confirm departure times with your hotel travel agent or with the airline a day or two before your flight. **Taxis** are available at the airport to take you into town; the cost is generally about 90,000d, but this price is usually negotiable.

BY TRAIN

Trains from all over Vietnam come into the **Hue Railway Station** (Ga Hue; ✉ On right bank at southwest end of Le Loi St.). The ticket office is open daily 7:30–5. Four trains depart daily for Ho Chi Minh City (24 hours, $60–$80 for a sleeping berth), and four depart daily for Hanoi (15 hours, $40–$50 for a sleeping berth).

Getting Around

BY BICYCLE

One of the easiest ways to get around Hue is by bicycle, which you can rent from the Century Riverside Inn (☞ Lodging, *above*).

BY BOAT

Many hotels in Hue can arrange dragon-boat rides, which shuttle you from one tomb and pagoda to the next along the Perfume River. The boat companies are either affiliated with the state-run Hue City Tourism or Thua Thien–Hue Tourism (☞ Travel Agencies, *below*), or they are run independently. You can also arrange for your own boat with guide at the pier across from the train station; a small boat, seating approximately six people, costs $15 a day. In addition, Lac Thanh Restaurant (☞ Dining, *above*) has its own mini–tourist company, which rents boats. Make arrangements at the restaurant or at the pier.

BY CAR OR MINIBUS

Cars or minibuses with drivers can be rented through hotels, booking offices, and government-run travel agencies (☞ Travel Agencies, *below*) for $40 and up per day, depending on the condition of the car. The cost of the services of a guide in addition to the car and driver is $25–$50. Keep in mind that some of the harder to reach monuments, such as the Tomb of Tu Duc, are more accessible if you hire a car and guide.

BY CYCLO

You can almost always find a cyclo outside hotels or cruising along the right bank. For 50,000d you should be able to get pretty much anywhere, although you will almost always have to negotiate to get down to this price. If you hate to bargain, the Century Riverside Inn (☞ Lodging, *above*) posts suggested cyclo prices, which the drivers follow.

BY TAXI

Taxis are metered. Expect to pay about $5–$10 for trips around town. Call **Hue Taxi ATC** (☎ 054/824–500 or ☎ 054/833–333) to arrange a ride, or just hail one on the street, though they are not always so easy to find. Taxi drivers will also take you anywhere you want to go for a prearranged price. A one-hour taxi trip should cost about $10.

Contacts and Resources

CURRENCY EXCHANGE

The Thua Thien–Hue branch of **Vietcom Bank** (ICBV; ✉ 21 Le Duy Don St., ☎ 054/822–281) changes money. It's open weekdays 7–11 and 1:30–3:30. You can also exchange money at most hotels in Hue.

DOCTORS AND HOSPITAL

In case of emergency, contact **Benh Vien Trung Uong Hue** (Hue General Hospital; ✉ 16 Le Loi St., ☎ 054/822–325). They do not speak English. If your illness is not life threatening, it may be better to seek assistance through your hotel staff.

GUIDED TOURS

Guided tours can be arranged through a number of different travel agencies (☞ Travel Agencies, *below*). Many hotels are affiliated with one of the government-run tourism agencies. The **DMZ Tour Office** (☞ *below*) arranges different types of tours: Guided city tours for $15 per day, including tours of the citadel and Imperial Tombs; and excursions to surrounding areas including the DMZ and the Bruor Van Kieu ethnic-minority village.

A number of agencies organize **boat trips** on the Perfume River, which include stops at the tombs and the Thien Mu Pagoda (☞ Getting Around by Boat, *above*). Most depart at 8 AM daily and cost 30,000d, excluding tomb and pagoda entry fees, which amount to about 50,000d each.

PHARMACY

The woman working at **Thuoc Tay** (✉ 5 Hung Vuong St.,) speaks better French than English, but she is very helpful, especially if you write down what you need. If she doesn't have what you're looking for, she will recommend someone else who does. On Hung Vuong Street, there are a number of other pharmacies near this one. Though the sign claims the pharmacy stays open 7:30 AM–10 PM, that's not true; it closes for lunch.

VISITOR INFORMATION AND TRAVEL AGENCIES

DMZ Tour Office (✉ 26 Le Loi St., ☎ 054/825–242) arranges minibus and car rentals that include a guide; tours of Hue by car; boat tours along the Perfume River; and trips to the DMZ. They also book train and air tickets. It's open daily 8–5.

Hue City Tourism (✉ 18 Le Loi St., ☎ 054/823–577) runs the Hue City Tourism Villas (☞ Lodging, *above*) and arranges visits to traditional theaters, bus tours of Hue and the Imperial Tombs, and trips to the DMZ. It's open daily 8–5.

Huong Giang Company (✉ 17 Le Loi St., ☏ 054/820–188, FAX 054/823–102) is a first-class travel agency that gives excellent tours of Hue (including a boat tour of the tombs in which you return by car) and organizes trips to the DMZ. One special feature is its cooking tours, during which you can learn to cook Vietnamese food. The agency is affiliated with the Houng Giang Hotel (☞ Lodging, *above*) but is in a separate location. It's open daily 7–noon and 1:30–5.

Thua Thien–Hue Tourism (Cong Ty Du Lich Thua Thien–Hue; ✉ 30 Le Loi St., ☏ 054/822–369, 054/822–288, or 054/822–355) is a government-run tourism agency. It offers services similar to those of other agencies in town. It's open daily 8–5.

DANANG AND ENVIRONS

Although Danang was once an important port town and a critical U.S. Air Force base during the Vietnam War, today it is a dreary, slightly run-down city with only one tourist attraction: its impressive museum of Cham culture. It's not the biggest tourist destination so there aren't many good hotels or restaurants, except for the Furama Resort in nearby China Beach. Danang also has a major regional airport, which makes it the arrival point for Hue, Hoi An, and other nearby cities. (Hue also has a smaller airport.) South of the city, on the way to Hoi An, are China Beach and the cave-temples of the Marble Mountains.

There is really no reason to spend more than a morning in Danang visiting the Cham Museum. But just outside Danang, en route to Hoi An, are the Marble Mountains and China Beach, where the Furama Resort opened in 1997. Both China Beach and the Marble Mountains can be seen as part of a single day trip from Danang (or Hoi An) or as stops on your way to Hoi An. A pilgrimage to My Son, Vietnam's most significant Cham ruins, also merits at least a half day, either from Danang or Hoi An.

Danang

15 *108 km (67 mi) south of Hue, 30 km (17 mi) north of Hoi An, and 972 km (603 mi) north of Ho Chi Minh City.*

Danang became an important port city at the end of the 19th century when silt filling up the Thu Bon River eliminated neighboring Hoi An's access to the sea. The French gained control of Danang (which they called Tourane) in 1888, taking it by force from Emperor Gia Long (he had promised it to them in exchange for their help but had reneged on his agreement). In its heyday, during the first half of the 20th century, the city was second only to Saigon as Vietnam's most cosmopolitan center.

During the Vietnam War, the city played a significant role: It was the first place U.S. marines landed in March 1965, and subsequently it became home to a large U.S. Air Force base. Only 200 km (124 mi) south of the DMZ (Demilitarized Zone), the city was an ideal location for launching bombing missions. The influx of army personnel brought enormous growth, numerous refugees, and all kinds of entertainment, including movie theaters, bars, and prostitution. Soldiers would take time off at the nearby R&R resort of China Beach (☞ *below*). By March 1975, Danang was in a state of total chaos as people tried to escape the fast-encroaching North Vietnamese army and had to fight for space on any boat or plane leaving the city. Today there are remnants of the American presence in the city, as well as vestiges of the French in the wide avenues and old villas. But Danang is not a place where you are likely to want to linger after visiting its hightlight, the Cham Museum.

Danang

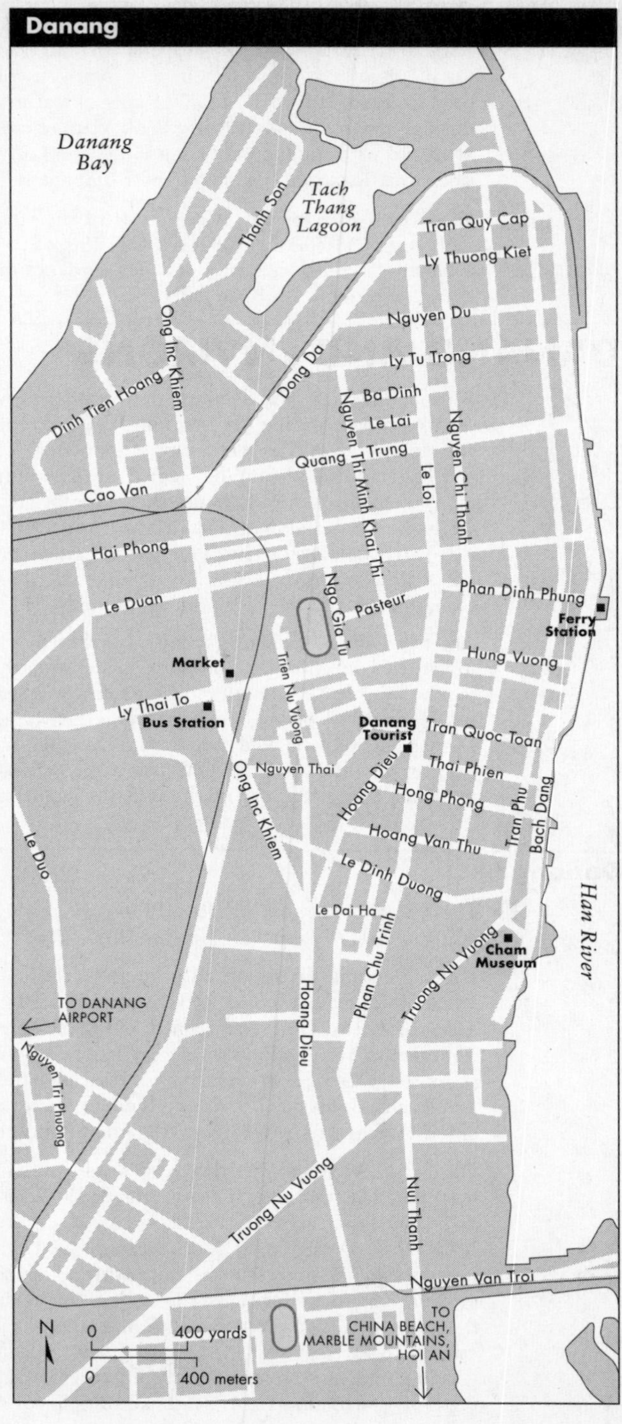
Danang Bay
Tach Thang Lagoon
Thanh Son
Tran Quy Cap
Ly Thuong Kiet
Nguyen Du
Ly Tu Trong
Ba Dinh
Le Lai
Quang Trung
Ong Inc Khiem
Dinh Tien Hoang
Dong Da
Nguyen Thi Minh Khai Thi
Le Loi
Nguyen Chi Thanh
Cao Van
Hai Phong
Le Duan
Ngo Gia Tu
Pasteur
Phan Dinh Phung
Ferry Station
Hung Vuong
Market
Ly Thai To
Bus Station
Trien Nu Vuong
Danang Tourist
Tran Quoc Toan
Thai Phien
Nguyen Thai
Hoang Dieu
Hong Phong
Hoang Van Thu
Tran Phu
Bach Dang
Le Duo
Le Dinh Duong
Le Dai Ha
Han River
Cham Museum
Truong Nu Vuong
Phan Chu Trinh
TO DANANG AIRPORT
Nguyen Tri Phuong
Hoang Dieu
Nui Thanh
Truong Nu Vuong
Nguyen Van Troi
N
0
400 yards
0
400 meters
TO CHINA BEACH, MARBLE MOUNTAINS, HOI AN

On display at the **Cham Museum** are artifacts from the Kingdom of Champa, which ruled this region for more than 1,000 years. The Cham religion combines native beliefs with elements of Indian culture and early Hindu thought (the god Shiva is often represented on Cham ruins). The Cham adopted many elements of Indian art and Sanksrit as their sacred language. Prevalent in an area stretching from the north of Hue south to the Mekong Delta in the 10th and 11th centuries, the Cham established a kingdom between the Khmer to the south and the Viet to the north. In the 12th century, the Cham were under frequent attack by the Khmer. In the 13th century, backed by the Chinese, the Viet attacked the northernmost Cham, but were defeated in 1377 when the Cham reached an agreement with the Chinese. The Cham had a substantial presence until the 1400s, when they were conquered by the Viet. After that, they had a much smaller presence in the area until they were finally completely overthrown by the Viet in the 1700s. Remnants of the sandstone-and-brick towers built for Hindu worship by the Cham can still be found along the central coast, and descendants of the Cham continue to live in the highlands.

The Cham Museum was founded by the French in 1915 to exhibit Cham sculptures and fragments of temples and towers found by archaeologists. Exhibits are arranged chronologically, reflecting the changing seats of power in the kingdom from Emperor Indrapura to Tra Kieu to My Son to Khuong My. The highly sensual, innovative, and expressive works from Tra Kieu's reign (7th century) and that of My Son (8th–9th centuries) and the abundant sandstone carvings of the god Shiva show the prosperity of the Kingdom of Champa.

As you walk through the museum, note that although Buddha is traditionally pictured seated in the lotus position, the Cham Buddha is displayed on a throne in an imperial pose, with his feet flat on the ground. This subtle difference in Buddha styles reflects the Cham belief in the spiritual continuum between crown and divinity—meaning that the nobility were thought to be "higher up" because they were more directly connected to God. The symbol of fertility Uroja (meaning woman's breast or female breast), which you will also see throughout the museum, reveals the esteem afforded women in Cham culture.

Keep in mind the following cast of characters as you look at the Cham sculptures: Vishnu, god of conservation and life; Garuda, the holy bird; Rama, god of creation and birth; Goddess Sarasvati, Rama's wife and goddess of sacred language, whose animal counterpart is a swan; Laksmi, Vishnu's wife and goddess of prosperity. Shiva, god of the dead, who is represented in phallic form (*linga*); Skanda, god of war and son of Shiva and Uma, who is often depicted as a peacock; Ganesha, god of peace and the son of Shiva and Uma, whose disobedience prompted Shiva to cut off his head. When Uma (Ganesha's mother and Shiva's wife) prayed to the gods for forgiveness and for a new head, they gave her a consolation prize of the head of the first animal she spotted. Hence you have the omnipresent elephant head and human body motif.

The central **Tra Kieu Altar** (in the Tra Kieu Room)—in the middle gallery, opposite the entrance and across the courtyard—illustrates in relief sculpture part of the Hindu *Ramayana* epic story. This is the museum's best-preserved relief. Beginning on the left panel and working clockwise, the narrative runs as follows: Rama successfully breaks the sacred bow; Rudra is granted the right to marry King Janak's daughter Princess Sita; the fathers, King Videha and King Dasaratha, interact; and the wedding festivities follow.

Although you may be offered a guided tour of the Cham Museum, you should make sure you understand what your potential guide is saying and that he or she is truly knowledgeable about the museum's contents before wasting your time and money. ✉ *Intersection of Tran Phu and Le Dinh Duong Sts., no phone.* 🎫 *20,000d.* ⏲ *Daily 8–11 and 1–5.*

OFF THE BEATEN PATH **MY SON** – About 70 km (43 mi) southwest of Danang are the My Son Cham ruins. Built between the 4th and 13th centuries, these temples and towers were dedicated to kings and divinities, particularly Shiva, who was considered the founder of the Kingdom of Champa. Unfortunately, not many of the brick structures remain—most were destroyed by B-52 bombings during the Vietnam War. Make arrangements for a car and driver through the Danang Travel Information Center (☞ *below*).

Lodging

$$$ **Marco Polo.** One of the nicest hotels in town and one of the only places that you would want to stay, the Marco Polo is a haven of Western-style efficiency (meaning: it has phones that work and an English-speaking staff). Rooms are large and tastefully decorated. ✉ *11 Quang Trung St.,* ☎ *0511/823–295,* FAX *0511/827–279. 28 rooms. Restaurant, bar, air-conditioning, IDD phones, minibars, refrigerators, TVs, room service, laundry service and dry cleaning, business services, travel services, car rental. AE, MC, V.*

Shopping

If you find yourself stuck in Danang for the day, fabric shops and tailors along **Hung Vuong Street** can make clothes for you cheaply and quickly. Shirts and pants should cost less than $10 apiece.

Marble Mountains

16 *11 km (7 mi) southwest of Danang, 19 km (12 mi) north of Hoi An.*

Five beautiful limestone peaks, known as the Marble Mountains, rise above the beach south of Danang and north of Hoi An. Tours from Danang en route to Hoi An generally stop here, and a visit here can easily be combined with a trip to China Beach (☞ *below*). The five Marble Mountains have been equated with the five basic elements of Chinese philosophy: Tho Son (earth), Thuy Son (water), Hoa Son (fire), Moc Son (wood), and Kim So (metal). Over the centuries the caves (*dong*) in the Thuy Son Peak have been turned into temples and shrines. The first to exploit them were the Cham, who used them as Hindu shrines. The Buddhists have since taken over, adorned, sanctified, and inhabited them.

Ever since the local government cracked down on solicitation—i.e., people hassling tourists for money—the Marble Mountains have become a very pleasant place to spend a few hours. The climb up the path leading to the various cave-pagodas is not particularly strenuous. Polite children in traditional schools uniforms (white shirt and blue trousers) may take you by the hand and give you a free guided tour of the various Buddhist cave sanctuaries. Since there is only one path, and there are enough people around, it is usually not a problem to have them accompany you. At the end of these tours, don't be surprised if they offer you the "best price. . . for you only" for marble souvenirs, such as miniature Marble Mountains. You shouldn't feel obliged to buy one, however.

After entering through **Ong Chon Gate,** the main entrance, you will see the **Linh Ong Pagoda,** a Buddhist shrine inside a cave, filled with a large collection of Buddhas. The hole at the top of the cave filters in an ethereal sort of natural light. As you continue on the main path, you will come to another temple, the **Tam Thai Tu Pagoda,** where monks still live. The path then leads to a spectacular view of the mountains and the surrounding countryside. ✉ *About 11 km (7 mi) south of Danang; 9½ km (6 mi) north of Hoi An off Hwy. 1.* 🎫 *Free, though donation may be requested at pagodas.*

China Beach

17 *12 km (7 mi) southwest of Danang, 45 km (28 mi) north of Hoi An.*

Yes, the TV show *China Beach* was based on this place, but the China Beach that was an R&R resort spot for U.S. soldiers during the Vietnam War is actually 5 km (3 mi) north of what is now called China Beach (Bac My An). China Beach's pristine and quiet sandy stretches are a welcome change from Danang's portlike atmosphere. Stop here on your way to or from Hoi An, make it a day trip from Danang or Hoi An, or stay at the Furama Resort (☞ Lodging, *below*); arrangements can be made through travel agencies in either town or in Ho Chi Minh City.

Activity on China Beach is limited to lazing on the sand and surfing. Surfboards can be rented from the China Beach Resort and the Furama Resort, where you can also rent surfing gear and bicycles. It's best to come between May and July, when the water is placid. Waves can be very big at other times—in fact, the first international surfing competition in Vietnam was held in China Beach in December 1992. With the opening of the Furama Resort, the atmosphere in China Beach is more inviting—and it means, thankfully, that there is somewhere to stay other than the state-run China Beach Resort.

Dining and Lodging

$$$ 🏨 **Furama Resort.** Right on the beach, this international, joint-venture resort, which opened in 1997, is made up of a group of French-Vietnamese–style villas surrounding a manmade tropical swimming lagoon. Rooms overlook either the lagoon or the ocean. The interior evokes the French-colonial era, with a Vietnamese influence: shuttered windows, cane furniture, ceiling fans, and Vietnamese pieces. The resort has a shuttle service from Danang's airport and can organize tours for you to Danang, Hue, and Hoi An. ✉ *68 Ho Xuan Huong St.,* ☎ *0511/847–333 or 08/821–1888 in Ho Chi Minh City,* FAX *0511/847–666. 200 rooms. 2 restaurants, 2 bars, air-conditioning, in-room safes, minibars, room service, pool, sauna, golf driving range, 4 tennis courts, health club, beach, surfing, bicycles, dry cleaning and laundry service, meeting rooms, travel services. AE, MC, V.*

$$$ ✕🏨 **China Beach Resort** (Non Nuoc). At the foot of the Marble Mountains, this glorified motel on the water is the only other lodging option in town. This ripe-for-the-wrecking-ball, 1960s concrete structure may be replaced by a new resort to be built by an American-Vietnamese joint venture at an unscheduled date in the future. If you must stay here, though, the resort has reasonably clean, utilitarian rooms with views of the sea. This is also one of the few places to eat in town with adequate Vietnamese food, although the environment is nondescript. ✉ *Non Nuoc, Danang,* ☎ *0511/836–216,* FAX *0511/836–335. 103 rooms with bath. 2 Restaurants, bar, air-conditioning, tennis courts, beach, laundry service, travel service, car rental.*

Danang and Environs A to Z

Arriving and Departing

BY CAR

China Beach and the Marble Mountains are easily accessible by car from Danang, as is Hoi An. You can make arrangements at most hotels and from the **Danang Travel Information Center** (✉ 3–5 Dong Da St., ☎ 0511/823–431). The trip shouldn't cost you too much. It is likely that you may stop at the Marble Mountains on your way from the airport in Danang to Hoi An.

BY PLANE

Vietnam Airlines (✉ 35 Tran Phu St., Danang, ☎ 0511/821–130, FAX 0511/832–759) flies to Danang's airport, 3 km (2 mi) southwest of the city, from Ho Chi Minh City (daily), Hanoi (daily), and Nha Trang (four times a week). To make arrangements in Danang, go to the Vietnam Airlines booking office, which also has a Vietcom Bank foreign exchange booth; it's open 7–11 and 1:30–4:30. Booking offices in Hoi An, including those in your hotel, can also make plane reservations. A regular taxi to the airport should cost no more than 50,000d; to reserve one, call **Airport Taxis** (☎ 0511/825–555), Danang's only taxi company.

Getting Around

BY CAR AND MOTORBIKE

See Arriving and Departing by Car, *above,* for information about renting cars with drivers; motorbikes can also be rented from many hotels and travel agencies.

BY TAXI

In Danang, the **taxi** drivers hanging out at the Cham Museum offer the cheapest rates in town—about 50,000d a day. They also provide transportation to Hoi An for about $10. Taxis are preferable to cyclos since the roads are bad, even in town, and the scenery is grim.

Contacts and Resources

CURRENCY EXCHANGE

Changing money at your hotel is the easiest option.

EMERGENCIES

Contact your hotel for medical assistance or if something has been stolen.

Travel Agency

Danang Travel Information Center (✉ 3–5 Dong Da St., ☎ 0511/823–298, 0511/824–555, or 0511/824–400; FAX 0511/823–431), which is affiliated with the Danang Hotel, can arrange guided tours and transportation in and around the city as well as to the airport.

HOI AN

Perhaps the most delightful of all Vietnamese towns, enchanting riverside Hoi An, 30 km (19 mi) south of Danang, defies the insidious pace of modernization. Preserved in pristine condition are its 18th-century houses, pagodas, and assembly halls built by the early Fukien, Canton, Chaozhou, and Hainan—Chinese communities living in Hoi An. Hoi An's bustling market also makes you feel as if you've gone back in time. The crowded streets are lined with souvenir vendors and shops selling the rice-paper canvases of local artists. You'll also find great cuisine, many tailors who can make you a nice suit in just one day, and a very pleasant sandy beach. The whole town can easily be navigated by foot in an hour, but plan to spend more time in Hoi An than you think you will want to, since it's easy to fall in love with the place.

Hoi An, or Faifo as it was called in previous centuries, is a composite of many foreign influences. From the 2nd to 10th centuries AD, the city was under the control of the Kingdom of Champa and was an important port town. During the 14th and 15th centuries, the Cham and the Vietnamese fought for control of Hoi An, and as a consequence the city ceased to be a trading center. Peace between the Cham and the Vietnamese in the 16th century once again made possible the accommodation of ships from all over Asia and Europe, bringing merchants in search of silk, porcelain, lacquer, and medicinal herbs. During the Tay Son rebellion in the 1770s, Hoi An was severely damaged by fighting.

After a speedy reconstruction, the town managed to sustain a two-century tenure as a major international port town where Chinese, Japanese, Dutch, and Portuguese merchants came to trade. During the off-season, seafaring merchants set up shop, and foreigners' colonies began to develop along Hoi An's riverfront. To this day, ethnic Chinese, who settled early in Hoi An, make up a significant portion of the population.

The French arrived in the late 1800s and made Hoi An an administrative post. They even built a rail line to Danang (then called Tourane). By this time, the Thu Bon River, which connected Hoi An to the sea, had begun to fill up with silt, making navigation almost impossible. Danang gradually eclipsed Hoi An as the major port town in the area, but when a 1916 storm washed away its railroad the town was never rebuilt. Fortunately, Hoi An was not destroyed during the Vietnam War.

The old town is made up of a combination of Vietnamese, Japanese, and Chinese architectural styles, and is strictly reserved for pedestrians, bicycles, and the occasional motorbike. It is the perfect place for a leisurely walk, with ancient structures on almost every corner. You can get a map from your hotel or from the local tourist office at the corner of Nguyen Hue Street and Phan Chu Trinh Street.

To get tickets to official monuments you must go to the central tourist office at the corner of Nguyen Hue Street and Phan Chu Trinh Street, rather than to the sites themselves. For 50,000d you get to choose from a "menu" of sights: one of three museums, one of three assembly halls, one of four old houses, and the Japanese Bridge or the Quan Cong Temple. Once you buy your first ticket from the tourist office, you may purchase an additional entry ticket there to any site for 10,000d (these are also available at most hotels).

A Good Walk

A good place to begin exploring Hoi An is at the tourist office on Nguyen Hue Street, close to the corner of Phan Chu Trinh Street. You can find an English- or French-speaking guide in the office for 50,000d.

After purchasing your ticket, start your walk at the small colonial-era **Museum of History and Culture** ⑱, approximately one block from the tourist office, at the corner of Tran Phu and Nguyen Hue streets. The entrance to the museum brings you to a collection of ancient ceremonial gongs and other religious objects. Walk across the courtyard filled with bird cages to get to **Quan Cong Temple** ⑲, dedicated to the deified Chinese general Quan Cong. Leave through the front entrance, and you'll find yourself directly in front of the **Central Market** ⑳, one of Vietnam's most pleasant and easy to navigate. Stay clear of the river unless you want to stumble onto the day's catch.

After leaving the market, make a left on Nguyen Hue Street, and continue past Hoang Dieu Street until you get to No. 178, the **Assembly**

Hall of the Hainan Chinese Congregation ㉑. Proceed east on Tran Phu Street, which turns into Nguyen Duy Hieu Street after it intersects with Hoang Dieu Street. Just past the intersection on the left, at No. 157, is the **Chaozhou Assembly Hall** ㉒, with its fine woodcarvings. Turn around and start walking down the street going west on Tran Phu Street. Continue until you get to the corner of Tran Phu and Tran Quy Cap Streets; cross over Tran Phu so that you are on the even-number side of the street, and continue walking until you hit Le Loi Street. Almost immediately on your right, at No. 46, is the colorful **Phuoc Kien Assembly Hall** ㉓, now a temple devoted to Thien Hau, the goddess of the sea. Just a few doors down is the **Assembly Hall of the Fujian Chinese Congregation** ㉔, also dedicated to Thien Hau. Continue along Tran Phu street until you come to No. 64, the **Chinese All-Community Assembly Hall** ㉕ on your right; as its name implies, it was used as a meeting place for all the Chinese communities in Hoi An. Farther along on your left will be the ancient **Quang Thang House** ㉖, at No. 77.

At No. 80 is the Diep Dong Nguyen House, which has been converted into the **Museum of Trade Ceramics** ㉗. At the intersection of Tran Phu and Nguyen Thai Hoc Streets on the north side, is the **Assembly Hall of the Cantonese Chinese Congregation** ㉘. Farther along Tran Phu Street, past a row of souvenir shops and the intersection with Nhi Trung Street, is the entrance to the red wooden **Japanese Bridge** ㉙. Keep going on Tran Phu Street, but note that the street name changes to Nguyen Thi Minh Khai Street. At No. 4 is the **Old House of Phung Hung** ㉚, where eight generations of one family have lived for more than 200 years. Turn around and head back east on Tran Phu Street. Take the small road that forks in front of the Japanese Bridge to get to Nguyen Thai Hoc Street. At No. 101 is the **Old House of Tan Ky** ㉛. Continue east until you arrive at Le Loi Street and make a left. Cross Phan Chu Trinh Street; on the corner is the **Tran Family Chapel** ㉜, where you can get a tour from members of the Tran Family.

TIMING

This walk will probably take you about five or six hours at a very leisurely pace. Visiting other sights outside of town (☞ Off the Beaten Path, *below*) will take about an hour each.

Sights to See

28 **Assembly Hall of the Cantonese Chinese Congregation.** The main altar of this hall, founded in 1786, is dedicated to Quan Cong, a revered General of the Chinese Han dynasty. ⊠ *176 Tran Phu St., at Nguyen Thai Hoc St.* 🎫 *Included in 50,000d tourist-office ticket.* ⏲ *Daily 8–5.*

24 **Assembly Hall of the Fujian Chinese Congregation.** Built as a meeting place for Chinese residents of Hoi An, this hall later became a temple dedicated to the Fujian goddess of the sea and protector of fishermen, Thien Hau. It is a reminder of how important fishing and trading were to the Chinese community in Hoi An. Thien Hau is represented in the mural near the entrance. Another mural depicts six Fujian families who fled from China to Hoi An in the 17th century. The gate is newer: it was constructed in 1975. ⊠ *Opposite 35 Tran Phu St.* 🎫 *Included in 50,000d tourist-office ticket.* ⏲ *Daily 8–5.*

21 **Assembly Hall of the Hainan Chinese Congregation.** This hall, founded by Chinese from Hainan, was constructed in 1883 in memory of more than 100 merchants who were mistakenly (some say purposefully) killed by a general in Emperor Tu Duc's army because they were thought to be pirates. ⊠ *178 Nguyen Duy Hieu St.* 🎫 *Included in 50,000d tourist-office ticket.* ⏲ *Daily 8–5.*

A. H. of the Cantonese Chinese Congregation, **28**
A. H. of the Fujian Chinese Congregation, **24**
A. H. of the Hainan Chinese Congregation, **21**
Central Market, **20**
Chaozhou A. H., **22**
Chinese All-Community A. H., **25**
Japanese Bridge, **29**
Museum of History and Culture, **18**
Museum of Trade Ceramics, **27**
Old House of Phung Hung, **30**
Old House of Tan Ky, **31**
Phuoc Kien A. H., **23**
Quan Cong Temple, **19**
Quang Thang House, **26**
Tran Family Chapel, **32**

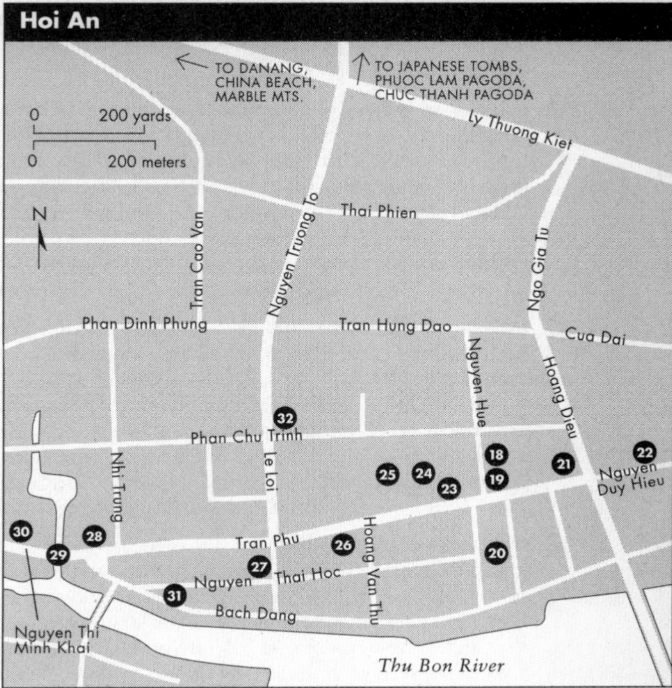

20 **Central Market.** Hoi An's Central Market is one of the most enjoyable markets in Vietnam. The merchants here are friendly and there is a large selection of merchandise available. The outer aisles of the market are lined with silk shops that can do custom clothing orders—pants, shirts, dresses, and even suits—all made for you in less than 24 hours. In the center aisles are fresh and dried fruit, flowers, and fresh tobacco. Walk toward the river to find the fish sellers with their daily catch. Miscellaneous items, such as batteries, pajamas, and bicycle pumps, pop up in stands throughout. ✉ *Intersection of Tran Quy Cap and Tran Phu Sts.* ⏲ *Daily 6–dusk.*

22 **Chaozhou Assembly Hall** (Trieu Chau). Constructed by the Chaozhou Chinese community in 1776, this assembly hall exemplifies Chinese wood carving of this period at its finest. Note the carved ceiling and the depiction of Chinese women on the doors in the front of the altar. ✉ *157 Nguyen Duy Hieu St.* 🎫 *Included in 50,000d tourist-office ticket.* ⏲ *Daily 8–5.*

25 **Chinese All-Community Assembly Hall** (Chua Ba). This assembly hall was built in 1773 as a meeting place for Cantonese, Chaozhou, Fujian, Hainan, and Hakka families living in Hoi An. ✉ *64 Tran Phu St.* 🎫 *Included in 50,000d tourist-office ticket.* ⏲ *Daily 8–5.*

29 **Japanese Bridge** (Cau Nhat, or Lai Vien Kieu). One of the city's landmarks and one of it's oldest structures, this red-painted, wooden bridge was originally built in 1593 by the Japanese to link their quarter of town to the Chinese quarter. It has been rebuilt a number of times since. At one end of the structure are statues of two dogs; at the other, statues of two monkeys—perhaps indicating the years when the bridge's construction was begun and completed. The small temple (Chua Cau) on the northern side of the bridge is dedicated to Tran Vo Bac De (God of the North), revered by sailors because he controls wind and rain. ✉ *Intersection of Tran Phu and Nguyen Thi Minh Khai Sts.* *Included in 50,000d tourist-office ticket.* *Daily 8–5.*

18 **Museum of History and Culture.** This small museum—housed in just one large room—provides a great introduction to Hoi An and its culture. On display are ancient bowls, cups, and other ceramics, many of them archeological artifacts. There is also a collection of traditional Chinese objects, including pagoda bells and the "watchful eyes" placed above doorways for protection. The courtyard is filled with bird cages, which makes for a pleasant atmosphere. ✉ *7 Nguyen Hue St., no phone.* *Included in 50,000d tourist-office ticket.* *Daily 8–5.*

★ 27 **Museum of Trade Ceramics.** The ancient Diep Dong Nguyen House has been converted into a terrific small museum dedicated to the history of ceramics in Hoi An. The collection includes ancient wares, some of them recovered from shipwrecks in the surrounding waters; and a large assortment of household objects, such as bowls and vases. There are also detailed architectural drawings of the house, with an explanation of its design and its Chinese, Vietnamese, and Japanese influences. ✉ *80 Tran Phu St.* *Included in 50,000d tourist-office ticket.* *Daily 8–5.*

30 **Old House of Phung Hung.** Ask the owner to explain in French, or his granddaughter to explain in English, the architectural significance of this house built in 1780. Eight generations of the Phung Hung family have lived here since that time. Note the Japanese influences in the roof, the Chinese influences in the balcony, and the Vietnamese architectural style of the walls. On the second floor is a bowl containing dice; if you roll a red one, it is said, your journey will be lucky; if not, you should probably postpone your trip. ✉ *4 Nguyen Thi Minh Khai St.* *Included in 50,000d tourist-office ticket.* *Daily 8–5.*

31 **Old House of Tan Ky.** One of the oldest private houses in Hoi An, this house has remained largely unchanged in the 200 years since it was built. Seven generations of the Tan Ky family have lived here. The house incorporates both Chinese and Japanese styles. Chinese poetry is engraved in mother-of-pearl on the walls. The back door was constructed to open onto the river so that water-borne goods could be easily transported into the house. ✉ *101 Nguyen Thai Hoc St.* *Included in 50,000d tourist-office ticket.* *Daily 8–5.*

23 **Phuoc Kien Assembly Hall.** Like so many of the structures in this port city, this colorfully decorated building, constructed in 1690 and redone in 1900, is dedicated to Thien Hau, the goddess of the sea. ✉ *46 Tran Phu St.* *Included in 50,000d tourist-office ticket.* *Daily 8–5.*

NEED A BREAK? Dine in a 200-year-old home at the **Yellow River (Hoang Ha) Restaurant** (✉ 38 Tran Phu St.), where the owner serves Chinese specialties and will happily tell you about his family.

19 **Quan Cong Temple.** Founded in 1653 by the Chinese community, this temple is dedicated to Quan Cong, a revered general of the Chinese Han dynasty. Come here to contemplate life inside the bright red interior of the temple or while watching the small school of fish that happily dart around in the pond out front. The carp, symbolic of patience in Chinese mythology, is displayed throughout. ✉ *168 Tran Phu St.* *Included in 50,000d tourist-office ticket.* *Daily 8–5.*

26 **Quang Thang House.** Another of Hoi An's ancient family homes—built about 300 years ago—this house has some beautiful wood carvings on the walls of the rooms that surround the courtyard. ✉ *77 Tran Phu St.* *Included in 50,000d tourist-office ticket.* *Daily 8–5.*

33 **Tran Family Chapel.** Built in 1802, this house is dedicated to the worship of the Tran family's deceased ancestors. The altar in the house faces west, the direction the Vietnamese believe their ancestors face. Behind the altar stands a box with pictures and names of dead relatives. Tours are given in English by members of the Tran family. ✉ *21 Le Loi St. and 77 Tran Phu St.* 🎫 *Included in 50,000d tourist-office ticket.* ⏲ *Daily 8–5.*

OFF THE BEATEN PATH

CHUC THANH PAGODA AND PHUOC LAM PAGODA – If you are interested in seeing even more pagodas, head north on Nguyen Truang To Street for approximately 1 km (½ mi) to the end, turn left, and follow the path until you reach the Chuc Thanh Pagoda, the oldest pagoda in Hoi An. Founded in 1454 by Minh Hai, a Chinese Buddhist monk, the pagoda contains several ancient religious objects, including several bells and gongs made of both stone and wood. On the way back stop at the Phuoc Lam Pagoda, this one built in the mid-17th century. Note the interesting Chinese architecture and the large collection of ceramics on its roof. Both pagodas are open daily 8–5.

JAPANESE TOMBS – Hire a motorbike and a driver to take you 3 km (2 mi) north of the city to see the few surviving tombs of Hoi An's old Japanese community. (Cars are not recommended since the tombs are at the end of a narrow, rugged path, and the tombs are almost impossible to find on your own.) The tombs were erected in the 1600s and are reminders of the early Japanese presence in the area. Although the tombs—tombstones, really—are not nearly as grand as those in Hue, it's worth the trek if only to see the "suburbs" of Hoi An. En route you will see families sitting in their front yards, and field workers harvesting rice. Buried in the first tomb along the dirt path—clearly visible in the front yard of a family home, although there are no signs—is a Japanese merchant named Masai. About another 1,500 ft ahead is the most famous of Hoi An's Japanese tombs, the burial place of another Japanese merchant named Yajirobei who died in 1647. Perched right in the middle of a working rice field, his tomb has an almost supernatural feel.

Dining and Lodging

$$ ★ ✕ **Café des Amis.** There is no menu at the Café des Amis. Instead, your waiter will ask if you want to eat a seafood or vegetarian meal and then he will start bringing you food. Expect five or six excellent courses. Funky Western background music and a waterfront location make for a great atmosphere. ✉ *52 Bach Dang St.,* ☎ *0510/861–616. No credit cards.*

$$ ✕ **Ving Hung Restaurant.** A peaceful oasis across the street from the Cantonese Assembly Hall, this restaurant serves superb seafood and local specialties such as White Roses, the delicious shrimp dumpling said to resemble a rose. Chinese lanterns and lacquered chairs decorate the place, which caters primarily to tourists. Sit outside on Chinese high-back wooden chairs, and watch your fellow travelers walk by. ✉ *1 Nguyen Hue St.,* ☎ *0510/862–203. No credit cards.*

$ ✕ **Faifoo.** Come here for refreshing fruit shakes, as well as a great multicourse sampler menu of chicken and pork dishes, all for next to nothing. You might want to avoid the "Pizza-Spaghetti-Guacamole," however, it's not one of Faifoo's better dishes. ✉ *104 Tran Phu St.,* ☎ *0510/861–548. No credit cards.*

$ ✕ **Ly Cafeteria 22.** Catering mostly to backpackers, this very friendly spot serves tasty local specialties such as *cao lau* (a noodle dish topped with pork and bean sprouts) and White Roses. This is a great place for a cheap lunch; it's also open for dinner. ✉ *22 Nguyen Hue St.,* ☎ *0510/861–603. No credit cards.*

$ ✕ **My Lac.** Excellent traditional Vietnamese and Chinese cuisine at unbeatable prices is served at this friendly, family-run establishment. ✉ *106 Tran Phu St.,* ☎ *0510/861–591. No credit cards.*

$ ✕ **Restaurant Thanh.** This restaurant makes a splendid flounder (or whatever white fish happens to be fresh that day) cooked in banana leaves, as well as a refreshing squid salad prepared with lemon, onions, peanuts, and cucumber. Unfortunately the open-air, candlelight riverfront ambience is frequently disrupted by persistent postcard vendors. ✉ *76 Bach Dang St.,* ☎ *0510/861–366. No credit cards.*

$$–$$$ **Hoai Thanh.** Slightly away from the center of town, the Hoai Thanh is the place to try when other, more centrally located properties fill up. Rooms are utilitarian but clean. ✉ *23 Le Hong Phong St.,* ☎ *0510/861–242 or 0510/861–171,* FAX *0510/861–135. 43 rooms. Restaurant, air-conditioning, fans, refrigerator, laundry service, travel services, car rental, free parking. No credit cards.*

$$–$$$ **Hoi An Hotel.** The most cheerful staff in all of Vietnam makes up for the lack of luxury in what is just about the only real hotel in Hoi An. It's also the only hotel that takes credit cards or traveler's checks. Rooms are comfortable, spotless, and spacious, if basic (there are hair dryers, though). The outstanding Hoi An tourist office is in the lobby; it runs tours of the city and makes travel arrangements for your next destination. ✉ *6 Tran Hung Dao St.,* ☎ *0510/861–445,* FAX *0510/861–636. 130 rooms. Restaurant, air-conditioning, fans, bicycles, laundry services, travel services, car rental. AE, MC, V.*

$$ **Cu Dai Hoi An Hotel.** One of the nicest and newest accommodations in town, this plush minihotel has spotless, sunny rooms, many with balconies. It's between the beach and the town center, and both are just a short bike ride away (you can rent bikes at the hotel). ✉ *18A Cua Dai St.,* ☎ *0510/861–722. 17 rooms. Restaurant, air-conditioning, fans, bicycles, laundry service, travel services. No credit cards.*

$$ **Sea Star.** Rooms at this newer hotel, just outside the town center on the way to the beach, are clean but basic. ✉ *15 Cua Dai St.,* ☎ *0510/861–589,* FAX *0510/861–858. 11 rooms. Restaurant, air-conditioning, laundry service, travel services, car rental. No credit cards.*

$$ **Thien Trung.** This hotel is very close to the bus station and only a short bike ride from the old town. Rooms are neat and bright. ✉ *63 Phan Ding Phung St.,* ☎ *0510/861–720 or 0510/861–769. 16 rooms. Restaurant, air-conditioning, fans, laundry service, travel services, car rental. No credit cards.*

$$ **Vinh Hung Hotel.** Not far from the Japanese Bridge, this Chinese-inspired hotel has dark wood carvings and a smiling Buddha in the lobby. Rooms are sunny and cheerfully decorated. ✉ *142 Tran Phu St.,* ☎ *0510/861–621,* FAX *0510/861–893. 12 rooms. Bar, air-conditioning, fans, laundry service, travel services. No credit cards.*

$ **Pho Hoi (Faifoo) Minihotel.** Close to the river and the Central Market, this hotel has a couple of brightly decorated, basic rooms with balconies overlooking the tree-lined street; ask for one these. Others don't have windows and aren't nearly as nice. ✉ *73 Phan Boi Chau St.,* ☎ *0510/861–453. 20 rooms. Air-conditioning, fans, bicycles, motorbikes, travel services, car rental. No credit cards.*

$ **Thanh Binh.** This centrally located hotel has clean rooms that get plenty of light. Get here early: the hotel often fills up by noon with budget travelers. ✉ *1 Le Loi St.,* ☎ *0510/861–740. 14 rooms. Air-conditioning, fans, laundry service, travel services, car rental, free parking. No credit cards.*

Outdoor Activities and Sports

For a low-impact, highly scenic workout, rent a **bicycle** and ride 20 minutes from the center of town to Cua Dai Beach, a splendid place to catch a breeze and relax in the sun. Bikes can be rented from a number of places in town (☞ Getting Around *in* Hoi An A to Z, *below*). To get to the beach, go 5 km (3 mi) east of the town center along Tran Hung Dao Street, which turns into Cua Dai Street, all the way to the beach. The price for parking your bicycle is often as much as for a day-long rental, but it is easily negotiable; you shouldn't pay more than 1,000d.

Short **paddleboat trips** along the Thu Bon (Cai River) can be arranged at Huang Van Thu Street or through young solicitors who hang out at the riverside cafés across from 50 Bach Dang Street. Hoi An Tourism (☞ Visitor Information and Travel Agencies, *below*) arranges **motorized boat trips,** including visits to a ceramics factory and a shipyard. Full-day boat trips to Cham Island and to My Son and Cam Kim islands can also be arranged at the dock across from 50 Bach Dang Street.

Shopping

Because it's a low-key place, Hoi An is perhaps the most pleasant town in all of Vietnam in which to shop for souvenirs and clothes—and the quality of items here is generally pretty high. Along **Tran Phu Street** are numerous shops selling everything from works of art and ceramics to clothing and opium paraphernalia. Though most ceramic objects are billed as antiques, only some are the real thing. Unless you are an antiques expert or do some serious comparative shopping—which usually means being duped into buying an "antique" and then having another shop owner let you know that you were fooled—it is often impossible to tell a phony from a real antique by the price since they often cost the same. Bargaining is advisable as quoted prices are generally largely inflated, especially for fine art.

For cheap casual clothing and same-day service on custom orders, the seamstress stalls at the **Central Market** (✉ 65 Nguyen Duy Hieu St.) are your best bet (there is very little ready-made apparel available in Hoi An). These stalls are overflowing with endless yards of Vietnamese, Japanese, and Chinese silks and cottons. Try stall **No. 10 Diep,** where the large staff of women uses a bit of English, fine-tuned charades, and stick-figure fashion drawings to deduce what you want made (they can make just about anything in only a few hours). Shirts cost as little as 30,000d and pants as little as 50,000d. The seamstresses at this stall seem to toil all day and all night, long after other stalls have closed. For slightly more elaborate articles of clothing, such as fitted jackets and formal attire, tiny **Phuong Huy II** (✉ 21B Tran Phu St.) can turn any order around in a day.

Hoi An A to Z

Arriving and Departing

BY CAR

The only way to get to Hoi An from Danang is by minibus or car, which takes about an hour due to poor road conditions, even though it's only a 30 km (19 mi) trip. The trip to Hoi An costs $5–$10, depending on the number of passengers, and is a very scenic drive through small towns and rice paddies. You can rent a car with a driver from **Danang Travel Information Center** (✉ 3–5 Dong Da St., Danang, ☎ 0510/823–431) or from any travel agency in Hoi An (☞ Contacts and Resources, *below*).

BY PLANE

The closest **airport** to Hoi An is the one in Danang, 30 km (19 mi) north. To get to Hoi An, rent a car with a driver in Danang.

Getting Around

The most enjoyable and most convenient means of getting around Hoi An are on foot, by bicycle (for 550d per day), and by motorcycle (for 5,500d–7,700d per day). There are only a few cyclos, but the town is so small that you probably won't need to take one. **Hoi An Tourism,** which operates out of the Hoi An Hotel (☞ Lodging, *above*), has a wide variety of bicycles and motorcycles for rent. You can also rent bikes from many hotels and cafés.

Contacts and Resources

CURRENCY EXCHANGE

Change money at your hotel or at the **Hoi An Bank** (✉ 4 Hoang Dieu St.).

EMERGENCIES

Contact your hotel in case of an emergency.

PRECAUTIONS

The streets of Hoi An are very dark at night, but the city is generally safe. Consider bringing a flashlight to help you find your way around.

TRAVEL AGENCIES

There are a number of booking offices along Le Loi and Tran Hung Dao streets handling train and plane reservations, car rentals, hotel arrangements, and excursions from Hoi An to the Marble Mountains and China Beach.

Hoi An Tourism Office (✉ 6 Tran Hung Dao St., ☎ 0510/861–373 or 0510/861–362, FAX 0510/861–636), the state-run travel agency operated out of the Hoi An Hotel, organizes tours following several different itineraries of the city, as well as excursions to the Marble Mountains and China Beach. The staff here speaks perfect English and provides excellent services.

5 The South-Central Coast and Highlands

Nha Trang and Dalat

Set aside a few days to escape to two of Vietnam's best-known resort towns, Nha Trang—by the sea—and Dalat—in the mountains. In Nha Trang, stroll along stretches of sandy beach, dance through the night at a waterfront disco, and explore ancient Cham ruins. Go to Dalat, a quiet mountain village, for long walks and to visit Emperor Bao Dai's summer palace along with the many Vietnamese honeymooners who favor this place.

By Sherrie Nachman with Pilar Guzman

THE SPRAWLING BEACHES OF NHA TRANG and the cool mountain refuge of Dalat are the reasons to come to south-central Vietnam. Nha Trang, the capital of Khan Hoa Province, and Dalat are two of the country's oldest resorts. Nha Trang has long been a favorite destination for Vietnamese, who come to frolic in the sea. Today it has numerous hotels and a crowded beachfront. Dalat has been a popular retreat since the French first started coming here at the beginning of the century. A mountain town in the midst of the central highlands, it has an abundance of natural beauty but few stellar attractions. Come here to catch a cool hilltop breeze, even in summer when the rest of the country is sweltering; play golf and go hiking; and visit the waterfalls along with the many Vietnamese who spend their honeymoons in Dalat.

Don't expect untouched beaches or mountain terrain in Nha Trang or Dalat, however. Both are established resort towns and are undergoing further development as new hotels are built and old ones renovated. One benefit of these hotels is their amenities such as golf courses, tennis courts, and swimming pools, all still uncommon elsewhere in Vietnam. Yet despite such attempts to lure a more international crowd, the bulk of foreign visitors seems to be backpackers who have come to hang out. Although there are several attractions to keep you busy in Nha Trang and Dalat, there are few cultural or historic sites of note. Visit these towns only if you have some extra time and want to spend a few days relaxing in a pleasant environment.

Pleasures and Pastimes

Beaches

Nha Trang's several miles of narrow, sandy beaches stretch from the center of town to its north end. Pick a spot to lounge on the beach, go swimming, and have a light meal at a waterfront café. Though the beaches are clean and pleasant, they are not isolated: Along the beach is the road on which sit most of the town's hotels—a reminder that Nha Trang is a resort town.

Dining

Nha Trang has numerous outstanding and reasonably priced seafood restaurants, including a few along the beachfront. Many serve whatever has been caught earlier in the day. Unusual for a town of its size, Nha Trang also has two restaurants serving Western-style food—which means that you won't have any trouble finding burgers or spaghetti and meatballs here. In contrast, the large agricultural center of Dalat has surprisingly poor and uninspiring restaurants. Dalat's only local specialties are dried deer meat, strawberry jam, and artichoke tea, though you can find plenty of basic Vietnamese food.

Lodging

For such a lovely place, Nha Trang has the dubious distinction of having the largest number of run-down and dreary hotels in Vietnam. Most larger properties were put up in the 1960s or '70s and look like they have hardly been touched since. In most places, expect peeling linoleum, see-through sheets, dirty towels, stained walls, and no sign that your room has been cleaned in the last year. Thankfully, however, there are a few good alternatives—several resorts and small hotels that have been built in the last few years. You're best off looking for a place with the most recent opening date. New hotels are obvious from their exteriors, or you can ask how long a place has been opened when you call. Dalat has one of Vietnam's only true luxury hotels outside Ho Chi

Minh City and Hanoi—the Sofitel Palace, which is reminiscent of a French château and has the added bonus of an adjacent tennis court and golf course. Other hotels in Dalat are clean and cheerful. Unless otherwise noted, every room has a private bathroom in the recommended hotels.

Nightlife

Nha Trang has quite an exciting nightlife for such a small Vietnamese city. Many bars and ice cream shops stay open well past midnight. You can play pool until breakfast time at the Nha Trang Sailing Club and dance until 4 AM at several bars and the local disco. Dalat, on the other hand, is the ideal place to crack open that book you've been carrying around because there is really nothing else to do at night.

Outdoor Activities and Sports

As resort towns, both Nha Trang and Dalat provide myriad activities. In Nha Trang you can go swimming, diving, sailing, and snorkeling, as well as participate in many other water sports. Dalat's mountains and lakes provide an ideal place for a long walk or a trip in a paddle boat.

Waterfalls

Consistent with its image as a honeymoon resort town, Dalat is home to several gushing waterfalls, including Cam Ly Falls, Datania Falls, and Prenn Falls. Though they don't compare in size to Niagara Falls, they are good places to spend a couple of hours wandering around.

Exploring the South-Central Coast and Highlands

Dalat is only about 120 km (74 mi) southwest of Nha Trang, but the trip can easily take at least seven hours by car. The driving is slow because the roads connecting the towns are winding, narrow, and badly paved. If you do go by car, you'll pass through lush countryside covered with rice fields and, closer to Dalat, coffee farms and strawberry fields. The easiest way to get to either city is to fly directly from Ho Chi Minh City; there are no direct flights between Nha Trang and Dalat.

Numbers in the text correspond to numbers in the margin and on the South-Central Coast and Highlands, Nha Trang, and Dalat maps.

Great Itineraries

IF YOU HAVE 3 DAYS

Choose either **Nha Trang** ①–③ or **Dalat** ⑧–㉑ as your destination; it takes too long and is too difficult to get to both in so short a time. Remember that this is the part of your trip when you get to relax, so you're probably better off visiting just one place. Spend one day sightseeing and the other days loafing around. With so short a time, you would definitely want to fly here from either Hanoi or Ho Chi Minh City.

IF YOU HAVE 6 DAYS

With six days you could see both **Dalat** ⑧–㉑ and **Nha Trang** ①–③. Drive to Dalat through the **central highlands** ④–⑦. Spend two days in Dalat. On the morning of the third day, wake up early and drive to Nha Trang. You should arrive by midafternoon and will have two days at the beach before flying home on the morning of the sixth day. Be sure to try as many restaurants as possible in Nha Trang.

TIMING

The best time to come to Nha Trang is between June and September, during the dry season. It rains frequently in October and November and can be chilly. Dalat provides the most relief from June through August, when the rest of the country is really hot.

The South-Central Coast and Highlands

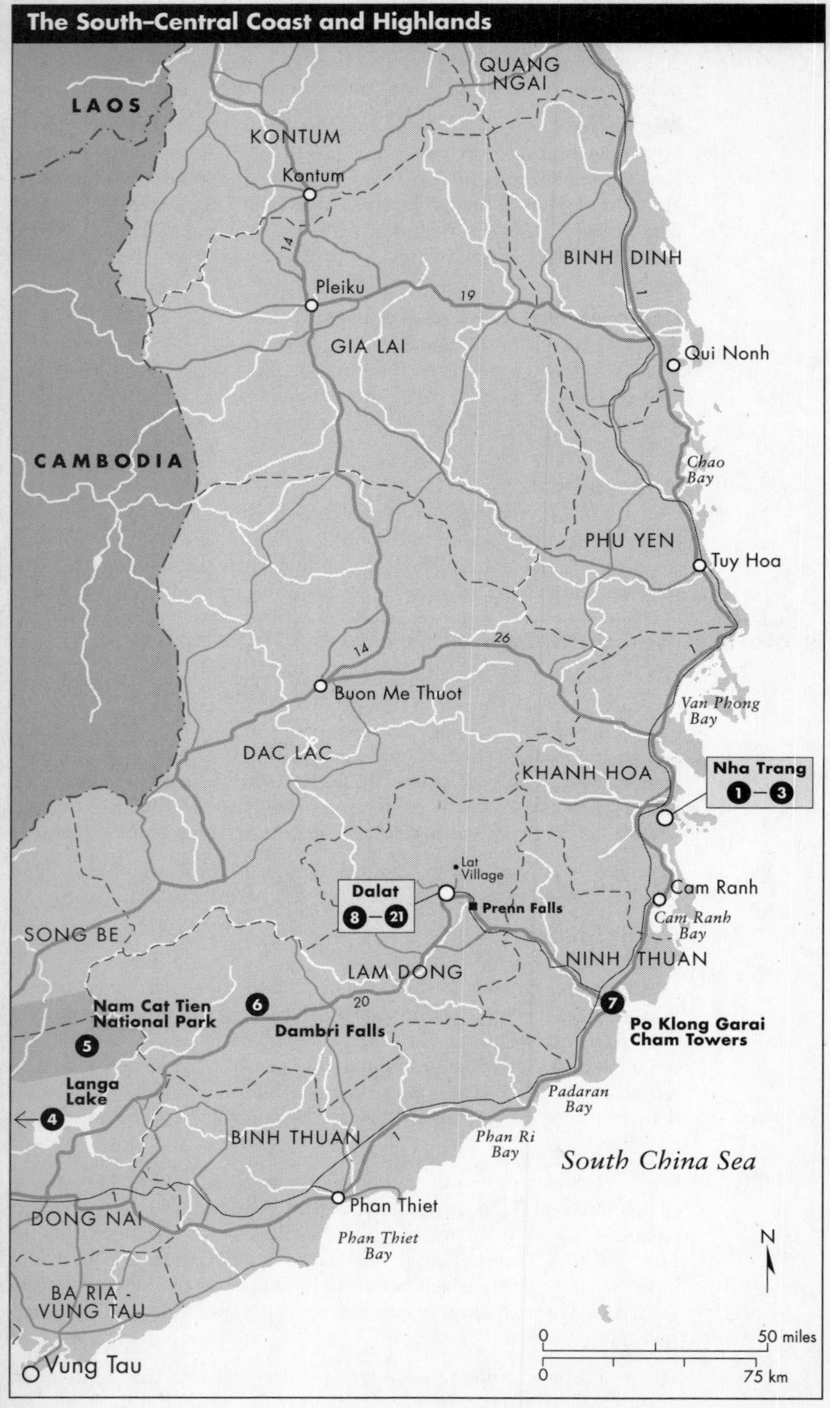

NHA TRANG

A bustling city with a long stretch of developed beachfront, Nha Trang is not an idyllic, deserted hideaway. Older hotels share the waterfront with an assortment of flashy, new, Western-style joint-venture establishments. But the beachfront still retains its charms: Swarms of high-school students bike to and from classes, and hordes of teenagers play soccer in the few waterfront lots that have not been turned into tourist sights. Recreational attractions include swimming, scuba diving, and snorkeling, and boat trips to neighboring Hon Tre (Bamboo Island), Mieu Island, Dao Khi (Monkey Island), and Hon Yen (Salangane Island)—lush enclaves with isolated beaches and groves of palm trees.

Exploring Nha Trang

The easiest way to get around town is by *cyclo* (pedicab). They're not hard to find; in fact, they'll probably find you first. Another way to see Nha Trang is by motorbike—with or without a driver. A third option is to hire a car and driver.

❶ The beautiful **Long Son Pagoda**, built in the late 19th century and reconstructed a number of times since, is the town's most famous. To reach it from town, follow Yerstin Street inland on foot, by bike, or by motorbike, about 2 km (1 mi) from the coast. When you come to No. 23 Thang 10 Street (called Thai Nguyen Street as you get closer to the water), make a right (continuing inland) to get to the pagoda. A giant Buddha beckons you up a flight of stairs, at the top of which is a panoramic view of Nha Trang. The entrance to the pagoda itself is down below. The resident monks happily give guided tours of the main sanctuary. ✉ *About 550 yards west of railroad station, opposite 15, 23 Thang 10.* ⏲ *Daily 8–noon and 2–4.*

Nha Trang is home to one of the better preserved Cham ruins in Viet-
❷ nam, the **Po Nagar Cham Towers** (Nha Trang Huu Duc), also known as the Mother Goddess or Lady of the City Towers. To reach them from the center of town, take Quang Trung Street, which turns into 2 Thang 4 Street (the name of the street, not an address), then cross the Cai River on the Ha Ra and Xom Bong bridges. Here there are colorful vignettes of postcard-perfect fishing-boat activity. As you cross the second bridge, you'll see the impressive towers jutting up from the hill on the left-hand side. As the walk is not that pleasant, consider taking a cyclo. The towers were originally a site of Hindu worship dating from the 2nd century; the present buildings were constructed between the 7th and 12th centuries. Today it is still an active shrine for Chinese and Vietnamese Buddhists. Of the original eight towers, four remain in various states of preservation. The North Tower (Thap Chinh), built during King Harivarman I's reign in AD 817, originally housed a *linga,* a phallic stone. After the linga was stolen and replaced, the stone statue of Uma that you see today was finally substituted for it. ✉ *On north side of Cai River over Hai Ra and Xom Bong bridges.* 🎫 *6,000d.* ⏲ *Daily 8–5.*

On the same side of the river as the Po Nagar Cham Towers (☞ *above*)
❸ is the **Hon Chong Promontory,** where there are good views of the coastline and the surrounding islands. From the Po Nagar ruins, head north on 2 Thang 4 Street and take a right on Nguyen Dinh Chieu Street. Climb up the promontory for a good view of Nha Trang and Hon Rua (Tortoise Island), both to the northeast. Look northwest to see Nui Co Tien (Fairy Mountain), said to look like a reclining fairy. ✉ *About ¾ km (¼ mi) from intersection of Nguyen Dinh Chieu and 2 Thang 4 Sts.* 🎫 *10,000d.* ⏲ *Daily 8–4.*

Hon Chong Promontory, **3**
Long Son Pagoda, **1**
Po Nagar Cham Towers, **2**

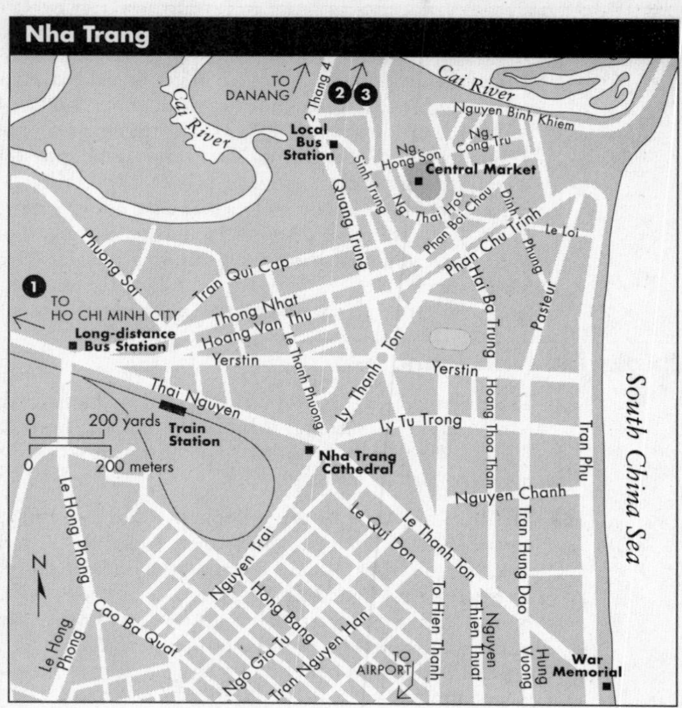

No trip to Nha Trang would be complete without a boat trip to the surrounding islands, such as Mieu Island (Tri Nguyen Island), Bamboo Island (Hon Tre), and Monkey Island (Dao Khi). Boat trips can be arranged through any number of hotels and travel agencies (☞ Contacts and Resources *in* Nha Trang A to Z, *below*). **Mama Hahn's Boat Trips** to these islands are reputed to be the most fun, with music, an endless supply of mulberry wine, and a Club Med mentality. Book through the Nha Trang Sailing Club (☞ Dining and Lodging *and* Nightlife and the Arts, *below*). Almost all boat trips serve an impressive feast of seafood for lunch as well as an amazing array of exotic fruits, all included in the $17 price.

North of town are two more isolated and less developed beaches, **Doc Let,** (30 km/19 mi), and **Dai Lanh,** (83 km/51 mi). To reach them it's best to hire a car and driver or simply catch a cab.

Dining and Lodging

$$$ ✕ **Casa Italia.** Chef Marco Russoni serves surprisingly authentic Italian food. This restaurant is a great place for a pasta lunch while sitting in a lounge chair facing the sea. ✉ *Tran Phu St., in Huong Duong Center,* ☎ *058/823–914,* FAX *058/825–768. No credit cards.*

$$ ★ ✕ **Nha Trang Sailing Club.** The most happening of all the seaside cafés/restaurants in town, the Sailing Club is popular with expats, locals, and tourists. It's the place to go if you're looking for something other than Vietnamese food: Burgers, fish-and-chips, and tomato soup are all on the menu. Westerners come for breakfast, lunch, and dinner. Boat trips can be arranged through the office just behind the restaurant. ✉ *72–74 Tran Phu St.,* ☎ *058/826–528,* FAX *058/821–906. No credit cards.*

$$ ★ ✕ **Ngoc Suong.** This establishment a block from the beach serves the best and the freshest seafood in town. It also has a friendly waitstaff. Fish salad, made from marinated local seafood, is the specialty. The rather daunting and rambling English-language menu also includes wild boar meat and testicles. But you're best off sticking to the fish dishes. ✉ *16 Tran Quang Khai St., not far from Tran Phu St.,* ☎ *058/954–516. No credit cards.*

$ ✕ **Lac Canh.** Here is your chance to hang out with locals. At each table in this smoke-filled restaurant is a charcoal grill on which you can make your own cheap and delicious marinated seafood and meat dishes. Just be prepared for one odd habit: The diners pile empty beer bottles and other leftovers on the floor after they're done with them. ✉ *11 Hang Ca,* ☎ *058/821–391. No credit cards.*

$ ✕ **Thanh Lich.** At this rustic family-run restaurant excellent fresh seafood specials are prepared before your eyes. The sublime squid in ginger comes to your table as a raw marinade and is cooked on a portable charcoal burner at your table, then lingers on your breath for the next two days. The marinated beef in lime juice, which arrives sizzling in a clay pot, is equally delicious. ✉ *8 Phan Boi Chau St.,* ☎ *058/821–955. No credit cards.*

¢ ✕ **Banana Split.** This small sidewalk café serves ice-cream sundaes, as well as Western-style dishes such as omelets, chicken, and burgers. Open for breakfast, lunch, and dinner, it's a destination for homesick Western travelers looking to meet other people. Boat trips and other travel arrangements can also be made here. ✉ *58 Quang Trung St.,* ☎ *058/829–115. No credit cards.*

¢ ✕ **Thanh The.** Locals and Vietnamese tourists pack this restaurant specializing in seafood and traditional Vietnamese fare. ✉ *3 Phan Chu Trinh St.,* ☎ *058/821–931. No credit cards.*

¢ ✕ **Vietnam Restaurant.** This family-run Vietnamese restaurant serves excellent seafood at low prices. Tasty unnamed fried fish is a specialty. ✉ *23 Hoang Van Thu St.,* ☎ *058/822–933. No credit cards.*

$$$ ★ **Ana Mandara Nha Trang Resort.** Completed in 1997, this beachfront resort is the classiest and most comfortable place to stay in Nha Trang. Reminiscent of Balinese- and Thai-style resorts, the hotel has private thatched cottages; local arts and crafts are hightlighted. Some are only footsteps from the ocean. There is also a small pool with a bar. ✉ *60 Tran Phu St.,* ☎ *058/829–829,* FAX *058/823–629. 68 rooms. Restaurant, TV, air-conditioning, in-rooms safes, minibars, room service, IDD telephones, pool, bicycles, motorbikes, library, laundry service and dry cleaning, meeting rooms, travel services. AE, MC, V.*

$$ **Bao Dai Villas.** Once the beach retreat of Emperor Bao Dai, this hotel has certainly seen better days. Stay here only if you are fond of giant cockroaches and stained towels. Its only redeeming qualities are its historical significance and its peaceful hilltop location, which makes it a good place to stop in for a drink on your way to sleep elsewhere. ✉ *Cau Da-Vinh Nguyen,* ☎ *058/881–471. 48 rooms, 45 with bath. Restaurant, air-conditioning, fans, room service, TV, tennis court, beach, snorkeling, boating, meeting rooms, travel services. No credit cards.*

$$ **Haiyen Hotel.** Though it caters to large cruise ships full of Asian tourists, this big waterfront hotel looks like it has not been touched since the '70s. Nonetheless, rooms are passable—meaning they are reasonably clean and have basic amenities such as TV. ✉ *40 Tran Phu St.,* ☎ *058/822–828,* FAX *058/821–902. 107 rooms. 2 bars, dining room, lobby lounge, outdoor café, air-conditioning, fans, minibars, refrigerators, room service, pool, beauty salon, massage, sauna, dance club, laundry service and dry cleaning, meeting room, travel services, car rental, parking. MC, V.*

$$ **Nha Trang Lodge Hotel.** This relatively new hotel across the street from the ocean has an incredibly tacky lobby and decor reminiscent of roadside motels across the Uniterd States. But rooms are perfectly clean and comfortable, and some have views of the sea. The hotel can exchange money. ✉ *42 Tran Phu St.,* ☎ *058/810–500,* FAX *058/828–800. 124 rooms. Restaurant, air-conditioning, room service, satellite TV, in-room safes, minibars, IDD telephones, laundry service and dry cleaning, travel services. AE, MC, V.*

$$ **Seaside Hotel.** A plush, new minihotel just south of town on the coast, this place has some of the most tastefully decorated rooms in Nha Trang; a number even have ocean views. No services are offered, however, and the staff sleeps in the lobby at night. Nonetheless, it is one of Nha Trang's best. ✉ *96 Tran Phu St.,* ☎ *058/821–178,* FAX *058/828–038. 15 rooms. Restaurant, air-conditioning, fans, laundry service. No credit cards.*

$–$$ **Vien Dong Hotel.** One of the first large hotels in Nha Trang, the Vien Dong, adjacent to the Haiyen Hotel (☞ *above*), is a hub of tourist activity. Though it's a popular place for Westerners to stay because it's close to the beach and has a pool, the hotel is slightly run-down and overpriced and the staff tends to be excessively impersonal. On the other hand, the travel service is very good, and you can use it even if you're not staying at the hotel. ✉ *1 Tran Hung Dao St.,* ☎ *058/821–606,* FAX *058/821–912. 86 rooms. Restaurant, bar, air-conditioning, fans, minibars, refrigerators, TV, pool, massage, laundry service, travel services, car rental. AE, MC, V.*

$–$$ **Duy Tan Hotel.** Overlooking the water, the Duy Tan is one of the best of the sparse choice of hotels in Nha Trang. Rooms are simple, efficient, and charmless, though not depressing. The staff, however, is unfriendly and speaks little to no English. ✉ *24 Tran Phu St.,* ☎ *058/822–671,* FAX *058/825–034. 90 rooms. Restaurant, lobby lounge, air-conditioning, fans, minibars, TV. No credit cards.*

$–$$ **Nam Long Hotel.** The Nam Long is in the center of town, not too far from the beach. Rooms are clean and nondescript. ✉ *7 Le Thanh Ton St.,* ☎ *058/827–714,* FAX *058/824–991. 25 rooms. Air-conditioning, fans, minibars, refrigerator, laundry service, travel services. No credit cards.*

$–$$ **Thanh Thanh Hotel.** This efficient, brightly lit minihotel overlooks the water and is just south of town. ✉ *98A Tran Phu St.,* ☎ *058/824–657,* FAX *058/823–031. 18 rooms. Restaurant, air-conditioning, minibars, refrigerators, room service, TVs, laundry service, travel services. No credit cards.*

Nightlife and the Arts

People tend to congregate on the beach or at beachfront bar-cafés like the **Coconut Grove** (✉ 40 Tran Phu St., no phone). **Zippo Bar** (✉ 2 Hung Vuong St., ☎ 058/827–296) is another popular nightspot, complete with several pool tables and a largely local crowd. The **Nha Trang Sailing Club** (✉ 72–74 Tran Phu St., ☎ 058/826–528) attracts homesick travelers and expatriates. You can hang out until dawn dancing, drinking, playing pool, and speaking English. It also acts as a surrogate gallery for a brilliant and friendly local photographer named Long Thanh, who works out of his home. Farther down the beach, the **Huong Duong Center Bar/Discotheque** (✉ Tran Phu St., ☎ 058/823–914), a hangout for Vietnamese teenagers, is a good place to get away from other travelers.

Outdoor Activities and Sports

Nha Trang has all kinds of seaside resort town activities, including snorkeling, jet skiing, scuba diving, and boating. The **Blue Diving Club** (✉ 40 Tran Phu St., Coconut Grove, ☎ 058/825–390, FAX 058/824–

214), a very well-run Professionally Approved Diving Institute (P.A.D.I.) center, offers beginning instruction in English and French and arranges guided excursions for all diving levels.

Nha Trang A to Z

Arriving and Departing

BY BUS

The Sinh Café (☞ Visitor Information and Travel Agencies *in* Ho Chi Minh City A to Z, Chapter 6) bus links Ho Chi Minh City with Dalat (80,000d) and Nha Trang with Danang (80,000d).

BY CAR

Nha Trang is 448 km (278 mi) north of Ho Chi Minh City along Highway 1 (20 hours by car) and 2,250 km (1,200 mi) south of Hanoi. Dalat is 120 km (74 mi) southwest of Nha Trang and takes 7–8 hours by car. Danang is 541 km (225 mi) north of Nha Trang (10 hours by car). A car and driver can be hired from hotels and from private and state-run travel agencies (☞ Contacts and Resources, *below*).

BY PLANE

The recommended way to get to Nha Trang is by plane. **Vietnam Airlines** (✉ 12B Hoang Hoa Tham St., Nha Trang, ☎ 058/823–797) flies daily between Nha Trang and Ho Chi Minh City (55 minutes; $60) and Hanoi (2½ hours; $100), and three times a week to Danang.

BY TRAIN

Nha Trang is served three times daily by both express and local trains from Hanoi and Ho Chi Minh City. A soft sleeper to Ho Chi Minh costs $25–$35; to Hanoi it costs $80–$100, depending on whether you take the express or the local train. The express train (15 hours) to from Ho Chi Minh City to Nha Trang is considerably faster than the local train (22 hours); from Hanoi to Nha Trang the express takes 24 hours and the local 32 hours. Note that the ticket office at **Nha Trang Railway Station** (✉ 26 Thai Nguyen St., ☎ 058/822–113) is open between 7 and 2 only.

Getting Around

BY BICYCLE

One of the best ways to get around Nha Trang is by bicycle. You can rent one at any travel agency (☞ Travel Agencies, *below*) and at most hotels for about 10,000d a day. A deposit may be required.

BY BOAT

Boat trips can organized through most hotels and travel agencies (☞ *below*). The most popular, **Mama Hahn's Boat Trips,** can be arranged through the Nha Trang Sailing Club (☞ Dining and Lodging *and* Nightlife and the Arts, *above*).

BY CAR

Hiring a car with a driver is one option for getting around Nha Trang but is unnecessary unless you want to go to one of the beaches outside of town. You can make arrangements at any of the travel agencies (☞ Travel Agencies, *below*) in town.

BY CYCLO

The easiest way to get around Nha Trang is by cyclo, which you can find all over town. For about 10,000d can you get you just about anywhere you want to go. Be sure to bargain to get the best rate.

BY MOTORBIKE

Renting a motorbike, with or without a driver, is another way to see Nha Trang and the surrounding areas. You can rent them at any travel agency (☞ Travel Agencies, *below*) and at most hotels for about 70,000d a day. A deposit may be required.

Contacts and Resources

CURRENCY EXCHANGE

Vietcom Bank (17 Quang Trung St.) exchanges money, as do many hotels.

EMERGENCIES

Contact your hotel.

POST OFFICE

The **Main branch** (2 Tran Phu Blvd.) sells stamps, as do many hotels.

TRAVEL AGENCIES

Khanh Hoa Tourism (✉ 1 Tran Hung Dao St., ☎ 058/822–753, FAX 058/824–206). **Nam-Viet** (✉ 2 Hung Vung St., ☎ 058/821–428, FAX 058/821–428). **Nha Trang Tourism** (✉ 3 Tran Hung Dao St., Hung Dao Hotel, ☎ 058/821–231).

THROUGH THE CENTRAL HIGHLANDS TO DALAT

En route to Dalat from Ho Chi Minh City is the region known as the central highlands, an unspoiled landscape dotted with ethnic minority villages and religious complexes. Part of the southern end of the Truong Son range, Vietnam's central highlands is a region of mountains, streams, lakes, and waterfalls covering the provinces of Lam Dong, Dac Lac (Dak Lak), Gia Lai, and Kon Tum. It is one of the few parts of the country where it is cool enough to wear a sweater, even in summer. The mountain resort of Dalat is the principal town of the region. Though Dalat town is somewhat tacky, the lovely scenery continues to make it appealing.

The Central Highlands

Difficult to get to, the western part of the central highlands is home to a large population of ethnic minorities. Known as Montagnards, from the French for "mountain people," these ethnic minorities live in tribal villages. Some of these tribes have lived in Vietnam for thousands of years, others came from neighboring Thailand several centuries ago. They are largely nomadic farmers who live an isolated existence. Bordering Cambodia and Laos, the strategic Buon Ma Thuot, Pleiku, and Kontum were major battlegrounds during the Vietnam War. Only now has the vegetation, including coffee trees, begun to recover from the napalm and defoliants rained on this area during the war.

Approximately 100 km (62 mi) north of Ho Chi Minh City along High-
4 way 20, **Langa Lake** supports a number of floating fishing villages. Although these may sound exotic, they are nothing more than several groups of low-end houseboats. There may or may not be a roadside food stand open if you're in need of a snack.

5 Often inaccessible due to poor road conditions, **Nam Cat Tien National Park,** 250 km (155 mi) northwest of Ho Chi Minh City, shelters the endangered Javanese rhino, as well as monkeys, elephants, tigers, and several bird species. *See* Side Trips from Ho Chi Minh City *in* Chapter 6 for more information.

About 233 km (149 mi) northwest of Ho Chi Minh City and 75 km (47
6 mi) southwest of Dalat, are the **Dambri Falls.** Steep, slippery steps lead to excellent views of the 300-ft waterfalls. 🎫 *10,000d.* ⏲ *Daily 7–5.*

West of Dalat on Highway 20, just beyond the semiarid twin cities of
7 Phan Rang–Thap Cham are the **Po Klong Garai Cham Towers.** This is the only site you may want to be sure to visit en route to Dalat. These four well-preserved Hindu temples are remnants of a 13th-century Cham temple built during the reign of Cham King Jaya Simhavarman III, one of the emperors of the Kingdom of Champa, which ruled this part of Vietnam from the 2nd to 15th centuries. Over the entrance to the tallest tower is an intact carving of a dancing Shiva. Inside the entrance is a statue of the bull Nadin, a symbol of agricultural riches. ⊠ *Off Hwy. 20.* 🎫 *20,000d.* ⏲ *Daily 8–5.*

Dalat

308 km (191 mi) north of Ho Chi Minh City; 205 km (127 mi) southwest of Nha Trang.

Named for the "River of the Lat Tribe," after the native Lat people, Dalat was "discovered" in the early part of this century by Dr. Alexandre Yersin (1863–1943), a protégé of Louis Pasteur (the first person to identify the plague bacillus). It quickly became a vacation spot for Europeans anxious to escape the infernal heat of the coastal plains, the big cities, and the Mekong Delta. During the Vietnam War the city, oddly, served as the favorite nonpartisan resting spot for both high-ranking North and South Vietnamese officers, before it capitulated to the North Vietnamese on April 3, 1975.

Dalat today is a favorite of Vietnamese honeymooners, and attempts are being made to transform it into an international tourist destination. An 18-hole golf course is already in place, new hotels are planned, and old colonial villas are being converted into guest houses.

Dalat bears a vague resemblance to a small French town and is blessed with lovely weather. If you like kitsch, Dalat offers it up in unspoiled, un-self-conscious abundance. The endless flora and fauna are mocked by plastic versions decorating the white cars of the wedding processions that pass two or three times a day. Panoramic views of majestic mountains and placid lakes are often interrupted by an incongruous Vietnamese dressed as an American cowboy offering a ride and a photo opportunity.

Exploring Dalat

Dalat's prime sight is its market, which ranks among Vietnam's best. Several places outside downtown Dalat are worth a visit, however. As these are spread out across hilly Dalat, it is a good idea to hire a car with a driver and a guide. Decide what you want to see and leave the exact itinerary to your guide.

8 Dalat lies northwest of the dam-generated **Xuan Huong Lake** (Ho Xuan Huong), named for a 17th-century Vietnamese poet known for her daring attacks on the hypocrisy of social conventions and the foibles of scholars, monks, mandarins, feudal lords, and kings. Circumscribed by a path and abutted by a beautiful 18-hole golf course, the lake is a hub of leisurely activity (including paddleboating). Although there's traffic nearby, the lake provides a pleasant place to walk and bike.

Just west of the lake is the official center of Dalat, with its picturesque
9 **Central Market** and its small collection of restaurants. Locals come here to buy and sell chickens, fruits and vegetables, and specialties such as dried strawberries. ⊠ *Nguyen Thi Minh Khai St.*

10 **Bao Dai's Summer Palace** (Biet Dien Quoc Truong), on the south side of the lake, is a wonderfully preserved example of modernist architec-

Bao Dai's Summer Palace, **10**
Cam Ly Falls, **13**
Central Market, **9**
Chu Linh Phong Pagoda, **18**
Crémaillère Railway, **16**
Dalat Flower Garden, **14**
Dalat University, **15**
Hang Nga Guest House and Art Gallery, **11**
Lake of Sighs, **21**
Lam Ti Ny Pagoda, **12**
Prenn Falls, **19**
Thien Vuong Pagoda, **17**
Valley of Love, **20**
Xuan Huong Lake, **8**

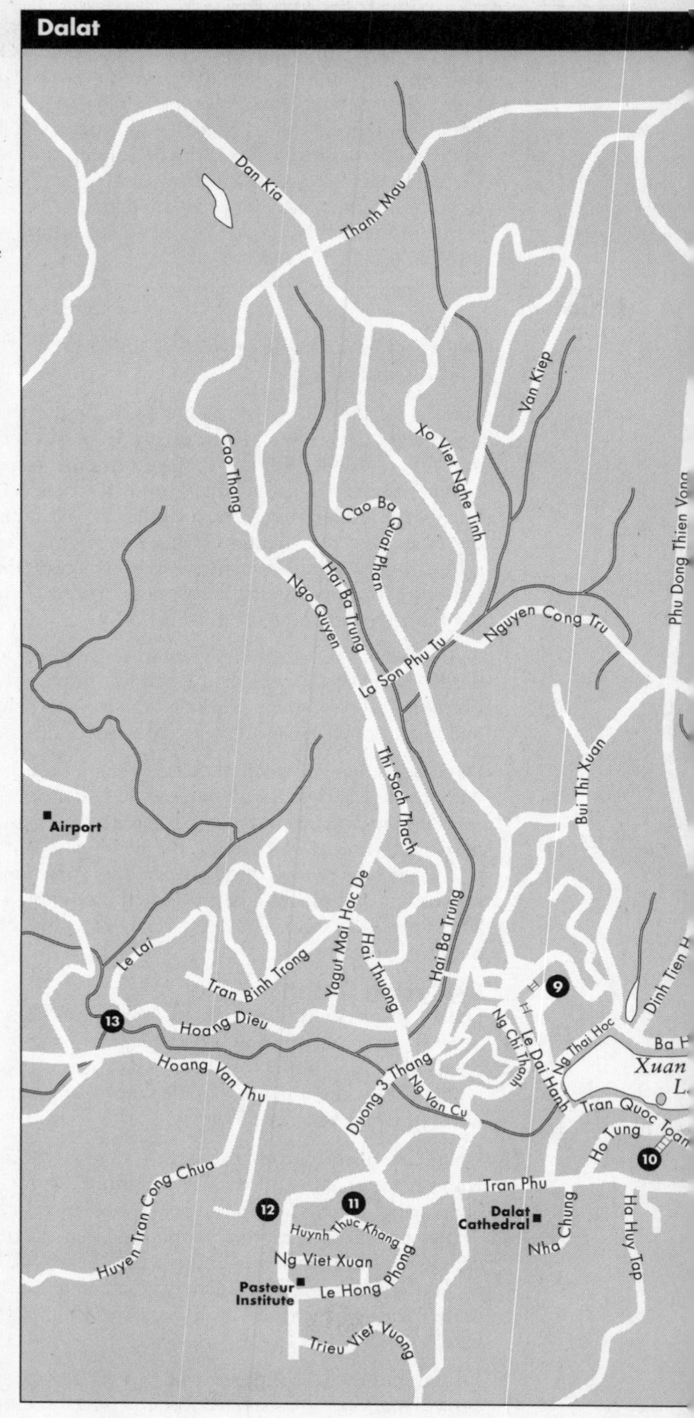

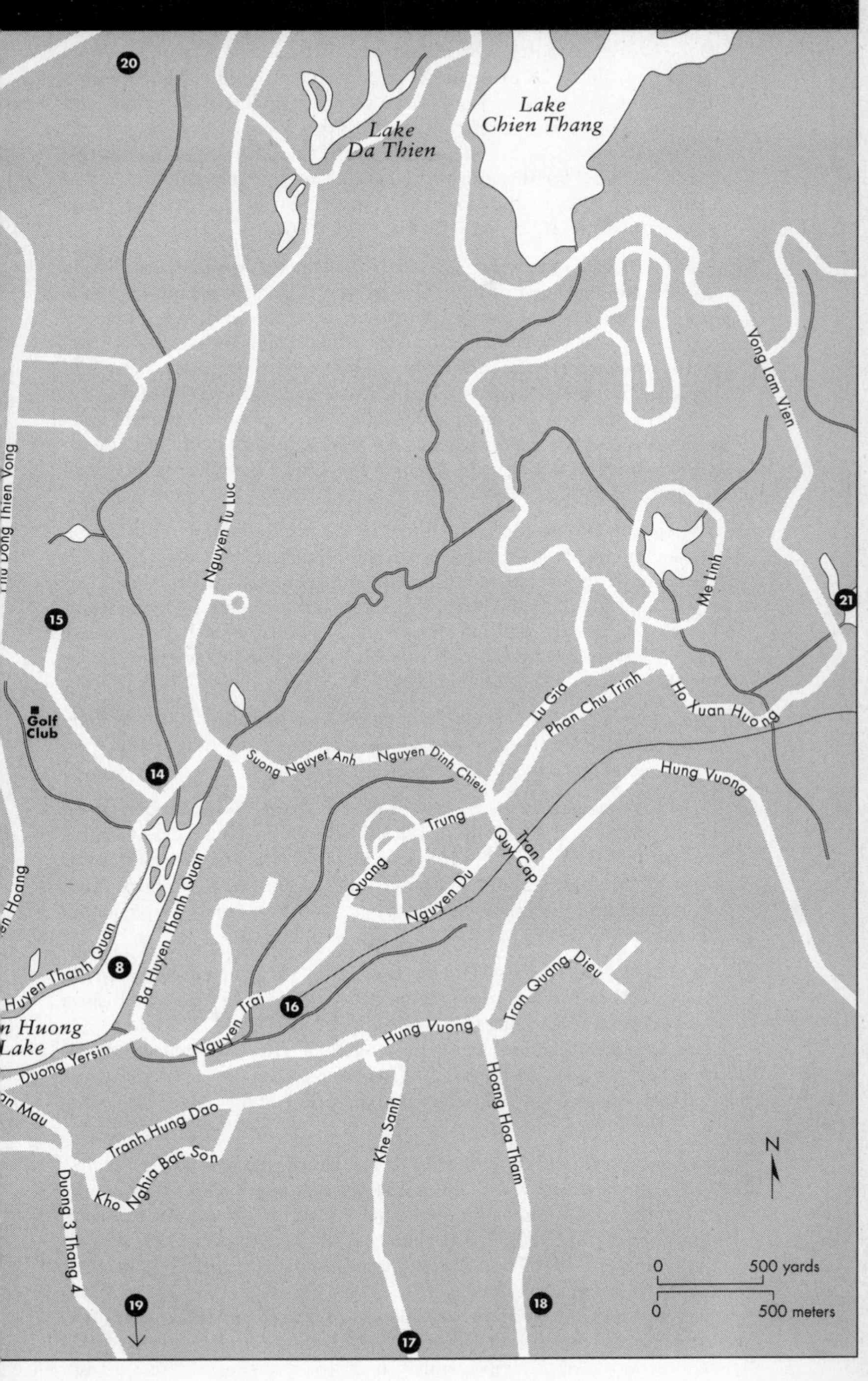

Lake Da Thien
Lake Chien Thang
Nguyen Tu Luc
Vong Lam Vien
Me Linh
Golf Club
Suong Nguyet Anh
Nguyen Dinh Chieu
Lu Gia
Phan Chu Trinh
Ho Xuan Huong
Hung Vuong
Trung
Quang
Tran Quy Cap
Nguyen Du
Ba Huyen Thanh Quan
Huyen Thanh Quan
n Huong Lake
Nguyen Trai
Tran Quang Dieu
Duong Yersin
Hung Vuong
Khe Sanh
Hoang Hoa Tham
Tranh Hung Dao
Kho Nghia Bac Son
Duong 3 Thang 4
N
0 500 yards
0 500 meters
20
15
14
8
16
21
19
17
18

ture—a yellow cement structure built in 1933. The palace houses the original 1930s French furnishings of Emperor Bao Dai, the last emperor of the Nguyen dynasty, who ruled from 1926 to 1945 with the support of the French. Stroll through the rooms and sit behind the emperor's desk. Your guide will no doubt have you pick up Bao Dai's phone and insist on taking your picture. The family sitting room holds military maps and family portraits, as well as chairs designated for each family member (as detailed on the description card). The room has a tactile immediacy, as if it were untouched and suspended in time. ✉ *Le Hong Phong St.,* ☎ *063/822–125.* 🎫 *10,000d.* ⏲ *Daily 7 AM–8 PM.*

11 A more offbeat experience is to be had at the **Hang Nga Guest House and Art Gallery,** west of Bao Dai's palace. In a strange building made out of a tree, the hotel and gallery are a fairy-tale landscape of wood-carved life-size fantastical creatures and real animals. It looks like Salvador Dalí meets the *Swiss Family Robinson.* Its Vietnamese owner and designer, Dang Viet Nga, studied architecture in Russia and has decorated the main dining room with a collection of photos of herself. Each room has its own wacky theme (*see* Dining and Lodging, *below,* for information on staying here). ✉ *3 Huynh Thuc Khang St.,* ☎ *063/822–070.* 🎫 *30,000d.* ⏲ *Daily 7 AM–8 PM.*

12 The **Lam Ty Ni Pagoda** is the home of the multitalented, multilingual resident monk Vien Thuc, known as the Mad Monk of Dalat. An artist, poet, landscape architect, craftsman, and religious scholar, Vien Thuc is a living legend. He will happily escort you through his rooms of watercolor paintings and may wrap up a picture even before you've agreed to buy it. Keep in mind that it is very hard to bargain with a monk. ✉ *2 Thien My St.* ⏲ *Daily 9–5.*

13 One of Dalat's smaller waterfalls, lovely **Cam Ly Falls** is unfortunately crowded with Vietnamese and western tourists and kids selling gum and dried meat, a local Dalat treat.

14 If you love gardens, go to the European-style **Dalat Flower Garden** (Vuon Hoa Dalat), on the northeast side of the lake. In January and February, around the time of Tet (the new year), its wide variety of orchids (*hoa lan*) are in full bloom. At other times, you'll see all kinds of flowers, including hydrangeas and fuchsias. ✉ *2 Phu Dong Thien Vuong St.,* ☎ *063/822–151.* 🎫 *8,000d (75¢).* ⏲ *Daily 7–5.*

15 **Dalat University** (Truong Dai Hoc Tong Hop), on the north side of town, was established as a Catholic university in 1957 by Hue's archbishop (and President Ngo Ding Diem's brother), Ngo Dinh Thuc. After 1975 it became a state school and is now one of Vietnam's intellectual centers. You can go onto the campus, wander around, and meet students eager to chat with you in English or French. ✉ *1 Phu Dong Thien Vuong St.* ⏲ *Daily 9–5.*

If you're a train buff or just want to see what Dalat was like in the first
16 half of the century, visit the **Crémaillère Railway** (Ga Da Lat), to the east of the lake. A movie-set quality pervades this picturesque train station built in the 1920s. From 1928 to 1964 Dalat was linked by train to the small town of Phan Rang–Thap Cham and to then-Saigon. Regular service was suspended in 1964 when Vietcong attacks forced it to shut down. These days the train goes only to **Trai Mat,** a small ethnic-minority village 8 km (5 mi) east of Dalat. Falsely advertised as a steam-train ride, the trip is only worth doing if you're with a group: Large groups, of up to 20 people, pay as little as $3, but small groups of about five or solo travelers have to pay $15 for a whole train car. On the ride to the Trai Mat village you can get a closer look at the area's bountiful fields full of such crops as strawberries, cabbage,

flowers, avocados, and rambutan. ✉ *½ km (⅓ mi) east of Xuan Huong Lake.* 🎟 *10,000d to view station itself.* ⏲ *Daily 8–5; trains leave for Trai Mat daily at 8* AM.

One of Dalat's most famous and popular monuments is the Chinese
17 **Thien Voung Pagoda** (Chua Tao Thien Voung), southeast of town, atop a steep mountain with great views of the surrounding area. The dirt path leading up to the pagoda is lined with stalls selling candied fruits—a local specialty—and souvenirs. The pagoda was built in 1958 by the Chaozhou Chinese congregation. Dominating the pagoda are three large, Hong Kong–made gilded-sandalwood sculptures—in the third of the three buildings. From left to right are Dai The Chi Bo Tat (an assistant of A Di Da, the Buddha of the past); Thich Ca Buddha (Sakyamuni, the historical Buddha); and Quan The Am Bo Tat (Avalokiteçvara, the Goddess of Mercy). Peaceful gardens surround the pagoda. ✉ *About 3 km (2 mi) southeast of center of town, following Khe Sanh St.* ⏲ *Daily 9–4.*

18 The **Chu Linh Phong Pagoda,** also known as the Su Nu Pagoda, is a serene Buddhist convent built in 1952. Out of respect, avoid visiting during lunchtime, when the nuns (who traditionally shave their heads) sing their prayers. ✉ *72 Hoang Hoa Tham St.* ⏲ *Daily 9–5.*

19 A favorite of Vietnamese honeymooners is **Prenn Falls** (Thac Prenn). In the crowded park surrounding the falls you can frolic over rope bridges and under the falls themselves. You can also hike up the short path to a makeshift zoo, where a few monkeys and birds sit in small cages. ✉ *South of Dalat on Hwy. 20; look for Prenn Restaurant.* 🎟 *50,000d.* ⏲ *Daily 8–4:30.*

20 The **Valley of Love** (Thung Lung Tinh Yeu), north of the lake, is another pilgrimage site for Vietnamese honeymooners. Once named the Valley of Peace by Emperor Bao Dai, the valley now has a name reflecting its transformation from a serene setting with lovely vistas into a magnet for newlyweds. On a walk around the lovely green valley you can see Vietnamese couples being photographed with locals on horseback dressed as cowboys. Rest on a heart-shape bench, chewing some of the dried deer meat sold everywhere, and you'll fit right in. ✉ *Approximately 3 km (2 mi) north of Xuan Huong Lake, following Phu Dong Thien Vuong St.* 🎟 *20,000d.* ⏲ *Daily 7:30–4.*

Evoking the story of the lovers Hoang Tung and Mai Nuong, the
21 **Lake of Sighs** (Ho Than Tho), northeast of town, is populated by Vietnamese dressed like cowboys and a slew of paddleboats. According to the *Romeo and Juliet*–like legend, Hoang Tung joined the army, but Mai Nuong thought she had been abandoned. Out of despair, she killed herself by jumping into the lake. On discovering her body, her lover did the same. ✉ *About 5 km (2 mi) northeast of Dalat, following Phan Chu Trinh St.* 🎟 *20,000d.* ⏲ *Daily 8–5.*

Dining and Lodging

$$ ✕ **Le Rabelais.** Imagine being a guest in a fabulous French country estate complete with chandeliers, period furniture, 3-foot-high floral arrangements, and a portrait gallery—you can almost believe it's true at the beautiful Rabelais. Flawless service and an impressive wine list make it worth dining in this restaurant. Unfortunately the French-influenced food doesn't live up to the setting, but it's decent. ✉ *In the Sofitel Dalat Palace, 12 Tran Phu St.,* ☎ *063/825–444. AE, V.*

$$ ✕ **Thanh Thanh.** If you're desperate for white tablecloths and napkins, this pleasant though unspectacular Vietnamese restaurant is one of the few formal establishments in Dalat. Because it's recommended by most of the local guides and hotel concierges, it's generally filled with Western tourists. One of the better dishes on the menu is the tasty sugarcane shrimp. ✉ *4 Tang Bat Ho St.,* ☎ *063/821–836. No credit cards.*

$ ✕ **Hoang Lan.** Come here for cheap and tasty traditional Vietnamese food served by a friendly waitstaff. Don't expect atmosphere, though—the restaurant is nothing more than a group of large tables and plastic-covered menus.✉ *118 Phan Dinh Phung St.,* ☎ *063/822–180. No credit cards.*

$$$$ ★ **Sofitel Dalat Palace.** Reminiscent of a French château, with 15-ft ceilings, ornate fireplaces, and huge public rooms, the Dalat Sofitel is one of the best hotels in Vietnam. Overlooking Xuan Huong Lake, the exquisite Dalat Palace Golf Club has been renovated to recapture the grandeur and elegance of its original 1922 French design. Spacious rooms with tasteful antique reproductions, original moldings, and unobtrusive modern conveniences, combined with impeccable service under the new international management, make this a great place to stay. ✉ *12 Tran Phu St.,* ☎ *063/825–444,* FAX *063/825–666. 43 rooms. Restaurant, café, lounge, piano bar, pub, in-room safes, minibars, no-smoking rooms, room service, 18-hole golf course, 2 tennis courts, mountain bikes, shops, baby-sitting, laundry service and dry cleaning, concierge, business services, meeting rooms, travel services, airport shuttle. AE, MC, V.*

$$ **Anh Dao Hotel.** Overlooking the Central Market, this hotel is in a prime location. Rooms are pleasant and modern; some have Western conveniences such as in-room refrigerators. ✉ *50–52 Hoa Binh Sq. (Nguyen Chi Thanh St.),* ☎ *063/822–384. 27 rooms. Restaurant, bar, minibars, room service, laundry service, dry cleaning, travel services. No credit cards.*

$$ **Hang Nga Guesthouse.** Choose from 18 unique rooms, each with its own offbeat theme, at this small guest house close to the center of town. The Bear Room has a life-size bear with eyes that light up when you turn on the lights and a small fireplace in his belly. Funky, too, are the Ant and Tiger rooms; the latter has a tiger with red lightbulbs for eyes staring at you in the middle of the room. This wacky architectural monument is a cheerful hotel alternative, although the rooms are quite small. ✉ *3 Huynh Thuc Khang St.,* ☎ *063/822–070. 18 rooms. Restaurant, travel services. No credit cards.*

$$ **Thanh Thuy.** This cozy "villa" right on Xuan Huong Lake is a small, charming hotel with pleasantly decorated, clean, bright rooms. ✉ *2 Nguyen Thai Hoc St.,* ☎ *063/822–262. 12 rooms. Restaurant, travel services. No credit cards.*

$$ **Xuan Tam Villa Hotel.** This out-of-the-way hilltop hotel recently opened to foreigners (previously only Vietnamese tourists were allowed to stay here) is close to the Bao Dai palace. The staff is helpful, and rooms are spacious and clean. ✉ *25 Le Hong Phong St.,* ☎ *063/823–142,* FAX *063/280–871. 14 rooms. Restaurant, travel services. No credit cards.*

Nightlife and the Arts

Barring a few Bohemian-type cafés, there isn't much to do at night unless you like karaoke, which you can find everywhere. **Café Tung** (✉ 6 Khu Hoa Bin St.) is a tiny spot where you can get coffee in the evening and swap travel tales. **Stop 'n Go Café** (✉ Kiosk 6 Hoa Binh Sq., ☎ 063/821–512) is small spot, open until 10, that is popular with travelers for meeting and exchanging information.

Outdoor Activities and Sports

Dalat's hilly terrain makes it a great place for gentle hikes. The Lake of Sighs and the Valley of Love are ideal places to spend an afternoon wandering—it is possible to escape the cowboys and honeymooners. **Dalat Tourist** (☞ Travel Agency *in* Dalat A to Z, *below*) has information on hiking in the Valley of Love and around the Lake of Sighs; it also arranges guided tours of these areas. The pristine **Dalat Palace Golf Club** (✉ Phu Dong Thien Vuong St, ☎ 063/821–201, FAX 063/824–325) has an 18-hole course overlooking Xuan Huong Lake. Fees are $88 for Sofitel Dalat Palace guests; non-guests pay $110. You can rent **paddleboats** from stands along Xuan Huong Lake for 20,000d an hour.

Dalat A to Z

Arriving and Departing

BY BUS

Dalat Tourist (✉ 4 Tran Quoc Toan St., Dalat, ☎ 063/822–125; ✉ 21 Nguyen An Ninh St., District 1, Ho Chi Minh City, ☎ 08/823–0227) runs daily minibus service from Dalat to Ho Chi Minh City, 308 km (191 mi) south. The trip costs 90,000d and takes 12 long hours. Try to go to the office one day in advance to reserve a seat.

Sinh Café (✉ 179 Pham Ngu Lao St., District 1, Ho Chi Minh City, ☎ 08/835–5601) sells an open bus ticket that connects Dalat to Ho Chi Minh City heading south and Dalat to Nha Trang heading north. The open-ended ticket allows you to get on the bus any day of the week. The daily trip to Dalat from Ho Chi Minh City, heading north, takes about 12 hours and costs $8; for an open ticket from Ho Chi Minh City to Hanoi, you pay $35 and can get on and off the bus any day you choose. (*See* Bus Travel *in* the Gold Guide for more information.)

BY CAR

Driving to Dalat from Ho Chi Minh City or Hanoi costs too much, takes too long, and is too complicated; you're better off taking either a plane, a bus, or a minibus.

BY PLANE

Vietnam Airlines has flights from Dalat's Lien Khuong Airport (30 km/19 mi south of town) to Hanoi (1½ hours, $110) and Ho Chi Minh City (one hour, $85) on Tuesday, Wednesday, Thursday, and Saturday. There are no direct flights between Dalat and Nha Trang; you would have to return to Ho Chi Minh City or Hanoi in order to get to Nha Trang. For ticket confirmation and reservations go to the **Vietnam Airlines office** (San Bay Lien Khuong; ✉ 5 Truong Cong Dinh St., ☎ 063/822–895).

Getting Around

BY CAR

The best way to get around Dalat is by car with a hired driver and guide. Be prepared for narrow, hilly, and hazardous roads; along the roadside are small shrines to motorists who have been killed. Drivers, however, are usually good. You can rent cars with drivers from Dalat Tourist (☞ Travel Agency, *below*).

Contacts and Resources

CURRENCY EXCHANGE

Exchange money at the **Agriculture Bank of Vietnam** (Nguyen Van Troi St.) and at most hotels.

EMERGENCIES

Contact **Sofitel Dalat Palace Hotel** (☞ Dining and Lodging *above*) if you need assistance.

POST OFFICE

For stamps, go to the **main branch** (14 Tran Phu St.) or ask at your hotel.

TRAVEL AGENCY

Dalat Tourist/Lamdong Tourist Company (✉ 4 Tran Quoc Toan St., ☎ 063/822–125, FAX 063/822–661) arranges cars with drivers and tours of the city.

6 Ho Chi Minh City

Ho Chi Minh City—Saigon to most—is a vibrant, bustling city that reflects Vietnam's past and its future. Its broad colonial boulevards leading to the Saigon River and its stucco buildings are remnants of the French colonial presence. Cholon, the city's Chinatown, is a reminder of the Chinese influence on the country. And the new office towers and international hotels changing the skyline overnight are symbols of tomorrow's Vietnam.

By Andrew Chilvers

ARRIVING IN HO CHI MINH CITY can be a bewildering experience. At the airport the endless customs paperwork can be confusing, and the throngs of taxi drivers competing for business outside can be jarringly disorienting when you're jet-lagged. But don't be put off—confusion and chaos are at the very heart of the city. If at first you feel like you are on a breathtaking roller-coaster ride moving at breakneck speed, you soon you get used to the feeling and may even grow to like it.

Once romantically referred to by the French as the Pearl of the Orient, Ho Chi Minh City is still called Saigon by almost everyone who lives here (and we use both names interchangeably throughout this book). The city has a more cosmopolitan feel than Hanoi, although much of the old French colonial city is vanishing beneath the rapidly rising skyline and the sheer weight of recent history.

History, however, has bequeathed the city a kaleidoscopic melting pot of styles. Only in Saigon can you get a ride in a '50s French Citroën, a '60s Ford Mustang, a '70s Russian Volga, or a brand-new Toyota. For dinner you have your choice of not only Vietnamese food but also hamburgers, fine French cuisine, or black caviar at one of the city's Russian restaurants. Afterward you can head to one of the new, sleek bars that are opening every month.

At the teeming markets, tropical fruits, king cobras, barbecued dogs, and a hundred other such items are for sale; the sidewalks are crammed with noodle stands, cafés, and vendors selling fresh glasses of beer (*bia hoi*) for as little as 25¢. The roads are often gridlocked with motorbikes, scooters, bicycles, *cyclos* (pedicabs), buses, and a few cars (for now). All kinds of people travel around by bicycle or motorbike: women dressed in traditional *ao dais,* long gloves, and conical hats; and whole families—mother, father, and two children—all squeezed on one seat. Everyone seems to be going somewhere, no matter what time of day. And even if people have nowhere to go, they simply cruise around until it's time to go to sleep.

Meanwhile, far above the din of street life, a new city is emerging amid the screech of jackhammers and pile drivers working on the newest Asian skyline. Since economic reforms—known as *doi moi*—were adopted over ten years ago, Ho Chi Minh City has witnessed furious growth. Starting in the early '90s, Ho Chi Minh City's economy has been expanding at the startling rate of 15% a year, and it is now the world's fastest-growing city.

Unfortunately, the flip side of all this success is rank failure, and many are being left behind in the struggle for self-enrichment. Homeless children roam the downtown streets, sometimes earning a living by shining shoes or by begging or pickpocketing. Limbless war veterans hobble behind wealthy tourists badgering them for small change. Women desperate for tourist dollars carry comatose infants and endlessly shuffle through the streets like specters. And after twilight prostitutes cruise downtown on their Hondas prowling for foreign customers. But, oddly, you grow accustomed to these tragic sights.

Ho Chi Minh City encompasses a large region, stretching all the way to Cu Chi, in Tay Ninh Province, and south to the upper reaches of the Mekong Delta. The part of the city known as Saigon is actually made up only of two districts: Districts 1 and 3 (there are 14 in Ho Chi Minh City). Bordered by the Thi Nghe Channel to the north, the Ben Nghe Channel to the south, and the Saigon River to the east, the city has served as a natural fortress and has been fought over by countless people during the past 2,000 years. The ancient empire of Funan used the area as a trading post, and the Khmer kingdom of Angkor transformed Prey Nokor, as Saigon was called, into a flourishing center of trade protected by a standing army. By the 14th century, while under Khmer rule, the city attracted Arab, Cham, Chinese, Malaysian, and Indian merchants. It was then known as the gateway to the Kingdom of Champa, the sister empire to Angkor.

In 1674 the Nguyen lords of Hue established a customs post at Prey Nokor to cash in on the region's growing commercial traffic. Saigon, as the Vietnamese called it, became an increasingly important administrative post. The building in 1772 of a 6-km (4-mi) trench on the western edge of old Saigon, in what is now District 5, marked the shift in control in the south from Angkor to Nguyen rule. Further Vietnamese consolidation came in 1778 with the development of Cholon, Saigon's Chinese city, as a second commercial hub in the area that is presently District 5.

In 1789 the Nguyen lords moved their power base from Hue to Saigon, following attacks from Tay Son rebels. Unhappy with the way the Nguyen lords had been running the country, the rebels massacred most of the Nguyen clan and took control of the government—briefly. In 1802, Prince Nguyen Anh, the last surviving heir of the Nguyen dynasty, defeated the Tay Son ruler—with French backing—regaining power and uniting Vietnam. He moved the capital back to Hue and declared himself Emperor Gia Long.

In quelling the Tay Son rebels, Gia Long's request for French assistance, which was readily provided, came at a price. In exchange for their help, Gia Long promised the French territorial concessions in Vietnam. Though the French Revolution and the Napoleonic Wars temporarily delayed any French claims, Gia Long's decision to seek help from France eventually cost Vietnam dearly. In 1859, the French seized Saigon, tired of waiting for the Vietnamese emperor to give them what they felt they deserved, and made it the capital of their new colony, Cochin China. This marked the beginning of an epoch of colonial-style feudalism and indentured servitude for many Vietnamese.

The catastrophe that was to overtake Saigon and the whole of Vietnam during the latter half of the 20th century was a direct result of French colonial interference. Despite France's role, however, to this day the Vietnamese people, both north and south, maintain deep sentimental ties with French culture and art, as is apparent across the country.

Without the threat of colonial interference or war, these days the Saigonese are living life to the fullest—and trying to make money. Saigon is the most Western of all the cities in Vietnam, with the greatest range of international cuisine, and Western-style high-rise buildings. But reminders of the past still poke through the headlong rush into capitalism. The Hotel Continental, immortalized in Graham Greene's *The Quiet American,* continues to stand on the corner of old Indochina's most famous thoroughfare, Rue Catinat (known to the American GIs as Tu Do Street and renamed Dong Khoi Street by the Communists). The city still has its central opera house and its old French City Hall, the Hôtel de Ville. You can still see the spires of Notre Dame Cathedral from the decks of the new cruise liners sailing up the Saigon River. And the city is still dotted with the bunkers and watchtowers of its more recent violent past.

Pleasures and Pastimes

Ho Chi Minh City is a modern city by Asian standards and has only been under firm Vietnamese control for a little more than 200 years. Consequently, there are few historic monuments or ancient sights to see. The city's character remains essentially French—with wide boulevards, colonial villas, and a café society—and resolutely Asian. Combined with a vivacious street life, the French influences have bred a charm all their own. But it is the people even more than the city that you will remember most.

Art

Nowhere is the French cultural influence clearer than in the works of Vietnamese artists. Ho Chi Minh City has countless art galleries, with many new ones opening each month, featuring a gamut of European-influenced art movements. The most common type of artwork you'll see throughout downtown Saigon is Impressionist knockoffs. Galleries are chock-full of copies of Monets and van Goghs, though some of the upscale galleries carry more serious works. Many of the tremendously talented artists represented in these galleries are French trained and are only now exhibiting their work to the world—and the world is beginning to take notice. So if you want to buy some art, now is the time, while the prices are still (relatively) low.

Cafés

In Ho Chi Minh City life is at its most colorful on the street, and the city's café society is at the center of this vivid spectacle. It is from a seat at one of the city's small cafés that you will really get to see the variety of urban life pass by. Order a strong, slow-filtered coffee or hot green tea, and spend an hour simply watching the street. It's hypnotic: You'll see cyclos crammed with dead pigs going off to market; chickens and ducks piled five deep and draped over the handlebars of bicycles; women selling noodle soup from bamboo baskets balanced on poles over their shoulders, singing their own distinctive tunes to attract customers; and young women wearing white ao dais riding motorbikes to school. You may also find that people are most relaxed and most sociable at the cafés, so don't be surprised if someone asks to join you for a drink.

Dining

Ho Chi Minh City has a plethora of Vietnamese and international restaurants, local cafés, and sidewalk noodle stalls. The French had a major influence on the city's cuisine, which means you can find many superb French-Vietnamese restaurants. In more recent years other types of international fare have appeared: Italian restaurants, Swiss eateries, American burger joints, fast-food spots, and even tapas bars. But most Vietnamese simply eat at street stalls, serving noodles, rice dishes, satays, kebabs, soups (*pho*), and other foods that are often as delicious and varied as at any of the more upscale establishments—at a fraction of the price. Note that the farther from the road (literally!), the more hygienic the establishment is likely to be. Though the city's air-conditioned restaurants are not always the most authentic places to eat, they are usually the most pleasant places to escape the heat.

Most international restaurants are in and around Districts 1 and 3, although there are several fine international restaurants in the city's suburbs. You can also find some good, inexpensive cafés serving Vietnamese and international cuisine along Pham Ngu Lao and De Tham streets in District 1. Most places are open for lunch and dinner but close in between, except cafés, which stay open all day and into the night. Most menus have English translations.

Meals are serious business, and between 11:30 AM and 2:30 PM the city shuts down to enjoy its collective repast and a post-lunch siesta, a tradition rooted in the French presence here. It's considered the height of bad manners to interrupt one of these naps. If your guide suddenly decides to sleep for an hour, it's advisable to let him be. It could make the difference between a good and a bad trip. Dinner is generally served any time between 6 PM and 1 AM.

Lodging

Ho Chi Minh City has had something of a hotel boom during the last few years, and new accommodations continue to open (including a Marriott, a Ramada, a Park Hyatt, and a Westin). Some of the grimmer state-run hotels have been replaced by new international joint-venture hotels, more of which are opening every month. Many "minihotels" have also opened; these family-run guest houses are excellent alternatives to the bigger hotels. Often only a third of the price of larger establishments, they are generally in good condition, are more sensitive to guests' needs, and have their own restaurants. The only drawback of minihotels is their lack of the facilities and services provided by international hotel chains.

A third option is to stay in one of the famous old colonial establishments that Saigon Tourist, the state tourism agency, has renovated. Though these old hotels certainly have their charms and some modern conveniences (IDD phones, fax machines), their renovations are often shoddy and service is sometimes lacking. If you're looking for service and amenities, you're better off staying at one of the international hotels—though it will cost you. But keep in mind that despite the number of facilities and conveniences at these newer hotels—fax machines, photocopiers, computer centers, health clubs, cable TVs, minibars, and marble bathrooms—the level of service will still probably not be what you've come to expect elsewhere. Vietnam's service industry is still in its infancy and often requires patience. Note that all hotels charging more than $10 a night have air-conditioning.

You may want to stay in Districts 1 and 3—the center of old Saigon—where most of the museums, galleries, restaurants, bars, and nightclubs are found. Most old colonial hotels are in Districts 1 and 3, as are many newer international hotels, though some are also in District 5 and in the Phu Nhuan District near the airport. Lower-price accommodations are clustered around Pham Ngu Lao, De Tham, and Bui Vien streets in District 1.

Find out if your hotel offers complementary airport pickup—most hotels, including minihotels, can arrange a driver for you. Call ahead and arrange to have someone from the hotel pick you up. If you've never been to Saigon, you may be overwhelmed by the general chaos of arriving and the crush of taxi drivers vying for your business. When you're jet-lagged, this is not a pleasant way to start your visit.

Museums

Several museums are peppered around the city, most housed in old colonial villas. Many were set up primarily to promote Communist Party propaganda, and the displays are less than memorable. Nevertheless, most are worth a visit, particularly the harrowing War Remnants Museum. The former presidential palace is also worth a visit: Here, on the grounds, is the tank that battered down the gates when the Communists took over Saigon in April 1975.

Shopping

In Ho Chi Minh City you can find all kinds of souvenirs of Vietnam—such as woodcarvings, lacquerware, paintings, ceramics, and T-shirts—

as well as idiosyncratic items such as imitation GI cigarette lighters. You can also get well-made designer gear at a fraction of the price of even Bangkok's markets and some of the most up-to-date electronic hardware at a steal. Be sure to spend an hour or two at the old colonial Ben Thanh Market in the city center and the Ben Tay Market in Cholon, where you can sample the city going about its daily business and buy a wide variety of items.

EXPLORING HO CHI MINH CITY

Ho Chi Minh City is not noted for its tourist attractions. Although there are several sights not to be missed, the particular appeal of the city is in its street life. From early morning to late at night, the streets and sidewalks are home to a startling range of activity—from street hawkers and barbers to noodle sellers and street artists. It's a kaleidoscopic maze, where Western-style commercial activity takes place alongside traditional practices.

The city has 14 districts, but most areas of interest are in either District 1 (downtown Saigon) or District 5 (Cholon). In District 1, major arteries such as Le Loi Boulevard, Ham Nghi Boulevard, and Pham Ngu Lao Street converge at the Ben Thanh Market, an important commercial and transportation hub. Northeast of the central market, at the intersection of Le Loi Boulevard with Nguyen Hue Boulevard and Dong Khoi Street, is a cluster of French colonial–style public buildings—the Hôtel de Ville (now the Ho Chi Minh City People's Committee); the Opera House (once again serving its original purpose after housing the former South Vietnam's National Assembly); and hotels like the Rex, the Continental, and the Caravelle, built by the French and made famous during the Vietnam War.

Saigon's waterways have traditionally served as a means of commercial transport as well as a natural moat. District 1 is bounded on the east by the Saigon River and on the south by the Ben Nghe Channel. Not only do the rivers provide an alternative way of getting around, they also serve as convenient landmarks. The city's rather daunting layout and chaotic traffic tend to discourage leisurely walking. The intermittent taxi, cyclo, or motorbike ride—ranging 6,000d–10,000d—is an unavoidable but enjoyable alternative. Any of the walks below could also be done as a cyclo ride, an option particularly recommended on hot days.

Numbers in the text correspond to numbers in the margin and on the Ho Chi Minh City, Cholon, and Ho Chi Minh City Environs maps.

Great Itineraries

IF YOU HAVE 1–2 DAYS

With one day you can see many of the city's major sights, though you have to be selective, especially if you want to visit a museum. Getting a cyclo or taxi to take you around can help you see the city more quickly. After you've seen the main sights on the first day, you'll have to go farther afield to find areas of interest. If on the first day you hired a cyclo driver you liked, you should use him again.

IF YOU HAVE 4 DAYS

With four days, you can see all the city's sights, go to one or two markets, and take a day trip—or even two—to surrounding areas including the Mekong Delta, the Cu Chi Tunnels, and the Caodai Holy See. Make arrangements for these excursions with one of the city's tourist agencies, or hire a car and driver (and maybe a guide) and go on your own.

When to Tour Ho Chi Minh City

The best time to visit the city is during the dry season, roughly between November and April, especially if you want to go down to the Mekong Delta. The rainy season runs from about May through October, during which outlying areas can become very flooded.

Central Saigon (Districts 1 and 3)

District 1 is the center of old Saigon. The broad Nguyen Hue and Le Loi boulevards converge at the Hôtel de Ville (now the People's Committee building), the historic Opera House, and the Hotel Continental. Dong Khoi Street, toward the eastern edge of District 1, is the neighborhood's historic main thoroughfare; it runs down to the Saigon River from Notre Dame Cathedral and the Central Post Office. Known as Rue Catinat during the French colonial era, Dong Khoi Street might be more easily recognized as Tu Do Street, its moniker when it was Saigon's red-light district in the 1960s and '70s. Since then, shops and restaurants have replaced the bars. Ben Thanh, an old colonial covered market, is on the western edge of District 1, and the former presidential palace (now called the Reunification Palace) is on the northern boundary of the area.

Numbers in the text correspond to numbers in the margin and on the Ho Chi Minh City map.

A Good Walk

Although slightly away from the center, the provocative **War Crimes Museum** ① makes a good starting point for this walk. From here head northeast on Vo Van Tan Street toward tree-lined Nam Ky Khoi Nghia Street. When you come to Nguyen Thi Minh Khai Street, you will see the grounds of the modern **Reunification Palace** ②. Directly behind it is the old French sports club, the Cercle Sportif, now known as **Cong Vien Van Hoa Park** ③; to enter the park, turn right off Nguyen Du Street, which is a one-way street running along the side of the palace. Walk through the park into the grounds of the palace; turn left on to Le Duan Boulevard, the street that intersects with Nam Ky Khoi Nghia Street at the palace entrance. After passing Pasteur Street, you'll see the back of **Notre Dame Cathedral** ④, with its pink spires. Continuing on Le Duan Boulevard, just a couple of blocks past Hai Ba Trung Boulevard, is the now-dilapidated former **U.S. Embassy** ⑤; it has remained untouched since being evacuated in 1975. With the renewal of U.S.-Vietnam relations, the site is going to be home to the new American consulate. Proceed about 1,000 ft down Le Duan Boulevard to get to the sprawling grounds of the **Zoo and Botanical Garden** ⑥ and the **History Museum** ⑦.

With your back to the main entrance of the complex, make a left onto Nguyen Binh Khiem Street and follow it to the intersection with Le Thanh Ton Street. Make a right, then take the first left at Ton Duc Thang Street, which runs along the Saigon River. Along the waterfront you can see the turn-of-the century **Hotel Majestic** ⑧, at the intersection of Ton Duc Thang and Dong Khoi streets. The hotel's rooftop bar provides magnificent views of the Saigon River and the Thu Thiem swamp district opposite. Turn right at Nguyen Hue Boulevard and make the first left onto Hai Trieu Street, also known as Whiskey Row. Take a right on Ham Nghi Street, where a bunch of international food stores (No. 64 is a good one) are jam-packed with Western specialties. Make a right onto Ton That Dang Street, where you can find everything from live eels to laundry detergent at the market that continues along intersecting Huynh Thuc Khang Street, a kind of electronics arcade. Continuing a block past Huynh Thuc Khang Street, you come to Ton That Thiep Street, in what has historically been the Indian quarter.

Art Museum, **19**
Ben Thanh Market, **17**
Central Post Office, **13**
Cong Vien Van Hoa Park, **3**
Emperor Jade Pagoda, **21**
History Museum, **7**
Ho Chi Minh City's People's Committee/ Hotel de Ville, **15**
Ho Chi Minh Museum, **18**
Hotel Caravelle, **9**
Hotel Continental, **10**
Hotel Majestic, **8**
Mariamman Hindu Temple, **16**
Municipal Theater, **11**
Museum of the Revolution **14**
Notre Dame Cathedral, **4**
Reunification Palace, **2**
Saigon Tourist, **12**
Ton Duc Thang Museum, **20**
U.S. Embassy, **5**
War Remnants Museum, **1**
Zoo and Botanical Garden, **6**

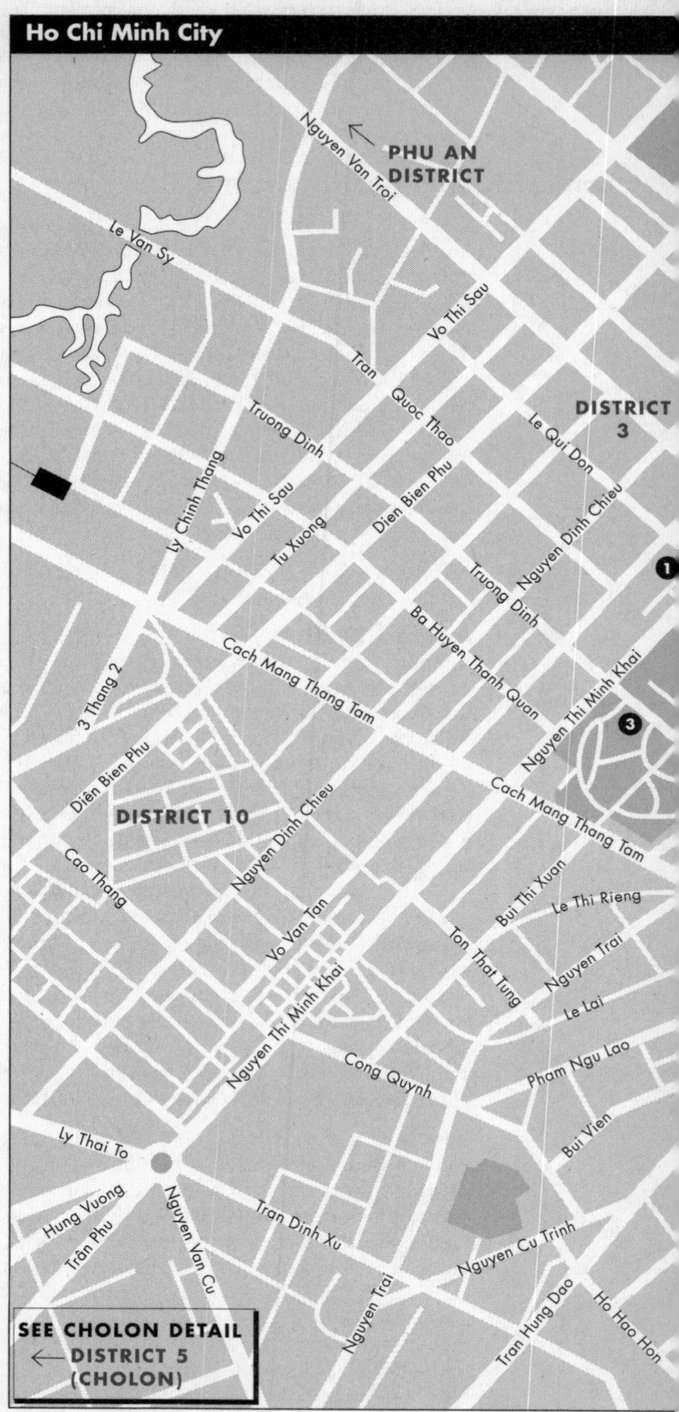

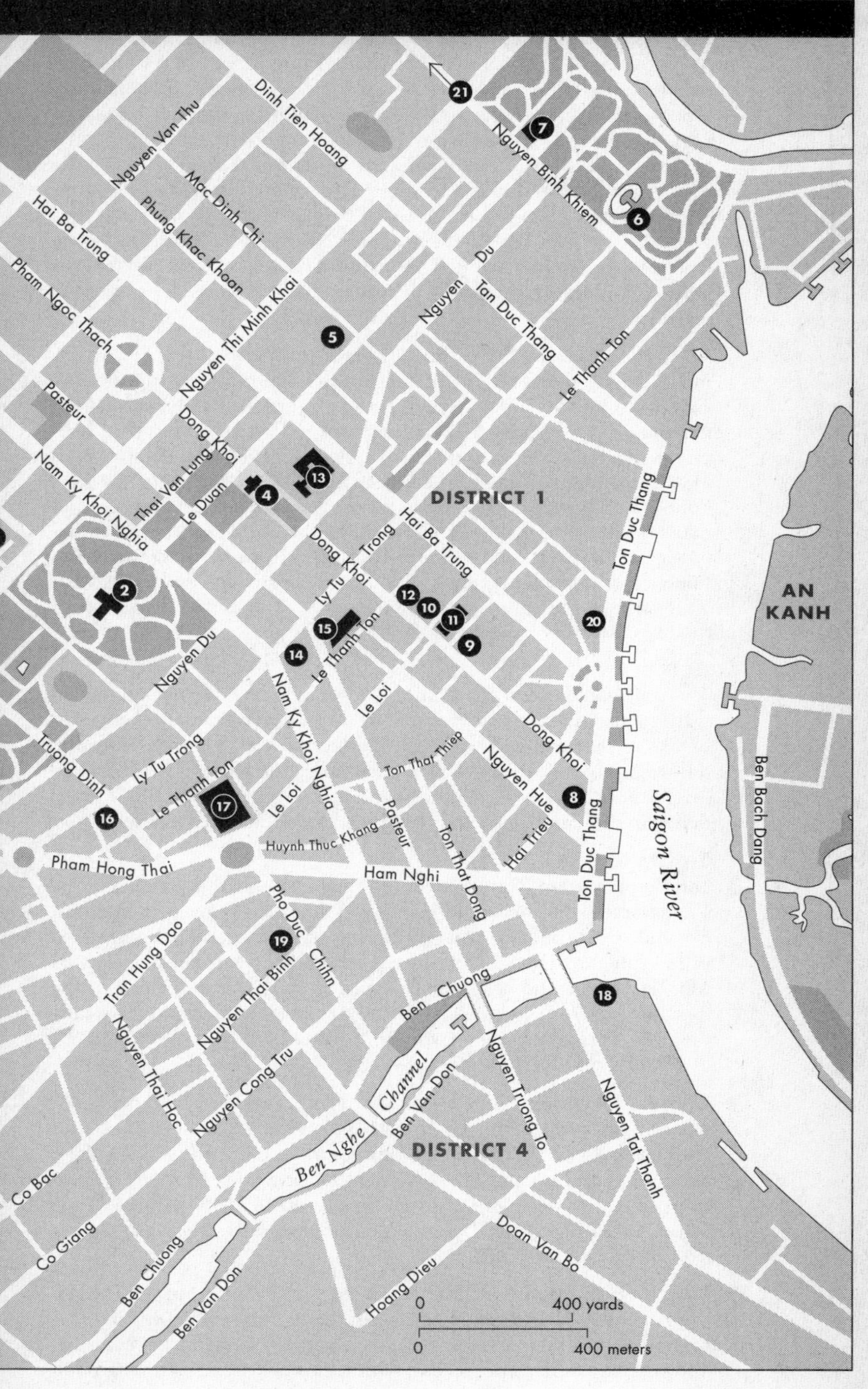

DISTRICT 1
DISTRICT 4
AN KANH
Saigon River
Ben Nghe
Channel
Dinh Tien Hoang
Nguyen Van Thu
Mac Dinh Chi
Hai Ba Trung
Phung Khac Khoan
Pham Ngoc Thach
Nguyen Thi Minh Khai
Nguyen Binh Khiem
Nguyen Du
Tan Duc Thang
Le Thanh Ton
Pasteur
Dong Khoi
Thai Van Lung
Le Duan
Nam Ky Khoi Nghia
Ton Duc Thang
Ly Tu Trong
Le Loi
Truong Dinh
Ton That Thiep
Nguyen Hue
Hai Trieu
Huynh Thuc Khang
Ton That Dong
Pham Hong Thai
Ham Nghi
Pho Duc Chinh
Tran Hung Dao
Nguyen Thai Binh
Ben Chuong
Nguyen Thai Hoc
Nguyen Cong Tru
Ben Van Don
Nguyen Truong To
Nguyen Tat Thanh
Ben Bach Dang
Co Bac
Co Giang
Doan Van Bo
Hoang Dieu
0
400 yards
0
400 meters

Make a right onto Ton That Thiep Street, crossing Nguyen Hue Boulevard, and turn left on to **Dong Khoi Street,** which extends from the river to Notre Dame Cathedral. Along Dong Khoi Street is the **Hotel Caravelle** ⑨, once a favorite haunt of war correspondents at cocktail hour. Opposite the Caravelle is the **Hotel Continental** ⑩. Although a shadow of its former self, it's still worth a visit. Sandwiched between the two at the end of Le Loi Boulevard is the **Municipal Theater** ⑪, recognizable by its inverted dome. Farther up Dong Khoi Street, past the Continental, is the main branch office of **Saigon Tourist** ⑫, on the corner of Le Thanh Ton Street. Next comes Notre Dame Cathedral—the front of the church this time. The beautiful French colonial **Central Post Office** ⑬ is on the right side of the square that opens up in front of the cathedral.

With your back to the cathedral, walk toward Nguyen Du Street, make a right, then take the first left onto Pasteur Street, and the first right onto Ly Tu Trong Street to get to the neoclassic **Museum of the Revolution** ⑭, or Army Museum. Return to Pasteur Street, then proceed down to Le Thanh Ton Street to get to the **Ho Chi Minh City's People's Committee** ⑮, built by the French as the Hôtel de Ville (City Hall). Follow Le Thanh Ton Street away from the People's Committee, and make a right on Truong Dinh Street. In the middle of the block between Ly Tu Trong and Le Thanh Ton streets is the **Mariamman Hindu Temple** ⑯, the last functioning Hindu house of worship in the city. With your back to the temple, make a left on Le Thanh Ton Street where the busy **Ben Thanh Market** ⑰ spills out into the surrounding street.

TIMING

The walk could take a day or more, depending on how much time you want to spend in the museums. Start in the morning and take lots of breaks in the small sidewalk cafés along the way. Consider splitting the walk into two parts, with a break after the History Museum. Be careful not to overexert yourself, and remember to drink a lot of bottled water: It can be hot and tiring walking around Saigon.

Sights to See

★ ⓱ **Ben Thanh Market** (Cho Ben Thanh). Every imaginable product of the Vietnamese economy is sold here—look for a cheap meal, a hat, even live snakes. The building that houses most of the market was constructed in 1914 by the French, who called it Les Halles Centrales (the Central Market Halls). The best time to visit the market is first thing in the morning, when stocks of produce are piled high and vendors are hustling. ✉ *At circular intersection of Le Loi Blvd., Pham Ngu Lao St., and Ham Nghi Blvd.* ⏲ *Daily 7–7.*

★ ⓭ **Central Post Office** (Buu Dien Truing Tam). This classic French colonial building was completed in 1891. Be sure to go inside to check out the huge map of old Indochina. Besides the usual mail services, there are phones and fax machines. To mail letters you need to use the entrance to the less romantic, Soviet-era expansion at 117 Hai Ba Trung Street. ✉ *At the top of Dong Khoi St. opposite Notre Dame Cathedral.* ⏲ *Daily 7:30–7:30.*

❸ **Cong Vien Van Hoa Park.** Known as the Cercle Sportif to the French, this park was the elite sporting club of the French bourgeoisie in colonial times, and Vietnamese people were actually barred from entering. Today there is still a sports club, with tennis courts, a swimming pool, a gym and weight room, and a colonial club house. To use the facilities will cost you no more than a dollar. These days the club is mostly frequented by young Vietnamese students eager to practice their English with any tourists who wander in. ✉ *Entrance on 115 Nguyen Du St.*

Dong Khoi Street. Once name Rue Catinat, Dong Khoi Street was Saigon's Fifth Avenue or Rodeo Drive in the French colonial era. During the Vietnam War this road was the center of the infamous red-light district and was known as Tu Do street. These days most of the old-time bars have been replaced by restaurants and shops (☞ Shopping, *below*). The street remains the center the old city, but this is the new Dong Khoi: A Hard Rock Cafe is in the works in the old Hotel Caravelle, and most shops are now oriented toward tourists.

NEED A BEEAK? The **Paris Deli** (☞ 31 Dong Khoi St. District 1, ☎ 08/829–7533) is a European-style café serving excellent cappuccinos and pastries.

7 **History Museum** (Vien Bao Tang Lich Su). Although the front door leads you right to a statue of the ubiquitous "Uncle Ho" (as Ho Chi Minh is known), this museum is dedicated to Vietnamese history from the earliest inhabitants to 1930, when the Communist Party was established. Half the museum covers the history of the nation as a whole, while the other half focuses on the art and artifacts of southern Vietnam; the ethnography section is particularly interesting. The neo-Vietnamese structure was built by the French in 1929, and much of the current collection was compiled by the French Far Eastern Institute. ✉ *2 Nguyen Binh Khiem, District 1,* ☎ *08/829–8146 or 08/829–0268.* 🎟 *10,000d.* ⏲ *Mon.–Sat. 8–11:30 and 1:30–4:30, Sun. 8:30–11:30.*

15 **Ho Chi Minh City's People's Committee.** Built by the French between 1901 and 1908 to be Saigon's Hôtel de Ville (City Hall), this yellow-and-white colonial-style building now houses the city's main governing body. Unfortunately, the building is not open to the public, so you can't get a peek at its ornate interior. ✉ *Intersection of Le Thanh Ton and Nguyen Hue Sts., District 1.*

9 **Hotel Caravelle.** This hotel was where most of the foreign correspondents stayed during the Vietnam War. During the 1968 Tet Offensive, several U.S. marines were killed here; journalists filmed the battle from the rooftop. The hotel is currently undergoing major renovation, with plans for a Hard Rock Cafe, and at press time (winter 1997) was scheduled to reopen by early 1998. ✉ *19–25 Lam Son Sq., no phone (at press time).*

★ 10 **Hotel Continental.** In French colonial days, the Hotel Continental's open terrace (now simply a sidewalk), shaded by broad tamarind trees, was the town's most sought-after lunch spot. During the Vietnam War, journalists and diplomats met on the terrace to discuss the latest events. Graham Greene's *The Quiet American* was set here. For information about staying at the hotel, *see* Lodging, *below.* ✉ *132–134 Dong Khoi St., District 1,* ☎ *08/829–9201.*

★ 8 **Hotel Majestic.** Built in the late 19th century, the Majestic was one of the first French colonial hotels, and it still has the elegant decor to show for it. Go to the rooftop bar for an excellent view of the Saigon River. For information about staying here, *see* Lodging, *below.* ✉ *1 Dong Khoi St., District 1,* ☎ *08/829–5514.*

16 **Mariamman Hindu Temple** (Chua Ba Mariamman). Vivid statues and colorful floral offerings at this temple, the last functioning Hindu house of worship in the city, create a microcosm of India in the streets of Saigon. Before its return in the early '90s to the Hindu community, the government used the temple as a factory for making joss sticks (incense) and processing dried fish. Today it serves a congregation of a mere 60 Tamil Hindus, but some Vietnamese and Chinese locals also revere it as a holy space. ✉ *45 Truong Dinh St.* ⏲ *Daily 7–7.*

11 **Municipal Theater** (Nha Hat Thanh Pho). This colonial-style theater was built by the French in 1899 as Saigon's opera house. Later it housed the National Assembly of South Vietnam, the congress of the South Vietnamese government. After 1975, when South Vietnam ceased to be, it became a theater again. For more information *see* Nightlife and the Arts, *below.* ✉ *Intersection of Le Loi Blvd. and Dong Khoi St., District 1,* ☎ *08/829–1249.*

14 **Museum of the Revolution** (Bao Tang Cach Mang). Constructed in 1886 as the residence for the French governor of Cochin China, the building is now a museum dedicated to the Vietnamese struggle against the French and Americans. Displays focus on famous marches, military battles, and anti-French and anti-American activists. Exhibits include photos of historical events, uprisings, student demonstrations, and the self-immolation of the monk Thich Quang Duc as a protest against the war. The collection also includes a lot of American GI paraphernalia—badges, lighters, helmets, and such—as well as a model of the Cu Chi Tunnels, the huge underground complex built by the Vietnamese Communists that allowed them to survive massive U.S. bombings and military sweeps (☞ Side Trips from Ho Chi Minh City, *below*). The displays are in Vietnamese, but you'll easily get the message. The building itself is as interesting as many of the exhibits inside: A neoclassic design, it has huge columns outside and high-ceilinged ballrooms from the 19th century inside. Beneath the building are concrete bunkers and tunnels connecting to the Reunification Palace. It was here that President Ngo Dinh Diem and his notorious brother Ngo Dinh Thuc hid before being caught and eventually executed in 1963, three weeks before the assassination of president John F. Kennedy. Outside on the grounds are Soviet tanks, a U.S. helicopter, and antiaircraft guns. ✉ *65 Ly Tu Trong St., District 1,* ☎ *08/829–9741.* 🎟 *Free.* ⏲ *Tues.–Sun. 8–4:30.*

4 **Notre Dame Cathedral** (Nha Tho Duc Ba). A prominent presence on the Saigon skyline, this neo-Romanesque cathedral was built by the French in 1880 on the site of an old fort. Spanish, Portuguese, and French missionaries introduced Catholicism to Vietnam as early as the 16th century. Today there are 9 million Catholics in Vietnam, the largest Christian population in Asia after the Philippines. The Mass celebrated at 9:30 AM on Sunday is quite a spectacle, as hundreds of faithful converge on the church and stand in the surrounding square. The service also includes short sections in English and French. ✉ *Top of Dong Khoi St.*

2 **Reunification Palace** (Hoi Truong Thong Nhat). This modern palace—the symbolic center of the South Vietnamese government—was the scene of the dramatic seizure of Saigon by the National Liberation Front in 1975, when tanks smashed down the gates and a NLF flag was draped over the building's balcony. The president's mansion was designed by a European-influenced modernist architect, Ngo Viet Thu, in 1962—and it is classic '60s architecture. It was built when South Vietnamese president Diem decided he had an "image problem" after his own air force bombed him in the old French palace in an assassination attempt. It succeeded a year later, so he never saw the palace finished. The former building on the site was called Norodom Palace and was the home of the French governor general of Cochin China. The present building still sits on large grounds, where there is a somewhat romanticized model of Ho Chi Minh's home.

There isn't much to see except the palace rooms: the cabinet room, the assembly room, the president's office, the war command room with maps and multicolored telephones, the dining rooms, the private quarters, and a bar-and-games room. You also get a look at the network of tunnels to which the government of South Vietnam would retreat in difficult times and the helicopter that bombed the building in 1975. It all sounds more interesting than it is, since there really isn't much in the rooms except some furniture. But the palace is worth a visit, if only to see a vestige of Vietnam's past. Be sure to stand out on the balcony for a view of the city down the long, tree-lined boulevard created by the French. Although tours are free to Vietnamese, foreigners must pay. ✉ *Visitors' entrance on 106 Nguyen Du St., District 1,* ☎ *08/823–3652 or 08/822–3673.* 🎫 *10,000d.* ⏲ *Daily 7:30–10:30 and 1–4.*

12 **Saigon Tourist.** This government-run travel service provides all kinds of visitor information and services (☞ Visitor Information and Travel Agencies *in* Ho Chi Minh City A to Z, *below*). ✉ *49 Le Thanh Ton St., District 1,* ☎ *08/823–0100.* ⏲ *Daily 7:30–6:30.*

5 **U.S. Embassy.** Although (at press time) the compound awaits reoccupation by the Americans now that diplomatic relations have been restored, the old U.S. embassy remains an architectural skeleton in the cupboard. Nicknamed "the bunker" because it resembles just that, the embassy was built in 1967 with little aesthetic appeal in mind. This is probably one reason why the new consulate may bulldoze it eventually. Although the building is nothing to get excited about architecturally, it still stands as one of the great landmarks of 20th-century history. This American symbolic stronghold was attacked during the 1968 Tet Offensive and was finally seized by the Vietnamese with the capture of Saigon in April 1975. The U.S. embassy was the site of one of the most memorable images of the war: the U.S. ambassador, an American flag clutched to his chest, rushing into a helicopter waiting on the roof, while Marine guards pushed back mobs of South Vietnamese who had been assured evacuation. You can't officially look into the compound or inside the building, but peering through the gates will give you a good look. ✉ *Intersection of Le Duan Blvd. and Mac Din Chi St.*

1 **War Remnants Museum** (Nha Trung Bay Toi Ac Chien Tranh Xam). You may instinctively shy away from this museum, which is dedicated to publicizing the horrors perpetrated by U.S. armed forces during the Vietnam War. You'll probably come away with mixed feelings about the one-sided propaganda—ashamed of the U.S. actions, angry about the Vietnamese inaccuracies in depicting them, or both. Nevertheless, it's a must-see if you're curious.

Although the museum has toned down slightly by changing its name from the Museum of American War Crimes to the War Crimes Museum and to, more recently, the War Remnants Museum, its coverage continues to be skewed. Conspicuous in its absence, for instance, is any mention of the division of the country into South Vietnam and North Vietnam throughout the Vietnam War. (The Communist government tends to overlook this division; instead it claims a puppet government backed by American imperialists illegally ruled in the South against the will of the people.) There are, however, photos of captured spies who attempted to infiltrate and overthrow the Communist regime.

Also missing is information about some of the horrors perpetrated by the National Liberation Front, particularly the 14,000 people massacred in Hue during the 1968 Tet Offensive. But there is a little information about civilian protests in Vietnam and in America against U.S. military actions, except for a few photos of antiwar demonstrators. Although photographs, the majority of items on display, accurately depict the horrors and details of the war, their presentations range from poignant to dull to obviously slanted. Along with these photos are gruesome displays documenting the effects of Agent Orange, napalm, and other weapons of mass destruction, as well as a mannequin of a rather dissolute looking American soldier (smoking Marlboros, of course) and a replica of a Con Dao prison cell. ✉ *28 Vo Van Tan St., District 3,* ☎ *08/829–0325.* 🎫 *10,000d.* ⏲ *Daily 7:30–11:45 and 1:30–4:45.*

6 **Zoo and Botanical Garden** (Thao Cam Vien). The fauna here does relatively well, and the flora thrives in its natural subtropical niche. In addition to the lackluster array of live animals, visit the eerie "taxidermy-go-round," where you can ride stuffed animals. As if this were not enough, the gardens have been filled with additional carnival-like attractions—a rather unfortunate addition, as the gardens were one of the first French building projects in Vietnam and once one of the finest such parks in all of Asia. ✉ *Nguyen Binh Khiem St. at Le Duan Blvd.* 🎫 *2,000d.* ⏲ *Daily 8–5:30.*

Circling Old Saigon

This tour covers the sights around the periphery of Old Saigon. South of District 1, on the broad waterfront along the Saigon River, is a less palatial section of the old city where the old docks and customs houses used to be. This was also the old banking district, and you can still see the colonial-era Hong Kong and Shanghai Banking Corporation, and Banque d'Indochine buildings. Most museums in this area are housed in the former customs houses and colonial buildings and predominantly contain collections dedicated to famous figures and moments in Vietnamese history. You might want to hire a cyclo to take you to some of the sights in this area.

Numbers in the text correspond to numbers in the margin and on the Ho Chi Minh City map.

A Good Walk

Start at the **Ho Chi Minh Museum** ⑱, in a converted French customs house on Saigon Port. From the museum follow Nguyen Tat Thanh Street across the bridge over the Ben Nghe Channel. Take your first left after the bridge, following the channel along Ben Chuong Street until you get to Pho Duc Chinh Street. Take a right to get to the **Art Museum** ⑲, in a grand old colonial building. After you've seen it, return to Ben Chuong street and continue back the way you came until you reach Ton Duc Thang street and the **Ton Duc Thang Museum** ⑳, dedicated to the first president of North Vietnam and later united Vietnam. From the museum take a cyclo along Ton Duc Thang Street, which turns into Dinh Tien Hoang Street, which leads to Dien Bien Phu Street. Take a left and proceed to No. 20; turn left onto Mai Thi Luu Street and follow it to the lovely **Emperor Jade Pagoda** ㉑. After looking around the pagoda, head right down Nguyen Binh Khiem Street and take another right along Nguyen Thi Minh Khai Street (you must use this route if going by cyclo because other roads are one-way or don't allow cyclos). This will bring you to the top of Dong Khoi Street (☞ *above*). Here you can either walk down the street toward the river or continue in your cyclo.

TIMING

Whether you travel by foot or cyclo, exploring this part of Saigon will probably take a day, including visiting the museums and the pagoda and browsing along Dong Khoi Street. All museums are open daily except Monday.

Sights to See

19 **Art Museum** (Bao Tang My Thuat). Considering its grand colonial setting, this museum is a disappointment. The building was designed in

a classic French-Vietnamese architectural style (European-type stucco and Asian designs), once common to those edifices built for rich French and Vietnamese families and officials. The collection on the first and second floors covers propaganda art of the Soviet socialist-realist variety—soldiers and peasants marching arm in arm to battle. At first it is interesting, but after a while you may start to feel bombarded by the number of images of war, Uncle Ho, and defeated foreign armies. The best reason to visit the museum is on the third floor—the antique statues and other relics of the pre-Vietnamese south. Also here are objects from the ancient Funan and Khmer civilizations as well as some of the best examples of Cham art outside the Central Highlands. ✉ *97A Pho Duc Chinh St., District 1,* ☎ *08/822–2577.* 🎫 *Free.* ⏲ *Tues.–Sun. 8:30–11:30 and 2–7.*

⓲ **Ho Chi Minh Museum** (Khu Luu Niem Bac Ho). The building itself, nicknamed the "Dragon House" (Nha Rong) for its architectural design, is actually far more interesting than most of the displays inside "Uncle Ho's Museum." It was constructed in 1863 as the original French customs house; any individuals coming to colonial Saigon would have had to pass through the building once they docked at the port. Ho Chi Minh (1890–1969) passed through here in 1911 on his way to his 30-year sojourn around Europe and America. Inside are some of his personal belongings, including his journals, fragments of his clothing, and his rubber sandals. Ho Chi Minh was an ascetic type of guy, known for only wearing sandals made from tires; these are now scattered at museums around the country (☞ Close-Up box: Meet Uncle Ho *in* Chapter 2, for more information on Ho Chi Minh's life). ✉ *On Saigon Port at 1 Nguyen Tat Thanh St., by quayside on Ben Nghe Channel at far end of Ham Nghi Blvd.,* ☎ *08/839–1060.* 🎫 *Free.* ⏲ *Tues.–Sun. 8:30–11:30 and 2–7.*

★ ㉑ **Emperor Jade Pagoda** (Chua Ngoc Hoang or Phuoc Hai Tu). Also known as the Tortoise Pagoda, this structure—the finest Chinese pagoda in Saigon—was built by the Cantonese community in 1909. A mixture of Taoist, Buddhist, and ethnic myths provide the sources for the pagoda's multitude of statues and carvings—everything from the *King of Hell* to a *Buddha of the Future.* Slowly strolling around the interior to view them may be preferable to attempting to decipher the significance of each of the numerous, distinct deities. Take a moment to note the main altar, the side panel's depiction of hell, and in the side room, the miniature female figures who represent the range of human qualities. ✉ *73 Mai Thi Luu St., District 3.*

⑳ **Ton Duc Thang Museum** (Bao Tang Ton Duc Thang). Housed in a characterless Soviet-era building on the waterfront by the Vietnamese navy barracks, this museum is unremarkable compared to the other museums in the city. It celebrates the life and times of president Ton Duc Thang (1888–1980), who succeeded Ho Chi Minh as head of North and later unified Vietnam after Ho Chi Minh's death in 1969. Inside are artifacts that Ton Duc Thang used in everyday life as well as photos of him taken during his incarceration by the French on Paulo Condor (now Con Dao Island) and propaganda pictures of him exhorting the people of Vietnam to fight the French and Americans. ✉ *5 Ton Duc Thang St., District 1,* ☎ *08/829–4651.* 🎫 *Free.* ⏲ *Tues.–Sun. 8:30–11:30 and 2–7.*

Cholon (District 5)

Southwest of central Saigon is Cholon, the city's Chinese sister city, otherwise known as District 5. Cholon was and is still the center of Chinese culture in Vietnam and a commercial mecca. The French supported the Chinese in Vietnam because of their success in commerce and their apolitical outlook, seldom supporting Vietnamese nationalist struggles. The Communists, on the other hand, saw Cholon as a bastion of capitalism, and the area suffered greatly after 1975. Later, in 1979, during the war between Vietnam and China, Cholon was again targeted since it was considered a potential center of fifth columnists (pro-Chinese agitators). Many of the first boat people were Chinese-Vietnamese from Cholon. (Ironically, they're now among Saigon's wealthiest returning émigrés, after making money in Australia, Canada, and the United States.)

Negotiate a price of about 55,000d with a cyclo driver to take you on a tour of the pagodas and mosques concentrated around Nguyen Trai Street and Tran Hung Dao Boulevard in Cholon. Bright blue, yellow, red, orange, and gold cover the pagodas in a dazzling display that would put mating peacocks to shame. Pagodas are seldom shut to the public, and most monks begin their prayers early in the morning, so you are generally welcome to enter a pagoda at any time of day. There are no admission fees, but it is traditional to put a donation of about 10,000d or so in the box at the altar in front of Buddha. Monks never hassle you for money, but they do look a little upset if you don't donate. When you've seen enough (the pagodas may start to look the same after a while), alert your guide or cyclo driver so you won't see every single one in the area.

Spend the rest of the day exploring Cholon's streets, markets, shophouses (stores that double as the owners' homes), and restaurants, with their distinctive Chinese appeal. Walk down the hundreds of small side streets, where the neighborhood is at its most colorful. And be sure to enter one of the many traditional medicine shops, which sell everything from herbal remedies being packaged for export to animals hoofs, antlers, and tails to sea horses and snake wine. What makes Cholon so special are the sights and sounds of its streets.

Numbers in the text correspond to numbers in the margin and on the Cholon map.

A Good Walk

Begin at the bustling **Binh Tay Market** ㉒, on Phan Van Khoe Street. Take a left out of the market and walk along Phan Van Khoe Street until you get to Phung Hung Street; take a left and follow it until you reach the **Ong Bon Pagoda** ㉓, where you can pay your respects to the guardian of happiness and virtue. Exiting the pagoda, take Hai Thuong Lan Ong Boulevard until you reach the old colonial **Post Office** ㉔. Walk straight up Chau Van Liem Boulevard to Tran Hung Dao Boulevard, the center of Cholon, with its street markets and old, small shophouses (and some newer, taller ones).

Keep walking straight ahead until you reach Nguyen Trai Street; take a right to get to Cholon's pagoda district. Continue on Nguyen Trai Street until you come to small Lao Tu Street, on your right, and the **Quan Am Pagoda** ㉕, which is known for its elaborately decorated scenes. Walk down Luong Nhu Hoc Street to the **Ha Chuong Hoi Quan Pagoda** ㉖, at No. 802, one of the many temples devoted to the goddess of the sea. Take a left on Nguyen Trai Street and walk along until you come to the **Thien Hau Pagoda** ㉗, at No. 710, where sailors used to come before they went out to sea. Farther along, past the intersection of Trieu Quang Phu Street, on the left at No. 678 is the **Nghia An Hoi Quan Pagoda** ㉘, famous for its detailed woodwork, and on the other side of the street, at No. 118, is the **Tam Son Hoi Quan Pagoda** ㉙, dedicated to the goddess of fertility. Keep going straight on Nguyen Trai Street, past the intersection of Ly Thuong Kiet Street, until

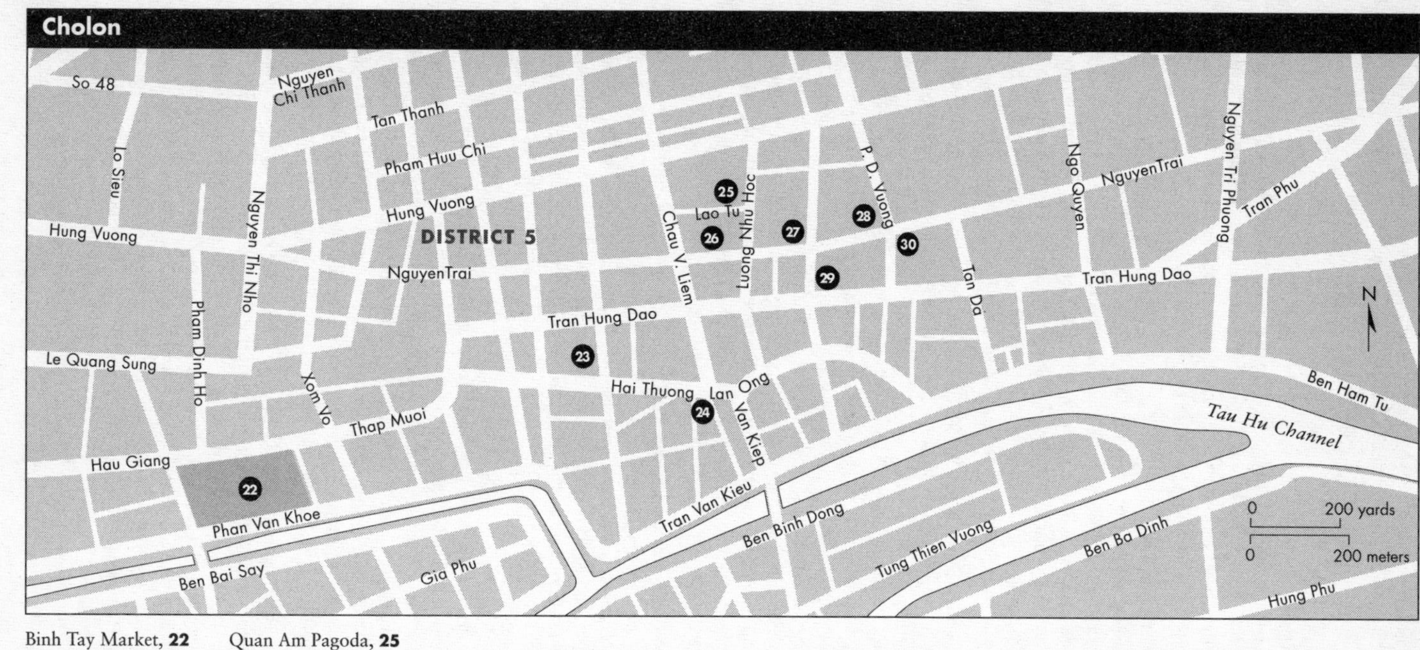

Binh Tay Market, **22**
Cholon Mosque, **30**
Ha Chuong Hoi Quan Pagoda, **26**
Nghia An Hoi Quan Pagoda, **28**
Ong Bon Pagoda, **23**
Post Office, **24**
Quan Am Pagoda, **25**
Tam Son Hoi Quan Pagoda, **29**
Thien Hau Pagoda, **27**

you reach the **Cholon Mosque** ㉚, used by Saigon's Muslim community. Go back to Ly Thuong Kiet Street and turn right onto Tran Hung Dao Boulevard. Take it to Luong Nhu Hoc Street, turn left, and you'll be back at the post office.

TIMING

Depending on how interested you are in pagodas, this walk could take up to three or four hours. If you have an interest in Chinese medicine, be sure to take time to explore the many stores along the small back streets surrounding the Binh Tay Market.

Sights to See

㉒ **Binh Tay Market** (Cho Binh Tay). Cholon's main market is in a colonial-era, Chinese-style building. The street outside is a frenzy of activity; inside can be a little calmer, though you have to wend your way through very narrow aisles. A variety of items are sold, including dried shrimp and fruit, aluminum kitchenware, baskets, plastic goods, barrettes, straw hats, and food. ✉ *On Hau Giang Blvd., District 6.*

㉚ **Cholon Mosque.** Built in 1932 by Tamil Muslims, the Cholon Mosque now serves Saigon's Indonesian and Malaysian Muslim community. It's interesting to see the difference in architectural styles between mosques and pagodas. Mosques have simpler domes and spires as compared to the exuberant ornamentation and bright colors that characterize pagodas. Most pagodas are decorated with dragons, lions, a wide variety of Buddhas, and other representations of spirits and deities, whereas mosques are generally far more restrained. In the Islamic tradition it is strictly forbidden to represent God or any animal or human. Hence decoration takes the form of abstract images and calligraphy. ✉ *641 Nguyen Trai St., at Ly Thuong Kiet Blvd.*

㉖ **Ha Chuong Hoi Quan Pagoda.** Like many pagodas built by Fujian congregations, this one is dedicated to Thien Hau, goddess of the sea and protector of fishermen and sailors. It has four stone pillars encircled by painted dragons; these were brought from China when the pagoda was constructed in the 19th century. Also note the scenes in ceramic relief on the roof and the murals next to the main altar. ✉ *802 Nguyen Trai St.*

㉘ **Nghia An Hoi Quan Pagoda.** Built by the Chaozhou Chinese congregation in 1872, this pagoda is worth seeing for its elaborate woodwork. There are intricately carved wooden boats and a large figure of the deified Chinese general Quan Cong's sacred red horse, as well as representations of Quan Cong himself with two guardians. A festival dedicated to Quan Ong is held every year on the 13th of the first lunar month. ✉ *678 Nguyen Trai St.*

★ ㉓ **Ong Bon Pagoda** (Chua Ong Bon or Nhi Phu Hoi Quan). Many deities are represented at this pagoda, but the main attraction is Ong Bon himself, the guardian of happiness and virtue. Ong Bong is also responsible for wealth, so people bring fake paper money to burn in the pagoda's furnace in his honor, hoping the year ahead will bring financial rewards to their families. The centerpiece of the pagoda is an elaborately carved, wood and gold altar and a finely crafted statue of Ong Bon. Be sure to note the intricately painted murals of lions, tigers, and dragons. ✉ *264 Hai Thuong Lai Ong Blvd. (parallel to Tran Hung Dao St.), at Phung Hung St.* 🎟 *Free.*

㉔ **Post Office.** This modernist building was constructed by the French in the 1920s. ✉ *Intersection of Hai Thuong Lai Ong Blvd. and Chau Van Liem Blvd.* ⏲ *Daily 7:30–7:30.*

25 **Quan Am Pagoda.** Dating from 1816, this pagoda was built by a congregation of Fujian refugees from China. It is notable for its busy array of scenes in lacquer, ceramic, gold, and wood illustrating traditional Chinese stories. Many legendary and divine beings, some dressed in elaborately embroidered robes, are portrayed, as are some simple rural scenes representing the birthplaces of the original members of the congregation. Be prepared for a stifling cloud of incense when you enter—this is still one of Cholon's most active pagodas. ✉ *12 Lao Tu St. (parallel to Huong Vuong Blvd. and Nguyen Trai St.).*

29 **Tam Son Hoi Quan Pagoda** (Chua Ba Chua). The Chinese Fujian congregation built this lavishly decorated pagoda dedicated to Me Sanh, the goddess of fertility, in the 19th century. Women—and some men—pray to the goddess to bring them children. Many other deities are represented here as well: Thien Hau, the goddess of the sea and protector of fishermen and sailors; Ong Bon, the guardian of happiness and virtue; and Quan Cong, the deified general, depicted with a long beard and his sacred red horse. ✉ *118 Trieu Quang Phuc St.*

27 **Thien Hau Pagoda** (Chua Ba). Built by the Cantonese congregation at the beginning of the 19th century, the pagoda is dedicated to Thien Hau, the goddess of the sea and protector of fishermen and sailors. Sailors used to come here to be blessed. On the main dais are three statues of the goddess, each flanked by two guardians. Note also the figure of Long Mau, guardian of mothers and babies. The turtles living on the grounds are considered sacred animals and are a symbol of longevity. ✉ *710 Nguyen Trai St.*

DINING

Central Saigon (Districts 1 and 3)

French

$$$$ ★ ✕ **Le Camargue.** One of the most romantic and tastefully done restaurants in Saigon, the French-influenced Le Camargue is an exciting culinary forum. The cuisine is a mix of East and West—with a good wine list to go along—and is very good, even by other cities' standards. Dine on the elegant, plant-filled terrace of a restored villa or indoors in the warmly-lit dining rooms. Sample dishes include pan-roasted sea bass on a bed of wasabi mashed potatoes and tamarind-glazed crab cake; the menu changes depending on what's available. The duck is also excellent (Vietnam is the number two exporter of ducks in the world). ✉ *16 Cao Ba Quat St., District 1,* ☎ *08/823–3148. Reservations essential. AE, DC, MC, V. No lunch.*

$$$$ ✕ **Le Caprice.** Stodgy but run like a Swiss timepiece, this landmark provides Saigon's expat elite with unoriginal but fine French cuisine, passé but well-maintained hotel decor, and a beautiful view of the Saigon River. If you don't actually get around to eating here, it's worth stopping by just to have a drink and take in the view. ✉ *Landmark Building, 5B Ton Duc Thang St., 15th floor, District 1,* ☎ *08/822–8337. AE, DC, MC, V.*

$$$ ✕ **Augustin.** Small, intimate, and filled with comfortably solo expats reading the newspaper at the bar, Augustin serves tasty French bistro food to a predominantly international crowd. ✉ *10 Nguyen Thiep St., District 1,* ☎ *08/829–2941. AE, DC, MC, V. No lunch Sun.*

$$ ✕ **Legros.** Outstanding, authentic French cuisine is cooked by a French chef who may offer you a liqueur on the house if you rave enough about his food. In fact, this place is so French that the menu is not in Vietnamese or English. However, this small show of nationalism is more

'A' The Russian Restaurant, **1**
Augustin, **14**
Blue Ginger, **22**
Bodhi Tree II, **20**
Café Mogambo, **9**
Le Camargue, **12**
Le Caprice, **10**
Chao Thai, **6**
Legros, **7**
Lemongrass, **15**
Liberty, **18**
Marine Club, **5**
May Ngan Phuong, **3**
Pho Hoa, **4**
Restaurant 13, **17**
Sapa, **13**
Sawaddee, **11**
Sekitei Japanese Restaurant, **2**
Shanti, **21**
Spices, **19**
Thi Sac Street Cafés, **8**
Vietnam House, **16**

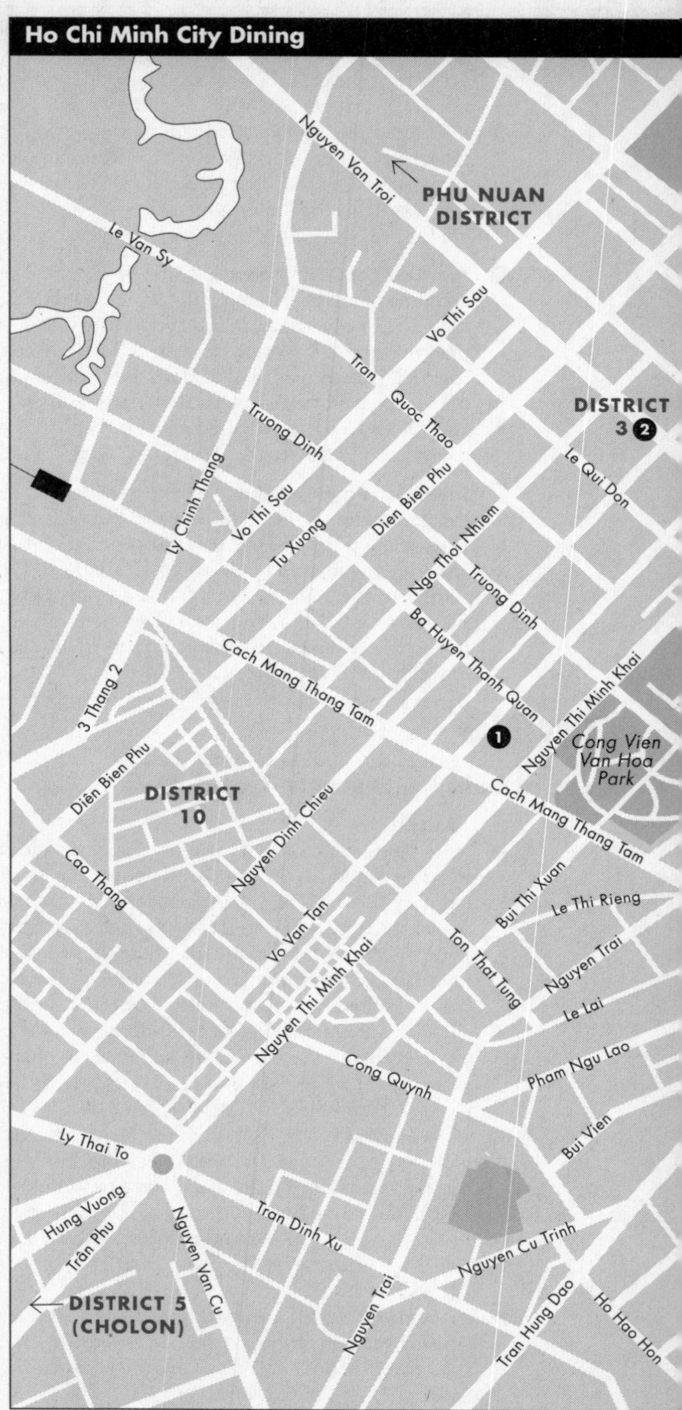

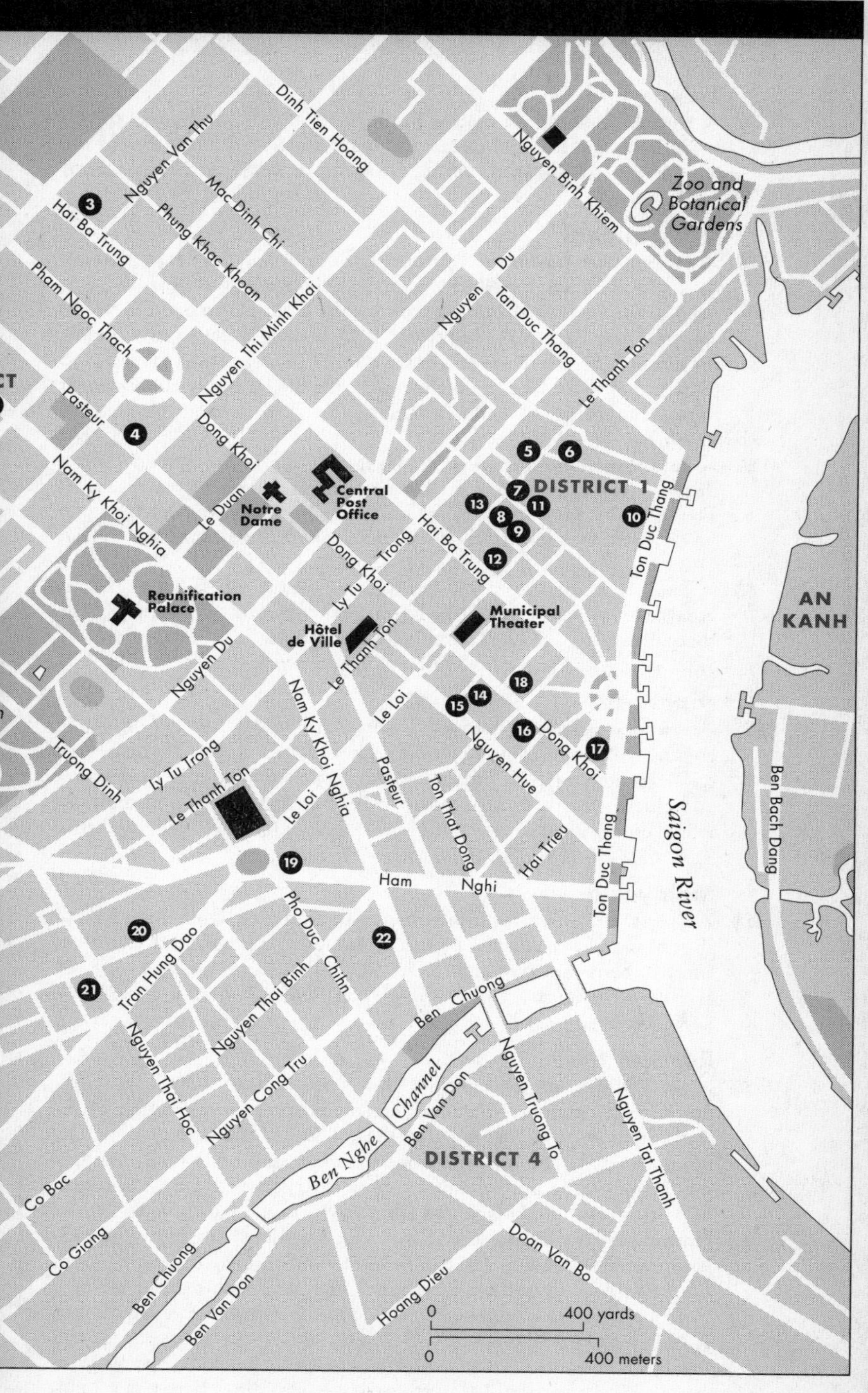

Dinh Tien Hoang
Nguyen Binh Khiem
Zoo and Botanical Gardens
Nguyen Van Thu
Mac Dinh Chi
Hai Ba Trung
Phung Khac Khoan
Pham Ngoc Thach
Nguyen Thi Minh Khai
Nguyen Du
Tan Duc Thang
Le Thanh Ton
Pasteur
Dong Khoi
Nam Ky Khoi Nghia
Le Duan
Notre Dame
Central Post Office
DISTRICT 1
Ton Duc Thang
Ly Tu Trong
Reunification Palace
Hôtel de Ville
Municipal Theater
AN KANH
Le Loi
Nguyen Hue
Truong Dinh
Ton That Dong
Hai Trieu
Ben Bach Dang
Saigon River
Ham Nghi
Pho Duc Chihn
Tran Hung Dao
Nguyen Thai Binh
Ben Chuong
Channel
Nguyen Truong To
Nguyen Thai Hoc
Nguyen Cong Tru
Ben Van Don
Nguyen Tat Thanh
Ben Nghe
DISTRICT 4
Co Bac
Co Giang
Doan Van Bo
Hoang Dieu
0
400 yards
400 meters

than compensated by the cuisine, which is as fine as any found in France. ✉ *267–269 Le Thanh Ton St., District 1,* ☏ *08/822–8273. MC, V. No lunch Sun.*

Indian

$ ✕ **Shanti.** The outdoor seating in the heart of Saigon's budget travelers' district and the very cheap and tasty Indian fare make up for the poor service. ✉ *236 De Tham St., District 1,* ☏ *08/835–6154. No credit cards.*

International

$$$ ✕ **Marine Club Restaurant.** Although more of a happening nightspot than a food mecca, the Marine Club has the only wood-burning pizza oven in Saigon. Expats gather here for the great piano bar and nautical paraphernalia and the hip and friendly management. Jeremy Hague, the amiable British manager, makes a point of welcoming everyone to his world. Beware: The late-night vodka-downing sessions can be a killer the next morning. ✉ *17A4 Le Thanh Ton St., District 1,* ☏ *08/829–2249. AE, DC, MC, V.*

$$ ✕ **Café Mogambo.** A quirky restaurant-cum-burger bar with an African theme, Mogambo is run by an American expat and his Vietnamese wife. The restaurant is a favorite for returning Vietnam War veterans and other Americans homesick for a good, inexpensive home-style meal. ✉ *20 Bis Thi Sach St., District 1,* ☏ *08/825–1311. MC, V.*

$$ ✕ **Sapa.** This airy Swiss-run bar and restaurant is best known for its breakfasts, which include fine bacon and eggs and hash browns. The Vietnamese-style chicken curry is also delicious. ✉ *26 Thai Van Lung St., District 1,* ☏ *08/829–5754. No credit cards.*

Japanese

$$$$ ✕ **Sekitei Japanese Restaurant.** The fresh fish flown in daily from Japan goes into the best sushi in Vietnam. Chefs Kori and Alex Ny also serve well-executed regional Japanese cuisine, such as a wonderful shiitake-and-chicken custard. Service is excellent and attentive, and the individual dining areas are romantic. ✉ *188 Nam Ky Khoi Nghia, District 3,* ☏ *08/825–1110. AE, DC, MC, V.*

Malaysian

$$$ ✕ **Spices.** One of the few Malaysian restaurants in Saigon, this is a good spot to try spicier cuisine. Be sure to sample the excellent dry chicken curry in banana leaves and the particularly delicate wonton soup. ✉ *Hai Van Nam Hotel, 132 Ham Nghi St. Blvd., District 1,* ☏ *08/821–1687. No credit cards.*

Russian

$$ ✕ **'A' The Russian Restaurant.** This is Saigon's premier Russian establishment, catering to the remaining members of the once-mighty Russian community, left behind after the collapse of the Soviet Union. Off the main road in an old villa complex, the restaurant has surprisingly good food—Siberian *pelmeni* (dumplings), kebabs from Uzbekistan, beef Stroganoff, and black and white caviar with black bread—at very reasonable prices. Also served are sweet Russian champagne and endless amounts of vodka. The frozen lemon vodkas are particularly good, but be sure to order them in advance. If you're with a group (from 3 to 15), you can hire out one of the two theme rooms for the night: One is designed like a Siberian hunting lodge, replete with moose heads and balalaikas; the other is like an aristocratic dining hall, modeled on 19th-century St. Petersburg. Almost everyone who dines here has a loud, raucous, and often drunken evening. ✉ *361/8 Nguyen Dinh Chieu St., District 3,* ☏ *08/835–9190. MC, V.*

Thai

$$$$–$$ ✕ **Chao Thai.** This sensational restaurant serves the finest Thai food in the city. The cuisine is equal to the setting: a mock Thai longhouse decorated with apsara dancers and wood carvings. If you love spicy Thai food you won't be disappointed, and if you don't you can request milder dishes. ✉ *16 Pai Van Lung St., District 1,* ☎ *08/824–1457. AE, MC, V.*

$ ✕ **Sawaddee.** Saigon has two Sawaddee locations, and both are well run and have simple, pleasant decor and authentic Thai dishes at very good prices. ✉ *29B Don Dat St., District 1,* ☎ *08/832–2494;* ✉ *252 De Tham St., District 1,* ☎ *08/822–1402. No credit cards.*

Vegetarian

¢ ✕ **Bodhi Tree II.** Bodhi serves delectable vegetarian delights in a quaint alley just off Pham Ngu Lao Street, next door to another unrelated vegetarian restaurant. The eggplant sautéed with garlic, the vegetable curry, and the braised tofu in a clay pot are superb. Don't miss out on the fresh-fruit shakes, which are like meals in themselves. ✉ *175 Pham Ngu Lao St., District 1,* ☎ *08/839–1545. No credit cards.*

Vietnamese

$$$ ★ ✕ **Blue Ginger.** Dine on excellent Vietnamese cuisine in an elegant setting with an international clientele. At night traditional music shows are performed at 7:30. ✉ *37 Nam Ky Khoi Nghia St., District 1,* ☎ *08/829–8676. AE, DC, MC, V.*

$$$ ★ ✕ **Lemongrass.** An expat and tourist favorite, Lemongrass serves excellent Vietnamese food in a French-bistro atmosphere. Almost everything on the short menu is delicious, but the spicy mixed-seafood soup deserves special praise. ✉ *4 Nguyen Thiep St., District 1,* ☎ *08/822–0496. AE, DC, MC, V. No lunch.*

$$$ ✕ **Liberty.** This spot combines a great Vietnamese menu (pricier Chinese and Western menus are also available) with a kind of *Star Search* live-entertainment ambience. It's definitely worth a visit, if only because of how kitschy it is. ✉ *80 Dong Khoi St., District 1,* ☎ *08/829–9820. AE, DC, MC, V.*

$$$ ✕ **Vietnam House.** Very popular with travelers and expats, Vietnam House serves a wide selection of hearty noodle dishes and other Vietnamese standards in a glossy Eurasian-style dining room. There are also performances of live traditional music every night upstairs. ✉ *93 Dong Khoi St., District 1,* ☎ *08/829–1623. MC, V.*

$ ✕ **Restaurant 13.** This local and expat hangout, on a quiet road just off Dong Khoi Street, serves delicious traditional local food in a no-nonsense setting. ✉ *11–17 Ngo Duc Ke St., District 1,* ☎ *08/829–1417. No credit cards.*

$ ✕ **Thi Sac Street Cafés.** Thi Sac Street is a must if you love seafood: Here you can great freshwater and saltwater fish. From 5 PM onward the top part of Thi Sac Street where it borders Le Thanh Ton Street is literally impassable with street restaurants. Best bets are the steamboat (boiling broth in which seafood and fish is cooked at your table), freshwater crabs, and colossal tiger prawns that are so huge that you order them by the gram. On a balmy Saigon evening, with the cacophony of street life carrying on all around, eating here can be a truly memorable experience. ✉ *Thi Sac St., District 1, no phone.*

¢ **May Ngan Phuong.** This very local, hole-in-the-wall Vietnamese eatery has delicious food and traditional live music performances (☞ Nightlife, *below*). Be prepared to point at whatever looks good at the next table, or bring a phrase book, as this place doesn't see many foreigners. ✉ *205 Nguyen Van Thu Si St., District 3,* ☎ *08/835–7322. No credit cards.*

¢ ✕ **Pho Hoa.** If you're not quite game for the sidewalk-food-stall eating experience, this open-air noodle kitchen is the next best thing. The homemade noodles and the vegetable and meat stocks are fresh and delicious. Just say "chicken," "beef," or "pork," or point to whatever looks good at the next table. ✉ *260C Pasteur St., District 3,* ☎ *08/829–7943. No credit cards.*

LODGING

Central Saigon (Districts 1 and 3)

$$$$ ★ **Hotel Continental.** If it's history you're after, stay at the French-colonial-style Continental. Graham Greene's classic *The Quiet American* was set here; it was also once the most sought-after lunch spot in colonial Saigon and the meeting place of journalists and diplomats during the Vietnam War. The hotel has a unique outdoor courtyard garden and dining area that dates from the late 19th century. The courtyard is still a superb place to while away a couple of hours having a beer below the frangipangi trees in which ong birds swing in cages hung on the branches. However, because the Continental was renovated by the state-run travel agency, Saigon Tourist, it remains only a shadow of its former self—the decor and finishing lack the finesse and expert renovations of the hotel's international counterparts. The bar, though a little dead, features a very fine cellist. Rooms facing the street are very noisy; ask for one overlooking the inner courtyard. ✉ *132–134 Dong Khoi St., District 1,* ☎ *08/829–9201,* FAX *08/829–9252. 87 rooms. 2 restaurants, lobby lounge, air-conditioning, in-room safes, minibars, no-smoking rooms, refrigerators, room service, laundry service and dry cleaning, concierge, business services, meeting rooms, travel services. AE, DC, MC, V.*

$$$$ ★ **New World Hotel Saigon.** Along with the Omni Hotel, the New World was one of Saigon's first international-chain hotels (it opened in 1994). Its central location—across the street from the Ben Thanh Market—makes it very popular, particularly with tour groups and business people. The front foyer can seem somewhat sterile, with its somnolent-looking pianist playing the same tunes throughout the day, but if you're jet lagged or just back from an exhausting day out at Cu Chi, it can seem like heaven. The Chinese restaurant is excellent, but the Western buffet is lackluster. If it's Western-style dining you're after, head to one of the French restaurants or to the Omni. ✉ *76 Le Lai St., District 1,* ☎ *08/822–8888,* FAX *08/823–0710. 541 rooms. 3 restaurants, bar, lobby lounge, air-conditioning, in-room safes, minibars, no-smoking floor, refrigerators, room service, in-room TVs, pool, sauna, massage, driving range, tennis court, exercise room, motorbikes, nightclub, piano, baby-sitting, laundry service and dry cleaning, concierge, business services, meeting rooms, travel services, airport shuttle, car rental. AE, DC, MC, V.*

$$$$ **Saigon Marriott Hotel.** At press time (winter 1997), the Saigon Marriott was set to open in early 1998. When it does, it is bound to be one of the best hotels in the city. Expect the high level of service that you expect from this international chain. It's certainly in a prime location overlooking the Saigon River. ✉ *2A–4A Ton Duc Thang St., District 1,* ☎ *08/823–3333 or 800/228–9290 in the U.S.,* FAX *08/823–2333. 278 rooms, 9 suites. 3 restaurants, 2 bars, café, lobby lounge, air-conditioning, minibars, room service, pool, health club, laundry service, dry cleaning, business services, meeting rooms. AE, MC, V.*

$$$$ ★ **Saigon Prince Hotel.** The Saigon Prince is one of the newer international luxury hotels, and entering it makes you feel like you have left Vietnam—for better or worse. Rooms are more spacious and have

higher ceilings and finer finishing touches than many other hotels in the city. But, unfortunately, it has fewer facilities. The staff is competent and pleasant. The lobby bar is a nice spot for a calm mid-afternoon break, whether you are staying at the hotel or not. ✉ *63 Nguyen Hue Blvd., District 1,* ☎ *08/822–2999,* FAX *08/824–1888. 203 rooms. Dining room, sushi bar, lobby lounge, air-conditioning, in-room safes, minibars, no-smoking rooms, refrigerators, room service, hot tub, massage, sauna, steam room, exercise room, nightclub, laundry service and dry cleaning, concierge, business services, meeting rooms, travel services. AE, DC, MC, V.*

$$$ ★ **Hotel Majestic.** The Majestic, on the waterfront overlooking the Saigon River, is one of Vietnam's truly great colonial hotels. As with the Continental, the hotel was renovated by Saigon Tourist, so it still lacks the service expertise of the international chains. Nevertheless, the hotel's charm and location more than make up for that. Be sure to have a gin and tonic in the rooftop breeze bar overlooking the river. Rooms, with their high ceilings and the original wooden trim, strike a delicate balance between airy and intimate. ✉ *1 Dong Khoi St., District 1,* ☎ *08/829–5514,* FAX *08/829–5510. 122 rooms. 2 restaurants, 2 bars, outdoor café, lobby lounge, air-conditioning, in-room safes, minibars, no-smoking rooms, refrigerators, room service, pool, massage, sauna, exercise room, piano, laundry service and dry cleaning, concierge, business services, meeting rooms, travel services. AE, DC, MC, V.*

$$$ **Kimdo International Hotel.** The elegant and central Kimdo had a Saigon Tourist–organized face-lift in 1994. The spacious rooms have high ceilings and exquisite French and Chinese antique reproductions that provide a warmth lacking in many modern luxury hotels. The staff seems somewhat inexperienced but is eager to please. ✉ *133 Nguyen Hue St., District 1,* ☎ *08/822–5914,* FAX *08/822–5913. 135 rooms. Dining room, outdoor café, lobby lounge, air-conditioning, in-room safes, minibars, no-smoking rooms, refrigerators, room service, massage, exercise room, nightclub, laundry service and dry cleaning, concierge, business services, meeting rooms, travel services. AE, DC, MC, V.*

$$$ **Mercury Hotel.** This modern hotel combines warmth and elegance with modern conveniences. Rooms are reasonably sized and are neatly decorated in a luxurious yet utilitarian and unoriginal style. The hotel is closer to the budget traveler's haven—Pham Ngu Lao Street—than to the congregation of upscale hotels and restaurants around Le Loi and Nguyen Hue boulevards. ✉ *79 Tran Hung Dao St., District 1,* ☎ *08/824–2555,* FAX *08/824–2602. 104 rooms. 2 restaurants, bar, lobby lounge, air-conditioning, in-room safes, minibars, no-smoking rooms, refrigerators, room service, massage, health club, laundry service, dry cleaning, baby-sitting, business services, meeting rooms, travel services. AE, DC, MC, V.*

$$$ ✕ **Rex Hotel.** The Rex stands as a monument to Saigon's recent history. Originally a French garage, it later became a hotel and then the base for American operations during the Vietnam War. Its conference room was the scene of the daily press briefings to journalists, or "five o'clock follies," as they were called. In 1976 the announcement by the former North Vietnam of the unification with South Vietnam was announced in the same room. Today the hotel is filled with kitsch: stuffed animals, Chinese furniture, statues, traditionally dressed dolls, and lamp shades shaped like crowns (the Rex's symbol). Even if you don't stay here, go up to the rooftop bar, which is an ideal setting to take in the view of downtown and have a drink amid statues, songbirds, topiary animals, and decorative lights. The restaurants, which you're best off skipping (except for the breakfast, which is satisfactory), specialize in Vietnamese cuisine with a touch of the French. ✉ *141 Nguyen Hue Blvd., District 1,* ☎ *08/829–2185,* FAX *08/829–1469. 207 rooms. 2 restau-*

Arc En Ciel Hotel, **23**
Asian Hotel, **5**
Cam Minihotel, **19**
Dong Khanh Hotel, **22**
Garden Plaza Hotel, **1**
Hanh Long Hotel, **21**
Hotel Continental, **17**
Hotel Equatorial, **24**
Hotel Majestic, **13**
Kimdo International Hotel, **14**
Mercury Hotel, **20**
Mogambo Guest House, **7**
Mondial Hotel, **10**
New World Hotel Saigon, **18**
Norfolk Hotel, **16**
Omni Saigon Hotel, **2**
Palace Hotel, **11**
Phuong Duong Hotel, **4**
Prince Hotel, **25**
Rex Hotel, **15**
Saigon Hotel, **9**
Saigon Marriott Hotel, **8**
Saigon Prince Hotel, **12**
Sol Chancery Saigon, **3**
Spring Hotel, **6**

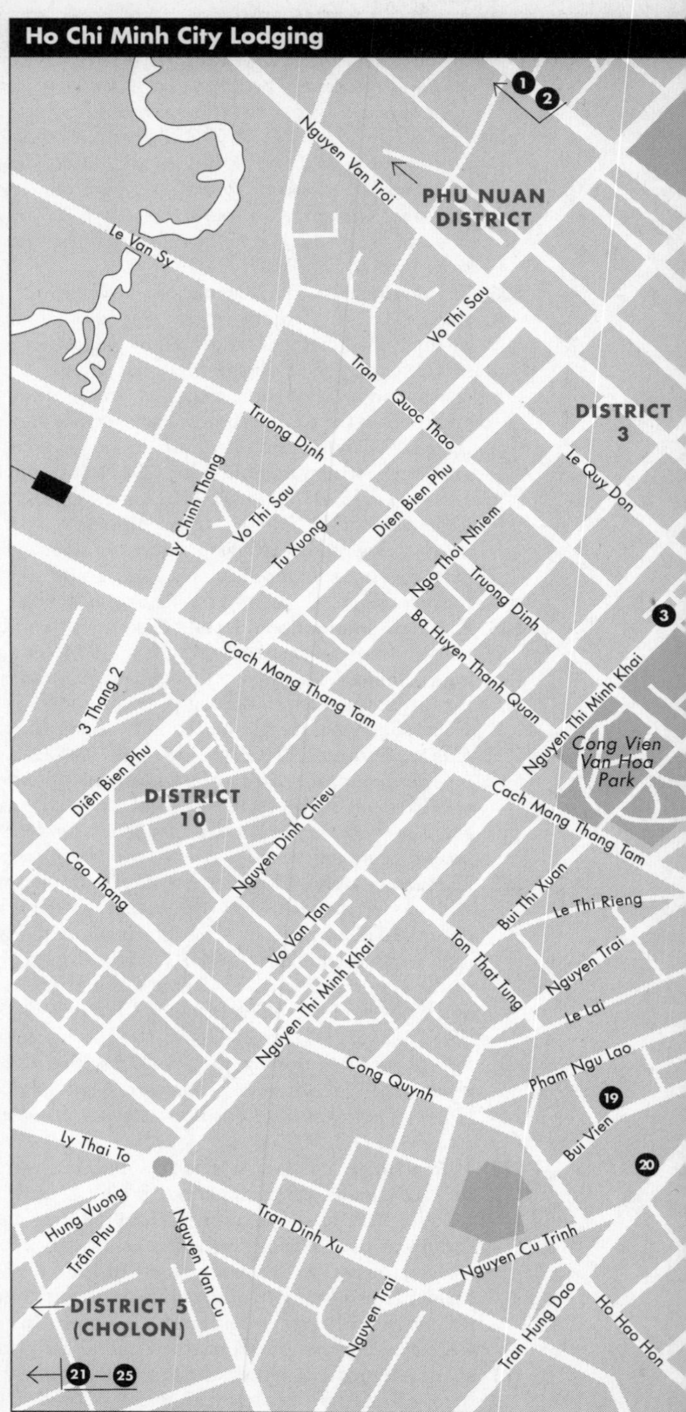

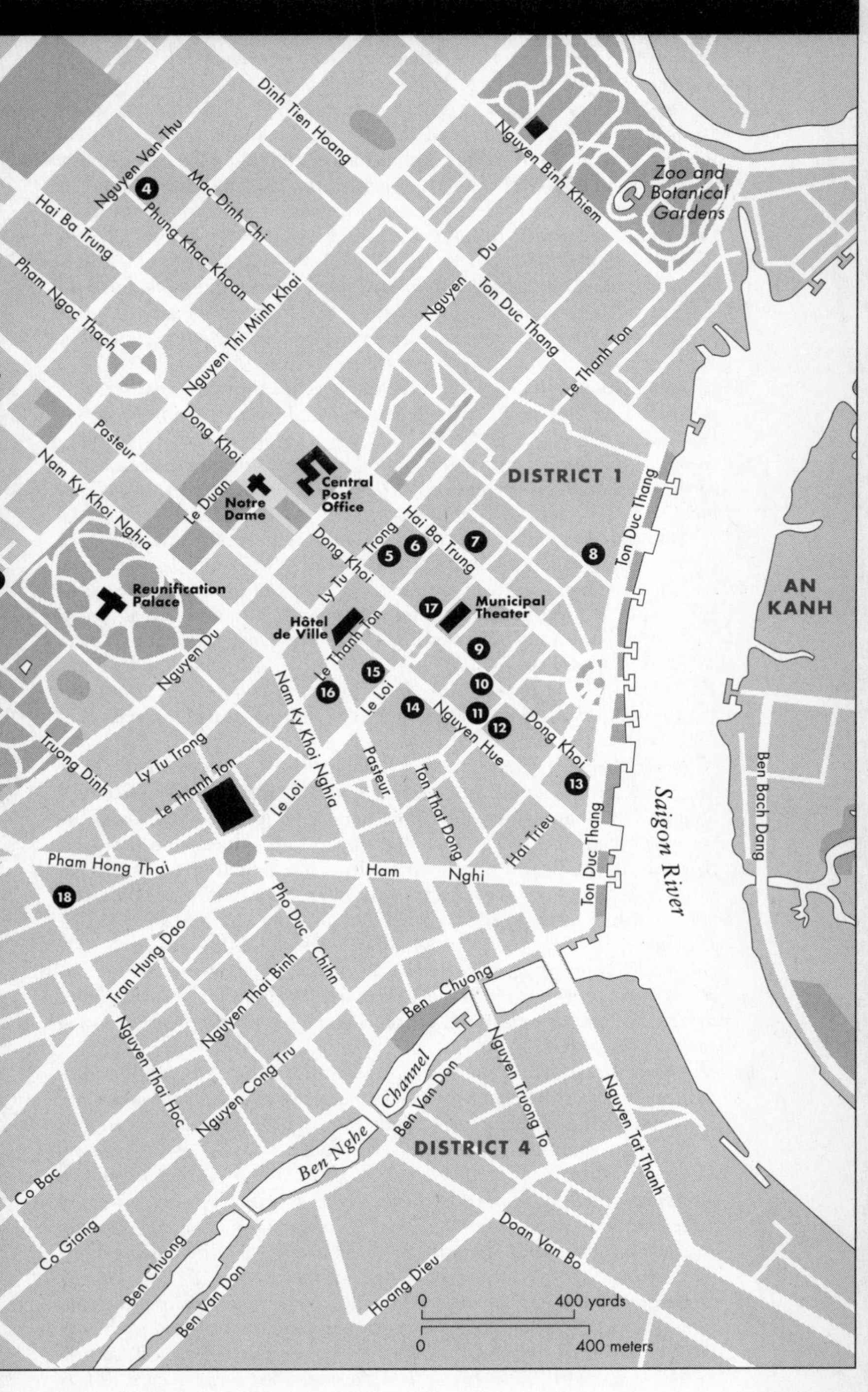
Dinh Tien Hoang
Nguyen Binh Khiem
Zoo and Botanical Gardens
Nguyen Van Thu
Mac Dinh Chi
Phung Khac Khoan
Hai Ba Trung
Pham Ngoc Thach
Nguyen Thi Minh Khai
Nguyen Du
Ton Duc Thang
Le Thanh Ton
Pasteur
Dong Khoi
Nam Ky Khoi Nghia
Le Duan
Notre Dame
Central Post Office
DISTRICT 1
Ly Tu Trong
Reunification Palace
Hôtel de Ville
Municipal Theater
AN KANH
Le Loi
Nguyen Hue
Truong Dinh
Ton That Dong
Hai Trieu
Saigon River
Ben Bach Dang
Pham Hong Thai
Ham Nghi
Pho Duc Chinh
Tran Hung Dao
Nguyen Thai Binh
Ben Chuong
Nguyen Thai Hoc
Nguyen Cong Tru
Channel
Ben Van Don
Nguyen Truong To
Nguyen Tat Thanh
DISTRICT 4
Ben Nghe
Co Bac
Co Giang
Doan Van Bo
Hoang Dieu
0
400 yards
400 meters

rants, lobby lounge, air-conditioning, in-room safes, minibars, no-smoking rooms, refrigerators, room service, pool, beauty salon, massage, sauna, steam room, nightclub, laundry service and dry cleaning, concierge, business services, travel services. AE, DC, MC, V.

$$$ **Sol Chancery Saigon.** This new all-suites hotel run by Grupo Sol of Spain has a kind of nouveau-French facade and many amenities. Rooms, though comfortable and neat, are afflicted with low ceilings and the kind of pastel, no-wood, antiseptic decor typically found in hotels that are constructed seemingly overnight. It is not too far from the War Remnants Museum and other points of interest. ✉ *196 Nguyen Thi Minh St., District 3,* ☎ *08/829–9152,* FAX *08/825–1464. 96 suites with bath. Restaurant, lobby lounge, air-conditioning, in-room safes, minibars, no-smoking rooms, refrigerators, room service, massage, sauna, exercise room, laundry service and dry cleaning, concierge, business services, meeting rooms, travel services. AE, DC, MC, V.*

$$ **Asian Hotel.** In the midst of the Dong Khoi shopping district, this no-frills hotel has small but tidy rooms. ✉ *146–150 Dong Khoi St., District 1,* ☎ *08/829–6979,* FAX *08/829–7433. 47 rooms. Bar, dining room, lobby lounge, air-conditioning, in-room safes, minibars, room service, laundry service and dry cleaning, business services, travel services. AE, DC, MC, V.*

$$ **Mondial Hotel.** The renovated Mondial has small, tidy standard rooms. Show this book and get a 10%–30% discount. In the lobby are various large bas-relief wooden sculptures of dragons and mythical Vietnamese warriors. The hotel's Skyview restaurant has traditional Vietnamese dancing and music nightly. ✉ *109 Dong Khoi St., District 1,* ☎ *08/835–2410,* FAX *08/835–2411. 40 rooms, most with bath. Restaurant, lobby lounge, air-conditioning, in-room safes, room service, nightclub, laundry service and dry cleaning, travel services. AE, DC, MC, V.*

$$ **Norfolk Hotel.** This superslick establishment is conveniently situated between the Ben Tranh Market and the Hôtel de Ville in central Saigon. White and chrome dominate, making it look like a cross between a cruise ship and a space ship. Rooms are impeccable and comfortable if small and simple. Facilities are oriented primarily to businesspeople; there is even a resident interpreter. With this book, you get a discount of up to 25%, depending on your length of stay. ✉ *117 Le Thanh Ton St., District 1,* ☎ *08/829–5368,* FAX *08/829–3415. 109 rooms. Restaurant, bar, sports bar, lobby lounge, air-conditioning, in-room safes, minibars, massage, sauna, health club, baby-sitting, laundry service and dry cleaning, business services, meeting rooms, travel services. AE, DC, MC, V.*

$$ **Palace Hotel.** The Palace is a pleasant but standard no-frills Vietnamese hotel in the center of town. The views of central Saigon are excellent. One drawback is the slightly unfriendly front-desk staff, but a plus is the breakfast included in the room rate. ✉ *56–66 Nguyen Hue Blvd., District 1,* ☎ *08/829–2840,* FAX *08/824–4229. 130 rooms. Restaurant, lobby lounge, outdoor café, air-conditioning, in-room safes, minibars, room service, pool, beauty salon, massage, sauna, steam room, nightclub, laundry service and dry cleaning, business services, meeting rooms, travel services, airport shuttle. AE, DC, MC, V.*

$$ **Saigon Hotel.** At the Saigon get a clean room overlooking the center of the city. The hotel betrays a '60s aesthetic despite modern black-lacquer furniture accents. ✉ *41–47 Dong Du St., District 1,* ☎ *08/824–4982,* FAX *08/829–1466. 103 rooms. Restaurant, café, lobby lounge, air-conditioning, in-room safes, minibars, room service, nightclub, laundry service and dry cleaning, business services, meeting rooms, airport shuttle. AE, DC, MC, V.*

$ ★ **Cam Minihotel.** In a cluster of family-run minihotels, in an alley between Pham Ngu Lao and Bu Vien streets, this place stands out because it's run with care compared to other budget hotels. It has a 24-hour gate post, mandatory shoe removal at the door, and simple, spotless, and well-maintained rooms. The extended family and friends who run the hotel are very friendly and helpful and speak English. ✉ *40/31 Bui Vien St., District 1,* ☎ *08/832–4622. 12 rooms. Air-conditioning, fans, refrigerators. No credit cards.*

$ **Mogambo Guest House.** This minhotel above the restaurant of the same name (☞ Dining, *above*) is run by an American and is very popular with—guess who?—Americans. Like most of these small establishments, this one is unexceptional-looking but has clean rooms that are suitable for a good night's sleep. Rooms have IDD phones and satellite TV. ✉ *20bis Thi Sach St., District 1,* ☎ *08/825–1311. 10 rooms. Restaurant, air-conditioning. MC, V.*

$ **Phuong Duong Hotel.** Another one of the city's minihotels, this one, too, is bare bones but comfortable and clean. Rooms have IDD phones and satellite TV. ✉ *55B Nguyen Van Thu St., District 1,* ☎ *08/822–2437,* FAX *08/822–1346. 10 rooms. Restaurant. MC, V.*

$ **Spring Hotel.** In the hub of a major dining and nightlife area in District 1, this cozy, new family-run minihotel has squeaky clean rooms with new moldings and fixtures made to look old. Some rooms have nice views of the street below, but the standard ones have no windows at all and are a lot less expensive. ✉ *44–46 Le Thanh Ton St., District 1,* ☎ *08/829–7362,* FAX *08/821–1383. 38 rooms. Bar, dining room, lobby lounge, air-conditioning, in-room safes, room service, travel services. AE, DC, MC, V.*

Cholon (District 5)

$$$$ **Hotel Equatorial.** This newer four-star hotel is in an odd location—on the edge of Cholon, about 15 minutes from the downtown area. To date, bookings have been somewhat scarce because of this, so the doormen seem to scramble when the sporadic guest arrives through the front entrance. Nonetheless, the hotel is one of the best in town. It also has Vietnam's nicest health club, with Jacuzzis, saunas, a very good gym, and a half-Olympic-size swimming pool with a poolside lounge area. In addition, the hotel has three fine restaurants, one serving Japanese, another Chinese, and a third with an international buffet. ✉ *242 Tran Binh Trong St., District 5,* ☎ *08/839–0000,* FAX *08/839–0011. 333 rooms. Bar, café, lobby lounge, air-conditioning, minibars, refrigerators, room service, pool, health club, nightclub, piano, laundry service and dry cleaning, business services, meeting rooms, travel services, car rental, free parking. AE, DC, MC, V.*

$$ **Arc En Ciel Hotel.** This neon-clad hotel is done up in a mishmash of modern, '60s, and Chinese interior decor, with accommodations on the higher end of utilitarian. But overall it's a good deal—if you're interested in staying in Cholon. The hotel has a pleasant rooftop garden café, which management takes great pride in, though it's not one of the best in the city. ✉ *52–56 Tan Da St., District 5,* ☎ *08/855–2550,* FAX *08/855–0332. 91 rooms. Bars, restaurant, lobby lounge, outdoor café, air-conditioning, in-room safes, room service, beauty salon, massage, sauna, exercise room, nightclub, laundry service and dry cleaning, concierge, business services, meeting rooms, travel services. AE, DC, MC, V.*

$$ **Dong Khanh Hotel.** In the heart of Cholon, the Dong Khanh sees mostly businessmen from Hong Kong and Taiwan. Although staff members speak little English, they know enough of that language to help you get by. The Chinese decor—wooden furniture with its char-

acteristic inlaid lacquerware and wall hangings with designs depicting dragons and landscapes—is bold but elegant. ✉ *Tran Hung Dao B Blvd., District 5,* ☎ *08/835–2410,* FAX *08/835–2411. 81 rooms. 2 restaurants, bars, café, lobby lounge, air-conditioning, in-room safes, minibars, no-smoking rooms, refrigerators, room service, massage, exercise room, nightclub, laundry service and dry cleaning, business services, meeting rooms, travel services. AE, DC, MC, V.*

$$ **Hanh Long Hotel.** In Cholon and not too far from District 1, the Hanh Long is another reasonable semiluxurious hotel. Rooms are spacious and have Chinese-style furnishings that are just slightly overbearing. ✉ *1027–1029 Tran Hung Dao St., District 5,* ☎ *08/835–0251,* FAX *08/835–0742. 48 rooms. Bars, dining room, lobby lounge, outdoor café, air-conditioning, in-room safes, minibars, room service, laundry service and dry cleaning, travel services. AE, DC, MC, V.*

$ **Prince Hotel.** Not to be confused with the Saigon Prince in District 1, this small-time "royal" lodging in the middle of Chinatown provides charm and efficiency cheaply. Unlike many hotel restaurants, the Prince's actually serves good food. ✉ *29 Chau Van Liem St., District 5,* ☎ *08/855–6765,* FAX *08/856–1578. 25 rooms. Bar, restaurant, lobby lounge, outdoor café, air-conditioning, in-room safes, minibars, refrigerators, room service, travel services. AE, DC, MC, V.*

Phu Nuan District

$$$$ **Garden Plaza Hotel.** Only about 10 minutes from the airport, this international establishment is one of the best (for now). Its sunken lobby and accompanying swimming pool are a departure from the hotel architecture usually seen in Vietnam. In fact, the hotel's style is more Thai or Balinese than Vietnamese. Its location could be a drawback for you (a good 15–20 minutes from downtown Saigon), but it's a boon if you're a businessperson eager to settle into town quickly. There are the usual facilities you'd expect with the prices of an international chain. ✉ *309 Nguyen Van Troi St., Phu Nhuan District,* ☎ *08/842–1111,* FAX *08/842–4370. 157 rooms. Restaurant, lobby lounge, pub, air-conditioning, in-room safes, minibars, no-smoking rooms, refrigerators, room service, in-room TVs, pool, sauna, massage, exercise room, motorbikes, shop, laundry service and dry cleaning, concierge, business services, meeting rooms, travel services, airport shuttle, car rental. AE, DC, MC, V.*

$$$$ **Omni Saigon Hotel.** Built out of the former CIA headquarters in Saigon with walls so thick mobile phones fail to work, the Omni is one of the city's finest hotels. It has the essence of French elegance mixed with a hint of glitz and a touch of '60s bunker architecture. More importantly, it's one of the few international hotels to have sent its staff abroad for training, and its service is some of the best in town. The restaurants serve first-class Japanese, Chinese, and international cuisine. Even if you don't stay here, come for the Sunday brunch, a bacchanalian frenzy of Belgian waffles and omelets. ✉ *251 Nguyen Van Troi St., Phu Nhuan District,* ☎ *08/844–9222,* FAX *08/844–9200. 248 rooms. 3 restaurants, lobby lounge, pub, air-conditioning, in-room safes, minibars, no-smoking rooms, refrigerators, room service, TVs, pool, beauty salon, sauna, massage, exercise room, motorbikes, nightclub, piano, baby-sitting, laundry service and dry cleaning, concierge, business services, meeting rooms, travel services, airport shuttle, car rental. AE, DC, MC, V.*

NIGHTLIFE AND THE ARTS

Saigon's thriving nightlife is a constant headache to the city's Communist leaders because most of it revolves around the sort of decadence they once promised to stamp out. Still, the city lacks the sort of entertainment that you take for granted almost everywhere else in the world. There are no multiplex cinemas, for instance: For ideological reasons, authorities tend to view contemporary films as containing polluted materials. The only movies available are videotapes of terrible quality, pirated from Bangkok. There are a few theaters, but the plays and operas presented are often dull, propaganda-filled discourses and are frequently incomprehensible to foreigners. Live theater is just now beginning to change, albeit slowly.

Rock music, too, is still very much in its infancy. Any rock band—local or international—wishing to perform in Vietnam has to go through endless red tape and even has to submit lyrics to the Ministry of Culture for approval. Over the last few years Sting and Air Supply both performed in Vietnam to very lackluster receptions (probably because tickets were far too expensive for the average Vietnamese, and many of the youth here prefer other types of Western music). Incidentally, Sting's song "Russians" was rejected by the Ministry of Culture for ideological reasons. Classical concerts are more common but still infrequent.

Mainly, the city's nightlife revolves around drinking at one of the many bars and discos—frequented predominately by expatriates—that have opened in the last few years. This may still be communist Saigon, but many of these bars are as raucous as their counterparts in Hong Kong, Manila, and Jakarta; only Bangkok has the edge on sleaze. Nonetheless, nightclubs in Saigon are subject to the erratic rules laid down by the authorities. One week they are open, and the next they are classified as social evils and are all shut down. But nightclub owners take this all in stride and just wait for the right moment to start up again. Most expatriate bars are open throughout the night and only close their doors when everyone has left (local bars tend to close around midnight). Check in the weekly English-language supplement, "Time Out," in the *Vietnam Investment Review* for information about what's going on around town.

Nightlife

Bars and Clubs

Apocalypse Now (✉ 2C Thi Sach St., District 1), one of the oldest clubs in Saigon, is loud, fun, and always packed with a cross section of expatriates and foreign tourists. Amiable pimps and local prostitutes shoot pool while hordes of foreigners drink tequila and vodka and dance until dawn. But remember these words of warning: Always take a taxi, *not* a cyclo, back to your hotel (cabs line up outside); cyclo drivers have been known to steal from drunken foreigners. Also you should leave any jewelry, including watches, at your hotel; there are pickpockets at this nightspot.

Bar Rolling Stones (✉ 177 Pham Ngu Lao St., District 1), in the backpacker area of town, is a rattan bar serving cheap beer. The place spills out onto the street with loud music. If you sit outside, be sure to hold your bag in your lap or wind the straps around your ankles. The children hanging around the bar are magicians at spiriting things away from right under your feet.

Café Latin (✉ 25 Dong Du St., District 1) is a multilevel tapas bar with constructivist decor that looks like something out of *The Jetsons,* and fine Australian and French wines. It's the hangout for a hip, foreign crowd.

Café Mogambo (✉ 20 Bis Thi Sach St., District 1), run by an American expat and his Vietnamese wife, is a kind of self-parodying Renostyle roadside stop where you can get good draft beer in a kitschy environment all dressed up with African decor (statues, headdresses, and wall hangings).

Le Camargue (✉ 16 Cao Ba Quat St., District 1), although really more of a French-influenced restaurant (☞ Dining, *above*), also has an excellent terrace bar where you can have a drink outside among tropical palms and creepers. It's an ideal first on your way to a night on the town. There's also a pool table and a downstairs bar.

Globo (✉ 6 Nguyen Thipe St., District 1, ☎ 08/822–8855) was designed by the same people that did the Café Latin, thus the constructivist decor made out of metal—iron stairwells, relief art, and even a burnished metallic toilet. The small place looks like it could be in Paris and it is very popular with the city's fashionable French set. Good French food is served and there is often live music on Friday nights.

Gossip (✉ 79 Tran Hung Dao St., District 1), in the Mercury Hotel, is one of the best discos in town. Its only problem is that it is periodically classed as a social evil and shut down. But when it's open, Gossip has all the glitz and glamour you could want from an international dance club—with drink prices to match. There is no admission charge for women, but men have to pay $8.

Hard Rock Café (✉ 24 Mac Thi Buoi St., District 1), though not official, does a booming business (plans, however, are in the works for a real one in the renovated Hotel Caravelle). It is particularly popular late at night with young foreign tourists and expats, especially the French. Occasionally there are late-night jazz band sessions.

Hard Rock Café (✉ in the Hotel Caravelle, 17–23 Lam Son Square, District 1, ☎ 08/829–3704), the real thing, was set to open in mid to late 1998.

Long Phi (✉ 163 Pham Ngu Lao St., District 1) is one of the few bars in town to attract expats, Vietnamese, *and* backpackers. It's a rattan affair—wicker armchairs and wicker tables—that spills out onto the street, with music blaring until dawn. There's also a pool table. As always, be sure to look after your valuables if you're sitting out on the street.

Marine Club (✉ 17A4 Le Thanh Ton St., District 1), another expat favorite, is a very nice piano bar tastefully done with nautical paraphernalia. It's a good place to start out the evening or to finish it up—there's often a drunken sing-along into the early hours of the weekend mornings. The fine wine list includes many French and Australian labels.

Q Bar (✉ In the side of the Municipal Theater, off Dong Khoi St.)—a hip spot that looks like it could be in New York, London, or Paris—has become one of Saigon's classics already. Expats come here to hang out, and movie stars have been known to stop by on their way through town. It's also one of the few bars where you can sit outside in the evening. Though it opens at about 7 PM, it only starts to liven up at around 10 PM. Bar food is served.

Dance Clubs and Karaoke

Catwalk (✉ 76 Le Lai St., District 1), in the New World Hotel, has private karaoke dens where you can sing to your heart's delight and a dance floor where dry ice creates a moody atmosphere.

Cheers (✉ 257 Pham Ngu Lao St., District 1) is a trendy Singaporean-run nightspot in the Vien Dong Hotel. It is popular with Vietnam's young nouveaux riches as well as the city's Asian expats. There are private karaoke rooms and a regular Filipino band that plays covers of American hits.

Europa (✉ 43 Truong Son St., Tan Binh District) in the Saigon Superbowl (☞ Outdoor Activities and Sports, *below*) is a new Singaporean-run club that is slowly beginning to fill up on weekends with locals. The place looks like a hamburger . . . or the bridge from the Starship Enterprise. Captain Kirk would have been quite at home, but other foreigners aren't so sure about it. It's also a long trip from the center of town—20 minutes by taxi—with which you may not want to bother.

Queen Bee (✉ 104 Nguyen Hue Blvd., District 1) is right in the heart of downtown, but the club is second rate compared to Gossip. The new Singaporean DJ is, however, sprucing up the outdated dance tunes. It's especially popular with expat men, who come to meet young Vietnamese women. Like many clubs, it gets closed down from time to time.

Stephanie's (✉ 14 Don Dat St., District 1) is a karaoke bar that is very popular with expatriate men.

Hotel Bars

A more civilized alternative to Saigon's bar scene is one of the many rooftop establishments at the city's hotels. Though drinks are more expensive than those of other places, you often get a panoramic view of the city for your money. Particularly noteworthy hotel bars include those in the **Caprice Hotel** (✉ Landmark Building, 513 Le Ton Duc Thang St., District 1) and the **Hotel Majestic** (✉ 1 Dong Khoi St., District 1); the fifth floor verandah at the **Rex Hotel** (✉ Khach San Ben Thanh St., District 1); and the piano bar at the **Saigon Prince** (✉ 63 Nguyen Hue Blvd., District 1).

The Arts

Music and Theater

Conservatory of Music (Nhac Vien Thanh Pho Ho Chi Minh; ✉ 112 Nguyen Du St., ☎ 08/839–6646) is the only regular venue in town for classical music performances. The theater's main season is September–June; it's generally closed in summer except when there are special concerts of visiting orchestras. Look in the daily *Vietnam News* for information on upcoming events.

Hoa Binh Theater (Nha Hat Hoa Binh; ✉ 14,3 Thang 2 Blvd., District 10, ☎ 08/865–5199), an ugly Soviet-era palace, is mostly used for local Vietnamese dramas, circus acts, and the occasional fashion show.

Municipal Theater (Nha Hat Thanh Pho; ✉ intersection of Le Loi and Dong Khoi Sts., District 1, ☎ 08/829–1249), built in 1899 by the French as an opera house, was later used as the home of the National Assembly of South Vietnam. It became a theater again in 1975. Most performances now are family shows with Vietnamese singers and dancers, though occasionally an international opera singer performs here.

OUTDOOR ACTIVITIES AND SPORTS

Parks and Farms

In and around Ho Chi Minh City's urban bustle, there are very few spots where you can find green, open spaces and enjoy the outdoors. One nice place in the city for a stroll, however, is **Cong Vien Van Hoa Park,** on the other side of the Reunification Palace. Try not to be put off by the stares from locals—they rarely see tourists in these parts. The **Zoo and Botanical Gardens** (✉ Nguyen Binh Khiem St. at Le Duan Blvd.) is another good place for a walk.

You might also consider a short escape outside the city, where orchid farms with thousands of plants and varieties abound. Ask your driver or get a taxi to take you to the **Artex Saigon Orchid Farm** (✉ 5/81 Xa Lo Vong Dai highway, which is better known as Xa Lo Dai Han, or the "Korean Highway" because it was built by the Koreans during the Vietnam War), 15 km (9 mi) outside the city. It's open daily and there is a 20,000d admission.

Participant Sports

Bowling

Saigon Superbowl (✉ 141, A43 Truong Son St., Tan Binh District, ☎ 08/885–0188), the biggest entertainment complex ever to hit Vietnam, opened in late 1996. Not only does it have state-of-the-art bowling facilities and an electronic games arcade—another one of the entertainments occasionally shut down for being a social evil—it also has a mall (with overpriced clothes from the West) and a Kentucky Fried Chicken. If you intend to go bowling here, you'll have to be patient: All the alleys are in constant use, and you often have to wait some time before getting to play. When you do get to play, be prepared for the crowds that may swarm around you—analyzing your bowling style and technique. The place opens at 7:30 AM and only closes when the last person leaves. Foreigners pay 55,000d per game, which is not cheap.

Golf

There are two 18-hole golf courses outside Saigon. **Vietnam Golf and Country Club** (☎ 08/825–2951), in the outlying district of Thu Duc, 10 km (6 mi) north of Saigon, costs about $50 a day for a game. **Song Be Golf Resort** (✉ 254B Nguyen Dinh Chieu St., ☎ 06/585–5802) is 20 km (12 mi) outside the city. Many of the club's facilities are still under construction but will eventually include swimming pools, tennis courts, restaurants, and television rooms where family members can hang out while they wait for their links-playing relatives. The cost for a day is $50.

Health Clubs and Swimming Pools

If it's fitness you're after, the city has some good health clubs, usually based in the newer hotels. It simply depends on how much you're willing to pay.

Cercle Sportif (✉ In Cong Vien Hoa Park) was once an elite French club but is now open to all. It has tennis courts, a swimming pool, and a gym with a weight room. You can use the facilities for less than 1$.

Hotel Equatorial (✉ 242 Tran Binh Trong St., District 5, ☎ 08/839–0000) has the best gym in town, with a half-Olympic-size pool, stationary bikes, a rowing machine, a step machine, a treadmill machine, and weights. The cost is $15 for the day.

Hotel Majestic (✉ 1 Dong Khoi St., District 1, ☎ 08/829–5514) has a small pool and gym, both available for use even if you're not a guest, as long as you order something from the bar.

New World Hotel Saigon (✉ 76 Le Lai St., District 1, ☎ 08/822–8888) charges $12 for use of its small pool and standard gym.

Rex Hotel (✉ 141 Nguyen Hue Blvd., District 1, ☎ 08/829–2185) has a small rooftop pool, which you can use for $2.

Jogging

Saigon isn't really a good city for jogging; it's generally too hot, too crowded, and too polluted, even in the parks. Some Vietnamese do, however, go out jogging in the streets in the very early morning (around 5) before the traffic begins. They also head for the parks and squares in the wee hours of the morning to do stretching exercises and play badminton. If you are set on running during your visit, contact the **Hash House Harriers running club,** which meets every Sunday outside the Century Hotel (✉ 68A Nguyen Hue Blvd.; for information call 08/845–3886).

Spectator Sports

Horse Racing

Pho Tho Racetrack (✉ 2 Le Dai Hanh St., District 11, ☎ 08/855–1205), built in 1900, was once an exclusive center of French colonial life. The track was shut down the day Saigon fell, on April 30, 1975—gambling was deemed a frivolous capitalist social evil by Hanoi—and wasn't reopened until 1989. After years of neglect, the building and track had fallen into disrepair and were only made suitable for racing again in 1994. They are still in fairly poor condition. Nonetheless, a weekend spent placing 5,000d bets can be a lot of fun. People go crazy when the racing starts: To get a grandstand view, they climb onto everything, including tops of buildings, telegraph poles, and even each other's shoulders. Most of the ponies racing are about half the size of racehorses you're probably used to seeing. They are a special type introduced by the French in the 19th century and are still being bred in villages outside Saigon. Notice how small the jockeys are, even compared to those in the West—that's because their average age is 9 or 10 years old. Watching these children racing tiny horses cheered on by thousands of spectators crowded onto nearby rooftops might just be one of your most memorable experiences in Saigon. Occasionally motorbike racing is also held at the track. It's open weekends from 1 PM on, and there's no admission. Check in the daily *Vietnam News* for more detailed schedule information.

SHOPPING

Ho Chi Minh City is a good place to have casual clothes made or to have designer apparel copied. In addition, the city is famous for its lacquerware (boxes, trays, etc.) and its wood carvings of all kinds. There's also a wide availability of inexpensive compact discs pirated from China.

Continuing a tradition first true when it was French Saigon's main shopping thoroughfare, Dong Khoi Street (formerly Tu Do Street and before that rue Catinat), between Le Loi Boulevard and the river, is lined with art galleries and shops selling jewelry, antique watches (or lookalikes), lacquerware, wood carvings, and other souvenirs to mostly tourists (which doesn't mean there aren't good finds). The galleries have some works by fine local artists, though you may end up paying more than you expected for something you love.

Ready-to-wear Western-style clothes and shoes are available near the central Ben Thanh Market, on Le Thanh Ton and Ly Tu Trong streets in District 1. Both the Ben Thanh Market in the center of the city and the Binh Tay Market in Cholon have all kinds of stuff for sale—clothes, wood carvings, shoes, plastic goods, kitchenware, food, and more. No matter where you shop, even if a place says it has fixed prices but you are purchasing a large number of items, be sure to bargain—it is part of shopping in Vietnam. But be polite—the debate over prices is expected to be a very civil and friendly process. Also, as is the case all over the country, most shops will either take dollars or dong and will often list prices in dollars only.

Department Stores

Nam Hai Yuan Shopping Plaza (✉ 39 Nguyen Trung Truc St., District 1, ☎ 08/823–1988), an enclosed mall, has vendors specializing in jewelry, wood carvings, and lacquerware; it primarily caters to Chinese tourists.

On the ground floor of the huge **Tax Department Store** (Cua Hang Back Hoa; ✉ intersection of Nguyen Hue St. and Le Loi Blvd, no phone) you can find all kinds of souvenirs as well as a place to change traveler's checks. But it's on the two upper floors that you can find the best bargains in Vietnam. Many designer clothes and sneakers, made in China but redirected to Vietnam on the black market, end up here at unbeatable prices. There are also nice (and very inexpensive) bags made of Chinese, Vietnamese, and Cham fabrics, as well as tailors who can make you clothes in 24 hours.

Markets

Clothing, shoes, bags, wood carvings, lacquerware, food, and more are available at the large **Ben Thanh Market** (Cho Ben Thanh), at the intersection of Tran Hung Dao, Le Loi, and Ham Nghi boulevards in the heart of District 1. Keep careful watch of your belongings; pickpockets have been known to strike in the thin aisles here. But don't let this stop you from exploring this busy market.

Cholon's **Binh Tay Market** (Cho Binh Tay), on Hau Giang Boulevard in District 6 (near District 5), has all kinds of wholesale items that can be purchased in small amounts by anyone—kitchenware, baskets, plastic goods (barrettes, magnets, toys, shopping bags, wigs, you name it), hats (traditional conical, straw, baseball caps, etc.), shoes, and food.

The charming open-air market on **Ton That Dam Street,** between Huynh Thuc Khang Street and Ham Nghi Boulevard, has everything from fish and produce to plastic toys and cleaning products for sale.

On the north side of **Ham Nghi Boulevard,** between Ho Tung Mau and Ton That Dam streets, you can find imported cheese, olive oil, and just about any international food at the tiny, jam-packed European-style specialty food shops.

For dirt-cheap pirated CDs and an assortment of electronic equipment, try **Huynh Thuc Khang Street,** Nguyen Hue Boulevard, and Pasteur Street.

Specialty Shops

Antiques

It's against the law for foreigners to take antiques out of Vietnam, and anyone found carrying antiques at the airport has to hand them over to the authorities. Vietnamese law specifies that any object more than 21 years plus one day old is an antique. This creates a vast gray area of what is and isn't an antique, and often it's up to the whims of individual customs officers to decide. If you buy a fake article that looks like an antique, be sure to get a receipt in Vietnamese with the shop owner's signature guaranteeing the object is not genuine. Without it, you'll run into big trouble at customs. If you do decide to spend big bucks on the real thing (genuine antiques don't come cheaply in Vietnam), be sure you know what you're buying. It's very difficult to distinguish between genuine and fake items, especially on Dong Khoi Street, where both sell at comparable prices. In particular, beware of restored antique timepieces, which often have a 1950s Rolex face, for example, covering the much cheaper hardware of a '70s Seiko.

Nguyen Freres (✉ 2A Le Duan Blvd., District 1, ☎ 08/821–3716) sells antique replicas, including prints of old colonial Saigon.

Art

Taking fine art out of the country isn't as problematic as taking antiques out of the country, but have a receipt for your purchase to show customs just in case. Many art galleries can be found on Dong Khoi Street and the surrounding area. Paintings and lacquerware by master artists Do Xuan Doan, Bui Xuan Phau, Quach Dong Phuong, and Truong Dinh Hao are available at a wide variety of galleries. Many of these artists base their work on French post-Impressionist styles, and their work is generally apolitical (still lifes and pastoral scenes, for instance). Canvases fetch as much as $15,000 and as little as $30. Following is a list of suggested galleries.

Anh (✉ 135 Nguyen Hue Blvd., District 1, ☎ 08/821–3716) sells ethnic folk art and material.

ATC (Art Tourist Services; ✉ 172 Nam Ky Khoi Nghia St., District 3, ☎ 08/829–6833, FAX 829–8947; ✉ 29B Dong Khoi St., District 1, ☎ 08/829–2695, FAX 08/829–8947; ✉ 2 Cong Truong Quoc St., District 3, ☎ 08/829–6833, FAX 08/829–8947) is a national art organization.

Fine Arts Museum (97A Pho Duc Chinh St., District 1, ☎ 821–0001).

Galerie Lotus (✉ 43 Dong Khoi St., District 1, ☎ 08/829–2695).

Hong Hac Art Gallery (✉ 9A Vo Van Tan St., District 3, ☎ 824–3160).

Phuong Dong Gallery (✉ 135 Nam Ky Khoi Nghia St., District 1, ☎ 822–1716).

Saigon Gallery (✉ 5 Ton Duc Thang St., District 1, ☎ 829–7102).

Clothing

Linh Phuong Maison de Couture (✉ 38 Ly Tu Trong St., District 1, ☎ 08/824–2985) is very reliable for custom-made clothing for adults and children. Though the English- and French-speaking staff specializes in creating Vietnamese and Japanese silk items, the store carries a wide variety of imported and domestic cottons. They copy designer clothes cheaply and very well.

Tropic (✉ 73A Le Thanh Ton St., District 1, ☎ 08/829–7452) carries contemporary and traditional clothing as well as some home furnishing items.

Zakka (✉ 23 Dong Khoi St., District 1, ☎ 08/829–8086), next to the Hotel Majestic, sells fabric and beautifully-designed clothing, shoes, and bags (with a Western influence). Although items are expensive compared to other shops in the city, you may not mind paying extra for the quality. You can also get clothes made for you in three days. Note, however, that you can get some things cheaper elsewhere.

Housewares

Home Zone (✉ 41 Dinh Tien Hoang St., District 1, ☎ 08/822–8022) sells stylish silverware, furnishings, and other housewares.

Mai Huong (✉ 73 Le Thanh Ton St., District 1, ☎ 08/829–6233) is the place to go for beautifully embroidered table clothes, napkins, and bed spreads, all made in Saigon.

Q Home (✉ 65 Le Loi St., 2nd floor, District 1, ☎ 08/821–4883) has brightly colored, western-style ceramics made in Vietnam.

Lacquerware

There are a number of galleries that sell lacquerware on Dong Khoi Street (from No. 137 to No. 145) and in the Phu Nhuan District on Nguyen Van Troi Street (and on its continuation, Cong Hoa Street).

Heritage (✉ 53 Dong Khoi St., District 1) has beautiful contemporary-looking lacquerware, outstanding replicas of antique Buddhas and statuary, silver jewelry, and ao dais made from traditional fabrics.

Tay Son (✉ 198 Bo Thi Sau St., District 3, ☎ 08/820–2524, FAX 08/820–2526) is a large lacquerware distributor with a very wide selection and good prices.

Musical Instruments

On the north side of Ham Nghi Boulevard between the circular intersection to the west and Nam Ky Khoi Nghia Street to the east are shops selling fake Fender Stratocasters and other cheap acoustic guitars that are actually not all that bad.

Shoes

Tran Van My (✉ 95 Le Thanh Ton St., District 1, ☎ 08/822–3041) is the place to go for ready-made, custom-made, embroidered, and leather shoes and sandals. The cobblers are quite adept at copying other shoes, but some of their own designs are also very nice. The quality of workmanship is very high, and the prices are low.

Wood Carvings

Not too far from the airport, in the Phu Nhuan District on Nguyen Van Troi Street and on its continuation, Cong Hoa Street (between Nos. 72 and 306), there are a number of shops where you can buy wood carvings (as well as lacquerware, rattan, etc.) and see the craftsmen at work.

SIDE TRIPS FROM HO CHI MINH CITY

When you find yourself ready to escape Ho Chi Minh City—or just want to see some of the countryside—make a short excursion outside the city. Some of the destinations around Ho Chi Minh City can be done as day trips; others may take a few days. Some excursions are more rugged, adventurous trips through forests and islands; others will take you to sandy beaches and new seaside resorts. The easiest way to plan a trip outside Ho Chi Minh City is to do it through a travel agency or one of the "tourist cafés" that organize tours (☞ Visitor Information and Travel Agencies *in* Ho Chi Minh City A to Z, *below*); almost all organize trips to various points in the region.

Numbers in the margin correspond to points of interest on the Ho Chi Minh City Environs map.

Cu Chi Tunnels

❶ *65 km (40 mi) northwest of Ho Chi Minh City via Hwy. 22.*

The Cu Chi Tunnels—a 250-km (155-mi) underground network of field hospitals, command posts, living quarters, eating quarters, and trap doors—stand as a symbol of the Vietcong's ingenuity in the face of overwhelming odds. (A note about the use of the term Vietcong: Vietcong is used throughout this book to refer to the opposition movement in the South because it is the term that is probably most familiar. However, Vietcong—which means, loosely, Vietnamese "Commies"—was the name given by the Americans and the Republic of South Vietnam to this opposition movement. The National Liberation Front [NLF] was the official name of the group fighting the southern government.

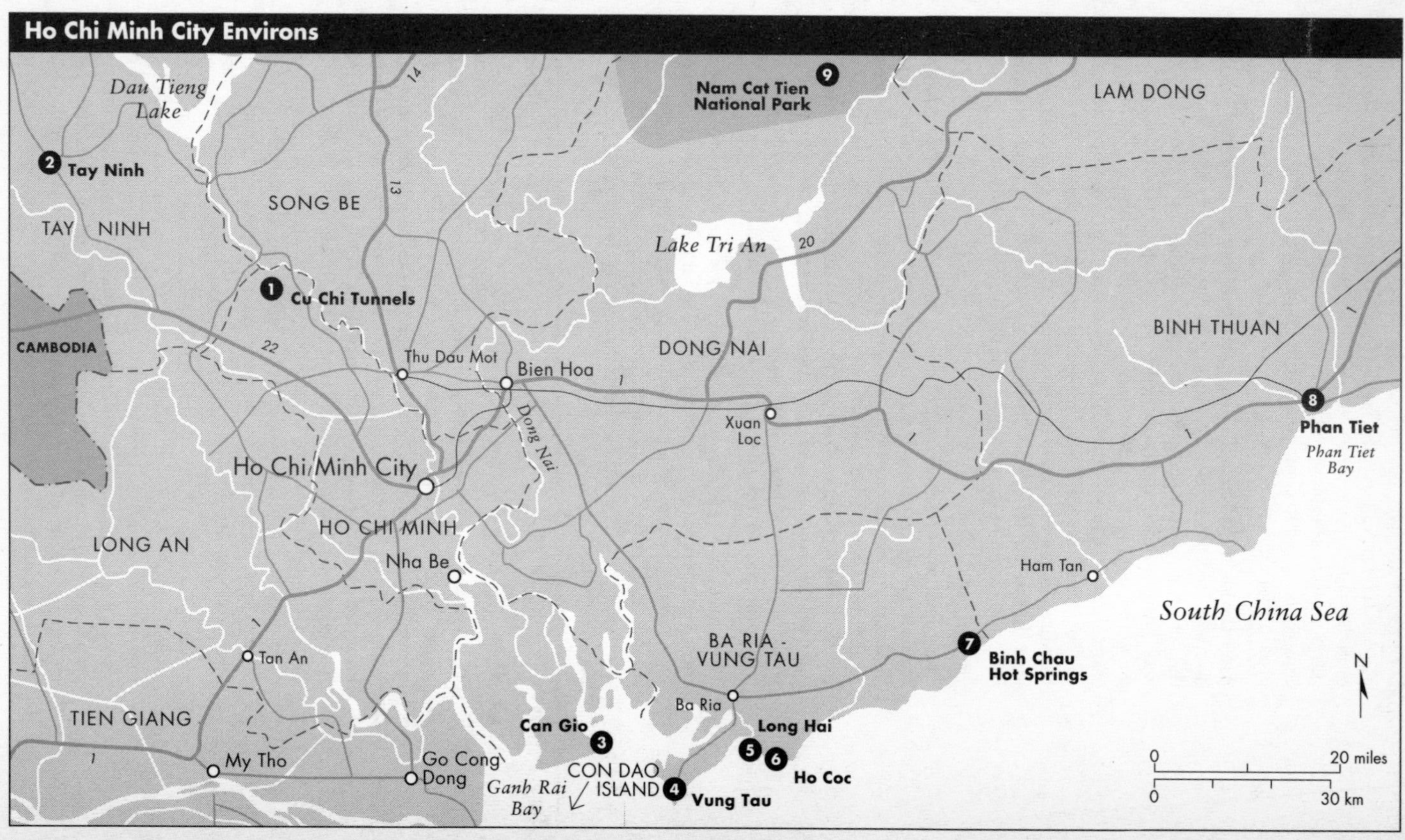
Ho Chi Minh City Environs
Dau Tieng Lake
2 Tay Ninh
TAY NINH
SONG BE
14
13
1 Cu Chi Tunnels
CAMBODIA
22
Thu Dau Mot
Bien Hoa
Dong Nai
Ho Chi Minh City
HO CHI MINH
LONG AN
Nha Be
Tan An
TIEN GIANG
My Tho
Go Cong Dong
Ganh Rai Bay
Can Gio
3
CON DAO ISLAND
4 Vung Tau
5
6
Long Hai
Ho Coc
Ba Ria
BA RIA - VUNG TAU
9 Nam Cat Tien National Park
Lake Tri An
20
DONG NAI
1
Xuan Loc
LAM DONG
BINH THUAN
8 Phan Tiet
Phan Tiet Bay
Ham Tan
7 Binh Chau Hot Springs
South China Sea
N
0
20 miles
0
30 km

For more history of these terms, *see* Vietnam at a Glance: A Chronology *in* Chapter 8.) First used in the late '40s to combat the French, the tunnels made it possible for the Vietcong in the '60s to not only withstand massive bombings and to communicate with other distant Vietcong enclaves but to command a sizable rural area that was in dangerous proximity (a mere 35 km/22 mi) to Saigon.

After the Diem regime's ill-fated "strategic hamlet program" of 1963, disenchanted peasants who refused to move fled to Cu Chi to avoid the aerial bombardments. In fact, the stunning Tet Offensive of 1968 was masterminded and launched from the Cu Chi Tunnels nerve center, with weapons crafted by an enthusiastic assembly line of Vietcong-controlled Cu Chi villagers. Despite extensive ground operations and sophisticated chemical warfare—and even after declaring the area a free-fire zone—American troops were incapable of controlling the area. In the late '60s B-52 bombing reduced the area to a wasteland, but the Vietnamese Communists and the National Liberation Front managed to hang on.

The guided tour of the Cu Chi Tunnels includes a film that documents the handiwork of "American monsters" (with, of course, no mention of South Vietnamese involvement) and an array of booby traps demonstrated by former Vietcong soldiers. If you are prone to claustrophobia, you might consider skipping the crawl through the hot, stuffy, and tight tunnels (though sections have been expanded to allow room for tourists' bigger bodies). Amazingly in these very same tunnels many Vietnamese survived for months and even years.

The easiest and best way to visit is on a tour arranged through one of the travel agencies or tourist cafés (☞ Travel Agencies *in* Ho Chi Minh City A to Z, *below*), since every agency—state-run and private—does the identical trip. A day trip, which will run you about $40 per person, will generally combine the tunnels with a visit to the Cao Dai Holy See, in neighboring Tay Ninh.

Tay Ninh

❷ *95 km (59 mi) northwest of Ho Chi Minh City via Hwy. 22.*

The town of Tay Ninh is home to Caodaism, an indigenous hybrid religion based on the major Eastern and Western religions—Buddhism, Confucianism, Taoism, Vietnamese spiritualism, Christianity, and ★ Islam—and its impressive brightly-colored temple, the **Caodai Holy See.** Founded in 1926 by a mystic named Ngo Minh Chieu, Caodaism is a fusion of a Mahayana Buddhist code of ethics with Taoist and Confucian components. Sprinkled into the mix are elements of Roman Catholicism, the cult of ancestors, Vietnamese superstition, and over-the-top interior decoration, encompassing a fantastic blend of Asian and European architectural styles.

Caodai has grown from its original 26,000 members to a present-day membership of 3 million. Meditation and communicating with spiritual worlds via earthly mediums or seances are among its primary practices. Despite its no-holds-barred decorative tendencies, Caodaism emphasizes abstinence from luxury and sensuality as well as vegetarianism as means of escaping the reincarnation cycle. Although the priesthood is strictly nonprofessional, clergy must remain celibate.

Perhaps most important, the Caodaists believe the divine revelation has undergone three iterations: God's word presented itself first through Lao Tse and other Buddhist, Confucianist, and Taoist players; then through a second set of channelers such as Jesus, Muhammad, Moses,

Confucius, and Buddha. Whether because of the fallibility of these human agents or because of the changing set of human needs, the Caodaists believe the divine transmission was botched. They see themselves as the third and final expression, the "third alliance between God and man." Since anyone can take part in this alliance, even Westerners like Joan of Arc, Victor Hugo, and William Shakespeare have been added to the Cao Dai roster.

It's worth noting that Caodaism's presence wasn't always so tolerated. Although it quickly gained a large following after its founding, including Vietnamese officials in the French administration, it soon became too powerful for some. By the 1930s the Caodaists had begun consolidating their strength in the region and recruiting their own army. Eventually the area became a mini-kingdom under the domain of the Caodaists. Needless to say, this didn't make the government very happy, and it did all it could to take away power from the region.

During World War II, the Caodaists were armed and financed by the Japanese, who the sect saw as also fighting the government. After the war, the Caodaists gained the backing of the French in return for their support against the Viet Minh. This collusion with the French, however, was not always so peaceful, and skirmishes often occurred between the Caodaists and the French. After the French left in the late '50s, the South Vietnamese government made a point to destroy the Caodaists as a military force, which caused many members of the sect to turn to the Communists, and the area became an anti–South Vietnamese stronghold. But when the Communists came to power in 1975, they repossessed the sect's land, and Caodaism lost most of its remaining power. Today the religion is tolerated but is not involved in politics as it once was.

The noon ceremony (others are held at 6 AM, 6 PM, and midnight) at the Caodai Holy See is one of the most fascinating and colorful religious vignettes to which you will ever be privy as a tourist. A finely tuned hierarchical procession of men and women of all ages parades through the temple's great hall, where great painted columns twined with carved dragons support sky-blue arched vaults; panels of stained glass with a cosmic-eye motif punctuate the walls. You are permitted to watch and take snapshots from the mezzanine. Ignore any feeling of complicity in what appears to be a collective voyeuristic sacrilege; the ceremony goes on as though you were not there.

Generally a visit to Tay Ninh is part of a day trip to the Cu Chi Tunnels (☞ *above*) arranged through one of the travel agencies in Saigon. A guide will accompany you, explain the history of the Caodai sect, and take you through the temple.

Can Gio

❸ *60 km (37 mi) south of Ho Chi Minh City.*

Officially a district of Ho Chi Minh City and only one hour from the city proper by car, Can Gio is an area the size of Singapore covered by a young 30-ft-high mangrove forest. The old forest was destroyed by aerial bombing and defoliants—primarily Agent Orange—during the Vietnam War. The forest had been a regular hiding place for the Vietcong who would fire mortars at the supply ships on the Saigon River. Residents of the area were forced to leave and it wasn't until 1978 that surviving Can Gio families returned, replanted the forest, and gradually resettled. Surprisingly, the area's wild animals also returned, and today there are monkeys, wild boars, deer, leopards, and even the odd crocodile. Can Gio is a maze of channels, inlets, and tiny fishing hamlets hidden among the swamp and forest. Make arrangements to get here with one of the travel agencies or tourist cafés in Ho Chi Minh City.

Vung Tau

4 *130 km (81 mi) west of Ho Chi Minh City.*

Called Cap St-Jacques during colonial times, Vung Tau was a popular beach resort for the French; some rundown, old colonial buildings still remain. During the Vietnam War it became a major U.S. and Australian army base. The area was later taken over by the Soviet Union as a concession for helping Hanoi win the war. The Soviets used the Vung Tau port as a navy base and drilled for oil off the coast. Many of the Stalinist-style concrete monstrosities dotting the town are a reminder of those postwar years. Following the collapse of the Soviet Union, many Russians left, though Vung Tau is still home to 2,000 (compared with Ho Chi Minh City, where only 200 Russians remain).

Vung Tau's beaches are the closest to Ho Chi Minh City, though they are not some of the country's nicest. But this is beginning to change—for better and worse—as the area is cleaned up for tourism and new hotels are built. There are a number of beaches in the town. The most popular, **Back Beach,** has had a face-lift and is now a very acceptable beach that stretches for miles up the coast. A part of this makeover is a new Disneyland-style park called Paradise, complete with the requisite turrets and posters of Mickey Mouse and Pluto, now under construction by the Taiwanese. It will also have an 18-hole golf course (☎ 06/485–9687 for information). Unfortunately, the whole place borders on the tacky. Back Beach is at its best during the week when it is quieter; on weekends it gets very crowded.

Bai Dau is a cramped beach below a huge, new road (still called Ha Long Street) completed in 1997. It's certainly not a place you would travel miles to see, but it is an acceptable tropical beach and the most secluded one in Vung Tau. However, it's fairly rocky and not ideal for swimming. **Front Beach** is the worst of them all—a dirty little beach strewn with fishing tackle and oil flotsam from the nearby rigs. But using a bit of imagination, you can picture how this beach and the old, broken seafront boulevard straddling it must have looked during the colonial era.

Worth visiting is the **White Villa** (✉ 12 Tran Phu St.), which at different times was the French governor's residence, the home of Emperor Bao Dai, and the South Vietnam presidential summer house. The villa, now a museum showing the opulence of the old regime, is a beautiful example of French colonial architecture, with classical columns, busts, and stucco decorations. Other sites of interest are the two small mountains crowned with pagodas and a giant statue of Jesus that overlook the town on a headland above. Interestingly, this hill is currently the site of a club of Japanese hang gliders, based in Saigon, who come here every weekend to fly the local skies. You can get a guide to take you along the mountain circuit around Vung Tau; the trip takes about four hours.

The best way to get to Vung Tau is by the new regular hydrofoil service from Saigon, which takes only about 45 minutes (☞ Getting Around by Boat *in* Ho Chi Minh City, *below*).

Long Hai

5 *170 km (105 mi) northeast of Ho Chi Minh City; 30 km (19 mi) northeast of Vung Tau.*

This beach is about a two-hour drive from Ho Chi Minh City and 40 km (25 mi) up the coast from Vung Tau, but it feels like it's worlds away. Local authorities recently designated Thuy Duong, just outside Long Hai, an international tourist resort and built a complex on the beach called the **Thuy Duong Resort.** The result is surprisingly tasteful, although you probably would just want to visit it for the day. Small kiosks and restaurants dot the bright, sandy beach, which runs for miles up the coast. Sit on the beach, which is equipped with deck chairs and umbrellas, and a waiter will take your order of fresh seafood. Thuy Duong is a popular day trip from Ho Chi Minh City; to get there, make arrangements through one of the travel agencies in Ho Chi Minh City.

Ho Coc

6 *190 km (118 mi) southeast of Ho Chi Minh City; 36 km (22 mi) east of Long Hai.*

Three hours from Ho Chi Minh City and farther up the coast from Long Hai is Ho Coc, the most beautiful beach in the area. It is a splendid retreat for anyone desperate to get away from the chaos of the city. The area is very remote, and consequently no public transportation reaches it. To get here, you need to hire a car and driver in Ho Chi Minh City. The only place to stay is the Ho Coc Guest House (☞ Lodging, *below*). There are a few small sidewalk cafés, but you're best off bringing your own food from Hanoi.

Lodging

¢ **Ho Coc Guest House.** This barebones but clean place has only five rooms, each sleeping two people. The bathrooms are basic—just a shower with cold water only and a toilet. But remember: You're not coming here for luxury but to enjoy the beautiful, secluded beach. ✉ *Ask for directions in town. No credit cards.*

Binh Chau Hot Springs

7 *150 km (93 mi) southeast of Ho Chi Minh City; 50 km (31 mi) north of Long Hai.*

About half an hour's drive from Ho Coc are the Binh Chau Hot Springs (Suoi Nuoc Nong Binh Chau), famous among the Vietnamese for their therapeutic properties. A veritable industry of acupuncture, massage, and other healing methods has grown up around the springs. People suffering from rheumatism or backaches come here to take the water. The springs are okay to use, though they can get very crowded on weekends and holidays. There are a few pho stands and some small cafés serving Vietnamese food. To get here, hire a car and driver or make arrangements with a travel agency in Ho Chi Minh City.

Lodging

¢ **Binh Chau Hotel.** This very basic hotel is the only worthwhile accommodation in town—for the moment. Hotels are going up so fast in Vietnam that you never know if there will be luxurious international spots in town the next time you show up (though it is unlikely here). ✉ *Ask for directions in town. No credit cards.*

Phan Tiet

8 *192 km (120 mi) northeast of Ho Chi Minh City.*

Phan Tiet is a lovely place to visit—miles of empty sandy beaches interrupted only by the odd lone fisherman and surrounded by lush, tropical palm forest. **Mui Ne Beach** is a particularly beautiful and pristine spot. The town itself has a large fishing industry and is known for its *nuoc mam,* the ubiquitous fish sauce served with most Vietnamese food. Dividing the town is the Phan Tiet River; the harbor is filled with small, colorful fishing boats. In the colonial era the French built homes on the north bank of the river, and everyone else lived on the south bank. Until 1692 the area was controlled by the Cham, and some of the present-day population are their descendants. More recently a golf course, the **Ocean Dunes Golf Club** (☎ 08/824–3729) opened 5 km (3 mi) away. A game starts at $60. Make arrangements to get to Phan Thiet through one of the travel agencies in Ho Chi Minh City.

Dining and Lodging

$$ ✕▣ **Co Co Beach.** A Swiss-run venture that opened in 1995, Co Co Beach has become one of the most popular destinations for Saigon's expats. It's regularly booked up weeks in advance, so call ahead to make reservations. The resort is made up of 20 bungalows on stilts, each with a bathroom and a sitting room. ✉ *Hai Duong Resort Ham Tien,* ☎ *062/848–401 or 062/848–402,* FAX *06/284–8493. 20 bungalows with bath. Restaurant, pool. MC, V.*

$$ ✕▣ **Pansea Resort.** This very popular place, about 5 km (3 mi) down the beach from Co Co Beach, is made up of 50 bungalows on stilts, built in Thai style. It's always a good idea to book in advance, especially during Christmas and Tet. The swimming pool and tennis courts are additional pluses. Beware, though, the service here is truly abysmal; patience is required. But the resort itself is worth it. ✉ *Pansea Resort Phu Hai, Phan Thiet, Binh Thuan,* ☎ *062/848–437, 062/848–438, or 062/848–439;* FAX *062/848–440. 50 bungalows with bath. Restaurant, pool, tennis courts. MC, V.*

Nam Cat Tien National Park

❾ *250 km (155 mi) northwest of Ho Chi Minh City.*

Often inaccessible due to poor road conditions, Nam Cat Tien National Park, northwest of Ho Chi Minh City and close to the Cambodian border, shelters the endangered Javanese rhino, as well as monkeys, elephants, tigers, and several bird species. The park also has one of Vietnam's only Banyan forests. With the encouragement of the regional tourist agency, Dong Nai Tourism, this national park is fast becoming the most popular adventure-travel location in the country. From Ho Chi Minh City, you may be able to arrange a two- to four-day jungle trip through one of the tourist agencies such as Vidotours (☞ Travel Agencies *in* Ho Chi Minh City A to Z, *below*). Dinner comes in your backpack, and accommodations are on a hammock—so this is only for you if you're a hardy traveler.

Con Dao Island

100 km (62 mi) off southern tip of Vietnam; about 40 min by plane from Ho Chi Minh City.

One of the most fascinating areas in Vietnam but also one of the most isolated, Con Dao Island (or Poulo Condore, as the French called it) is actually an archipelago of 14 islands. Although it's closer to the Mekong Delta region (☞ Chapter 7), Con Dao Island is most easily accessible by plane from Ho Chi Minh City.

The largest of the islands, known as Con Dao or Con Son, was used as a penal settlement by the French for more than a hundred years: it was the Devil's Island of the South China Sea. You can still see the solid French prison, with its infamous open "tiger cages"—where the guards would stand above the cells watching the prisoners pacing (if there was enough room) below—and the communal cells where sometimes over 100 prisoners were manacled to the walls. Most of the prison is now surrounded by creeping jungle.

The South Vietnamese took over the prison in 1954, incarcerating their own political prisoners. The Americans, with the South Vietnamese, built a prison camp here during the Vietnam War. Today there is only a rotting reminder of the camp next to the old French prison, with its iron watchtowers corroding with age. All told, thousands of people died miserable deaths on Con Dao—Nationalist and Communist prisoners as well as revolutionary insurgents and criminals from all over the French empire. Only one of Con Dao's cemeteries still exists; it alone has 20,000 graves, victims of the struggles from the 1940s to the 1970s. The population of the island currently stands at about 1,000—including many local fishermen and their families.

The attractive French town of Con Dao has been left intact, with the prison officers' quarters now occupied by Vietnamese fishing families. The prison governor's mansion is now a museum. Hours depend on when you show up—they'll open it especially for you if no one else is around. Along the rotting seafront boulevard are the remains of old, crumbling French villas where Saigon's wealthy used to fly in for weekend visits in the shadow of the gulag.

These days local authorities are trying to attract visitors to the island. A South Korean company has plans to build a hotel, and Saigon Tourist intends to renovate the few seafront villas that are still inhabitable. The island itself is a dream, with its beautiful but empty beaches, glistening coral in the water; and forests teeming with wildlife and rare sea mammals. Unfortunately, at present the only feasible means of transportation to the island is an expensive (Russian-made) helicopter charter from VASCO (☞ Arriving and Departing by Plane *in* Ho Chi Minh City A to Z, *below*), the domestic arm of Vietnam Airlines. The only other transportation option to the island is by boat, a 14-hour ride from Vung Tau, with departures just twice a week. But this is not advised, as the boats are generally in bad shape and the trip is extremely unpleasant.

Lodging

¢ **Con Dao Guest House.** Presently the only place to stay on the island (though this may quickly change as the island gets developed as a tourist destination), this guest house, next to the museum in the town of Con Dao, is very run-down. Rooms are communal, as is the one shower, and there is no air-conditioning. Be aware that as a foreigner and a tourist, you will probably be charged an outrageous $25 a night for the barest of accommodations. But there is no alternative if you want to stay on Con Dao. ✉ *Ask for directions in the town of Con Dao, no phone.*

Angkor Wat Complex, Cambodia

10 km (6 mi) from Siem Reap, and 260 km (161 mi) from Phnom Penh, which is about 300 km (186 mi) from Ho Chi Minh City.

Only a couple of hours by plane from Ho Chi Minh City is the famous Angkor Wat Complex in Cambodia, built in the 7th–14th centuries by the Kingdom of Angkor for Hindu worship. Here you will find not only the stunning Angkor Wat but also the ancient palace of Angkor Thom, the Bayon Temple, the Terrace of the Elephants, and the Terrace of the Leper Kings. Spend a day exploring the complex, then drive up the Phnom Bakheng hill to watch the sun set over Angkor Wat—one of the most magnificent sights in the world. At the very least, you need two whole days to see the complex.

Getting to the temple takes some planning—and some flexibility. The political situation in Cambodia is not very stable, and you may not be able to go when planned. From Ho Chi Minh City you will need to fly into Phnom Penh on Vietnam Airlines and then continue on to Siem Reap on Royal Air Cambodge. Visas for Cambodia are granted at the airport, though you can certainly arrange to get one beforehand. You need a visa to get back into Vietnam, which can sometimes take a few days or more (and sometimes only 24 hours), so you might consider flying to Bangkok after visiting the temple and not returning to Vietnam.

You may want to—or have to—spend a day or two in Phnom Penh, and two or three days in Siem Reap, depending on how much time you want to spend at the temple. There is a lot more to see and do in Phnom Penh than in Siem Reap, but it is the jumping off point for getting to the temple complex. Your hotel can arrange for a car with a driver and a guide to take you around the complex; or you can make arrangement with a travel agency in Ho Chi Minh City before you leave.

Lodging

PHNOM PENH

$$$ **Intercontinental.** This international luxury hotel, completed in late 1997, is one of the best in Phnom Penh. Be sure to make reservations in advance. ✉ *Regency Square, 296 Mao Tse Toung Blvd.,* ☎ *(855)23/720–888,* FAX *(855)23/720–885. 354 rooms. Restaurant, bar, pub, air-conditioning, pool, dry cleaning, laundry service, business services. AE, MC, V.*

$$$ **Sofitel Cambodiana.** This classy hotel is right on the bank of the Mekong River at Sisowath Quay. A popular choice in town, it is frequently booked. Rooms are large and modern, though a bit overpriced for what you get. ✉ *Sisowath Key,* ☎ *(855)23/426–288,* FAX *(855)23/426–392. 267 rooms. 2 restaurants, bar, air-conditioning, pool, tennis court, casino, health club, business services. AE, MC, V.*

SIEM REAP

$$$ **Grand Hotel d'Angkor.** This beautiful, classic colonial hotel was built in the 1920s by the French. It's being renovated by the Raffles Hotel chain and, at press time, was set to open in 1998. *Contact the Raffles Hotel chain headquarters in Singapore for information,* ☎ *65/339–7650.*

$–$$ **Angkor Village.** Traditional wood houses built on wooden stilts, this place is the most well known in Siem Reap and is often booked. Be sure to make reservations in advance. Rooms are small but pleasant. Siem Reap's best hotel. ✉ *Ask for directions in town,* ☎ *(855)015/916–048. 20 rooms. Restaurant, bar, air-conditioning, fans. MC, V.*

HO CHI MINH CITY A TO Z

Arriving and Departing

By Bus

Traveling by bus around Vietnam is not recommended. They are usually overcrowded, hot, and uncomfortable, and they often breakdown. Schedules, too, are arbitrary. You're better off taking one of the minibuses that leave from the bus stations, and even preferable is going on a bus organized by one of the travel agencies or tourist cafés (☞ Travel Agencies *below*). But if you do plan on taking the bus, Ho Chi Minh City has a number of bus stations:

Cholon Station (✉ close to the Binh Tay Market on Tran Hung Dao B St., District 5) serves routes to the Mekong Delta. **Mien Dong Station** (✉ National Highway 13, Binh Thanh District) serves points north of

Ho Chi Minh City. **Mien Tay Station** (✉ just off Hung Vuong St, Binh Chanh District) also serves towns in the Mekong Delta. **Tay Ninh Station** (✉ Le Dai Hanh St., Tan Binh Station), near the airport, is where you get buses to Tay Ninh and Cu Chi. **Van Thanh Station** (✉ 72 Dien Bien Phu St., Binh Thanh District) services Dalat and Vung Tau.

By Car

One of the best ways to travel around Vietnam is by a car with a driver (☞ Car Rental *in* the Gold Guide). Most hotels and high-end travel agencies such as Saigon Tourist and Vietnam Tourism (☞ Travel Agencies, *below*) rent private air-conditioned cars (Mercedes Benzes, Mazdas, Renaults) with a driver for about $35 a day (under 100 km/62 mi; extra miles cost more). At budget agencies like Ann's Tourist and Sinh Café (☞ Travel Agencies, *below*), you can hire a car and driver for about $20–$30, depending on the season. You may want to be driven to sights around Saigon, though you will need a car mainly for excursions outside the city.

By Minibus

You should make reservations for minibus trips in or out of the city a day in advance through your hotel concierge, a travel agent, or a travel café.

By Plane

Major international airlines with flights to and offices in Ho Chi Minh City include: **Air France** (✉ 127 Tran Quoc Thao St., District 3, ☎ 08/829–0981). **Cathay Pacific Airways** (✉ 58 Dong Khoi St., District 1, ☎ 08/822–3203). **China Airlines** (✉ 132–134 Dong Khoi St., District 1, ☎ 08/825–1388). **EVA Air** (✉ 32 Ngo Duc Ke St., District 1, ☎ 08/822–4488). **Japan Airlines** (✉ 143 Nguyen Van Troi St., Phu Nhuan District, ☎ 08/842–4462). **KLM Royal Dutch Airlines** (✉ 244 Pasteur St., District 3, ☎ 08/823–1990). **Lufthansa** (✉ 132–134 Dong Khoi St., District 1, ☎ 08/829–8529). **Quantas Airways** (☎ 08/829–3249). **Royal Air Cambodge** (✉ 343 Le Van Sy, Tan Binh District, ☎ 08/844–0126). **Singapore Airlines** (☎ 08/231–1583). **Thai Airways** (✉ 65 Le Loi St., 5th floor, District 1, ☎ 08/821–4660). **United Airlines** (☎ 08/823–4755) has an office in Ho Chi Minh City, though it doesn't yet fly directly here.

Vietnam Airlines (✉ 116 Nguyen Hue St., District 1, ☎ 08/823–0696), the Vietnamese national carrier, has international flights from Ho Chi Minh City as well as domestic flights to the following destinations: Buon Ma Thuot, Cantho, Dalat, Danang, Haiphong, Hanoi, Hue, Nha Trang, Phu Quoc, Pleiku, and Qui Nhon. Prices range from $60 to $150. It's best to book several days in advance and to reconfirm your flight; you can always change your reservation at branch offices all over the city.

For information about helicopers run by **VASCO,** the domestic arm of Vietnam Airlines, inquire at the Vietnam Airlines office (☞ *above*).

AIRPORT

Tan Son Nhat Airport (✉ Hoang Van Thu Blvd., Tan Binh District, ☎ 08/844–3179), 7 km (4 mi) from central Saigon, is small and navigable. Depending on the officer behind the counter, getting through passport control is intermittently hassle-free. The airport tax on a domestic flight is 15,000d or $2 (you can pay in either currency); internationally it's 80,000d or $10.

BETWEEN THE AIRPORT AND DOWNTOWN

Take advantage of the complimentary hotel shuttle service provided by many of the middle to high-end hotels. Otherwise you will have to deal with the throngs of taxi drivers outside the city airport, all trying to get your business. But don't be put off: Just choose an official-looking one and be on your way. From Ho Chi Minh City's airport fixed-price and metered taxis are the best ways to get into the city center. Despite the advent of taxi meters, you should still try to negotiate a price before getting into the cab: about $7–$10 (you can pay in dong or dollars), depending on the number of passengers and pieces of luggage. The ride takes 10- to 20-minutes depending on traffic.

By Train

From Ho Chi Minh City there is local train service to Nha Trang, Qui Nhon, and Hue. The faster train (if only by a little), the Reunification Express, goes to many of the larger coastal towns north of Ho Chi Minh City, from Phan Rang–Thap all the way north to Hanoi (☞ Train Travel *in* the Gold Guide). This is not the fastest way to go or always the most comfortable, but it certainly is one of the most interesting modes of getting around the country.

Trains connecting Ho Chi Minh City with coastal towns to the north arrive and depart from the **Saigon Railway Station** (Ga Saigon; ✉ 1 Nguyen Thong St., District 3, ☎ 08/823–0105), about 1 km (½ mi) from central Saigon. It is best to ask a travel agent to call for ticketing and information, though you could try contacting the **Saigon Railway ticketing office** (✉ 275C Pham Ngu Lao St., District 1, ☎ 08/832–3537) yourself instead of having an intermediary do it; it's open daily 7:15–11 and 1–3. Note that Saigon Tourist does not provide any train service information.

Getting Around

By Bicycle

Bicycles can often be rented from your hotel; or ask there for a suggestion. Those available from shops on the street are generally unreliable.

By Boat

Boats touring the Saigon River start at 50,000d an hour and are available at the riverside on Ton Duc Thang Street, between Ham Nghi Boulevard and Me Linh Square. Choose any of the boats lining the river; almost all are family owned, and you must negotiate an exact price with the owners before boarding the boat. They will take both individuals and groups. Ask at travel agencies for advice about which are the best trips.

The **hydrofoil to Vung Tau** departs from the waterfront opposite Nguyen Hue Boulevard (for information: ✉ 6A Nguyen Tat Thanh St., ☎ 08/825–3888, FAX 08/825–3333) at 6:30, 8, and 2:30. The returning hydrofoil leaves from Vung Tau for Ho Chi Minh City at 1, 4, and 5:30. These times may change depending on demand, so check with a travel agency. If you are traveling on a weekend, be sure to book your ticket a day or so in advance. On Friday and Saturday the hydrofoil is usually filled with Vietnamese going to Vung Tau's new resorts.

By Bus

Public buses are the cheapest way to get around the around town, though not the fastest, most convenient, nor most pleasant way to travel. Service is often erratic and painfully slow, and the buses generally have no air-conditioning and are crammed full of people at busy times. You're better off taking a cyclo or a taxi, either of which is faster, more efficient, and not too expensive. If you do decide to take a bus, it is important to know about the Saigon–Cholon line, which you are most likely to use; it starts in Me Linh Square at the Tran Hung Dao intersection and ends up at Cholon's Binh Tay Market. Tickets, available on board, cost 2,000d. The Mien Dong–Mien Tay line offers transportation between these two bus stations for 4,000d. The Van Thanh–Mien Tay line travels between the Van Thanh eastern bus station and the Mien Tay western bus station. You can pick up all these buses at Me Linh Square or at stops marked *xe buyt* (bus stop).

By Car

Renting a car with a driver and even a guide makes the most sense for day trips outside Ho Chi Minh City (☞ Arriving and Departing, *above*). To get around the city, use taxis or cyclos.

By Cyclo

Although cyclos, or pedicabs, are only supposed to charge 2,000d per kilometer, 5,000d–10,000d is a decent rate (this includes the tip) for just about any destination within the same district. Going to districts in the outer suburbs obviously will cost you more. Cyclo drivers, often former South Vietnamese soldiers, frequently speak English very well and can provide informative city tours for a small price (a generous half-day rate is about 30,000d–55,000d)—bargaining is advised. Drivers will wait for you when you visit sights, just don't leave any valuables in the cyclo. If you are happy with your cyclo driver, you can make arrangements to have him pick you up the next day; he will certainly ask if you would like him to do so. Though cyclos are slower than taxis (☞ *below*), they are an excellent way to experience Saigon's street life.

By Motorbike

One of the quickest ways around the city is riding on the back of a motorbike taxi, known as an *Honda om* or a *xe om.* This service usually costs about 20,000d. Motorbike drivers are everywhere—they'll just drive up alongside you and ask where you're going and if you're interested in a ride. It's relatively safe to travel on motorbikes; unfortunately, the same can't be said for the roads, especially at rush hour.

You can also rent your own motorbike from any number of cafés, restaurants, and travel agencies, especially Sinh Café and Ann's Tourist. Daily rates usually start at about 50,000d–100,000d. But beware: Don't part with your deposit until you are convinced the place is legitimate. Legitimate establishments usually have a line of motorbikes for rent and a standard ticket they give to all customers.

By Taxi

Taxis are available in front of all major hotels. Many cluster around the Hotel Continental; at the intersection of Le Loi and Nguyen Hue streets, near the Rex Hotel and Hotel Caravelle; along Pham Ngu Lao Street; and outside the New World Hotel, near the Ben Thanh Market intersection. Nowadays most taxis have meters, and most drivers speak a little English. An average journey across town starts at 30,000–60,000d. The best taxi companies are: **Vina Taxi** (☎ 08/822–2990 or 08/842–2888), which is run by a British company with a French manager; and **Saigon Taxi** (☎ 08/844–8888); it's a good idea to book their taxis in advance. Other recommended taxi companies include: **Airport Taxi** (☎ 08/844–6666); **Cholon Taxi** (☎ 08/842–6666); **Giadinh Taxi** (☎ 08/822–6699); and **Saigon Tourist** (☎ 08/822–2206).

Contacts and Resources

Consulates

Australia (✉ 5B Ton Duc Thang St., District 1, ☎ 08/829–6035). **Canada** (✉ 203 Dong Khoi St., District 1, ☎ 08/824–2000). **New Zealand** (✉ 41 Nguyen Thi Minh Khai St., District 1, ☎ 08/822–6907). **United Kingdom** (✉ 21 Le Duan Blvd., District 1, ☎ 08/829–8433). **United States** (✉ 51 Nguyen Dinh Chieu, District 1, ☎ 08/822–9433).

Currency Exchange

Although they don't always offer the best exchange rate, hotels are usually the easiest places to change money; they can also change traveler's checks. Banks, too, don't always have the best rates; they offer the official rate, which isn't as good as the black-market rate (☞ Money *in* the Gold Guide for an explanation).

Major banks in Ho Chi Minh City include: **ANZ Bank** (Australia New Zealand Bank; ✉ 11 Me Linh Square, District 1, ☎ 08/829–9316); **Citibank** (✉ 8 Nguyen Hue St., District 1, ☎ 08/824–2118); **Standard Chartered Bank** (✉ 203 Dong Khoi St., District 1, ☎ 08/829–8383); and **Vietcom Bank** (✉ 29 Chuong Duong St., District 1, ☎ 08/823–0310). **ATMs** can be found at ANZ Bank and Hong Kong Bank.

Doctors and Hospitals

Round-the-clock medical treatment is available at **Asia Emergency Assistance** (AEA; ✉ Han Ham Building, 65 Nguyen Du St., District 1, ☎ 08/829–8520), a clinic run by Western doctors who treat minor illnesses and injuries, do dental work, and take care of emergency evacuations. **Cho Ray Hospital** (✉ 201B Nguyen Chi Thanh St., District 5, ☎ 08/855–8074) has regular and 24-hour emergency treatment. **International SOS Assistance** (✉ 151 bis Vo Thi Sau St., District 3, ☎ 08/829–8520) can help you with emergency medical care.

SOS (✉ 151 Vo Thi Sau St., District 3, ☎ 08/829–4386) is a small Western-run clinic open 24 hours where you can have minor illnesses and injuries treated as well as get help with evacuations.

Emergencies

Ambulance (☎ 15). **Police** (☎ 13).

LOST CREDIT CARDS AND PASSPORTS

If you have lost your credit cards, contact **Vietcom Bank** (☎ 08/829–3068 or 08/822–5413), which is affiliated with Western banks. For passport problems, contact your consulate (☞ Consulates, *above*).

English-Language Bookstores

There are a few bookstores in Ho Chi Minh City selling English-language books. Many traveling street vendors are also well equipped with English–Vietnamese phrase books and dictionaries, as well as travel guides, Graham Greene's *The Quiet American*, and other books on Vietnamese culture and history.

Quoc Su (✉ 20 Ho Huan Nghiep St., District 1), occupying a tiny space off Dong Khoi street, not too far from the river, is jam-packed with lots of photocopied bootleg political literature. It also sells guides to Southeast Asian cities dating from the '20s and '30s. French translations abound, but English-language literature is scarcer.

Xuan Thu (✉ 185 Dong Khoi St., District 1, ☎ 08/822–4670), Ho Chi Minh City's first foreign-language bookstore, is definitely lacking in the English literature department, but it sells quite a few international newspapers and periodicals. You can also get Vietnamese–English phrase books and dictionaries here.

Xunhasaba (✉ 76E Le Thanh Ton St., District 1), the largest foreign magazine and newspaper distributor in town, doubles as a tailor shop. Nice, cheap art books and some novels (mostly classics) in English are also available.

Guided Tours

Guided tours that only cover Ho Chi Minh City itself are virtually nonexistent, which is just as well. Since no one travels to Ho Chi Minh City just for its sights, but rather for the whole cultural experience, the few half-day major-sight tours, which cost around $35–$50, are ultimately not that worthwhile. Furthermore, though advertised as "English speaking," guides are often unintelligible in that language. You're better off exploring the city on your own or hiring an English-speaking cyclo driver (just make sure you can understand *his* English first).

On the other hand, do take advantage of the guided tours outside the city. For excellent tours to the Mekong Delta and the Cu Chi Tunnels and for various customized trips—some for as little as $5 per day with lunch included—check itineraries and schedules at the Saigon Tourist budget office or at any number of cafés and small travel agencies on Pham Ngu Lao Street (☞ Travel Agencies, *below*).

Late-Night Pharmacies

My Chau Pharmacy (✉ 389 Hai Ba Trung St., District 1, ☎ 08/822–2266) comes recommended by the Travel Medical Consultancy. The pharmacy is open daily 7:30 AM–10 PM.

Post Office

The **Central Post Office** (✉ 2 Cong Xa Paris St., District 1), next to Notre Dame Cathedral, is open daily 7:30–5:30. Here you can buy stamps, send faxes, and use the phones.

Precautions

In Ho Chi Minh City, as in any other city worldwide, you need to be aware of what is going on around you. Don't wear jewelry—or at least showy pieces—and keep a firm grip on your bag. Not only are there pickpockets, but robbers on motorbikes have been known to drive by and grab bags from people walking down the street. It's relatively safe to walk around the city at night—even for women—but, of course, you need to stay on guard and avoid walking down dark, deserted streets.

Travel Agencies

All these agencies can help you organize tours of Ho Chi Minh City as well as trips to sights such as the Cu Chi Tunnels, the Caodai Holy See, and the Mekong Delta (☞ Chapter 7), a few hours from the city.

Ann's Tourist (✉ 58 Ton That Tung St., District 1, ☎ 08/833–2564, FAX 08/832–3866) could very well be your only tourist-information stop. The company arranges tours both around Ho Chin Minh City and throughout the entire country, rents cars and makes flight arrangements, does visa extensions, and provides all the historical, cultural, and orientation material you could ever possibly need. Besides offering a wide array of travel services, Ann's also has a great story behind it: After the fall of Saigon in 1975, Tony and his brother were separated from their mother, Ann, and removed to the United States. Ann founded Ho Chi Minh City's first privately run travel agency with the intention of finding her sons. Reunited as a family, they became a professional unit; Tony now runs the company full time. It's open Monday–Saturday 8–6, and Sunday 9–11.

Exotissimo (✉ 28 Dinh Tien Hoang St., District 1, ☎ 08/825–1723, FAX 08/825–1684) is a more upscale, international inbound tour operator headquartered in Hanoi but with an office in Saigon. It's run by a helpful Frenchman.

Peregrine Tours (✉ 24/9 Pham Ngoc Thach St., District 3, ☎ 08/829–6086 or 08/822–8464, FAX 08/829–6158) is run by Australian John Powell and specializes in adventure tours as well as the more common package trip.

Saigon Tourist (✉ main office: 49 Le Thanh Ton St., District 1, ☎ 08/823–0100, FAX 08/822–4987; budget office (in Café Apricot): ✉ 187

Pham Ngu Lao St., 08/835–4535), a government-run travel service, owns an enormous number of luxury hotels, restaurants, and tourist attractions in and around Ho Chi Minh City. It can arrange tours and accommodations in Ho Chi Minh City and throughout the country; provide maps, brochures, and basic tourist information; book domestic and international flights on Vietnam Airlines; and arrange car rental. A word about Saigon Tourist: The company basically operates as two separate agencies—one for budget travel and the other for standard or first-class excursions. Besides the price, the only difference seems to be the size of the bus; the main office arranges for large groups to cruise on colossal buses for five times the cost. Although many budget touring companies will cancel a trip if they haven't filled their bus, Saigon Tourist's budget division has a no-cancellation policy (just on their end—you are permitted to cancel), so a minibus will depart on schedule even if you are the only passenger. It's open daily 7:30–6:30.

Vidotours (✉ 41 Dinh Tien Hoang St., District 1, ☎ 08/829–1438, FAX 08/829–1435), a successful, privately-run Vietnamese tour company, specializes in package and individual trips all over the country. It is one of the most upscale of the Vietnamese tour operators and consequently one of the most expensive. But Vidotours provides excellent personal service and English-speaking guides with an intimate knowledge of Vietnam.

Other offices and agencies include: **Getra Tour Company** (✉ 86 Bui Vien St., District 1, ☎ 08/835–3021); **Thanh Thanh Travel Agency** (✉ 205 Pham Ngu Lao St., District 1, ☎ 08/836–0205); and **Vietnam Tourism** (✉ 234 Nam Ky Khoi Nghia St., District 3, ☎ 08/829–0776, FAX 08/829–0775).

TOURIST CAFÉS

Kim's Cafe (✉ 272 De Tham St., District 1) organizes inexpensive trips to regions such as the Mekong Delta.

Sinh Café Travel (✉ 179 Pham Ngu Lao St., District 1, ☎ 08/835–5601) is by far the best tourist café in Saigon, specializing in budget travel. This agency has Vietnam's greatest travel deal: a $35 open-ended ticket good for bus travel the length of the country (☞ Bus Travel *in* the Gold Guide). The café is open daily 7 AM–11 PM. It also serves food, though you're better off eating at Kim's Café nearby.

7 The Mekong Delta

The Mekong Delta is a patchwork of waterways, tropical fruit orchards, mangrove swamps, and brilliant green rice-paddy fields that run their way into the emerald-colored South China Sea. It's a land touched by ancient and modern cultures, from the Funanese to the Khmer, Cham, and Vietnamese, today all living side by side after centuries of strife. If you're looking for wild frontiers, head south to the farthest reaches of the Mekong Delta—it doesn't get much more isolated than this.

By Andrew Chilvers

LUSH, BEAUTIFUL, AND FLAT, the Mekong Delta, Vietnam's southernmost region, is—unlike the many more-mountainous parts of the country—usually just 6 to 20 ft above sea level. The result is that the region is often flooded during the rainy season. Rivers and canals cross the land, functioning as waterways that transport people and goods.

In the northern part of the delta region, fruit grows in abundance: orchards full of mangos, jackfruit, lemons, custard fruit, dragon fruit, pineapples, durians, and papayas make the area Vietnam's Garden of Eden. The climate, which is hot and humid year-round, is ideal for cultivating tropical fruit. Rice also grows throughout the region. In the Mekong's southern section, steamy mangrove swamps and thick palm forests thrive on the flat, flooded delta, making the area difficult to navigate.

Traveling through the heart of the delta is the Mekong River, also known as Song Cuu Long, or River of the Nine Dragons. Every second the river carries with it from 2,500 to 50,000 cubic yards of fertile soil deposits; this flow of soil created the delta and continues to make it grow. Descending from the Tibetan plateau, the Mekong River runs through China, separates Burma from Laos, skirts Thailand, passes through Cambodia, and flows through Vietnam into the South China Sea. As it enters Vietnam, the river divides into two arteries: the Tien Giang (Upper River), which splinters at My Tho and Vinh Long into several seaward tributaries; and the Hau Giang (Lower River), which passes through Chau Doc, Long Xuyen, and Can Tho to the sea. The river is filled with islands that are particularly famous for their beautiful fruit gardens and orchards.

Fifteen million people live in the Mekong Delta's 11 provinces. Most subsist by fishing or rice farming. Dotting the endless fields of rice paddies, poor peasant farmers, shadowed by their limpet-shape hats, evoke the classic image of Vietnam. These days enough rice is produced to feed the country *and* to export abroad. Vietnam is now the world's third-largest rice exporter, after the United States and Thailand—a remarkable feat considering that less than 10 years ago the country was importing rice.

The northern delta, centered around Can Tho and My Tho, is far more accessible than the remote southern delta. Encompassing the Ca Mau peninsula that juts into the sea from Soc Trang, the lower delta is wild country. Isolated fishing communities live along the tributaries running through the area. In the southernmost province of Minh Hai, the ancient mangrove forests are home to monkeys, wildcats, boars, and even crocodiles. Around U Minh, on the Cau Mau Peninsula, is Vietnam's only large cajeput forest, which can only be seen by boat.

Throughout the delta are small settlements that are sometimes very isolated and can only be reached by boat. These villages are often haphazard affairs, made up of rickety wooden structures atop unsteady bamboo stilts. This is the local solution to living above the twice-daily swelling tides. In the heavy flooding of monsoon season, however, from May to September, these vulnerable homes often collapse.

Over the centuries the Mekong Delta has provided refuge to people fleeing wars and chaos farther north. The region was first mentioned in Chinese scholarly works as a part of the ancient kingdom of Funan, or the Oc Eo civilization, which had its capital near the modern-day city of My Tho. The Funan civilization was influenced by Indian,

Hindu, and Buddhist cultures and flourished between the 1st and 5th centuries AD. It was well known by Malay, Arab, and Chinese traders and was even large enough to warrant Chinese ambassadorial status. However, in the 6th century the Funan kingdom inexplicably disappeared. The Mekong Delta was settled by the Cham and the Khmer in the 7th century and was annexed by the Khmer civilization based at Angkor between the 9th and 10th centuries. Some Vietnamese settlers lived in the area even under Khmer rule, but with the defeat of the Cham in the late 15th century, more Vietnamese moved south. In the 17th century some of the Chinese fleeing one of the many northern dynastic autocrats appeared in the Mekong Delta. The Tay Son rebellion and the Lords of Hue retributions in the late 18th century brought even more Vietnamese into the region.

The Mekong Delta's modern borders were drawn up by the French in 1954. Before this time the region's boundaries were relatively fluid: People living in Vietnam and Cambodia mixed and settled in different parts of the region without knowing in which country they resided. Under the French, Indochina was a fairly loosely administered region comprising Laos, Cambodia, Cochin China, Annam, and Tonkin (now northern Vietnam) under one governor general based in Hanoi. Allegiances were based on ethnicity—Cham, Khmer, Vietnamese, and so on—rather than on nationality. And there was feuding: The Khmer believed that over the centuries the Vietnamese had taken away their land, and they wanted it back.

French colonialism briefly put a stop to the disputes—and later contributed to them. The French encouraged the Vietnamese and the Chinese, who were much more hardworking than the Khmer, to continue settling here. As more Vietnamese moved south, more Khmer left. Uncertainty over who would have sovereignty over the Mekong Delta lasted until 1954, when the French bequeathed the area to the new country of South Vietnam. The Khmer were not consulted, and they've been disgruntled ever since. Under Pol Pot's rule in Cambodia, the Khmer again laid claim to the delta as their ancestral land, and there were frequent skirmishes between Khmer Rouge and Vietnamese soldiers along the border.

Other social upheavals over the last 50-some years have also contributed to the region's further settlement. During the Japanese occupation of Vietnam in the 1940s, colonial French and Vietnamese families fled from towns and villages farther north to avoid the fighting. But the fighting eventually spread to the Mekong Delta, and these refugees were forced to fan out into the previously uninhabited mangrove swamps, hacking them down as they went. During the Vietnam War defoliants like Agent Orange destroyed huge areas of natural wilderness. These were later settled in the '60s and '70s after the trees had regrown.

Today the Mekong Delta is still populated with a variety of cultures. The majority of people living in the area are Vietnamese, with the Khmer comprising the second-largest ethnic group. Nearly 2 million Khmer people live in the vicinity of the city of Soc Trang and on the Cambodian border, and the Mekong Delta is still often referred to as Khmer Krom by Cambodians. A small number of Cham also live close to the Cambodian border, but these Cham, unlike their counterparts in the central highlands, are Muslim not Hindu. The southern Cham were converted to Islam by Malay and Javanese traders who skirted the coast several hundred years ago. The northern Cham contemptuously call the southern Cham the "New Cham," and the groups don't really mix with each another.

Pleasures and Pastimes

Dining

For a region that produces so much fruit (which you can sample at one of the area's many orchards), the Mekong Delta has the least varied cuisine in Vietnam. Not surprisingly, rice is the diet staple and is usually accompanied by fairly bland boiled or grilled chicken, pork, or beef. For a relatively gastric-problem–free holiday, stick to a diet of plain boiled rice and grilled chicken or pork, or French bread and pâté, which you can bring with you from Saigon or buy in larger towns in the delta. The best places to eat throughout the Mekong Delta are restaurants in hotels or guest houses—the seafood there should be fine (at least in the northern delta). You can also get some satisfactory meals in bigger towns such as My Tho and Can Tho.

If in doubt, ensure that vegetables are properly boiled before eating them; many local vegetables are sprayed with toxic insecticides and are often only washed in local tap water. Watch your food being prepared, if necessary. In addition, avoid some of the local fish, particularly catfish and shrimp, especially in the far reaches of the southern delta—they tend to be raised on human and other excrement in small trenches below farmers' houses.

If you're adventurous, try more exotic dishes—snake (usually cobra or python), turtle, deer, monkey, and even rat, more readily available in the southern delta. Cobra meat is quite tasty and sweet, but python meat is tough and chewy and best avoided, as are turtle and monkey. Although turtle is delicious, it is also difficult and potentially dangerous to eat; it's usually cooked inside its own shell, so eating it involves biting into potentially sharp, deadly fragments of bone. Monkeys are an endangered species in the delta, and they carry rabies.

Lodging

It can't be overemphasized that much of the Mekong Delta is a remote, undeveloped region, which means it has some of the most primitive accommodations in Vietnam. It's possible to find cheap rooms in most towns, but they're often so basic that you may want to pay more for the best hotel in the area or go to the nearest town with better hotels. Around Can Tho, however, hotel standards are improving because of the growing number of tourists, though this doesn't mean accommodations are as nice as they are elsewhere in Vietnam. Keep in mind that the least expensive rooms probably won't have air-conditioning or adequate fans—and you'll definitely want a cool room after a scorching day outside. All hotels and most guest houses in the delta are state owned, which means prices are fixed and generally far too expensive for what you get. But for $30 or more per night, you can usually get an adequate room with air-conditioning and a private bathroom. Rooms vary in grade from standard (which often have a fan and a communal bathroom) to deluxe (which generally have air-conditioning and a private bathroom), so be sure to make your request known when you book your room. Check the different options around town—new hotels and guest houses are opening all the time—before you make a decision.

Exploring the Mekong Delta

The Mekong Delta stretches from the Plain of Reeds in the northern reaches to the wet mangrove forests of Ca Mau at the southernmost tip. A sprawling region, much of it isolated and totally undeveloped, the Mekong Delta can be somewhat difficult to travel around. Can Tho is the capital of the Mekong Delta and the best base for traveling around the northern part of the region. Southeast of Can Tho is Soc Trang, the center of Khmer culture, and northwest is Long Xuyen, famous for its relics from the Funan kingdom. Farther north is the Plain of Reeds, marshlands controlled throughout the French-Indochina War and the Vietnam War by the Vietminh and the Vietcong and by the Hoa Hao religious sect. (A note on the term Vietcong: Vietcong is used throughout this book to refer to the opposition movement in the South because it is the one that is probably the most familiar. However, the history of this term is a complex one; *see* Vietnam at a Glance: A Chronology *in* Chapter 8 for further explanation).

On the Cambodian border is the center of Cham culture, Chau Doc. The highest peak in the Sam mountain range is also just a few miles from the border. Farther down the coast is the Mekong's only resort town, Ha Tien, although you would be hard pressed to call it a real resort. Along the southernmost tip are remote fishing villages, which are often cut off from the main roads and rivers much of the year because of flooding and so are difficult to get to. Few tourists venture this far into the lower delta, but if you do, the journey can be rewarding. Most likely you will visit the region with a tour arranged through a travel agency in Ho Chi Minh City; many of these include prepaid boat trips.

Numbers in the text correspond to numbers in the margin and on the Mekong Delta map.

Great Itineraries

Tours of the Mekong Delta vary in length from 1 to 10 days. For example, it's possible to just take a day trip from Ho Chi Minh City to My Tho, in the Tien Giang Province, and go on a boat trip to an island orchard. Or you can travel around the region for longer.

IF YOU HAVE 2–3 DAYS

My Tho ① is only two hours from Saigon, so it's possible to make a day trip of it or to visit as part of a longer tour. While in My Tho, go to both the Island of the Coconut Monk, where the island's namesake set up a religious sanctuary, and Tan Long Island, to see some of the area's orchards. Just outside My Tho, on the road back to Saigon, is the Dong Tam Snake Farm, which probably won't take you more than a half hour to see. That evening, head to **Can Tho** ②. Go to the Floating Market at the crack of dawn, then take a ride through the channels surrounding the city. Stop in at the Munirangsyaram Pagoda, a Khmer temple. The next day, make an excursion to **Vinh Long** ③, a river island with abundant fruit gardens and orchards, and the large Chinese Van Thanh Mieu Pagoda.

IF YOU HAVE 4–6 DAYS

After covering the upper and lower Mekong River areas around **My Tho** ① and **Can Tho** ②, head west to **Long Xuyen** ④, once a center of Funanese civilization. The Long Xuyen Catholic Cathedral, one of the largest churches in the Mekong Delta, is worth seeing. From Long Xuyen travel up through Dong Thap Province to the Plain of Reeds and explore the area by boat. On the fourth day, head down to **Chau Doc** ⑤, one of the more cosmopolitan towns in the Mekong Delta. Spend a morning visiting the Chau Giang Mosque, the religious center of the local Cham community, and go to shrine-covered Sam Mountain. You can see Cambodia from its peak when the weather is good. From Chau Doc drive down to the coastal city of **Ha Tien** ⑥ to relax on the beach.

IF YOU HAVE 10 DAYS

A visit to the lower delta—Minh Hai and U Minh—takes more time. You could go to this area on a separate journey or tack it onto a trip

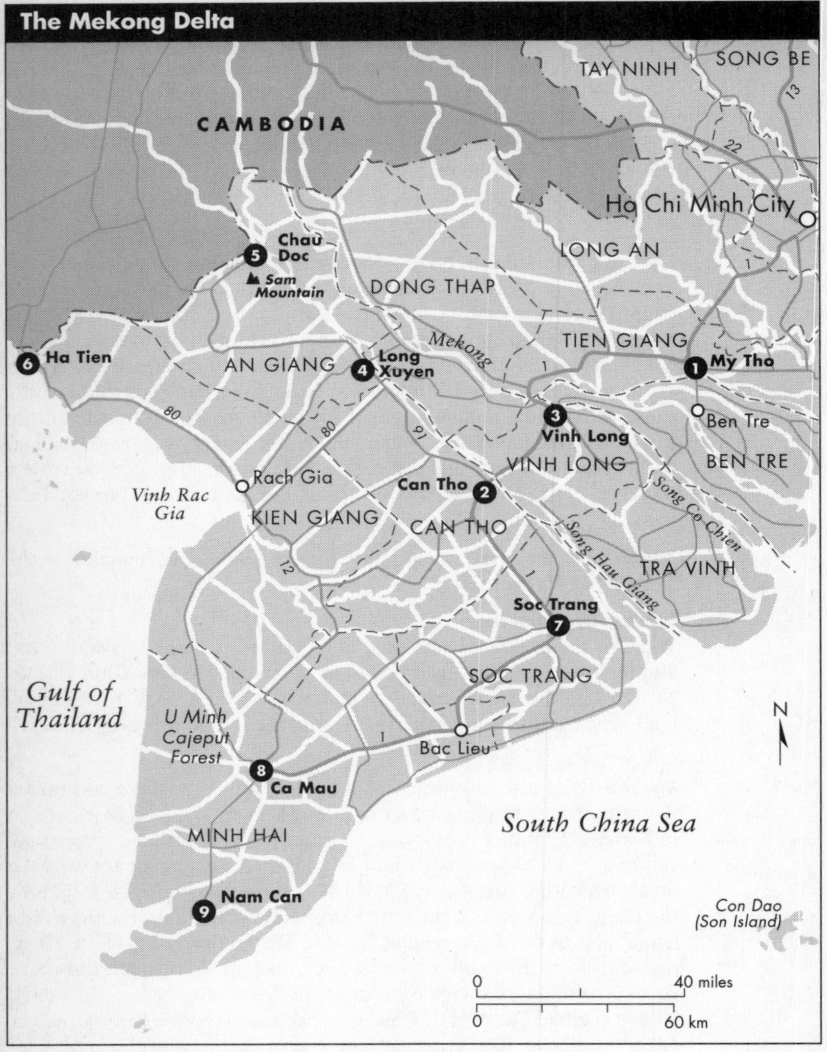

to the upper and western delta regions around **Can Tho** ②. About an hour and a half southeast of Can Tho is the Khmer city of **Soc Trang** ⑦, where there are many beautiful pagodas, a museum of Khmer culture, and a large Catholic church. Spend a day in Soc Trang, then travel to **Ca Mau** ⑧, the last big town on the southernmost tip of Vietnam. Use Ca Mau as a base for getting to the bird sanctuaries in Dan Dai, where you can see exotic feathered creatures, and for exploring the large U Minh Cajeput Forest and the Minh Hai Mangrove Forest. On the second day in Ca Mau, take a boat down the Ngang River to **Nam Can** ⑨, the last town in Vietnam before the sea.

When to Tour the Mekong Delta

The best time to tour the Mekong Delta is during the dry season, from October to May. During the rainy season, from May to September, a large portion of the region is under water and inaccessible.

My Tho

❶ *70 km (43 mi) south of Ho Chi Minh City.*

My Tho is the only port city along the upper Mekong River and the first ferry stop in the Mekong Delta. It is a good place to stop for lunch if you are coming from Ho Chi Minh City for a day of touring along one of the Mekong River's tributaries by boat (with a stop at one of the tropical fruit orchards on the river islands). With a population of about 150,000, it's one of the largest cities in the delta and one of the least attractive. Houses in My Tho are of the ugly, modern, concrete variety that are all over Vietnam (they are often called tube houses because they're long and thin and have no windows on the sides). To find quaint wooden longhouses and cottages on stilts you have to travel farther south.

My Tho was the center of the ancient civilization of Funan from the 1st to 5th centuries AD, and then the culture disappeared—no one really knows what happened. Today Funan relics are still being unearthed. The modern-day city was established by Chinese refugees fleeing Taiwan (then known as Formosa) in the 17th century. During the Vietnam War My Tho was one of the centers of operations for American and Australian troops. The largest battle in the Mekong Delta was fought in 1972 at Cai Lai only 20 km (12 mi) outside the city. My Tho is now known for its fruit and fish markets, a major food source for Ho Chi Minh City.

About 2 km (1 mi) from My Tho, on the Mekong River, is Phung Island (Con Phung), better known as the **Island of the Coconut Monk** (Ong Dau Dua). A religious sanctuary before the war, the island once had a garish, eclectic complex (in a similar style to the Cao Dai Holy See in Tay Ninh). It was built in the 1940s by a monk named Nguyen Thanh Nam, who was nicknamed the Coconut Monk by locals because he was reputed to have once lived for years on nothing but coconuts. The monk presided over a small community of followers, teaching a religion that was a mix of Buddhist and Christian beliefs. He was imprisoned repeatedly, first by the Saigon regime and later by the communists for antigovernment activities; he died in 1990. All that is left of the monk's utopian dreams are some dragons and gargoyles and columns with mythic creatures wrapped around them. ✉ *Take boat from Trung Trac St., next to Mekong tributary.*

Like many of the islands in the Mekong River and its tributaries, **Tan Long Island** is covered with fruit gardens and large orchards. A pretty island with little walkways and paths, it's a haven of peace and tranquillity only a few minutes from the bustle of My Tho's docks. You're likely to be invited into someone's house for refreshments. The island is usually a stop on tour itineraries. ✉ *Take boat from Trung Trac St., next to Mekong tributary.*

The **Dong Tam Snake Farm,** 10 km (6 mi) northwest of My Tho, is on an old U.S. military compound that lay deserted for years until a northern Vietnamese general decided to take over the land and develop it into a for-profit snake farm. The restaurant on the farm, which not surprisingly mostly serves snake dishes, is extremely popular with Vietnamese families on weekend day trips from My Tho. The farm specializes in cobras, which are prodded and poked for reactions by delighted Vietnamese youths. The most dangerous are the king cobras, which, according to the farm, still have their venom sacs. Probably hard to believe, but if in doubt, keep your distance. Even the kids shy away from the cobras, which can spit poison over some distances when angry. There are also a bunch of relatively docile pythons and a selection of rather miserable animals—many of them rare—such as monkeys, bears, wildcats, and pangolins, locked in tiny cages. These animals, too, suffer from the prodding of visiting children. Animals lovers will definitely want to stay away. ✉ *On road between My Tho and Vinh Long.* 🎫 *10,000d.* ⏲ *Daily 8–5.*

Can Tho

❷ *170 km (105 mi) southwest of Ho Chi Minh City, 108 km (67 mi) southwest of My Tho.*

Can Tho is the capital of the Mekong Delta and the region's gateway. Residents of Can Tho are quick to label themselves the friendliest and most helpful people in Vietnam, and judging by the relaxed atmosphere of the city, you may agree. Can Tho retains a French cosmopolitan feel—it was once one of the largest French colonial trading ports. Elegant villas can still be found throughout the city and along the shores of the surrounding river islands. Many have been renovated and are now occupied by rich Vietnamese merchants, though others are falling to pieces. During the Vietnam War Can Tho was almost constantly surrounded by hostile Vietcong forces, but the city itself stayed loyal to the Saigon regime and many U.S. and South Vietnamese troops were based here. It was the last city to fall to the North Vietnamese army, on May 1, 1975, a day after the fall of Saigon, as North Vietnamese forces moved south.

For a great day-long excursion from Can Tho, take a boat trip around the tiny islands in the river and canals surrounding the city. You can rent boats of various sizes from the quay along Hai Ba Trung Street; all come with a captain and a guide. Negotiate the price yourself, or let your tour guide do it for you.

Markets in the port and on the nearby rivers sell produce from the delta—mainly for markets in Ho Chi Minh City and for export. Can Tho has several floating markets—where people buy and sell from boats all jostling each other—but the **Floating Market at Phung Hiep,** 7 km (4 mi) southeast of the city by boat, is the largest and most picturesque. A bridge overlooking the market gives you a good view of the whole scene. Trading begins at dawn and carries on for much of the day. Goods are tied to poles to indicate what's for sale. A mango seller, for instance, will attach a mango to the top of his pole; others put grapes, pineapples, and other fruits on their poles. You can buy fruit here, but be sure to haggle over the price—it's all part of the process. The market is included on almost all tour itineraries.

Another of Can Tho's highlights is the **Munirangsyaram Pagoda,** a Khmer temple built in the 1940s to serve and provide spiritual well being to Can Tho's dwindling Khmer community, the pagoda is an emblem of one of the numerous ethnic groups that live side by side in the Mekong Delta. Unlike many of the more highly decorated, almost gaudy Vietnamese pagodas, this temple reflects the more spare Khmer sensibility. ✉ *36 Hoa Binh St.*

Lodging

$$$ **Saigon-Can Tho Hotel.** Not only is this hotel the best in Can Tho, it is also the best in the whole Mekong Delta. Completed in 1986 as a joint venture between Saigon Tourist and Can Tho Tourist, the hotel has clean, good-sized rooms and an elevator. But it also has the usual borderline-tacky Formica furnishings, and its view—of the street—is not the most appealing. The restaurant serves an evening buffet of acceptable Vietnamese food, as well as burgers and fries. There is also karaoke nightly. The hotel is next to the main market and downtown

shopping area. Ask about ongoing special offers, such as tours of the area or shopping trips, when you book. ✉ *55 Phan Dinh Phung St.,* ☎ *071/825–831 or 071/822–318,* FAX *071/823–288. 46 rooms with baths or showers. Restaurant, air-conditioning, satellite TVs, IDD phones, travel services. MC, V.*

$$ **Cuu Long Hotel.** Just off the waterfront and overlooking the main street is your basic state-run hotel, with nylon bedspreads and curtains, gaudy furnishings, pictures of castles and landscapes in the lobby, and the pervasive smell of dampness. Service is terrible, as it is in most state-run places. Nonetheless, this hotel is clean and one of the few options in Can Tho. Only the deluxe rooms have air-conditioning; the others have fans. ✉ *52 Quang Trung St.,* ☎ *071/820–300,* FAX *071/826–157. 100 rooms with bath or shower. Restaurant, travel services. MC, V.*

$$ **Hau Giang Hotel.** Built in 1996, this newer hotel is basic but comfortable. It's popular with budget travelers, though there are cheaper rooms in town. Only the superior and deluxe rooms have private bathrooms, and only the deluxe rooms have air-conditioning. Stay here only if every other place in town is booked. In the evenings there is karaoke. ✉ *34 Nam Ky Khoi Ngia St.,* ☎ *071/821–851 or 071/821–139,* FAX *071/821–806. 34 rooms, some with bath. Restaurant, travel services. No credit cards.*

$$ **Ninh Kieu Hotel.** This hotel on the corner of a street overlooking a small boat jetty has the best views of the river. Rooms vary in grade from standard to deluxe, as in most hotels in the area; only those in the upper ranges have private baths and air-conditioning. To get the best views of the bustling waterfront, try to book ahead and ask for a room overlooking the river. These come with balconies, which are a great place to unwind after a long day. ✉ *2 Hai Ba Trung St.,* ☎ *071/821–171 or 071/825–285,* FAX *071/821–104. 31 rooms, some with bath. Restaurant, travel services. No credit cards.*

$$ **Quoc Te (International) Hotel.** The Quoc Te is one of the best of the many hotels along the waterfront. It touts itself as an international hotel, which it definitely is not, but it's clean and if you want a good view of the river this is the place. Top and middle range rooms have private baths and air-conditioning. The restaurant serves Vietnamese food. ✉ *10–12 Hai Ba Trung St.,* ☎ *071/822–079 or 071/822–080,* FAX *071/821–039. 39 rooms, some with bath. 2 restaurants, travel services. No credit cards.*

$ **Can Tho Hotel.** One of the newest hotels to open along the waterfront, this place has basic but clean and inexpensive rooms. If you're on a budget backpacker trip, then this is definitely the hotel for you. The deluxe rooms have air-conditioning and private bathrooms. ✉ *16–18 Hai Ba Trung St.,* ☎ *071/822–218. 15 rooms, 3 with bath. Restaurant, travel services. No credit cards.*

Vinh Long

❸ *34 km (21 mi) north of Can Tho; 170 km (105 mi) southwest of Ho Chi Minh City.*

Of all the river islands in Can Tho Province, Vinh Long is the best known. Lushly covered in thick palm forest and fruit orchards, it is a beautiful place to explore by boat its canals and tributaries. On much of the island's coast are crumbling—and some newly renovated—French villas, which were abandoned in the late 1940s as the Viet Minh overran the territory south of Saigon. The locals are so hospitable that almost everyone will offer you tea and fruit at no expense if you happen to dock near their home. The most popular stop on tours of the island is at the **Binh Thuan hamlet,** where you eat lunch among the bonsai trees and fruit orchards of an eccentric old Francophone artist named

Nguyen Thanh Gia. The fruit orchards and gardens are the island's main attraction. **Vinh Long** is also the name of the island's main town, but the town is not attractive enough to warrant a special visit.

Five km (3 mi) from the town of Vinh Long is the **Van Thanh Mieu Pagoda,** a large Chinese Confucian temple built in the mid-19th century. It's decorated with multicolor dragons and statues of Confucius, which is odd because the monks here practice Buddhism. Added to the original structure is a different style of hall built in honor of a local fighter against colonialism, Phan Tanh Gian, who committed suicide in the 1930s rather than submit to French rule. Often the locals refer to the temple by his name, so try both names if the boat guide seems confused.

Long Xuyen

4 *190 km (118 mi) southwest of Ho Chi Minh City; 62 km (38 mi) northwest of Can Tho.*

Long Xuyen, like My Tho, was founded by the ancient Funanese, or Oc Eo, civilization. Until 1975 it was also the center of the Hoa Hao Buddhist sect, which, like the Cao Dai, had its own standing army to protect its interests against other sects and armies of the time. The Hoa Hao Buddhists often refer to themselves as Vietnamese Buddhists (that is, practicing a version of Buddhism distinct to Vietnam). Hoa Hao are very proud and fiercely independent people; during the 1950s and '60s they fought both the Saigon regime and the Vietcong with their own army. They were disarmed after the reunification of Vietnam. Their faith lives on, however, in their communities like Long Xuyen.

The city is the birthplace of Ton Duc Thang, North Vietnam's president after Ho Chi Minh's death and the first president of the unified country after 1975. In Long Xuyen, communists are eager to remind you that Ton Duc Thang was born in the area. If you have a few hours to spare, visit his birthplace, on **My Hoa Hung Island,** accessible by boat from town. There isn't much more there than a small shrine with a plaque in Vietnamese explaining that the island is—surprise!—Ton Duc Thang's birthplace, but if you're a Vietnam history buff, it's worth a trip.

Long Xuyen is also home to one of the largest cathedrals in the Mekong Delta. The **Long Xuyen Catholic Cathedral** is a relatively new church—it was completed only in 1973. Its most distinguishing feature is its huge bell. ✉ *2 Nguyen Hue St., at Tran Hung Dao St. and Huong Vuong St.*

The **Plain of Reeds** (Rung Tram) is the main reason to come to Long Xuyen. This swamp and marshlands interspersed with clumps of mangrove forest—much of which is impassable—covers the region on either side of the Dong Thap and Long An provinces. The area is also home to the **Tam Nong Nature Reserve,** famous for its rare wild birds. It's a great place to visit if you're an avid bird-watcher; but if you want to see the rare herons, note that many migrate out of the region for much of the rainy season. The Plain of Reeds and the reserve are both 45 km (28 mi) from Long Xuyen and Cao Lanh (east of Long Xuyen), an utterly forgettable, newly built modern town, and accessible from either. The reserve and the Plain of Reeds are both included in tours of the area; have the guide who has accompanied you from Ho Chi Minh City or from your hotel in the Mekong region organize the trip for you. Be aware that there are mosquitoes carrying many types of dangerous diseases, including dengue fever, malaria, and Japanese encephalitis; take precautions like using mosquito repellent and wearing long-sleeve shirts and pants.

Lodging

$$ 🏨 **Mekong Hotel.** This hotel is the best in town, but don't expect silver service, as it is state run. You'll find the standard nylon curtains, nylon bedspreads, and smell of dampness that come with Mekong Delta accommodations. But this place is about as comfortable as you're going to get in this very rural region. Request one of the top-end rooms; they are the most comfortable. ✉ *21 Nguyen Van Cung St.,* ☎ *076/841–265,* FAX *076/843–176. 18 rooms with bath or shower. Restaurant, air-conditioning, satellite TV. No credit cards.*

$ 🏨 **Long Xuyen Hotel.** At this state-tourist-authority-operated hotel, rooms are comfortable but no frills. The lower-end rooms are extremely cheap and come only with a fan and the use of a communal shower. Ask for one of the deluxe rooms—these come with private toilet and shower and air-conditioning. There is some talk of adding satellite TV in the near future. ✉ *17 Nguyen Van Cung St.,* ☎ *076/841–927. 38 rooms, some with shower. Restaurant, travel services. MC, V.*

$ 🏨 **Thai Binh Hotel.** Rooms are surprisingly comfortable at this inexpensive hotel favored by backpackers. Upper-range rooms have air conditioning. There is karaoke in the room behind the lobby. Only breakfast is served at the restaurant. ✉ *12–14 Nguyen Hue St.,* ☎ *076/841–184. 27 rooms with bath or shower. Restaurant, travel services. No credit cards.*

Chau Doc

❺ *245 km (152 mi) west of Ho Chi Minh City; 119 km (74 mi) northwest of Can Tho.*

Chau Doc is a port town on the Hau Giang River only a few miles from the Cambodian border. It is well known for its ethnically mixed population, made up of Chinese, Cham, and Khmer minority groups, as well as Vietnamese. Each ethnic group has built its own distinctive temples—Khmer wats, Cham mosques, and Vietnamese and Chinese pagodas. In addition to the three major ethnic groups, Chau Doc has large populations of Hoa Hao, Catholics, Buddhists, and Muslims, all coexisting peacefully together. In the late 1970s the town was notorious as a target of brutal border raids by the Khmer Rouge under the guise of seeking to reclaim land. There haven't been any raids in a long time, but if you're hoping to use Chau Doc as a jumping-off point to Cambodia, forget it. Not only are the Vietnamese military border posts unsympathetic to travelers, but the Cambodian side is still rife with dangerous bandits and smugglers.

The religious center for the local Cham community is the **Chau Giang Mosque.** As with other mosques in Vietnam, this one is starkly simple, with only some minarets and colonnaded entrances as embellishment, in contrast to the many brightly decorated Buddhist pagodas and temples. The mosque is on the river bank opposite Chau Doc, so you have to take a ferry (✉ Ferry terminal: Tran Hung Dao St.) to get here.

South of Chau Doc is **Sam Mountain** (Nui Sam), which is touted as the region's highlight. In fact, the mountain is more like a hill and thus a huge anticlimax. Nonetheless, it is worth visiting as long as you understand it will be a little less magical and a little tackier than claimed. At the base of the mountain are cafés and food stalls, as well as street children begging for money. The walk up to the summit skirts several pagodas and a park with—oddly—plastic scale models of dinosaurs. The **Tomb of Thoai Ngoc Hau** is the most interesting shrine on Sam Mountain. Built in the early 19th century for Thoai Ngoc, an official of the Nguyen dynasty, the tomb is one of the few still-existing precolonial structures put up by the Vietnamese in the Mekong Delta. The tomb also served as the last resting place of various other lesser functionaries of the time. When you reach the top of the mountain, there are splendid views into Cambodia—on a good day. Let your guide organize an excursion to Sam Mountain.

Lodging

$ **Chau Doc Hotel.** Consider this no-frills, cheap backpacker hotel a place to stay, and no more. There isn't much difference in price between the nicest and the shabbiest room, though the least expensive ones don't have private bathrooms or air-conditioning; be sure to ask for the most expensive. All, however, come with nylon bedspreads and curtains, which are standard issue in state-run hotels. Make sure the hotel staff supplies you with a mosquito net if your room doesn't have one. ✉ *17 Doc Phu Thu St.,* ☎ *076/866–484. 33 rooms, 6 with bath. Restaurant, fans, travel services. No credit cards.*

$ **Hang Chau Hotel.** Closed for renovation at press time, this hotel is worth a try in the future. ✉ *Le Loi St.,* ☎ *076/866–196,* FAX *076/867–773.*

Ha Tien

❻ *206 km (128 mi) south of Can Tho; 206 km (128 mi) southwest of Ho Chi Minh City.*

This resort town has untouched stretches of beach and limestone formations. The coastal area is a pleasant diversion from the flatness of the rest of the delta and is a good place to spend a day or two just hanging out. The water is crystal clear and the beaches a brilliant sandy white. You can go snorkeling, diving, and fishing here, though you have to bring your own gear.

With its crumbling French colonial villas and busy waterfront, the town is surprisingly charming. Today fishing is the main enterprise. Under Khmer rule the town was a thriving port; in the 17th century the Nguyen lords gave it to a Chinese lord, Mac Cuu, as a private, protected fiefdom. For the next 40 years the Khmer, Siamese, and Vietnamese all struggled for control of the port and the trade that would come with it. Ha Tien finally became an outpost of the Vietnamese Lords of Hue in 1780. The town's most famous site is the grave of the original Chinese lord, Mac Cuu, and his ancestors.

Lodging

$ **Dong Ho Hotel.** This no-frills establishment, run by the local state tourist agency, is a typically adequate and clean state-run hotel—nylon bedspreads, pictures of European castles, and small rooms that smell damp. Only the more expensive rooms have air-conditioning and private bathrooms, so you probably want to request one of these. ✉ *Tran Hau St.,* ☎ *077/852–141,* FAX *077/862–111 (c/o Kien Giang Tourist). 19 rooms, 7 with shower. No credit cards.*

$ **Hon Trem Hotel.** Very basic but comfortable and clean, this small state-owned minihotel is good enough for an overnight stay. Air-conditioning comes with the higher-price rooms; ask for one of these because it can get really hot. ✉ *Nga Ba Hon St., Binh An,* ☎ *077/845–331,* FAX *077/862–111 (c/o Kien Giang Tourist). 13 rooms, 3 with shower. Restaurant. No credit cards.*

Soc Trang

❼ *63 km (39 mi) south of Can Tho.*

Soc Trang is the center of Khmer culture in Vietnam. Many inhabitants are either Buddhist monks or—oddly—Catholic nuns. It was once a provincial capital of the Angkor Empire, which covered much of Indochina from the 9th to the 15th centuries. Vietnamese settlers did not appear here until the 17th century, encouraged to come by the French, who sought to develop agricultural production in the region. Even though there is a fairly large Vietnamese population, Khmer culture is still very much present. Soc Trang's architecture is a mix of French colonial and Khmer styles. Although many buildings are dilapidated, they are still impressive.

On November 15 the town's Khmer community takes to the water to race traditional Khmer boats—long, slim rowing vessels, often with a half-man, half-bird figurehead—during the Ghe Ngo Water Festival, a celebration of fertility. In April the Khmer New Year is celebrated with another water festival. Many roads in the town have no names, and inquiring about them only produces puzzled stares from passersby. However, the town is so small that finding your way around is not a problem.

One of the most beautiful Khmer structures in Vietnam is the **Kleang Pagoda.** The pagoda and nearby communal longhouse and meditation center are off the road behind graceful palm groves and huge banana trees. Originally constructed in the 16th century, the pagoda was rebuilt in the French-Khmer style at the turn of the 20th century. It's an almost ethereal photo opportunity if you can persuade monks to pose in the foreground—a request they're willing to comply with once convinced. Watch out for their enthusiasm, though; local Khmer monks are often so delighted to see you that they may drag you to the nearby monastic school to introduce you to their friends and have you teach them a little English. ✉ *Nguyen Chi Thanh St.*

The **Khmer Museum** is housed in a large stucco French-Khmer colonial-style building with classical colonnades, Khmer flutes and eaves around the roof, and half-man, half-beast Khmer figures on the walls and stairways leading to the entrance. The structure was originally built as a Khmer school in the 19th century. During the French-Indochina War the building was the headquarters for the local French militia, and during the Vietnam War it was a headquarters for American troops. The museum's collection includes Khmer statues and clothing, antique pots and utensils, and two long racing boats painted in vivid greens and reds. Across the street from the museum are Khmer religious schools. ✉ *Nguyen Chi Thanh St.* 🎫 *Free. Tues.–Sun. 8–4:30.*

Built early in the 20th century, the large, active **Catholic church** and nearby convent are classic examples of French colonial neoclassical architecture. The church is the largest structure in town and can be seen from everywhere. ✉ *Hai Ba Trung St.*

The **Clay Pagoda** (Dat Set Pagoda) is a vibrantly decorated Vietnamese temple built entirely out of clay. Even the statues, dragons, and gargoyles inside are fashioned from clay and painted bright colors. This is the most popular temple with the town's Vietnamese population. Inside are candles so big and so broad—each about 40 ft high and so wide that two people extending their arms around it can barely reach each other—that they can burn continuously for 30–40 years. ✉ *Hai Ba Trung St.*

The **Matoc (Bat) Pagoda,** 6 km (4 mi) from Soc Trang, is the most interesting of the hundreds of Khmer temples and wats in the countryside around the town. Legend has it that about 400 years ago Khmer monks constructed the pagoda to honor the big bats that live in the mango trees surrounding it. In the Buddhist religion bats are considered sacred and, above all, lucky. Despite the effects of war in the region, these bats survived. Strangely, the bats don't eat the fruit of the trees on which they live but feed on fruit from forests several miles away. Many Chinese from the Cholon district of Ho Chi Minh City make two-day pilgrimages to the pagoda to gather good fortune from the bats. The best time to see these night creatures is dawn or dusk. After visiting the pagoda, take a walk through the surrounding Khmer villages. The first village is about 55 yards from the pagoda, hidden by a small copse of fruit trees. The next village is nearby. People in the villages tend to be very friendly and may invite you to have a cup of tea with them. ✉ *Hai Ba Trung St.*

Twelve kilometers (7 mi) outside town, in the village of Dai Tan, is the **China Bowl Pagoda** (Xa Lon), the largest Khmer pagoda and religious school (for novice monks) in the area. The original pagoda was destroyed during the Vietnam War and was rebuilt using China clay ceramic tiles, hence the name.

En Route After leaving Soc Trang, on the way to Ca Mau (☞ *below*), you will pass through the village of **Vinh Loi** (20 km/12 mi away), where incense is made. It's easy to spot the village from the road—you'll see thousands of incense sticks drying along its sides.

Lodging

$$ **Khanh Hung Hotel.** Though not the best in town, the Khanh Hung is a basic, relatively comfortable place to spend a night or two. Don't be put off by the overlit and rather bleak-looking lobby; the better rooms are large, bright, and airy. Be sure to ask for one of the eight rooms with shower and private bathroom; the cheapest ones share a toilet down the hall, though they do have their own showers. ✉ *15 Tran Hung Dao St.,* ☎ *079/821–0267. 55 rooms, 8 with toilet and shower. Restaurant, air-conditioning. No credit cards.*

$$ **Phuong Lan Hotel.** This hotel is Soc Trang's best; it's in the center of town and fairly comfortable. Rooms are large and have the standard state-run hotel decor of nylon curtains and bedspreads. ✉ *124 Dong Khoi St.,* ☎ *079/824–229. 19 rooms. Restaurant, air-conditioning, satellite TVs. MC, V.*

Ca Mau

8 *179 km (111 mi) south of Can Tho, 350 km (217 mi) southwest of Ho Chi Minh City.*

On the Dai Dong River at the Phung Hiep Canal, some 50 km (31 mi) from the South China Sea, Cà Mau is the heart of Vietnam's Wild West. An isolated, rough-and-tumble kind of territory, it evokes what the American West must have been like long ago. People even wear beat-up old hats that look like cowboy hats. But everyone is very friendly, even if they do unabashedly stare at you. Most of the population of about 40,000 subsists on fishing. Tourists seldom come here because it's not very easy to get to. The town is inaccessible for much of the year because of the monsoons, and the old U.S. air base that now serves as an airport is sometimes hazardous, even in the dry season. Although the airport advertises two flights a week to and from Saigon, the solitary ground staff has no idea when the next flight will actually arrive, if indeed there is a next flight.

But it's worth trying to get here, whether by boat, by car, or bus from Can Tho or all the way from Saigon (a 13-hour trip). The town has an almost medieval atmosphere, with its chaotic collection of wooden houses leaning over the Dai Dong River, 20 ft below. Also running through the town are tributaries and canals that feed off the river. Along the river banks are lush mangrove forests and palm groves with a fascinating panoply of river life: people fishing, sleeping, working, washing, and drinking. Boat trips from Ca Mau's waterfront cost about $70 a day on a private boat and $100 a day on a state-owned boat. Have your guide—either the person you've brought from Ho Chi Minh City or someone from a local hotel—ask around about boats. They range in size from small ones for a few people to larger ones for up to 20. If you want to take a boat trip from **Nam Can** (the next town down the river) to the sea or spend more than a day in the U Minh Cajeput Forest (☞ *below*), set aside another full day. The U Minh Forest can be approached from Ca Mau or Nam Can, but to reach the sea, you have to stay in Nam Can overnight. From Nam Can the sea is between 5 km (3 mi) and 30 km (19 mi) away, depending on the season and who's giving you the information.

One of the highlights of a trip to Ca Mau is the **U Minh Cajeput Forest**, 35 km (22 mi) from town and reachable only by boat. This forest of pearl-white cajeput trees is in a swamp, so the boat has to wind its way through the sometimes thick undergrowth. Nevertheless, the journey through the forest is quite breathtaking and eerily quiet. But beware of mosquitoes. Make arrangements for boat trips—or let your guide or hotel do it—in Ca Mau.

Another daylong boat trip from Ca Mau will take you to the **Minh Hai Mangrove Forest**, one of the largest mangrove forests in the world and a truly primeval experience. The growth is so dense that it's almost unnavigable, but the boats manage to weave their way around the outskirts of the forest or to take wide channels through it. Often the most accessible areas are bordered by lone military outposts on the rivers and estuaries flowing to the sea. Most local soldiers live on their own or with their families in wooden houses above the wash on the muddy banks. Arriving tourist boats combat boredom, and often for no fee these soldiers will take you along the edge of the forest and, if possible, into the interior. Watch out for marauding monkeys and the odd crocodile.

Forty kilometers (25 miles) west of Ca Mau by boat is a series of riverine settlements called **Dan Dai.** The area is well known for its privately owned bird sanctuaries on 2 to 120 acres of small mangrove reserves. Not only can you see rare birds, but you can also find wild cats, monkeys, and deer. Beware: The owners of the reserves often ask for money *after* the fact, sometimes as much as $100, so be sure to negotiate a fee before you enter (you shouldn't pay more than $2 per person). To get to the sanctuaries, take a small boat from Ca Mau.

Lodging

$ 🏨 **Ca Mau Hotel.** Considering the town's frontierlike atmosphere, the quality of this hotel is surprising. In fact, it's actually one of the better hotels in the Mekong Delta. Rooms have many amenities, including air-conditioning, private showers, and satellite TVs. There is karaoke. ✉ *20 Phan Ngoc Hien St.,* ☎ *078/834–8834. 30 rooms, some with bath. Restaurant, IDD phones, satellite TVs, travel services. MC, V.*

$ 🏨 **Phuong Nam Hotel.** Another pleasant surprise in Cau Mau, the Phuong is a large and rather busy hotel filled with Vietnamese tourists. It has a small ornamental rock pool and spacious rooms with balconies as well as satellite TVs. Request one of the deluxe rooms, as there is a variety of cheaper and more basic accommodations. ✉ *91 Phan Dinh Phung St.,* ☎ *078/83–1752,* FAX *078/834–402. 39 rooms, with shower. Restaurant, air-conditioning, IDD phones, satellite TVs, travel services. MC, V.*

Side Trip to Nam Can

9 **Nam Can,** 45 km (28 mi) mi south of Ca Mau by boat along the Dan Dai River, is the last settlement of any size in Vietnam before the sea. About 5,000 people live in the town, which consists of a series of lean-tos and old, abandoned boats used as homes. Although there is some fishing here, the town exists mainly to smuggle in commodities from all over, including consumer goods, fish, and rice. Many of the Vietnamese "boat people," who left the country between 1975 and 1979, departed from Nam Can, and they bought many of the wretched vessels they used for their escape right here in town. The locals are very friendly.

There isn't much to do in town, but there is a daily market on the riverfront, with caged rats, as well as chickens, dogs, and cats, for sale as food; shellfish, vegetables, household goods, and clothing. Though the market is fascinating, the best part of Nam Can is the return journey to Ca Mau up the Ngang Canal, which is without doubt one of the most beautiful and exotic stretches anywhere in the delta region. Thick palm and mangrove forests line the water's edge, and tiny fishing and fruit hamlets sell goods from boats along the route.

THE MEKONG DELTA A TO Z

Arriving and Departing

There are only two ways to get to the Mekong Delta, both of which must be arranged from Ho Chi Minh City—hiring a private car with driver and guide through a travel agency or participating in an organized tour. All guides speak English. A private car can be expensive ($300–$500), but it enables you to plan your own trip and go farther into the Mekong Delta than you might be able to on a tour. Guides can make all necessary travel arrangements, including boat trips. **Vidotours** (☞ Travel Agencies, *below*) organizes trips for individuals, and many of its tours and treks can take you to the most far-flung places.

Getting Around

By Boat

The most scenic parts of the Mekong Delta are accessible only by boat. Boat trips can be prearranged by your tour company, hired by your guide, or arranged through your hotel for as little as US$2 an hour at every dock in every town. Be sure to keep an eye on your bags and valuables during your trip. Can Tho is the departure point for riverboat trips the river islands.

By Car

Private cars with drivers and tours can be arranged only in Ho Chi Minh City.

By Guided Tour

Group tours that travel via tour bus and boat are available through the Sinh Café or Kim's Café (☞ Travel Agencies, *below*), as well as through more upscale (though not necessarily better) state-run agencies such as **Saigon Tourist. Vidotours** is the best agency for tours of the region.

By Motorbike

If you want to see the Mekong Delta by motorbike, rent one from the **Sinh Café** (☞ Travel Agencies, *below*) in Saigon; there are special discount rates if you rent one for longer periods. Be sure to ask for the motorbike's documents, and try to get a newer Honda. Many of the scooters rented here—such as older Lambrettas from the '50s and '60s—break down almost immediately. Take your motorbike for a test drive before you venture on your way with it.

Contacts and Resources

Currency Exchange

It's a good idea to bring cash, though if you need to change dollars or traveler's checks your hotel can probably do so.

Precautions

If you're planning to travel in the Mekong Delta for 10 or more days, make sure you're adequately prepared. There are malaria-carrying mosquitoes all over the delta and in some of the forests. Other mosquitoes carry diseases such as Japanese encephalitis (or Japanese B). Typhus is also a major health problem (it's water borne). However, it's almost unheard of for a tourist to contract any of these diseases; nevertheless, take precautions. Bring along mosquito coils and mosquito repellent for longer stays; malaria pills are generally a waste of time. Hotels generally provide mosquito netting. Try to cover your body at all times by wearing long-sleeve shirts and pants—day and night—and never drink anything but bottled or boiled water. *See* Health *in* the Gold Guide for more information on health precautions.

Travel Agencies

IN HO CHI MINH CITY

The following agencies arrange private and group tours from Ho Chi Minh City to the Mekong Delta:

Kim's Cafe (✉ 272 De Tham St., District 1, Ho Chi Minh City). **Saigon Tourist** (Main office, ✉ 49 Le Thanh Ton St., District 1, Ho Chi Minh City, ☎ 08/823–0100, FAX 08/822–4987; budget office, in Café Apricot, ✉ 187 Pham Ngu Lao St., ☎ 08/835–4535). **Sinh Café** (✉ 179 Pham Ngu Lao St., District 1, Ho Chi Minh City, ☎ 08/835–5601). **Vidotours** (✉ 41 Dinh Tien Hoang St., District 1, Ho Chi Minh City, ☎ 08/829–1438, FAX 08/829–1435).

IN THE MEKONG DELTA

Can Tho Tourist (Cong Ty Du Lich Can Tho; ✉ 20 Hai Ba Trung St., Can Tho, ☎ 071/821–853, FAX 071/822–719). **Tien Giang Tourism** (Cong Ty Dy Lich; ✉ On riverfront at intersection of Rach Gam and Trung Trac Sts., My Tho, ☎ 073/872–154 or 071/872–105).

8 Portraits of Vietnam

Vietnam at a Glance: A Chronology

Riding the Dream

Getting Down to Business

Books and Videos

VIETNAM AT A GLANCE: A CHRONOLOGY

Early History

Around 1300 BC The Dong Son, the earliest recorded civilization in what is now Vietnam, emerge in the Red River delta in the region that would later become Hanoi. This culture is known for its elaborate bronze drums.

208 BC The loosely organized feudal lords, the Lac Viet, of the Red River Delta are conquered by a renegade Chinese general who claims the title of Nam Viet (emperor of the Viet people in the south). The region north of Champa is called Dai Co Viet.

111 BC The Han Chinese invade and conquer Tonkin and Annam (what is now northern Vietnam). Through about 100 BC, the Han dynasty pursues a policy of administrative and cultural incorporation of Tonkin and Annam into the Chinese empire.

40 AD The Trung Sisters lead a successful rebellion against the Chinese: After the Chinese execute a high-ranking Vietnamese feudal lord, the lord's widow and her sister mobilize the disorganized Vietnamese chieftains against the Chinese governor. After a quick victory the sisters are proclaimed queens of the newly independent Vietnamese state.

43 AD Chinese forces reconquer the new Vietnamese state. The Trung sisters choose to commit suicide rather than accept defeat.

100–500 AD The Funan Kingdom rules the southern part of Vietnam (later known as Cochin China). This Indianized kingdom has major trading centers in the region near what is today Kien Giang. Archaeologists have found evidence of trade links between Funan, China, Indonesia, India, and Persia. Discovery of a Roman medallion in Funan dating from 152 AD indicates the Funanese may have had trade networks extending as far as ancient Rome. Although not much is known about this kingdom, many believe it was either the progenitor of or a sister state to the later Khmer Empire.

Around 100 AD The Champa Kingdom emerges near present-day Danang in southern Annam. Like the Funan Kingdom, the Kingdom of Champa was based on strong trade links with India. The Cham culture adopted Indianized art forms and architectural styles as well as written Sanskrit. The Cham ruins in central Vietnam today are evidence of these influences.

166 AD The first documented direct contact between Vietnam and the West occurs when Roman travelers arrive in the Red River Delta.

Early Dynasties

939–970 The Annamese Ngo dynasty ousts the Chinese and establishes an independent state in the Red River Delta.

967–980 Dinh dynasty: Emperor Dinh Bo Linh ascends the throne and renames the independent state Dai Co Viet.

980–1009 Early Le dynasty.

1010–1225 Ly dynasty: Established by Emperor Ly Thai To, this dynasty is known for promoting a Chinese-style Mandarin education system, symbolized by the construction of Van Mieu, the Temple of Literature, in Hanoi. The dynasty is also known for promoting Buddhism over Confucian values and for expanding the Vietnamese state's territory southward into Cham lands through the promotion of agricultural development and the creation of Vietnamese villages.

1225–1400 First Tran dynasty: This dynasty is known for increasing the nation's population and its cultivated land. Its most celebrated single achievement is the repulsion of invading Mongol forces in the mid-13th century. In a brilliant naval victory in the Bach Dang River, Tran Hung Dao lured a superior Mongol fleet into the mouth of the estuary. He patiently held the Mongols at bay, positioning them in a vulnerable area in which their ships were impaled on steel-tipped poles planted by Vietnamese forces and the crews massacred when low tide arrived.

1400–1406 Ho dynasty: In 1400 Tonkinese leader Ho Quy Le overthrows the Tran. Tran loyalists and the Chams, who had been fighting their Tonkinese northern neighbors, encourage the Chinese to intervene and reinstate the Tran.

Later Dynasties

1407–1413 Later Tran dynasty: After being reinstated, the Tran reign briefly.

1413–1428 The Chinese Ming Empire reconquers Vietnam and occupies the country.

1428–1786 Later Le dynasty: The Chinese officially recognize Vietnam's independence following a revolt led by Emperor Le Loi, who establishes the Le dynasty. It lasts until 1786.

1460–98 Under the rule of Emperor Le Thanh Tong, a comprehensive legal code is introduced and Vietnamese domination extended farther southward into Cham territory.

1516 Portuguese traders land in the port of Danang.

1527 Dominican missionaries from Portugal arrive in Danang to gain converts among the people living there.

1545 As Le rulers' authority weakens, civil strife splits the country for nearly two centuries. The Le dynasty continues its official rule, but warring lords who accept Le rule operate largely independent of the emperor. Much of the conflict is between the Trinh lords, who dominate the north from Tonkin, and the Nguyen lords, who rule from Hue to the south. Although neither achieves dominance, the Nguyen establish control over the Khmer areas of the Mekong Delta and populate the area with Vietnamese settlers.

1615 French Jesuit missionaries expelled from Japan arrive in Vietnam.

1627 Alexandre de Rhodes, a French Jesuit missionary, adapts spoken Vietnamese to the Roman alphabet, leading to the current Vietnamese script. He creates a Vietnamese dictionary in 1651.

1700 The country splits into the Trinh dynasty north of Hue and the Nguyen dynasty including Hue and lands to the south.

1771–1802 Tay Son rebellion: After years of a weak central government and warring factions, a rebellion starts in the village of Tay Son, near present-day Qui Nhon in south-central Vietnam. Led by the three sons of a wealthy merchant, the Tay Son rebels capture central and southern Vietnam by 1783, sending the surviving Nguyen lord, Prince Nguyen Anh, into exile in Thailand. In retaliation, Prince

Nguyen Anh asks the French for their assistance in his return to Vietnam to defeat the Tay Son rebels. Meanwhile, the Tay Son conquer the Trinh in the north and pledge allegiance to the weak Le dynasty. The Le emperor, however, asks the Chinese to help him control the Tay Son. Mobilizing popular support against the Chinese, one of the Tay Son brothers proclaims himself emperor and leads the Vietnamese in an overwhelming defeat of the Chinese forces near Hanoi in 1789. But soon after, Prince Nguyen Anh, with support from French-trained forces, returns to southern Vietnam and moves north against the Tay Son.

French Influence

1802–1945 In 1802 Prince Nguyen Anh proclaims himself Emperor Gia Long, officially beginning the Nguyen dynasty. When Gia Long captures Hanoi from the Tay Son rebels, it marks the first time in 200 years that Vietnam is united, with Hue as its capital. French missionary activity begins to spread, as the Nguyen develop a mutually tolerant relationship with the French.

1847 The first clash occurs between Emperor Thieu Tri, successor to the Nguyen throne, and the French, after the French attack Danang Harbor in retaliation for a Vietnamese crackdown on Catholic converts. Also in this year Nguyen emperor Tu Duc ascends the throne and continues the struggle against the French.

1861 French colonial forces win the battle of Ky Hoa and take Saigon. Defeated, Tu Duc's forces disband. But unhappy with the prospect of French rule, local elites continue resistance, using anti-French guerrilla tactics in the south.

1862 Emperor Tu Duc negotiates a treaty with the French, giving broad religious, economic, and political concessions: permission for missionaries to proselytize throughout the country; the opening of ports to French and Spanish trade; surrender of the three eastern provinces of Cochin China; and payment of a large indemnity to the French.

1863 The French expand into Cambodia.

1867 The French name the southern part of the country Cochin China and take over its administration after a final French offensive breaks Vietnamese resistance.

1872 French merchant Jean Dupuis seizes Hanoi. In an effort to preserve the fragile French–northern Vietnamese relationship, the French send gunships to subdue him. But instead they demand tribute from local Vietnamese leaders. In response, the Co Den, a band of unallied Vietnamese, Chinese, and Hill tribe mercenaries subdue the French forces and begin pirating local villages. Chaos reigns in the north.

1883 After Tu Duc's death, French forces take the Imperial City in Hue and impose the Treaty of Protectorate on the Imperial Court. The French give protectorate status—as an independent government subject to French policy—to the north, which they designate Tonkin, and central Vietnam, which they designate Annam, and rule Cochin China as a colony administered directly by France.

1887 The French create the Indochinese Union in order to end Vietnamese expansion into Cambodia and Laos, thereby officially ending a unified Vietnamese state. The Union includes Tonkin, Annam, Cochin China, Cambodia, and the Port of Qizhouwan in China.

1890 Ho Chi Minh is born as Nguyen Ai Quoc (meaning "Nguyen who loves his country") in Nghe An Province in north-central Vietnam.

1911 Ho Chi Minh leaves Vietnam and begins his world travels. Over the next 30 years he works in France and spends time in Moscow, becoming involved with the growing communist movement.

1919 Ho Chi Minh tries to petition American president Woodrow Wilson, at the Versailles peace conference held at the end of World War I, for self-determination for Vietnam and is refused.

1920 Ho Chi Minh joins the French Communist Party.

1930 Ho Chi Minh and his colleagues form the Indochinese Communist Party in Hong Kong, where they are free from French repression.

1932 Bao Dai, the nominal emperor of Vietnam, returns from his education in France to take over the Nguyen dynasty throne under French guidance.

1940 Rather than risk a full-scale confrontation, the Nazi-backed, French Vichy government peacefully capitulates to Japanese troops' invasion of Vietnam. The Japanese leave the French administration in place as the most efficient way of controlling the region.

1941 Ho Chi Minh returns to Vietnam and forms the Vietnamese Independence League, commonly known as the Vietminh nationalist movement, to resist both the Japanese and the French.

1944 General Vo Nguyen Giap forms the Vietminh army in the north with military funding and arms from the U.S. Office of Strategic Services (OSS) to fight the allied Japanese and French.

1945 In March as a major Vietminh military offensive gets started, the Japanese take over by force the administration of Indochina from the French in response to growing French discontent with the Japanese presence. Backed by Tokyo, Emperor Bao Dai proclaims Vietnam an independent state under Japanese auspices. In August as Japan's war machine crumbles, the Vietminh takes over large portions of the country. During that month the Japanese also transfer control of Indochina to Vietminh forces under Ho Chi Minh and Vo Nguyen Giap. Bao Dai abdicates in an attempt to maintain some national unity. Ho proclaims the area north of the 18th parallel the Democratic Republic of Vietnam; south of the parallel is declared an associated state within the French union by the allies, with Bao Dai as supreme counselor. Japanese policies of planting industrial crops and requisitioning rice to feed the Japanese army as well as bad flooding combine to cause famine throughout the north, killing 2 million of the north's 10 million inhabitants.

The French-Indochina War and the Vietnam War

1946 In March the French and Vietminh reach a peace accord, determining that Vietnam will be a "free state" within the French Union. In June the French violate the agreement by proclaiming a separate government for Cochin China. In November, as tensions grow, the French navy bombs Haiphong. In December Vietminh forces withdraw from Hanoi after attacking the French garrison, retreating to build their movement in rural areas. The French-Indochina War begins. Bao Dai flees to France as hostilities increase.

1947 In France Bao Dai reaches an understanding with the French on recognizing limited Vietnamese independence.

1949 Bao Dai returns to Vietnam after three years of self-imposed exile in France to designate Vietnam as an "associated state" of France. France retains control of defense and finances but grants administrative authority to the Vietnamese.

1950 Ho declares that the Democratic Republic of Vietnam is the only legal government. The Democratic Republic of Vietnam is recognized by the Soviet Union and China. The United States and Britain join the French in recognizing Bao Dai's government as the legitimate one. The Chinese begin to supply weapons to the Vietminh. President Truman authorizes $15 million in military aid to the French in Indochina to fight the Vietminh.

1953 Laos and Cambodia gain greater independence from France. French forces occupy Dien Bien Phu. The Vietminh pushes into Laos. Ho says he is ready to discuss peace with the French.

1954 The Vietnamese defeat the French at Dien Bien Phu, which marks the end of the French-Indochina War. Eisenhower decides against American intervention on behalf of the French. Bao Dai selects Ngo Dinh Diem, who has strong ties to the American government, as prime minister. Agreement is reached among France, Britain, the United States, and the Soviet Union as part of the Geneva Accords to cease hostilities in Indochina and to divide Vietnam temporarily at the 17th parallel until national elections determine a single government. The country is divided into the Democratic Republic of Vietnam in the north and the Republic of Vietnam in the south. Seeing a threat to his power, Bao Dai denounces the agreement. As part of the agreement, French forces leave Hanoi. U.S. government affirms support of Prime Minister Diem with pledge of $100 million in aid. Hundreds of thousands of refugees, mostly Vietnamese Catholics worried that religious tolerance will not be practiced in the Vietminh-controlled north, flee to the south with U.S. Navy assistance.

1955 The United States begins to provide direct aid to the Saigon government and to train the South Vietnamese army. Diem rejects the Geneva Accords and refuses to participate in nationwide elections. He becomes president of South Vietnam and begins cracking down on suspected Vietminh members in the south. The Vietminh begins to show communist tendencies as it promotes social upheaval and radical land reforms in the north. During this period many landlords are required to go before "people's tribunals" designed to punish the wealthy classes of Vietnamese society.

1957 The Soviet Union proposes the permanent division of Vietnam at the 17th parallel. Southern-based Vietminh Nationalists and northern Communists strengthen ties in their opposition to the southern regime.

1959 As the Vietminh Nationalists from the south and the communists from the north continue to strengthen ties, Diem increases repression against suspected communists and dissidents in the south.

1960 The remaining southern Vietminh members changes the name of their movement to the National Liberation Front (NLF), known to the South Vietnam government and the Americans as and popularly called the Vietcong. (The term Vietcong is generally used throughout this book in reference to the opposition movement in the south because it is probably the most familiar term. However, Vietcong—which means, loosely, Vietnamese communists—was the name given by the Saigon government and the Americans to this opposition movement. The National Liberation Front (NLF) was the official name of the coalition of groups fighting the southern government.) As Diem's public popularity wanes, southern army officers stage an unsuccessful coup against him.

1961 Close advisers to President John F. Kennedy visit Vietnam and recommend American military intervention disguised as flood relief on behalf of the weak southern regime. Kennedy rejects the idea but provides military "advisers" and more equipment. Indirect American military support increases over the next few years.

1963 Thich Quang Duc, a Buddhist monk from Hue, is the first of many monks to commit suicide through self-immolation in Saigon, protesting Diem's repressive tactics. With American support, Saigon generals murder Diem. By this time American aid is up to approximately 15,000 military advisers and $500 million.

1964 American-backed general Nguyen Khanh seizes power in Saigon. Pentagon strategists refine plan to bomb North Vietnam, which is increasing support for the southern revolutionaries with equipment and personnel. An unconfirmed attack on U.S. destroyers in the Tonkin Gulf prompts passage of the Gulf of Tonkin resolution in Congress, permitting the Americans to respond by bombing North Vietnam for the first time. Years later it is determined that the incident may have been staged by the U.S. government.

1965 The first American combat troops arrive in Danang. Sustained bombing of North Vietnam by American planes begins. Nguyen Cao Ky takes over the weak Southern government. By the end of the year 200,000 American troops are in Vietnam.

1966 President Charles de Gaulle of France calls for U.S. withdrawal from Vietnam. The number of American troops reaches 400,000.

1967 Nguyen Van Thieu is elected president of South Vietnam, and Nguyen Cao Ky becomes vice-president. Americans begin to fortify Khe Sanh, a hamlet in the Central Highlands, in preparation for a major North Vietnamese assault. After heavy fighting at Khe Sanh, U.S. troops withdraw from the area, leaving the battle-scarred hillsides bare. Later the United States realizes that Khe Sanh was a ploy to divert U.S. forces from the Tet Offensive. By the year's end American forces number 500,000.

1968 During the Tet Offensive southern insurgents and northern forces orchestrate coordinated attacks on southern towns and cities. Although tactically a failure, the offensive proves that South Vietnam and U.S. strategists have seriously underestimated the strength of the NLF. American troops massacre South Vietnamese civilians in the village of My Lai. In part because of the Tet Offensive and My Lai, opposition to the war in Vietnam on the part of the American public and politicians increases. American forces number 540,000.

1969 Paris peace talks expand to include the Saigon government and NLF representatives. The U.S. government begins secret bombing of Cambodia to root out suspected NLF bases there. In response to growing domestic opposition and military frustrations, the American government says it will "Vietnamize" the war and begins withdrawing troops. Ho Chi Minh dies of natural causes in Hanoi.

1970 U.S. national security adviser Henry Kissinger begins secret talks with Le Duc Tho, the acting North Vietnamese foreign minister. President Richard Nixon announces that U.S. forces have attacked NLF sanctuaries in Cambodia, provoking a major upsurge of antiwar action in the United States. American troops in Vietnam number 280,000 at year's end.

1971 South Vietnamese forces enter Laos in an attempt to cut off the Ho Chi Minh Trail. This network of supply roads stretching from north to south Vietnam, a critical lifeline for the NLF, winds through the mountainous areas on the border between Vietnam, Laos, and Cambodia and is very difficult for Saigon troops to control. During the year the number of American troops is reduced to 140,000.

1972 President Nixon announces that Kissinger has been in secret negotiations with North Vietnam. Northern forces cross the 17th parallel. Americans resume the bombing of the north and mine Haiphong Harbor. Kissinger and Le Duc Tho make progress on a peace agreement, but South Vietnamese president Thieu resists a cease-fire.

1973 Kissinger and Tho sign a cease-fire agreement in Paris in January. The last American troops leave Vietnam in March. The United States halts the bombing of Cambodia.

1974 Thieu declares a continuation of war. The NLF further builds up supplies and troops in the south.

1975 North Vietnamese and NLF forces each capture key strategic towns. Thieu flees Vietnam for Taiwan before settling in Britain. The remaining Americans and their key Vietnamese colleagues in Saigon are evacuated to U.S. Navy ships in April. Images of the last overpacked U.S. helicopters lifting from the American embassy in Saigon are emblazoned in the public mind as the United States—after 30 years in Vietnam—makes a hasty retreat. Communist forces capture Saigon on April 30 and accept the surrender of the government of South Vietnam, thereby unifying the north and the south. The U.S. government does not recognize the legitimacy of a reunified Vietnam. The U.S.-led economic embargo on North Vietnam, in place since the '60s, is extended to the whole of reunified Vietnam. The Soviet Union increases support for the newly unified Vietnam.

The Postwar Years to the Present

1977 Talks begin between the United States and Vietnam about official recognition of Vietnam by the U.S. government. Due to the increasing links between Hanoi and Moscow, these talks eventually grind to a halt until the early '90s.

1978 Vietnam joins COMECON (the Soviet-influenced Eastern European economic community). Relations between Vietnam, Cambodia, and its Chinese benefactor deteriorate as skirmishes along the Vietnamese-Cambodian border increase. Hanoi signs a friendship pact with the Soviet Union. Following Khmer Rouge border incursions at Chau Doc and the growing China-Cambodia alliance, Vietnam responds and is involved in armed conflict with Cambodia until 1989, effectively ending the "killing fields," the brutal murder of more than a million Cambodians by the Pol Pot regime.

1979 In partial retaliation for Vietnam's conflict in Cambodia, China invades Vietnam but is quickly repulsed by the battle-hardened People's Army of Vietnam.

1986 Hanoi selects reform-minded Nguyen Van Linh as general secretary of the Communist Party of Vietnam, signaling a cautious opening to the West. This year is generally seen as the period in which Vietnam commits to *doi moi*, the reform of socialist economic policies into a more market-oriented system.

1989 Vietnamese forces withdraw from Cambodia, ending a 50-year period of almost continuous war between the two countries. General Secretary Linh reaffirms that although economic reforms are moving the country away from a traditional communist system, they are in no way an endorsement of pluralism and a multiparty system.

1991 Ailing general secretary Linh is replaced by Prime Minister Do Muoi, who vows to continue the economic reforms begun by Linh. The Politburo and the Central Committee of the Vietnamese Communist Party undergo a major shift; aging, conservative leaders are replaced by younger, more liberally oriented members. Prime Minister Vo Van Kiet and Do Muoi visit Beijing in an attempt to heal relations.

1994 The U.S. ends its economic embargo on Vietnam, which helps the country begin to rebuild its economy and infrastructure through International Monetary Fund (IMF) and World Bank loans and greatly increased foreign investments.

1997 The beginning of normalization of relations between Vietnam and the United States. The U.S. embassy officially opens in Hanoi, a U.S. consulate opens in Ho Chi Minh City, and the Vietnamese embassy officially opens in Washington.

1998 General Le Kha Phieu assumes the top position of the Vietnamese Communist Party from General Secretary Do Muoi. Neither a committed advocate of liberal reforms nor the conservative line, Secretary Phieu takes over the reins of power amidst a sense of uncertainty about the direction that Vietnam will continue to head.

— By Jim Spencer

RIDING THE DREAM

THE FIRST THING about Vietnam that struck me was how familiar it seemed. The second was how unique it was. The third thing that struck me was a Honda Dream motorbike—carrying a family of four through the chaos of midday traffic. Vietnam is a little surprising like that.

You, too, may find Vietnam oddly familiar, perhaps because you spent years glued to TV's images of U.S. helicopters skimming over rice paddies in the Mekong Delta, American soldiers creeping through the thick jungles of the central highlands, and Vietnamese refugees passing trucks bringing GIs to the front; or maybe because you saw Hollywood's version of these events in movies like *Apocalypse Now* and *Platoon*; or maybe you even went to Vietnam yourself. The images of a familiar past may come flooding back to you as you approach the airport in Hanoi over a landscape speckled with craters left by U.S. bombs, or touch down at the airport in Saigon where American-built tarmac and hangars are still in use.

The desire to come looking for remnants of the war is understandable, especially for those of us from countries whose histories are linked with Vietnam's. And as someone who grew up in New York with a Vietnamese mother educated in America and an American father, surrounded by Vietnamese culture, I had yet another reason for wanting to understand how and why the United States became involved with Vietnam. On my first trip to Vietnam in 1990, I went to discover all I could about what life was like during the Christmas bombing of Hanoi in 1972, and what it was like living in the Vinh Moc underground tunnels. I visited the rooftop bar at the Rex Hotel to see where wartime journalists gathered nightly to reflect on the day's events.

What I found were only a few visible remnants of the war and its aftermath: Soviet-style memorials and cemeteries; towns where famous battles were fought; airplanes, helicopters, and artifacts on display in museums; and underground tunnel systems like those at Cu Chi, which are now open to tourists. The bomb craters at the Hanoi airport have been made into fish ponds, and the hangars at Saigon's have become storage sheds.

I also discovered that although many people are willing to talk with foreigners about the war, they are more often interested in reviewing the finer points of the latest American music videos, price fluctuations of the Toyota Camry, or the semi-automatic clutch on their new Honda Dream motorbikes—the latest in Vietnamese conspicuous consumption—than they are in rehashing the Battle of Khe Sanh. Others are understandably reluctant to talk about this painful history.

Younger people especially have little time for reflections on what they increasingly see as grandpa's old war stories. After years of strife and isolation, they are ready for greater economic and cultural opportunities. The economic reforms instituted in 1986, *doi moi,* has been one of the major factors in bringing Vietnam out of isolation and onto a global stage where it once danced with the world's most powerful nations.

Until 1991 Vietnam was under the influence of the Soviet bloc and severely crippled by the U.S.-led economic embargo. As a result, the country has only been able to chart an independent course for a very short time. And for better or worse, the Vietnamese have decided that the road ahead lies with a free-market economy. As the country begins the journey toward becoming the next Southeast Asian "tiger"—a status that former Vietnamese foreign minister Nguyen Co Thach cautioned had to be preceded by becoming a "small cat"—Vietnam is at a critical point in its history. To comprehend why, you must first understand something about its history of conflict and synthesis.

As a crossroad of global trading, Vietnam has for over 2,000 years been an object of desire of the major European and Asian powers. From the early Chinese, Cham, and Khmer empires competing for a piece of what is currently Vietnam right up to the French, Americans, and Soviets vying for political and cultural influence, Vietnam has been a contested land. All who have come have left their mark on the country, resulting in a culture that is an amalgamation of many foreign elements yet one that is uniquely Vietnamese. There are markedly few places in the world where you can find Catholic church spires poking out of the tropical rain forest, indigenous hill tribe leaders speaking French and English, and farmers piling their Japanese and East German motorcycles high with Chinese-made dishes on their way home from the market.

It would be a mistake, however, to say that Vietnam has compromised its identity by assimilating elements of these invading cultures. This paradox is best summed up by the comments of an aging revolutionary who graciously welcomed me into his home when I first visited the country. Once a high-ranking member of the diplomatic team that negotiated the peace agreement with the Americans in 1973, he had been without question a thorn in the side of both the French and American governments. Strangely, though, on numerous occasions, while sipping French Cognac postdinner, he looked me in the eye and—in impeccable French—made sure I understood one thing: "*Je ne suis pas un Francophile, mais je suis vraiment un Francophone* (I am not a Francophile, but I am very much a Francophone)." Though he felt no lost love for his former colonizers, he did celebrate that he was himself a product of French culture. This kind of cultural adoption predates the French and has come to define a Vietnamese culture of adaptation.

The Conquering Chinese, and the Cham and Khmer Empires

From about 200 BC to 938 AD, Vietnam was subject to heavy Chinese influence, and consequently made a national pastime of kicking out invaders from the north. For a thousand years Hanoi and Beijing danced in a cycle of liberation and domination until the Chinese were finally kicked out for good in the early 10th century.

The Chinese invaders influenced every aspect of Vietnam, from agriculture to architecture to education to cuisine, particularly in the north. In the 3rd century BC, the Chinese began to promote intensive rice paddy farming in the Red River Delta, replacing nonintensive dryland crops. Over the centuries this system spread throughout the country and eventually came to symbolize the Vietnamese way of life. The Chinese also established an educational system in Vietnam modeled on the Chinese Mandarin system. The system was embraced by the Vietnamese and thrived in Vietnam long after the Chinese had abandoned it in their own country.

Other Chinese elements include temples replete with dragons, words in the Vietnamese language, and, more recently, a taste for monosodium glutamate, which rumor has it was imported during wartime from China to add flavor to spare diets. Mahayana Buddhism and Confucianism, too, came to Vietnam from the north, and you can readily see their influence in today's Vietnam. These influences, however, never overshadowed the most Vietnamese form of religious practice in the country: *ban tho,* the altar to family ancestors that graces almost every Vietnamese home from Saigon to Son La to San Jose.

The Chinese influence wasn't as strong in the south, where they had competition. Beginning around 100 AD, the Funan Kingdom ruled what is now southern Vietnam and the Kingdom of Champa controlled the central region. Both Indianized kingdoms have had a major impact on this part of Vietnam and contributed to some of the regional differences found there.

Although attempts have been made to claim only one history for Vietnam, many believe these regions have as much in common with Cambodia, Thailand, the Philippines, and Indonesia as they do with China. Many point to the stronger social and economic roles of women, a warmer disposition, and a less regimented way of life in the south and central regions as vestiges of this earlier period. Since the Cham and Khmer were not as meticulous at imposing and institutionalizing social norms, their influences have not survived as well as those imported from China. Instead, the Indianness of *Indo*-China is mostly felt in the old Cham towers that pepper the central coast with images of Vishnu and Shiva, the Khmer temples in the Mekong Delta, and names of places such as Sadec, Kontum, and Daklak, which harken back to non-Chinese origins.

The Paternalistic French

The Chinese, the Khmer, and the Cham were merely the first to come. Centuries later the French burst onto the scene with their French bread, espresso coffee, and "*mission civilisatrice*" (civilizing mission), in an effort to make the Vietnamese into little brown Frenchmen. As with the Chinese before them, the French had their own policies of domination and integration, and they saw Vietnam as fertile ground for the expansion of French culture.

For better or worse, the French administration took quite seriously the task of making Vietnam an economically productive Southeast Asian province of France. In doing so, the French extended the tentacles of their complicated and convoluted educational system into the tropics. Under this system, throughout the early part of the century elite young Vietnamese traveled to France and other French colonies, gaining exposure to Western ideas, culture, and people. In addition, the Vietnamese elite were educated at French lycées in Vietnam. Ironically, at the Marie Curie School in Saigon, for instance, young Vietnamese girls were taught Vietnamese as a foreign language. And though many were impressively knowledgeable about which French province produced the finest French wine, they were unable to say which Vietnamese province grew the best rice.

Both Ho Chi Minh, the Nationalist-turned-Communist revolutionary, and his monarchist-counterpart Bao Dai, the dilettante last emperor of Vietnam, spent many of their early years in France absorbing the culture that would later influence their politics. Perhaps because both ends of the political spectrum of this generation of leaders were educated under the French, elements of French culture have survived Vietnam's tumultuous past three decades: the mildewed colonial villas lining the boulevards of both Hanoi and Saigon, the beret gracefully sported by the occasional man over 50, the excellent French bread hawked on almost every street corner, and the cafés serving espressolike coffee.

The Americans Arrive

Although most people associate U.S. involvement in Vietnam from the time the first marines landed in Danang in 1965, the American government had been interested in Vietnam since the end of World War II. In 1945 the U.S. government sent agents from the Office of Strategic Services (OSS) to gather information in northern Vietnam on the transfer of power following the withdrawal of the Japanese from Southeast Asia. During the mission, code-named Deer, OSS agents went to live in Ho Chi Minh's camp in the northern highlands. Finding Ho on death's door, plagued by malaria and dysentery, the Americans treated him and probably saved his life.

The OSS officers were so impressed with Ho that they supplied him with arms and other materials, ultimately recommending that the United States back his nationalist forces against the French. Ho, in turn, also had respect for the Americans. This relationship, no doubt, prompted Ho to have OSS officers by his side when he signed the declaration of independence of the Democratic Republic of Vietnam in Hanoi's Ba Dinh Square on September 2, 1945.

For political reasons, however, Washington chose to back its long-standing allies, the French, instead of Ho. Rather than alienate Paris by siding with the Vietnamese Nationalists, President Truman supported President Charles de Gaulle's efforts to regain Vietnam. From 1945 to 1954 the U.S. government provided substantial military aid to the French and set the stage for a protracted American presence in Vietnam that would splatter across headlines for the next 20 years.

After the French were officially defeated in 1954, the U.S. government continued its anticommunist efforts by contributing military advisors who trained and sometimes fought alongside South Vietnamese troops. But it wasn't until 1965 that Uncle Sam's troops landed in Vietnam, bringing billions of dollars in military hardware; thousands of American GIs; and a robust dose of '60s culture. This time, however, the Americans were not there to support the Nationalist forces, but rather Ho Chi Minh's archrival Ngo Dinh Diem, president of a struggling southern regime based in Saigon.

Remnants of the American presence survive today in many forms, even if these don't always inspire the same nostalgic enthusiasm from the Vietnamese as do French bread and espresso. In the south, Zippo lighters still spark cigarettes among the elite, and GMC trucks form the basis of the Vietnamese trucking industry—though mostly only the engines are left; the bodies have long been rebuilt and repainted with "GMC," "Desoto," or "Ford." Even more apparent today is the inundation of contemporary American culture, especially in Saigon: for instance, videos of American movies and compact discs of American bands are sold in shops; and American-style bars and restaurants have replaced some of the less competitive noodle shops.

But there is yet another side to America's relationship with Vietnam: Throughout the war both Nationalist and Communist Vietnamese leaders always recognized that the United States comprised both a government and a people. To this day they often speak with great appreciation about the Americans who protested the war. Less controversial yet perhaps more telling is that during a 35-year-plus era of strained and nonexistent official relations, American and Vietnamese people-to-people organizations have had long, respectful relationships. These positive legacies of an American influence on Vietnam are what many Vietnamese appreciate and remember. Today, too, they are more than happy to put the past behind them and to begin a new relationship with America.

The Eastern-Bloc Years

After the last overloaded helicopter took off from the roof of the U.S. embassy in Saigon in 1975, another superpower stepped in: the Soviet Union. For the next 15 years Vietnam was overrun with Volgas—the boxy Russian-made cars—and thousands of Soviet advisers, engineers, and tourists.

This Soviet influx was part of a multibillion-dollar aid package to build up Vietnam's infrastructure and provide education for Vietnamese in Eastern-Bloc countries. However, in 1991, with the disintegration of the Soviet Union and the rest of the Eastern Bloc nearly complete, Soviet aid dried up, and the Vietnamese were left to rebuild their war-torn economy with no major benefactor. Despite this withdrawal and the financial vacuum it has left, Hanoi's leaders can be relieved that doi moi, their version of *perestroika,* has not led to the kind of social upheaval that the Soviets faced.

The Soviets have left Vietnam, and Vietnamese children have stopped shouting "Lien Xo" (the Vietnamese word for Soviet person)—as they did with me when I first visited in 1990—at any passing Westerner. Nevertheless the Eastern bloc has left a legacy of its own. Thousands of young Vietnamese—educated in everything from civil engineering to commercial baking in Moscow, Budapest, and Havana—speak Russian, Hungarian, and Spanish. Their expertise and international experience have been an important and undervalued tool for helping Vietnam rebuild its infrastructure, schools, and economy after 40 years of devastation. The most visible remnants of the Soviet contribution, however, are the dour, concrete-block apartment buildings in neighborhoods around Hanoi and Saigon. Although probably the least appreciated foreigners to visit Vietnam this century, the Soviets have also contributed to the current culture that is Vietnam.

The Vietnamese Melting Pot

With its history of invasions, perhaps it was inevitable that Vietnam would end up reflecting a melange of cultural influences. But by incorporating these foreign elements without compromising its identity, the country has created a culture that is uniquely Vietnamese.

An excellent way to get a sense of this melting pot is simply to explore the country. Walk through the streets of Hanoi and Saigon past the French colonial villas, American- and Russian-built monoliths (most notably the old U.S. embassy in Saigon), Chinese-style pagodas, and shiny, new, glass-fronted high-rise office buildings. Take a trip to Hue to see the old Imperial City, the former home of the Vietnamese emperors. Though it was modeled on the Forbidden City in Beijing, it is actually relatively new: it was built in the early 19th century by the French architect Olivier de Puymanel, who was influenced by that greater builder of French forts, Vauban. Go to Dalat and wander through Emperor Bao Dai's French colonial–style summer palace. The last emperor of Vietnam, Bao Dai (1914–97) had a reputation for dilettantism matched only by his love of French culture—an attitude reflected in this Dalat retreat.

The most distinctive example of Vietnam's cultural syncretism is to be found at the temple of the Caodai sect, in Tay Ninh

Province northwest of Saigon. The sect was founded in the Mekong Delta in the 1920s by Ngo Minh Chieu, a civil servant for the French, who claimed to receive revelations from God. Through the French, Chieu was exposed to a variety of Western philosophies. Caodaism was his attempt to create a universal religion based on the major Eastern and Western religions—a fusion of Buddhism, Confucianism, Taoism, Vietnamese spiritualism, Christianity, and Islam.

By the 1950s and '60s the sect had become so strong that it provided an alternative to both the National Liberation Front or the American-backed Saigon regime. As the Caodai strived to maintain its control over the western part of the Mekong Delta, it grew increasingly politically active and heavily armed. After the war, however, the Caodai took on a lower profile and declined in both numbers and firepower. Today the Caodai faithful are concentrated mainly at the home of their Holy See, the Tay Ninh, although temples can be found throughout the Mekong Delta and even in the United States and France.

Decorated in a wild array of colors, the massive structure has towering ceilings like those found in a cathedral. But the tile floors, no-shoes policy, and monks in white robes give it a distinctly pagodalike feel. The most telling sign of Caodai's syncretic nature, however, greets you in the bright, open, main room: a mural of the Caodai pantheon, which includes such diverse notables as Buddha, Jesus Christ, Muhammad, Sun Yat-sen, Victor Hugo, and others. The Caodai believe these leaders have all made great contributions to world culture, and that their religious, political, and literary traditions have all been unified in a religion that is neither contradictory nor faddish.

Another example of this melange of cultures is reflected in the Vietnamese language itself. A history of foreign influences is revealed: wherever you go, look at the signs. For example, many inscriptions on buildings are written in Chinese, as are many of Vietnam's oldest history books. Vietnamese began as a distinct language, with its own indigenous vocabulary and sentence structure but no widespread written form. With the coming of the Chinese and the Mandarin educational system, Chinese characters came to be the dominant written language. Throughout this period many Chinese words (known as *Han Viet,* or words derived from Chinese) were integrated into the Vietnamese language (known as *Nom Viet,* those words derived from indigenous Vietnamese roots).

In 1627 a French missionary named Alexandre de Rhodes adapted spoken Vietnamese to Roman script in order to facilitate the conversion of the Vietnamese to Catholicism. Rhodes's system took hold, so Vietnam, unlike most of its neighbors, uses a Roman-based alphabet. But don't be fooled: Although the language is recognizable to Westerners, spoken Vietnamese is based on a tonal system not easily reflected in the Roman script. Tones are denoted by accents placed above or below words and provide clues to pronunciation. Be careful: a recognizable script doesn't make learning to say words correctly any easier, however, and you still may end up insulting someone's mother.

Today the language continues to change; most recently there have been efforts to "Vietnamize" Vietnamese. But the difficulty in doing so is manifest in the tenacity of such words as *tam biet,* the Han Viet word for *chao* in Nom Viet (goodbye in English); and *banh ga-to,* the Vietnamese word for western-style cake, which is derived from the French word for cake, *gateau.* These words reflect the unique synthesis now a part of the Vietnamese language. In what other language can you read a Chinese word in a Franco-Roman script that is unlikely to be understood by someone from either country?

One word that is universally understood, however is *ca phe,* from the French word, café, or coffee. Unlike most other countries in Asia, good coffee is ever-present in Vietnam, served espresso-style in almost every café. A tradition adopted from the French, the café takes different forms in Vietnam—both the familiar French indoor-outdoor style and a Vietnamized version—tables on the sidewalk surrounded by small plastic stools.

Although Vietnamese coffee is reminiscent of the strong, dark brew found in Paris, its method of preparation is uniquely Vietnamese. Order a *ca phe den* (black coffee) and you'll get a filtration device perched on top of a small espresso cup. You must then patiently wait for the coffee to drip through the filter into your cup until you are left with a rich, dark brew. An even better choice is a *cafe sua,* the Vietnamese version of a cappuccino (though the iced version is more like a shake)—coffee mixed with sweet, condensed milk.

While you sip your coffee, watch people go by—elderly women heading to market weighted down by poles bearing baskets filled with fruit; old men on bicycles sporting green pith helmets, remnants of the North Vietnamese army uniform; and young women on motorbikes wearing T-shirts and jeans, long gloves, and conical hats or traditional *ao dais* (pronounced "ow yai" in the south and "ow zai" in the north), the elegant, straight-cut silk gowns worn over flowing pants.

A hybrid of the old and the new, this gown is the perfect emblem for Vietnamese culture. It is said that it was adapted from a Chinese dress called the *cheong sam,* which was modernized in the 1930s by two Vietnamese painters, Cat Tuong and Le Pho, who were influenced by French styles. Tailors took their paintings and produced this new style of gown. The gloves, too, are a Western influence: They came into style in the late 1950s after Madame Ngo Dinh Nhu, the sister-in-law of then President Diem, started wearing them.

It is this ability to synthesize what has been forced upon it that has made Vietnam so resilient. Now, after such a long history of conflict and hardship, the Vietnamese are welcoming the chance to chart their own course. This is why people fantasize about the future so readily, and why, finally, they are more excited about their Honda Dreams than they are about revisiting a painful history. Although only time will tell, there is little doubt that they will be able to adapt this time around as well.

—Jim Spencer

An amateur anthropologist and international development consultant, Jim Spencer has researched the consequences of Agent Orange in Vietnam, looked at the effects of environmental policy in the Mekong Delta, and worked with NGOs in Vietnam, Cambodia, and Laos. His preferred research methods include slurping a bowl of soup at a streetside noodle stand, enjoying a postsoccer-game beer with Vietnamese friends, and test driving Honda Dream motorbikes.

GETTING DOWN TO BUSINESS

IN THE MID-1980S Vietnam's government began opening the country to foreign investment to save it from bankruptcy. Twenty years before, following the fall of Saigon on April 30, 1975, the entire country was reorganized to follow Hanoi's ideological strictures requiring an economy based on Marxist-Leninist precepts. Some business and factory owners were imprisoned or sent off for political reeducation, their operations closed, their savings taken, and their enterprises nationalized. Overnight in the southern part of the country banks collapsed, and the capitalist system was abolished. The educated elite fled the country. To make matters worse, Cholon, the economic heart of Saigon with its huge entrepreneurial Chinese population, was effectively closed down; its population was later branded as fifth columnists and forced out to sea during the Vietnamese-Chinese border war of 1979.

By the mid-1980s Vietnam's economy was in dire straits. Following nearly a half century of war and later acute mismanagement, Vietnam could no longer even feed itself—despite being one of the world's rice bowls. In 1986 the government set about trying to rebuild the country by setting in motion free-market regulations and inviting foreign investment. The catch phrase *doi moi* (openness) was used to echo Gorbachev's *perestroika* movement in the former Soviet Union: it promised economic reforms without political compromise.

But by the early 1990s the Vietnamese watched nervously as their benefactors in Moscow were overthrown and their partners in the old Eastern Bloc were forced to grapple with pluralism and capitalism. Suddenly, besides its old enemy China and the self-reliant but failed and isolated economy of North Korea, Vietnam's only reliable Communist ally was distant Cuba.

Consequently, today's economic revival in Vietnam has come as a huge relief for the government, its economic woes overcome and political fears waylaid—for the moment at least. The results of more than 10 years of reforms are clearly visible on the streets of Hanoi and Ho Chi Minh City. More and more tall, glass-fronted office buildings and world-class hotels are opening each month. Honda Dream motorcycles, a symbol of the new affluence, cruise the streets. Although much of the countryside is still very poor, new wealth can be seen in the cities and along the highways where new homes are going up. Still, this transition from a closed to an open economy is not easy—witness contemporary Russia or China. It's unclear what Vietnam's prospects are in the longterm or what path it will continue to take as a new cadre of Vietnamese leaders take over both the government and the party and economic changes affect the region.

The Economy Today

Since the start of the reforms, Vietnam has attracted more than $25 billion in pledged foreign investment. Inflation for 1996 was at an all-time low of 5%, and in general individual incomes are rising throughout the country. Since 1990 the country has had an average annual GDP growth rate of 8%, while Ho Chi Minh City has grown by up to 15%—a runaway figure that has caused some alarm among local and foreign bankers. Nevertheless, foreign investors and international corporations are playing a pivotal role in Vietnam's jump from moribund, bankrupt state to emerging tiger economy.

However, economic strides still far outstrip political changes, a vexing problem for foreign businesspeople. The government's occasional lapses into hard-line socialist dogma and xenophobia, campaigns that baffle and dismay many foreign business leaders in the country, are a result of the recent disasters to hit Vietnam's former communist partners. Vietnam's Communists are nothing if not resilient, and whatever happens elsewhere, the party intends to hold the reins of power for some time to come.

Vietnam's per capita GDP is roughly estimated at $300 per year, a figure that woefully deceives foreign observers about the real picture of what is happening in the country. Today many of the country's private businesspeople cruise around in $100,000 Mercedes Benz limos, and a Honda Dream motorbike (Vietnam's equivalent of the family sedan) costs about $3,000. Even the Minsk, a rural, rough-road motorbike imported from Belarus, is $500—theoretically almost two years' wages. Yet most urban families own a Honda, and many rural families own a Minsk—and even young entrepreneurs are buying limos.

Privatization

The number of private businesses in Vietnam has increased every year since 1990. In the past the government's disdain for the "ill-gotten gains" of capitalism could land someone in prison for years. But these days everyone is at it, from tiny workshops dealing in scrap metal to phenomenally successful silk fashion shops netting thousands of dollars a week.

Furthermore, many Vietnamese often have more than one job and almost always underreport their income. There is an understandable deep-seated suspicion of banks and of revealing exactly how much you earn. Few Vietnamese flaunt their wealth, and cash is allowed to accumulate over the years, literally at home under the mattress, guarded by Granny. The overseas Vietnamese community, once reviled by the Communists as puppets of the United States, also now contributes up to $800 million a year to their families in Vietnam. Increasingly, these *Viet Kieu* (Vietnamese living overseas) are coming back, often armed with MBAs and thus bringing back expertise and know-how. The result has been a booming economy and a growing consumer class.

Like many other emerging markets cocooned by years of communist control, Vietnam's economy currently lies somewhere between open and state-controlled. The former is gradually displacing the latter—but not without turmoil at all levels of government and business. Vietnam's managers of state-owned enterprises (SOEs) are accustomed to their privileges and positions, but few have ever had any experience as company managers on the open market. Many acquired their positions for being loyal to the party.

In direct conflict with these managers are the owners of new private businesses. They see it as essential to privatize or dismantle completely many of the SOEs that have set productivity targets at a fraction of their potential. Until now the concept of competition was irrelevant; the enterprises were subsidized by the government. Even though Vietnam's gradual and methodical approach toward a market economy tends to inhibit entrepreneurs, this caution also helps maintain high GDP growth rates, relatively low inflation and unemployment, and a relatively stable local currency. The reduction of radical swings in the economy to date has enabled local companies and foreign-invested companies to begin getting down to business.

Vietnam, however, still has no stock market, although one has been promised for several years now. It is unlikely to happen until after 2000. Nevertheless, several large state companies have been listed for privatization (or "equitization," as the government calls it), which means the company will be turned into a corporation that can sell shares to investors, including foreign ones. But the question of stocks, shares, and a financial market is still some way off.

Consumption

In terms of trade and consumerism, Vietnam's economy has been booming like never before. The country's distribution companies, almost all privately owned, respond quickly to market demand, whether for French pharmaceuticals, Australian cheese, or American cosmetics. Many consumer items can be found in Ho Chi Minh City and Hanoi; ironically some can be found only in Vietnam—countries like Japan and South Korea use the country as a testing ground before trying to negotiate trade agreements with the West. In Ho Chi Minh City, for example, new mini-CD video equipment can be purchased for a steal long before it hits the streets of New York or London at three times the cost.

Vietnam is awash with information about consumer trends, generated by the many major international advertising agencies now operating in Ho Chi Minh City, the center of the consumer boom. Billboards are going up by the day and are now all along the banks of the Saigon River. Foreign ad agencies have brought in art directors and producers from outside Vietnam to cope with their clients' increasing demands for high-quality product exposure. Regardless of gripes by expatriate investment fund managers, real estate dealers, and financial speculators, Vietnam is clearly in the throes of a consumer boom.

Manufacturing

Vietnam's manufacturing industry is still in a terminally ill position, however. Consumers want more, but the country continues to fail to come up with locally produced goods for local consumption. The result is a colossal trade deficit. Although the trade ministry asserts that the many imports of machinery it has recently made will help boost manufacturing of exportable goods, huge deficits in Vietnam's balance of payments are inevitable until the end of the century.

Most goods will continue to be imported to meet demand. Although the government imposes high tariffs intended to keep out many imported products, the goods arrive in the country regardless, smuggled through the thousands of miles of sea and land border. Smuggling is and will remain the greatest problem for Vietnam for years to come, sucking away at its economic lifeblood and remaining a thorn in the side of foreign trading partners.

But there are local manufacturers that have been trying against all odds—and the odds have been considerable. For example, power-supply problems have dogged industry. During the past decade some of Vietnam's largest state companies could manufacture at only a fraction of their capacity because there was not enough power. Lack of credits to help keep businesses running and an insufficient supply of materials, especially with the dissolution of the Soviet Union and the Eastern Bloc, have only added to Vietnam's woes. In the mid-'80s there were still only nine international phone lines out of the country. Even in the early '90s many foreign investors were put off by the condition of infrastructure in the country.

Recently, however, Vietnam's power supply, especially electricity, has improved considerably. Power outages are still a nuisance, but they no longer cause the days or even weeks of disruptions that were so common just a few years ago. As for telecommunication problems, international telecommunications companies have tried to take up some of the slack. The rise, too, of industrial parks outside Hanoi and Ho Chi Minh City (in the Song Be and Dong Nai provinces) is going some of the way toward offering more reliable infrastructure and lower manufacturing costs to local and foreign businesses. Although the Ministry of Planning and Investment is still restricting the operations of 100% foreign-owned enterprises (FOEs), this is changing.

But local and foreign manufacturers still have much to do. Although the country is starting to establish an infrastructure, rules concerning the hiring of local people to replace expatriates and technology transfer policies require manufacturers to plan carefully in order to reap any substantial profits. Most businesspeople, local and foreign, expect the granting of Most Favored Nation (MFN) status to change the picture entirely. MFN would grant Vietnam's access to U.S. markets for most sectors of the country's manufacturing base and probably change the way Japan, Taiwan, South Korea, and Singapore do business with Vietnam.

Business Protocol

Other Asian countries have, in general, been most successful in Vietnam because they are familiar with practices there. They have also been willing to take risks—and have had the capital to do so.

One mistake many Western businesspeople have made is wanting to sit down quickly to sign a contract rather than spending time to get to know their potential partners. They have treated business relationships in Vietnam as merely that rather than as longterm relationships to be developed. But Vietnamese businesspeople want to know the background of an organization—and its people—with which they are dealing. They are wary of "cowboy investors" who quit after making a few bucks. If they think you are a cowboy, then all negotiations will fail at the first fence.

Many Vietnamese have very high standards of protocol, and they need to feel comfortable before taking on any serious business. This often means spending the first hour or so of any meeting discussing many subjects other than the one at hand.

Business cards are a way of life in Vietnam and are proffered on all occasions. After the initial pleasantries, offer the most senior person at the meeting your business card with both hands and a slight bow. Accept the host's name card with both hands as well, and be sure to have enough cards for everyone else present. Following this exchange, sit down and be prepared to drink several cups of tea and talk about personal matters like family, country, and impressions of Vietnam. Sometimes people even get more personal and ask how old you are and how many children you have. Don't be put off by these inquiries, they are just part of the process.

When using an interpreter, address the person with whom you are talking, not the interpreter. If you can, it is a good idea to take along your own interpreter. Many young English speakers working for state firms tend to overstate their language abilities, then fail to understand exactly what you are trying to say in meetings. The resulting misunderstandings can be embarrassing. Your own interpreter will already be familiar with your speech style and with your objectives before the meeting.

Many Vietnamese businesspeople still lack experience when it comes to dealing with the language of detailed corporate strategies and objectives. (Using charts and graphs in meetings helps to clarify matters.)

The situation is starting to change, however, particularly in Ho Chi Minh City, as more and more Vietnamese people in their twenties and thirties get MBAs at home and overseas. Many Vietnamese are now winning scholarships to top western universities like Oxford and Harvard, as well as to lesser-known business schools; until the late 1980s they would have received their college degrees from Marxist-Leninist institutes in Moscow and Dresden. Vietnamese universities have also begun several new MBA programs for private businesspeople and government officials.

In Vietnam change is often viewed with deep skepticism, especially among the older generation. This is where a young, dynamic local manager with an MBA can play a significant role. Keep in mind that it is important to show a sense of vision to your partner and your client and to emphasize that change is the only way to succeed regionally, nationally, and globally in Vietnam.

Understanding Vietnam's history and its numerous wars is also essential for doing business in the country (☞ Vietnam at a Glance: A Chronology, *above, and* Books and Videos, *below*). Many Vietnamese are extremely proud of their struggle for freedom against the Chinese and later the Mongols. For instance, mention of Emperor Tran Hung Dao's historic defeat of the Mongols during their 13th-century invasion will earn you great respect.

In addition, it helps to learn some basic Vietnamese. Like Chinese, Vietnamese is a tonal language, but unlike Chinese it is written in Roman script—making it easier to learn than Mandarin or Cantonese. To be able to speak conversational Vietnamese takes time and patience, but to be able to get by in the language on a daily basis usually takes only a matter of weeks. And it is worth learning. Few cyclo or *xe om* (motorbike taxi) drivers speak English, and most taxi drivers speak very little. Most people in markets and shops will bargain with you over prices, so it is a good idea to know some Vietnamese so you can get a better deal.

To do business in Vietnam today is a unique experience. It is to witness the renaissance of a proud and resilient Asian culture where week by week you can see the urban landscape changing. More high-rises spring up, while more cars gridlock the roads. It's also probably one of the few remaining places in Asia where you will see such a transformation from the old to the new, from international pariah to Asian tiger.

— Andrew Chilvers

BOOKS AND VIDEOS

Books

Of the numerous books written about Vietnam, most concern the Vietnam War and its aftermath. Some of the most comprehensive histories of the Vietnam War—already considered classics—are David Halberstam's *The Best and the Brightest*, Stanley Karnow's *Vietnam: A History*, Neil Sheehan's *A Bright Shining Lie*, and George C. Herring's *American's Longest War: The United States and Vietnam, 1950–1975*. Marilyn Young's *The Vietnam Wars: 1945–1990* and Frances Fitzgerald's *Fire in the Lake* provide histories of the war from both the American and Vietnamese perspectives. Other insightful accounts of the war include Jonathan Schell's *The Real War* and Michael Herr's *Dispatches*.

A number of moving personal narratives (some fictionalized) have been written about the war, including *A Rumour of War* by Philip Caputo, *In Pharoah's Army* by Tobias Wolff, *Nam* by Mark Baker, *Fields of Fire* by James Webb, *Chickenhawk* by Robert Mason, and *The Things They Carried* and *Going After Cacciato* by Tim O'Brien. For images of the war look for *Requiem*, a collection of war pictures by photographers who died while in Vietnam. A more recent account of the war is Robert McNamara's *In Retrospect: The Tragedy and Lessons of Vietnam*, in which he reexamines the war with 20-years' perspective.

Tom Mangold's *The Tunnels of Cu Chi* describes the Vietcong movement based in the tunnels around Cu Chi. *PAVN: People's Army of Vietnam* by Pike Douglas is a history of the war from the North Vietnamese point of view. Michael Lanning's *Inside the VC and the NVA* is a look at the workings of the North Vietnamese army and the Vietcong. *When Heaven and Earth Changed Places* is Le Ly Haslip's story of her life before, during, and after the Vietnam War; it was the basis for Oliver Stone's film *Heaven & Earth*. Truong Nhu Tan's *A Vietcong Memoir* is a narrative of the war as told by a former member of the Vietnamese National Liberation Front.

For a history of the French role in Vietnam read Bernard Fall's *Street Without Joy* and Roy Jules' *The Battle of Dienbienphu*. Graham Green's literary classic *The Quiet American* is a prophetic tale of America's involvement in Vietnam. *The Lover*, by Marguerite Duras, is a fictionalized autobiographical tale of a French girl coming of age in 1930s Indochina.

To learn more about contemporary Vietnam read Henry Kamm's *Dragon Ascending: Vietnam and the Vietnamese* and Neil Sheehan's *After the War Was Over: Hanoi and Saigon*, in which the author discusses his impressions today of the place that he covered during the Vietnam War. Look for an account of traveling through Vietnam by train in Paul Theroux's *The Great Railway Bazaar*. For a sense of Vietnam in pictures before you go, take a look at the stunning *Passage to Vietnam: Through the Eyes of Seventy Photographers*; there is also a CD-ROM version.

Two literary anthologies that address postwar Vietnam are *The Other Side of Heaven: Postwar Fiction by Vietnamese and American Writers*, which includes short stories by Tim O'Brien, Philip Caputo, and John Edgar Wideman; and *Aftermath: An Anthology of Post-Vietnam Fiction*. Robert Olen Butler's *A Good Scent from a Strange Mountain* is a collection of short stories about Vietnamese living in America.

Videos

Countless films have been made about the Vietnam War. *Apocalypse Now* is Francis Ford Coppola's powerful look at the Vietnam War based on Joseph Conrad's *Heart of Darkness*; it stars Martin Sheen, Marlon Brando, and Dennis Hopper. Oliver Stone's *Platoon*, with Charlie Sheen, Willem Dafoe, and Tom Berenger, is a harrowing, first-person tale of a young soldier's experience in the war. Stone's *Born on the Fourth of July* is the stirring story of Ron Kovic, played by Tom Cruise, a gungho solider who is paralyzed during the war and becomes an antiwar activist. Brian de Palma's *Casualties of War* focuses on two soldiers in the same platoon, Michael J. Fox and Sean Penn, who battle over moral issues. *The Deer Hunter* is a Michael Cimino film about three steelworkers from Pennsylvania who go off to fight in Vietnam, starring Robert de Niro, Christopher Walken, and Meryl Streep. Stanley Kubrick's *Full Metal Jacket* is an unblinking look at the realities of the Vietnam War through the perspective of a U.S. army journalist. *The Green Berets* is a cliched but classic movie with John Wayne as a Green Beret. *Hamburger Hill,* a John Irvin film, follows a group of infantrymen from training to combat.

Barry Levinson's *Good Morning, Vietnam* is a more humorous look at the Vietnam-War era, with Robin Williams as a U.S. Army Radio DJ. *Heaven & Earth,* another Oliver Stone film about Vietnam, portrays the odyssey of a young Vietnamese woman, Le Lyn, from 1953 through the war and after in America. Eric Weston's *The Iron Triangle,* starring Beau Bridges, attempts to show the conflict from both the Vietnamese and American sides. For an inside look at the making of *Apocalypse Now,* see the documentary *Hearts of Darkness: A Filmmaker's Apocalypse.* Abill Couturie, in his documentary about the Vietnam War, *Dear America: Letters Home From Vietnam,* uses newsreels, amateur footage, and letters read by Robert de Niro, Sean Penn, and others to portray soliders' experiences. The *War at Home* is a documentary about the anti-war movement, focusing on activity in Madison, Wisconsin.

A number of films address the experience of Vietnam veterans after the war. Martin Scorsese's disturbing *Taxi Driver* stars Robert De Niro as Travis Bickle, an alienated Vietnam veteran who is a New York City taxi driver. *Birdy* is a film by Alan Parker, with Nicholas Cage and Matthew Modine as a Vietnam veteran suffering post-traumatic stress disorder who believes he is a bird. In Hal Ashby's *Coming Home,* Jane Fonda is a career soldier's wife who falls in love with a wheelchair-bound veteran played by John Voight. *First Blood,* directed by Ted Kotcheff, is an action thriller starring Sylvester Stallone as Vietnam veteran John Rambo.

The Quiet American is Joseph L. Mankiewicz's cinematic portrayal of Graham Greene's classic. *The Lover,* a Jean-Jacques Annaud film based on the Marguerite Duras book, is the tale of a young French woman coming of age in colonial Vietnam and her relationship with her Vietnamese lover. Régis Wargnier's *Indochine,* starring Catherine Deneuve, is another film set in Vietnam during the French colonial era; some of it was filmed in beautiful Halong Bay. Contemporary Vietnamese filmmaker Tran Anh Hung's *The Scent of Green Papaya* follows the life of a young serving girl who comes to work for an upper-class Saigon family. For a gritty look at present day Ho Chi Minh City, see Tran Anh Hung's *Cyclo.*

VIETNAMESE VOCABULARY

In the mid-17th century, the Vietnamese language, which had been based on Chinese characters, was Romanized by the French Jesuit, Alexandre de Rhodes. This change made the tonal language easier for Westerners to read, but not much easier to pronounce. Vietnamese has six tones, which can significantly change the meaning of a word spelled the same way. Within a certain context, however, Vietnamese people will understand what you are trying to say even if you get the tones wrong. A bit of body language also helps get your point across.

Keep in mind that vocabulary and pronunciation varies from region to region. For example, a spoon in northern Vietnam is a *thìa* but it is a *muỗng* in the south. The soft "d" and soft "gi" are pronouced like a "z" in the north but change to "y" in the south.

Also remember that there is an "honorific" system of address, so what you call someone depends on their relation to you. There are many specific titles of address but the five listed below are all you need in a pinch. Use *ông* for an older man, *anh* for a younger man, and *em* for a boy. Use *bà* for an older woman, *cô* for a younger woman, and *em* for a girl.

Words and Phrases

	English	Vietnamese	Pronunciation
Basics			
	I	Tôi	doy
	We	Chúng tôi	choong doy
	Yes/No	Có/Không	caw/kawm
	Please	Làm ơn	lamb un
	Thank you	Cám ơn	cam un
	That's all right	Không có chi	kawm caw chee
	Excuse me, sorry	Xin lỗi	seen loy
	Hello	Xin chào	seen chow
	Goodbye	Tạm biệt	tom be-it
	Mr. (older man)	Ông	awm
	Mrs. (older woman)	Bà	bah
	Miss (younger woman)	Cô	co (like co-op)
	Mr. (young man)	Anh	ine / un(s)
	Young person	Em	em
	Pleased to meet you	Hân hạnh được gặp (ông)	haan hine dook gup (title)
	How are you?	(Ông) có khoẻ không?	(ông) caw Kway kawm?
	Very well, thanks	Khoẻ, cám ơn	kway, cam un
	And you?	Còn (ông)?	cawn (ông)?
Numbers			
	one	một	moat
	two	hai	hi
	three	ba	bah
	four	bốn	bown

five	năm	num
six	sáu	sow (like cow)
seven	bảy	by
eight	tám	tom
nine	chín	chin
ten	mười	moy
eleven	mười một	moy moat
twelve	mười hai	moy hi
thirteen	mười ba	moy bah
fourteen	mười bốn	moy bown
fifteen	mười năm	moy num
sixteen	mười sáu	moy sow
seventeen	mười bảy	muoi by
eighteen	mười tám	moy tom
nineteen	mười chín	moy chin
twenty	hai mươi	hi moy
twenty-one	hai mốt	hi moat
thirty	ba mươi	bah moy
forty	bốn mươi	bown moy
fifty	năm mươi	num moy
sixty	sáu mươi	sow moy
seventy	bảy mươi	by moy
eighty	tám mươi	tom moy
ninety	chín mươi	chin moy
one hundred	một trăm	moat chum
one thousand	một nghìn (n)	moat nyin
	một ngàn (s)	moat nyan
one million	một triệu	moat chew

Colors

black	đen	den
blue	xanh	sine
brown	nâu	no
green	xanh lá cây	sine la kay
orange	cam	cahm
pink	hồng	hawm
purple	tím	teem
red	đỏ	daw
white	trắng	chaang
yellow	vàng	vang

Days of the Week

Sunday	chủ nhật	chu nyat
Monday	thứ hai	two hi
Tuesday	thứ ba	two ba
Wednesday	thứ tư	two tu
Thursday	thứ năm	two num
Friday	thứ sáu	two sow
Saturday	thứ bảy	two by

Months

January	tháng một	tang moat
February	tháng hai	tang hi
March	tháng ba	tang ba

April	tháng tư	tang tu
May	tháng năm	tang num
June	tháng sáu	tang sow
July	tháng bảy	tang by
August	tháng tám	tang tom
September	tháng chín	tang chin
October	tháng mười	tang moy
November	tháng mười một	tang moy moat
December	tháng mười hai	tang moy hi

Useful Phrases

Do you speak English?	(Ông) có nói tiếng Anh không?	(ông) caw noy ting ine kawm?
I don't speak Vietnamese	Tôi không biết nói tiếng Việt	doy kawm byet noy teng Viet
I don't understand	Tôi không hiểu	doy kawm hue
I understand	Tôi hiểu	doy hue
I don't know	Tôi không biết	doy kawm byet
I'm American/British	Tôi là người Mỹ/Anh	doy la noy mee/ine
What's your name?	Tên (ông) là gì	ten (ong) la zee (southern=yee)
My name is . . .	Tôi tên là . . .	doy ten la . . .
How old are you?	(Ông) bao nhiêu tuổi	bow nyoo toy
What time is it?	Mấy giờ rồi?	may zuh zoy (n) may yuh roy (s)
How?	Bằng cách nào?	bong cack now?
When?	Bao giờ?	bow zuh? (n) bow yuh? (s)
Yesterday	Hôm qua	home kwa
Today	Hôm nay	home ny (like hi)
Tomorrow	Ngày mai	ny my
This morning/	Sáng nay/	sang nye
afternoon	trưa nay	chewa nye
Tonight	Đêm nay/tối nay	dem nye/doy nye
Why?	Tại sao?	tie sow (like cow)
Who?	Ai?	eye
Where?	Ở đâu	uh doe
Where is	. . . ở đâu?	uh doe
Train station	Ga tàu Ga xe lửa	gah tow (n) gah say luh-ah (s)
Bus station	Bến xe	ben say
Bus stop	Trạm xe buýt	chum say boot
Airport	Sân bay	sun bye
Post office	Bưu điện	boo dien
Bank	Ngân hàng	nun hang
Hotel	Khách sạn	kack san
Temple	Chùa	chew-a
Restaurant	Nhà hàng	nya hang

Store	Cửa hàng	kua hang
Market	Chợ	chuh
Museum	Bảo tàng	bow taang
Art museum	Bảo tàng mỹ thuật	bow taang me twut
Gallery	Phòng tranh	fowm chine
Theater	Nhà hát	nya hat
Movie theater	Rạp cine	zap see-nay
Beach	Bãi biển	bye be-in
Lake	Hồ	hoe
Park	Công viên	cowm vee-in
Street	Phố (n)/Đường (s)	foe/dooahng
Hospital	Bệnh viện	ben vee-in
Telephone	Điện thoại	dee-in twai
Restroom	Nhà vệ sinh/toilette	nya vay sing
Here/there	ở đây/đằng kia	uh day/dang kee-uh
Left/right	trái/phải	chy/fye (as in 'bye')
Is it far?	Có xa không	caw sah kowm
Go	Đi	dee
Stop	Dừng lại	zoong lie
Slow	Chậm chậm	chum chum
Straight ahead	Thẳng	tang
I'd like . . . a room the key a newspaper magazine a stamp	Tôi muốn . . . một phòng chìa khóa tờ báo tạp chí con tem	doy mun . . . moat fong cheah kwa tuh bow tup chee cawn tem
I'd like to buy . . . cigarettes matches dictionary soap city map envelopes writing paper postcard	Tôi muốn mua . . . thuốc lá diêm (n) bật lửa (s) từ điển xà phòng/xà bông (s) bản đồ thành phố phong bì giấy viết thơ bưu thiếp	doy mun moo-a . . . twook la zee-im but luh-ah tuh dien sa fong/sa bowm ban doe tine foe fawm bee zay vee-it tuh yay vit tuh (s) boo tip
How much is it? Expensive/cheap A little/lot More/less Too much/enough Too expensive	Bao nhiêu? Đắt/rẻ ít/nhiều Nhiều hơn/ít hơn Nhiều quá/đủ rồi Đắt quá	bow nyew dut/zay /ray (s) eat/nyew nyew huhn/eat huhn nyew kwa/ doo zoy doo roy (s) dut kwa
Change money	Đổi tiền	doy tee-in
I am ill	Tôi bị ốm	doy be awm

Call a doctor	Gọi bác sỹ	goy back see
Help!	Cứu tôi!	ku doy
Stop!	Dừng lại!	zoong lie
Fire!	Cháy nhà!	chay nyah
Caution!/look out!	Coi chừng!	coy chung

Dining Out

A bottle of	Chai	chye
A glass of	Cốc (n)/Ly (s)	cup/lee
Bill/Check please	Tính tiền	ting tee-in
Bowl	Bát (n)/Tô (s)	baht/toe
Bread	Bánh mỳ	bine mee
Breakfast	Ăn sáng	ahn sang
Butter	Bơ	buh
Chopsticks	Đũa	doo-a
Delicious	Ngon	nawn
Dinner	Bữa tối	booa doy
Eat	Ăn cơm	ahn come
Fork	Dĩa	zee-a
Hot/cold	Nóng/lạnh	nawm/line
thirsty	Khát nước	cat nooc
Fish sauce	Nước mắm	nooc mum
Knife	Dao	zow
Lunch	Ăn trưa	ahn chewa
Menu	Thực đơn	took duhn
Napkin	Giấy ăn	zay ahn/yay ahn (s)
Pepper	Tiêu	tyew
Plate	Đĩa	dee-a
Please give me . . .	Cho xin . . .	chaw seen . . .
Rice	Cơm	come
Salt	Muối	moo-ee
Shrimp paste	Mắm tôm	mum tome
Spicy	Cay	kai (as in eye)
Too spicy!	Cay quá	kai (as in eye) kwa
Spoon	Thìa (n)/Muỗng (s)	tee-ah/moong
Sugar	Đường	dooahng
Sweet	Ngọt	naught
Bon appetit	Chúc ăn ngon	chook ahn nawn
Bottoms up!	Trăm phần trăm	chum fun chum
I am a vegetarian	Tôi ăn chay	doy ahn chai (as in eye)
I am hungry	Tôi đói	doy doy
I cannot eat . . .	Tôi không biết ăn . . .	doy cawn bee-it ahn . . .
To your health	Chúc sức khoẻ	chook soo kway

MENU GUIDE

Vietnamese	English

Soups

Vietnamese	English
Canh	Soup, broth
Canh chua	Sour soup
Bún	Round rice noodles
Bún Riêu	Freshwater crab soup
Cháo	Congee, or rice porridge
Cháo cá	Congee with fish
Phở	Flat rice noodle soup
Phở bò	Beef noodle soup
Phở gà	Chicken noodle soup
Phở xào	Fried rice noodles
Miến	Vermicelli
Miến lươn	Vermicelli eel soup
Miến gà	Vermicelli chicken soup
Mỳ ăn liền	Instant noodles

Salads/Các loại gỏi

Vietnamese	English
Gỏi đu đủ xanh	Green papaya salad
Gỏi ngó sen	Lotus stem salad
Nộm hoa chuối	Banana flower salad

Fish and Seafood/Đồ biển

Vietnamese	English
Cá	Fish
Cá chép	Carp
Cá thu	Cod
Cá trê	Catfish
Cua	Crab
Ếch	Frog
Lươn	Eel
Mực	Squid
Tôm	Shrimp
Tôm hùm	Lobster

Meat/Thịt

Vietnamese	English
Bít tết	Beefsteak
Bò	Beef
Chả	Grilled meat patties
Chó	Dog
Dê	Goat
Giò	Processed meat roll
Heo(s)	Pork
Lợn (n)	Pork
Ốc	Snail
Rắn	Snake
Sóc	Squirrel
Sườn	Pork ribs

Poultry/Chim

Vietnamese	English
Chim cút	Quail
Gà	Chicken
Trứng	Egg

ốp-la/rán	Fried
ốp lếp	Omelet
luộc	Boiled
Vịt	Duck

Vegetables/Các loại rau

Bắp cải	Cabbage
Cà chua	Tomato
Cà pháo	Baby eggplant
Cà tím	Eggplant
Đậu đũa	Stringbean
Đậu phụ (n) Tàu hũ (s)	Tofu
Giá	Bean sprouts
Gừng	Ginger
Hành	Onion
Khoai	Potato
Lạc	Peanuts
Măng	Bamboo shoots
Nấm	Mushroom
Ớt	Chili pepper
Rau cải	Mustard greens
Rau dền	Amaranth
Rau muống	Water convolvulus
Su hào	Kohlrabi
Súp lơ	Cauliflower
Tỏi	Garlic
Xả	Lemongrass

Methods of preparation

Chiên	Fried
Hấp	Steamed
Kho	Braised, with caramelized sauce
Kho tộ	Claypot
Lẩu	Steamboat
Luộc	Boiled
Nhúng dấm	Dipped in hot vinegar
Nướng	Grilled
Quay	Roasted
Rút xương	Filleted
Sống	Raw
Xào	Sauteed
Xốt	Sauce

For example: Gà xào nấm = chicken sauteed with mushrooms
Cá hấp bia = fish steamed with beer
Đậu phụ xốt cà chua = tofu with tomato sauce

Fruit/Hoa Quả

Cam	Orange
Chanh	Lemon
Chôm chôm	Rambutan
Chuối	Banana
Đu Đủ	Papaya
Dưa hấu	Watermelon
Dừa	Coconut

Dứa	Pineapple
Khế	Starfruit
Măng cụt	Mangosteen
Mít	Jackfruit
Na	Custard apple
Nhãn	Longan
Sầu riêng	Durian
Táo	Apple
Thanh Long	Dragon Fruit
Vải	Lychee
Vú Sữa	Milkfruit
Xoài	Mango

Miscellaneous delicacies

Bánh chưng (n)/Bánh tết (s)	Stuffed sticky rice cake
Bánh cuốn	Rice noodle crepe
Bánh xèo	Meat & shrimp crepe
Gỏi cuốn	Summer rolls
Nem (n)/Chả giò (s)	Spring rolls
Xôi	Sticky rice

Drinks/Đồ uống

Bia	Beer
Có đá	With ice
Không đá	Without ice
Nước cam	Orange juice
Nước chanh	Lemonade
Nước dừa	Coconut milk
Nước khoáng	Mineral Water
Nước	Water
Rượu Vang	Wine
Rượu	Alcohol
Sinh tố	Smoothie
Sô-đa chanh	Soda-water lemonade
Sô-đa	Soda
Sữa tươi	Fresh milk
Chè/Trà (s)	Tea
Trà đá	Iced tea
Cà phê	Coffee
Cà phê đen	Black coffee
Cà phê sữa	Coffee with sweetened milk
Cà phê đá	Iced coffee

Dessert/Tráng Miêng

Bánh flan/kem caramen	Flan
Bánh ngọt	Sweet cakes
Chè đậu đen	Black-bean compote
Chè đậu xanh	Green-bean compote
Chè thập cẩm	Assorted compote
Kem	Ice cream
Kẹo	Candy
Sữa chua	Yogurt

INDEX

✕ = *restaurant*, 🏨 = *hotel*

A

A Dong Hotel 1 🏨, *133*
A Dong 2 Hotel 🏨, *133*
Adventure trips, *xl*
Air travel. ☞ Plane travel
Al Fresco ✕, *46*
Ambassador's Pagoda, *28*
Am Phu ✕, *131*
Ana Mandara Nha Trang Resort 🏨, *157*
Angkor Village 🏨, *214*
Angkor Wat Complex, *213–214*
Anh Dao Hotel 🏨, *166*
Antique shops, *204–205*
Arc En Ciel Hotel 🏨, *197*
Architecture, *5–7, 121*
Army Museum, *34–35*
Art, *7*
Artex Saigon Orchid Farm, *202*
Art galleries and museums
Dalat, 164
Hanoi, 16–17, 35
Ho Chi Minh City, 172, 182–183
Art Museum (Ho Chi Minh City), *182–183*
Art shops
Hanoi, 64–65
Ho Chi Minh City, 205
Asian Hotel 🏨, *196*
Assembly Hall of the Cantonese Chinese Congregation, *144*
Assembly Hall of the Fujian Chinese Congregation, *144*
Assembly Hall of the Hainan Chinese Congregation, *144*
'A' The Russian Restaurant ✕, *190*
ATMs (automated teller machines), *xxxii*
Auberge Hotel 🏨, *115*
Augustin ✕, *187*
Au Lac Café ✕, *43*

B

Ba Be Guest House ✕, *107*
Ba Be Hotel 🏨, *107*
Ba Be Lakes, *107*
Bac Ha, *116*
Back Beach, *210*
Bai Dau, *210*
Banana Split ✕, *157*
Banh Khoai ✕, *132*
Bao Dai's Summer Palace, *161, 164*
Bao Dai Villas 🏨, *157*
Bao Tang Cach Mang (Hanoi), *30*
Bao Tang Cach Mang (Ho Chi Minh City), *180*
Bao Tang Ho Chi Minh, *36, 38*
Bao Tang Lich Su, *29–30*
Bao Tang My Thuat (Hanoi), *35*
Bao Tang My Thuat (Ho Chi Minh City), *182–183*
Bao Tang Quan Doi, *34–35*
Bao Tang Thanh Pho Hai Phong, *92*
Bao Tang Ton Duc Thang, *183*
Bars and pubs
Haiphong, 95
Hanoi, 56–57
Ho Chi Minh City, 199–200, 201
Basketball, *61*
Bat Pagoda, *233–234*
Ba Vi Mountain, *68*
Beaches, *7*
China Beach, 141, 142
Ho Coc, 211
Long Hai, 210–211
Nha Trang, 152, 156
Phan Tiet, 211–212
Tra Co, 101
Vung Tau, 210
Ben Thanh Market, *178*
Bicycling, *xvi*
Haiphong, 95
Hanoi, 61, 75
Ho Chi Minh City, 216
Hoi An, 149
Hue, 135
Nha Trang, 159
rules of the road, xxv
tours, xl
Biet Dien Quoc Truong, *161, 164*
Binh Chau Hotel 🏨, *211*
Binh Chau Hot Springs, *211*
Binh Minh (Hue) 🏨, *133*
Binh Minh Hotel (Mong Cai) 🏨, *101*
Binh Tay Market, *186*
Binh Thuan, *229–230*
Blue Ginger ✕, *191*
Boat travel, *xvi*
Halong Bay, 97–98
Hanoi, 61
Ho Chi Minh City, 216
Hoi An, 149
Hue, 135
Mekong Delta, 236
Nha Trang, 156, 159
Northern Vietnam, 104
Bodhi Tree II ✕, *191*
Bong, *72*
Books on Vietnam, *257*
Bookstores. ☞ English-language bookstores
Border crossings, *xvi*
Botanical Garden (Hanoi), *35*
Bowling, *202*
Buffalo Fighting Festival, *13, 96*
Bun Bo Hue ✕, *132*
Business hours, *xvii–xviii*
Business travel, *xvii, 253–256*
Bus travel, *xvi–xvii*
Dalat, 167
Hanoi, 73
Ho Chi Minh City, 214–215, 216–217
Hue, 135
Nha Trang, 159
Northern Vietnam, 103
Buu Dien Truing Tam, *178*

C

Café des Amis ✕, *147*
Café Moca ✕, *31*
Café Mogambo ✕, *190*
Café 252 ✕, *43*
Ca Mau, *234–235*
Ca Mau Hotel 🏨, *235*
Cambodia, *213–214*
Cameras and camcorders, *xviii*
Cam Ly Falls, *164*
Cam Minihotel 🏨, *197*
Can Gio, *209–210*
Can Tho, *228–229, 237*
Can Tho Hotel 🏨, *229*
Caodai Holy See, *208–209*
Car rentals, *xviii–xix*
Car travel, *xxiv–xxv*
Dalat, 167
Danang, 142
Hanoi, 73–74, 75
Ho Chi Minh City, 215, 217
Hoi An, 149
Hue, 135
Mekong Delta, 236
Nha Trang, 159
Northern Vietnam, 103–104, 108, 116–118
Casa Italia ✕, *156*
Casinos, *95–96*
Cat Ba Island, *99–100, 104*
Cau May Hotel 🏨, *115*
Cau Nhat, *145–146*
Caves
Hoa Lu, 70
Lang Son, 102
Marble Mountains, 140
Son La, 110
Cemeteries
Dien Bien Phu, 112
Lang Son, 102
Central coast, *4, 121.* ☞ Danang; Hoi An; Hue
art and architecture, 121
dining, 122
itineraries, 122–123
lodging, 122
outdoor activities, 122
when to tour, 123
Central highlands, *160–161*
Central Market (Dalat), *161*
Central Market (Hoi An), *145*

Central Market (Hue), *127*
Central Post Office (Ho Chi Minh City), *178*
Century Riverside Hotel Restaurant ✕, *131*
Century Riverside Inn 🏨, *132*
Cha Ca La Vong ✕, *47*
Chains First Eden Hotel 🏨, *51*
Chambers of commerce, *xvii*
Cham Museum, *139–140*
Chan Vu Quan, *41*
Chao Thai ✕, *191*
Chaozhou Assembly Hall, *145*
Chau Doc, *231–232*
Chau Doc Hotel 🏨, *232*
Chau Giang Mosque, *231*
Chie Japanese Restaurant ✕, *93*
Children and travel, *xix*
Haiphong, 91
Hanoi, 35, 58, 60
Ho Chi Minh City, 178, 182, 202
My Tho, 227–228
Children's Park, *91*
China Beach, *141, 142*
China Beach Resort 🏨, *141*
China Bowl Pagoda, *234*
Chinese All-Community Assembly Hall, *145*
Chinese congregation halls, *144, 145, 146*
Cho Ben Thanh, *178*
Cho Binh Tay, *186*
Cholon Mosque, *186*
Chua Ba (Ho Chi Minh City), *187*
Chua Ba (Hoi An), *145*
Chua Ba Chua, *187*
Chua Ba Mariamman, *179*
Chua Hang, *92*
Chua Mot Cot, *39*
Chua Ngoc Hoang, *183*
Chua Ong Bon, *186*
Chua Quan Su, *28*
Chua Quan Thanh, *41*
Chua Tao Thien Vuong, *165*
Chua Tran Quoc, *41–42*
Chua Ve, *93*
Chuc Thanh Pagoda, *147*
Chu Linh Phong Pagoda, *165*
Churches
Haiphong, 92
Hanoi, 30–31
Ho Chi Minh City, 180
Long Xuyen, 230
Phat Diem, 71
Soc Trang, 233
Cinemas, *58–59*
Circus, *58*
Citadels
Co Loa, 67–68
Hue, 125–127
City Theater, *92*
Clay Pagoda, *233*
Climate, *xliii–xliv*
Clothing shops
Hanoi, 65
Ho Chi Minh City, 205
Club Garden ✕, *131*
Club Opera ✕, *43*
Coca Cola Restaurant ✕, *100*
Co Co Beach 🏨, *212*
Co Loa Citadel, *67–68*
Computers, *xviii*
Con Dao Guest House 🏨, *213*
Con Dao Island, *212–213*
Cong Fu Restaurant ✕, *116*
Cong Vien Thieu Nhi, *91*
Cong Vien Van Hoa Park, *178*
Consolidators, *xiv*
Consulates. ☞ Embassies and consulates
Consumer protection, *xx*
Cot Co, *127*
Cot V3 tower, *110*
Coupon books, *xxiii*
Credit cards, *xx, xxiii–xxiv, xxxii*
Crémaillère Railway, *164–165*
Crime concerns, *xxxv*
Cu Chi Tunnels, *206, 208*
Cuc Phuong National Park, *71–72*
Cu Dai Hoi An Hotel 🏨, *148*
Cung Chu Tich, *39*
Cung Van Hoa Viet-Xo, *31*
Currency, *xxxi*
Customs, *xx–xxi*
Cuu Dinh O The-Mieu, *128*
Cuu Long Hotel 🏨, *229*
Cyclos, *xxi*
Haiphong, 95
Hanoi, 75–76
Ho Chi Minh City, 217
Hue, 136
Nha Trang, 159

D

Dac Kim Bun Cha ✕, *48*
Dai Lanh, *156*
Dalat, *161*
currency exchange, 167
dining, 165–166
emergencies, 167
exploring, 161–165
lodging, 166
mail service, 168
nightlife, 166
outdoor activities and sports, 167
transportation, 167
travel agencies, 168
Dalat Flower Garden, *164*
Dalat University, *164*
Dambri Falls, *160*
Danang, *137–138*
currency exchange, 142
emergencies, 142
exploring, 139–140
lodging, 140
shopping, 140
side trips, 140–141
transportation, 142
travel agencies, 142
Dance clubs
Haiphong, 95
Hanoi, 57–58
Ho Chi Minh City, 200–201
Dan Chu Hotel 🏨, *51*
Dan Dai, *235*
Da Tano ✕, *46–47*
Dat Set Pagoda, *233*
Dengue fever, *xxvii*
Den Nghe, *92–93*
Den Ngoc Son, *25–26*
Diarrhea, *xxvii*
Dien Bien Hotel 🏨, *94*
Dien Bien Phu, *111–112, 117, 118*
Dien Huu Pagoda, *39*
Dining, *xxi–xxii, 7–8.* ☞ *Specific cities*
Fodor's Choices, 10–11
Disabled travelers, *xxii–xxiii*
Discounts and deals, *xxiii–xxiv*
Diving, *158–159*
DMZ (Demilitarized Zone), *130*
Doc Let, *156*
Doctors and hospitals. ☞ Emergencies
Dong A Hotel 🏨, *102*
Dong Da Hotel 🏨, *133*
Dong Dang, *102*
Dong Ho Hotel 🏨, *232*
Dong Khanh Hotel 🏨, *197–198*
Dong Loi Hotel 🏨, *133*
Dong notes, *xxxi*
Dong Tam Snake Farm, *227–228*
Dong Xuan Market, *24*
Do Son, *13, 95–97*
Driving. ☞ Car travel
Du Hang Pagoda, *92*
Duties, *xx–xxi*
Duyet Thi Duong, *127*
Duy Tan Hotel (Hue) 🏨, *133*
Duy Tan Hotel (Nha Trang) 🏨, *158*

E

Eating and drinking precautions, *xxi–xxii*
Eden Hotel 🏨, *55*
Edo ✕, *49*
Electricity, *xxv*
E-mail, *xxv–xxvi*
Embassies and consulates
Hanoi, xxvi, 77–78
Ho Chi Minh City, xxvi, 217
Embroidery shops, *65–66*
Emergencies, *xxvi*
Dalat, 167
Danang, 142
Haiphong, 105
Hanoi, 77, 78
Ho Chi Minh City, 218
Hoi An, 150

Hue, 136
medical assistance, xxx–xxxi
Nha Trang, 160
Emperor Jade Pagoda, *183*
English-language bookstores
Hanoi, 78
Ho Chi Minh City, 218
Etiquette, *xxvi–xxvii*
Exchanging money, *xxxi.* ☞ *Specific cities*

F

Faifoo ✕, *147*
Fansipan Restaurant ✕, *115*
Festivals and seasonal events, *xxvii–xxviii, 12–13, 96*
Fine Arts Museum, *35*
Five Royal Fish ✕, *46*
Flat Tower, *127*
Floating Market at Phung Hiep, *228*
Fodor's Choices, *10–11*
Forbidden Purple City, *127*
Forestry Research Center, *110*
Forests, *235*
French architecture, *6*
French penal colony (Son La), *110*
Friendship Gate, *102*
Front Beach, *210*
Furama Resort 🏨, *141*

G

Ga Da Lat, *164–165*
Galaxy Hotel 🏨, *54*
Galleon Steak House ✕, *47*
Garden Plaza Hotel 🏨, *198*
Gardens
Dalat, 164
Hanoi, 35
Ho Chi Minh City, 182
Gas stations, *xxiv*
Gift-giving, *xxvi–xxvii*
Golf, *8*
Dalat, 167
Hanoi, 61–62
Ho Chi Minh City, 202
Phan Tiet, 212
Grand Hotel d'Angkor 🏨, *214*
Green Bamboo 🏨, *115*
Group tours, *xl*
Guided tours, *xxiv.* ☞ *Specific cities*

H

Ha Chuong Hoi Quan Pagoda, *186*
Hai Au Hotel 🏨, *96*
Haiphong, *90–91*
children, attractions for, 91
currency exchange, 105
dining, 93–94
emergencies, 105
exploring, 91–93
lodging, 93, 94
mail service, 106
nightlife, 94–95
transportation, 95, 103, 104, 105
travel agencies, 106
Haiphong Museum, *92*
Haiyen Hotel 🏨, *157*
Halong Bay, *97–99, 103, 104, 106*
Halong Bay Hotel 🏨, *98*
Halong City, *97*
Halong I Hotel 🏨, *98*
Halong Plaza Hotel 🏨, *98–99*
Ham Rong Hotel 🏨, *116*
Handicraft shops, *66*
Hang Chau Hotel 🏨, *232*
Hang Nga Art Gallery, *164*
Hang Nga Guesthouse 🏨, *166*
Hanh Long Hotel 🏨, *198*
Han Kook Kwan ✕, *93*
Hanoi, *4, 15–16*
the arts, 58–60
cafés, 17
camera and watch repair, 78
children, attractions for, 35, 58, 60
climate, xliv
currency exchange, 76–77
dining, 17, 42–50
embassies, xxvi, 77–78
emergencies, 77, 78
English-language bookstores, 78
exploring, 18–42
film developing, 78
French Quarter, 26–31
Hang Bac Street, 24
Hang Dao Street, 25
Hang Gai Street, 25
Hang Ma Street, 25
Hang Quat Street, 25
Hoan Keim District, 43, 46–48, 50–51, 54–55
Ho Chi Minh Mausoleum area, 31–40, 49–50, 55–56
itineraries, 19
Lenin Park area, 48–49, 55
lodging, 18, 50–56
mail service, 78
nightlife, 56–58
Old Quarter, 22–26
outdoor activities and sports, 61–63
shopping, 18, 63–66
side trips, 66–73
tourist cafés, 80
Tran Hung Dao Street, 31
transportation in, 75–76
transportation to, 73–75
travel agencies, 79
West Lake area, 40–42, 50, 56
when to tour, 22
Hanoi Daewoo Hotel 🏨, *55*
Hanoi Flag Pillar, *35*
Hanoi Hilton (prison), *29*
Hanoi Horison Hotel 🏨, *55–56*
Hanoi Hotel 🏨, *55*
Hanoi Opera Hilton 🏨, *50*
Hanoi Sheraton Hotel 🏨, *56*
Ha Thanh Restaurant ✕, *48*
Ha Tien, *232*
Hau Giang Hotel 🏨, *229*
Hawaii Hotel 🏨, *55*
Health clubs
Hanoi, 62
Ho Chi Minh City, 202
Health concerns, *xxvii*
Helicopter travel, *104*
Heritage Halong 🏨, *99*
Hiking
Cat Ba Island, 100
Northern Vietnam, 84
Sapa, 114–115
History Museum (Ho Chi Minh City), *179*
History of Vietnam, *239–252*
H'mong Spring Festival, *12–13*
Hoa Ban Hotel 🏨, *111*
Hoa Binh Hotel (Haiphong) 🏨, *94*
Hoa Binh Hotel (Hanoi) 🏨, *51*
Hoa Hong Hotel II 🏨, *132*
Hoa Hong I 🏨, *134*
Hoai Thanh 🏨, *148*
Hoa Lo Prison, *29*
Hoa Lu, *70*
Hoang Lan ✕, *166*
Hoang Thanh, *128*
Hoan Kiem Lake, *25*
Hoa Sua ✕, *43*
Ho Chi Minh, biographical note on, *37*
Ho Chi Minh City, *4–5, 170–171*
the arts, 198–199, 201
cafés, 172
Central Saigon (Districts 1 and 3), 175–182, 187–197
children, attractions for, 178, 182, 202
Cholon (District 5), 183–187, 197–198
climate, xliv
consulates, xxvi, 217
currency exchange, 218
dining, 172–173, 187–192
Dong Khoi Street, 179
emergencies, 218
English-language bookstores, 218
exploring, 174–187
guided tours, 218–219
itineraries, 174
lodging, 173, 192–198
mail service, 219
nightlife, 198–201
Old Saigon, 182–183
outdoor activities and sports, 201–203
pharmacies, 219
Phu Nuan District, 198
safety concerns, 219
shopping, 173–174, 203–206

side trips, 206–214
transportation in, 216–217
transportation to, 214–216
travel agencies, 219–220
when to tour, 175
Ho Chi Minh City's People's Committee, *179*
Ho Chi Minh Mausoleum, *35–36*
Ho Chi Minh Museum (Hanoi), *36, 38*
Ho Chi Minh Museum (Ho Chi Minh City), *183*
Ho Chi Minh's Residence, *38–39*
Ho Coc, *211*
Ho Coc Guest House 🏨, *211*
Ho Guom, *25*
Ho Hoan Kiem, *25*
Hoi An, *142–143*
currency exchange, 150
dining, 147–148
emergencies, 150
exploring, 143–147
lodging, 148
outdoor activities and sports, 149
shopping, 149
transportation, 149–150
travel agencies, 150
Hoi An Hotel 🏨, *148*
Hoi Truong Thong Nhat, *180–181*
Holidays, *xxvii–xxviii*
Hon Chong Promontory, *155*
Hon Trem Hotel 🏨, *232*
Horse racing, *203*
Ho Tay Villas 🏨, *56*
Hotel Caravelle, *179*
Hotel Continental 🏨, *179, 192*
Hotel du Commerce 🏨, *94*
Hotel Equatorial 🏨, *197*
Hotel Majestic 🏨, *179, 193*
Hotel Phuong Huyen 🏨, *112*
Hotel Victoria Sapa 🏨, *115*
Ho Than Tho, *165*
Ho Tinh Tam, *128*
Hot springs
Binh Chau, 211
Son La, 110
Houseware shops
Hanoi, 66
Ho Chi Minh City, 205
Ho Xuan Huong, *161*
Huan Vu Hotel 🏨, *134*
Hue, *123–125*
currency exchange, 136
dining, 130–132
emergencies, 136
exploring, 125–130
guided tours, 136
lodging, 132–134
pharmacies, 136
shopping, 134
side trips, 130
transportation in, 135–136
transportation to, 134–135
visitor information, 136–137
Hue City Tourism Villas 🏨, *133*
Hue Hotel 🏨, *134*
Hue Restaurant ✕, *48*
Hung Vuong Hotel 🏨, *134*
Huong Giang Hotel 🏨, *132*
Huong Giang Hotel Restaurant ✕, *131*
Huong Giang Tourist Villa 🏨, *132–133*
Huu Nghi Hotel 🏨, *94*

I

Il Grillo ✕, *49*
Il Padrino Wine Bar and Delicatessen ✕, *46*
Immunizations, *xxvii*
Imperial City, *128*
Imperial Museum, *128*
Imperial Tombs, *128–130*
Incense-making, *234*
Indochine ✕, *47*
Insurance, *xxviii*
Intercontinental 🏨, *214*
Internet service, *xxv–xxvi*
Island of the Coconut Monk, *227*
Itineraries, *9–10*

J

Japanese Bridge, *145–146*
Japanese Tombs, *147*
Jeep trips, *84*
Jogging
Hanoi, 62
Ho Chi Minh City, 202–203

K

Karaoke clubs
Haiphong, 94
Ho Chi Minh City, 200–201
Khai Dinh, *Tomb of, 129–130*
Khanh Hung Hotel 🏨, *234*
Khazana ✕, *49*
Khe Sanh, *130*
Khmer Museum, *233*
Khu Biet Thu Garden Resort 🏨, *97*
Khu Luu Niem Bac Ho, *183*
Kimdo International Hotel 🏨, *193*
Kinh Thanh, *127*
Kleang Pagoda, *233*

L

Lac Canh ✕, *157*
Lacquerware shops, *206*
Lac Thanh Restaurant ✕, *131*
Lai Vien Kieu, *145–146*
Lake of Sighs, *165*
Lakes
Ba Be, 107
central highlands, 160
Dalat, 161, 165
Hanoi, 17–18, 25, 40–42
Hue, 128
Lam Nghiep (Forestry) **Hotel** 🏨, *97*
Langa Lake, *160*
Lang Chu Tich Ho Chi Minh, *35–36*
Lang Son, *102, 103–104, 105*
Language, *xxviii–xxix*
Lan Ty Ni Pagoda, *164*
La Paix ✕, *49–50*
La Primavera ✕, *46*
Large Cathedral, *92*
La Villa Blanche 🏨, *94*
Learning vacations, *xli*
Le Camargue ✕, *187*
Le Caprice ✕, *187*
Legros ✕, *187, 190*
Le Loi Hue Hotel 🏨, *134*
Lemongrass ✕, *191*
Le Rabelais ✕, *165*
Le Splendide ✕, *43*
Liberty ✕, *191*
Libraries
Hanoi, 78
Hue, 128
Lien Westlake Hotel 🏨, *56*
Linh Ong Pagoda, *140*
Lodging, *xxix–xxx.* ☞ *Specific cities*
discount services, xxiii
Fodor's Choices, 11
Long Hai, *210–211*
Long Son Pagoda, *155*
Long Xuyen, *230–231*
Long Xuyen Hotel 🏨, *231*
Luggage, *xxxiv*
Ly Cafeteria 22 ✕, *147*

M

Madison's ✕, *48–49*
Mai Chau, *109–110, 117*
Mai Chau Guest House 🏨, *110*
Mai Huong ✕, *131*
Mail service, *xxx.* ☞ *Specific cities*
Malaria, *xxvii*
Maps, *xxiv*
Marble Mountains, *140–141, 142*
Marco Polo 🏨, *140*
Mariamman Hindu Temple, *179*
Marine Club Restaurant ✕, *190*
Matoc Pagoda, *233–234*
May Ngan Phuong ✕, *191*
Mealtimes, *xxi*
Medical assistance, *xxx–xxxi*
Mediterraneo ✕, *47*
Mekong Delta, *5, 222–223*
currency exchange, 237
dining, 224
exploring, 224–236
guided tours, 236
health concerns, 237
itineraries, 225–226
lodging, 224

transportation, 236–237
travel agencies, 237
when to tour, 226
Mekong Hotel 🏨, *231*
Mercury Hotel 🏨, *193*
Metropole Hotel Sofitel 🏨, *50*
Mid-Autumn Festival, *13*
Minh Hai Mangrove Forest, *235*
Minh Mang, Tomb of, *130*
Minibus travel
Hanoi, 74
Ho Chi Minh City, 215
Hue, 135
Northern Vietnam, 105
Miró ✕, *43, 46*
Mogambo Guest House 🏨, *197*
Mondial Hotel 🏨, *196*
Money, *xxxi–xxxii*
Mong Cai, *101–102, 103*
Mosques
Chau Doc, 231
Ho Chi Minh City, 186
Mosquito bites, precautions against, *xxvii*
Motorbiking, *xxxii–xxxiii*
Danang, 142
Haiphong, 95
Hanoi, 76
Ho Chi Minh City, 217
Mekong Delta, 236–237
Nha Trang, 159–160
Northern Vietnam, 117
rules of the road, xxv
Mt. Fansipan, *114–115*
Mui Ne Beach, *211*
Mui Ngoc, *101*
Municipal Theater, *180*
Municipal Water Puppet Theater, *60*
Munirangsyaram Pagoda, *228*
Museum of History, *29–30*
Museum of History and Culture, *146*
Museum of the Revolution (Hanoi), *30*
Museum of the Revolution (Ho Chi Minh City), *180*
Museum of Trade Ceramics, *146*
Museums. ☞ Art galleries and museums
ceramics, 146
Champa Kingdom, 139–140
in Danang, 139–140
in Dien Bien Phu, 112
in Haiphong, 92
in Hanoi, 29–30, 34–35, 36, 38
history, 29–30, 92, 146, 179
Ho Chi Minh, 36, 38, 183
in Ho Chi Minh City, 173, 179, 180, 181–182, 183
in Hoi An, 146
in Hue, 128
Khmer culture, 233
military history, 34–35
prisons, 29
Revolution, 30, 180
royalty, 128
in Soc Trang, 233
Ton Duc Thang, 183
Vietnam War, 181–182
in Vung Tau, 210
Music
Hanoi, 60
Ho Chi Minh City, 201
Musical instrument shops
Hanoi, 66
Ho Chi Minh City, 206
My Hoa Hung Island, *230*
My Lac ✕, *148*
My Son Cham ruins, *140*
My Tho, *227–228, 237*

N

Nam Can, *236*
Nam Cat Tien National Park, *160, 212*
Nam Long Hotel 🏨, *158*
Nam Phuong ✕, *47–48*
Nam Phuong Hotel 🏨, *54*
National parks
Cuc Phuong, 71–72
Nam Cat Tien, 160, 212
Nature reserves. ☞ National parks
Dan Dai, 235
Long Xuyen, 230
Sapa, 114
Navy Guest House 🏨, *94*
New World Hotel Saigon 🏨, *192*
Nghe Temple, *92–93*
Nghia An Hoi Quan Pagoda, *186*
Ngoc Anh ✕, *131*
Ngoc Son Temple, *25–26*
Ngoc Suong ✕, *157*
Nha Bac Ho, *38–39*
Nha Hat Lon, *30*
Nha Hat Thanh Pho (Haiphong), *92*
Nha Hat Thanh Pho (Ho Chi Minh City), *180*
Nha Tho Duc Ba, *180*
Nha Tho Lon, *30–31*
Nha Trang, *155*
the arts, 158
beaches, 152, 156
currency exchange, 160
dining, 156–157
emergencies, 160
exploring, 155–156
lodging, 157–158
mail service, 160
nightlife, 158
outdoor activities and sports, 158–159
transportation in, 159–160
transportation to, 159
travel agencies, 160
Nha Trang Huu Duc, *155*
Nha Trang Lodge Hotel 🏨, *158*
Nha Trang Sailing Club ✕, *156*
Nha Trung Bay Toi Ac Chien Tranh Xam, *181–182*
Nhi Phu Hoi Quan, *186*
Nhi Tam Thanh, *102*
Nine Dynastic Urns, *128*
Ninh Kieu Hotel 🏨, *229*
Norfolk Hotel 🏨, *196*
Northern Vietnam, *5, 82–83.* ☞ Haiphong
dining, 83–84
exploring, 85–87
Far North, 106–108
guided tours, 106
itineraries, 86–87
lodging, 85
Northeast, 87–106
Northwest, 108–119
outdoor activities, 84
shopping, 85
transportation, 103–105, 108, 116–118
when to tour, 87
Notre Dame Cathedral, *180*
Nui Hoang Lien Nature Reserve, *114*
Nui Sam, *231–232*

O

Old House of Phung Hung, *146*
Old House of Tan Ky, *146*
Omni Saigon Hotel 🏨, *198*
One-Pillar Pagoda, *39*
Ong Bon Pagoda, *186*
Ong Dau Dua, *227*
Ong Tao ✕, *131*
Ong Tao Festival, *12*
Opera, *59*
Opera House, *30*
Orchid farms, *202*
Outdoor activities, *xxxiii.* ☞ *Specific cities and activities*

P

Package deals, *xxiv, xl*
Packing for Vietnam, *xxxiii–xxxiv*
Pagodas, *6*
Can Tho, 228
Dalat, 164, 165
Fodor's Choices, 11
Haiphong, 92, 93
Hanoi, 28, 39, 41–42
Hanoi area, 68–69
Ho Chi Minh City, 183, 186, 187
Hoi An, 147
Hue, 128–129, 130
Marble Mountains, 140–141
Nha Trang, 155
Soc Trang, 233–234
Vinh Long, 230
Palace Hotel 🏨, *196*
Palace of Supreme Harmony, *128*

Palaces
Dalat, 161, 164
Hanoi, 31, 39
Ho Chi Minh City, 180–181
Hue, 128
Pansea Resort 🏨, *212*
Paris Deli ✕, *179*
Parking, *xxiv*
Passports, *xxxiv–xxxv*
Pedicabs. ☞ Cyclos
People's Committee Guest House 🏨, *100*
Perfume Pagoda, *69*
pilgrimage to, 12
Phan Thai Hotel 🏨, *54*
Phan Tiet, *211–212*
Phat Diem, *70–71*
Phnom Penh, *Cambodia, 214*
Pho Hoa ✕, *192*
Pho Hoi (Faifoo) **Minihotel** 🏨, *148*
Phong Lan Hotel 🏨, *111*
Pho Tho Racetrack, *203*
Phu Dong, *13*
Phung Island, *227*
Phuoc Hai Tu, *183*
Phuoc Kien Assembly Hall, *146*
Phuoc Lam Pagoda, *147*
Phuong Duong Hotel 🏨, *197*
Phuong Lan Hotel 🏨, *234*
Phuong Nam Hotel 🏨, *235*
Piano Restaurant & Bar ✕, *48*
Pissing Cow Waterfall, *102*
Plain of Reeds, *230*
Planet Hotel 🏨, *54*
Plane travel, *xiii–xv*
airfares, xiv
airports, xv–xvi
baggage allowances, xxxiv
with children, xix
consolidators, xiv
Dalat, 167
Danang, 142
discount services, xxiii
Hanoi, 74
Ho Chi Minh City, 215–216
Hoi An, 150
Hue, 135
major airlines and low-cost carriers, xiii–xiv
Nha Trang, 159
Northern Vietnam, 104, 118
overbooking by airlines, xv
tips for, xv
travel agencies for, xiv
Po Klong Garai Cham Towers, *161*
Po Nagar Cham Towers, *155*
Post Office (Ho Chi Minh City, *Cholon District*), *186*
Prenn Falls, *165*
Prescription drugs, *xxxiv*
Presidential Palace, *39*
Press Club ✕, *46*
Prices, *xxxii*
Prince Hotel (Hanoi) 🏨, *51*
Prince Hotel (Ho Chi Minh City) 🏨, *198*
Prisons
Con Dao Island, 212–213
Hanoi, 29
Son La, 110
Public transportation, *xxxvi*
Puppetry, *60*

Q

Quan Am Pagoda, *187*
Quan Cong Temple, *146*
Quan Gio Moi ✕, *48*
Quang Thang House, *146*
Quan Sake ✕, *93–94*
Quan Thanh Temple, *41*
Quoc Te (International) **Hotel** 🏨, *229*

R

Railways, *164–165*
Ram Thang Bay summer festival, *13*
Restaurant Gaulois ✕, *100*
Restaurant Thanh ✕, *148*
Restaurant 13 ✕, *191*
Reunification Palace, *180–181*
Rex Hotel 🏨, *193, 196*
Roads, *xxiv–xxv*
Royal Library, *128*
Royal Theater, *127*
Rung Tram, *230*

S

Saigon. ☞ Ho Chi Minh City
Saigon-Can Tho Hotel 🏨, *228–229*
Saigon Hotel (Hanoi) 🏨, *50–51*
Saigon Hotel (Ho Chi Minh City) 🏨, *196*
Saigon Hotel (Hue) 🏨, *134*
Saigon Marriott Hotel 🏨, *192*
Saigon Prince Hotel 🏨, *192–193*
Saigon Sakura ✕, *47*
Saigon Thien Bao ✕, *94*
Saigon Tourist travel service, *181*
St. Joseph's Cathedral, *30–31*
Sam Mountain, *231–232*
Sampan ✕, *49*
Sao Mai Hotel 🏨, *116*
Sapa, *113–116, 117, 118*
Sapa ✕, *190*
Sawaddee ✕, *191*
Scooters, *xxxii–xxxiii*
Seaside Hotel 🏨, *158*
Seasons of Hanoi ✕, *50*
Sea Star 🏨, *148*
Sekitei Japanese Restaurant ✕, *190*
Senior-citizen travel, *xxxvi*
Shanti ✕, *190*
Shoe shops, *206*
Shopping, *xxxvi–xxxvii, 8–9.* ☞ *Specific cities*
Fodor's Choices, 11
Siem Reap, *Cambodia, 214*
Single travelers, *xl*
Smiling Café ✕, *48*
Snake farms, *227–228*
Soccer, *63*
Soc Trang, *232–234*
Sofitel Cambodiana 🏨, *214*
Sofitel Dalat Palace 🏨, *166*
Soho Cafe and Deli ✕, *49*
Sol Chancery Saigon 🏨, *196*
Son La, *110–111*
South-central coast and highlands, *5, 152.* ☞ Dalat; Nha Trang
central highlands, 160–161
dining, 152
itineraries, 153
lodging, 152–153
nightlife, 153
outdoor activities and sports, 153
Spices ✕, *190*
Sports, *xxxiii.* ☞ *Specific cities and sports*
Spring Hotel 🏨, *197*
Street addresses, *xxxvii*
Student and youth travel, *xxxvii*
Su Nu Pagoda, *165*
Suoi Nuoc Nong Binh Chau, *211*
Swimming
Hanoi, 62
Ho Chi Minh City, 202

T

Tam Dao Hill Station, *72–73*
Tam Nong Nature Reserve, *230*
Tam Son Hoi Quan Pagoda, *187*
Tam Ta Toong Caves, *110*
Tam Thai Tu Pagoda, *141*
Tandoor ✕, *43*
Tan Long Island, *227*
Tan Trao, *107–108*
Taxes, *xxxvii*
Taxis, *xxxvii–xxxviii*
Danang, 142
Haiphong, 95
Hanoi, 76
Ho Chi Minh City, 217
Hue, 136
Tay Ninh, *208–209*
Tay Phuong Pagoda, *68–69*
Telephone service, *xxxviii*
Temple of Literature, *39–40*
Temples, *6.* ☞ Pagodas
Angkor Wat Complex, 213–214
central highlands, 161
Fodor's Choices, 11
Haiphong, 92–93
Hanoi, 25–26, 39–40, 41

Ho Chi Minh City, 179
Hoi An, 146, 147
Tay Ninh, 208–209
Tennis, *63*
Tet Doan Ngu Festival, *13*
Tet Festival, *12*
Tet Trung Nguyen Festival, *13*
Thac Prenn, *165*
Thai Binh Hotel ⊞, *231*
Thai Binh Lau, *128*
Thai Hoa Dien, *128*
Thang Loi Hotel ⊞, *56*
Thang Long Hotel ⊞, *51*
Thang Nam Hotel ⊞, *94*
Thanh Binh ⊞, *148*
Thanh Lich ✕, *157*
Thanh Minh Festival, *12*
Thanh Thanh ✕, *165–166*
Thanh Thanh Hotel ⊞, *158*
Thanh The ✕, *157*
Thanh Thuy, *166*
Thao Cam Vien, *182*
Thay Pagoda, *68–69*
Theater
Hanoi, 59
Ho Chi Minh City, 201
Theater buildings
Haiphong, 92
Ho Chi Minh City, 180
Hue, 127
Theme trips, *xl–xli*
Thien Hau Pagoda, *187*
Thien Mu Pagoda, *128–129*
Thien Trung ⊞, *148*
Thien Vuong Pagoda, *165*
Thi Sac Street Cafés ✕, *191*
Thit De Restaurant ✕, *111*
Thoai Ngoc Hau, Tomb of, *231–232*
Thung Lung Tinh Yeu, *165*
Thuy Duong Resort, *211*
Tinh Tam Lake, *128*
Tipping, *xxxviii–xxxix*
Tombs
Chau Doc, 231–232
Hanoi, 35–36
Hoi An, 147
Hue, 128–130
Ton Duc Thang Museum, *183*
Tong Phuc Nen ✕, *131*
Tortoise Pagoda, *183*
Tour operators, *xxxix–xli*
for disabled travelers, xxiii
Towers
Hanoi, 35
Hue, 127
Nha Trang, 155
Son La, 110
Tra Co, *101*
Trai Mat, *164*
Train travel, *xli*
Hanoi, 74–75
Ho Chi Minh City, 216
Hue, 135
Nha Trang, 159
Northern Vietnam, 105, 118
Tra Kieu Altar, *139*
Tran Family Chapel, *147*
Tran Quoc Pagoda, *41–42*
Travel agencies, *xli–xlii.* ☞ *Specific cities*
for disabled travelers, xxiii
for plane tickets, xiv
tour bookings with, xl
in Vietnam, xlii
Travel clubs, *xxiii*
Traveler's checks, *xxxii*
Travel gear, *xlii–xliii*
Travel insurance, *xxviii*
Trieu Chau, *145*
Tri Huong Restaurant ✕, *96*
Trung Hoa Restaurant ✕, *94*
Trung Thap Festival, *13*
Trung Thu Festival, *13*
Truong Dai Hoc Tong Hop, *164*
Tu Cam Thanh, *127*
Tu Doc, Tomb of, *130*
Tu Hieu Pagoda, *130*

U

U Minh Cajeput Forest, *235*
Universities, *164*
Urns, *128*
U.S. Embassy compound (Ho Chi Minh City), *181*
U.S. government travel briefings, *xliii*

V

Valley of Love, *165*
Van Mieu, *39–40*
Van Thanh Mieu Pagoda, *230*
Ve (Drawing) **Pagoda,** *93*
Vegetarian Restaurant Com Chay Nang Tam ✕, *47*
Verandah ✕, *46*
Videos on Vietnam, *257–258*
Vien Bao Tang Lich Su, *179*
Vien Dong Hotel ⊞, *158*
Vietnam Circus, *58*
Vietnam House ✕, *191*
Vietnam Restaurant ✕, *157*
Vietnam veterans, services for, *xli, xliii*
Vietnam War sites
Cu Chi Tunnels, 206, 208
DMZ and Khe Sanh, 130
Hanoi, 29, 42
Ho Chi Minh City, 179, 181–182
Viet Xo Cultural Palace, *31*
Ving Hung Restaurant ✕, *147*
Vinh Hung Hotel ⊞, *148*
Vinh Loi, *234*
Vinh Long, *229–230*
Vinh Quang Hotel ⊞, *54*
Visas, *xxxiv–xxxv*
Visitor information, *xliii*
Vu Lan Festival, *13*
Vung Tau, *210*
Vuon Bach Thao, *35*
Vuon Dao Hotel ⊞, *99*
Vuon Hoa Dalat, *164*

W

Walking in cities, *xxv*
War Memorial, *42*
War ordnances, unexploded, *xxxvi*
War Remnants Museum, *181–182*
Waterfalls
central highlands, 160
Dalat, 164, 165
Lang Son, 102
South-central coast and highlands, 153, 160
Water for drinking, *xxii, xxvii*
Water puppetry, *60*
West Lake, *40–42*
When to go, *xliii–xliv*
White Thai Villages ⊞, *110*
White Villa, *210*
Win Hotel ⊞, *54–55*
Wood carving shops, *206*

X

Xa Lon, *234*
Xuan Huong Lake, *161*
Xuan Tam Villa Hotel ⊞, *166*

Y

Yellow River Restaurant ✕, *146*

Z

Zoo and Botanical Gardens (Ho Chi Minh City), *182*

NOTES

Fodor's Special Series

Fodor's Best Bed & Breakfasts

America

California

The Mid-Atlantic

New England

The Pacific Northwest

The South

The Southwest

The Upper Great Lakes

Compass American Guides

Alaska

Arizona

Boston

Chicago

Colorado

Hawaii

Idaho

Hollywood

Las Vegas

Maine

Manhattan

Minnesota

Montana

New Mexico

New Orleans

Oregon

Pacific Northwest

San Francisco

Santa Fe

South Carolina

South Dakota

Southwest

Texas

Utah

Virginia

Washington

Wine Country

Wisconsin

Wyoming

Citypacks

Amsterdam

Atlanta

Berlin

Chicago

Florence

Hong Kong

London

Los Angeles

Montréal

New York City

Paris

Prague

Rome

San Francisco

Tokyo

Venice

Washington, D.C.

Exploring Guides

Australia

Boston & New England

Britain

California

Canada

Caribbean

China

Costa Rica

Egypt

Florence & Tuscany

Florida

France

Germany

Greek Islands

Hawaii

Ireland

Israel

Italy

Japan

London

Mexico

Moscow & St. Petersburg

New York City

Paris

Prague

Provence

Rome

San Francisco

Scotland

Singapore & Malaysia

South Africa

Spain

Thailand

Turkey

Venice

Flashmaps

Boston

New York

San Francisco

Washington, D.C.

Fodor's Gay Guides

Los Angeles & Southern California

New York City

Pacific Northwest

San Francisco and the Bay Area

South Florida

USA

Pocket Guides

Acapulco

Aruba

Atlanta

Barbados

Budapest

Jamaica

London

New York City

Paris

Prague

Puerto Rico

Rome

San Francisco

Washington, D.C.

Languages for Travelers (Cassette & Phrasebook)

French

German

Italian

Spanish

Mobil Travel Guides

America's Best Hotels & Restaurants

California and the West

Major Cities

Great Lakes

Mid-Atlantic

Northeast

Northwest and Great Plains

Southeast

Southwest and South Central

Rivages Guides

Bed and Breakfasts of Character and Charm in France

Hotels and Country Inns of Character and Charm in France

Hotels and Country Inns of Character and Charm in Italy

Hotels and Country Inns of Character and Charm in Paris

Hotels and Country Inns of Character and Charm in Portugal

Hotels and Country Inns of Character and Charm in Spain

Short Escapes

Britain

France

New England

Near New York City

Fodor's Sports

Golf Digest's Places to Play

Skiing USA

USA Today The Complete Four Sport Stadium Guide